Taxation of Crypto Assets

Taxation of Crypto Assets

Edited by

Niklas Schmidt
Jack Bernstein
Stefan Richter
Lisa Zarlenga

Wolters Kluwer

Published by:
Kluwer Law International B.V.
PO Box 316
2400 AH Alphen aan den Rijn
The Netherlands
E-mail: international-sales@wolterskluwer.com
Website: lrus.wolterskluwer.com

Sold and distributed by:
Wolters Kluwer Legal & Regulatory U.S.
7201 McKinney Circle
Frederick, MD 21704
United States of America
Email: customer.service@wolterskluwer.com

ISBN 978-94-035-2350-7

e-Book: ISBN 978-94-035-2351-4
web-PDF: ISBN 978-94-035-2352-1

Editors

Jack Bernstein is the Senior Tax Partner at Aird & Berlis LLP in Toronto and Chair of the firm's International Tax practice. Jack is well known in international tax planning, mergers and acquisitions, corporate restructuring, reorganizations and financing. He is experienced in dealing with public and private corporations and has advised hedge funds, venture capital funds and real estate funds. He also has extensive experience in advising high-net-worth private clients on international, cross-border and domestic estate and tax planning. An authority on multijurisdictional matters and a prolific writer and speaker, Jack regularly contributes to leading tax publications globally, including Tax Notes International. He has been actively involved at a senior level in several international and Canadian tax organizations, including being a past Governor of the Canadian Tax Foundation, former Chair of the American Bar Association Foreign Lawyers Forum, former Global Co-Chair of the International Bar Association Taxation Committee, and former Member of Council of the International Fiscal Association (Canadian Branch). Jack is internationally recognized by leading legal publishers, including Chambers and Partners, Who's Who Legal, The Legal 500, Best Lawyers, Martindale-Hubbell and Lexpert. As a result of his outstanding leadership and contributions to the field of tax law, Jack was honoured with the 2020 Ontario Bar Association Award for Excellence in Taxation Law. **Email:** jbernstein@airdberlis.com.

Stefan Richter is a tax partner at SMP heading the tax practice with more than twenty years of experience in M&A and tax structuring consulting. He specializes in providing advice on corporate transactions, structuring and tax planning of token-based business models as well as tax-driven reorganizations in an international context. In addition, Stefan has longstanding experience in advising national and international law firms regarding their own ongoing and structural tax matters. Stefan formerly was a partner with Deloitte. He is a lecturer at the Bucerius Law School, a board member of the Hamburger Steuerdialog e.V., and a frequent speaker at tax conferences. **Email:** stefan.richter@smp.law.

Niklas Schmidt is a Tax Partner with WOLF THEISS in Austria. He has completed studies in Vienna, Barcelona, Munich and Oxford and has been admitted in Austria both as a lawyer and as a tax adviser. Before joining WOLF THEISS in the year 2000, he had previously worked for several years at a 'Big Four' accounting firm and as a research assistant at the University of Vienna. Niklas has written various books (including a recent book on crypto assets and blockchains in German), is frequently engaged as a speaker at law conferences, is a member of several international legal organizations and networks and has top rankings in international directories. Currently, Niklas is a chair of the Private Client Tax Committee of the International Bar Association (IBA). **Email:** niklas.schmidt@wolftheiss.com.

Lisa Zarlenga is a Tax Partner at Steptoe & Johnson, LLP, where her practice focuses on corporate transactional and planning matters as well as tax policy issues. She advises clients on structuring tax-free and taxable acquisitions and dispositions. Drawing on her experience as Tax Legislative Counsel at the Treasury Department, she also helps clients advocate for and resolve tax policy issues before Treasury and the Internal Revenue Service involving proposed and pending regulations and other administrative guidance, and before Congress involving legislation. She has also assisted clients during the rulemaking process, including preparing comment letters and meeting with policymakers. Lisa has combined her policy and transactional backgrounds to advise clients on certain specialized tax issues, such as blockchain and digital currency. She advises clients on conducting digital currency transactions and conversions, token offerings, and different investment and entity structures. Lisa is a frequent speaker, and she is active in the Tax Section of the American Bar Association, currently serving as the chair of the Committee on Government Submissions. **Email:** lzarlenga@steptoe.com.

Contributors

Tomás Bailey is a Senior Associate in the corporate tax department at Matheson currently based in the firm's London office. Tomás advises Irish and multinational clients on corporate and international tax, mergers and acquisitions, tax controversy and transfer pricing. Tomás advises clients in relation to tax-effective structures for inbound and outbound investment and has advised on numerous cross-border reorganizations. Tomás also advises on state aid in the context of taxation matters. **Email:** tomas.bailey@matheson.com.

Ákos Baráti is a lawyer and an economist. Ákos obtained his law degree at the Law Faculty of the University of Pécs in 2010. He obtained a Diploma in Economics at the Budapest Corvinus University in 2012. He is a certified tax advisor and a certified public accountant. Before joining Jalsovszky law firm in 2014 Ákos has gained more than four years of professional experience at international 'Big4' consulting firms, where his main areas of expertise were international tax planning and corporate tax advisory. In addition to tax planning, Akos assists his clients with regulatory matters. **Email:** abarati@jalsovszky.com.

Joachim M. Bjerke is a Partner in the law firm BAHR and heads the firm's tax and VAT department. Joachim works with a broad range of national and international corporate tax questions, including transfer pricing, oil and gas taxation and structuring of M&A transactions. He is one of the leading advisers in Norway with respect to transfer pricing and his work spans from advisory services to dispute resolution. He has also written one of the few Norwegian books on transfer pricing. Together with BAHR-partner Jan B. Jansen he has written a book with an introduction to the Norwegian oil taxation regime, which is used as course material at the University of Oslo. **Email:** jmb@bahr.no.

Miri Bickel co-heads Shibolet & Co.'s tax practice. Miri is a dual-qualified accountant and lawyer, with particular expertise in international tax planning and transactions, blockchain and smart contracts, and international taxation of venture capital funds. Miri has extensive experience in all tax aspects relating to complex cross-border M&A,

corporate restructurings, financing, public offerings, employee stock option plans, hi-tech companies and their employees, underwritings, executive interests, and many other financial instruments. She is also recognized as a leading attorney in both civil and criminal tax litigation (income tax, real estate taxation and VAT), and regularly appears before the Appellate-level Courts. **Email:** m.bickel@shibolet.com.

Louis Botha ((BCom *cum laude*, LLB *cum laude*, LLM (Tax Law), University of Pretoria) is a Senior Associate in the Tax and Exchange Control practice of Cliffe Dekker Hofmeyr Inc. in South Africa. Louis' experience includes the areas of corporate income tax, individual income tax, employees' tax and the application of exchange control laws in the context of various transactions. **Email:** louis.botha@cdhlegal.com.

Emil Brincker (BCom *cum laude*, LLB *cum laude*, LLM *cum laude*, LLD, University of Stellenbosch, HDip (Tax) *cum laude*, University of Johannesburg) is a Director and National Head of the Tax and Exchange Control practice of Cliffe Dekker Hofmeyr Inc. in South Africa. Emil's experience includes the areas of corporate finance, corporate reorganization and restructuring, exchange control, export finance, funding, general banking and commercial including derivative transactions, empowerment transactions, JSE Ltd and Takeover Regulations Panel, project finance and tax law, including income tax, tax controversy, VAT, stamp duties, PAYE, capital gains tax (CGT), and other fiscal statutes. **Email:** emil.brincker@cdhlegal.com.

Reuben Buttigieg is the Managing Director and Founder of Erremme Business Advisors, a business and management consultancy firm servicing local and international clients. Reuben also has a direct immersion in the Corporate Finance and consultancy services within the Firm. He holds an MBA from Warwick, is a Fellow Member of the Association of Chartered Certified Accountants and a Member of the Malta Institute of Management, Islamic Banking Institute and a Member in the Worshipful Company of International Bankers. Reuben holds the Presidential position within the Malta Institute of Management. The Institute represents among others Edinburgh Business School and the Chartered Institute of Taxation. Reuben has been the pioneer in the discussions on Islamic Finance in Malta and has prepared various papers and articles on the subject being published in esteemed research journals and participates regularly as a speaker in International Islamic Finance conferences. Reuben acts as a consultant on various Islamic Finance transactions in Malta and abroad. Reuben shares his knowledge and contributes to the academic society by lecturing Islamic Finance at the University of Malta and the Malta College for Arts, Science and Technology. Before establishing Erremme Business Advisers, Reuben worked with two of the Big Four accountancy and audit firms, namely, Ernst & Young (Malta and Milan) and KPMG. Reuben has conducted various corporate finance and due diligence assignments as well as audits and consultancy work both in Malta as well as in Milan. During the Euro Changeover process in Malta, Reuben was a member in the National Euro Changeover Committee and chaired the Pricing Task Force within the said committee which falls under the umbrella of the Ministry of Finance. Reuben has vast experience in the Euro changeover as he acted as consultant even during the changeover in first wave countries. **Email:** rmb@erremme.com.mt.

Juan Camilo Sánchez is a Principal Tax Associate with broad experience in international tax law and private equity transactions. He currently forms part of the Garrigues Digital group, a team specialized in advising start-ups and entrepreneurs in the technology and digital economy sectors. **Email**: juan.camilo.sanchez@garrigues.com.

Vivien Chan is the Founding and Senior Partner of Vivien Chan & Co., with over forty years of experience in M&A, information technology, intellectual property and related tax issues. Vivien was awarded the Lifetime Achievement Award in 2017 by the American Chamber of Commerce in Hong Kong and was recently recognized as WIPR Leaders 2019 of Trademark and Patent. She was also awarded the Bronze Bauhinia Star (BBS) in 2008 and Silver Bauhinia Star (SBS) in 2014 by the HKSAR Government for her outstanding contributions to Hong Kong. Vivien is a Justice of the Peace and is the Past President of the Inter-Pacific Bar Association. She also is a notary public, a notarial attesting officer in China, and an arbitrator at the China International Economic and Trade Arbitration Commission, Shanghai International Arbitration Center and the Shenzhen Arbitration Commission. Ms Chan received her law degree from King's College, University of London, and is admitted as a solicitor in England and Wales, Hong Kong, Australia and Singapore. She is fluent in English, French, Mandarin and Cantonese. **Email:** vivchan@vcclawservices.com.

Maria Chang is a Senior Foreign Attorney in the Bae, Kim & Lee LLC firm's tax practice group. Her main practice areas involve cross-border tax structuring, international trade and customs, tax dispute resolutions and general tax and customs-related advisory services. Prior to joining Bae, Kim & Lee LLC in 2009, Maria Chang worked at the Seoul office of PricewaterhouseCoopers from 2006 to 2009, specializing in various customs matters relevant to multinational clients. **Email:** maria.chang@bkl.co.kr.

Aseem Chawla is the Practice Leader at ASC Legal, Solicitors & Advocates in New Delhi. He is a Member of Bar Council of India and Fellow Chartered Accountant and certificate holder of Comparative Tax Policy & Administration from Harvard Kennedy School. He is a candidate for the prestigious '*Vienna Certificate in Double Tax Treaties*' under the auspices of WU Vienna University of Economics and Business, Austria. He has extensive experience in advising on a variety of tax matters, including international tax, inbound and outbound investment structuring and cross-border tax issues, corporate and business advisory, exchange control and regulatory and money laundering laws. He is an accredited Trust & Estate Practitioner (''TEP'') and a member of the Society of Trust & Estate Practitioners (STEP), UK. Aseem is well regarded for estate planning, inheritance & family governance, trusts and private clients, including national and international clients, high net-worth individuals and trustees and family offices. He is also a Visiting Faculty at the Institute of Chartered Accountants of India (ICAI) on International Taxation, economic offences and money laundering laws. He is regularly invited to address various domestic and international forums and industry bodies. He is actively involved in the leadership capacities of various professional associations and industry chambers. He is the Vice-Chair of the South Asia/Oceana and India Committee, Section of International Law (ABA) and is an Officer at ABA International Tax Committee. He is the outgoing Secretary of the Taxes Committee of the International Bar Association (IBA) and Vice-Chair of the Task Force for Legal Services of the Confederation of Indian Industry (CII). Aseem is the Chairman of the Financial Services & Taxation Committee of the Indo American Chamber of Commerce (IACC). **Email:** aseem@aseemchawla.com.

Michel Collet is a Partner of the international tax department of CMS Francis Lefebvre Avocats. He assists mainly multinational enterprises (MNEs), investment and sovereign funds and banks on cross-border transactions, financing, or restructuring. Michel also assists and represents high net worth individuals including international sportsmen and artists. He is a former officer of the International Bar Association (IBA). He is also an active member of the American Bar Association (ABA) and International Fiscal Association (IFA) and is in charge of taxation in the working group of the Association Française des Fiduciaires (French Association of French equivalent of Trustees). Michel was in charge of the New York office of the firm from 2002 to 2007. He also sits on the board of the Jeanine Manuel International School in Paris. **Email:** michel.collet@cms-avocats.com.

Marta Cura is a Research Associate in the Blockchain and Digital Assets practice group at SMP. She studied law at the University of Coimbra School of Law in Portugal and at Fordham University School of Law in New York, where she completed an LLM in International Business and Trade Law. She is an attorney admitted in the state of New York. Before joining SMP, she previously worked for international law firms in London, Lisbon, and Hamburg. **Email:** marta.cura@smp.law.

Roberto de Castro Mendonça is a Member of the Stibbe Luxembourg Tax practice. Roberto specializes in international tax planning, the tax aspects of public and private M&A, corporate reorganizations, intellectual property, structured and hybrid finance, as well as tax litigation. He is a correspondent and author at the International Bureau of Fiscal Documentation (IBFD). **Email**: roberto.decastromendonca@stibbe.com

Álvaro de la Cueva is a partner in the tax practice area, with extensive experience in the provision of advice on international tax matters to Spanish and foreign multinationals, and with a particular focus on the technology, telecommunications, and crypto assets industries. **Email:** alvaro.delacueva@garrigues.com.

Barney Cumberland, Partner, leads the taxation practice at Simpson Grierson. With twenty-two years of practice, Barney has accumulated a broad range of experience in all fields of New Zealand's domestic and international tax law. He is a Member of the Taxes Committee of the International Bar Association, the New Zealand Branch of the International Fiscal Association and of the New Zealand Law Society Tax Law Committee. **Email:** barney.cumberland@simpsongrierson.com.

Bridget English is an English Qualified Associate in the London office of Gibson, Dunn & Crutcher and a member of the firm's Tax Practice Group. Bridget is an experienced tax adviser with a broad practice. She advises on a wide range of domestic and cross-border matters, including in relation to mergers and acquisitions, private equity, corporate reorganizations, real estate, corporate finance, and capital markets. **Email:** BEnglish@gibsondunn.com.

Ben Fryer is a Partner in the London office of Gibson, Dunn & Crutcher and a member of the firm's Tax Practice Group. Ben is an experienced tax adviser with a broad practice. He advises on a wide range of domestic and cross-border matters and transactions, including in relation to banking, capital markets, corporate finance, corporate reorganizations, debt restructuring, mergers and acquisitions, private equity, real estate and structured finance. He also guides clients on general corporate tax planning and risk management matters. **Email:** BFryer@gibsondunn.com.

Stephanie Gabriel is a Senior Associate at Tiberghien. She assists in various aspects of national and international wealth and inheritance tax planning, covering both private and professional clients. Over the years she has developed a thorough knowledge in providing advice on asset structures, e.g., Cayman tax law and data exchange. She is also a member of the BATL and is the author of several articles on tax issues. **Email:** stephanie.gabriel@tiberghien.com.

André Geest is a Researcher at the Wharton School of the University of Pennsylvania and at the UCL Centre for Blockchain Technologies. At the Wharton School he is co-organizing the Reg@Tech working group and the Blockchain governance project. His research focus is on the governance and regulation of decentralized financial technologies and the transformation towards decentralized finance. Before joining the Blockchain and Digital Assets practice group of SMP, he was a research assistant at the Institute for Computer Science at the University of Innsbruck. Currently, he is pursuing a PhD degree at Ludwig Maximilian University in Munich researching at the interface of financial market regulation and DLT/Blockchain. **Email:** andre.geest@smp.law.

Angelo Gentile is a Partner at the Tax Group at Aird & Berlis LLP. His practice focuses on tax litigation and commodity tax, including goods and services tax/harmonized sales tax (GST/HST) and provincial sales taxes. Angelo excels at resolving tax disputes at the early stages of the tax dispute process, although where litigation is necessary, he has experience litigating in the Tax Court of Canada and the Federal Court of Appeal on a wide range of tax disputes. **Email**: agentile@airdberlis.com.

Gerd D. Goyvaerts is a Partner at Tiberghien. His tax practice covers professional and private estate taxation of the Belgian entrepreneur and high net-worth individuals, international corporate and private tax planning, death duties and estate planning and tax inspired migration from and into Belgium. He developed a special interest in tax issues relevant to Anglo-Saxon trusts, foundations and settlements and voluntary disclosure proceedings, anti-money laundering legislation and regulations especially in a world where banking secrecy is shrinking. He is a regular speaker on (inter)national seminars and author of various articles on tax issues in leading journals such as *Tijdschrift voor Fiscaal Recht*, *Fiscale Actualiteit*, *Trusts & Trustees* and *Vermogensplanning in de Praktijk*. He is a member of the IBA anti-money Laundering Action Group. Gerd is president of the Belgian Association of Tax Lawyers (BATL) and International

Fellow at ACTEC and member to TIAETL. He is the former President and Vice President of the Tax Commission of AIJA (Association Internationale des Jeunes Avocats), where he is now an honorary member. Gerd is ranked as a 'Band1 Private Wealth Lawyer' in the Chambers HNW 2019/2020 rankings. Gerd is also mentioned as a 'Global Leader' in Tax Advisory and Private Clients by Who's Who Legal 2019. **Email:** gerdd.goyvaerts@tiberghien.com.

Gian Gualberto Morgigni is a Senior Associate of the Tax and Tax Planning department at Chiomenti in Italy. He has completed his studies in Rome and Milan and has been admitted to the Italian Bar Association. He joined Chiomenti in 2011. Gian Gualberto focuses on family estate restructuring, taxation of business operations, taxation of financial transactions and corporate restructurings. He regularly advises clients on issues related to international taxation, M&A, private equity and financing operations. Gian Gualberto has authored several publications in tax matters and is a speaker at tax conferences and seminars. **Email:** giangualberto.morgigni@chiomenti.net.

Benjamin J. Hamnes is an associate in the law firm BAHR and is a part of the firm's department for energy and natural resources. Benjamin works with both advisory services and dispute resolution in the field of national and international corporate tax and transfer pricing. He has previously worked at EY, where he specialized within the field of transfer pricing and intangible value chains. **Email:** beham@bahr.no.

Anders Oreby Hansen has more than twenty-five years of experience and has primarily represented US, EU, Scandinavian and other multinational groups and high net-worth individuals investing in or conducting business in Denmark. His experience covers assistance to international corporate clients on matters involving strategies and dispute resolution in relation to Danish transfer pricing issues, group restructurings, international taxation issues, M&A Real Estate and corporate consulting. His experience also covers partner-owned and family businesses. Anders furthermore has experience as an arbitration judge and as an expert witness on Danish tax legislation before the High Court in London. Anders is a member of the Danish Bar & Law Society, the Danish Tax Lawyers Association, ABA, IFA and the Danish Tax Scientific Society. He is also co-author/author of several books and numerous articles in Danish and international publications. His field of specialties include M&A Real Estate, group restructurings, transfer pricing, international taxation issues, corporate consulting and partner-owned and family businesses. **Email:** aoh@lundgrens.dk.

Nils Harbeke is the Head of Pestalozzi's Tax Practice Group. He has a particular strength in cross-border tax work and tax work for international clients, both inbound and outbound. Prior to becoming a partner with Pestalozzi, Harbeke led a team of tax advisors at PwC. He has gained special experience and knowledge in tax work for regulated industries. He frequently works for leading Swiss and international financial institutions and life sciences companies. He is the co-chair of the Tax Chapter of the Zurich Bar Association and is recognized in Chambers, Legal500, Who's Who Legal and Best Lawyers in Switzerland. On behalf of the Swiss Bar Association, Nils Harbeke was called to the Swiss government's working group 'Justitia 4.0', an experts group set up to prepare a full digitization of the Swiss justice system. Nils Harbeke was awarded for outstanding academic achievements: 'Best 3' Swiss Certified Tax Experts graduates award and 'Best 10 achieving law students' in his year of graduation. **Email:** nils.harbeke@pestalozzilaw.com.

Yushi Hegawa is a Tax Partner at Nagashima Ohno & Tsunematsu. As a specialist in tax law, he has broad practical experience on all spectrum of Japanese taxation, such as tax-free reorganizations, tax-efficient mergers and acquisitions and financing/capital markets transactions, taxation of wealthy individuals, international taxation on inbound investment by foreign-owned businesses and outbound investment by Japanese businesses, and transfer pricing. He also represents many foreign-owned taxpayers before Japanese courts and tax tribunals in many tax controversy cases and has secured successful results. Mr Hegawa receives high market recognitions from media such as Chambers Asia-Pacific (Band 1), Legal 500 and Nikkei. Mr Hegawa received his LLB from the University of Tokyo and LLM from Harvard Law School, and is admitted to practice in Japan and New York. **Email**: yushi_hegawa@noandt.com.

Pál Jalsovszky is a lawyer and economist who specializes in tax planning and M&A. He founded his own law firm, Jalsovszky in 2005 and currently employs more than thirty people. The firm's client base mainly consists of multinational and domestic small and medium-sized businesses, providing corporate, real estate and commercial law consulting services in addition to tax, tax structuring and tax litigation matters. Since 2019, the firm has been dealing with litigation as well. He gained his professional experience at international law firms. Pál obtained his degree at the Law Faculty of Eötvös Loránd University Budapest in 1997. Previously, he obtained an MA at the University of Economics in Budapest, and an LLM in International Taxation at Leiden University in 2002. He regularly publishes in various professional journals. Pál is recognized as leading tax lawyer by legal professional publications, such as *Legal500* and *Chambers Europe*. He has been awarded as Tax Advisor of the Year 2012 by Best Lawyers. Since 2015, he has been a member of the Supervisory Board at the Budapest Festival Orchestra. **Email:** info@jalsovszky.com.

Louise Kotze (BCom *cum laude*, LLB *cum laude*, University of Pretoria) is an Associate in the Tax and Exchange Control practice of Cliffe Dekker Hofmeyr Inc in South Africa. **Email:** louise.kotze@cdhlegal.com.

Bradley Kruger is the Lead Partner of Ogier's Corporate team in the Cayman Islands. He advises on IPOs, SPACs and M&A transactions, start-up businesses and fund formations. He is a member of the firm's Digital, Blockchain and Fintech group, working with blockchain companies, token issuers, technology companies and cryptocurrency fund managers on a regular basis. **Email:** bradley.kruger@ogier.com.

Johan Leonard leads the Stibbe Luxembourg Tax practice. Johan specializes in national and international tax law, providing structuring and transactional advice to investment funds, private equity firms, real estate conglomerates, financial institutions, and multinational groups. He also assists clients in the context of tax litigation and has broad experience in advising clients on the tax aspects of multi-jurisdictional transactions and restructurings. Johan holds a master's degree in law from the Université catholique de Louvain and a Master of Laws (LLM) in International Taxation from New York University. **Email:** johan.leonard@stibbe.com.

Antti Lehtimaja is a Tax Partner and Head of the tax practice group at Krogerus. He completed his Master of Laws at the University of Helsinki in 1998 and was admitted to the Finnish Bar Association in 2003. Before joining Krogerus in 2010, he had previously worked for several years in the tax department of another leading Finnish law firm, completed one year of trainee service as a judge in a district court and worked at the Finnish Tax Administration as a corporate tax specialist as well as a presenting officer at the Central Tax Board, a body that gives advance tax rulings in Finland. He has written numerous taxation-related articles and lectures frequently. He is a member of both the International Bar Association (IBA) and the International Fiscal Association (IFA). **Email:** antti.lehtimaja@krogerus.com.

Ricardo Leon Santacruz is Sánchez Devanny's Managing Partner. He is a tax attorney with more than twenty-five years of experience. He has a broad-based transactional tax practice focused on Mexican inbound and outbound tax planning and transfer pricing; tax treaties, their application and limitations; anticipation of anti-deferral and anti-abuse legislation; and overall Income Tax and VAT rationalization. His expertise allows him to structure tax-efficient domestic and cross-border acquisitions, mergers, reorganizations, spin-offs, redemptions, liquidations, post-acquisition integrations and business restructurings. Ricardo's transfer pricing experience allows him to proactively advise clients on the design and implementation of intellectual property, financing, e-commerce, procurement and distribution of goods and performance of services transactions. His experience and sensitivity have afforded Ricardo prominent recognition in the market as a trusted private family advisor that can render guidance on tax optimization and multigenerational planning family governance. He is the Co-chair of the Taxes Committee of the International Bar Association. **Email:** rls@sanchezdevanny.com.

Alicia Lim was a trainee with GSM Law LLP and joined the firm as an associate after being called to the Singapore Bar in 2017. **Email**: alicia@gsmlaw.com.sg.

Wendy Lim is an Associate in MinterEllison's national tax practice, specializing in income tax, capital gains tax, international tax, and employment tax. Wendy's work spans a range of industries, including real estate, mining and financial services. In 2019, Wendy was the runner-up in the International Bar Association's Taxes Committee Scholarship on the topic of whether corporate taxes should be based on residence, source or another concept. **Email**: Wendy.Lim@minterellison.com.

Foo Yong Lim was a trainee with GSM Law LLP and joined the firm as an associate after being called to the Singapore Bar in 2019. **Email**: yonglim@gsmlaw.com.sg.

David Dingfa Liu is an International Partner of Duan & Duan. His practice is focused on cross-border mergers and acquisitions, tax, customs and commercial matters affecting cross-border investment. He also represents high net-worth individuals in their estate and tax planning matters. **Email:** david.liu@duanduan.com.

Jorge Lopez Lopez has more than ten years of legal experience. His practice is primarily focused on national and international corporate tax issues as well as wealth management issues. He has experience in a variety of tax matters, including M&A, corporate restructurings, transfer pricing and audit management and defence. His experience also comprises tax litigation and the implementation of defence strategies before tax and judicial authorities. Jorge is a candidate for a Master of Laws (LL.M.) in International Taxation from the University of Florida and has a Master of Laws in Tax from the Universidad Panamericana. **Email**: jlopez@sanchezdevanny.com.

Margriet Lukkien is a Tax Partner and advises multinationals (especially North-American-based), financial institutions and sovereign wealth funds on Dutch corporate tax and dividend tax aspects and accompanying international tax aspects. Her expertise includes international structuring/restructuring taking into account the OECD and EU developments on BEPS. Margriet is an active member of the International Tax Affairs Section of the Dutch Association of Tax Advisers (NOB). In addition she has been an active member of the International Bar Association (IBA), since she won the 2010 IBA Taxation Scholarship. Margriet has been an officer of the IBA Taxes Committee since 2013, and she has taken up the role of co-chair of the IBA Taxes Committee for 2019 and 2020. **Email:** Margriet.Lukkien@loyensloeff.com.

Suvrat Mehta is a Litigation Associate at ASC Legal, Solicitors & Advocates, New Delhi, India. Mr Mehta is the Member of Bar Council of India and has over four years of experience in the field of Advisory and Litigation in Cybercrime, Data Protection Law, AI, Blockchain, Fintech, E-commerce, Financial & EOW crimes, Privacy Law, Trade-marks, Copyright and Consumer & Electronic Evidence. He is the first Indian to have contributed in the Data Breach Investigation Report (DBIR), 2017, released by Verizon that presents findings from security incident investigations and has also showcased his research skills on various Indian Cyber Law books published. **Email:** suvrat.mehta@aseemchawla.com.

Ban Su Mei is a tax and private client lawyer in practice since 1999. After graduating from the National University of Singapore in 1998, she joined the Tax and Private Client department of a large Singapore law firm and eventually rose through the ranks to become equity partner before co-founding GSM Law LLP. **Email:** ban@gsmlaw.com.sg.

Alina Miyake is an Associate at Machado Meyer in São Paulo. Alina holds a bachelor's degree from the Faculty of Law of the University of São Paulo (USP). She is specialist in tax law, more specifically on the provision of consultancy related to direct taxes and international taxation. Her practice encompasses tax planning, merger and acquisition transactions, corporate restructurings in general, and international taxation. **Email:** amiyake@machadomeyer.com.br.

Doron Mutai leads Shibolet & Co.'s international tax practice. Doron specializes in all areas of income tax, with a focus on international tax, M&A transactions, taxation of activities in the capital markets, blockchain and smart contracts. Doron's expertise relates to all aspects of Israeli income tax, while he has extensive knowledge of other tax systems as well. His vast experience in this field allows him to advise Israeli residents on the tax aspects of their activities in Israel and abroad, and to advise non-Israeli residents on their activities and investments in Israel. In this respect, Doron consistently advises non-Israeli multinationals that acquire Israeli hi-tech companies, non-Israeli banks that operate in Israel, companies of the Oil & Gas industry that operate in Israel's Exclusive Economic Zone and hi-tech companies on their activities in Israel and abroad. **Email**: d.mutai@shibolet.com.

Vikram Nagrani is a Partner of Hassans International Law Firm, Gibraltar's leading law firm for over two decades. Vikram has a profound knowledge in a range of core topics in distributed ledger technology ('DLT'), which range from token issuances, security token offerings, and other DLT matters including licence applications under Gibraltar's DLT Providers Regulations. He has also assisted with the development of the DLT regulatory framework in Gibraltar, including being involved in the drafting of Regulatory Guidance Notes to Gibraltar's Distributed Ledger Technology Regulations and assisting with the draft regulatory framework for Tokens in Gibraltar. Vikram has co-authored two manuals on virtual currencies for the United Nations Office on Drugs and Crime, intended as training and educational material for law enforcement agencies and for regulators. He has attended the European Commission's Blockchain Observatory and Forum, and is an inaugural member of the advisor board of the European Law Observatory of New Technologies. He has also contributed to various international events and initiatives as a speaker and is considered a thought leader in the space. Vikram is also very experienced in all aspects of corporate and commercial legal work, including large M&A transactions, and a variety of financing transactions and structures. He also advises high net-worth individuals and families on their wealth and estate planning structures as a fully qualified Trusts and Estate Practitioner and is a practising notary public. **Email:** vikram.nagrani@hassans.gi.

Saam Nainifard is an Associate in the Tax Group at Aird & Berlis LLP. He advises on all aspects of income taxation, with a particular focus on corporate taxation and reorganizations, mergers & acquisitions and international tax matters. Saam is also a member of the Blockchain group at Aird & Berlis LLP. He has a wide variety of experience in representing clients in the crypto asset space, including structuring foreign investments in crypto mining operations in Canada representing investors in tax disputes with the Canada Revenue Agency involving crypto asset transactions. **Email:** snainifard@airdberlis.com

Elias Neocleous is the Managing Partner of Elias Neocleous & Co LLC and a specialist in tax law, tax planning, and advanced business structuring. He completed his studies at Oxford University in the UK and was called to the UK Bar in 1992 and to the Cyprus Bar in 1993. He has been a partner in the legacy firm since 1995. He has extensive experience in advising international organizations on tax and tax planning issues and is recognized as a leading tax advisor to high net-worth individuals. Elias is a frequent speaker at international events and has numerous publications to his credit. He is a member of several international legal and business networks including the International Tax Planning Association and is a highly rated lawyer in all key international directories. In addition, Elias is currently a board member of the Cyprus Investment Promotion Agency and the Honorary Consul of Portugal. **Email:** elias.neocleous@neo.law.

Raquel Novais is a Senior Tax Partner at Machado Meyer in São Paulo, Brazil. Raquel holds a bachelor's degree from Faculdade de Direito de Franca and a Master's in Tax Law from Pontifícia Universidade Católica de São Paulo. She has ample experience in both domestic and international taxation, as well as tax controversy. Raquel's practice is divided between tax consultancy and high-end technical tax conflicts settlement. She is frequently engaged as a speaker at tax law conferences, is a member of several international legal organizations and networks and has top rankings in several international directories. **Email:** rnovais@machadomeyer.com.br.

Raul-Angelo Papotti is a Partner and Head of the Tax and Tax Planning department at Chiomenti in Italy. He has completed his studies in Milan and Leiden and has been admitted to the Italian Bar Association. Before joining Chiomenti in 2007, Raul-Angelo has previously worked in a leading law firm in London. He advises Italian and international clients on tax law and tax planning, cross-border taxation and transfer pricing, M&A transactions, private wealth management, trusts and estate planning matters. His clients include leading global investment banks, Italian and foreign multinationals, and prominent high net-worth individuals, families and family offices. He is author of many publications on international tax matters and is a frequent speaker at domestic and international congresses. Raul-Angelo is a member of several international legal organizations and networks and he is ranked as a leading expert in international tax law in the foremost international legal guides such as Chambers, Legal 500 and Who's Who Legal. **Email:** raul.papotti@chiomenti.net.

Leandro M. Passarella is a founder of Passarella Abogados, where he leads its tax practice. He obtained his law degree in 1995 with honours and his joint LLM degree and International Tax Program certificate at Harvard Law School in 1998, where he was also recognized for his thesis on the source rule of income from derivative financial instruments. After being a member and heading tax practices of other law firms, he founded his boutique tax law firm, Passarella Abogados, in 2010. Since then, both Leandro and his firm have received awards and recognitions by international tax publications. Leandro also participates as panel co-chair or speaker regularly in conferences of his specialty, with active participation at the International Bar Association. Since 2004, he has been a Professor of 'Basic Income Taxation' for the Master's in Tax Law of Universidad Torcuato Di Tella (Buenos Aires, Argentina). **Email:** lmp@palegal.com.ar.

Pepijn Pinkse is a Tax Lawyer and Senior Associate, advising Dutch and foreign listed multinationals as well as large privately owned companies, on corporate income tax, mergers and acquisitions, reorganizations and IPOs. In the case of privately owned companies, he is also involved in advising the shareholders. He is a member of the Fintech Team and regularly advises clients across a range of financial technology fields, including payments, identity and security and data analytics. He also has a focus on initial coin offerings (ICOs), cryptocurrencies and distributed ledger technology (DLT) in the broad sense. **Email**: Pepijn.pinkse@loyensloeff.com.

Joanna Prokurat is a certified tax adviser with almost fifteen years of experience. She advises clients on Polish and international tax law, particularly on corporate income tax, VAT, international tax planning, tax optimization, and taxation of transactions. She specializes in tax advisory for new technology sector, including cryptocurrencies, gaming, fintech as well as tax optimization solutions for innovation taxpayers (including IP Box, R&D tax relief, R&D centres, etc.). Ms. Prokurat is completing her LLM in Poland. **Email**: joanna.prokurat@wardynski.com.pl.

Diogo Ortigão Ramos is a Partner and Head of Cuatrecasas' tax practice in Portugal. He focuses his practice on EU, national and international taxation, particularly regarding M&A, buyouts, corporate restructuring, financial transactions, real estate investment structuring and transactions, and tax and customs litigation. He is a member of the Portuguese Bar Association (since 1989), the Portuguese Tax Association, the International Fiscal Association, the Portuguese Association of Tax Consultants, the International Bar Association and the American Bar Association, and has been acknowledged by the Portuguese Bar as a specialist tax lawyer. Diogo is a member of the European Tax Law Group, Tax Associates Meeting and of the Europe VAT Group, the members of which are renowned European law firms, leaders in their respective jurisdictions. He is the Portuguese representative of the Foreign Lawyers Forum of the American Bar Association. Diogo obtained his law degree from Universidade Lusíada (1989) and postgraduate degree in taxation from ISG – Business & Economics School (1995). **Email:** dortigaoramos@cuatrecasas.com.

Daniel Resas is an Associated Partner at the German law firm SMP where he is heading the firm's Blockchain and Digital Assets practice group. He advises all range of clients on tokenization and blockchain-related business models, transactions and regulatory policy. In addition, he is a Senior Fellow at the Wharton School of the University of Pennsylvania and co-founder of regular international working groups on blockchain regulation/Decentralized Finance as well as blockchain governance hosted by the Wharton School. **Email:** daniel.resas@smp.law.

Michael Robinson is a Senior Associate of Ogier's Corporate team in the Cayman Islands. He specializes in Cayman corporate matters and, in particular, mergers and acquisitions, restructurings, reorganizations, public listings, and migrations. He also advises technology companies, ICO/STO/IEO issuers and cryptocurrency funds and is a member of the firm's Digital, Blockchain and Fintech group. **Email:** michael.robinson@ogier.com.

Monica Reyes Rodriguez is the Founding Partner in Reyes Abogados Asociados in Bogota, Colombia. She obtained a major in Law from Universidad del Rosario in Bogota, and specialized in taxes in the same university. She attended LLM courses in London School of Economics and obtained a diploma in International Tax Law at the Kennedy University in Switzerland. Ms. Reyes worked at the Colombian National Tax Administration and at Occidental Petroleum Inc. For ten years, she served as the Partner in charge of the fiscal practice in the Colombian law firm Brigard & Urrutia Abogados. Ms. Reyes has taught tax law master's degree courses at Universidad del Rosario and Universidad Externado de Colombia and is currently teaching in Universidad de los Andes in Bogota. She is part of the Editorial Committee of the Magazine on Taxes published by Legis S.A. She was president of the Colombian Chapter of the International Fiscal Association and is a member of the Colombian Tax Law Institute and of the Tax Sections in the American Bar Association and the International Bar Association. **Email:** mreyes@reyesaa.com.

Daria E. Romanova specializes in Tax Law, currency regulations, complex evaluation of tax risks and consulting in tax planning. Daria has experience in legal consulting since 2009. Before joining AT Lawyers, she had been working with Russian law firm 'FDP United Consultants' where she specialized in legal support of budget investments in construction and development, VAT taxation, other complex tax issues and representation of clients in disputes with tax authorities. Daria holds a master's degree (LLM in Maritime Law) awarded by the Oslo University, Norway. She has also graduated with honours from the Moscow State University. **Email:** romanova@atlawyers.com.

João Pedro Russo has been at Cuatrecasas since 2019, working in this firm's tax practice. He focuses his practice on EU, national and international taxation, particularly regarding M&A, buyouts, corporate restructuring, financial transactions and transfer pricing. João obtained his law degree and postgraduate degree in Tax Law and Regulation of Financial Markets from Universidade de Lisboa (2013). **Email:** joao.russo@cuatrecasas.com.

Matthieu Sabonnadiere has been a Senior Associate with the international tax department of CMS Francis Lefebvre Avocats since 2019. He assists mainly MNEs on cross-border transactions, financing, restructuring and tax litigation. Before joining the firm, he practised during three years with Baker McKenzie Paris. He holds an LLM in International Taxation (class 2015) from New York University and Master's in Corporate Taxation (class 2013) from Université Paris Dauphine. **Email:** matthieu.sabonnadiere@cms-avocats.com.

Gurbachan Singh is regarded as one of Singapore's leading tax lawyers, who began his career as a Legal Officer with the Inland Revenue Authority of Singapore almost forty years ago. He was a Judicial Officer at the Subordinate Courts prior to joining private practice, and was Managing Partner of one of the largest firms in Singapore prior to founding GSM Law LLP. **Email:** guru@gsmlaw.com.sg.

Theodoros Skouzos, born in 1975, is a practising advocate, registered in the Athens Bar Association, Greece and Managing Partner of the law firm Iason Skouzos & Partners. He has published several articles in Greek and English about tax topics, and has participated in tax law panels at the IBA annual conference and other international conferences. He is a member of the International Tax Specialist Group (www.itsgnetwork.com) and chairman of the Tax Committee of the Hellenic Association of Law Firms. He is ranked as a leading Greek tax law practitioner in international directories. He graduated from the University of Northumbria at Newcastle in 1998 with an LLB and a *License en droit* from the *Universite d' Orleans* in France, having completed the programme 'LLB exempting with French Law'. In 1999 Theodoros was awarded the LLM in European Union Business Law by the University of Amsterdam. **Email:** tskouzos@taxlaw.gr.

Tapasi Sharma is a Research Associate at ASC Legal Solicitors & Advocates, New Delhi, India. Miss Sharma holds a merit degree in LLM in International Commercial Law from London, United Kingdom, and she is also a recipient of various accolades during her Masters in London. Miss Sharma is Member of Bar Council of India and has three years of post-qualification experience in both UK and India in the field of investigation, GDPR, research, commercial and taxation matters. **Email:** tapasi.sharma@aseemchawla.com.

Kevin Smith is a Partner in the Tax Practice of Matheson and is also a member of the Structured Finance and Derivatives Group. Kevin advises financial institutions, investment banks, investment managers and institutional investors on all tax aspects of financial services in Ireland, including securities transactions, debt capital markets, cross-border financing and derivative transactions. Kevin also advises many of the world's largest aircraft leasing companies on tax aspects of carrying on aircraft leasing business in or from Ireland. **Email:** kevin.smith@matheson.com.

Nicholas Warren has a strong professional background with over sixteen years of work experience which complement his qualifications which include a Masters in Strategic Planning, a Bachelor of Commerce (B.Com.) Honours focused in Banking & Finance from the University of Malta, ACCA qualified as well as Certificates in Islamic Finance. Throughout his career he has focused his attention predominantly towards providing counsel, guidance and consultancy to international clients on the various possibilities presented by Malta as a Financial Services Centre. He commenced his passion for financial services as a manager with the Malta Financial Services Authority, focusing on Professional Investor Funds, UCITS Schemes and Investment Services Licence Holders (MiFID) and has also assumed management positions at two large fund management companies. He expanded his horizons in the fields of banking, payment services and financial institutions, capital markets as well as blockchain. **Email:** nicholas@fjvassallo.com.

Robert Yunan is a Special Counsel in MinterEllison's national tax practice, specializing in income tax matters. He acts for taxpayer clients of all sizes and is adept at advising on transactions across all stages of the business life cycle, from establishment, restructuring and expansion to operation and exit. He has acted extensively for inbound and outbound medium-sized to large corporate entities, government and major international funds. His work involves assisting with capital gains tax, tax consolidation, international tax (including funding and repatriation) and executive remuneration. Yunan is also a qualified chartered accountant. **Email:** Robert.Yunan@minterellison.com

Summary of Contents

Overview

1. Country Guides
   1.1 [Country Name]
      1.1.1 Applicable Tax Law, Guidance, and Case Law
         (a) Which laws, regulations, and other administrative guidance exist dealing with crypto assets?
         (b) Which court cases exist dealing with crypto assets?
      1.1.2 Income and Capital Gains Taxes
         (a) How are crypto assets classified for income and capital gains tax purposes?
         (b) What are the income/capital gains tax consequences of selling crypto assets against fiat currency?
         (c) What are the income/capital gains tax consequences of exchanging crypto assets against other crypto assets?
         (d) If a distinction is made between business assets and non-business assets, when does trading in crypto assets lead to a trade or business?
         (e) What are the income/capital gains tax consequences for an employee receiving wages or salaries in crypto assets?
         (f) What are the income/capital gains tax consequences for a merchant receiving payment in crypto assets?
         (g) What are the income/capital gains tax consequences of a loss of crypto assets?
         (h) What are the income/capital gains tax consequences of a loss in value of crypto assets?
         (i) What are the income/capital gains tax consequences of forks of crypto assets?
         (j) What are the income/capital gains tax consequences of airdrops of crypto assets and are the tax consequences different if the airdropped tokens are unwanted?

- (k) What are the income/capital gains tax consequences of (solo, pool, and cloud) mining?
- (l) What are the income/capital gains tax consequences of staking crypto assets?
- (m) What are the income/capital gains tax consequences of an indirect investment in crypto assets?
- (n) How is income from crypto assets to be treated under double tax treaty law?
- (o) What are the income/capital gains tax consequences of selling crypto assets in an ICO/STO/IEO?

1.1.3 Other Taxes

- (a) What are the value added tax/sales tax consequences of selling crypto assets?
- (b) Are payments in crypto assets subject to withholding taxes?
- (c) Does payment of compensation in crypto assets give rise to payroll tax consequences?
- (d) Do transactions with crypto assets trigger any transfer taxes?
- (e) Are firms operating in the crypto space subject to digital service taxes?
- (f) Are crypto assets subject to gift, inheritance, estate, or wealth taxes?
- (g) Are crypto assets subject to exit tax?
- (h) Can mining trigger gambling tax?

1.1.4 Compliance and Documentation Obligations

- (a) What documentation requirements exist for taxpayers regarding crypto assets and are there best practices in recordkeeping to support representations made in tax returns?
- (b) What is the evidentiary burden of supporting tax positions when a digital wallet address is lost or shared with other persons?
- (c) Are crypto asset exchanges and wallet providers subject to reporting obligations?
- (d) Are taxpayers holding crypto assets subject to reporting obligations apart from the filing of income tax/capital gains tax returns?
- (e) Are crypto asset exchanges and wallet providers subject to CRS/FATCA reporting?

1.1.5 Civil and Criminal Tax Enforcement

- (a) What powers do the tax authorities have to compel the disclosure of information by third parties, such as exchanges or wallet providers, and have these been used in the past?
- (b) What measures have the tax authorities undertaken in the past to ensure crypto tax compliance?
- (c) Are the tax authorities cooperating with tax authorities in other jurisdictions on enforcement?

List of Abbreviations

CbC MCAA	Multilateral Competent Authority Agreement on the Exchange of Country-by-Country Reports
CMAA	Convention on Mutual Administrative Assistance in Tax Matters
CRS MCAA	Multilateral Competent Authority Agreement on Automatic Exchange of Financial Account Information
CRS	Common Reporting Standard
FATCA	Foreign Account Tax Compliance Act
FIFO	First-In-First-Out
GST	Goods and Services Tax
ICO	Initial Coin Offering
IEO	Initial Exchange Offering
LIFO	Last-In-First-Out
OECD	Organisation for Economic Co-operation and Development
STO	Securities Token Offering
VAT	Value Added Tax

Introduction*

Jack Bernstein, Marta Cura, André Geest, Saam Nainifard, Daniel Resas, Stefan Richter, Niklas Schmidt & Lisa Zarlenga

This book contains guides for the taxation of crypto assets in thirty-nine separate countries. The organization of each guide is the same so that users can easily locate the information they seek. The authors anticipate three main types of users of this book: (1) tax advisors who may not be well versed in the technical aspects of crypto assets; (2) crypto asset enthusiasts who may not be well versed in tax laws; and (3) tax advisors who are also crypto asset enthusiasts. Sections 1 and 2 of this Introduction present certain concepts that will be necessary to fully understand the country guides.

For users in the first category, section 1 introduces the concept of cryptocurrency and crypto assets, including a discussion of blockchain technology and smart contracts, how crypto assets are generally classified for tax, accounting, and other regulatory purposes, and specialized transactions involving crypto assets.

For users in the second category, section 2 introduces certain general tax concepts that are addressed in the country guides, including the computation of gain or loss, different types of taxes, tax reporting requirements, and tools for enforcement of tax laws.

For users in the third category who are interested in a jurisdiction-by-jurisdiction analysis, feel free to skip ahead to the country guides. All information provided there is in general current as of 1 October 2020.

* Section 1.1 of the Introduction was provided by Niklas Schmidt, sections 1.2.1, 1.2.2, and 1.3 by Daniel Resas, André Geest and Marta Cura, sections 1.2.3 and 1.2.4 by Stefan Richter, and section 2 by Jack Bernstein, Lisa Zarlenga, and Saam Nainifard.

1. INTRODUCTION OF CRYPTO ASSETS

1.1 From Bitcoin to Crypto Assets

1.1.1 History of Bitcoin

Bitcoin was invented by the pseudonymous Satoshi Nakamoto and presented on an internet mailing list in October 2008. The nine-page paper *Bitcoin: A Peer-to-Peer Electronic Cash System* describes the theoretical foundations of this electronic money. Not everything in the paper is completely new; there are numerous previously existing ideas and concepts on which bitcoin was based. It is significant that Satoshi Nakamoto's paper was presented in Autumn 2008, i.e., at the height of the global banking and financial crisis. After the Lehman Brothers bankruptcy, general confidence in banks was at a low point. Bitcoin can be seen as a reaction to a crisis caused by banks, insofar as it is a new monetary system that makes intermediaries such as banks superfluous. In the cryptography community, Satoshi Nakamoto's theoretical concept was seen as a breakthrough. Over the next few months, he and other people programmed the first version of the bitcoin software together. This was finally switched on in January 2009. At that point in time, bitcoin was an experiment, known only to a few people, but it was to become more and more popular over time.

Nobody knows who the person is behind the pseudonym. Satoshi Nakamoto only communicated by electronic means. Nobody has ever met him personally or spoken to him on the phone. While many attempts have been made, Satoshi Nakamoto has not yet been identified. There is plenty of speculation as to who Satoshi Nakamoto could be, as well as a few conspiracy theories. Newsweek magazine, for example, in 2014 dug out an engineer in California by the name of Dorian Satoshi Nakamoto, who ultimately denied being the founder of bitcoin. A few members of the cryptography community are often listed as possible founders of bitcoin, such as Nick Szabo (whose initials correspond to those of Satoshi Nakamoto) or Hal Finney (who received the first bitcoin payment from Satoshi Nakamoto). The Australian Craig Wright has outed himself as Satoshi Nakamoto, but without providing any credible evidence, which has earned him the nickname 'Faketoshi'. There is also a theory that Satoshi Nakamoto is an acronym derived from the names Samsung, Toshiba, Nakamichi, and Motorola; according to this theory, there is not an individual behind the pseudonym, but rather a consortium of companies. Due to the publication of an earlier paper by three United States ('US') National Security Agency cryptographers on electronic money, some people believe that this agency developed bitcoin. Most recently, the eccentric American programmer and businessman John McAfee claimed to know the founder of bitcoin and to reveal his identity (alas, this never happened). It will probably not be possible to find out who Satoshi Nakamoto really is. At any rate, if the inventor of bitcoin is an individual (rather than a group of people), then he must be an extremely talented person with outstanding expertise in the areas of cryptography, computer science and economics.

The most important milestones in the early years of bitcoin, when this new money was only known to, and used by, a very small group of cryptography experts, were as follows: In mid-2010, Satoshi Nakamoto withdrew from the project and handed over the website and control of the bitcoin source code to several prominent members of the bitcoin community, who from then on continued the development of bitcoin. In May 2010, the first documented purchase took place in which bitcoins were used as a means of payment (two pizzas for 10,000 bitcoins). In February 2011, the bitcoin/US Dollar exchange rate reached parity. In June 2011, the whistleblowing platform WikiLeaks was boycotted by payment systems such as VISA and PayPal (apparently at the instigation of the US Government) and announced its intention to accept donations in the form of bitcoins. In October 2013, the operator of an illegal marketplace called 'Silk Road' (which offered drugs and other illegal goods and services, for payment in bitcoins) was arrested, with the US Federal Bureau of Investigation managing to secure around 144,000 bitcoins, which were later sold in an auction. In February 2014, Mt. Gox, the largest bitcoin exchange at the time through which around 70% of all bitcoin trading was processed, filed for bankruptcy in Tokyo, Japan, since approximately 850,000 bitcoins had apparently been lost. It was not until 2017 that bitcoin finally arrived in the mainstream, with the price of one bitcoin reaching USD 20,000 at the end of the year. In February 2018, the price quickly fell back to around USD 7,000. In August 2020, bitcoin has still not reached its all-time high, but is back at USD 12,000.

1.1.2 Blockchains

Satoshi Nakamoto not only invented bitcoin, but also its underlying transactional database system, the blockchain. Blockchain technology makes uses of cryptography, game theory, and peer-to-peer networks. A blockchain is a digital ledger of transactions that is distributed across a network of computers, rather than being maintained by a single, centralized authority. The participants at each node of the network can access an identical copy of the ledger, and any changes or additions made to the ledger are reflected and copied to all nodes. As a result, there is no single point of failure (e.g., due to attacks from hackers, technical problems or the intervention of a regulator). Transactions can be made without the need for intermediaries or third-party administrators. They are validated, lumped together in 'blocks' and added to an already existing 'chain', giving rise to the name 'blockchain'. Once a transaction has been added to the blockchain, it generally cannot be altered or removed.

In simplified terms, one can imagine the relationship between bitcoin and blockchain as follows: A blockchain is like an operating system (e.g., Windows). Bitcoin is like a program (e.g., Word, Excel, or Powerpoint) that runs on it. Thus, a blockchain cannot only be used for money; any type of transaction can be recorded on a blockchain, e.g., transactions relating to tangible assets (such as cars, real estate, or diamonds) or intangible assets (such as shares, receivables, patents, documents, voting rights, or identities). The development of blockchain technology and blockchain-based applications has begun to revolutionize the way transactions are done in numerous industries, from new ways to process financial transactions, to new ways to manage supply chains, to new ways to trade equity and debt. Sometimes the terms 'blockchain technology' and 'distributed ledger technology' ('DLT') are used interchangeably. This is technically speaking not totally correct, since blockchains are just one type of DLT.

Following is a summary of how blockchain technology works, using bitcoin as an example.

- When a transaction (i.e., the sending of bitcoins from one address to another address) is initiated by a user, the software on the user's smartphone or computer connects to one of the nodes on bitcoin's peer-to-peer network.
- This node initially checks whether this amount has already been spent in the past and whether the user is authorized to spend the bitcoins by using the correct private key.
- If the transaction is legitimate from these two points of view, it is forwarded to the other nodes connected to that node, which in turn proceed in the same way. Ultimately, all nodes in the network will learn about this transaction and will put it into a pool of pending transactions (i.e., the memory pool, a kind of waiting room for transactions).
- Approximately every ten minutes (i.e., the block time) special nodes (i.e., miners) pick transactions from the memory pool to fill a so-called candidate block of transactions, which will possibly be appended to the existing blockchain. A block has a capacity of 1 megabyte, and since the memory pool will normally be a lot larger, the candidate blocks prepared by miners contain a selection of transactions from the memory pool. Also, all candidate blocks prepared by the miners will slightly differ. Every candidate block contains a cryptographic summary (i.e., hash) of the previous block, thus linking to the previous block and creating a chain.
- At the end of the day, only one of these prepared candidate blocks will actually be added to the blockchain. In order for the candidate block of a certain miner to be used, this miner must be the first one to solve a computationally intensive mathematical puzzle. The puzzle can only be solved by continuous trial and error. The more computing power a miner has at his disposal, the greater his chances to win. As soon as a miner has solved his puzzle, he quickly sends his candidate block to the other miners, who verify the correctness of the candidate block and the puzzle.
- If this is the case, each node attaches the candidate block of the successful miner to his copy of the blockchain. It takes a few seconds until the new block has arrived in the whole network and the blockchain has become one block longer.
- At this moment all unsuccessful miners discard their unfinished candidate blocks. Then the game starts all over again: The miners try to extend the blockchain by attaching a new block to the last block in the blockchain.
- A transaction, which is in the memory pool, is an unconfirmed transaction. Only when it has been included in a block that has been added to the blockchain, is it called a confirmed transaction, meaning that the transaction is completed and that the recipient may dispose of the bitcoins credited to his

address. After six confirmations, i.e., if five more blocks have been added to the blockchain after the block containing the transaction, a transaction is considered entirely irreversible.
- The miner who successfully mined a block receives a remuneration in newly created bitcoins (currently 6.25 bitcoins per block) and any transaction fees from the transactions contained in the block. This remuneration solves two fundamental problems: First, the miners are incentivized to keep the blockchain. Second, because they typically sell a portion of the bitcoins received (e.g., to pay their electricity bills), they cannot hoard them but rather regularly have to bring them into circulation.
- If a miner creates a block with incorrect transactions, he does not receive any remuneration and suffers a loss due to the electricity costs caused by having to maintain the mining operation. From a game theory point of view, it therefore makes no sense to cheat as a miner. The cost-intensive use of work creates an incentive to include only correct entries in the blockchain.

1.1.3 Cryptocurrencies

Bitcoin is an open source and has spawned numerous direct competitors (e.g., Bitcoin Cash, Litecoin, Dash, and Monero). These are called cryptocurrencies, that aspire to fulfil the functions of money (medium of exchange, store of value and unit of account), typically run on their own blockchain, and have certain features that distinguish them from conventional ('fiat') money:

- Fiat money is issued centrally by a central bank. Cryptocurrencies are issued by a decentralized network of computers.
- Fiat money has a money supply based on decisions by humans. Cryptocurrency supply is based on an algorithm. For example, one can know how many bitcoins will be in circulation, e.g., in a month, a year or in a decade from now.
- Fiat money can be multiplied at will, has no upper limit and consequently may one day be worthless. Certain cryptocurrencies have a limited supply. For example, there will ever only be 21 million bitcoins, of which 18.5 million have been created as of August 2020.
- Fiat money can only be transferred in an electronic manner by using intermediaries (e.g., banks, credit card companies, PayPal, Apple). With cryptocurrency, there are no intermediaries; everyone is his or her own bank and payments are made directly from one user to another user.
- Since fiat money is transferred electronically through intermediaries, a transaction may be prevented by an intermediary, often for legal reasons (e.g., the application of money laundering regulations, sanctions or restrictions on capital movements). Since cryptocurrencies are transferred without using intermediaries, nobody can prevent a transaction from occurring, so that this payment system is censorship-resistant.

- Opening a bank account for fiat money is a lengthy process, due to, among other things, the need to comply with legal provisions on money laundering and taxation. In contrast, with cryptocurrency, the generation of an address (which is similar to a bank account number) and the corresponding private key (which is similar to a PIN code securing the bank account) is a mathematical operation, which does not require the consent of a third party.
- With fiat money, bank balances can be lost through seizure, expropriation or insolvency of the bank. Cryptocurrencies, on the other hand, are not claims against an intermediary and as long as the private key is not disclosed, the cryptocurrency cannot be accessed (this is different when a user decides to entrust an exchange to hold the cryptocurrency).
- With fiat money, transfers abroad are slower and more expensive than domestic transfers. Cryptocurrencies are electronic money systems that know no national boundaries; there is no distinction between domestic and foreign addresses.
- In the case of fiat money, remittances are often reversible. With cryptocurrencies, on the other hand, transactions are mostly irreversible.
- With fiat money, there is no database that tracks the fate of every single bill and coin. On the other hand, transactions with cryptocurrencies are recorded in a public ledger (the blockchain).
- Fiat money is divisible to two decimal places (to hundredths). In contrast, bitcoins are divisible to eight decimal places (to hundred millionths), with the smallest unit being called a 'Satoshi' or a 'Sat' in honour of the pseudonymous founder.
- The security of fiat currencies is maintained by central banks, the police, the public prosecutor's office, courts, safes, money transporters, and specialized printing presses. In contrast, the security of cryptocurrencies is purely based on mathematics (cryptography).

1.1.4 Smart Contracts and Tokens

Smart contracts were first made possible on the Ethereum blockchain. Ethereum was developed in 2014 by Vitalik Buterin, a Russian-Canadian programmer and co-founder of 'Bitcoin Magazine', who was frustrated by the limited programmability of bitcoin (a feature, not a bug in the view of hard-core bitcoiners). He wanted an open blockchain platform, where all types of assets (so-called tokens) could be created and where all sorts of programming logic could be implemented. Ethereum is a platform based on bitcoin, but instead of storing money on the blockchain, programs (i.e., smart contracts) can be stored there. In order to run a smart contract on this infrastructure, a user has to pay for this service, with the native currency of Ethereum being called ether.

The smart contracts that are stored on the Ethereum blockchain cannot be changed, run fully automatically (i.e., without any possibility of interference by the parties themselves or by third parties), can dispose of crypto assets stored on the blockchain and contain 'if-this-then-that' instructions. In the simplest case, Party A transfers crypto assets to a smart contract to be paid out to Party B if a condition defined in advance is met.

There are numerous examples of the use of smart contracts:

- A smart contract could be used to replicate a trust (or a foundation). Instead of transferring assets to a trustee, which manages these and pays out monthly amounts to certain beneficiaries, a smart contract could be set up and crypto assets sent to its address. The smart contract would then make monthly payments to the beneficiaries' addresses. The beneficiaries would thus no longer be dependent on the trustee fulfilling his obligations.
- The payment of taxes could be automated by smart contracts. If a merchant has an incoming payment in crypto assets at a defined address, the corresponding amount of value added tax ('VAT') or sales tax contained therein could be deducted and sent to the address of the tax office.
- A smart contract could be used as a substitute for a will. It could be provided that if a certain person dies, crypto assets stored at an address (including for example tokens on a blockchain representing real estate held by the deceased) will be automatically transferred to an heir. In a similar vein, life insurance proceeds could be paid out automatically upon proof of death via smart contract.
- Smart contracts could also be used to replicate financial transactions, such as lending and borrowing, insurance and derivatives. This is commonly referred to as decentralized finance ('DeFi').

Smart contracts have several advantages. First, they make intermediaries (such as escrow agents) obsolete, which reduces costs and complexity. Second, legal disputes can be avoided by completely excluding the possibility of non-performance by a party of its obligations. Finally, obligations of the parties are immediately fulfilled as soon as the relevant requirements are met, which means that transactions can be processed more quickly.

However, there are also some disadvantages of smart contracts. First, just as contracts written by humans can be inaccurate or incomplete, this is of course also the case with computer programs written by humans. Second, most people can understand the contents of a contract without the help of a lawyer; in contrast, very few people can understand a computer program without the assistance of a programmer. Third, conventional contracts often contain vague terms such as 'force majeure', 'within a reasonable period of time', 'usual', 'necessary' or 'reasonable', which help to react flexibly to unforeseeable events; with smart contracts, on the other hand, it is not possible to use vague language. In addition, often data from the real world (e.g., how high was the temperature on a certain day or which team won a football match) must be integrated into a smart contract. Finally, the conclusion of contracts can typically be challenged on the grounds of bad faith, error, or compulsion; contesting smart contracts on these grounds is in itself contrary to the concept of freedom from interference and is thus not possible.

A token contract is a special type of smart contract that describes how a token (a type of digital good on the Ethereum platform) is generated, how it can be transferred from one address to another, whether it is divisible, whether it is fungible, etc. Every token contract is a smart contract, but not every smart contract is also a token contract. There are certain standards for token contracts, such as ERC-20. These are used to standardize tokens and make them easier to administer, e.g., through exchanges.

As discussed at a later point, tokens can have many uses. The term 'tokenization' refers to real goods (such as real estate, cars, gold bars, works of art, intellectual property rights, receivables, shares or participation rights) being represented by asset-backed tokens recorded on a blockchain. The token is thus the digital representation of the real good. There are certain advantages of the token compared to the real good:

- It is easier and faster to transfer the token than the underlying good (e.g., sending a gold bar is complicated and slow).
- It is easier to store the token than the good (e.g., storing uranium cannot be done by anybody).
- It is possible to hold only a fraction of the underlying good with the token (e.g., it is not possible to break a work of art into parts).
- The token may have more liquidity than the underlying good (e.g., a share of an intellectual property right is not very liquid).
- Holding the token on a public blockchain gives a higher transparency than holding the underlying good (e.g., there is no public register of the owner of a claim).

1.1.5 Crypto Assets

In the following, we will be using the term 'crypto asset' for all digital assets which are based on: (1) a computer program containing the rules regarding the generation and transfer of this asset; (2) a cryptographically secured blockchain database that contains all transactions with units of this asset; and (3) an open and decentralized network that operates the database and periodically supplements it according to the rules of the computer program. This definition encompasses both coins (i.e., crypto assets running on their own blockchain, such as Bitcoin and most other cryptocurrencies) and tokens (crypto assets not running on their own blockchain, such as those assets created on Ethereum).

1.2 Regulation of Crypto Markets and Participants

1.2.1 Market View

Conventional financial systems are increasingly under pressure from various directions, while Blockchain-based crypto assets have been gaining traction since 2014. The markets for crypto assets are moving at a rapid pace though. What started with a digital currency used by a fringe set of the population developed into a sometimes overhyped means for early stage funding of decentralized protocols (so-called Initial Coin Offerings, or 'ICOs'), and nowadays has turned into so-called DeFi with products representing a completely interoperable stack of financial products. Decentralized exchanges, DLT-based payment systems, stablecoins, crypto-lending, derivatives platforms, and tokenization solutions seek to reinvent the financial ecosystem on a distributed blockchain foundation. These systems, alone and in combination, raise a number of challenges not only for financial regulators and policy makers, but also for tax authorities and law-makers of tax-relevant rules.

Crypto and DeFi products and their underlying business models are highly flexible by design and consist of a multilayer architecture, with each layer serving different purposes. The common characteristics of these novel products usually are: (1) built upon public permissionless protocols; (2) decentralized trust-minimized operation; (3) programmability; and (4) service composability. The ecosystem includes both assets (tokens) and decentralized applications ('DApps') operating on-chain, as well as organizations and services constituted off-chain. Some have similar characteristics and a corresponding business model in the conventional finance space and some are potentially completely new, such as flash loans.[1]

The next Blockchain-based innovation can already be seen on the horizon. Although private forms of money have been around for quite some time, new DLT-based payment systems and stablecoin initiatives backed by large firms with access to huge networks of users pushed the discussions on shaping the future of money and payment to a new level. Concepts of decentralized payment systems are increasingly maturing, including stablecoins, tokenized fiat, and central bank digital currencies ('CBDCs'). It is very likely to see DLT-based payment solutions scaling to new levels of adoption in areas beyond what has been considered the 'crypto space' so far. Computable means of payment are considered to be the missing part in on-chain delivery versus payment transactions, essential to leverage the full potential of tokenized equity and debt products.

As a consequence of this development, traditional intermediaries such as central banks and commercial banks are looking to redefine their roles. Central banks around the world actively research on CBDCs challenging traditional concepts such as the two-tier banking system or the dollar as the world's prime reserve currency. In addition, commercial banks and other traditional financial institutions have started to explore options to engage in these novel alternative asset markets, gaining their customers' access to crypto assets in its various forms.

1. For more information on flash loans, *see Qin/Zhou/Livshits/Gervais*, Attacking the DeFi Ecosystem with Flash Loans for Fun and Profit (2020), available at https://arxiv.org/pdf/2003.03810; *Boado*, Aave Protocol Whitepaper v1.0. (2020), 15, available at https://github.com/aave/aave-protocol/blob/master/docs/Aave_Protocol_Whitepaper_v1_0.pdf; *Gudgeon/Perez/Harz et al.*, The Decentralized Financial Crisis: Attacking DeFi (2020), 9, available at https://arxiv.org/pdf/2002.08099.pdf.

1.2.2 *Regulatory Classification*

(a) General

The regulatory classification is the starting point for the application of every regulatory regime. Several terms have arisen in practice and in legal literature for the classification of blockchain-based representations of rights or values, such as crypto assets, virtual currencies, crypto tokens and digital assets, to name a few.[2] Understood in their broadest sense, crypto assets are digital representations of any right or value on a blockchain-based ledger. Similar to a book-entry system, the allocation of rights and values does not require a physical document in the form of a certificate, but instead the allocation of rights or values is registered by entries on a decentralized ledger.

As the underlying smart contracts govern the issuance and transfer of crypto assets and are freely programmable, crypto assets demonstrate a high degree of flexibility as to their possible structure and design.[3] The rights or values represented by crypto assets can therefore vary immensely. There is neither one single type nor a clear set of categories of crypto assets, instead they are characterized by their broad spectrum of possible features, serving different functions. For example, they can be assigned economic, voting, participation, consumptive, utilization rights or may have no tangible value except for the expectation that they may serve as a means of exchange or payment.[4]

To understand and classify crypto assets accordingly, a two-fold approach has emerged: a classification from (1) a commercial perspective and (2) a regulatory perspective. From a commercial perspective, crypto assets are evaluated based on their economic functionality, examining the purpose they serve between participants and the network. In contrast, the regulatory perspective is determined by the legal assessment of their functionality and the significance of crypto assets in a supervisory law context. Despite the commercial classification (to a certain extent) pre-determining the regulatory one, these two perspectives may be very distinct.[5]

---

2. *Blandin/Cloots/Hussain/Rauchs et al.*, Global Cryptoasset Regulatory Landscape Study, University of Cambridge Faculty of Law Research Paper No. 23/2019 (2019), 35 et seq., available at https://www.jbs.cam.ac.uk/wp-content/uploads/2020/08/2019-04-ccaf-global-cryptoasset-regulatory-landscape-study.pdf
3. *Fußwinkel/Kreiterling*, Blockchain Technology – Thoughts on Regulation, BaFin Perspectives 1/2018 (2018), 54, available at https://www.bafin.de/SharedDocs/Downloads/EN/BaFinPerspektiven/2018/bp_18-1_digitalisierung_en.html.
4. *Rohr/Wright*, Blockchain-Based Token Sales, Initial Coin Offerings, and the Democratization of Public Capital Markets, Hastings Law Journal (Feb. 2019), Volume 70, Issue 2, 463, 468; *ESMA*, ESMA Advice on Initial Coin Offerings and Crypto-Assets (9 Jan. 2019), 8, available at https://www.esma.europa.eu/sites/default/files/library/esma50-157-1391_crypto_advice.pdf.
5. Cf. *Gurrea-Martínez/Léon*, The Law and Finance of Initial Coin Offerings, in Brummer, Cryptoassets: Legal, Regulatory and Monetary Perspectives (2019), 120.

(b) *Commercial Classification*

Crypto asset classifications have evolved in practice over time and, as such, a single official or harmonized taxonomy for crypto assets does not exist. However, there is a high degree of agreement as to the nomenclature used in international practice. Even some regulatory authorities around the world have adopted a taxonomy based on commercial aspects to understand and compare the features, nature, and economic function of crypto assets. Although across jurisdictions and supervisory authorities, the terms used for these categories can differ slightly,[6] crypto assets can usually be sorted into the following three categories:

(1) **Cryptocurrencies (payment or currency tokens)** are crypto assets that are intended to be used, now or in the future, as a means of payment for acquiring goods or services or as a means of money or value transfer external to the blockchain ecosystem that they are built on.[7] They tend not to have any intrinsic value.[8] Cryptocurrencies do not give rise to any claims on the issuer and only develop the necessary functionality and become accepted as a means of payment over a period of time.[9] Cryptocurrencies are not considered legal tender and due to their high volatility do not necessarily serve the functions of money from an economic standpoint, lacking the function of unit of account and storage of value.[10]

(2) **Security tokens (equity, debt, or asset-backed tokens)** are crypto assets that resemble financial instruments. Security tokens can represent, for example, membership rights, a share in future company earnings, future cash flows or interest earnings. In terms of their economic function, these crypto assets are analogous to equities, bonds, or derivatives. Crypto assets that enable underlying physical assets to be traded on the blockchain also fall within this category.[11]

---

6. *Blandin/Cloots/Hussain/Rauchs et al.*, Global Cryptoasset Regulatory Landscape Study (2019), 37 et seq., available at https://www.jbs.cam.ac.uk/fileadmin/user_upload/research/centres/alternative-finance/downloads/2019-04-ccaf-global-cryptoasset-regulatory-landscape-study.pdf.
7. *ESMA*, Advice on Initial Coin Offerings and Crypto Assets (9 Jan. 2019), 43, available at https://www.esma.europa.eu/sites/default/files/library/esma50-157-1391_crypto_advice.pdf.
8. *Fußwinkel/Kreiterling*, Blockchain Technology – Thoughts on Regulation, BaFin Perspectives 1/2018 (2018), 57, available at https://www.bafin.de/SharedDocs/Downloads/EN/BaFinPerspektiven/2018/bp_18-1_digitalisierung_en.html.
9. *FINMA*, Guidelines for enquiries regarding the regulatory framework for initial coin offerings (ICOs) (16 Feb. 2018), 3, available at https://www.finma.ch/en/news/2018/02/20180216-mm-ico-wegleitung/.
10. From an economic standpoint money serves three purposes: it functions as a medium of exchange, a unit of account, and a store of value. Bitcoin arguably satisfies the first criterion, because a growing number of network participants accept it as payment. But it performs poorly as a unit of account and a store of value., cf. *Yermack*, Bitcoin Lacks the Properties of a Real Currency, MIT Technology Review (18 Feb. 2014), available at https://www.technologyreview.com/2014/02/18/173917/bitcoin-lacks-the-properties-of-a-real-currency/.
11. *FINMA*, Guidelines for enquiries regarding the regulatory framework for initial coin offerings (ICOs) (16 Feb. 2018), 3, available at https://www.finma.ch/en/news/2018/02/20180216-mm-ico-wegleitung/.

(3) **Utility tokens** are crypto assets that provide some 'utility' or consumption rights.[12] They can only be used in the issuer's network or platform to buy products or give digital access to an application or service.[13] Utility tokens come in various structures and designs, but can best be described as digital vouchers.

As crypto assets are freely programmable and therefore flexible by design, they can embody a combination of the aforementioned features, e.g., a crypto asset can bear coinciding exchange and investment characteristics, in which case it is referred to as a **hybrid token**.[14] An archetype of hybrid tokens are so-called stablecoins, which aim to eliminate the high volatility of crypto assets by pegging their value to a national currency 1:1 and thus removing the speculative aspect.[15] Stablecoins can be designed to achieve parity in many different ways.[16] As such they are a subset of asset-backed tokens, as they derive their value from an underlying asset, and classify as cryptocurrencies as they serve as a means of payment.

As the functionality of a crypto asset may gradually change over its lifecycle, so may the commercial classification over time. For this reason, a crypto asset's classification is always contingent upon the time of assessment. The same can be true for the regulatory classification. Given the dynamic evolvement of a crypto asset's economic functionality (e.g., shifting from a capital raising mechanism to a means of payment or utility), depending on the jurisdiction, it is possible that also a crypto asset's regulatory

12. *ESMA*, ESMA Advice on Initial Coin Offerings and Crypto Assets (9 Jan. 2019), 8, available at https://www.esma.europa.eu/sites/default/files/library/esma50-157-1391_crypto_advice.pdf; *FINMA*, Guidelines for enquiries regarding the regulatory framework for initial coin offerings (ICOs) (16 Feb. 2018), 3, available at https://www.finma.ch/en/news/2018/02/20180216-mm-ico-wegleitung/.
13. *Fußwinkel/Kreiterling*, Blockchain Technology – Thoughts on Regulation, BaFin Perspectives 1/2018 (2018), 57, available at https://www.bafin.de/SharedDocs/Downloads/EN/BaFinPerspektiven/2018/bp_18-1_digitalisierung_en.html; *FINMA*, Guidelines for enquiries regarding the regulatory framework for initial coin offerings (ICOs) (16 Feb. 2018), 3, available at https://www.finma.ch/en/news/2018/02/20180216-mm-ico-wegleitung/.
14. *Blandin/Cloots/Hussain/Rauchs et al.*, Global Cryptoasset Regulatory Landscape Study (2019), 37, available at https://www.jbs.cam.ac.uk/fileadmin/user_upload/research/centres/alternative-finance/downloads/2019-04-ccaf-global-cryptoasset-regulatory-landscape-study.pdf.
15. Regarding different operating models for stablecoin arrangements, *see FSB*, Annex 1, Consultative document: Addressing the regulatory, supervisory and oversight challenges raised by 'global stablecoin' arrangements (14 Apr. 2020), available at https://www.fsb.org/wp-content/uploads/P140420-1.pdf; for the impact of global stablecoins, *see G7 Working Group on Stablecoins* (Oct. 2019), available at https://www.bis.org/cpmi/publ/d187.pdf.
16. Parity can be maintained by collateralizing stablecoins with fiat (Tether, USDC or Gemini Dollar), other crypto assets or algorithmic trading (MakerDAO) based on price movement to stabilize price fluctuations, *see Rauchs/Blandin/Klein/Pieters/Recanatini/Zhang*, 2nd Global Cryptoasset Benchmarking Study (Dec. 2018), 48, available at https://www.jbs.cam.ac.uk/fileadmin/user_upload/research/centres/alternative-finance/downloads/2018-12-ccaf-2nd-global-cryptoasset-benchmarking.pdf.

classification may correspondingly evolve over time.[17] Such a dynamic classification would be a novel concept for most jurisdictions.[18]

(c) *Regulatory Classification*

(i) General

The relevant regulatory classification depends on the regulatory regime that is being assessed. Each regulatory regime attempts to mitigate specific risks. Financial regulation aims to guarantee investor protection and the integrity of the financial market. The traditional rationale for financial services and market regulation is the correction of market failures related to asymmetric information and to externalities, notably systemic risks, in order to support market efficiency and efficient resource allocation.[19] Similar risks can also materialize in markets in crypto assets. If crypto assets are classified as financial instruments, this triggers financial markets regulation and, depending on the nature of the financial instrument, specifically securities laws (including prospectus requirements and market abuse regulations), banking law (e.g., licensing regimes for certain financial activities), collective investment schemes law, payment regulation and anti-money laundering ('AML')/know-your-customer ('KYC') regulation. As the regulatory classification and terminology depends on the respective regimes, crypto assets must be examined from the individual viewpoint of these regimes.

(ii) Regulatory Approaches to Crypto Assets

Due to the flexible nature of crypto assets, most supervisory authorities have adopted a case-by-case approach, meaning that the characteristics of each asset are assessed individually and that the commercial classification does not preclude the legal classification.[20] As there are numerous ways in which crypto assets can be designed and as they embody a wide range of technical properties,[21] they must be assessed individually

17. Cf. *FSB*, Consultative document: Addressing the regulatory, supervisory and oversight challenges raised by 'global stablecoin' arrangements (14 Apr. 2020), 15.
18. This was discussed at large after the statement of William Hinman (SEC Director, Division of Corporate Finance), 'Putting aside the fundraising that accompanied the creation of Ether, based on my understanding of the present state of Ether, the Ethereum network and its decentralized structure, current offers and sales of Ether are not securities transactions' (14 Jun. 2018), available at https://www.sec.gov/news/speech/speech-hinman-061418. This statement is even coined 'the Hinman test' by the crypto community, which statement is interpreted as an admission that sufficient decentralization can alter the legal classification of a previous security.
19. *Moloney*, The Oxford Handbook of Regulation (Sep. 2010), 437.
20. *Blandin/Cloots/Hussain/Rauchs et al.*, Global Cryptoasset Regulatory Landscape Study, University of Cambridge Faculty of Law Research Paper No. 23/2019 (2019), 36, available at https://www.jbs.cam.ac.uk/fileadmin/user_upload/research/centres/alternative-finance/downloads/2019-04-ccaf-global-cryptoasset-regulatory-landscape-study.pdf.
21. *Fußwinkel/Kreiterling*, Blockchain Technology – Thoughts on Regulation, BaFin Perspectives 1/2018 (2018), 54, available at https://www.bafin.de/SharedDocs/Downloads/EN/BaFinPerspektiven/2018/bp_18-1_digitalisierung_en.html.

according to the specificities of each case and classified into the conventional or, if existing, into a novel crypto-specific financial framework.

From a financial regulatory standpoint, most jurisdictions have not yet adopted bespoke crypto-specific frameworks.[22] Instead, they utilize the existing financial market regulation[23] in a technology-neutral manner, which also enables these jurisdictions to react accordingly to unorthodox instruments such as crypto assets. Regulators worldwide have, since the rise of crypto assets, garnered extensive administrative experience and have a sound level of expertise when applying conventional rules to crypto assets, their underlying business models, and related financial activities. However, despite the technology-neutral approach, not every constellation in this dynamic environment can be covered by the conventional framework and regulatory gaps may become apparent. As a result, there is a rising tendency to enact crypto-specific tailored rules and fill these regulatory gaps.[24] In this spirit, some jurisdictions have adopted crypto-specific regulation, among which are Gibraltar, Malta, Germany, Liechtenstein, the State of New York, and the State of Wyoming.

(iii) Legal Assessment of Economic Functionality of Crypto Assets

As mentioned above, the financial regulatory classification depends on the crypto asset's legal functionality. The rights conferred by crypto assets can be divided into financial and non-financial rights. Financial rights can be equity or debt-like. Equity rights can be differentiated between membership rights (e.g., voting rights, rights to participate in the management of the community) and cash-flow rights (dividend rights, annual profit participation rights). Financial rights comparable to debt involve the right to a repayment after a certain time and, in addition, usually an interest payment. Non-financial rights can provide, in a voucher-like form, the right to an existing or yet to be developed service or product or merely represent the expectation to be able to transfer the crypto asset and using it as a means of payment. Not surprisingly, similar to the commercial classification, there is also no clear-cut assessment as to the legal functionality, as crypto assets can represent several financial and non-financial rights in a novel way and thus combine a myriad of legal features. As a

22. *Blandin/Cloots/Hussain/Rauchs et al.*, Global Cryptoasset Regulatory Landscape Study, University of Cambridge Faculty of Law Research Paper No. 23/2019 (2019), 41 et seq., available at https://www.jbs.cam.ac.uk/fileadmin/user_upload/research/centres/alternative-finance/downloads/2019-04-ccaf-global-cryptoasset-regulatory-landscape-study.pdf.
23. Alternatively, they subject crypto assets to 'related neighbouring regulatory regimes', *see Dimitropoulos*, Global Currencies and Domestic Regulation: Embedding through Enabling?, in Hacker/Lianos/Dimitropoulos/Eich, Regulating Blockchain: Techno-Social and Legal Challenges (2020), 126.
24. With regard to the European Union ('EU') and the European Economic Area ('EEA'), the European Securities and Markets Authority ('ESMA') criticized such national gap filling and is concerned that bespoke national rules do not provide for a level playing field in the EU single market. Therefore, ESMA advocates for an EU-wide approach, especially considering the cross-border nature of crypto assets, *see ESMA*, Advice Initial Coin Offerings and Crypto-Assets (9 Jan. 2019), 5, available at https://www.esma.europa.eu/sites/default/files/library/esma50-157-1391_crypto_advice.pdf.

result, depending on the jurisdiction, crypto assets may fall under multiple regulatory classifications as shown below:[25]

Legal Assessment of Crypto Assets' Economic Functionality				
Financial Rights			*Non-financial Rights*	
Equity-like: membership rights and/or cash-flow rights	Debt-like: repayment after time plus interest payment	Asset-backed: underlying physical assets	Right to existing or yet to be developed product or access to digital service	Using as a means of payment

(iv) Classification Regarding Financial Regulatory/Securities Law

Securities are the most prominent subgroup of financial instruments (besides money-market instruments, units in collective investment undertakings, options, futures and swaps). Finding common characteristics with regard to securities regulation from a comparative, cross-jurisdictional perspective, is rather complex. Depending on the jurisdiction, the scope of application of the securities definition and delineation to other financial instruments can differ. However, looking at it from a high-level view, two different regulatory approaches can be observed.

Jurisdictions with a common law background tend to take a more principle-based or functional approach, which is determined by case law, and classify unorthodox instruments closely to the commercial classification. This results in a broad scope of application and leaves limited room for regulatory gaps. Other jurisdictions with a civil law background tend to codify different 'types' of securities and compare unorthodox instruments with these conventional, codified ones. Some jurisdictions combine aspects of both common law and civil law backgrounds.

Both approaches are technology-neutral and generally follow a 'substance over form' approach.[26] Therefore, ultimately, the outcome of classifying unorthodox instruments such as crypto assets may be very similar.[27] This can be exemplified by the securities framework applied in the US under the 'investment contract' definition, whose elements were stipulated by the *Howey* test,[28] and in the European Union / European Economic Area (EU/EEA) under the 'transferable securities' definition

25. *FSB*, Consultative document: Addressing the regulatory, supervisory and oversight challenges raised by 'global stablecoin' arrangements (14 Apr. 2020), 19.
26. Cf. *Hacker/Thomale*, The Crypto-Security: Initial Coin Offerings and EU Securities Regulation, in Hacker/Lianos/Dimitropoulos/Eich, Regulating Blockchain: Techno-Social and Legal Challenges (2020), 230.
27. *Maume/Fromberger*, Regulation of Initial Coin Offerings: Reconciling US and EU Securities Laws, Chicago Journal of International Law (2019), Volume 19, Issue 2, 548, 584.
28. In the 1946 case *SEC v. W.J. Howey Co.*, 328 U.S. 293, 298-99 (1946), the Supreme Court stated that an instrument is an 'investment contract' if it involves an (1) investment of money, (2) in a common enterprise, (3) with the expectation of profits, (4) to be derived solely from the efforts of others. *See also Choi/Pritchard*, Securities Regulation, Cases and Analysis (2019), 183-195.

pursuant to the Markets in Financial Instruments Directive ('MiFID II'),[29] serving as paradigms for these two systems.

The definition of investment contract is principle-based and its elements can take various criteria into account to determine whether a crypto asset fulfils an investment purpose (including how a crypto asset is marketed),[30] whereas the securities definition of MiFID II relies on a comparability to conventional equity, debt, or derivative instruments, such as shares in companies or bonds. In the US, the investment contract definition serves as a catch-all clause, but the US Securities and Exchange Commission ('SEC') has concluded that any crypto asset to be sold for capital raising purposes can potentially be classified as securities in the US.[31]

By contrast, in the EU, the scope of applicability is prima facie narrower due to the need for comparability to the enumerated conventional security instruments. However, it is worth noting that in strong contrast to the US, there is a complete absence of case law from the European Court of Justice ('ECJ') on what constitutes transferable securities.[32] As the essence of conventional equity, debt, and derivative instruments remains unclear, there is no common understanding of the element of comparability. As a result, the element of comparability is a rather vague one and, depending on the interpretation ascribed to it by Member States and their supervisory authorities, the transferable securities definition can be similar to the investment contract definition, giving ample discretion when it comes to classifying crypto assets.[33]

---

29. 2004/39/EC. Art. 4 No. 1 (44) MiFID II defines 'transferable securities' as classes of securities which are negotiable on the capital market, with the exception of instruments of payment, such as: (1) shares in companies and other securities equivalent to shares in companies, partnerships or other entities, and depositary receipts in respect of shares; (2) bonds or other forms of securitized debt, including depositary receipts in respect of such securities; (3) any other securities giving the right to acquire or sell any such transferable securities or giving rise to a cash settlement determined by reference to transferable securities, currencies, interest rates or yields, commodities or other indices or measures.
30. *See* cease and desist order against Munchee Inc., where the SEC concluded that the investor's expectations were primed by Munchee's marketing of the MUN token offering, SEC Release No. 33-10445 (11 Dec. 2017), 9, available at https://www.sec.gov/litigation/admin/2017/33-10445.pdf.
31. *See SEC,* Framework for 'Investment Contract' Analysis of Digital Assets, available at https://www.sec.gov/corpfin/framework-investment-contract-analysis-digital-assets#_ednref5; *see also* complaint against Telegram Group Inc. (11 Oct. 2019), available at https://www.sec.gov/litigation/complaints/2019/comp-pr2019-212.pdf.
32. *Klöhn/Parhofer/Resas,* Initial Coin Offerings: Economics and Regulation (26 Nov. 2018), 29, available at https://ssrn.com/abstract=3290882.
33. ESMA undertook a survey of Member States' National Competent Authorities in summer of 2018, using a sample set of crypto assets to understand under which circumstances crypto assets may qualify as financial instruments. Three key takeaways are: (1) Member States, in the course of transposing MiFID into their national laws, have defined the term 'financial instrument' differently. Some employ a restrictive list of examples to define transferable securities, and others use broader interpretations. This creates challenges to both the regulation and supervision of crypto assets. (2) Regulatory gaps with regard to crypto assets were identified. If a crypto asset is not a financial instrument or non-financial instrument under EU rules, it is still possible that consumer/investor risks might exist. (3) For crypto assets that do not qualify as MiFID II financial instruments, Member States can set up bespoke rules at the national level for (a subset

For the avoidance of doubt, it should be clarified that crypto assets that do not fall within the scope of securities laws can still be subject to financial regulation, if they fall within the broader categories of other financial instruments, either conventional or crypto-specific ones.

(v) Classification Regarding Payment Regulation

Crypto assets may fall within the scope of payment regulation (which deals with payment services and payment service providers) if they are considered non-cash payment instruments or in particular electronic money in the respective jurisdiction.[34] The definition of payment instruments is even more fragmented across jurisdictions than the securities definition. From a regulation standpoint, jurisdictions face two main challenges.

First, the applicability of payment regulation mostly relies on the existence of a central issuer. Depending on the business model and protocol design, the generation and distribution of cryptocurrencies may be fully decentralized, as they are generated by the protocol itself and distributed automatically to the validators.[35]

Second, depending on the jurisdiction, the classification of electronic money may depend on the instrument representing a claim on the issuer, which usually consists of a redemption right to exchange electronic money for fiat currency.[36] Depending on the design of the cryptocurrencies, such a claim might not be existent or excluded.[37] Therefore, a majority of cryptocurrencies might fall outside the scope of payment regulation, as those that are issued in a decentralized manner do not have an issuer, and those that are issued centrally do not constitute a claim.

If crypto assets do not fall within the scope of payment regulation, apart from being subject to AML Regulation, they will otherwise be unregulated from a financial supervisory standpoint. This does not mean, however, that they are completely unregulated. Crypto assets are still subject to private law regimes such as contract law or consumer protection law.

---

of) crypto assets. *See ESMA*, Advice Initial Coin Offerings and Crypto-Assets (9 Jan. 2019), 5, available at https://www.esma.europa.eu/sites/default/files/library/esma50-157-1391_crypto_advice.pdf.

34. For an overview of key features and uses of digital currencies, *see Bank for International Settlements (BIS)*, Committee on Payments and Market Infrastructures, Report on digital currencies (Nov. 2015), 4 et seq., available at https://www.bis.org/cpmi/publ/d137.pdf.
35. *Shcherbak*, How Should Bitcoin Be Regulated?, European Journal of Legal Studies (2014), Volume 7, Issue 1, 45, 61.
36. *See* Art. 2 No. 2 Directive 2009/110/EC (E-Money Directive), which defines electronic money as 'electronically, including magnetically, stored monetary value as represented by a claim on the issuer which is issued on receipt of funds for the purpose of making payment transactions [...], and which is accepted by a natural or legal person other than the electronic money issuer'; *FSB*, Consultative document: Addressing the regulatory, supervisory and oversight challenges raised by 'global stablecoin' arrangements (14 Apr. 2020), 15.
37. 'Libra does not appear to qualify as e-money, as it does not embody a claim of its holders against the Libra Association', Speech by *Yves Mersch*, Member of the Executive Board of the ECB, at the ECB Legal Conference, Frankfurt am Main (2 Sep. 2019), available at https://www.ecb.europa.eu/press/key/date/2019/html/ecb.sp190902~aedded9219.en.html.

(vi) Classification Regarding AML Regulation

The aim of AML Regulation is to protect the monetary system from money laundering and to combat terrorism finance. As these risks do not only arise with services around financial instruments, AML Regulation has a broader scope of applicability than financial regulation and co-exists independently alongside it. To keep up with emerging new trends based on modern technology services and to cope with evasive movements, AML Regulation must constantly evolve to seal regulatory gaps.[38]

From an AML standpoint, crypto assets have been understood, from a very early stage, to pose a significant risk to the safeguards put forth by AML Regulation. Existing money laundering and combating terrorism finance rules regulate intermediaries, such as banks or credit card companies, which serve as gateways to the monetary system.[39] They maintain a record of the transactions and collect information about the identity and transactions of their customers. In decentralized, peer-to-peer payment technologies, network participants do not rely on such conventional intermediaries to transact.[40] However, a full disintermediation has not taken place, instead the technology spawned new intermediaries, in particular, custodial wallet providers and crypto exchanges.

In June 2015, the Financial Action Task Force ('FATF')[41] provided for the initial guidelines to address money laundering and terrorist financing risks associated with so-called virtual currencies.[42] The scope was limited to *convertible* virtual currencies, which were defined as a virtual currency that 'has an equivalent value in real currency and can be exchanged back-and-forth for real currency'.[43] This limited scope was justified in that 'in the near-term, only convertible [virtual currency], which can be used to move value into and out of fiat currencies and the regulated system, is likely to

38. Recital 2 Directive (EU) 2018/843.
39. *Covolo*, The EU Response to Criminal Misuse of Cryptocurrencies: The Young, Already Outdated 5th Anti-Money Laundering Directive (13 Dec. 2019), 4, available at https://ssrn.com/abstract=3503535.
40. For an overview on how cryptocurrency works as a payment mechanism, *see FATF*, Appendix B, Guidance for a Risk-Based Approach to Virtual Currencies (Jun. 2015), 35.
41. FATF is an independent intergovernmental body initially established by the G7 in 1989 developing and promoting policies to protect the global financial system against money laundering and terrorist financing. FATF currently has 39 members and over 200 jurisdictions around the world have committed to the FATF rules. The mandate of FATF is to set standards and to promote effective implementation of legal, regulatory, and operational measures for combating AML and terrorist financing. The FATF Recommendations provide for 40 recommendations setting out requirements and are complemented by their interpretive notes and a glossary of the applicable definitions.
42. *FATF*, Guidance for a Risk-based approach: Virtual Currencies (Jun. 2015), available at https://www.fatf-gafi.org/media/fatf/documents/reports/Guidance-RBA-Virtual-Currencies.pdf.
43. Definitions already used in *FATF*, FATF Report, Virtual Currencies: Key Definitions and Potential AML/CFT Risks (Jun. 2014), 4, available at https://www.fatf-gafi.org/media/fatf/documents/reports/Virtual-currency-key-definitions-and-potential-aml-cft-risks.pdf.

present [money laundering/terrorist financing] risks'.[44] As a consequence, only cryptocurrencies were covered by the definition of convertible virtual currencies.

In October 2018, FATF extended its definition from virtual currencies to virtual assets, which are defined as 'digital representations of value that can be digitally traded, or transferred, and can be used for payment or investment purposes'.[45] By including the 'investment purpose' element, the scope of application was expanded to also capture security tokens, and those utility tokens, which to some degree serve an investment purpose, leaving only a very negligible amount of crypto assets unregulated from an AML perspective (e.g., non-tradeable electronic vouchers).

In June 2019, FATF published more detailed advice and guidelines on the application of the risk-based approach in relation to virtual assets.[46] In addition, FATF extended the so-called *travel rule* (Recommendation 16) to Virtual Assets Service Providers ('VASPs'), which comprise crypto exchanges, custodial wallet providers, and financial service providers related to offer and sale of virtual assets.[47] The travel rule requires VASPs to collect and *transmit* to each other information about the originator and beneficiary of a transaction, in much the same way as traditional financial institutions. Furthermore, for effective supervision, FATF requires all its members to introduce a registration or licensing regime for VASPs. It is in the discretion of the national authorities to decide under which category of regulated activities VASPs should be regulated, e.g., as a financial institution, designated non-financial business and professions or other, distinct categories.

About five months before the October 2018 FATF recommendations were published, the 5th Anti-Money Laundering Directive ('AMLD5')[48] was adopted on 30 May 2018, rendering it partly outdated in light of the following FATF recommendations.[49] Generally speaking, AMLD5 imposes specific monitoring and verification obligations on certain persons and companies with a typically higher risk of being involved in money laundering or terrorist financing activities. Following the FATF 2015 Guidance, AMLD5 requires Member States to make custodian wallet providers and custodial fiat-to-crypto exchanges subject to certain requirements relating to 'virtual currencies'.[50] Virtual currencies are defined under AMLD5 as *'a digital representation*

44. *See FATF,* Guidance For a Risk-Based Approach to Virtual Currencies (Jun. 2015), 6, available at https://www.fatf-gafi.org/media/fatf/documents/reports/Guidance-RBA-Virtual-Currencies.pdf.
45. *FATF,* The FATF Recommendations (Jun. 2019), 126.
46. *FATF,* Guidance for a Risk-based approach, Virtual Assets and Virtual Asset Service Providers (Jun. 2019), available at http://www.fatf-gafi.org/media/fatf/documents/recommendations/RBA-VA-VASPs.pdf.
47. *FATF,* The FATF Recommendations (2012, updated Jun. 2019), available at https://www.fatf-gafi.org/media/fatf/documents/recommendations/pdfs/FATF%20Recommendations%202012.pdf.
48. Directive (EU) 2018/843 of the European Parliament and of the Council of 30 May 2018 amending Directive (EU) 2015/849 on the prevention of the use of the financial system for the purposes of money laundering or terrorist financing, and amending Directives 2009/138/EC and 2013/36/EU.
49. *Covolo,* The EU Response to Criminal Misuse of Cryptocurrencies: The Young, Already Outdated 5th Anti-Money Laundering Directive (13 Dec. 2019), 4, available at https://ssrn.com/abstract=3503535.
50. Article 2(1)(g) and (h) AMLD5.

of value that is not issued or guaranteed by a central bank or a public authority, is not necessarily attached to a legally established currency and does not possess a legal status of currency or money, but is accepted by natural or legal persons as a means of exchange and which can be transferred, stored and traded electronically'.[51] As a directive, AMLD5 must be implemented by the EU/EEA Member States.

(vii) Outlook Regarding Regulatory Classification

Attempting a global outlook on the regulatory classification of crypto assets, it is possible that, in the future, cryptocurrencies and the majority of so-called utility tokens could also be classified as financial instruments in their respective jurisdictions. After the financial crisis, the G20 committed itself at the summits in Pittsburgh and London in 2009 to the regulatory approach that in the future no financial market player, no financial market product and no financial market should be without appropriate regulation or supervision. As crypto assets can pose similar risks to conventional financial instruments, it is fair to say that on a political level we can expect the same desire in relation to crypto assets.[52]

1.2.3 Accounting Classification

(a) IFRS/IAS

(i) General

There is no specific guidance under the text of the International Financial Reporting Standards ('IFRS') on how to classify and account for crypto assets. The International Accounting Standards Board is aware of the developments in the realm of crypto assets, but has decided not to engage in specific standard setting (yet). This means that crypto assets must be qualified under the existing standards using a principle-based approach that is sensitive to the specificities of the respective case at hand. Since no crypto assets are the same, there is no 'one size fits all' solution. The most important standards[53] to be considered when dealing with crypto assets are the following:

- IAS 2 Inventories;
- IAS 7 Statement of Cash Flows;

51. Article 3(18) AMLD5.
52. *European Commission*, Consultation document: An EU framework for markets in crypto-assets (19 Dec. 2019), available at https://ec.europa.eu/info/files/2019-crypto-assets-consultation-document_en; Non-Paper on the possible content of a proposal for an EU framework for markets in crypto-assets (14 May 2020), available at https://www.politico.eu/wp-content/uploads/2020/05/May-14_3.pdf.
53. International Accounting Standards ('IAS') are an older set of standards that were issued by the International Accounting Standards Committee. Since 2001, the newer set of standards has been issued by the International Accounting Standards Board and are known as IFRS. In case of a conflict, the requirements of IFRS prevail over IAS. Currently, the United States, Japan, and China are the only major capital markets that have not adopted IFRS.

- IAS 32 Financial Instruments: Presentation;
- IAS 38 Intangible Assets;
- IFRS 9 Financial Instruments; and
- IFRS 15 Revenue from Contracts with Customers.

The only official classification of crypto assets stems from an agenda decision of the IFR Interpretations Committee ('IFRIC') from 2019. The decision only covers cryptocurrencies and does not relate to other crypto assets. The considerations relating to these categories are discussed below.

(ii) Standards Applicable to Cryptocurrencies

Under the IFRIC decision, cryptocurrencies are defined as having the following characteristics:

- a digital or virtual currency recorded on a distributed ledger that uses cryptography for security;
- not issued by a jurisdictional authority or other party; and
- does not give rise to a contract between the holder and another party.

The IFRIC concluded that cryptocurrencies fall within the definition of intangible asset under IAS 38. Intangible assets are identifiable non-monetary assets without physical substance. Cryptocurrencies fall under this definition, because they are separately transferable and therefore identifiable, and do not give rise to a right to receive a fixed or determinable number of units of currency, i.e., are non-monetary. According to the committee, cryptocurrencies are not financial assets within the meaning of IAS 32.11, which include cash. Cryptocurrencies are not cash since they are not (yet) a medium which is used to measure all other transactions in financial statements. The committee did not give further guidance on the exact treatment of cryptocurrency under IAS 38, so the general rules would apply.

There are circumstances, however, under which cryptocurrencies can constitute inventories within the meaning of IAS 2, which would mean that IAS 38 is not applicable. This would be the case if an entity holds cryptocurrency for sale in the ordinary course of business. Crypto assets held as inventory are to be measured at the lower of cost and net realizable value. The committee noted that the broker-trader exception under IAS 2.3(b) might apply to those 'who buy or sell commodities for others or on their own account'. The committee therefore implicitly clarified that cryptocurrencies could constitute commodities.

The committee also discussed the disclosure requirements for holding cryptocurrencies under the IFRS rules. It noted that for cryptocurrencies accounted for under IAS 2, the disclosure requirements under IAS 2.36-39 will apply and for such accounted for under IAS 38 the requirements under IAS 38.118-128. If cryptocurrencies are measured at fair value, the respective disclosure requirements under IFRS 13.91-99 must be followed. Finally, the committee made reference to the general disclosure requirements under IAS 1.122 and IAS 10.21, which obligate entities to disclose essential judgments made in accounting and significant events after the reporting period which could influence the economic decisions of a reader of the financial statements. It gave the example that an entity might have to disclose strong price fluctuations in cryptocurrencies which occurred after the reporting period.

Additional to the IFRIC decision, some further conclusions can be drawn for the classification of cryptocurrencies:

- As long as cryptocurrencies do not constitute cash within the meaning of IAS 32, they can also be ruled out as functional currency or presentation currency in the sense of IAS 28.8, since the terms 'currency' and 'cash' are used synonymously in IFRS.
- Cryptocurrencies could be classified as cash equivalents under IAS 7.6 if they are 'readily convertible to a known amount of cash and be subject to an insignificant risk of changes in value'. The IFRIC has clarified that the amount of cash received from the conversion of the investment must be known already at the time of the investment. Since cryptocurrencies are subject to strong price fluctuations, they will not fulfil this requirement and therefore not constitute cash equivalents.
- If an entity offers goods or services to customers in exchange for cryptocurrency, the cryptocurrency constitutes non-cash consideration under IFRS 15.48(d) and 15.66 and is to be measured at fair value.

(iii) Standards Applicable to Other Crypto Assets

In its agenda decision, the IFRIC specifically stated that it only wanted to deal with cryptocurrencies under the definition above. This means that the classification of other crypto assets requires further discussion.

Even though cryptocurrencies do not meet the definition of financial instruments within the meaning of IAS 32.11, this may be the case for security tokens, which have security-like characteristics. As discussed above, the two archetypes of security tokens are equity tokens, which grant equity-like participation and dividend rights and debt tokens, which work similar to classical debt capital. Because of their characteristics, security tokens may qualify as financial assets, specifically as equity instruments or contractual rights to receive cash or other assets. IAS 32.11 defines an equity instrument as 'a contract which evidences a residual interest in the assets of an entity after deducting all of its liabilities'. If an equity token grants such right, it can therefore qualify as a financial asset. Debt tokens can qualify as contractual rights to receive cash or other financial assets and therefore as financial assets as well. Such classification would mean that the issuer equivalently would have to account for a financial liability. Yet, it should be noted that these tokens will only be classified as financial instruments if they grant enforceable rights against the issuer, which might not always be the case.

For asset-backed tokens, the accounting treatment depends on the specificities of the token and the underlying asset. Some asset-backed tokens might give rise to a right to receive a cash equivalent at the value of the underlying asset and would therefore meet the definition of a financial asset under IAS 32.11. Some tokens might represent the legal ownership of the underlying asset and should therefore be accounted for as the asset itself.

The treatment of utility tokens depends on the rights these tokens grant. A utility token that gives the right to access a platform or service might meet the definition of an intangible asset under IAS 38.8. This may be the case as well for utility tokens that grant no enforceable right if future economic benefits can be expected from them nevertheless. IFRS 15 will usually not apply for the holder of utility tokens. This is because even if the relationship between the holder and the issuer qualifies as a contract, the standard would only cover the issuer.

(iv) Crypto Assets Held on Behalf of Third Parties

If an entity holds crypto assets on behalf of a third party, e.g., as a custodian, the main accounting question is whether the entity has to account for the assets on its balance sheet, typically in conjunction with a respective liability. This depends on the nature of the relationship between the entity and the third party. Important issues to consider are whether the entity has the right to use the assets for its own purposes and whether the third party would have preferential claims for the assets in case the entity is liquidated.

(b) EU

Under EU law, different accounting rules exist, which can be subdivided into non-IFRS accounting and IFRS accounting.

Directive 2013/34/EU, known as the 'Accounting Directive', requires Member States to implement certain non-IFRS accounting requirements for limited liability companies doing business in the EU. The requirements are mostly of a general nature and do not specifically deal with crypto assets. Since Member States have leeway in transposing the Directive into national law, the specific effects on crypto assets can be found in the respective country guides of this book.

Additionally, Regulation (EC) 1606/2002 requires listed companies to provide financial reporting under IFRS. New IFRS standards are added to the regulation by the European Commission following an endorsement process. All IFRS/IAS standards discussed above have been transposed into EU law in that manner. This means that the treatment of crypto assets is not different from the general application of IFRS as described above.

1.2.4 Tax Classification

In comparison to other areas affected by DLT, the examination of its effects on taxes is scarce in international organizations.

Relative to other players, the Organisation for Economic Co-operation and Development ('OECD') is the most active in the field. It has identified blockchain as an important issue and has established a 'Global Blockchain Policy Centre', which deals with the policy implications of DLT. In its scope of work, the Centre specifically includes tax implications. Such implications are also discussed on the annual Blockchain Policy Forum, which is hosted by the OECD in Paris and are mentioned en passant in different official documents, including reports on the OECD/G20 Base Erosion and Profit Shifting ('BEPS') project. These mentions are however of a rather general nature. The OECD has not yet issued a comprehensive discussion of DLT from a tax point of view, which would allow for specific conclusions.

Other major international organizations have also yet to weigh in on the tax implications and classifications of crypto assets. The United Nations Committee of Experts on International Cooperation in Tax Matters has not discussed DLT yet. A similar paucity of concrete statements regarding tax implications prevails at the EU level and at the World Trade Organization.

It will be an important task for these organizations to foster standard setting and the identification of best practices for the tax treatment of crypto assets, in order to facilitate the development of a legal framework and provide guidance for this nascent industry.

1.3 Crypto Transactions

1.3.1 Capital Raised Through Token Sales

(a) General

Token sales such as ICOs, Security Token Offerings ('STOs'), and Initial Exchange Offerings ('IEOs') differ in their respective structure but share the same common denominator in that they are all measures of raising capital. Capital is either raised in other cryptocurrencies (mostly in bitcoin or ether, which developed into reference currencies) or in fiat money. In exchange, users/investors receive native crypto assets on the respective network or DApp of the invested projects. These crypto assets can have different functions:

- They can have the function of a general means of payment for the purchase of goods and services (currency tokens or payment tokens).
- They may entitle the holder to use the goods and services of the project itself (i.e., the company issuing the token) and thus resemble vouchers, receipts or admission tickets (utility tokens).
- They can give the buyers a share in the profits of the project, possibly also with voting rights, and thus be similar to shares (security tokens, investment tokens or equity tokens).
- They can grant a say in a project (governance tokens).
- They may be linked, and confer a right, to assets (such as gold or real estate), whereby if they are returned to the issuer, the latter will surrender the underlying asset (asset-backed tokens).

The investment phase is followed by the crypto assets being generated and distributed (token generating event), which may be performed in different ways. In the context of token sales, crypto assets are usually generated beforehand by the issuer ('pre-mined'). If the funding goal is reached and once the network or DApp is launched, the crypto assets are distributed by being transferred to the wallets of the respective users/investors. As a variant to this procedure, crypto assets can also be generated directly into the wallets of the respective users/investors by writing the opening balances into the first block ('genesis block') without transferring them per se.[54] Crypto assets can also be generated and distributed in a decentralized manner by the protocol itself (e.g., as a mining reward in the Bitcoin protocol). In this scenario, new crypto assets are generated and distributed once a new block is created, following the rules of the protocol. The latter generating and distribution method will be covered in the next section.

The terms 'ICO', 'STO', and 'IEO' do not follow an official taxonomy or predetermine a regulatory classification, but instead have derived from practice. The demarcation between ICOs and STOs usually follows an asset-based distinction. ICOs are a way of raising capital for decentralized business models that do not generate traditional cash flows comparable to conventional companies, instead crypto assets derive their value from positive network effects and the scarcity of the crypto assets.[55] By contrast, security tokens issued through STOs are backed by and derive their value from underlying real world assets, such as conventional cash flows of a business or fractional ownership of physical assets. Examples for the latter can be real estate or collectibles, e.g., art or classic cars. Security tokens are thus very similar to traditional equity or debt instruments.

The demarcation between ICOs, STOs on the one side and IEOs on the other side follows an issuer-based distinction. Whereas in ICOs and STOs the project itself assumes the role of the issuer and distributor, in IEOs, similar to the role of crowdfunding platforms, crypto exchanges as intermediaries administer and facilitate the fundraising process and conduct the initial placement of the crypto assets to their users. The issued crypto assets are immediately listed on the trading platform of the respective exchange, thus leading to a strong convergence of primary and secondary market.

54. *See Van Valkenburgh*: 'This first block could list certain amounts of tokens as belonging to addresses already generated by the developers as a self-bestowed reward for their work to develop the new network software, or it could assign new tokens to addresses created for investors who financed these development efforts.', What Are Cryptocurrency Forks, Airdrops, and What's the Difference?, Coin Center (17 Oct. 2019), available at https://coincenter.org/entry/what-are-cryptocurrency-forks-airdrops-and-what-s-the-difference.

55. *Klöhn/Parhofer/Resas*, Initial Coin Offerings (ICOs): Economics and Regulation (26 Nov. 2018), 9, available at https://ssrn.com/abstract=3290882.

(b) ICOs

ICOs evolved into a novel method of raising capital comparable to investment or product crowdfunding.[56] The issuance of crypto assets is not conducted through traditional channels, such as investment banks, but instead conducted directly on a blockchain.[57] Even though some predecessors financed themselves through token sales,[58] the launch of the Ethereum Blockchain in 2014 with its smart contract functionality paved the way for projects and companies to finance themselves through ICOs, mostly utilizing the so-called ERC-20 token standard.[59] As a result, it is possible for anyone to issue a crypto asset using less than 100 lines of smart contract code.[60]

This led to a surge in ICOs with an overall capital raised of almost USD 24.9 billion by the end of 2019.[61] Some of the most funded ICOs include EOS (USD 4.2 billion), Telegram (USD 1.7 billion), Filecoin (USD 262 million), Tezos (USD 234 million), and Polkadot (USD 144 million).[62] The most funded ICOs were projects with developments on the protocol layer instead of on the application layer, as the belief is that the development of value concentrates at the shared protocol layer and only a fraction of that value is distributed along at the application layer (this is also referred to as the Fat Protocol Thesis).[63] ICOs were a very popular fundraising method between the years 2016–2018, overtaking venture capital funding as a fundraising method for blockchain-based businesses.[64] However, the market cooled down drastically in 2018–2019, when the value of many cryptocurrencies plunged and many projects could not deliver on their promises. Partly this was also due to the increased scrutiny by regulatory authorities such as the SEC in the US.

The vast majority of ICOs takes place at a very early stage in the project's development. Start-ups with often nothing more than an idea and a promise of a product or service access, for their fundraising needs, a financial market very much

56. *Rohr/Wright*, Blockchain-Based Token Sales, Initial Coin Offerings, and the Democratization of Public Capital Markets, Hastings Law Journal (Feb. 2019), Volume 70, Issue 2, 463, 470.
57. *Gurrea-Martínez/Léon*, The Law and Finance of Initial Coin Offerings, in Brummer, Cryptoassets: Legal, Regulatory and Monetary Perspectives (2019), 119.
58. Mastercoin (Jul. 2013), NextCoin (Sep. 2013); cf. *M. Mendelson*, From Initial Coin Offerings to Security Tokens: A U.S. Federal Securities Law Analysis, Stanford Technology Law Review (Jan. 2019), Volume 22, Issue 1, 52, 61.
59. The ERC-20 Token is a standard program code that is used to create tokens within the Ethereum blockchain. The ERC-20 smart contract enables its creator to set a supply of tokens, facilitates the transmission and receipt of tokens between parties participating in the Ethereum network, and maintains a record of token holders. If complying with the standard, the tokens can then be used in all wallets as long as they are compatible with Ethereum. *See* ERC20 Tokenstandard, The EthereumWiki, https://en.bitcoinwiki.org/wiki/ERC20.
60. *Rohr/Wright*, Blockchain-Based Token Sales, Initial Coin Offerings, and the Democratization of Public Capital Markets, Hastings Law Journal (Feb. 2019), Volume 70, Issue 2, 463, 468.
61. *See* https://sci.smithandcrown.com/ico-tracker.
62. *See* https://sci.smithandcrown.com/ico-tracker.
63. *Monegro*, Fat Protocols, Union Square Ventures Blog (8 Aug. 2016), available at https://www.usv.com/writing/2016/08/fat-protocols/.
64. *Klöhn/Parhofer/Resas*, Initial Coin Offerings (ICOs): Economics and Regulation (26 Nov. 2018), 3, available at https://ssrn.com/abstract=3290882.

similar to a capital market, which can best be described as a pre-product IPO.[65] In the past, project initiators raised high amounts of funding with nothing more than the promise of developing a final product or service, explaining their project and its envisioned development in a document generically referred to as 'whitepaper'. Whitepapers have become widely accepted disclosure documents, in which details of the projects are communicated.[66] Next to containing explanatory information, whitepapers are also used for marketing and soliciting purposes. A seemingly unregulated way of communication, whitepapers vary heavily in their quality and truthfulness.[67]

Even though some of the underlying business models funded through ICOs were at the very least questionable,[68] the potential of the underlying blockchain technology became apparent. Through a combination of scarcity and positive network effects, a higher demand for crypto assets results directly in a higher crypto asset price. In contrast to traditional financial instruments, an increase in demand for the network reflects directly in the crypto asset price, whereas in traditional finance the share value is always a function of the expected cash flows of the intermediary.[69] Consequently, depending on the token economics, even a small peak in demand can result in a strong increase to the crypto asset price. This combination of features made it possible, for the first time, to finance and monetize open source development in a sustainable way.[70] Furthermore, the tokenization of rights and values creates highly tradeable representations of projects in the form of crypto assets without having to rely on traditional intermediaries, such as investment banks, for the issuance of these crypto assets. Such disintermediation leads to a radical reduction of transaction costs.[71] Additionally, unlike investment crowdfunding, which has not provided investors with liquid secondary markets, crypto assets can be easily and cheaply traded on crypto exchanges.[72] However, crypto exchanges conglomerate a high market power, as listing crypto assets on a crypto exchange is essential for their tradability and therefore for a potential price

65. For an overview of the differences and similarities between ICOs and other sources of financing, *see Gurrea-Martínez/León*, The Law and Finance of Initial Coin Offerings, in Brummer, Cryptoassets: Legal, Regulatory, and Monetary Perspectives (2019), 126–128.
66. ICOs which are not issuing financial instruments do not trigger disclosure regimes such as prospectus requirements. Even they are subject to disclosure regimes it is not clear how the conventional disclosure requirements apply to blockchain-based business models of start-ups.
67. *Brummer/Kiviat/Massari*, What should be disclosed in an initial coin offering, in Brummer, Cryptoassets: Legal, Regulatory, and Monetary Perspectives (2019), 167.
68. *Satis Group*, Cryptoasset Market Coverage Initiation: Network Creation (11 Jul. 2018), according to which the vast majority of ICOs were fraudulent, available at https://research.bloomberg.com/pub/res/d28giW28tf6G7T_Wr77aU0gDgFQ.
69. *Klöhn/Parhofer/Resas*, Initial Coin Offerings (ICOs): Economics and Regulation (26 Nov. 2018), 11, available at https://ssrn.com/abstract=3290882.
70. *Lipusch*, Initial Coin Offerings – A paradigm Shift in Funding Disruptive Innovation (23 Mar. 2018), 7, available at https://ssrn.com/abstract=3148181.
71. Cf. *Catalini/Gans*, Initial Coin Offerings and the Value of Crypto Tokens, Working Paper 24418, NBER Working Paper Series (Mar. 2018, revised Mar. 2019), available at www.nber.org/papers/w24418.
72. *Klöhn/Parhofer/Resas*, Initial Coin Offerings (ICOs): Economics and Regulation (26 Nov. 2018), 3, available at https://ssrn.com/abstract=3290882.

increase. In the past, this led to exchanges requesting listing fees of up to USD 1 million during the ICO boom of 2017–2018.[73]

(c) STOs

Over the past few years, the market has seen a shift from ICOs towards STOs, denoting that the focus of projects and investors has shifted from the utility and consumptive aspects of a crypto asset to the investment side of it. From an investor's perspective, many ICOs struggled to live up to their expectations, and it is still quite a challenge to issue an instrument that properly captures the value of a decentralized network. Against this background, it is no surprise that investors, especially those with a traditional investment background, looking for new investment opportunities, have shifted their focus to crypto assets that are more similar to traditional assets.[74]

From a legal perspective, a once seemingly unregulated method of capital raising has moved into a regulated setting. Crypto assets issued in STOs are, in contrast to ICOs, intentionally securities and fall within the ambit of the respective securities law regime. Consequently, the issuance as well as financial services around security tokens will be regulated. If security tokens are publicly offered, issuers must comply with the conventional disclosure regimes and draft a prospectus that will need to receive approval by the jurisdiction's financial supervisory authority in which they are operating. However, jurisdictions usually have safe harbour or private placement rules in place, under which no prospectus is needed if certain investor-related or threshold-related exemptions are met.[75]

Over the past few years, the first approved STOs in Europe and the US have started to emerge. Public STOs in Europe include NEX (Liechtenstein), Hydrominer (Austria), Envion (Switzerland), Bitbond (Germany), StartMark (Germany), and Fundament (Germany). However, issuing an STO does not automatically mean that the underlying business model is successful. This could be seen first-hand in projects like Envion or Hydrominer, which have been subject to bankruptcy and even criminal law related procedures.

From a commercial perspective, STOs share many of the advantages discussed under ICOs and are in many ways superior to conventional securities offerings. For issuers, the advantage consists of reducing transaction costs by relying on fewer

73. *Wilmoth*, Here's What It Costs to get Your ICO Token Listed on an Exchange, CCN (4 Apr. 2018), based on a study undertaken by Autonomous Next.

74. Unlike ICOs, where there still is no widely accepted methodology to value the price of a token due to the decentralized business models of the funded projects, traditional valuation methods can be applied to STOs.

75. In the United States, safe harbour/private placement regimes are Reg A + , Reg D, Reg CF. For a detailed overview, *see M. Mendelson*, From Initial Coin Offerings to Security Tokens: A U.S. Federal Securities Law Analysis, Stanford Technology Law Review (Jan. 2019), Volume 22, Issue 1, 52, 87. It is worth noting that the US system of regulation differs from a number of other countries that an exemption must exist both for the initial distribution and for the subsequent transfer of securities, *see Meade/Tyshow*, United States of America, in Calkoen, Securities Word: Jurisdictional Comparisons, 4th edition (Sep. 2014), 479. In the European Union, the Prospectus Regulation (Regulation (EU) 2017/1129) provides for various exemptions.

intermediaries as a consequence of the disintermediation capabilities of blockchain technology.[76] The programmability of smart contracts can be leveraged to integrate automatic corporate actions and integrated compliance. For investors, the representation of real assets by securitizing them at a low cost in the form of crypto assets lowers the threshold to invest in asset classes that would usually only be available to privileged investor classes (e.g., real estate or art). The possibility of fractional ownership in these assets makes them available to the general public, which increases the liquidity of the overall market in these underlying assets.[77]

(d) IEOs

In the wake of many fraudulent ICOs and as exchanges seek new sources of revenue and opportunities to monetize their user base, a variant in the form of IEOs emerged. The main difference between ICOs and IEOs is the involvement of an exchange as a middleman between projects and investors during the fundraising process.[78] In contrast to ICOs, where project initiators themselves conduct the fundraising, in IEOs, it is the exchange who administers the fundraising process and conducts the initial placement of crypto assets to its users, assuming a role similar to that of an underwriter in traditional finance.[79]

IEOs promise mainly three advantages over ICOs. From an investor's perspective, the advantage is that the projects offered on the platform of the exchange are subject to a screening and verification process by the exchange itself. In principle, this should endorse high-quality projects and therefore reduce the risk for investors from investing in low-quality or fraudulent projects.[80] The exchange is, at least in theory, incentivized to perform a thorough due diligence as it is staking its reputation behind the projects, comparable to a conventional equity crowdfunding platform.[81] However, as with any reputation-based system, its effectiveness is contingent on the existence of an active and pluralistic competition. The project's reliability and quality depends heavily on the actual due diligence performed by the exchange. Furthermore, the investment process is technically simpler for investors, as the IEO is conducted on an exchange's

76. For a comparison between tokenization and securitization, *see Wandmacher/Wegmann*, Tokenization and Securitization – A Comparison with Reference to Distributed Ledger Technology, in Thorhauer/Kexel, Facetten der Digitalisierung (2020), 157–174.
77. *Amsden/Schweizer*, Are Blockchain Crowdsales the New 'Gold Rush'? Success Determinants of Initial Coin Offerings (16 Apr. 2018), 11, available at http://www.fmaconferences.org/NewOrleans/Papers/ICO_final.pdf.
78. Binance (https://launchpad.binance.com/) and Bitfinex (https://tokensales.bitfinex.com/token-sales) are the most popular exchanges to offer IEOs.
79. *Gras*, What Token Issuers and Exchanges should consider when undertaking an Initial Exchange Offering (IEO), Flag Theory (28 May 2019), available at https://flagtheory.com/initial-exchange-offering-ieo/.
80. *Y. Chen/C. Bellavitis*, Blockchain Disruption and Decentralized Finance: The Rise of Decentralized Business Models, Journal of Business Venturing Insights (2020), Volume 13, 5.
81. *Agrawal/Catalini/Goldfarb*, Some Simple Economics of Crowdfunding, NBER Working Paper No. 19133 (Jun. 2013), 22–24, available at http://nber.org/papers/w19133.

fundraising platform, where users can easily browse through admitted projects and purchase crypto assets with funds directly from their exchange account.[82]

From a project's perspective, project initiators get access to the large user database of the exchange and therefore expose it to a larger set of potential investors, possibly reducing their marketing costs.[83] In contrast to ICOs, the compliance and regulatory burden, e.g., with regard to KYC/AML procedures is at least partly shifted to the exchange conducting the IEO.[84] Finally, crypto assets become immediately listed on the exchange, thus eliminating the uncertainty for investors and projects of whether they would get listed. As mentioned before, a successful listing is a crucial component for tradability and the potential for appreciation of the crypto asset price. To summarize, IEOs are designed to minimize risks, liquidity problems and a delay in listing crypto assets at the end of the token sale.[85]

Through the involvement of exchanges in the fundraising process, a conversion between primary market and secondary market takes place, blurring the distinctive lines between new projects and the role of exchanges as gatekeepers. As a result, IEOs lead to a more centralized form of capital raising, as they pool together projects with the exchange's user base.

From a regulatory perspective, exchanges facilitating token sales can potentially be a suitable access point for future regulation comparable to crowdfunding platforms or broker-dealers.[86] If the crypto assets that are being distributed are considered securities, then the exchange, by brokering these crypto assets, already may need to be registered as a financial service provider in the jurisdiction in which it is marketing the IEO.[87]

(e) More Complex Crypto Related Investment Products

There are different ways to invest into crypto assets to participate in their performance. As mentioned before, an investor can directly purchase crypto assets through a token sale or on the secondary market. Additionally, there are indirect ways to invest into

82. *Miglo*, Choice Between IEO and ICO: Speed vs. Liquidity vs. Risk (Apr. 2020), 2, available at https://mpra.ub.uni-muenchen.de/99600/1/MPRA_paper_99600.pdf.
83. *Myalo/Glukhov*, Comparison Analysis of ICO, DAOICO, IEO and STO, Case study (4 Sep. 2019), 13, available at https://ssrn.com/abstract=3447974.
84. *Gras*, What Token Issuers and Exchanges should consider when undertaking an Initial Exchange Offering (IEO), Flag Theory (28 May 2019), available at https://flagtheory.com/initial-exchange-offering-ieo/.
85. *Myalo/Glukhov*, Comparison Analysis of ICO, DAOICO, IEO and STO, Case study (4 Sep. 2019), 1, available at https://ssrn.com/abstract=3447974.
86. Cf. *Ashley Fox MEP*, Draft Report on the proposal for a regulation on the European Parliament and of the Council on European Crowdfunding Serve Providers (ECSP for Business (COM(2018)0113 – C8-0103/2018 – 2018/0048(COD)) (10 Aug. 2018), available at https://www.europarl.europa.eu/doceo/document/ECON-PR-626662_EN.pdf?redirect.
87. Valerie Szczepanik (SEC): 'Platforms seeking to list these tokens for a listing fee or bring buyers to the table for issuers are probably engaging in broker-dealer activity', *see Baydakova/Hochstein*, SEC's Crypto Czar Says Exchanges That List IEOs May Face Legal Risks, Coindesk (13 May 2019), available at https://www.coindesk.com/secs-crypto-czar-says-exchanges-that-list-ieo-tokens-may-face-legal-risks.

crypto assets by purchasing conventional financial instruments that mirror the value of the underlying crypto assets. This is a way for investors, particularly institutional investors, to invest in this asset class without having to hold crypto assets directly.[88] One way to do so is by investing in an investment vehicle that holds the crypto assets, such as exchange traded funds ('ETFs') or non-listed funds, such as alternative investment funds, trusts or venture capital funds.[89] More recently, derivatives in the form of futures, options and contracts for difference have developed, which are structured on crypto assets such as Bitcoin or Ether.[90]

Besides conventional financial instruments being structured around crypto assets, financial products in the form of crypto assets are also developing. Very similar to the development of traditional markets over the last few decades, where conventional financial instruments became progressively more complex, financial products represented by crypto assets are also becoming more sophisticated and complex. The technology provides for a broad range of flexibility. This ongoing evolution goes beyond blockchain-based lending business models to more sophisticated investment strategies based on rather complex derivative products that have been synthesized in a way to simulate other instruments while altering key characteristics. These complex crypto derivatives can be tailored to suit the needs of the investor, e.g., based on certain maturities or risk profiles. However, the pace at which this development is taking place is astonishing and could surpass the known patterns of conventional financial products. The flexibility of blockchain technology makes it very accessible and prone to the creation of such products, as potentially anyone who can code is able to structure such novel financial products.

1.3.2 *Tokens Received Without Consideration*

(a) *General*

Apart from receiving crypto assets for consideration through token sales such as ICOs, STOs or IEOs or by purchase on secondary markets, crypto assets can also be received without consideration. Crypto assets can either be distributed free of charge by projects themselves via so-called airdrops, by the protocol itself when a hard fork is occurring or as a reward for validation services through mining or staking.

88. *Patti*, The Regulation of Financial Product Innovation Typified by Bitcoin-Based Derivative Contracts (31 Dec. 2018), 8, available at https://ssrn.com/abstract=3380770.
89. *Lautenschläger*, A Beginner's Guide to Crypto Investing, Medium (6 May 2020), available at https://medium.com/the-capital/a-beginners-guide-to-crypto-investing-9ebfacd5402e.
90. Cf. *Autorité des Marchés Financiers (AMF)*, Analysis of the Legal Qualification of Cryptocurrency Derivatives (23 Mar. 2018), available at https://www.amf-france.org/en/news-publications/news/analysis-legal-qualification-cryptocurrency-derivatives; *Chimienti/Kochanska/Pinna*, Understanding the Crypto-Asset Phenomenon, Its Risks and Measurement Issues, ECB Economic Bulletin 5/2019 (2019), 100, 104.

(b) Airdrops

The terms 'fork' and 'airdrop' are not clearly defined and not consistently used within the crypto community.[91] An airdrop is a distribution of crypto assets by blockchain projects (both at an early phase of the project as well as for established blockchain-based enterprises and services) free of charge.[92] There are different ways to become eligible to receive airdrops. Some airdrops happen without the user having to engage beforehand, in any form, with the project and are completely free of charge. Users just have to hold a particular crypto asset or have a wallet address on a particular blockchain at a particular point in time. However, airdrops can also serve as a reward for engaging in marketing measures of the project, e.g., for performing certain tasks to show engagement and support the community, similar to a loyalty or referral programme. Airdrops can be pre-announced to heighten the interest around a project, but can also happen unannounced, surprising users as they find the new crypto assets in their wallets, potentially stirring up conversation about it.

In contrast to token sales, airdrops are not a way of raising capital. The motivation for airdrops can vary, but mostly they serve as a token distribution method to raise awareness to the project, diversify and increase the number of holders and encourage the crypto asset's adoption.[93] Due to the decentralized business models underlying such projects, the distribution should lead to an increased demand of the crypto asset and thus directly increase its value.[94]

It is worth mentioning that from a regulatory perspective, if a security token is distributed via an airdrop, even though this takes place free of charge, it could potentially fall within the scope of securities law and be regarded as a securities offering.[95]

91. *Van Valkenburgh,* What Are Cryptocurrency Forks, Airdrops, and What's the Difference?, Coin Center (17 Oct. 2019), available at https://coincenter.org/entry/what-are-cryptocurrency-forks-airdrops-and-what-s-the-difference.
92. *Katalyse.io,* What Are 'Airdrops' in Crypto World? (15 Feb. 2018), Medium, available at https://medium.com/the-mission/what-are-airdrops-in-crypto-world-a345725c75e0; *Dell'Erba,* From Inactivity to Full Enforcement. The Implementation of the 'Do Not Harm' Approach in Initial Coin Offerings, Michigan Technology Law Review (May 2019), Volume 26, Issue 2, 175, 188, available at https://repository.law.umich.edu/mtlr/vol26/iss2/2/.
93. *Dell'Erba,* From Inactivity to Full Enforcement. The Implementation of the 'Do Not Harm' Approach in Initial Coin Offerings, Michigan Technology Law Review (May 2019), Volume 26, Issue 2, 175, 188, available at https://repository.law.umich.edu/mtlr/vol26/iss2/2/.
94. *Sockin/Xiong,* A Model of Cryptocurrencies, NBER Working Paper No. 26816 (Mar. 2020), 1, available at https://ssrn.com/abstract=3550965.
95. *Van Valkenburgh,* A Token Airdrop May Not Spare You from Securities Regulation, Coin Center (20 Sep. 2017), available at https://coincenter.org/link/a-token-airdrop-may-not-spare-you-from-securities-regulation.

(c) Forks

Forks must be clearly distinguished from airdrops, even though from a user's perspective the result may be the same, as the crypto assets are received free of charge.[96] From a technical standpoint, it is important to understand that the software underlying blockchain networks is open source, and thus can be duplicated and modified at will, which is referred to as a 'fork' of the software.[97] In terms of blockchain technology, these modifications can either be compatible with the initial network ('soft fork') or not compatible ('hard fork').[98] Changes regarding the consensus mechanism of a network can happen both through soft and hard forks. The consensus mechanism is the entirety of rules that designates how entries are written into the ledger.[99] Changes tightening the consensus rules are backwards-compatible and can be implemented through soft forks, changes loosening the rules, e.g., increasing the block size of a protocol and therefore allowing more transactions within a block, are not backwards-compatible and can only be implemented through hard forks.[100] In general, a distinction can be drawn between three forms of hard forks:[101]

(1) A 'temporary' or 'non-contentious' hard fork occurs when participants fail to update their software, leading to a temporary divergence of the nodes. The blockchain forks because the two sides of the network as per the rules governing the consensus mechanism no longer recognize each other as valid participants. This is also referred to as a consensus failure. Once all participants update, the non-updated chain ceases to exist.

(2) A 'contentious hard fork' occurs when an unresolvable dispute between network participants exists over which software version should be used. If this dispute persists, it will permanently result in two different blockchains, with two distinctive crypto assets where only one existed before. Both blockchains recognize all transactions that happened before the block where the fork occurred, but after it, the nodes will only include transactions that are valid according to their consensus rules. Examples of such hard forks are the split between Bitcoin and Bitcoin Cash and Ethereum and Ethereum Classic.

96. *Harrigan/Shi/Illum*, Airdrops and Privacy: A Case Study in Cross-Blockchain Analysis, IEEE International Conference on Data Mining Workshops (2018), 13, available at https://arxiv.org/pdf/1809.05360.pdf.
97. *Haque/Silva-Herzog/Plummer/Rosario*, Blockchain Development and Fiduciary Duty, Stanford Journal of Blockchain Law & Policy (28 Jun. 2019), 139, 148.
98. *Finck*, Blockchain Regulation and Governance in Europe (2018), 202.
99. Cf. *Brummer*, Introduction, in Brummer, Cryptoassets: Legal, Regulatory, and Monetary Perspectives (2019), 2.
100. *Haque/Silva-Herzog/Plummer/Rosario*, Blockchain Development and Fiduciary Duty, Stanford Journal of Blockchain Law & Policy (Jun. 2019), Volume 2, Issue 2, 139, 162 et seq.; *Lombrozo*, Forks, Signaling and Activation, Medium (18 Jun. 2017), available at https://medium.com/@elombrozo/forks-signaling-and-activation-d60b6abda49a.
101. *Van Valkenburgh*, What Are Cryptocurrency Forks, Airdrops, and What's the Difference?, Coin Center (17 Oct. 2019), available at https://coincenter.org/entry/what-are-cryptocurrency-forks-airdrops-and-what-s-the-difference.

(3) A 'codebase hard fork' creates a completely new cryptocurrency on a new blockchain.[102] In this case the new blockchain does not recognize any former transactions of the blockchain the fork was based on. These forks do not split the blockchain but instead merely use the underlying codebase of a blockchain to create a new one. There are various examples for such forks where the underlying codebase of Bitcoin was used to create alternative cryptocurrencies (also called altcoins), e.g., Litecoin and Dogecoin.

Only contentious hard forks permanently give the user a new crypto asset based on holding crypto assets of the original blockchain. In a contentious fork, both networks recognize as valid the transactions before the fork happened. Therefore, from the perspective of the user, he will, by no action of his own, have access to two different crypto assets of equal amount on both networks after the fork. However, this does not mean that both crypto assets are valued the same. The valuation of a network and hence of the crypto assets after a fork is extremely complex and depends on how many participants back the initial and forked version.[103]

Even though the outcome might be similar to an airdrop, airdrops and forks are technically and commercially completely different. In an airdrop, crypto assets are transferred from the project initiators to the eligible wallets, whereas in a fork, the new crypto assets are distributed in a decentralized manner by the new protocol itself, comparable to distribution of new crypto assets as a reward for validation work (see below).

Another difference between forks and airdrops is that from a technical standpoint, after a fork, users do not automatically gain access to the new crypto assets. Users holding their own private keys in self-custody will only gain control over crypto assets of a new blockchain once they choose to install the software of the forked version.[104] If, on the other hand, a user has entrusted his private keys to a cryptocurrency exchange or a custodial wallet provider, then the exchange or custodial wallet provider will be the one who gains access to newly forked crypto assets. These service providers can then choose whether to give their customers the benefit of these new assets.

(d) Rewards for Validation: Mining and Staking

Mining and staking are integral parts of consensus mechanisms. Although in practice, a wide variety of consensus mechanisms have developed, the common denominator is that through a well-designed combination of reward and penalty mechanisms, the

102. *Lombrozo*, Forks, Signaling and Activation, Medium (18 Jun. 2017), available at https://medium.com/@elombrozo/forks-signaling-and-activation-d60b6abda49a.
103. For an in-depth analysis of forks as a governance mechanism subject to coordination failures, *see Barrera/Hurder*, Blockchain Upgrade as a Coordination Game (17 Oct. 2018), available at https://ssrn.com/abstract=3192208.
104. *Van Valkenburgh*, What Are Cryptocurrency Forks, Airdrops, and What's the Difference?, Coin Center (17 Oct. 2019), available at https://coincenter.org/entry/what-are-cryptocurrency-forks-airdrops-and-what-s-the-difference.

behaviour of validators as decentralized intermediaries is influenced.[105] The two most significant consensus mechanisms used are proof of work ('PoW') and proof of stake ('PoS').

In the case of PoW, validators compete to update the blockchain in a manner comparable to a race. The competition consists in solving a mathematical puzzle, where the success of mining the next block depends upon the computational power (hashing power) of the validator. The validator who solves the mathematical puzzle first is rewarded with newly minted crypto assets of the particular blockchain, which is referred to as the 'mining reward'. In other words, validators compete through the use of hardware and energy expenditure. The crypto assets forming the mining reward are created in the same moment that the new block is registered on the blockchain and distributed by the protocol itself, not relying on a central issuer. In addition to the mining reward, the validators also receive a transaction fee in form of crypto assets that users can add to their transactions. For this reason, miners have a financial incentive to prioritize the validation of transactions with a higher fee.[106] If a miner does not behave according to the rules of the protocol and wants to include a fraudulent block, the other nodes will disregard his proposed block and he will not receive the mining reward, thus not being able to recover the costs invested in the operation of the mining infrastructure beforehand.

There are no admission requirements to become a miner of bitcoin. As designed by Satoshi Nakamoto, the bitcoin blockchain is an open source blockchain, so anyone who has the appropriate equipment can download the bitcoin software and become a miner. Miners can enter or exit the system at any time without affecting the system: If it is economically attractive (e.g., high bitcoin price and low electricity costs), new miners will enter the system. If it is economically unattractive (e.g., declining bitcoin price and high electricity costs), miners will withdraw from mining. Thus, the number of miners (and the computing power they provide) is not constant, but constantly fluctuates. Mining is a tough business and some miners do not mine alone ('solo mining'), but instead join other miners in forming a mining pool ('pool mining'). Other miners might not even have their own equipment, but might rent computing power from the operator of a data centre ('cloud mining').

PoS[107] attempts to solve the energy expenditure problem and promises a higher degree of scalability.[108] In PoS, the protocol uses a pseudo-random election process, based on a combination of factors randomly selecting the next validator from a pool of

105. For a detailed insight into the game-theoretical background behind consensus mechanism, *see* *Werbach*, Trust, but Verify: Why the Blockchain Needs the Law, Berkeley Technology Law Journal (2018), Volume 33, Issue 2, 487, 504.
106. *Xu/Weber/Staples*, Architecture of Blockchain Applications (2019), 28.
107. PoS is used, for instance, by DASH and NEO. Ethereum wants to upgrade in the future to PoS through the Casper upgrade. The other form of PoS is Delegated Proof of Stake, in which users signal their support through other participants of the network.
108. Cf. *Saleh*, Blockchain Without Waste: Proof-of-Stake (14 May 2020), 9, available at https://ssrn.com/abstract=3183935; *Catalini/Jagadeesan/Kominers*, Market Design for a Blockchain-Based Financial System (18 Jun. 2019), 4, available at https://ssrn.com/abstract=3396834.

validators, who 'staked' a certain number of crypto assets.[109] In technical terms, validators lock their crypto assets in smart contracts as collateral. The most decisive factor is the amount of crypto assets that has been staked. Validators who staked more crypto assets have a higher chance to be chosen by the protocol. So instead of competing for the next block with heavy computational work, PoS validators are selected based on the amount of crypto assets they are committing to stake. Different from PoW and depending on the PoS system used, validators in PoS mostly do not receive a 'mining reward' from the protocol itself, but instead just the transaction fee from the transacting users. Although PoS systems have their own combination of set of rules, they all have in common that if a validator suggests a fraudulent block, the block is rejected by the other nodes and the previously staked crypto assets will be destroyed (so-called slashing).

In addition to being used as an incentivization method within consensus mechanisms on the network layer, staking is also a common practice within DApps to encourage value-creating activities among their users.[110] Generally, staking crypto assets may enable network participants to potentially receive access to exclusive features of the platform, partake in business activities, or receive status recognition.

1.3.3 Decentralized Finance

Recently, DApps and open protocols have been challenging traditional financial business models that developed over the last century. DeFi aims to increase financial inclusion, security and transparency and to build an integrated and standardized economic system.[111] Financial intermediaries have been playing a significant role in mediating and structuring economic transactions that could otherwise not be executed due to high transaction costs.[112] The increasing level of digitization lowers transaction costs significantly, which results in an increased effectiveness of the underlying procedures. However, digitization does not remove the need for intermediaries; instead traditional intermediaries, such as financial institutions, are replaced by novel ones, such as technology companies. Blockchain technology provides the means to allow a further disintermediation between market participants and may constitute the next stage of this development.[113]

The use of blockchain technology is not exhausted by its application to decentralized fundraising. This technology offers a comprehensive spectrum of potential use cases and novel business models, which may facilitate a more open financial system.[114]

109. *Brummer*, Introduction, in Brummer, Cryptoassets: Legal, Regulatory, and Monetary Perspectives (2019), 3.
110. *Cong/Li/Wang*, Tokenomics: Dynamic Adoption and Valuation (26 Feb. 2020), 40, available at https://papers.ssrn.com/sol3/papers.cfm?abstract_id=3222802.
111. *See* https://consensys.net/blockchain-use-cases/decentralized-finance/.
112. *Y. Chen/C. Bellavitis*, Blockchain Disruption and Decentralized Finance: The Rise of Decentralized Business Models, Journal of Business Venturing Insights (2020), Volume 13, 1.
113. *Y. Chen/C. Bellavitis*, Blockchain Disruption and Decentralized Finance: The Rise of Decentralized Business Models, Journal of Business Venturing Insights (2020), Volume 13, 1.

The following is a non-exhaustive list of such use cases:[115]

Application	*Description*	*Use Case*	*Examples*
Decentralized fundraising	Project initiators can raise capital from the general public without relying on conventional intermediaries	Token sales such as ICOs, STOs, IEOs	EOS, Telegram, Polkadot
Second-layer protocols: state channels/sidechains	Second-layer protocols do not immediately settle every transaction on the underlying blockchain	Offer faster transactions and provide liquidity (possibility of off-chain micropayment network)	Lightning Network, Liquidity Network, OMG Network
Account aggregation	Applications aggregating core DeFi infrastructure provide a single point of integration to access various DeFi protocols	Aggregation applications allow customers easier access, better monitoring, and in general, better usability	Zerion, InstaDapp, Defi Watch
Lending/borrowing	Lending crypto assets and receiving interest in a peer-to-peer manner	Ability to short crypto assets, borrow utility, create leverage, use arbitrage possibilities	Compound, Aave
Decentralized payment instruments, stablecoins	Stablecoins are pegged to a fiat currency or other external reference with an established value. Parity can be maintained by collateralizing stablecoins with fiat, other assets or crypto assets or by algorithmic trading	Cryptocurrency with minimal volatility, unit of account to compare the value of various crypto assets	Tether, Dai, USDC, Libra

114. *Zetsche/Arner/Buckley*, Decentralized Finance, IIEL Issue Brief 02/2020 (2020), 8, available at https://ssrn.com/abstract=3539194.
115. For further examples, *see John/Lundy-Bryan*, Outlier Ventures: Mapping Decentralized Finance (DeFi) (Jun. 2019), available at: https://outlierventures.io/research/mapping-decentralised-finance-defi/; *Schär*, Decentralized finance: On Blockchain- and Smart Contract-based Financial Markets (8 Mar. 2020), available at https://ssrn.com/abstract=3571335.

Application	*Description*	*Use Case*	*Examples*
Decentralized exchanges	Decentralized alternative to trade crypto assets	Crypto assets can be exchanged without relying on a centralized trading platform	Uniswap, 0x, IDEX, Kyber, Oasis
Derivatives, exotic assets and prediction markets	Decentralized alternative to complex financial instruments like put and call options, index trackers and futures	Derivatives can be tailored to suit the needs of the investor, e.g., based on certain maturities or risk profiles	dYdX, UMA project, Synthetix, TokenSet, Augur, Gnosis
Insurance	Insurance against systemic and idiosyncratic risks	Insure against a variety of risks: volatility risk, counterparty risk, technical risk, network risk	Etherisc, Opyn

Courtesy of and based on von Wachter/Sandner, Decentralized Finance (DeFi): What Do You Need to Know? (9 December 2020), Medium, available at https://medium.com/@philippsandner/decentralized-finance-defi-what-do-you-need-to-know-9cd5e8c2a48.

DeFi and the blockchain technology (as a whole) remain emerging technologies, but the number of DeFi projects developed and in development is exponentially rising. On 7 February 2020, DeFi broke the threshold of USD 1 billion locked in decentralized finance protocols.[116] In July 2020, it already surpassed USD 4 billion; at the time of writing, the total value locked in DeFi is close to USD 10 billion.[117] Compared to the value locked in conventional financial markets this number is still minimal, thus confirming that there is still a long way for DeFi projects to go. Despite their increased popularity, DeFi products are still in their infancy and a niche-product that has not yet reached the general public. Most of these DeFi products are still in the technical experiment and innovation stages, bearing significant technical and operational risks, which a non-sophisticated investor might not be willing to commit to. As the market stands today, some of the constraints that DeFi faces are volatility, usability, speed, scalability concerns, low liquidity hindering efficient pricing and regulatory uncertainty.[118]

116. *DeFi Pulse*, DeFi breaks $1 Billion Total Value Locked (TVL) (7 Feb. 2020), available at https://defipulse.com/blog/1-billion-tvl-in-defi/; for the most recent amount *see* DeFi Pulse at https://defipulse.com.
117. *Di Salvo*, The Amount of Value Locked in DeFi Just Hit $4 Billion (25 Jul. 2020), Decrypt, available at https://decrypt.co/36730/defi-closing-in-fast-on-4-billion-mark.
118. *Cf. Zetsche/Arner/Buckley*, Decentralized Finance, IIEL Issue Brief 02/2020 (2020), 10, available at https://ssrn.com/abstract=3539194.

2. INTRODUCTION OF TAX CONCEPTS

2.1 General

Most jurisdictions represented in the following country guides have not amended their tax laws to specifically address the treatment of crypto assets, though Poland and South Africa are exceptions.[119] As a result, general principles of the jurisdiction's tax law will apply to crypto assets. However, the tax authorities of a number of countries have issued some administrative guidance on the how the general tax laws will apply to crypto assets.

Several countries have provided a framework for addressing different types of crypto assets, showing that a consistent taxonomy is beginning to emerge – France, Germany, Singapore, and Hong Kong have classified crypto assets as payment tokens, utility tokens, or security tokens. Similarly, Malta and Poland have classified payment tokens (otherwise known as cryptocurrency or coins) separately from other tokens.

Although cryptocurrency and other payment tokens are intended to be used as a medium of exchange, a unit of account, and/or a store of value, similar to a currency, very few tax authorities have indicated that cryptocurrency will be treated as a currency for tax purposes. Of the countries in the following country guides, only Italy and Malta have ruled that cryptocurrency is treated as a foreign currency for tax purposes. Other countries treat crypto assets as some form of property, though the classification of that property differs from country to country. Thus, in these countries, transactions in crypto assets (whether they are exchanges of crypto assets for fiat or other crypto assets, payment of compensation in crypto assets, payment to merchants in crypto assets, etc.) are subject to the general tax rules. In many cases, this means the transactions are taxable, but some countries discussed in this book provide exceptions to the taxation of personal or investment activities of individuals.

2.2 Types of Taxpayers

Most tax systems distinguish between private investors or consumers, on the one hand, and trades or businesses or companies, on the other. In some countries, such as Brazil, Portugal, Spain, and Switzerland, there are different laws governing corporate income tax and personal income tax. In most other countries reflected in the country guides, a distinction is made between business activities and non-business, or investment, activities. Generally, business entities are deemed to be engaged in business activities, but individuals are subject to a facts-and-circumstances test to determine whether their activities rise to the level of a trade or business, considering such factors as the

119. It should be noted that some countries have proposed or enacted legislation to make certain aspects of crypto assets illegal, such as Belgium (which bans commercialization of financial derivatives in virtual currency by private non-professionals), China (which bans payments in cryptocurrency and the operation of crypto asset exchanges), and India (which has proposed legislation to ban crypto assets).

frequency and size of the transactions and whether the transactions are engaged in with an investment or speculative intent.

Personal or investment activities are often taxed as capital gains or may be taxed at progressive rates for individual taxpayers. Business activities are usually taxed consistently with business profits, which in some countries, such as Germany and Switzerland, depends on the financial accounting treatment.

As discussed above, some countries provide exceptions to the taxation of personal or investment activities of individuals. For example, Austria, Germany, Luxembourg, and Singapore do not tax long-term investments; Australia and Ireland exempt smaller transactions from tax; and Greece, Portugal, and Switzerland completely exempt individuals from tax on their investment gains.

2.3 Types of Taxes

2.3.1 Income Tax

Income taxation is generally the primary method through which governments raise revenues to finance public expenditures and obligations. Generally, a person (i.e., individual, corporation, trust, etc.) who is resident in a particular jurisdiction is subject to income taxation in that jurisdiction on the person's worldwide income (i.e., income from sources inside and outside of the person's country of residence). There are, however, some jurisdictions that do not impose any income tax at all.

The income tax system is generally applied in a progressive manner for individuals where tax rates increase on every dollar earned above certain thresholds. A progressive tax system is premised on the notion that it is fair for an individual to pay more income tax as the individual earns more income.

Some jurisdictions may tax specific sources of income in a more preferential manner (i.e., at a lower rate) compared to other sources of income. For example, a particular jurisdiction may tax active business income more favourably than passive investment income to encourage business investment in the jurisdiction. In Austria, investment income (e.g., interest and dividends) is taxed at a lower rate than business income.

The liability of a business for income tax on business profits will ultimately depend on how the business is organized under the domestic business association laws. For example, the business income of a fiscally regarded entity such as a corporation, trust, and self-employed individual is taxed in the entity's hands while, on the other hand, business income earned by a fiscally transparent entity, such as a partnership, is reported by the members or owners who have an interest in the entity and the corresponding income tax is owed by the members or owners. The tax treatment of crypto funds and their investors is highly dependent on how the fund is organized under business association laws.

An income tax is generally assessed on the taxable income of a person's tax year. Taxable income is computed under the domestic tax laws of the person's country of residence and is generally reported on an income tax return, which is filed with the tax authority for assessment. In cases where income is earned in a foreign country, a person may be subject to foreign income tax on such foreign-source income based on the foreign country's laws. If the person is subject to tax both in their country of residence and a foreign country, relief from potential double taxation is possible based on treaties.

2.3.2 Capital Gains Tax

Capital gains tax is a tax levied on gains realized on the sale of capital assets. Capital assets are to be distinguished from inventory. Generally, the question of whether an asset is a capital asset or inventory is a question of fact.

A capital gain is generally the difference between the original purchase price and the sale price of capital property. For example, if a person acquired one Bitcoin in 2015 as capital property for USD 300 and later sold the Bitcoin in 2017 for USD 15,000, the person would realize a capital gain of USD 14,700. In some jurisdictions, the tax on capital gains is simply an ordinary income tax that applies to a fraction of a capital gain (e.g., 50% or 75% of a capital gain), while in other jurisdictions the tax is more specialized and is based on a variety of factors including the entity disposing of the property and the length time the asset was held before its disposition.

If a capital asset is sold for less than its original purchase price, a capital loss may be realized. For example, if a person acquired one Bitcoin in 2017 as capital property for USD 15,000 and later sold the Bitcoin for USD 8,000 in 2020, the person would realize a capital loss of USD 7,000. Generally, capital losses may be deducted only against taxable capital gains realized in the year, and any balance remaining may be carried back to prior years or forward to future yèars to be applied against taxable capital gains realized in those years. In keeping with the foregoing example, if the person had a taxable capital gain of USD 3,500 in 2018, a net capital loss of USD 3,500 may be carried back from 2020 to be applied against the capital gain in 2018.

Generally, capital gains are realized when a capital asset is sold or disposed. Accordingly, capital gains tax generally does not apply on unrealized gains.

2.3.3 Sales/Use Tax

A sales/use tax is a tax levied on the consideration paid by an end-user or consumer of taxable goods and services. In general, and subject to a myriad of specific exceptions, the person ultimately responsible for paying sales/use tax is the end-user or consumer of the goods or services. This means that sales/use taxes are not levied at each stage of the supply chain (contrary to value added taxes ('VAT'), discussed below), but rather are intended to be charged to the end consumer. However, unlike for VAT, taxable inputs used in the supply chain that are not resold as inventory will generally be subject to sales/use tax and are generally not recoverable in the form of input tax credits, and so the tax becomes embedded throughout the supply chain.

Whether a vendor must register to charge and collect sales/use tax will depend on the degree of connection (or 'nexus' in the US state sales/use tax context) to that jurisdiction; however, specific rules may apply, particularly in the realm of online sales. Where vendors are not required to register to collect sales/use taxes, purchasers of goods in jurisdictions that impose such taxes may nevertheless have self-assessment obligations in respect of that sales/use tax.

2.3.4 VAT/GST

A VAT, or a goods and services tax ('GST'), as it is referred to in many jurisdictions, is also a tax levied on the consideration paid by recipients of taxable goods and services. However, unlike sales/use taxes, a VAT is imposed at each stage of the supply chain, and VAT-registered purchasers who are not end consumers are generally entitled to recover that VAT in the form of input tax credits. Accordingly, and subject to certain exceptions, the VAT is generally not embedded in the cost of goods or services as it moves along the supply chain, and ultimately the end consumer (that is not engaged in any commercial activity) bears the ultimate economic burden for paying the VAT as it cannot recover any input tax credits in respect of that VAT.

The requirement to register for and collect the VAT will vary depending on whether the seller is resident or non-resident in a jurisdiction. Residents will be required to register when selling taxable goods and services above a certain minimum threshold. Non-residents will be required to register when certain additional conditions are met (e.g., whether it is carrying on business for VAT purposes in that VAT jurisdiction; whether special rules apply with respect to online or digital sales).

2.3.5 Payroll Tax

A payroll tax is a tax that is generally applied against an employee's salary, wages, commission, and tips. The tax is deducted from the employee's earnings by the employer and remitted directly to the applicable tax authority on behalf of the employee. In some cases, payroll taxes include programme-specific charges, such as unemployment insurance, government pension plan premiums, and medical insurance premiums. In the context of crypto assets, payroll taxes can be of relevance if employees are remunerated not in cash, but by payment in crypto.

2.3.6 Withholding Tax

A withholding tax is applied (apart from the payroll tax cases mentioned above) primarily to non-residents to ensure that taxes are paid on income sources from within a country. A person who pays an amount to the non-resident is required to deduct and withhold the appropriate amount of tax and remit the amount to the appropriate tax authority on behalf of the non-resident. If the payor does not remit the amount, the payor is generally liable for the tax. Generally, non-residents are required to pay tax in a jurisdiction on investment income (e.g., dividends, interest, rent, royalties) from sources in another country and the payor of the income is required to withhold and remit the tax. Withholding tax may also apply to payments to a non-resident for services.

Practical difficulties may arise if payments to a non-resident are made in crypto assets and the payment falls within the scope of a country's withholding tax regime. Tax authorities currently do not accept payment for withholding taxes in the form of crypto assets. Accordingly, it is incumbent on the payor of amounts that are subject to withholding tax to withhold a sufficient amount of crypto assets from the payment that will give rise to enough after-tax sales proceeds to satisfy the withholding tax liability of the non-resident. The payor should liquidate those crypto assets (which itself is a taxable event) and remit the after-tax sales proceeds to the appropriate tax authority on account of the non-resident's withholding tax. This may not be feasible in all circumstances, especially if illiquid crypto assets are involved.

2.3.7 Stamp Duty

A stamp duty is a tax that a government imposes on the execution of legal documents. In the context of crypto assets, stamp duties are normally not of relevance.

2.3.8 Transfer Tax

A transfer tax is a tax levied on the transfer of legal or beneficial ownership of property from one person to another (e.g., a transfer of title of real estate from a vendor to a purchaser). Generally, transfer taxes do not apply to transfers of crypto assets from one person to another.

2.3.9 Digital Services Tax

A digital services tax is a tax imposed on the gross revenues of digital businesses that generally provide advertising services, sell user data for advertising purposes, or perform certain intermediation services. Digital services taxes generally apply to businesses that meet or exceed specific revenue thresholds. Often these revenue thresholds are large (e.g. USD 1 billion in worldwide revenue and USD 40 million in local revenue, determined on a consolidated basis), which ensures that smaller businesses are not affected by the tax.

Digital services taxes are aimed at taxing large multinational businesses that derive value from the customer base of a particular jurisdiction but avoid income taxation in that jurisdiction. Businesses involved in the crypto space generally will not be subject to digital services taxes because of the high revenue thresholds involved.

2.3.10 Gift/Estate/Inheritance Tax

A gift tax is applied to an individual that transfers property with value to another person without consideration. Typically, the giftor is required to pay a tax on the fair market value of the gift, although in some cases the giftee is liable for the tax. In some jurisdictions, there are exemptions from the gift tax for gifts of certain property or gifts with a value less than a specified threshold or gifts made to certain individuals (e.g., spouses).

An estate tax is a tax on the fair market value of an estate that is left by a deceased person. The estate tax liability crystallizes as a result of the death of the individual and the individual's estate is generally responsible for paying the tax. Estate taxes typically apply above a threshold amount, with estates with values less than the specified threshold not subject to an estate tax. There may be some exceptions to the estate tax, such as estates that are left to a surviving spouse. However, when the surviving spouse of the estate dies, the surviving spouse's estate may then owe estate taxes if the estate exceeds the threshold limit.

Inheritance taxes are similar to estate taxes, except the person who inherits the assets from the deceased's estate must pay the tax on the amount by which the value of the inherited asset exceeds the exemption threshold. The rate of the inheritance tax may depend on the relationship between the person who inherits the assets and the deceased.

Crypto assets should normally be included when calculating, gift, estate, or inheritance tax, but there may be practical issues of valuation.

2.3.11 Wealth Tax

A wealth tax is a tax based on the value of assets, net of liabilities, owned by an individual, including cash, private and public company stocks, bonds, and real estate. The value of crypto assets held by an individual should also be included in the base of assets to which a wealth tax is applicable (note, however, that the value of crypto assets may be difficult to determine in some circumstances).

2.3.12 Exit Tax

An exit tax is a tax that is assessed on the fair market value of assets held by an individual, corporation, or trust at the time the individual, corporation, or trust ceases to be resident in a particular jurisdiction. Certain property may be exempted from the exit tax, such as real estate situated in the particular jurisdiction, but generally all property held before the time of exit is subject to the exit tax including crypto assets (other than, perhaps, asset-backed crypto assets that derive their value from real state situated in the particular jurisdiction). The purpose of the exit tax is to ensure that taxes on gains that accrue while the person is resident in a particular jurisdiction are taxed in that jurisdiction.

2.3.13 Gambling Tax

A gambling tax applies to a person's earnings from gambling. If a person undertakes gambling activities with a certain degree of commerciality, the gambling activities may constitute a business and as such, the gambling earnings may be subject to income tax instead of gambling tax. Crypto asset mining activities involve a certain degree of random chance and, therefore, some commentators have argued that the earnings from crypto asset mining may be gambling earnings to which a gambling tax applies (in jurisdictions that assess a gambling tax). However, in most jurisdictions earnings from crypto asset mining are characterized as business profits and taxed accordingly.

2.4 Valuation Aspects

2.4.1 General

Because gain or loss is generally calculated as the value received less cost basis, both fair market value and basis are important concepts. The value received from a sale or exchange of property is generally computed as the total amount of money received plus the fair market value of other property and services received. The concept of basis in a number of jurisdictions is, in effect, the starting cost – i.e., how much the investor purchased the asset for less any allowable costs. Both of these concepts can be challenging when dealing with a new class of assets – crypto assets. In addition, the taxation of gain often depends on whether the asset is capital or ordinary and how long the asset was held.

2.4.2 Valuation

In terms of determining value received, the current guidelines from many jurisdictions discussed in the following country guides suggest using the prices that were used to buy and sell as per the exchange where the crypto assets were acquired. Most reputable exchanges will provide a report of the transaction history for each of their clients. This information should have all relevant data such as price, volume, and date/time stamp, thus allowing the investor to calculate gains and losses. The value of crypto assets generally must be determined in the taxpayer's local currency. If, for example, the exchange only quotes a crypto asset in US dollars and the investor has a UK tax domicile, then the investor would need to conduct an additional step to calculate the British pounds sterling/US dollar exchange rate at the time of transacting.

However, because exchanges are not connected or tied to a standard currency, prices will vary across the exchanges depending on the buy and sell activity on each one. This means that larger exchanges may yield more market-relevant prices. In addition, different exchanges charge different transaction fees. A lot of news or pricing services, such as Cointelegraph or Coin360, use an aggregate average price of cryptocurrency based on popular exchanges. Some countries, such as Luxembourg, Norway, and Switzerland, publish official exchange rates to use in determining fair market value.

When a taxpayer receives crypto assets in exchange for property or services, and the crypto assets are not traded on any cryptocurrency exchange and does not have a published value, then the fair market value of the crypto assets received may be treated as equal to the fair market value of the property or services exchanged for the crypto assets when the transaction occurs.

2.4.3 Basis

The concept of basis in a number of jurisdictions is, in effect, the starting cost - i.e., how much the investor purchased the asset for less any allowable costs, which may include:

- transaction fees paid to add the transaction to a blockchain;
- advertising for a purchaser or vendor;
- professional costs to draft a contract for the acquisition or disposal of the crypto assets; or
- costs of obtaining a valuation or apportionment to be able to calculate gains or losses.

If the taxpayer is selling a unit of cryptocurrency (or fraction of a unit), he or she may need to identify which basis is being recovered. This may not be so easy, if the investor trades in high volumes and the price is volatile, for example. Different methods have been used to identify fungible items that are sold, such as specific identification, which means the seller picks which unit he or she is selling, or certain assumptions about the flow of assets may be used (e.g., first-in-first-out ('FIFO'), last-in-first-out ('LIFO'), or weighted average basis). Other jurisdictions, such as the United Kingdom, adopt pooling concepts to compute basis, which effectively does away with the requirement to match the specific asset sold to that purchased. Under pooling, assets of the same type (e.g., shares of the same company) can be placed in a separate pool to those of a different type, and prices paid for multiple purchases can be netted. Portugal actually adjusts the basis for inflation if the crypto asset is held for more than two years, which has the effect of eliminating gain.

2.5 International Tax Aspects

2.5.1 Appropriate Taxing Jurisdiction

When a resident of one state invests in another state, a key question arises as to which state has the right to tax the income earned from the investment. Does the state in which the investment is made (the 'Source State') have the right to tax the investment, or does the jurisdiction to tax the income extend to the state in which the investor is resident (the 'Residence State')? Surely, an international tax system that enables the taxation of the same income twice by two different states is both inefficient and unfair from the perspective of the person who earned the income.

States around the world have overcome these issues by negotiating income tax treaties that allocate taxing rights and reduce or eliminate certain taxes, among other things. A tax treaty is a bilateral agreement made by two countries to resolve issues involving double taxation of passive and active income of each of their respective residents by allocating taxing rights between the two countries. Under these treaties, residents of foreign countries may be eligible to be taxed at a reduced rate or exempt from income taxes on certain items of income they receive from the Source State. Tax treaties generally do not reduce the taxes of the Residence State.

Some countries are regarded as 'tax havens'. Generally, a tax haven is a jurisdiction that does not impose an income tax or imposes a very low level of tax. Tax havens typically do not enter into tax treaties.

If a tax treaty does not cover a particular kind of income, or if there is no treaty between the Residence State and the Source State, the income will be subject to tax under the domestic laws of both jurisdictions and, consequently, may be subject to double taxation.

There should be available in the country in which the person is resident a foreign tax credit to avoid double taxation.

2.5.2 Double Tax Treaty Application

Generally, the right of a Source State to tax the income of a person is based on the person's status as a resident of a contracting state for purposes of the applicable treaty signed between the Source State and Residence State. The applicable treaty determines whether a person is resident in a contracting state for treaty purposes.

Generally, a resident of a contracting state means any person who, under the laws of that state, is liable for tax therein by reason of the person's domicile, residence, place of registration, place of incorporation, place of management or any other criterion of a similar nature. Tie-breaker rules are included in tax treaties to help determine which country has the right to tax an individual as the country of residence in case the individual qualifies as a resident (for tax purposes) under the domestic laws of both countries. If a person is resident in a contracting state for purposes of the treaty, the person will generally be entitled to the benefits under the treaty.

In some treaty jurisdictions, a resident of a contracting state does not include a person that is only liable for tax in that jurisdiction under a specific limited tax regime (i.e., not taxed on their worldwide income, as for example, in the United Kingdom under their non-domiciled resident regime).

Many of the jurisdictions discussed in the following country guides have based their double tax treaties on the OECD Model Tax Convention on Income and on Capital ('OECD Model Convention'). Crypto assets are not mentioned in the OECD Model Convention, which means that the treatment and classification for tax treaty purposes must be made under the existing rules. The application of a tax treaty based upon the OECD Model Convention will depend on specific facts and circumstances and the characteristics, especially rights represented by or attributed to the crypto asset at hand.

It is however important to note that the treatment and classification of crypto assets in the context of double tax treaties does not only depend on the treaty itself. Article 3(2) OECD Model Convention determines that a term not defined by the Convention is, unless context otherwise requires or the competent authorities have agreed differently, to be interpreted pursuant to the meaning of that term under national (tax) law of the member state applying the Convention.

2.5.3 *Base Erosion and Anti-Avoidance*

The OECD underwent the so-called Base Erosion and Profit Shifting ('BEPS') programme, which is a multilateral project to tackle multinational tax abuses.

BEPS refers to tax planning strategies that exploit gaps and mismatches in tax rules to artificially shift profits to low or no-tax locations where there is little or no economic activity or to erode tax bases through deductible payments such as interest or royalties. Most of the schemes used are not illegal, but some perceive that these strategies undermine the fairness and integrity of tax systems because businesses that operate across borders can use BEPS to gain a competitive advantage over enterprises that operate at a domestic level. Moreover, it has been argued that when taxpayers see multinational corporations legally avoiding income tax, it undermines voluntary compliance by all taxpayers.

To combat the perceived abuse, the OECD launched the BEPS programme in 2013, which is a multilateral project to tackle multinational tax abuses. The initiative received unprecedented attention from governments and the private sector. The BEPS project brought together over 135 countries and jurisdictions to collaborate on the implementation of the BEPS package. The BEPS package was released in 2015 and provided fifteen Actions that equip governments with the domestic and international instruments needed to tackle tax avoidance. The OECD has only designated four Actions as part of the minimum standard that countries should adopt. Countries adopting the minimum standards – a condition of joining the BEPS Inclusive Framework – are required to introduce measures to remove any 'harmful' tax provisions from their domestic tax regimes, amend their treaty rules to prevent treaty abuse, implement country-by-country reporting rules and exchange these reports with other countries, and work with other countries to improve cross-border tax dispute resolution mechanisms. Alongside the minimum standards, there were identified a number of best practices and areas for greater alignment.

The fifteen Actions included in the Final Report of the BEPS project are:

- Action 1 – Addressing the tax challenges of the digital economy;
- Action 2 – Neutralising the effects of hybrid mismatch arrangements;
- Action 3 – Designing effective controlled foreign company rules;
- Action 4 – Limiting base erosion involving interest deductions and other financial payments;
- Action 5 – Countering harmful tax practices more effectively, taking into account transparency and substance;
- Action 6 – Preventing the granting of treaty benefits in inappropriate circumstances;
- Action 7 – Preventing the artificial avoidance of permanent establishment status;
- Actions 8–10 – Aligning transfer pricing outcomes with value creation;

- Action 11 - Measuring and monitoring BEPS;
- Action 12 -Mandatory disclosure rules;
- Action 13 - Guidance on transfer pricing documentation and country-by-country reporting;
- Action 14 - Making dispute resolution mechanisms more effective; and
- Action 15 - Developing a Multilateral Instrument to modify bilateral tax treaties.

The OECD Multilateral Convention to Implement Tax Treaty Related Measures to Prevent BEPS (Multilateral BEPS Convention) can affect the taxation of crypto assets. The Instrument provides for modifications of existing double tax treaties which are in force bilaterally between the respective parties. However, many signatories to the Instrument have not yet deposited their instruments of ratification, acceptance, or approval and only such treaties that were actively selected by both concerned states are affected. Hence, the scope of covered double tax treaties is limited as of now. Nevertheless, the modifications set out in the Instrument have an impact on the definition of a permanent establishment, hybrid mismatches in the application of a treaty, and activities considered treaty abuse.

2.6 Compliance and Documentation Aspects

2.6.1 Recordkeeping

Most of the jurisdictions discussed in the following country guides do not have specific documentation requirements for taxpayers holding crypto assets. Instead, such taxpayers must comply with general requirements to maintain records sufficient to establish amounts reported on the tax return. A few jurisdictions, such as Australia, Brazil, Singapore, the United Kingdom, and the US, have provided administrative guidance indicating the type of data that should be documented regarding crypto assets, including receipts and dispositions of crypto assets, wallet addresses, and the fair market value or exchange rate of the crypto asset at the time received or transferred.

2.6.2 Information Reporting

Most of the jurisdictions discussed in the following country guides have not adopted specific rules to require information reporting for crypto asset transactions. Payment of employees or merchants in crypto assets is treated in most of these countries as any other payment in kind and subject to any associated reporting requirements. However, there are generally not any tax information reporting requirements imposed on crypto asset exchanges or wallets, though Brazil is a notable exception. In addition, some countries, such as Gibraltar, Italy, Malta, and the Netherlands, impose non-tax registration and reporting requirements on exchanges or wallets.

Taxing authorities of a number of countries discussed in this book have the authority to request information from crypto asset exchanges or wallets in conjunction with their audit of a particular taxpayer. Some taxing authorities, such as Australia, New Zealand, and the US, have the authority to request information on a broader range of taxpayers fitting certain criteria, rather than a specific taxpayer under audit.

The Foreign Account Tax Compliance Act ('FATCA') is a US law that generally requires foreign financial institutions to register with the Internal Revenue Service and to comply with certain information reporting, withholding, and due diligence requirements with respect to 'financial accounts' maintained by US persons. The US has negotiated intergovernmental agreements with many other countries to implement FATCA. These countries have incorporated the FATCA requirements into their local laws and may apply their own penalties for non-compliance. Few, if any, jurisdictions have provided guidance on how FATCA applies to crypto assets, thus resulting in inconsistent interpretations by taxpayers and their advisors.

Similarly, the Common Reporting Standard ('CRS') is an information standard for the automatic exchange of information regarding financial accounts between tax authorities. The OECD developed CRS in 2014 to combat tax evasion, with countries beginning to report in 2017 and 2018. CRS sets out the financial account information to be exchanged, the financial institutions required to report, the different types of accounts and taxpayers covered, as well as common due diligence procedures to be followed by financial institutions.

2.6.3 Exchange of Information

Almost all the countries discussed in this book have a network of bilateral agreements, including double tax treaties or tax information exchange agreements, which facilitate the exchange of tax information with foreign countries.

In addition, the Convention on Mutual Administrative Assistance in Tax Matters ('CMAA') was developed jointly by the OECD and the Council of Europe in 1988. The CMAA facilitates international cooperation in the assessment and collection of taxes, including the automatic exchange of information and the recovery of foreign tax claims. Currently, 137 jurisdictions participate in the CMAA, including all G20 and OECD countries. Article 6 of the CMAA requires the Competent Authorities of the parties to mutually agree on the scope of the automatic exchange of information and the procedure to be complied with. Additional agreements have been developed pursuant to this Article – the Multilateral Competent Authority Agreement on the Exchange of Country-by-Country Reports (the 'CbC MCAA'), for the automatic exchange of Country-by-Country Reports, and the Multilateral Competent Authority Agreement on Automatic Exchange of Financial Account Information (the 'CRS MCAA'), for the automatic exchange of financial account information pursuant to the CRS.

2.7 Civil and Criminal Tax Enforcement Aspects

It is difficult to know the extent of civil and criminal tax enforcement by tax authorities, as many jurisdictions discussed in the following country guides do not make public their enforcement activities. However, at least a few of these countries, including Canada, France, and Japan, are engaging in active audit activity relating to crypto assets, and others, such as India, Spain, and the US, have sent notices to taxpayers. Some countries, including Australia, the United Kingdom, and the US have used their third-party summons authority to collect information from exchanges and wallet providers to identify noncompliant taxpayers.

Some countries are beginning to collaborate on criminal enforcement activities. In July 2018, tax authorities from five countries joined forces to form the Joint Chiefs of Global Tax Enforcement (known as the 'J5'), which targets transnational tax crime through increased enforcement collaboration. The J5 comprises the Australian Criminal Intelligence Commission and Australian Taxation Office, the Canada Revenue Agency, the Netherlands Fiscale Inlichtingen- en Opsporingsdienst, Her Majesty's Revenue and Customs in the United Kingdom, and the Internal Revenue Service Criminal Investigation Division in the US.

3. OVERVIEW OF COUNTRY GUIDES

1. COUNTRY GUIDES
   - 1.1 Country Name
     - 1.1.1 Applicable Tax Law, Guidance and Case Law
       - (a) Which laws, regulations and other administrative guidance exist dealing with crypto assets?
       - (b) Which court cases exist dealing with crypto assets?
     - 1.1.2 Income and Capital Gains Taxes
       - (a) How are crypto assets classified for income and capital gains tax purposes?
       - (b) What are the income/capital gains tax consequences of selling crypto assets against fiat currency?
       - (c) What are the income/capital gains tax consequences of exchanging crypto assets against other crypto assets?
       - (d) If a distinction is made between business assets and non-business assets, when does trading in crypto assets lead to a trade or business?
       - (e) What are the income/capital gains tax consequences for an employee receiving wages or salaries in crypto assets?
       - (f) What are the income/capital gains tax consequences for a merchant receiving payment in crypto assets?
       - (g) What are the income/capital gains tax consequences of a loss of crypto assets?

(h) The loss of a private key to a crypto asset may be deductible for purposes of assessing the income tax, whether the crypto asset is held as a business asset or for investment purposes, with the limitations referred to in Section 1.1.2 (b) above. However, to claim that deduction, the taxpayer should properly document the occurrence of the loss. It is unclear under current rules how this requirement would be met. In addition, this loss may have implications for wealth tax purposes when the affected person is an individual. Please see Section 1.1.3 (f) below.What are the income/capital gains tax consequences of a loss in value of crypto assets?

(i) What are the income/capital gains tax consequences of forks of crypto assets?

(j) What are the income/capital gains tax consequences of airdrops of crypto assets and are the tax consequences different if the airdropped tokens are unwanted?

(k) What are the income/capital gains tax consequences of (solo, pool, and cloud) mining?

(l) What are the income/capital gains tax consequences of staking crypto assets?

(m) What are the income/capital gains tax consequences of an indirect investment in crypto assets?

(n) How is income from crypto assets to be treated under double tax treaty law?

(o) What are the income/capital gains tax consequences of selling crypto assets in an ICO/STO/IEO?

1.1.3 Other Taxes

(a) What are the value added tax/sales tax consequences of selling crypto assets?

(b) Are payments in crypto assets subject to withholding taxes?

(c) Does payment of compensation in crypto assets give rise to payroll tax consequences?

(d) Do transactions with crypto assets trigger any transfer taxes?

(e) Are firms operating in the crypto space subject to digital service taxes?

(f) Are crypto assets subject to gift, inheritance, estate or wealth taxes?

(g) Are crypto assets subject to exit tax?

(h) Can mining trigger gambling tax?

1.1.4 Compliance and Documentation Obligations

(a) What documentation requirements exist for taxpayers regarding crypto assets and are there best practices in recordkeeping to support representations made in tax returns?

(b) What is the evidentiary burden of supporting tax positions when a digital wallet address is lost or shared with other persons?
(c) Are crypto asset exchanges and wallet providers subject to reporting obligations?
(d) Are taxpayers holding crypto assets subject to reporting obligations apart from the filing of income tax/capital gains tax returns?
(e) Are crypto asset exchanges and wallet providers subject to CRS/FATCA reporting?

1.1.5 Civil and Criminal Tax Enforcement

(a) What powers do the tax authorities have to compel the disclosure of information by third parties, such as exchanges or wallet providers, and have these been used in the past?
(b) What measures have the tax authorities undertaken in the past to ensure crypto tax compliance?
(c) Are the tax authorities cooperating with tax authorities in other jurisdictions on enforcement?

Country Reports

Argentina

Leandro M. Passarella

1. COUNTRY GUIDES

1.1 Argentina

1.1.1 Applicable Tax Law, Guidance, and Case Law

(a) Which laws, regulations, and other administrative guidance exist dealing with crypto assets?

In late 2017, Argentina incorporated rules dealing with 'digital currencies' to its income tax law as part of a reform that overhauled the Argentine federal tax system.[1] For that purpose, it included rules on sourcing of income from crypto assets, offset of losses and valuation, as well as those dealing on the assessment of the tax properly. Subsequently, regulations under AITL were amended to adapt them to the new system after the tax reform, and a few rules on digital currencies were added thereto.[2]

However, neither AITL nor its Regulations define what a 'digital currency' is for purposes of their rules. Neither do they state whether 'crypto assets' are included therein. Moreover, no other rules of the Argentine legal system define what a 'digital currency' is. Rather, the wording included in the AITL referring to crypto assets differs from the definition used by other government agencies dealing with them. For

1. Law No. 27430 (B.O. 29 Dec. 2017), amending Law No. 20628 (B.O. 31 Dec. 1973, as then reinstated by Decree No. 649/1997, B.O. 6 Aug. 1997; hereinafter 'AITL'). All references to AITL will be to its text reinstated by Decree No. 824/2019 (B.O. 6 Dec. 2019).
2. Decree No. 1170/2018 (B.O. 27 Dec. 2018), amending Decree No. 1344/1998 (B.O. 25 Nov. 1998, hereinafter 'Regulations' or 'AITL Regulations'). All references to Regulations or AITL Regulations will be to Decree No. 862/2019 (B.O. 9 Dec. 2019), which replaced Decree No. 1344/1998.

instance, the Argentine Financial Information Unit (*Unidad de Información Financiera*)[3] refers to '*monedas virtuales*' or 'virtual currencies' to require reporting transactions dealing with crypto assets for anti-money laundering purposes since 2014.[4] Likewise, when issuing its warning to investors on the risks of participating in 'Initial Coin Offerings' or ICOs in December 2017,[5] the Argentine Securities and Exchange Commission (*Comisión Nacional de Valores* or 'CNV') referred to initial offerings of 'virtual currencies' or 'tokens', without mentioning 'digital currencies' or crypto assets. Adding to this variety of definitions and references addressing crypto assets, when restricting exchange controls in late 2019, the Argentine Central Bank directly required its prior consent to permit foreign currency remittances to acquire 'crypto assets', being the first governmental body that includes this term in its rules.[6]

Based on this different terminology, some scholars have put into question whether the new AITL rules on 'digital currencies' reach virtual currencies (including crypto assets) or not.[7] If they did not, crypto assets (or at least some of them) would still be out of the income tax's reach in some cases.[8] Notwithstanding this construction, we understand that the AITL reference to 'digital currencies' is meant to be broader than 'virtual currencies', so as to comprise crypto assets, as well as other forms of digital assets that can be transacted electronically, as long as they do not fall within another asset category (e.g., certain security tokens; please refer to section 1.1.2(a) below). Otherwise, AITL rules on crypto assets would be empty and inapplicable. In addition, the lack of definition may help tax authorities to reach transactions of any assets created digitally or through blockchain in the future. Based on this situation, all references to 'crypto assets' in this chapter should be understood to be made with

3. The Argentine Financial Information Unit or *Unidad de Información Financiera* is the anti-money laundering authority.
4. Resolution (UIF) No. 300/2014 (B.O. 10 Jul. 2014). The definition provided herein states that:

   > *se entenderá por 'monedas virtuales' a la representación digital de valor que puede ser objeto de comercio digital y cuyas funciones son la de constituir un medio de intercambio, y/o una unidad de cuenta, y/o una reserva de valor, pero que no tienen curso legal, ni se emiten, ni se encuentran garantizadas por ningún país o jurisdicción.* (it is understood that 'cryptocurrency' is the digital representation of value that may be the subject of digital commerce and whose functions are to constitute a means of exchange, and/or a unit of account, and/or a reserve of value, but which has no legal tender, nor are they issued, nor are they guaranteed by any country or jurisdiction.)

5. Comisión Nacional de Valores, Prensa, *Alerta al Publico Inversor sobre ofertas iniciales de monedas virtuales o tokens*, https://www.cnv.gov.ar/SitioWeb/Prensa/Post/1204/1204-alerta-al-publico-inversor-sobre-ofertas-iniciales-de-monedas-virtuales-o-tokens. Comisión Nacional de Valores stated that, subject to further analysis, ICOs may imply a public offering that would require its authorization, and that lack of such authorization may result in the application of sanctions.
6. Comunicación A 6823 (B.O. 4 Nov. 2019).
7. Ricardo Mihura Estrada, *Las 'Monedas Digitales' y el Bitcoin en el Nuevo Impuesto a las Rentas Financieras*, Doctrina Tributaria ERREPAR (DTE) XXXIX:233 (Jan.-Mar. 2018). Daniel Rybnik, *Últimos Reductos de la Teoría de la Fuente*, IMP - Práctica Profesional 2018-XXVI, 44 (2018). These authors claim that the new rules do not apply to cryptocurrencies, or if they do, they do it with limited application.
8. *See* Daniel Rybnik, *supra* n. 7. He states that the new rules do not reach virtual currencies, but only security tokens.

reference to 'digital currencies', as stated in AITL rules. However, this should not be construed in the sense that it is assumed that current AITL rules on crypto assets provide the necessary solutions to this economic phenomenon. On the contrary, certain additional hurdles have been created as a result of the adoption of these rules.

Having adopted a position in favour of the validity and applicability of the new AITL rules on crypto assets, the tax reform – which became effective in fiscal year 2018 – was aimed at taxing individuals dealing with crypto assets held for investment purposes. Until then, those transactions were outside of the scope of the income tax. Likewise, the reform provided new and clearer rules to Argentine taxpayers that had been holding crypto assets as business assets before Law No. 27430 was enacted and, consequently, have already been subject to tax pursuant to Argentine general income tax rules.

On the other hand, unlike the income tax, no other Argentine tax laws (whether federal or provincial) deal with crypto assets. Consequently, taxes such as value added tax, provincial gross receipts taxes and so on may apply on crypto assets transactions depending on whether they fall within their respective scopes.

(b) Which court cases exist dealing with crypto assets?

Argentine courts have not dealt with cases involving crypto assets so far. Likewise, we are not aware that Argentine tax authorities have consistently audited transactions dealing with crypto assets yet.

1.1.2 Income and Capital Gains Taxes

(a) How are crypto assets classified for income and capital gains tax purposes?

Crypto assets are classified as intangible assets, subject to the same treatment applicable to bonds or other debt securities.[9] However, they are not included in the definition of 'securities' provided by the AITL Regulations.[10] In addition, they are assets that give rise to Argentine source or foreign source income or gains, depending

9. AITL Articles 2(4) and 67.
10. AITL Regulations Article 9. 'Securities' are defined as any values that are susceptible of generalized and impersonal trade in stock exchanges authorized by the Argentine Securities and Exchange Commission. Based on this definition, security tokens would not be per se 'crypto assets' when they fall within this definition. Rather, they should be treated as securities for AITL purposes. *See* Ricardo Mihura Estrada, *supra* n. 7. However, the classification of security tokens as 'securities' would not imply a different income tax treatment in practice, because crypto assets and 'securities' are taxed in the same way. The difference steps on the fact that gains from trades of publicly offered 'securities' in Argentine stock market are exempt from Argentine tax when realized by Argentine resident individuals that hold them for investment purposes, or by non-residents. However, as of the date hereof, no filings have been made with the Argentine Securities and Exchange Commission to request authorization of public offering of any security tokens. Consequently, unless otherwise noted, security tokens are included in the concept of 'crypto assets' for purposes of this analysis.

on whether the issuer is in Argentina or abroad, respectively.[11] This rule may not be problematic in the context of centralized crypto assets. Crypto assets produced by an Argentine person will generate Argentine source income, while those created by non-Argentine persons will give rise to foreign source income. However, there is no guidance as to how to determine the location of an 'issuer' of a decentralized crypto asset.[12] Could a miner be considered the 'issuer' of decentralized crypto assets? Based on current rules, such miner may fall within the category of 'issuer'. Therefore, Argentine miners would produce decentralized crypto assets located in Argentina.[13] As a result, income and gains deriving from them would be sourced therein. This solution, however, poses new questions, some of which are listed below:

(1) How can the miner of a decentralized crypto asset be identified?
(2) Would the decentralized crypto asset carry a specific feature that would help determining that it has been created by an Argentine (or non-Argentine) miner?
(3) How can it be determined where the miner of a decentralized crypto asset is located when creating it?
(4) What happens if miners create the decentralized crypto assets using technology located in a jurisdiction different from the one where they are located?
(5) Where is the source of a decentralized crypto asset created by a pool of miners located in different countries?
(6) How can decentralized crypto assets be tracked once they are created to determine whether Argentine income tax is to be assessed on each and all trades involving them?

AITL or its Regulations do not provide answers to these questions, which may not be the only ones arising from this AITL source rule.[14] Please refer to sections 1.1.2(b), (k) and (l) *infra* for further analysis of these questions and the issues they present when solved with current AITL rules. These issues might have been avoided by considering that income and gains from crypto assets are sourced in Argentina when derived by an Argentine resident taxpayer.

At the same time, there is no *a priori* distinction of crypto assets between business assets and non-business assets. While corporate taxpayers are always deemed to hold

11. AITL Article 7.
12. *See* Marcos Zocaro, *Algunos Aspectos Problemáticos de la Gravabilidad de las Monedas Digitales en el Impuesto a las Ganancias*, IMP – Práctica Profesional 2019-LII, 26, Buenos Aires, Argentina (2019).
13. *See* Ricardo Mihura Estrada, *supra* n. 7. This author argues that miners would not fall within the definition of 'issuer' because crypto assets that they generate are their reward for solving mathematical algorithms. Therefore, according to his interpretation, source of income from crypto assets would be determined based on AITL general sourcing rule. While this interpreta tion might have some grounds, it should be considered that without mining activity, new crypto assets would not be created or issued. That is the reason to understand the term 'issuer' broadly to include miners.
14. Please refer to n. 21 *infra*. Further analysis of decentralized crypto assets' background and features should be performed by the Argentine regulator (and, possibly, the Argentine Congress) to adjust AITL rules to those of crypto assets' reality.

these assets for business purposes, individuals may be deemed to hold crypto assets as business or non-business assets depending on how they acquire those assets and transact them thereafter. Thus, individuals that receive crypto assets as consideration for their trade or business (including mining for crypto assets) would be required to treat those assets as part of their business. On the other hand, those receiving crypto assets as consideration for the performance of personal or professional services only would be able to treat them as non-business assets, subject to fulfilling certain requirements.[15] This has implications in the way the individual's income tax is to be assessed upon the crypto assets' transfer.

(b) What are the income/capital gains tax consequences of selling crypto assets against fiat currency?

Pursuant to AITL Article 3, transfers of assets for any consideration are deemed 'sales' for Argentine income tax purposes. In addition, transfers of crypto assets give rise to taxable gain or loss, regardless of the tax residence of the person obtaining this result. Consequently, while Argentine tax residents are taxed on their gains (or losses) from trades in crypto assets created worldwide, non-residents may only be taxed on their gains from crypto assets created or issued by Argentine persons.

Resident taxpayers' gain or loss is assessed by subtracting the crypto assets' tax basis from the value received in exchange for them, using the 'First In First Out' (FIFO) method of accounting.[16] Gains or losses are assessed in Argentine currency by the following features: Crypto assets created or issued by Argentine persons may give rise to gains or losses in Argentine or foreign currency, while those gains or losses realizing from crypto assets created or issued by non-Argentine persons are to be accounted for in the currency of the creator or issuer.[17] Pursuant to AITL Article 2(4), this gain or loss is taxable or deductible (pursuant to certain offset rules), respectively. Once the result of their sales is assessed, their income tax treatment and calculation depend on three factors: (a) who the taxpayer is (i.e., is it an individual or corporate taxpayer?), (b) whether crypto assets have been acquired for investment purposes or business reasons and (c) where the source of the income is located.[18] In addition, sales of crypto assets trading in foreign currency may also give rise to foreign exchange gains (or losses)

15. Providers of personal or professional services receiving assets (including crypto assets) as consideration can treat them as non-business assets if they do not complement their services with commercial activities (AITL Articles 53 and 82). For instance, a veterinarian or a physician would be deemed to render professional services only if either of them does not combine their services with commercial activities (e.g., the sale of pet food or owning a clinic, respectively). Likewise, a carpenter would have a trade or business if she creates and manufactures furniture for sale, while she would not reach that threshold if she only performs jobs at their clients' request and according to their indications and preferences.

    When fulfilling this general requirement, individuals are also required to hold the assets received for at least two years prior to their disposition to be entitled to apply the tax treatment of non-business assets upon their transfer. If sold before the two-year term, gains are treated as part of the consideration for their personal or professional services. Therefore, those gains are subject to tax at progressive rates (AITL Regulations Article 185).
16. AITL Article 67.
17. AITL Articles 98 and 151. AITL Regulations Article 245.
18. AITL Articles 1, 2(2), 2(4) and 7.

resulting from the difference in exchange rates of the Argentine currency to the relevant foreign fiat currency in effect both at the time of the crypto assets' acquisition and subsequent sale. These gains may or may not be taxable, depending on the type of taxpayer disposing the crypto asset. It is unclear whether capital gains from the disposition of crypto assets could be characterized solely as foreign exchange gains, because it is uncertain whether crypto assets would qualify as 'currency' under Argentine law.[19]

The simpler tax implications are for corporate taxpayers. They are subject to corporate income tax on any gains from sales of crypto assets for fiat currency at the corporate income tax rate (currently set at 30%, to be lowered to 25% for fiscal years starting as of 1 January 2021).[20] This tax treatment applies to sales of crypto assets, whether they have been acquired for investment purposes or not. Corporate taxpayers' tax basis in crypto assets created or issued by Argentine persons is their acquisition price (if sold in the same year of acquisition) or their fair market value at the beginning of the fiscal year in which they are sold (if bought in a previous year).[21] Tax basis in crypto assets created or issued by non-Argentine persons is always their acquisition price.[22] Foreign exchange gains (or losses) from sales of crypto assets created or issued by Argentine persons are taxable on an accrual basis when they are denominated in foreign currency.[23] On the other hand, those arising from crypto assets created or issued by foreign persons are taxable income (or deductible losses) when the fiat currency received for the crypto asset is in any way disposed of, or the funds are transferred to Argentina.[24]

Individuals, on the other hand, may be subject to different income tax treatments:

- Individuals that acquire crypto assets in the course, or as a result, of their business activities are required to assess the gains from sales of crypto assets as if they were corporate taxpayers. Crypto assets are deemed business assets in their hands. This tax treatment also applies to individuals that receive crypto assets as consideration for sales of goods or the performance of services complemented with commercial activities (including mining of crypto assets).[25] Consequently, any gains from their subsequent transfer would be subject to income tax at progressive rates. Crypto assets created by non-Argentine persons generate foreign source income, which would be added on top of their Argentine source income for purposes of assessing their income tax

19. *See* Ricardo Mihura Estrada, *Tenencias y ganancias (y pérdidas) de criptoactivos en las declaraciones juradas personales*, Doctrina Tributaria ERREPAR (DTE) XL:831 (August 2019). This author argues that cryptocurrencies, such as Bitcoin, should be deemed 'currency' for Argentine legal purposes. There is no indication that Argentine authorities or courts concur with this construction.
20. AITL Article 73. Law No. 27541 Article 48 (B.O. 23 Dec. 2019).
21. AITL Article 67.
22. AITL Article 149.
23. Argentine corporate taxpayers are required to mark-to-market their holdings of crypto assets created or issued by Argentine persons as of each year end (AITL Articles 106(a)(8) and 107(c)). *See* s. 1.1.2(h) below.
24. AITL Articles 151 and 155.
25. AITL Articles 2(2) and 53.

liabilities at progressive rates. Thus, such gains may be subject to higher tax rates. Sourcing rules are also relevant in the event of loss realization, as discussed below.

- In turn, individuals that acquire crypto assets with cash for investment purposes are subject to income tax at rates of 5% or 15% upon the disposition of crypto assets created or issued by an Argentine person.[26] Likewise, gains from the transfer of crypto assets created or issued by foreign persons are subject to income tax, although at a 15% rate. These tax rates apply whether the gain is short or long term. Sourcing the gain is also relevant in the event of the realization of losses, as discussed below. Sales of crypto assets received as consideration for the performance of personal or professional services that are not complemented with commercial activities also give rise to gains subject to the 5% or 15% income tax, unless they are disposed of within two years of their receipt. If sold within the two-year term, gains (including foreign exchange gains) are deemed part of the consideration of those services.[27] Therefore, they are subject to income tax at progressive rates, as stated above. The source of the gain is also relevant in case of realizing losses, as well as in the event of disposing the crypto asset before the two-year term elapses.
- In all cases, taxable gain (or deductible loss) is assessed as the excess of the crypto assets' sales price over their tax basis. Tax basis of crypto assets that are business assets in individuals' hands is determined applying the same rules of corporate taxpayers. On the other hand, crypto assets' acquisition price is their tax basis when held for investment purposes. In that regard, crypto assets created by Argentine persons can be 'denominated' in Argentine or foreign currency pursuant to AITL Article 98. Therefore, taxable gain is to be assessed in the fiat currency of these crypto assets' 'denomination'. On the other hand, in the case of crypto assets created or issued by foreign persons, taxable gain is to be assessed in the fiat currency with legal tender in the jurisdiction where the crypto assets' creator or issuer is located.[28] In addition, foreign exchange gains are exempt when realized from the disposition of crypto assets held as non-business assets.[29] As a result, any foreign exchange gains or losses resulting from the fluctuation in value of Argentine and foreign currencies that

26. AITL Article 98 provides that gains from the disposition of crypto assets are subject to income tax at a 15% rate. However, AITL Regulations Article 245 states that a 5% tax rate applies to the disposition of crypto assets 'denominated' in Argentine currency, while the 15% tax rate is applied to crypto assets 'denominated' in Argentine currency that have an adjustment feature or in foreign currency directly. The tax treatment under the AITL Regulations differs from the one established under AITL Article 98. In addition, it refers to crypto assets 'denominated' in fiat currency, when they may not have any reference to another currency, whether Argentine or foreign. *See* Marcos Zocaro, *supra* n. 12.
27. Cristina del Carmen Mansilla, *Tratamiento Fiscal de las Monedas Digitales*, IMP – Práctica Profesional 2019-LXVI, 24.
28. AITL Article 143.
29. AITL Articles 26(t) and 134(c).

are realized upon crypto assets' transfers may not be relevant for purposes of assessing the individuals' income tax liability.[30]

References to 'fiat currency denomination' and 'location of the issuer or creator' in the rules for assessing gains from transfers of crypto assets create additional tensions: how are gains assessed when crypto assets do not have a 'denomination' in fiat currency? Which fiat currency is used for purposes of such assessment? Moreover, in the context of creation of decentralized crypto assets, would they be denominated in Argentine currency when created by Argentine miners? Would the same crypto asset have different fiat currencies as references, depending on the location of the miners? What happens if the miner location is unknown? These questions might not have arisen if these rules had stated that gains from transfers of crypto assets are to be assessed in the fiat currency that they are usually traded for.

Losses realized from sales of crypto assets can only be offset against capital gains from sales of crypto assets, as well as gains realized from sales of shares, bonds and other securities.[31] Like in the case of gains, losses are to be determined in the fiat currency of its denomination (if the crypto asset's creator or issuer is Argentine) or of the creator's location (if it is non-Argentine), and then converted to Argentine currency. In addition to this specific basket, losses must be classified according to their source (i.e., losses from Argentine sources or from foreign sources), as they would only be offset against gains from the same sources. Therefore, gains from sales of crypto assets created or issued by foreign persons cannot offset losses from sales of crypto assets created or issued by Argentine persons, and vice versa.[32] In all cases, unused losses expire if they do not offset gains realized in the same fiscal year or the following five fiscal years. This treatment is applicable to both individuals that hold crypto assets for investment purposes, as well as those that hold them as business assets, whether corporate or individual taxpayers.

When individuals hold crypto assets for investment purposes, their income tax treatment on gains from trades with those assets is less favourable than the one applicable to foreign exchange gains from conversions of foreign currency into Argentine currency, which are exempt from income tax.[33] A similar situation may arise with respect to crypto assets referenced to other physical assets, such as precious metals, collectibles and so on: direct transfers of those kinds of assets do not give rise to taxable gains under current AITL rules, while transfers of crypto assets are taxed.[34] Consequently, compared to other foreign currencies and some types of valuable assets

30. If crypto assets were created or issued by persons located in foreign jurisdictions, Argentine individual taxpayers may only be required to recognize foreign exchange gains or losses from foreign sources if crypto assets were traded for a fiat currency different from the one with legal tender in the jurisdiction where their creator or issuer is located. In that case, however, those foreign exchange gains or losses would be exempt from Argentine income tax, and they would have to be reported in that way when assessing the individuals' income tax liabilities (AITL Article 134(c) and Decree No. 895/2016 (B.O. 28 Jul. 2016) Article 20).
31. AITL Article 25.
32. AITL Article 132.
33. AITL Article 26(v).
34. AITL Article 2.

that may offer asset and/or value protection, crypto assets are less favourably treated from a tax perspective. Therefore, individuals may not have an incentive to acquire crypto assets if tax is the main driver for the investment decision.

Non-residents are, generally, taxed on their Argentine source income on a gross basis at an effective rate of 13.5 %. Nonetheless, they can opt to be taxed on their actual capital gains if they can prove their basis in the crypto assets.[35] In that case, the applicable rate is 15 %. This tax treatment applies if they traded crypto assets created by Argentine persons (if any),[36] whether the purchaser is an Argentine person or not. If sold to an Argentine person, the Argentine purchaser would be liable to assess the tax by way of withholding. On the other hand, when sold to another non-resident, the non-resident seller would be required to assess the Argentine tax and remit it to the Argentine tax authorities via international wire transfer.[37] This rule, which is also applicable in the case of sales of other Argentine assets from one non-resident to another (e.g., shares in Argentine companies), poses compliance issues: Argentine tax authorities have no mechanisms available under current domestic or treaty law to enforce the collection of unpaid taxes from non-residents. Please *see* section 1.1.5 (c) below.[38]

In all cases, taxes are to be paid in Argentine currency. Therefore, amounts in crypto assets must be converted to the fiat currency of the relevant crypto asset's creator or issuer, and then to Argentine currency. In case of decentralized crypto assets, this method of conversion may not be applicable. It might have been preferable that, for transactions with this type of crypto assets, different rules had been provided to ease the individuals' income tax assessment. A possible solution might have been – and still might be – to use the main fiat currency in which such decentralised crypto asset is traded to assess the Argentine tax appropriately. Besides this issue, please refer to sections 1.1.2(e)–(h) below for additional income tax implications from certain transactions with crypto assets.

(c) What are the income/capital gains tax consequences of exchanging crypto assets against other crypto assets?

As mentioned above, transfers of assets for consideration are deemed sales for Argentine income tax purposes. Consequently, the exchange of crypto assets for crypto assets is also deemed a taxable transfer, giving rise to the different implications discussed in section 1.1.2(b) above. In this case, however, the result of these exchanges is assessed as the excess of the fair market value of the crypto assets received at the time of the exchange over the exchanged crypto assets' tax basis (as previously

35. AITL Article 98.
36. Please refer to the discussion on the issues arising from sourcing decentralized crypto assets created by Argentine persons in s. 1.1.1(a) *supra*.
37. General Resolution (AFIP) No. 4227 (B.O. 12 Apr. 2018) Article 9(b).
38. This is an area that should be revisited by a future tax reform, not only with respect to transfers of crypto assets, but also in general.

defined).[39] Fair market value of both crypto assets must be assessed in fiat currency. As previously mentioned, foreign exchange gains or losses would be relevant in the event of exchanges performed by corporate taxpayers, as well as individuals that receive the exchanged crypto assets in the course, or as a result, of engaging in a trade or business.

(d) *If a distinction is made between business assets and non-business assets, when does trading in crypto assets lead to a trade or business?*

As stated in section 1.1.2(a) above, there is no *a priori* distinction between business crypto assets and non-business crypto assets. Rather, that distinction would have been the result of the context in which crypto assets have been acquired (i.e., during the course of a trade or business or not). Consequently, such a classification would be relevant only with respect to individuals to determine how they are to be taxed on the gains resulting from their trading in crypto assets.

However, it might have been argued that, pursuant to AITL general rules, individuals trading in crypto assets held for investment purposes prior to the tax reform by Law No. 27430 might have had a trade or business of trading in crypto assets if they entered into those transactions periodically.[40] In that case, crypto assets would have been business assets for them. Consequently, they would have been subject to personal income tax on their gains from those trades at progressive rates, under the rules for assessing gains applicable to corporate taxpayers (i.e., mark-to-market rules, taxation of foreign exchange gains, etc.). However, there has not been – and there is not yet – any guidance as to when any investment activities performed by an individual, with respect to any type of assets, are periodic or sporadic for purposes of determining whether the 'trade or business' threshold is reached.[41] Therefore, it would have been contentious to affirm when speculative trades in crypto assets held for investment purposes had created a trade or business. This discussion has ended with the incorporation of rules on crypto assets to the AITL: now individuals trading in crypto assets for speculative purposes are subject to tax, whether they do it periodically or sporadically, and the discussion of the existence of a trade or business is no longer relevant, because they are deemed held for investment purposes (whether for a short or a long term).

(e) *What are the income/capital gains tax consequences for an employee receiving wages or salaries in crypto assets?*

Wages and salaries paid in crypto assets are subject to the same income tax treatment in the employees' hands as those paid in cash. In that case, the amount of income is to be set at the crypto assets' fair market value at the time of payment, converted to fiat

39. AITL Regulations Article 71.
40. AITL Article 2(1).
41. *See* Rafael Brave, Argentine Supreme Court of Justice, 15 Oct. 1947, 209 Fallos 129.

currency and then, if necessary, to Argentine currency.[42] This value will be the employees' tax basis in the crypto assets pursuant to general AITL rules. The location of the crypto assets' creator or issuer determines the source of the gain that employees may realise thereafter, as well as the form to assess the amount of gain or loss.

In that regard, unlike individuals receiving crypto assets as consideration for the performance of personal or professional services that are not complemented with commercial activities,[43] employees are entitled to treat crypto assets received as payment of their salaries or wages as non-business assets since their acquisition. Consequently, any gains resulting from their subsequent sale would not be subject to tax at progressive rates at any time.

(f) What are the income/capital gains tax consequences for a merchant receiving payment in crypto assets?

Merchants receiving crypto assets as consideration for their sales of goods or services would be required to treat them as business assets. The tax basis in those crypto assets would be equal to be value of the goods or services sold, which would be documented in the corresponding invoices. If crypto assets received have been created or issued by non-Argentine persons, the tax basis should be converted, on the date of the crypto assets' acquisition, to Argentine currency at the exchange rate of the currency with legal tender in the jurisdiction where such creator or issuer is located. When selling those crypto assets thereafter, merchants will be subject to the income tax treatment referred to in section 1.1.2(b) above. Therefore, they will be immediately subject to tax on the gain (i.e., the increase in the crypto assets' value) arising from their transfer, while the foreign exchange gains (i.e., the fluctuation in exchange rates since acquisition until disposition) will be taxable when the fiat currency is in any way disposed of, or transferred to Argentina.

(g) What are the income/capital gains tax consequences of a loss of crypto assets?

The loss of a private key to a crypto asset may be deductible for purposes of assessing the income tax, whether the crypto asset is held as a business asset or for investment purposes, with the limitations referred to in section 1.1.2(b) above. However, to claim that deduction, the taxpayer should properly document the occurrence of the loss. It is unclear under current rules how this requirement would be met. In addition, this loss may have implications for wealth tax purposes when the affected person is an individual. Please *see* section 1.1.3(f) below.

42. AITL Article 82. AITL Regulations Articles 71 and 177.
43. Please refer to *supra* n. 15.

(h) *What are the income/capital gains tax consequences of a loss in value of crypto assets?*

Argentine tax treatment of crypto assets' loss (or increase) in value differs depending the type of taxpayer and the source of the crypto assets' income.

Corporate and individual taxpayers that hold crypto assets as business assets are required to mark-to-market their holdings on an annual basis when crypto assets are issued by Argentine persons.[44] This mark-to-market should be made in Argentine currency. Any gains or losses must be considered for purposes of assessing the taxpayers' inflation adjustment. It implies a step-up or step-down in those taxpayers' tax basis in the crypto assets created by Argentine persons. Such annual revaluation does not apply with respect to crypto assets created by foreign persons. On the other hand, individual taxpayers are not required to mark-to-market their crypto assets, whether created by Argentine or foreign persons, when they are held for investment purposes. Consequently, they would only realize a decrease or increase in value upon a realization event, and any foreign exchange gain (or loss) would not be taxable (or deductible), as previously mentioned.

(i) *What are the income/capital gains tax consequences of forks of crypto assets?*

There is no guidance as to how forks, whether soft or hard, are to be treated under AITL or its Regulations. Considering that they imply debates within the community of the relevant crypto asset resulting in a full or partial consensual upgrade in the blockchain and the creation of a new crypto asset, forks may be deemed contracts among owners of the same crypto asset. Under that interpretation, they may not imply necessarily a disposition or exchange of crypto assets. Therefore, owners of the relevant crypto asset should not be deemed to realize gains or losses from the fork. This does not mean that, for those minority owners that do not consent to the upgrade, a subsequent loss in value of the old crypto asset may occur as a result of the fork. In that case, if the crypto asset were to become worthless, those owners should properly document the reasons to claim the loss when assessing their income tax liabilities.

Since there would not be a disposition of the crypto asset, the tax basis in the new crypto asset should be determined. In general, tax basis in the old crypto asset should be either maintained in the forked crypto asset (if a new one is created) or rolled over to its replacement. Since Argentina does not have rules on tax basis of stripped assets, and AITL rules on tax-free reorganisation rules apply to entities, rather than assets,[45] the tax basis in the new crypto asset may be zero.[46] However, when a new crypto asset is created, whether as a replacement of or to coexist with the old one, community members that may have invested economic resources for the fork to happen may have

44. AITL Article 107.
45. AITL Articles 80–81.
46. Ricardo Mihura Estrada, *supra* n. 7.

a claim to take a deduction for the amount of their investment (provided that they can prove such amount).[47] In that case, at least two questions may arise from this scenario:

(1) Regarding the timing to claim a deduction, is such investment an expense that would be immediately deductible or an improvement that should be added to the tax basis in the upgraded crypto asset, to be recovered upon the transfer of the crypto asset? Although there is no guidance, the upgrade in the crypto asset may initially seem to be an improvement. Therefore, it should be added to the cost of the upgraded crypto asset, or directly attributed, whether wholly or partially, to the new crypto asset's tax basis.
(2) Regarding the amount of the deduction, are those community members entitled to a full recovery of their investment, or can they claim a deduction only for the portion of their investment that can be attributed to their upgraded or newly created crypto assets? In this case, it could be argued that the full amount of the investment should be recovered by those community members that invested in making the fork possible. Community participants agreeing to the fork without making any economic investments may benefit from an unrealized increase in value in their holdings, whether the fork implies a substitution of the new crypto asset for the old one or the creation of a new one that coexists with the old crypto asset. In other words, the improvement in the crypto asset may not necessarily imply an immediate realization of income by owners that only agree to, or benefit from, the fork. However, those passive community participants will be taxed on the gains to be realized from the sale of the new crypto assets created as a result of the activity of those that invested economic resources to make it possible.

Further analysis should be performed to provide more definitive answers to these questions, as well as answers to additional questions that may arise from this analysis.

(j) *What are the income/capital gains tax consequences of airdrops of crypto assets and are the tax consequences different if the airdropped tokens are unwanted?*

From a tax perspective, airdrops imply the realization of an unexpected, and sometimes unwanted, gain. If crypto assets were held by individuals for investment purposes, airdrops would be exempt income.[48] Nonetheless, those individuals would be required to value the newly received crypto assets at the acquisition cost of the person giving up the airdropped crypto assets. If such acquisition cost is unknown, the individuals' tax basis in the airdropped crypto assets would be their fair market value.[49]

On the other hand, corporate taxpayers and individuals treating the crypto assets as business assets would be required to treat the airdropped crypto assets as taxable

47. Marcos Zocaro, *supra* n. 12.
48. AITL Article 26(s).
49. AITL Article 4.

income. The amount of income to be recognized would be their fair market value at the time of the airdrop, which would be their acquisition price for purposes of assessing the tax basis, as previously discussed in section 1.1.2(b) above.[50]

(k) *What are the income/capital gains tax consequences of (solo, pool, and cloud) mining?*

Mining activities imply the creation of crypto assets by actively decoding mathematical problems. Under that characterization, income from mining activities can be classified as business income. If derived by individuals, it would be taxed at progressive rates. Consequently, based on the source rule provided in AITL Article 7, mining activities performed in Argentina give rise to Argentine located crypto assets. This would not create a problem in the scenario of solo mining: Owners of those crypto assets will derive Argentine source income and capital gains.

On the other hand, when grouping with other miners in a pool, it is unclear where the creation of the crypto asset occurs. The same question arises when the hardware necessary for mining activities is in another jurisdiction (i.e., cloud mining): where is the crypto asset created? Considering the Argentine source rule for crypto assets, this is not a question to be overlooked. Could a crypto asset be partially sourced in Argentina? It may be impractical. At the same time, as previously said, it may be difficult for tax authorities of any jurisdictions to determine where a decentralised crypto asset is created. This may lead to further developments in the regulations on the matter.

(l) *What are the income/capital gains tax consequences of staking crypto assets?*

Unlike mining, staking crypto assets does not imply an active operation to create crypto assets. Consequently, it could be argued that income from staking should be classified as investment income. Therefore, if derived by individuals, it would be subject to income tax at a 15% rate. In this case, however, the issue of determining the location of the creation of crypto assets also arises: Does an Argentine person staking crypto assets create crypto assets that should be deemed located in Argentina? Or is it created as a result of the stake and the Argentine person receives a return on its investment? As previously said, further investigation of this phenomenon should be performed to design or redesign the rules adequately.

(m) *What are the income/capital gains tax consequences of an indirect investment in crypto assets?*

Indirect investment in crypto assets may give rise to different tax implications, depending on the type of instrument or vehicle that is used for the indirect investment,

50. AITL Regulations Article 71.

the investor's tax residence and the location of the source of income from crypto assets under AITL rules.

Regarding the type of instrument or vehicle used for the indirect investment, if it were through debt instruments or derivative contracts, both Argentine resident and non-resident taxpayers should be deemed to have an investment in those assets, rather than in crypto assets. Consequently, they should be taxed according to AITL rules applicable to debt instruments and derivative contracts.

On the other hand, if the investment were made through a vehicle (e.g., a company) or other legal structure (e.g., trusts, funds), the tax treatment of crypto assets may still be applicable under AITL. Thus, Argentine resident taxpayers are deemed to own crypto assets indirectly held (i.e., as if the foreign vehicle or legal structure does not exist) if two conditions are met: (1) the vehicle or legal structure is located outside Argentina and (2) Argentine tax transparency rules apply. Argentine tax transparency rules apply in the following cases:

- In the case of foreign trusts or foundations, when Argentine taxpayers control the assets under those structures (e.g., the structures are revocable, settlors or founders are beneficiaries, or they have some other form of control over the investment and disinvestment in the underlying assets).[51]
- In the case of foreign legal entities with no fiscal personality in their home jurisdictions.[52]
- In the case of foreign legal entities with fiscal personality, when the following requirements are simultaneously met:[53]
  - Income obtained by those foreign companies is not subject to another specific tax computation rules.
  - Argentine taxpayers have direct or indirect control over the foreign companies, whether by capital, voting power, control rights on the assets or the appointment or removal of the persons managing those assets.
  - Foreign companies have no substance or derive passive income (i.e., dividends, interest, capital gains from the sale of shares and other equity participations, bonds, other securities, as well as crypto assets)[54] for more than 50% of their annual gross revenues.
  - Foreign companies effectively pay income tax in their home jurisdictions at a rate lower than 18.75%.

In turn, non-residents will be subject to Argentine tax on the disposition of their indirect investments in crypto assets created or issued by Argentine persons if these assets are held through foreign companies or other foreign legal structures (e.g., trusts, funds) that have substantial assets located in Argentina. For the Argentine tax to apply on indirect transfers, the following conditions must be met simultaneously: assuming that the investment is held through a foreign company: (a) at any time during the last

51. AITL Article 130(d).
52. AITL Article 130(e).
53. AITL Article 130(f).
54. AITL Regulations Article 292.

twelve months prior to the sale, at least 30% of the fair market value of the non-resident's investment in the foreign company comes from assets located in Argentina (e.g., crypto assets created or issued by Argentine persons); (b) the non-resident sells a portion of the investment in such foreign company, held whether directly or indirectly, that has represented at least 10% of such foreign company's assets at any time during the last twelve months prior to the sale; and (c) the non-resident's investment in the foreign company has been made after 31 December 2017. Like in the case of direct transfers, non-resident sellers must assess the Argentine tax on the gross amount of the price (in this case, on the portion attributable to the Argentine located assets indirectly held) at an effective rate of 13.5%, or - at the non-resident seller's option - on the actual capital gain at a 15% rate.

While it seems that the tax treatment applicable to indirect sales is identical to the one applicable to direct sales of crypto assets, they differ in one critical point: When opting to be taxed on the actual capital gain, it is unclear which tax basis is to be selected to assess the Argentine tax appropriately. Is the purchase price paid by the intermediary company to acquire the underlying Argentine located assets (i.e., the crypto assets created or issued by an Argentine person), or is the amount paid for the participations or interests being sold? Further clarification is needed on this matter, which affects indirect transfers of several other Argentine located assets in addition to the crypto assets. This would be the main issue for assessing the Argentine tax on actual gains from indirect transfers of centralized crypto assets created or issued by Argentine persons. When decentralized crypto assets are indirectly held, the indirect capital gains tax would only apply if it were possible to determine that the crypto asset has been created or issued by an Argentine person. Until a mechanism to deal with decentralized crypto assets is implemented, the application of the indirect capital gains tax to transfers of companies holding these assets may be difficult.

(n) How is income from crypto assets to be treated under double tax treaty law?

The Argentine competent authority for the interpretation of Argentina's double tax treaties does not issue public statements with its position on matters concerning their application. Therefore, it is not known whether the taxation of transactions with crypto assets in the context of tax treaties has been already analysed. Nonetheless, this type of transaction gives birth to the following situations covered by double tax treaties:

- Whether transfers of crypto assets created or issued by Argentine persons should be subject to tax pursuant to the treaty article on capital gains or the one dealing with other income.
- In case of crypto asset mining, whether there would be a permanent establishment in case of pool mining or cloud mining because one miner or hardware is in Argentina.
- Whether staking Argentine crypto assets, if any, should be treated as a loan, with newly created crypto assets being characterized as Argentine source interest income.

(o) What are the income/capital gains tax consequences of selling crypto assets in an ICO/STO/IEO?

ICO and initial exchange offerings ('IEO') imply the creation of utility crypto assets, while security token offerings ('STO') are made for the issuance of crypto assets backed with an underlying asset. Based on this distinction, proceeds obtained in an ICO or an IEO should be ultimately treated as income derived by the crypto asset creators, whether directly or indirectly, once the available services are used by the utility token holder. Until then, utility token creators should register a liability in their records. Once the service is used, that income will offset expenses incurred in the creation of the inventory of crypto assets issued. On the other hand, funds obtained in an STO may have to be classified partly as income (for the proceeds to be used in the creation of the crypto asset) and partly as a liability (for the acquisition of the underlying asset or a position to hedge the exposure to it), provided that purchasers of this crypto asset are entitled to exchange the underlying asset for the cryptocurrency at any time. If no such exchange for the underlying were possible, issuers in an STO might also have to treat the proceeds received as taxable income as in the case of an ICO or an IEO. The issue in this case may be that funds used to hedge the exposure to the underlying asset may not be immediately deductible for issuers. Therefore, their tax burden might be excessive.

1.1.3 Other Taxes

(a) What are the value added tax/sales tax consequences of selling crypto assets?

Crypto assets are intangible assets. Consequently, their trades are outside the scope of the Argentine value added tax, which is levied on transfers of tangible personal property and the performance of services.[55]

On the other hand, provinces may levy their gross receipts taxes on transactions with crypto assets if they are entered into by taxpayers that are engaged in business activities within their jurisdictions.[56] Therefore, individual investors in crypto assets would not be within the scope of this provincial tax. In turn, business taxpayers would be subject to gross receipts tax on the payments in crypto assets they receive. These payments would have to be converted to Argentine currency, as in the case of the income tax. Fluctuations in the value of crypto assets thereafter would not be within the scope of the gross receipts tax of the merchant receiving the crypto assets, until

55. Law No. 23349 (B.O. 25 Aug. 1986, as reinstated by Decree No. 280/1997, B.O. 15 Apr. 1997) Article 1.
56. As examples, please *see* Law (Ciudad Autónoma de Buenos Aires) No. 541 (B.O. Buenos Aires Ciudad 22 Jan. 2001, as reinstated by Decree (Ciudad Autónoma de Buenos Aires) No. 104/2019, B.O. Buenos Aires Ciudad 15 Mar. 2019; hereinafter 'CF CABA') Articles 173–275; and Law (Provincia de Buenos Aires) No. 10397 (B.O. Provincia de Buenos Aires 3 Jul. 1986, as reinstated by Resolution (Ministerio de Economía Provincia de Buenos Aires) No. 39/2011; hereinafter 'CF PBA') Articles 182–227.

crypto assets are transferred. A similar treatment would apply to persons engaged in the business of buying and selling crypto assets. In that regard, crypto asset mining activities performed in Argentina could be deemed a business activity subject to gross receipt tax. In both cases, the gross receipts tax would be assessed on the gross amount of revenues generated from the sale of the crypto assets or their creation, respectively. The assessment of the tax would be ruled by the laws of the province where the taxpayer is deemed to be engaged in business activities.

(b) Are payments in crypto assets subject to withholding taxes?

Payments in crypto assets made by Argentine persons would be treated as made in kind. Thus, liability to assess withholding taxes on these payments varies depending on who the beneficiary of the payment is.

If payments are made to resident taxpayers, withholdings made by the payor are on account of these beneficiaries' tax liabilities.[57] Therefore, the payor may either deduct the amount of the withholding (assessed in fiat currency) from the crypto assets to be remitted or pay its obligation in full with crypto assets. In the second situation, the payor should report the transaction to the Argentine tax authorities, informing the impossibility to withhold.[58] In turn, the beneficiary of the payment may be required to self-assess the amount of withholding that the payor should have assessed and remit it to the Argentine tax authorities.[59]

On the other hand, the withholding tax on payments to non-residents is final. Therefore, non-residents are not required to self-assess the Argentine withholding tax and remit it to the Argentine tax authorities if the Argentine payor fails to do it. In that case, Argentine tax authorities will pursue payment of any unpaid withholding taxes from the Argentine person that made the payment with crypto assets. In any event, when assessing the withholding tax, Argentine payors must also deduct the amount of the withholding tax (assessed in fiat currency) from the crypto assets to be remitted. If the amount of crypto asset paid is net of the Argentine withholding tax, it must be increased to account for the appropriate amount of Argentine withholding tax that should have been deducted, as if payment had been made after such tax has been assessed and withheld.[60]

Withholding taxes, like any other taxes, must be paid in Argentine currency.

(c) Does payment of compensation in crypto assets give rise to payroll tax consequences?

Payment of salaries and wages in cryptocurrency would also be deemed payments in kind, triggering the applicable payroll taxes and social security contributions.

57. AITL Article 42. General Resolution (AFIP) No. 830 (B.O. 28 Apr. 2000; hereinafter 'RG 830').
58. RG 830 Article 35.
59. RG 830 Article 37.
60. AITL Article 102.

(d) *Do transactions with crypto assets trigger any transfer taxes?*

Provincial stamp taxes would be applicable to any transactions involving crypto assets if they are documented in a written agreement that is either executed in any Argentine province or expected to have effects therein. On the other hand, agreements documenting transactions with crypto assets executed or with effects outside Argentina are excluded from provincial stamp taxes. Stamp taxes are triggered by the execution of the written agreement in any physical format. The City of Buenos Aires is the only jurisdiction that levies its stamp tax on agreements executed with digital signatures.[61]

(e) *Are firms operating in the crypto space subject to digital service taxes?*

At the time of writing this chapter, Argentina does not levy a digital service tax. Neither are there discussions as to whether such a tax would be created.

(f) *Are crypto assets subject to gift, inheritance, estate, or wealth taxes?*

Argentina does not levy a gift, inheritance or estate tax at the federal level. Only the province of Buenos Aires levies such a tax.[62] In that case, beneficiaries residing in the province would be required to pay the gift or inheritance tax when they receive the crypto asset.[63] Non-residents are subject to the gift and inheritance tax only on their assets located within the province.[64] Consequently, they would be subject to the provincial tax if the crypto assets were created or issued by a person located within the province of Buenos Aires. The crypto asset must be valued at its fair market value at the time of the gift or death.[65] Applicable tax rates vary depending on the type of beneficiary, and they are annually set – together with the exempt amounts – by the provincial legislature annually.

While Argentina does not levy a tax on gratuitous transfers, it does levy an annual wealth tax on individual taxpayers only.[66] In the case of resident taxpayers, this tax is assessed on assets located within Argentina or abroad.[67] Under current law, assets located in Argentina are subject to wealth tax at a marginal rate of 1.25%, while those located outside Argentina may be subject to wealth tax at a marginal rate as high as 2.25%.[68] Non-resident individuals are subject to the wealth tax on their assets located in Argentina at a rate of 0.5%.[69] Argentine persons holding those assets on behalf or at

61. CF CABA Article 452.
62. CF PBA Articles 306–327.
63. CF PBA Article 306.
64. *Id.*
65. CF PBA Article 315(24).
66. Law No. 23966 (B.O. 20 Aug. 1991; hereinafter 'AWTL').
67. AWTL Article 17. Law No. 27541 Article 30.
68. AWTL Article 25.
69. AWTL Article 26.

the request of non-residents are required to assess and pay the wealth tax, with the right to claim the reimbursement of the amounts paid.[70]

It is unclear whether crypto assets would be subject to wealth tax.[71] The AWTL does not rely on a comprehensive and overreaching definition of assets or wealth. Rather, it lists the assets that are subject to tax, without including a category of 'other assets' for those that are not previously listed. Consequently, wealth taxation of crypto assets in Argentina depends on the legal nature of these assets. Crypto assets could not arguably be deemed 'currency', because they are not created or issued by a State. Therefore, they do not have legal tender. As a result, they may not be included as 'cash or equivalent' for purposes of wealth tax assessment. Similarly, the wealth tax definition of 'security' is narrower than the one used by AITL. It refers to securities that represent participation in the equity or equivalent.[72] Perhaps, security tokens may be included in that category when the underlying asset is a stock. In turn, utility tokens could be classified as 'credits' because Argentine holders are entitled to receive something from the issuer in the future. But other crypto assets would most likely be classified as intangible assets, which are exempt from wealth tax, whether they are created or issued by Argentine or foreign persons.[73] This lack of clarity may result in future discussions with the Argentine tax authorities, who will likely pursue payment of the wealth tax, although it is not certain the legal grounds for their assessments.

(g) Are crypto assets subject to exit tax?

Argentina does not levy an exit tax.

(h) Can mining trigger gambling tax?

Gambling taxes are levied on earnings that depend purely on luck,[74] rather than on the activity of the winner. Mining, on the other hand, implies an activity performed by one or more persons trying to solve mathematical problems to create a new block in the chain. Therefore, the reward for mining activity might be assimilated more to a success fee than to a reward from gambling.

70. *Id.*
71. *See* Ricardo Mihura Estrada, *supra* n. 19.
72. AWTL Articles 19(j) and 20(f).
73. AWTL Article 21(d) and Decree No. 127/1996 (B.O. 16 Feb. 1996) Article 11.
74. Law No. 27346 (B.O. 27 Dec. 2016) Article 5 (specific tax on wagers) and Article 6 (indirect tax on online gambling).

1.1.4 *Compliance and Documentation Obligations*

(a) What documentation requirements exist for taxpayers regarding crypto assets and are there best practices in recordkeeping to support representations made in tax returns?

There are no specific documentation requirements regarding crypto assets. Consequently, general rules on recordkeeping apply to taxpayers holding this type of assets. In that regard, they should gather all relevant and true documentation supporting their transactions with crypto assets, including invoices, receipts, receipts of wire transfers, to furnish Argentine tax authorities in the event of an audit. If the dealing is through Argentine wallet providers, tax authorities will also have the information available as per their reporting obligation, as discussed in section 1.1.4(c) *infra.*

(b) What is the evidentiary burden of supporting tax positions when a digital wallet address is lost or shared with other persons?

Argentine tax law requires taxpayers to keep supporting documentation of their transactions subject to tax to prove that taxes are correctly assessed.[75] Consequently, as a general rule, taxpayers should keep physical backup of their transactions with crypto assets. This requirement must be complied with for five years after the statute of limitation expires.[76] In the event of a loss of a digital wallet address, the taxpayer will have to gather all the documentary evidence to prove that the loss occurred. Depending on the facts and circumstances, tax authorities may or may not accept the taxpayer's position. If the loss were not the consequence of a crime, taxpayers may not be in a position to prove it, unless and until another person claims ownership of that asset, if that ever happens. If the loss of a digital wallet address is the result of a crime, the affected taxpayer should report the crime to the authorities, and evidence of this report and its subsequent investigation would serve the taxpayer as evidence of the loss.[77]

If digital wallets are shared, taxpayers should provide evidence as to who the other owners of the wallet are. In the case of Argentine wallet providers, they are required to report when wallets are shared, listing all persons holding the wallet. Therefore, tracking transactions per wallet owner may be possible.

75. Law No. 11683 (B.O. 12 Jan. 1933, as reinstated by Decree No. 821/1998, B.O. 20 Jul. 1998; hereinafter 'ATPL') Article 33.
76. Decree No. 1397/79 (B.O. 3 Aug. 1979) Article 48.
77. AITL Article 86.

(c) *Are crypto asset exchanges and wallet providers subject to reporting obligations?*

So far, no reporting requirements have been established on crypto asset exchanges. On the other hand, Argentine wallet providers are subject to a monthly reporting obligation[78] that requires them to report who their clients are, their countries of residence, their tax ID numbers, as well as to report all transactions made (deposits, withdrawals, transfers, etc.), and their monthly balances expressed in Argentine currency, foreign currency and crypto asset, considering the exchange rate of each relevant foreign currency or crypto asset as of the last business day of the month.

(d) *Are taxpayers holding crypto assets subject to reporting obligations apart from the filing of income tax/capital gains tax returns?*

Argentina has many reporting requirement regimes in effect through which Argentine tax authorities collect information from third parties regarding its taxpayers' consumption and investment behaviours. However, Argentine taxpayers do not have any reporting obligation to disclose their transactions in crypto assets, other than the necessary information when assessing their income tax and, when applicable, wealth tax liabilities. When making those filings, taxpayers must identify their holdings, amounts, values, etc., which should be properly supported with the appropriate documentation. On the other hand, if crypto assets are indirectly held, as discussed in section 1.1.2(m) *supra*, they will be required to report them pursuant to the reporting requirement applicable under the Registry of Passive Entities.[79]

(e) *Are crypto asset exchanges and wallet providers subject to CRS/FATCA reporting?*

Argentina does not have an inter-governmental agreement in effect with the United States (US) for purposes of FATCA reporting. Therefore, there is no automatic exchange of financial information mechanism with the US. On the other hand, it exchanges financial information automatically in accordance with the OECD's Multilateral Competent Authority Agreement on Automatic Exchange of Financial Account Information. Based on this Agreement, which set the Common Reporting Standard or 'CRS', Argentine financial institutions regulated by the Argentine Central Bank are the only Argentine taxpayers required to gather financial information to remit to the Argentine tax authorities for Argentina to be able to fulfil its obligations under the Agreement.[80] Crypto assets exchanges or wallet providers are not required to comply with any reporting requirements for CRS purposes. However, as mentioned in section 1.1.4(c) *supra*, Argentine wallet providers are subject to a reporting obligation.

78. General Resolution (AFIP) No. 4614 (B.O. 25 Oct. 2019).
79. General Resolution (AFIP) No. 4697 (B.O. 15 Apr. 2020).
80. General Resolution (AFIP) No. 4056 (B.O. 22 May 2017).

Therefore, Argentine tax authorities have information that they may share with foreign authorities, although not necessarily automatically.

1.1.5 *Civil and Criminal Tax Enforcement*

(a) What powers do the tax authorities have to compel the disclosure of information by third parties, such as exchanges or wallet providers, and have these been used in the past?

Argentine tax authorities would only have powers to compel disclosure of information to Argentine crypto assets exchanges or wallet providers.[81] Pursuant to their audit powers, they may require any of those persons to furnish information of a certain taxpayer under audit.[82] There is no information publicly available of the tax authorities having used these powers in the context of audits of taxpayers dealing with crypto assets so far.

(b) What measures have the tax authorities undertaken in the past to ensure crypto tax compliance?

Argentine tax authorities have implemented the reporting requirement to wallet providers to ensure crypto asset compliance.[83] Pursuant to this regime, Argentine tax authorities gather information on community participants, both resident and non-resident, and the transactions they make and their monthly balances. Argentine financial institutions and mutual funds are exempt from providing this information under this reporting requirement, because they are subject to their own reporting requirements.[84]

(c) Are the tax authorities cooperating with tax authorities in other jurisdictions on enforcement?

Argentina's cooperation on enforcement with foreign tax authorities results from twenty double tax treaties, twenty-six tax information exchange agreements and the Convention on Mutual Administrative Assistance in Tax Matters, effective since 1 October 2013. Through these instruments, Argentina can provide tax information on non-Argentine persons dealing with crypto assets in Argentina to tax authorities in foreign jurisdictions, so that they can enforce their tax laws. For purposes of the Convention on Mutual Administrative Assistance in Tax Matters, Argentina has made reservations not to: (i) provide information on taxes levied by political subdivisions, (ii) assist in the collection of taxes and administrative fines, and (iii) notify or transfer

81. ATPL Article 108.
82. *Id.* Articles 33 and 35.
83. Please refer to *supra* n. 62.
84. General Resolution No. 4298 (B.O. 29 Aug. 2018).

documents relating to any tax claim. Consequently, Argentina's assistance is limited to providing information to foreign tax authorities, providing no support in the collection of any unpaid taxes abroad.

Australia

Robert Yunan & Wendy Lim

1. COUNTRY GUIDES

1.1 Australia

1.1.1 Applicable Tax Law, Guidance and Case Law

(a) Which laws, regulations and other administrative guidance exist dealing with crypto assets?

The tax implications relating to crypto assets are not specifically addressed by Australian income tax,[1] goods and services tax (GST)[2] and stamp duty[3] laws and associated regulations. As such, analysing the tax implications of transactions involving crypto assets is a matter of applying existing principles to new technology, with the assistance of guidance issued by the Australian Taxation Office (ATO). Such guidance includes a general guide on the income tax treatment of crypto assets in transactions and business[4] and GST guidance relating to the use of crypto assets in business.[5] Guidance provided on the ATO's website is generally non-binding, whereas taxation determinations (issued publicly) and private rulings (issued to particular taxpayers) by the ATO are binding.

1. The main assessment acts for federal income tax in Australia are the *Income Tax Assessment Act 1936* (Cth) (ITAA36) and the *Income Tax Assessment Act 1997* (Cth) (ITAA97).
2. The key goods and services tax legislation is *A New Tax System (Goods and Services Tax) Act 1999* (Cth) (GST Act).
3. Each of the six States and two Territories of Australia has their own stamp duty legislation.
4. *See* https://www.ato.gov.au/General/Gen/Tax-treatment-of-crypto-currencies-in-Australia---specifically-bitcoin/ (accessed on 23 Jan. 2020).
5. *See* https://www.ato.gov.au/business/gst/in-detail/your-industry/financial-services-and-insurance/gst-and-digital-currency/ (accessed on 23 Jan. 2020).

In 2014, the ATO published a series of taxation determinations to provide public advice regarding the income tax treatment of bitcoin and other crypto assets bearing the same characteristics as bitcoin.[6] The ATO has also issued a number of private rulings concerning the income tax treatment of bitcoin and other crypto assets. Most of these private rulings were issued from 2018, coinciding with the surges in popularity and market valuation of crypto assets at that time. Although a private ruling is only binding in respect of the particular taxpayer that applied for it, private rulings can be a useful guide as to how the ATO will treat similar fact patterns.

The ATO also has a dedicated online forum called the 'ATO Community' where members of the general public, registered tax practitioners and ATO representatives can discuss a range of tax issues. There are a number of conversation threads on the ATO Community forum discussing crypto assets. The views expressed in this online forum by ATO representatives are not binding on the ATO.

(b) *Which court cases exist dealing with crypto assets?*

No Australian case law exists, at the time of writing this chapter, on the taxation treatment of crypto assets. However, a number of Australian cases have dealt incidentally with crypto assets in the context of breaches of directors' duties,[7] breaches of the *Australian Securities and Investments Commission Act 2001* (Cth)[8] and criminal offences.[9]

1.1.2 *Income and Capital Gains Taxes*

(a) *How are crypto assets classified for income tax and capital gains tax purposes?*

Crypto assets are 'CGT assets' for the purposes of Australian capital gains tax (CGT). A 'CGT asset' is defined as any kind of property or any legal or equitable right that is not property.[10] Crypto assets consist of a bundle of rights and are, effectively, a digital representation of value.

---

6. These taxation determinations are:

   - TD 2014/25 *Income tax: is bitcoin a 'foreign currency' for the purposes of Division 775 of the Income Tax Assessment Act 1997?*
   - TD 2014/26 *Income tax: is bitcoin a 'CGT asset' for the purposes of subsection 108-5(1) of the Income Tax Assessment Act 1997?*
   - TD 2014/27 *Income tax: is bitcoin trading stock for the purposes of subsection 70-10(1) of the Income Tax Assessment Act 1997?*
   - TD 2014/28 *Fringe benefits tax: is the provision of bitcoin by an employer to an employee in respect of their employment a property fringe benefit for the purposes of subsection 136(1) of the Fringe Benefits Tax Assessment Act 1986?*

7. *Matter Technology Ltd v. Mrakas; Mrakas v. Matter Technology Ltd* [2018] NSWSC 507.
8. *Noicos v. Dawson* [2019] FCA 2197.
9. *Day v. R* [2019] WASCA 60.
10. Section 108-5 of the ITAA97.

The current view of the ATO is that bitcoin holding rights (i.e., the bundle of rights comprising a bitcoin) are property rights.[11] This conclusion is based on the fact that:

- bitcoin has a value;
- bitcoin is used to transact;
- the owner of a bitcoin can exclude others from accessing/using that bitcoin; and
- bitcoin can change ownership.

On this basis, a bitcoin meets the definition of personal property.[12] This view should also be applicable to crypto assets other than bitcoin (provided they have the same or similar characteristics set out in the points mentioned above).

Although crypto assets are CGT assets, this does not necessarily mean that they are taxed under Australia's CGT rules. Crypto assets may have 'revenue' tax consequences which take precedence over the CGT regime.[13] This will be the case if the crypto asset is a revenue account asset (i.e., is used in a profit-making venture) or trading stock (i.e., is held for sale in the ordinary course of a business). The tax treatments of revenue account assets and trading stock are broadly the same, but the timing at which profits are brought to account differ. Alternatively, a crypto asset may be a 'personal use asset', the disposal of which is not subject to tax.

The sections below discuss the different classifications of crypto assets.

Capital asset

Assets that are held for long-term investment on capital account are subject to Australia's CGT regime. Such capital assets are retained for a significant period of time as a long-term store of value or with an expectation of capital appreciation over a long-term horizon. Capital gains made on the disposal of capital assets are eligible for the CGT discount of 50% where they are held by an individual or through a trust for at least twelve months. CGT on assets of a partnership is paid by the partners in their respective proportions.

Revenue account assets

Crypto assets will be revenue account assets where they are used speculatively with a view to making profit in a transaction that is organized in a commercial manner. This can be an isolated transaction or a series of transactions. A profit-making purpose can exist even if a crypto asset is held for a significant time period.

11. *See* Taxation Determination TD 2014/26 at paragraph 12.
12. The case of *National Provincial Bank Ltd v. Ainsworth* [1965] AC 1175 sets out various tests for determining whether an asset is personal property.
13. Section 118-20 of the ITAA97.

The ATO has published factors which it considers are relevant for determining whether a transaction has a profit-making character.[14] These factors include:

- the nature of the entity undertaking the transaction;
- the nature and scale of other activities undertaken by the entity;
- the amount of money involved and the scale of the profit sought or obtained;
- the nature, scale and complexity of the transaction;
- the length of time over which the transaction occurs; and
- whether the property had any other use other than as an object of trade (e.g., can the crypto asset be used as a medium of exchange or to buy services only available on the blockchain).

The ATO gives an example of crypto assets being a revenue account asset in the following circumstances:

- The taxpayer is employed or engaged in a profession other than full-time crypto trading and undertakes crypto trading as a side project.
- The taxpayer has identified an arbitrage opportunity involving multiple crypto asset pairs. To take advantage of this opportunity, the taxpayer has also developed strategies to reduce the risk of losses, including fast response programmes to adjust for events occurring during the series of transactions and offsetting option arrangements.
- To maximize profits from the transactions, the taxpayer undertakes back-to-back transactions on the same day.

Capital assets and revenue account assets are similar in the sense that they are both held to make a gain. The distinction is that capital assets often are a passive investment (in a 'set-and-forget' style), whereas revenue account assets require effort and time to be expended to exploit an identified advantage. In a crypto asset context, this generally means identifying an arbitrage and often undertaking other transactions (often simultaneously) to make a margin. Assets held on revenue account are taxed on disposal or under the trading stock rules. The primary difference is that capital gains made on capital assets may attract a discount, whereas revenue gains do not. We provide further detail below.

Trading stock

Bitcoin (or any crypto asset which is 'property') can be a trading stock for tax purposes where it is held for the purpose of sale or exchange in the ordinary course of a business.[15]

14. ATO webpage, 'Cryptocurrency Used in Business', QC 42159 (last modified 18 Jun. 2019, accessed 28 Jan. 2020), available at: https://www.ato.gov.au/General/Gen/Tax-treatment-of-crypto-currencies-in-Australia---specifically-bitcoin/?anchor=Cryptocurrencyusedinbusiness#Isolatedprofitmakingbusinessorcommercial.
15. *See* Taxation Determination TD 2014/27 at paragraph 3.

Examples of businesses that involve crypto assets include crypto asset trading, mining and exchange businesses (including ATMs).

Paragraph 14 of Taxation Determination TD 2014/27 clarifies this further as follows:

> Bitcoin held by a taxpayer carrying on a business of mining and selling bitcoin, or a taxpayer carrying on a Bitcoin exchange business will be considered to be trading stock. Further bitcoin received as a method of payment by any business that sells goods will also be considered to be trading stock of that business where the bitcoin is held for the purposes of sale or exchange in the ordinary course of the business.

Not all people acquiring and disposing of crypto assets will be carrying on businesses. To carry on a business, a taxpayer will usually:

- carry on their activities for commercial reasons and in a commercially viable way, with repetition and regularity;
- undertake activities in a business-like manner that would typically include preparing a business plan and acquiring capital assets or inventory in line with the business plan;
- prepare accounting records and market a business name or product; and
- intend to make a profit or genuinely believe that they will eventually make a profit.[16]

Where a crypto asset is the 'trading stock', gains or losses on the disposal of that crypto asset will be subject to tax under the trading stock rules in Division 70 of the ITAA97 on revenue account. This can result in a higher rate of tax applying on gains, as revenue gains (including gains on trading stock) are not eligible for the CGT discount of 50% that may apply to capital assets.

Personal use assets

Personal use assets are assets (other than collectables) that are used or kept mainly for the personal use or enjoyment of the taxpayer or the taxpayer's associates.[17]

Generally, intangible assets are not considered to be personal use assets. An exception to this may be where an intangible asset is used to directly acquire an asset held mainly for personal use and enjoyment.

Capital gains that are made on the sale of personal assets are disregarded if they were originally acquired for less than AUD 10,000.[18] This is true regardless of the quantum of the gain, although the exemption will only apply if the crypto continues to be held on capital account. It should also be noted that where a taxpayer disposes of personal use assets individually and those assets would ordinarily be disposed of as

16. ATO webpage, 'Cryptocurrency Used in Business', QC 42159 (last modified 18 Jun. 2019, accessed 28 Jan. 2020), available at: https://www.ato.gov.au/General/Gen/Tax-treatment-of-crypto-currencies-in-Australia---specifically-bitcoin/?anchor=Cryptocurrencyusedinbusiness#IsolatedprofitmakingbusinessorCommercial.
17. Section 108-20 of the ITAA97.
18. Section 118-10 of the ITAA97.

part of a set, the exemption will only apply where the entire set was acquired for less than AUD 10,000.[19] This rule may apply, for example, to newer types of crypto assets that are linked or grouped as packs.

In the context of crypto assets, the ATO has issued a public ruling stating that bitcoins will be kept or used mainly for personal use where they are kept or used predominantly to make ordinary purchases of items for personal use or consumption. However, if the bitcoins were instead purchased to facilitate the acquisition of income producing investments, they would not be considered to be personal use assets.[20]

An asset cannot be a personal use asset if the purpose of its acquisition is to keep it or use it as an investment, as part of a business or for a profit-making purpose. Personal use and investment use are mutually exclusive.[21]

The ATO has issued a private ruling stating that in determining whether an asset is a personal use asset, the ATO will consider:

- the taxpayer's initial intention (e.g., whether the crypto asset was acquired to be held as a speculative investment or not);
- the use and intention during the period owned (e.g., whether the taxpayer, after acquisition, subsequently developed an intention to hold the crypto asset as a speculative investment, having regard to the increase in value of the crypto asset);
- the length of time the asset was owned; and
- the circumstances of the subsequent disposal of the crypto asset.[22]

It appears from the private rulings that the ATO is generally more likely to consider that a crypto asset is a personal use asset where it is used to directly acquire a product or service for the taxpayer's personal use and enjoyment, such as online subscriptions[23] and online purchases of clothing and music.[24]

The ATO broadly considers that the longer the period of time that a crypto asset is held, the less likely it is that it will be a personal use asset. This is because the taxpayer is likely to be holding the crypto asset with the intention of selling it at an opportune time (to convert it into fiat currency) based on a favourable rate of exchange.

This notion is supported by a private ruling issued by the ATO stating that factors tending against the characterization of crypto assets as personal use assets include:

- the maturity of the crypto market and ecosystem, as evidenced by the existence of exchanges where crypto assets can be readily bought and sold; and

19. Section 108-25 of the ITAA97.
20. Taxation Determination TD 2014/26 *Income tax: is bitcoin a 'CGT asset' for the purposes of subsection 108-5(1) of the Income Tax Assessment Act 1997?*
21. Private ruling EVA 1051537413985 (dated 9 Jul. 2019).
22. Private ruling EVA 1051537413985 (dated 9 Jul. 2019).
23. Private ruling EVA 1051537413985 (dated 9 Jul. 2019).
24. Taxation Determination TD 2014/26 *Income tax: is bitcoin a 'CGT asset' for the purposes of subsection 108-5(1) of the Income Tax Assessment Act 1997?*

- the amount spent on purchases of crypto assets seen in the context of the taxpayer's level of income and personal expenditure. Particularly where significant dollar amount purchases are being made, the taxpayer is more likely to have a substantial aspect of seeking an exchange gain or at least storing value, as opposed to personal use or enjoyment.[25]

(b) *What are the income/capital gains tax consequences of selling crypto assets against fiat currency?*

If crypto assets are sold for fiat currency, the tax consequences will depend on the classification of the crypto assets (discussed above).

Capital assets

Crypto assets that are capital assets will be subject to the CGT rules. Under these rules, a capital gain will arise where the cash proceeds exceed the cost base of the crypto asset. The cost base is broadly the amount paid to acquire the original asset plus any costs of acquisition and disposal.[26] A capital gain made on the disposal of a crypto asset can be discounted by 50% where held by an individual or through a trust for at least twelve months prior to disposal.

Where there is a holding of identical crypto coins or tokens and they cannot be distinguished from one another, generally a 'first-in first-out' rule should apply to identify which crypto asset is disposed. This is consistent with the ATO's guidance that where separately unidentifiable shares in a company (of the same class and acquired over a period of time) have been disposed of, 'first-in first-out' is a reasonable basis of identification.[27]

Revenue account assets

On disposal of a crypto asset that is a revenue account asset, any net profit (gross receipts minus expenses) will be taxable as ordinary income to the taxpayer that is disposing of the crypto asset.[28] This net profit cannot be reduced by the CGT discount for assets held for at least twelve months prior to disposal. A net loss is deductible to the taxpayer.[29]

25. Private ruling PBR 1013139758672 (dated 15 Dec. 2016).
26. *See* Division 110 of the ITAA97.
27. Taxation Determination TD 33.
28. Section 6-5 of the ITAA97 and Taxation Ruling TR 96/4 *Income tax: valuing shares acquired as revenue assets*.
29. Section 8-1 of the ITAA97.

Trading stock

Sale proceeds from trading stock are included in the assessable income of a taxpayer and expenses incurred in carrying on the business (including acquisition costs of the stock) are deductible to the taxpayer.

A taxpayer carrying on a business must compare the value of all trading stock on hand at the beginning of the income year (opening value) with the value of all trading stock on hand at the end of the income year (closing value).[30] If the closing value exceeds the opening value, the excess is assessable.[31] If the opening value exceeds the closing value, the excess is deductible.[32] In accounting for crypto assets held as trading stock that have increased in value, it would generally be more favourable to value the crypto assets at cost price (rather than the market selling value (MSV) or the replacement value). Where values are declining, the other alternatives may be used to bring forward tax deductions.

Even if a taxpayer does not dispose of its crypto assets, an increase in the total trading stock value at the end of the year is treated as assessable income (while a decrease is treated as an allowable deduction). This can result in some timing distortions where the value of crypto assets greatly varies year to year.

Personal use assets

Capital gains that are made on the sale of personal use assets are disregarded if they were originally acquired for less than AUD 10,000.[33] This is true regardless of the increase in value, although the asset would still need to be held on capital account to attract the exemption. A good example of this is crypto asset held to be used as currency, that is, for the purpose of exchange for goods and services.

(c) What are the income/capital gains tax consequences of exchanging crypto assets against other crypto assets?

There is no specific roll-over provision for crypto asset exchange gains or losses.

The exchange of one crypto asset for another is likely to give rise to Australian tax implications.[34] The implications will depend on the circumstances giving rise to the exchange.

Capital asset

Where the crypto asset is a capital asset, the exchange will be subject to the CGT rules. On exchange, the market value of the replacement crypto asset will need to be determined in Australian Dollars. A capital gain, which is subject to tax,[35] will arise

30. Section 70-35(1) of the ITAA97.
31. Section 70-35(2) of the ITAA97.
32. Section 70-35(3) of the ITAA97.
33. Section 118-10 of the ITAA97.
34. *See* 'Transacting with Cryptocurrency' on the ATO's website, at https://www.ato.gov.au/General/Gen/Tax-treatment-of-crypto-currencies-in-Australia---specifically-bitcoin/?page=2#Transacting_with_cryptocurrency (accessed on 23 Jan. 2020).
35. *See* Division 100 of the ITAA97.

where the market value of the replacement crypto asset exceeds the cost base of the crypto asset disposed of. The cost base is broadly the amount paid to acquire the original asset plus certain costs of acquisition and disposal.[36]

Capital losses arise where the value of the replacement crypto asset is less than the reduced cost base of the original crypto asset disposed of.[37] Capital losses may only be offset against current year capital gains or, subject to certain loss recoupment rules, carried forward for use against future capital gains.[38] There is no carry back available in Australia for capital losses.[39]

If the exchange gives rise to a capital gain, it is eligible for a discount of up to 50% where the original crypto asset has been held by an individual or trust for at least twelve months prior to disposal.

Revenue account asset

If the crypto asset is a revenue account asset (as opposed to being a capital asset), then the exchange gain should be assessable and any loss on the exchange should be deductible.[40] The monetary value of the crypto asset will be deemed to have been paid to the seller as a result of the exchange, which will be the basis on which the exchange gain or loss is to be calculated.[41]

Trading stock

Trading stock includes assets that are held for exchange. Where coin-to-coin transactions are regular, the coins are held as trading stock for the purpose of exchange within the ordinary course of business.

An exchange is generally treated as a disposal of the trading stock, giving rise to income based on the value of the replacement coins. The tax treatment is best demonstrated using the following table, for example:

Transaction	*$*
Purchase a bitcoin for AUD 70 as trading stock. Claim a deduction for the AUD 70 expense on acquisition.	-70
Exchange the bitcoin for ether. The market value of the ether is AUD 100, and this amount is assessable at the time of the exchange.	+ 100
Gain (subject to the ether being treated as trading stock)	$30

If the ether is subsequently used as trading stock, the market value of the ether can be deducted at the point it becomes trading stock.

36. *See* Division 110 of the ITAA97.
37. Section 104-10 of the ITAA97.
38. Sections 102-5, 102-10, 102-15 of the ITAA97, subdivision 165-CA of the ITAA97 and Division 36 of the ITAA97. Note that the loss recoupment rules do not apply to capital losses of trusts.
39. Loss carry back was repealed effective on 30 Sep. 2014 and applied to the 2013–2014 and previous financial years.
40. Section 6-5 of the ITAA97 and section 8-1 of the ITAA97.
41. Section 21 and 21A of the ITAA36.

(d) *If a distinction is made between business assets and non-business assets, when does trading in crypto assets lead to a trade or business?*

As discussed above at section 1.1.2(b), there is a difference between crypto assets held as capital assets (non-business) and crypto assets held as revenue account assets or trading stock (business assets). The classification will depend on whether the taxpayer is carrying on a business in relation to their crypto assets or uses their crypto assets in a profit-making arrangement.

The distinction between revenue account assets and trading stock (discussed above at section 1.1.2(a)) is generally that trading stock is held as part of a business, whereas revenue account assets are not required to be.

Crypto assets are likely to be characterized as revenue account assets when a speculative profit-making purpose begins to develop in their trading, either in an isolated transaction or across a series of transactions which does not amount to a business. The speculation could be in exploiting an identified arbitrage opportunity.

On the other hand, crypto assets are likely to be characterized as trading stock when the trading becomes so repetitive and regular that it can be said that the crypto assets are held for the purpose of sale or exchange in the ordinary course of a business. There is generally a higher degree of organization in the trading and an expectation of profit compared to an arbitrage opportunity.

Where an entity is operating a business of trading in crypto assets, the crypto assets will likely be trading stock of the business. If an entity (including an individual) is not operating a business, then the crypto asset will not be trading stock, however, can still be revenue account assets and taxed accordingly on disposal.

The tax treatments of revenue account assets and trading stock are broadly the same, but the timing at which profits are brought to account differ and the valuation rules which apply to trading stock do not apply to revenue account assets.

In relation to trading stock, to be carrying on business, a taxpayer will usually:

- carry on their activities for commercial reasons and in a commercially viable way, with repetition and regularity;
- undertake activities in a business-like manner; this would typically include preparing a business plan and acquiring capital assets or inventory in line with the business plan;
- prepare accounting records and market a business name or product; and
- intend to make a profit or genuinely believe that they will eventually make a profit.[42]

42. ATO webpage, 'Cryptocurrency Used in Business', QC 42159 (last modified 18 Jun. 2019, accessed 28 Jan. 2020), available at: https://www.ato.gov.au/General/Gen/Tax-treatment-of-crypto-currencies-in-Australia---specifically-bitcoin/?anchor=Cryptocurrencyusedinbusiness#IsolatedprofitmakingbusinessorcommerciaI.

(e) *What are the income/capital gains tax consequences for an employee receiving wages or salaries in crypto assets?*

The consequences will depend on whether the employee has a valid salary sacrifice agreement in place.

Broadly, a valid salary sacrifice agreement must be in writing and apply prospectively to salary.[43] This means, for example, if an employee has already earned their salary or wages and then asks to be paid in crypto assets instead then there is no valid salary sacrifice arrangement in place, and the employer will need to withhold and remit amounts to the ATO under the Pay As You Go (PAYG) system,[44] which will be creditable against the taxpayer's tax liability arising from the deemed receipt of the wages.

Where an employee has a valid salary sacrifice arrangement with their employer to receive crypto assets as remuneration instead of Australian Dollars, the payment of the crypto asset is a fringe benefit (specifically a property fringe benefit whose value is established at the time of provision of the benefit).[45] In these circumstances, the employer is subject to fringe benefits tax, which is a tax imposed on employers for providing certain non-cash benefits to employees or associates of employees. Fringe benefits are specifically exempt from income tax for the employee.

(f) *What are the income/capital gains tax consequences for a merchant receiving payment in crypto assets?*

The merchant will need to include the value of the crypto assets in Australian Dollars as part of their ordinary income where the merchant receives crypto assets as payment for goods or services that the merchant provides as part of their business. This is the same process as receiving any other non-cash consideration under a barter transaction. One way of determining the value in Australian Dollars is the fair market value which can be obtained from a reputable crypto exchange.[46]

When the merchant exchanges the crypto assets received into fiat currency, the tax treatment will depend on whether the merchant held the crypto asset as a capital asset, revenue account asset or trading stock.

43. The requirements of a valid salary sacrifice arrangement are set out in Taxation Ruling TR 2001/10.
44. The 'Pay As You Go' (PAYG) rules provide the basis for withholding payments as source and are set out in Schedule 1 to the *Taxation Administration Act 1953* (Cth) (TAA53).
45. ATO webpage, 'Cryptocurrency Used in Business', QC 42159 (last modified 18 Jun. 2019, accessed 28 Jan. 2020), available at: https://www.ato.gov.au/General/Gen/Tax-treatment-of-crypto-currencies-in-Australia---specifically-bitcoin/?anchor=Cryptocurrencyusedinbusiness#Isolatedprofitmakingbusinessorcommercial.
46. ATO webpage, 'Cryptocurrency Used in Business', QC 42159 (last modified 18 Jun. 2019, accessed 28 Jan. 2020), available at: https://www.ato.gov.au/General/Gen/Tax-treatment-of-crypto-currencies-in-Australia---specifically-bitcoin/?anchor=Cryptocurrencyusedinbusiness#Isolatedprofitmakingbusinessorcommercial.

(g) *What are the income/capital gains tax consequences of a loss of crypto assets?*

A crypto asset is lost where the owner loses the private key associated with the wallet address where the crypto asset is stored or the crypto asset is stolen. The ATO considers that a crypto asset is lost where the owner no longer has access to the particular crypto asset.[47]

The treatment of a lost crypto asset depends on its tax classification, as follows:

- Capital asset: a capital loss can be claimed.
- Revenue account asset: a deduction can be claimed.
- Trading stock: the value of the lost crypto asset will be taken into account in working out the value of closing stock. Where the value of opening stock exceeds the value of closing stock at the end of an income year, the difference can be claimed as a deduction.
- Personal use asset: any capital loss made on a personal use asset must be disregarded and cannot be used to offset any capital gain.

The ATO has provided guidance that a taxpayer must be able to provide the following kinds of evidence to substantiate the loss of a crypto asset:[48]

- when the taxpayer acquired and lost the private key;
- the wallet address to which the private key relates;
- the cost the taxpayer incurred to acquire the lost or stolen crypto asset;
- the amount of crypto asset lost; and
- that the wallet was controlled by the taxpayer (e.g., either that the taxpayer is in possession of the hardware that stores the wallet or the taxpayer can demonstrate that there are transactions to the wallet from a crypto exchange for which the taxpayer holds a verified account or which is linked to their identity).

(h) *What are the income/capital gains tax consequences of a loss in value of crypto assets?*

Broadly, Australian tax rules will not recognize a reduction in the value of crypto assets until there has been a disposal or exchange.[49] However, if the crypto asset is a trading stock, there is a possibility that the loss can be deductible.

47. ATO webpage, 'Transacting with Cryptocurrency: Loss or Theft of Cryptocurrency', QC 42159 (last modified 18 Jun. 2019, accessed 28 Jan. 2020), available at: https://www.ato.gov.au/general/gen/tax-treatment-of-crypto-currencies-in-australia---specifically-bitcoin/?page=2#Lossortheftofcryptocurrency.
48. ATO webpage, 'Transacting with Cryptocurrency: Loss or Theft of Cryptocurrency' available at: https://www.ato.gov.au/general/gen/tax-treatment-of-crypto-currencies-in-australia---specifically-bitcoin/?page=2#Lossortheftofcryptocurrency.
49. *See* 'Cryptocurrency as an Investment' available at https://www.ato.gov.au/General/Gen/Tax-treatment-of-crypto-currencies-in-Australia---specifically-bitcoin/?page=2#Exchangingacryptocurrencyforanothercrypt (accessed on 23 Jan. 2020).

Under the trading stock rules,[50] an entity that operates a business must compare the value of trading stock on hand at the start of the income year to the value of trading stock on hand at the end of the year. Any increase in the value of trading stock is included in assessable income, whereas any decrease is treated as deductible.[51]

For these purposes, there are specific trading stock valuation elections available to taxpayers, which would apply to crypto assets held as trading stock.

While the opening value of trading stock must be equal to the closing value of trading stock from the previous tax period,[52] the value of trading stock at year end can be valued under any of the following methods, which may vary from year to year (although the closing value for one year must equal to the opening value for the next year):[53]

- historic cost;
- replacement value; and
- MSV.

Accordingly, where the value of a trading stock has decreased, a net deduction may be available in the current year where the stock is valued down to MSV.

There is no requirement to permanently adopt any of the three valuation methods. The method for determining the closing value of trading stock can vary from year to year. For example, a taxpayer may value stock at cost and, in the next income year, value the stock at MSV.

Additionally, a taxpayer is allowed to value each item of trading stock at its historic cost, replacement value or MSV. There is no requirement to use the same method for determining the closing value of all items of trading stock.

(i) What are the income/capital gains tax consequences of forks of crypto assets?

Where a taxpayer receives a new crypto asset as a result of a chain split (such as bitcoin cash being received by bitcoin holders), the tax consequences for the taxpayer will depend on whether the new crypto asset is held as an investment or a trading stock in a business.

Where a taxpayer receives new crypto assets in respect of crypto assets that are held as investments, the taxpayer does not derive ordinary income or make a capital gain at that time as a result of receiving the new crypto assets.[54] The cost base of a new crypto asset received as a result of a chain split is zero, as the taxpayer will not pay any

50. Particularly section 70-35 of the ITAA97.
51. Subsection 70-35(2) and subsection 70-35(3) of the ITAA97.
52. *See* section 70-40 of the ITAA97.
53. Section 70-45 of the ITAA97.
54. Private ruling EVA 1051532101397 (dated 5 Jul. 2019) and ATO webpage, 'Transacting with Cryptocurrency: Chain Splits', QC 42159 (last modified 18 Jun. 2019, accessed 30 Jan. 2020), available at: https://www.ato.gov.au/General/Gen/Tax-treatment-of-crypto-currencies-in-Australia---specifically-bitcoin/?page=2#Chainsplits.

money or give any property to acquire the new crypto asset.[55] The taxpayer will make a capital gain when they dispose of the new crypto asset.[56] The taxpayer (if an individual or trust) may be entitled to apply a 50% CGT discount to halve the capital gain, where the taxpayer holds the new crypto asset as an investment for twelve months or more beginning from the date when the taxpayer became the owner of the new crypto asset (i.e., the date of receipt).[57]

Prior to the ATO confirming the above treatment, there were discussions in industry about the possibility of new crypto assets being treated analogously to company demergers where a cost base adjustment takes place with the new shares taking on some value of the original shares' cost base and the original shares' cost base reduced by the same amount. The ATO is not of the view that new crypto assets should be given demerger treatment on the basis that generally where a fork happens the original blockchain continues despite the formation of a new blockchain. As the original crypto asset has not changed, its cost base is unaffected.[58]

Where a taxpayer receives a new crypto asset as a result of a chain split in relation to crypto assets held in a business carried on by the taxpayer, the new crypto asset will be treated as trading stock (assuming it is held for sale or exchange in the ordinary course of the business). No tax deduction will be available for the acquisition of the new crypto asset, as no expenditure or outlay is incurred by the taxpayer to obtain the new crypto asset. Like other items of trading stock held by the taxpayer, the value of the new crypto asset must be brought to account at the end of the income year under the trading stock rules. This effectively results in the value of the crypto received under the chain split being assessable in the year in which it is received.[59]

Importantly, the characterization of new crypto assets as capital assets or trading stock depends on the purpose for which the new crypto assets are held (and not the purpose for which the original crypto assets were held).

(j) What are the income/capital gains tax consequences of airdrops of crypto assets and are the tax consequences different if the airdropped tokens are unwanted?

An airdrop of crypto assets occurs where new tokens are given to existing token holders as a way of increasing the supply of tokens. In these circumstances, the money

55. Private ruling EVA 1051532101397 (dated 5 Jul. 2019) and ATO webpage, 'Transacting with Cryptocurrency: Chain Splits', QC 42159 (last modified 18 Jun. 2019, accessed 30 Jan. 2020), available at: https://www.ato.gov.au/General/Gen/Tax-treatment-of-crypto-currencies-in-Australia---specifically-bitcoin/?page=2#Chainsplits.
56. ATO webpage, 'Transacting with Cryptocurrency: Chain Splits', QC 42159 (last modified 18 Jun. 2019, accessed 30 Jan. 2020), available at: https://www.ato.gov.au/General/Gen/Tax-treatment-of-crypto-currencies-in-Australia---specifically-bitcoin/?page=2#Chainsplits.
57. Private ruling EVA 1051532101397 (dated 5 Jul. 2019).
58. Private ruling EVA 1051532101397 (dated 5 Jul. 2019).
59. ATO webpage, 'Transacting with Cryptocurrency: Chain Splits', QC 42159 (last modified 18 Jun. 2019, accessed 30 Jan. 2020), available at: https://www.ato.gov.au/General/Gen/Tax-treatment-of-crypto-currencies-in-Australia---specifically-bitcoin/?page=2#Chainsplits.

value of an airdropped token is ordinary income of the recipient at the time it is derived.[60]

The ATO provides the following example:[61]

(2) *Merindah has held TRX tokens since December 2018, entitling her to receive monthly BTT airdrops from February 2019.*

The money value of the BTT tokens Merindah receives as a result of holding her TRX tokens is assessable income of Merindah at the time the tokens are derived.

The cost base of Merindah's airdropped BTT tokens will be their market value at the time they were derived.

It is irrelevant whether the airdropped tokens are wanted or unwanted by the recipient.

(k) What are the income/capital gains tax consequences of (solo, pool, and cloud) mining?

The consequences of mining depend on whether the mining activities involve the carrying on of a business.

During the early stages of the existence of crypto assets, the ATO was more likely to have considered that mining was a hobby or recreational activity and accordingly coins obtained via mining were not taxable.

However, it is now more likely that the ATO will consider that taxpayers involved in mining are carrying on a business, having regard to the maturity of the crypto ecosystem and the fact that mining has now become more difficult due to its resource intensiveness and so requires a systematic approach. With regard to pools, the ATO's view as indicated in private rulings is that the higher difficulty of solo mining has led to the need to use pool mining. Pool mining involves cooperation in order to obtain something of value, which means it is more likely to be a commercial activity.[62]

Where a taxpayer is in the business of mining crypto assets, a crypto asset acquired from mining is treated as trading stock. When the taxpayer acquires the mined crypto asset, the value of the mined crypto asset is not assessable upfront. However, any income derived from the transfer of the mined crypto asset to a third party is assessable. Further, any increase in the total value of the mined crypto assets that are not sold (i.e., the taxpayer's remaining trading stock) at the end of the year

60. ATO webpage, 'Transacting with Cryptocurrency: Staking Rewards and Airdrops', QC 42159 (last modified 30 Mar. 2020, accessed 11 May 2020), available at: https://www.ato.gov.au/general/gen/tax-treatment-of-crypto-currencies-in-australia---specifically-bitcoin/?page=2#Stakingrewardsandairdrops.
61. ATO webpage, 'Transacting with Cryptocurrency: Staking Rewards and Airdrops', QC 42159 (last modified 30 Mar. 2020, accessed 11 May 2020), available at: https://www.ato.gov.au/general/gen/tax-treatment-of-crypto-currencies-in-australia---specifically-bitcoin/?page=2#Stakingrewardsandairdrops.
62. Private ruling PBR 1013139758672 (dated 15 Dec. 2016).

(compared with the opening value) is treated as assessable income (while a decrease compared to the opening value is treated as an allowable deduction). This means that in practice, if the crypto asset is mined and not sold, the value of the crypto asset at year end is treated as assessable income. Any expenses incurred in respect of the mining activity (e.g., electricity costs) may be deductible against other income, subject to integrity rules. The cost of capital assets (e.g., hardware and software) can be depreciated over their effective lives.[63]

In contrast, if a crypto miner undertakes mining activities but does not carry on a mining business, the mined coins would be capital assets obtained by the miner (and their value will not be assessable income). This means that the CGT rules would apply, so tax is essentially deferred until disposal of the coins. However, no deductions would be allowable for expenses incurred by the miner, although these costs may form part of the cost base. The CGT rules would need to be applied on the disposal of the coin.

The ATO's view is that a coin obtained via mining can only be treated as a personal use asset (and therefore exempt from the CGT rules) if the coin is acquired and then kept only temporarily in order to obtain personal use items.[64]

(l) What are the income/capital gains tax consequences of staking crypto assets?

In March 2020, the ATO confirmed that coins and tokens earned through staking are assessable as ordinary income, as follows:[65]

> Proof of Stake is a form of 'consensus mechanism' that requires forgers (similar to miners) to hold units of a cryptocurrency so they can validate transactions and create new blocks. Forgers participate in consensus by staking their existing tokens.
>
> A forger who is selected to forge a new block is rewarded with additional tokens when the new block has been created. The additional tokens are received from holding the original tokens. The money value of those additional tokens is ordinary income of the forger at the time they are derived.
>
> Other consensus mechanisms that reward existing token holders for their role in maintaining the network will have the same tax outcomes. This would include rewards derived through Proof of Authority and Proof of Credit mechanisms by Validators, Agent Nodes, Guardian Nodes, Premium Stakers and other entities performing comparable roles.

---

63. *See also* ATO webpage, 'ATO Community: Mining Cryptocurrency' (dated Apr. 2018, accessed 3 Feb. 2020), available at: https://community.ato.gov.au/t5/Tax/Mining-cryptocurrency/ta-p/4599.
64. ATO webpage, 'ATO Community: Mining Cryptocurrency' (dated Apr. 2018, accessed 3 Feb. 2020), available at: https://community.ato.gov.au/t5/Tax/Mining-cryptocurrency/ta-p/4599.
65. ATO webpage, 'Transacting with Cryptocurrency: Staking Rewards and Airdrops', QC 42159 (last modified 30 Mar. 2020, accessed 11 May 2020), available at: https://www.ato.gov.au/general/gen/tax-treatment-of-crypto-currencies-in-australia---specifically-bitcoin/?page=2#Stakingrewardsandairdrops.

Token holders who participate in 'proxy staking' or who vote their tokens in delegated consensus mechanisms, and receive a reward by doing so, also derive ordinary income equal to the money value of the tokens they receive.

Example 1

Anastasia holds 50,000 NULS tokens, which she stakes to a NULS pool as a premium staker. Anastasia receives additional NULS tokens when her pool participates in consensus, including a small payment of tokens from the node leader for supporting their node.

The money value of the additional NULS tokens Anastasia receives is assessable income of Anastasia at the time the tokens are derived.

The cost base of Anastasia's additional NULS tokens will be their market value at the time they were derived.

(m) What are the income/capital gains tax consequences of an indirect investment in crypto assets?

Indirect investments in crypto assets have tax consequences at the vehicle level and at the shareholder/beneficiary level. There is no particular Australian tax regime targeting indirect investments in crypto assets. Ordinary tax principles apply.

For crypto assets held in an Australian resident vehicle such as a company or trust (e.g., shares in Digitalx Ltd, a listed company on the Australian Stock Exchange), the tax consequences of the crypto assets (at the vehicle level) will depend on their classification in the hands of the company or trust, based on the principles outlined at section 1.1.2(a) above. Notably, the 50% CGT discount is not available to companies, but can flow through a trust to an Australian resident beneficiary.

In order to extract profits made on the crypto assets out of the company or trust, dividends or trust distributions will need to be made to the shareholders or beneficiaries. The tax consequences of such dividends and trust distributions are governed by the particular Australian tax regimes for companies and trusts and the tax residency of the recipient (which are topics beyond the scope of this chapter).

(n) How is income from crypto assets to be treated under double tax treaty law?

The ATO has not issued any particular views regarding the treatment of income derived from crypto assets under double tax treaty law. The existing principles in Australia's double tax agreements (DTAs) with partner countries will apply to activities involving crypto assets in Australia. Australia's DTAs are largely based on the Organisation for Economic Co-operation and Development (OECD) Model Convention.

The key DTA issue for a foreign entity seeking to undertake crypto activities in Australia is whether its activities in Australia could give rise to an Australian permanent establishment (PE). If so, the foreign entity would need to register with the ATO in Australia and should be taxable in Australia on the business profits that are attributable to its Australian PE.

The PE and profit attribution rules were developed at a time during which businesses had physical locations, used tangible resources, and required manual labour. Accordingly, these rules do not apply well to new technologies. Although a foreign crypto business may have a virtual/digital presence in Australia, it is possible for the business to avoid having a PE in Australia (such as a place of management, branch, or office) where the business is located offshore in a DTA partner country (often a crypto-friendly jurisdiction) and the business does not have personnel on the ground in Australia. PE avoidance has been made more difficult by the introduction of specific anti-avoidance rules, however the scope of those rules is generally limited to large global businesses and not individual traders.

(o) What are the income/capital gains tax consequences of selling crypto assets in an ICO/STO/IEO?

There will be income tax implications for both issuers and token holders in an initial coin offering (ICO). The contentious aspects are whether the issuer should be taxed on the proceeds and, if so, on what basis the issuer should be taxed.

In January 2019, the Australian Treasury released an Issues Paper[66] as part of its consultation process on ICOs. The Issues Paper focuses on the Australian tax treatment of ICOs and regulatory frameworks in Australia.

The Issues Paper noted:[67]

- The current tax treatment of ICOs follows from the attributes of the tokens that are issued. For example, some ICOs offer tokens with equity-like characteristics (e.g., voting rights and profit participation) while other ICOs offer tokens that give rights to the future use of a distributed ledger technology (DLT) platform. As a result, like any other transaction or event, how ICO proceeds are taxed in the hands of the issuer will depend on a number of factors, including whether the ICO is structured similarly to an offer of shares, an offer of derivatives or as a non-cash payment facility (with the promise of future services to be provided by the issuer).
- There is no single manner in which ICO proceeds are taxed to issuers. For example, where tokens are economically equivalent to debt or equity interests, the proceeds may not be assessable upfront to the issuer (analogous to a company issuing notes or shares). However, if the issuer makes regular transactions in tokens, the proceeds could be seen as income derived from trading activity and subject to tax on this basis. Where tokens are issued as a prepayment for a service (e.g., access to and use of the DLT), the proceeds are likely to be assessable to the issuer.
- The tax implications for token holders acquiring tokens in an ICO are the same as for tokens acquired in other ways.

66. Australian Treasury, 'Initial Coin Offerings Issues Paper, January 2019', available at https://treasury.gov.au/sites/default/files/2019-03/c2019-t353604-Issues_Paper-1.pdf (Issues Paper).
67. Issues Paper at p. 17.

As at the date of this chapter, the Australian Treasury has not yet published its conclusions, but submissions made during the consultation period are publicly available.[68]

1.1.3 *Other Taxes*

(a) *What are the value added tax/sales tax consequences of selling crypto assets?*

The GST is Australia's value added/sales tax.

Prior to 1 July 2017, sales and purchases of crypto assets (such as bitcoin) were subject to GST. Taxpayers that were registered for GST had to pay GST and were entitled to GST credits on any transactions relating to crypto assets. Additionally, a supply of crypto assets in exchange for goods or services was treated as a barter transaction for GST purposes.

From 1 July 2017, sales and purchases of crypto assets are not subject to GST. This means that taxpayers do not charge GST on their sales of crypto assets and are not entitled to GST credits for purchases of crypto assets. This treatment is the same for personal, business and investment transactions. The reason for the change in law was to remove the potential for double GST which could arise when consumers purchased a crypto asset and subsequently used it in exchange for other goods and services subject to the GST.[69]

However, from 1 July 2017, sellers of crypto assets may be entitled to a full GST credit (if they are under certain thresholds) or a reduced (75%) GST credit for certain costs relating to crypto asset sales. Such costs include:

- commission, brokerage costs or arranging services provided by entities that facilitate buying and selling of crypto assets; and
- costs in relation to transaction processing, account maintenance, and report generation services.[70]

(b) *Are payments in crypto assets subject to withholding taxes?*

There are no specific withholding taxes applicable to payments in crypto assets. However, where a non-cash benefit (such as the transfer of crypto assets) is provided in circumstances where a payment of cash would give rise to a withholding obligation,

68. Australian Treasury webpage, 'Initial Coin Offerings', available at: https://treasury.gov.au/consultation/c2019-t353604.
69. *See* Australian Government Treasury, 'Backing Australian FinTech' 2016 Report, available at https://treasury.gov.au/publication/backing-australian-fintech.
70. ATO webpage, 'GST and Digital Currency', QC 54048 (last modified 16 Mar. 2018, accessed 4 Feb. 2020), available at: https://www.ato.gov.au/business/gst/in-detail/your-industry/financial-services-and-insurance/gst-and-digital-currency/.

the provider of the non-cash benefit must pay an amount in cash to the Commissioner of Taxation.[71]

(c) *Does payment of compensation in crypto assets give rise to payroll tax consequences?*

Yes, the money value of crypto assets would be treated as 'wages' for the purposes of the relevant State and Territory payroll tax provisions and consequently subject to payroll tax, unless an exemption applied.[72]

(d) *Do transactions with crypto assets trigger any transfer taxes?*

The transfer of crypto assets themselves is not subject to any stamp duty or similar transfer taxes in Australia. However, if crypto assets are used as consideration for a dutiable transaction (e.g., the sale of shares in an entity with significant landholdings), then stamp duty in the ordinary manner is payable (generally by the purchaser).

(e) *Are firms operating in the crypto space subject to digital service taxes?*

Australia does not currently have a digital services tax (DST).[73] Following a consultation process on the digital economy, the Australian government announced on 20 March 2019[74] that it has no plans to introduce a unilateral DST and prefers to wait for the current OECD consultation process (under Action 1 of the Base Erosion and Profit Shifting Project) to address the taxation of the digital economy using a multilateral solution.[75]

(f) *Are crypto assets subject to gift, inheritance, estate, or wealth taxes?*

Australia does not have any gift, inheritance, estate, or wealth taxes. However, a transfer of crypto assets would result in a CGT event for the transferor,[76] and there is potential that if the transfer is undertaken on a non-arm's length basis, the transferor

71. *See* section 12-10 and Division 14 of Schedule 1 to the TAA53.
72. Payments in kind are treated as wages for payroll tax purposes – *see* for example paragraph 13(2)(b) of the Payroll Tax Act 2007 (Vic). Similar provisions exist in the legislation of other Australian jurisdictions.
73. *See* https://www.aph.gov.au/About_Parliament/Parliamentary_Departments/Parliamentary_Library/FlagPost/2019/August/Digital_Services_Taxation (accessed 29 Jan. 2020).
74. Media release on 20 Mar. 2019 by the Hon Josh Frydenberg MP (Treasurer), 'Government Response to Digital Economy Consultation', available at: https://parlinfo.aph.gov.au/parlInfo/search/display/display.w3p;query=Id%3A%22media%2Fpressrel%2F6568787%22.
75. *See* https://www.aph.gov.au/About_Parliament/Parliamentary_Departments/Parliamentary_Library/FlagPost/2019/August/Digital_Services_Taxation (accessed 29 Jan. 2020).
76. *See* CGT event A1 under section 104-10 of the ITAA97.

will be deemed to have received (and will be taxed on) the market value of the crypto assets transferred.[77]

(g) *Are crypto assets subject to exit tax?*

An 'exit tax' is a tax on persons who cease to be tax resident in a country. This often takes the form of a capital gains tax on unrealized gains attributable to the period in which the taxpayer was a tax resident of the country in question.

If an individual ceases to be an Australian tax resident, under Australian tax law he/she is deemed to have disposed of all of their CGT assets (other than Australian land interests) for market value.[78] CGT assets will include crypto assets. This deemed disposition results in the individual being taxed on the capital gains on these assets up to the date they stop being an Australian tax resident. To avoid this tax treatment, the individual can make an election to only be taxed on capital gains on the assets when they are actually sold (i.e., keep the assets in the Australian CGT net).[79]

(h) *Can mining trigger gambling tax?*

There is no gambling tax in Australia. However, there are a range of betting taxes that apply at the State and Territory level to specific types of gambling operators. Crypto mining does not fall in any of the specific types.

1.1.4 Compliance and Documentation Obligations

(a) *What documentation requirements exist for taxpayers regarding crypto assets and are there best practices in recordkeeping to support representations made in tax returns?*

Beyond the ordinary record keeping requirements for taxpayers under the Australian tax law, there are no specific documentation requirements for taxpayers holding crypto assets.

However, the ATO's guidance is that taxpayers should generally keep the following records for their crypto asset transactions:

- the date of the transactions;
- the value of the crypto assets in Australian Dollars at the time of the transaction (which can be taken from a reputable online exchange); and

77. *See* the market value substitution rule in section 116-30 of the ITAA97.
78. Under CGT event I1 in section 104-160 of the ITAA97.
79. Section 104-165 of the ITAA97.

- what the transaction was for and who the other party was (a wallet address is sufficient).[80]

The sorts of records that taxpayers should keep include:

- receipts of purchase or transfer of crypto assets;
- exchange records;
- records of agent, accountant and legal costs;
- digital wallet records and keys; and
- software costs related to managing their tax affairs.[81]

It is also prudent for taxpayers to maintain records of various crypto assets they hold to enable them to demonstrate an overall gain or loss on their crypto transactions if requested to by the tax authorities, noting the taxpayer bears the burden of proof.

(b) What is the evidentiary burden of supporting tax positions when a digital wallet address is lost or shared with other persons?

The taxpayer bears the burden of proof in establishing any tax position and on appeal to a court must show that an assessment is excessive or otherwise incorrect.[82] This is no different in the case of transactions involving crypto assets compared with the position for transactions involving fiat currency.

To discharge the burden in respect of the loss of digital wallet addresses, the taxpayer will likely need to keep the records referred to above in section 1.1.2(g). It is difficult to conceive of any case where the taxpayer can discharge its burden without complete and contemporaneous records of the items set out above at section 1.1.2(g).

(c) Are crypto asset exchanges and wallet providers subject to reporting obligations?

There are no specific rules in Australia which require crypto asset exchanges and wallet providers to report crypto balances to the ATO. However, the ATO possesses a broad range of powers which can be exercised to obtain information from these parties about the tax affairs of a person that uses their services.[83] These powers are discussed in more detail at section 1.1.5 below.

80. ATO webpage, 'Tax Treatment of Crypto-currencies in Australia - Specifically Bitcoin: Record Keeping' (QC 42159, last modified 18 Jun. 2019, accessed 3 Feb. 2020), available at: https://www.ato.gov.au/General/Gen/Tax-treatment-of-crypto-currencies-in-Australia---specifically-bitcoin/?page=4#Record_keeping
81. ATO webpage, 'Tax Treatment of Crypto-currencies in Australia – Specifically Bitcoin: Record Keeping' (QC 42159, last modified 18 Jun. 2019, accessed 3 Feb. 2020), available at: https://www.ato.gov.au/General/Gen/Tax-treatment-of-crypto-currencies-in-Australia---specifically-bitcoin/?page=4#Record_keeping.
82. Section 14ZZO of the TAA53.
83. This includes an information gathering notice under Division 353 of Schedule 1 to the TAA53 or its foreign counterparty under section 264A of the ITAA36.

The efficacy of such powers will, however, depend on whether the crypto asset exchange or wallet providers are within Australia – there are obvious practical difficulties in seeking to compel the production of information from parties outside the jurisdiction who have no assets or agents within Australia.

(d) *Are taxpayers holding crypto assets subject to reporting obligations apart from the filing of income tax/capital gains tax returns?*

Taxpayers holding crypto assets are not currently subject to tax related reporting obligations apart from the filing of tax returns.[84]

(e) *Are crypto asset exchanges and wallet providers subject to CRS/FATCA reporting?*

The ATO has not issued any guidance on whether Australian crypto asset exchanges and wallet providers are subject to CRS and FATCA reporting.

FATCA and CRS do not provide explicit guidance on the classification and the required reporting of crypto assets. As such, there may be some difficulty in seeking to apply FATCA and CRS to crypto assets.

One difficulty is that there is a possibility that a particular crypto asset may not be classified as a *financial asset*.[85] The term '*financial asset*' is defined non-exhaustively in the CRS to include a variety of asset types. However, the asset types that are explicitly listed are traditional in nature (e.g., shares, notes, swaps, futures and partnership interests). It could be argued that crypto assets are not analogous to these classes of traditional financial assets and so should not be included in the definition. However, the ATO provides the following guidance which suggests that a broad interpretation should be given to the term '*financial asset*':[86]

---

84. In this regard, cyptocurrency assets are not treated differently than any other assets. Australia does not have any rules which require reporting of foreign account balances such as FBAR in the United States.
85. Section VIII(A)(7) of the OECD, *Standard for Automatic Exchange of Financial Account Information in Tax Matters*, 2nd ed. defines the term 'Financial Asset' as follows:

> The term 'Financial Asset' includes a security (for example, a share of stock in a corporation; partnership or beneficial ownership interest in a widely held or publicly traded partnership or trust; note, bond, debenture, or other evidence of indebtedness), partnership interest, commodity, swap (for example, interest rate swaps, currency swaps, basis swaps, interest rate caps, interest rate floors, commodity swaps, equity swaps, equity index swaps, and similar agreements), Insurance Contract or Annuity Contract, or any interest (including a futures or forward contract or option) in a security, partnership interest, commodity, swap, Insurance Contract, or Annuity Contract. The term 'Financial Asset' does not include a non-debt, direct interest in real property.

86. ATO webpage, 'Automatic Exchange of Information – CRS and FATCA: Financial Accounts' (QC 48683, last modified 29 Aug. 2019, accessed 4 Feb. 2020), available at: https://www.ato.gov.au/General/International-tax-agreements/In-detail/International-arrangements/Automatic-exchange-of-information---CRS-and-FATCA/?page=3.

> The term 'financial asset' is intended to encompass *any assets* that may be held in an account maintained by a financial institution, except a non-debt, direct interest in real property. It does not include physical goods.

Another difficulty is that although some crypto asset exchanges are registered as financial institutions on the IRS FFI List (e.g., Coinbase UK, Ltd.), reporting is only required where the exchange maintains financial accounts for its customers. Where the exchange only provides exchange services, without accepting deposits or holding financial assets for or on behalf of customers, no reporting would be required even if crypto assets were to be considered as financial assets.[87]

We are unaware of any Australian crypto asset exchanges and wallet providers that are undertaking CRS and FATCA reporting. However, Bitfinex (registered in the British Virgin Islands) is reporting both FATCA and CRS information to the British Virgin Islands' Government.[88]

Aside from CRS and FATCA reporting, Australia's *Anti-Money Laundering and Counter-Terrorism Financing Act 2006* (AML/CTF Act) may apply to businesses that issue or sell crypto assets characterized as financial products, issuers of stored value cards, remitters, digital currency exchange providers and payment platform operators. The AML/CTF regime has cross-border application where designated services are provided by a subsidiary of an Australian company or are provided in Australia by a foreign company.

In 2017, the AML/CTF Act was amended to introduce new designated services, specifically capturing digital currency exchange providers. Beyond this, providers of services relating to crypto assets are caught by the AML/CTF Act only to the extent such assets fall within the scope of the existing concepts and definitions relating to financial services, bullion, and gaming or gambling designated services.

Most reporting entities, including registered digital currency exchanges, will be required to:

- enrol (and in some circumstances, register) with the Australian Transaction Reports and Analysis Centre (AUSTRAC);
- adopt and maintain a compliant AML/CTF programme;
- implement know-your-customer processes to verify the identity of their customers; and
- comply with continuous obligations to monitor and report suspicious and large transactions.

Exchange operators are also required to keep certain records relating to customer identification and transactions for up to seven years.[89]

87. Noam Noked, *Tax Evasion and Incomplete Tax Transparency*, 7(3) Laws 31 (23 Aug. 2018); doi:10.3390/laws7030031.
88. Webpage, 'Cointelegraph: Bitfinex Requires Customer Tax Info which It 'May Exchange' with Gov't, Tax Authorities' (dated 18 May 2018, accessed 4 Feb. 2020), available at: https://cointelegraph.com/news/bitfinex-requires-customer-tax-info-which-it-may-exchange-with-govt-tax-authorities.
89. Part 10 of the *Anti-Money Laundering and Counter-Terrorism Financing Act 2006* (Cth). Section 286 of the *Corporations Act 2001* (Cth) also requires companies and other disclosing entities

1.1.5 *Civil and Criminal Tax Enforcement*

(a) What powers do the tax authorities have to compel the disclosure of information by third parties, such as exchanges or wallet providers, and have these been used in the past?

The ATO has statutory information gathering powers including the ability to issue formal notices, colloquially referred to as 'Section 353-10 notices'.[90] Such notices may require the production of information and documents, the attendance of nominated persons for interview or a combination of the above. Section 353-10 notices are limited in scope to documents and personnel in Australia, however, the ATO may also issue 'Section 264A' offshore information notices to overseas entities.[91]

Taxpayers failing to meet the requirements of Section 353-10 notices may be subject to a fine, and in extraordinary cases, imprisonment, though such enforcement is quite rare. No penalties or criminal sanctions are applicable for failure to comply with a Section 264A notice, however, refusing or failing to provide the requested information will mean that the same information is subsequently inadmissible in judicial proceedings challenging assessments, without the consent of the ATO.

The ATO is currently undertaking a crypto asset data matching programme for the financial years from 2014–2015 to 2019–2020[92] due to the significant growth in participation of crypto assets in recent years. Under this programme, the ATO is seeking to:

- rely on Section 353-10 notices to obtain data relating to crypto transactions from Australian crypto asset designated service providers (DSPs), such as exchanges and wallet providers; the data will be collected throughout the period March 2019 to July 2020;
- identify the buyers and sellers of crypto assets and quantify the related transactions;
- match the data provided by the DSPs against ATO records to identify individuals who may not be meeting their registration, reporting, lodgement, filing and/or payment obligations; and
- contact individuals to give them the opportunity to verify the information collected by the ATO before the ATO takes compliance action.

(whether or not they are financial institutions) to keep for seven years financial records that correctly record and explain their transactions and financial position and performance and would enable true and fair financial statements to be prepared and audited.

90. Section 353-10 of Schedule 1 to the TAA53.
91. Section 264A of the ITAA36.
92. *See* heading 'At a glance' on ATO webpage, 'Cryptocurrency: 2014–15 to 2019–20 Financial Years Data Matching Program Protocol' (QC 58683, last modified 29 Apr. 2010, accessed 31 Jan. 2020), available at: https://www.ato.gov.au/General/Gen/Cryptocurrency-2014-15-to-2019-20-financial-years/.

The programme applies only to DSPs that operate businesses in Australia and are governed by Australian law.[93] This reflects the fact that Section 353-10 notices can only be used to compel the production of documents and information by Australian persons. This obviously leaves an informational gap as overseas-based DSPs (such as Binance, Coinbase, Bitfinex, and Kraken) are not compellable. To address this gap, the ATO is working in a joint international effort as part of the Joint Chiefs of Global Tax Enforcement (J5), aimed at investigating cross-national crypto asset-related tax evasion, cybercrime, and money laundering.[94] The J5 is discussed in more detail at section 1.1.5(c) below.

At a domestic level, the ATO is working with other Australian regulators, in particular AUSTRAC and the Australian Securities and Investment Commission to ensure that tax law requirements align with a whole of system approach.[95]

(b) What measures have the tax authorities undertaken in the past to ensure crypto tax compliance?

Prior to the ATO's crypto data matching programme for the financial years from 2014–2015 to 2019–2020, the ATO did not have a dedicated crypto tax compliance programme. When the data matching programme was launched in April 2019, the ATO noted that 'the ATO has limited data on the level of investment, gains, losses, transactions made by Australian taxpayers and other information relating to crypto assets as there are limited obligations for taxpayers and third parties to provide this information'.[96]

(c) Are the tax authorities cooperating with tax authorities in other jurisdictions on enforcement?

The ATO is a member of the J5 which was formed on 1 July 2018 in response to a call to action from the OECD for countries to be more proactive in tackling the enablers of

93. *See* heading 'Data Providers' on ATO webpage, 'Cryptocurrency: 2014–15 to 2019–20 Financial Years Data Matching Program Protocol' (QC 58683, last modified 29 Apr. 2010, accessed 31 Jan. 2020), available at: https://www.ato.gov.au/General/Gen/Cryptocurrency-2014-15-to-2019-20-financial-years/.
94. ATO webpage, 'ATO Receives Cryptocurrency Data to Assist Tax Compliance' (QC 58687, last modified 30 Apr. 2019, accessed 31 Jan. 2020), available at: https://www.ato.gov.au/Media-centre/Media-releases/ATO-receives-cryptocurrency-data-to-assist-tax-compliance/.
95. ATO webpage, 'ATO Receives Cryptocurrency Data to Assist Tax Compliance' (QC 58687, last modified 30 Apr. 2019, accessed 31 Jan. 2020), available at: https://www.ato.gov.au/Media-centre/Media-releases/ATO-receives-cryptocurrency-data-to-assist-tax-compliance/.
96. *See* heading 'At a glance' on ATO webpage, 'Cryptocurrency: 2014–15 to 2019–20 Financial Years Data Matching Program Protocol' (QC 58683, last modified 29 Apr. 2010, accessed 31 Jan. 2020), available at: https://www.ato.gov.au/General/Gen/Cryptocurrency-2014-15-to-2019-20-financial-years/.

tax crime. The J5 focuses on crypto asset-related crimes such as tax evasion and money laundering and is working to share intelligence and data in near real time.[97]

The group brings together the leading tax, offshore tax evasion, crypto asset, and cyber experts from Australia, the United Kingdom, the United States, Canada, and the Netherlands.[98] Apart from the ATO, the following agencies are included in the J5:

- Her Majesty's Revenue and Customs from the United Kingdom;
- Internal Revenue Service Criminal Investigations from the United States;
- Canadian Revenue Agency from Canada; and
- Dutch Fiscal Information and Investigation Service from the Netherlands.

On 24 January 2020, the J5 had a globally coordinated day of intelligence and information collection activities, as part of a series of investigations in multiple countries into an international financial institution located in Central America, whose products and services are believed to be facilitating money laundering and tax evasion for customers across the globe.[99] Further to this, the tax chiefs from the J5 countries met in Sydney, Australia on 17–21 February 2020 to share information about common mechanisms, enablers, and structures that are being exploited to commit transnational tax crime.[100] On 17 February 2020, the Dutch Fiscal Intelligence and Investigation Service arrested two men in connection with two criminal investigations on suspicion of money laundering using crypto assets as a result of the J5's efforts.[101]

97. ATO webpage, 'One Year In, J5 Making a Difference' (QC 59256, last modified 6 Jun. 2019, accessed 31 Jan. 2020), available at: https://www.ato.gov.au/Media-centre/Media-releases/One-Year-In,-J5-Making-a-Difference/.
98. ATO webpage, 'Joint Chiefs of Global Tax Enforcement' (QC 61181, last modified 24 Jan. 2020, accessed 31 Jan. 2020) available at: https://www.ato.gov.au/General/The-fight-against-tax-crime/Our-focus/Joint-Chiefs-of-Global-Tax-Enforcement/?anchor=AbouttheJ5#AbouttheJ5.
99. ATO webpage, 'Global Tax Chiefs Undertake Unprecedented Multi-country Day of Action to Tackle International Tax Evasion' (QC 61182, last modified 24 Jan. 2020, accessed 28 Feb. 2020), available at https://www.ato.gov.au/Media-centre/Media-releases/Global-tax-chiefs-undertake-unprecedented-multi-country-day-of-action-to-tackle-international-tax-evasion/.
100. ATO webpage, 'J5 Tax Chiefs Closing the Net on Global Tax Evasion' (QC 61479, last modified 19 Feb. 2020, accessed 28 Feb. 2020), available at https://www.ato.gov.au/Media-centre/Media-releases/J5-tax-chiefs-closing-the-net-on-global-tax-evasion/.
101. Inland Revenue Service, 'Arrests Made in Two Investigations into Money Laundering Using Cryptocurrencies' (media release dated 18 Feb. 2020, accessed 28 Feb. 2020), available at https://www.irs.gov/pub/irs-utl/j5-media-release-2-18-2020.pdf.

Austria

Niklas Schmidt

1. COUNTRY GUIDES

1.1 Austria

1.1.1 Applicable Tax Law, Guidance, and Case Law

(a) Which laws, regulations, and other administrative guidance exist dealing with crypto assets?

Austrian tax legislation – in particular the Austrian Income Tax Act,[1] the Austrian Corporate Income Tax Act[2] and the Austrian Value Added Tax Act[3] – as well as the tax regulations promulgated thereunder do not explicitly mention crypto assets in general or bitcoins in particular.[4] In terms of administrative guidance issued by the Austrian Ministry of Finance, the Austrian Income Tax Guidelines[5] and the Austrian Value Added Tax Guidelines[6] deal with certain tax aspects relating to crypto assets. Also, the

1. *Einkommensteuergesetz 1988*, as amended.
2. *Körperschaftsteuergesetz 1988*, as amended.
3. *Umsatzsteuergesetz 1994*, as amended.
4. Actually, the only Austrian law that explicitly deals with crypto assets is the Austrian Financial Markets Money Laundering Act (*Finanzmarkt-Geldwäschegesetz*) which imposes registration and anti-money laundering obligations on providers of certain services in respect of virtual currencies. This law was passed in order to implement Directive (EU) 2018/843 of the European Parliament and of the Council of 30 May 2018 amending Directive (EU) 2015/849 on the prevention of the use of the financial system for the purposes of money laundering or terrorist financing, and amending Directives 2009/138/EC and 2013/36/EU.
5. Austrian Ministry of Finance, Austrian Income Tax Guidelines (*Einkommensteuerrichtlinien 2000*), as amended, in particular paras 628a, 6143 and 6201.
6. Austrian Ministry of Finance, Austrian Value Added Tax Guidelines (*Umsatzsteuerrichtlinien 2000*), as amended, in particular para. 759.

Austrian Ministry of Finance has published a ruling dealing with the applicability of double tax treaties to cloud mining.[7]

(b) Which court cases exist dealing with crypto assets?

There exist no cases of the Austrian Federal Tax Court[8] or of the Austrian Administrative Court[9] dealing with crypto assets. There is, however, a decision of the European Court of Justice (ECJ) dealing with value added tax in relation to bitcoins.[10]

1.1.2 Income and Capital Gains Taxes

(a) How are crypto assets classified for income and capital gains tax purposes?

For Austrian income and capital gains tax purposes, a crypto asset is treated as a commodity (*Wirtschaftsgut*), this being defined by jurisprudence as an asset of any kind which - in the prevailing view - can be appraised in commercial intercourse on a standalone basis.[11] Furthermore, crypto assets are seen as intangible and as not subject to wear and tear (*nicht abnutzbare unkörperliche Wirtschaftsgüter*).[12] Crypto assets can qualify as fixed assets (*Anlagevermögen*) or as current assets (*Umlaufvermögen*), depending on whether they are being held for the long or for the short term.[13] Crypto assets used as means of payment will typically qualify as current assets; crypto assets held as an investment can be fixed or current assets, depending on the circumstances.[14] Finally, it is important to note that crypto assets such as bitcoins never qualify as investment assets pursuant to section 27(3) of the Austrian Income Tax Act,[15] this being assets that lead to investment income.

(b) What are the income/capital gains tax consequences of selling crypto assets against fiat currency?

The tax treatment of gains and losses from the sale of crypto assets against fiat currency depends on whether such crypto assets are being held as non-business assets (*Privatvermögen*) or as business assets (*Betriebsvermögen*).[16]

7. Austrian Ministry of Finance, EAS Ruling of 30 Apr. 2018, BMF-010221/0042-IV/8/2018; *cf.* section 1.1.2(n), *infra*.
8. *Bundesfinanzgericht*.
9. *Verwaltungsgerichtshof*.
10. ECJ, 22 Oct. 2015, C-264/14, *Hedqvist*; *cf.* section 1.1.3(a), *infra*.
11. *Steinhauser/Egger* in *Urnik/Fritz-Schmied*, Jahrbuch Bilanzsteuerrecht 2018 (2018), 43. This applies irrespective of whether the asset is used in the context of a business or not.
12. *Schmidt*, Kryptowährungen und Blockchains (2019), 130.
13. Austrian Ministry of Finance, Austrian Income Tax Guidelines, para. 628a.
14. *Schmidt*, Kryptowährungen und Blockchains (2019), 125.
15. The Austrian tax authorities do not share this view in the case of lending of crypto assets; *cf.* Austrian Ministry of Finance, Austrian Income Tax Guidelines, para. 6143. *See also* the discussion in *Schmidt*, Kryptowährungen und Blockchains (2019), 131.
16. *Cf.* section 1.1.2(d) regarding this distinction.

If crypto assets are held as non-business assets, the following applies:

- If the period between the acquisition and the disposal of the crypto assets is more than one year, gains and losses are not relevant for tax purposes. This means that gains are not taxable and that losses cannot be utilized for tax purposes. In the case of crypto assets acquired free of charge, the acquisition date of the previous owner (e.g., donor in case of a gift or testator in case of an inheritance) is to be taken into account when calculating the one-year holding period.
- In all other cases, gains and losses qualify as income from speculative transactions (*Einkünfte aus Spekulationsgeschäften*).[17] To determine the income, the acquisition costs must be deducted from the proceeds of the sale. In the case of crypto assets acquired free of charge, the acquisition costs of the previous owner (*e.g.*, donor or testator) must be deducted from the proceeds of sale. Transaction costs and custody fees are tax deductible. The balance from all transactions leading to income from speculative transactions is tax-free up to an exemption limit of EUR 440 per year. If the balance exceeds this exemption limit, the entire income is taxable and subject to the progressive income tax rate of up to 55%. If the balance is negative, it cannot be offset or carried forward (*i.e.*, the loss cannot be further utilized for tax purposes). An interesting question arises if crypto assets have been acquired in several tranches at different acquisition costs and if a part of these crypto assets are then sold: Pursuant to the views of the Austrian Ministry of Finance, the taxpayer can freely determine which tranche was sold, provided that the holdings of crypto assets are completely documented in terms of acquisition dates and acquisition costs. If this is not the case, the FIFO (First In First Out) method is to be applied (meaning that those tranches acquired first are deemed to have been sold first).[18]

In case crypto assets are held as business assets, gains realized are always taxable (*i.e.*, independent of the one-year speculation period mentioned above) as income from an active trade or business (*Einkünfte aus Gewerbebetrieb*).[19] The income is subject to the progressive income tax rate of up to 55%. Losses can be fully offset against other income and may also be carried forward. In order to determine the gain or loss on disposal, the acquisition costs (or the book value in case of double entry bookkeeping) must be deducted from the sales proceeds.

17. Section 31 of the Austrian Income Tax Act.
18. *Schmidt*, Kryptowährungen und Blockchains (2019), 133.
19. Section 23 of the Austrian Income Tax Act. Depending on the circumstance, the income might alternatively be such from agriculture and forestry (section 21 of the Austrian Income Tax Act) or from self-employed work (section 22 of the Austrian Income Tax Act).

(c) *What are the income/capital gains tax consequences of exchanging crypto assets against other crypto assets?*

The Austrian Ministry of Finance regards the exchange of one crypto asset against another crypto asset as a taxable exchange:[20] A taxpayer exchanging, for example, bitcoins into another crypto asset and then exchanging such crypto asset back into fiat currency triggers two potentially taxable exchanges (rather than only one on the second transaction). From a tax perspective, the exchange of assets involves both an acquisition and a disposal:[21] the sale price of the transferred asset and the acquisition cost of the asset acquired is the fair market value (*gemeiner Wert*) of the transferred asset. This realization of profits is problematic in view of the high volatility of crypto assets and the resulting possibility of reporting paper profits. In contrast thereto, exchanging a fiat currency into another fiat currency will only be a taxable exchange if the gain has been locked in, meaning if the taxpayer receives Euros or a fiat currency which is pegged to the Euro.[22]

(d) *If a distinction is made between business assets and non-business assets, when does trading in crypto assets lead to a trade or business?*

Trading in crypto assets can, for tax purposes, take place within the context of an active trade or business (*Gewerbebetrieb*)[23] or outside of a business (*Vermögensverwaltung*).[24] There are no clear-cut rules distinguishing these two types of activities, and certainly not for crypto assets. It seems reasonable to apply the guidelines applying to securities trading analogously.[25] Consequently, the following indicia would suggest that a taxpayer engaged in crypto asset trading is carrying out a business and thus earning income from an active trade or business, rather than having non-business income:

- the taxpayer exercises its trading activity as a main occupation;
- the taxpayer maintains an office or an organization to carry out the transactions;
- the taxpayer exploits market opportunities by using relevant professional securities trading experience;
- the taxpayer concludes transactions also on behalf of third parties;
- the taxpayer carries out a high number of purchases and sales (*e.g.*, through the use of trading bots); and
- the taxpayer finances its acquisitions through debt.

20. *Schmidt*, Kryptowährungen und Blockchains (2019), 133.
21. *Cf.* section 6(14)(a) of the Austrian Income Tax Act. This applies in respect of business assets and non-business assets.
22. Austrian Ministry of Finance, Austrian Income Tax Guidelines, para. 6201.
23. *Cf.* section 28 of the Austrian Federal Fiscal Procedures Act (*Bundesabgabenordnung*).
24. *Cf.* section 32 of the Austrian Federal Fiscal Procedures Act.
25. *Schmidt*, Kryptowährungen und Blockchains (2019), 131.

(e) *What are the income/capital gains tax consequences for an employee receiving wages or salaries in crypto assets?*

If a taxpayer (*e.g.*, a developer) is remunerated for work carried out under an employment agreement and if such remuneration consists of crypto assets, then taxable income from employment[26] arises at the point in time when the crypto assets are received (thus, not only at the point in time of the exchange of such crypto assets into fiat currency).[27] Regarding the valuation of the crypto assets received, the provisions of section 15 of the Austrian Income Tax Act on benefits in kind are to be applied. This would mean that an average exchange rate of several exchanges (such as the quotation listed on www.coinmarketcap.com or on www.coingecko.com) should be used; alternatively, the exchange rate of the exchange on which the taxpayer typically sells his or her crypto assets could be used.[28] Normally, wage withholding tax would be due.[29] Should the taxpayer at a later point in time sell the crypto assets received as wages or salaries, then the acquisition costs[30] of the crypto assets should be equal to the value used for purposes of calculating the income from employment (*i.e.*, no double taxation).

(f) *What are the income/capital gains tax consequences for a merchant receiving payment in crypto assets?*

According to the views of the Austrian Ministry of Finance, the supply by a merchant of goods and services, which are remunerated through crypto assets, are to be treated in the exact same way as supplies whose remuneration is paid in fiat currency.[31] Thus, for income tax purposes, the fair market value of the goods or services constitute the merchant's taxable income.[32] Once the merchant exchanges the crypto assets received into fiat currency, another taxable transaction will occur.

(g) *What are the income/capital gains tax consequences of a loss of crypto assets?*

The loss of crypto assets - meaning the loss of the private key associated with an address at which crypto assets are stored - is not relevant in case they were to qualify as non-business assets. In particular, such circumstances do not lead to negative income from speculative transactions,[33] the reason being that the total extinction or

26. *Cf.* section 25 of the Austrian Income Tax Act.
27. *Schmidt*, Kryptowährungen und Blockchains (2019), 140.
28. *Schmidt*, Kryptowährungen und Blockchains (2019), 137.
29. *Cf.* section 1.1.3(c), *infra*.
30. *Cf.* section 1.1.2(b), *supra*.
31. *Schmidt*, Kryptowährungen und Blockchains (2019), 134.
32. *Cf.* section 6(14)(a) of the Austrian Income Tax Act.
33. *Cf.* section 1.1.2(a), *supra*.

destruction of an asset is not seen as a sale.[34] In contrast thereto, the loss of crypto assets qualifying as business assets can lead to a tax deductible expense.[35]

(h) *What are the income/capital gains tax consequences of a loss in value of crypto assets?*

The loss in value of crypto assets, which has not been realized through a sales transaction, is normally not relevant when crypto assets qualify as non-business assets; however, in exceptional cases, a depreciation for extraordinary technical or economic deterioration could be possible.[36] In the case of an active trade or business, taxpayers subject to the requirements of double entry bookkeeping may write down assets to the fair market value.[37]

(i) *What are the income/capital gains tax consequences of forks of crypto assets?*

There exist no statements of the Austrian tax authorities on blockchain forks (i.e., cases where a blockchain splits into two blockchains, so that a taxpayer holding crypto assets on the original blockchain then additionally holds the same number of crypto assets on the new blockchain). Most likely, forks are to be treated in a similar manner as cases where a listed corporation spins off assets into a separate entity by way of a demerger.[38] Thus, the acquisition costs of the original (forked) crypto asset are to be allocated to the original crypto asset and to the newly received crypto asset, pursuant to the ratio of the fair market values of these two assets at the time of the fork. Additionally, the date of acquisition of the original crypto asset is relevant for the newly received crypto asset.[39] This applies equally to crypto assets held within and outside of an active trade or business. Consequently, the fork itself should not have any tax consequences; these would only occur when the newly received crypto assets were sold.[40] Determining the fair market value of the newly received crypto asset at the time of the fork can be difficult, and in extreme cases its fair market value can be zero.

---

34. *Kanduth-Kristen* in *Kanduth-Kristen/Laudacher/Lenneis/Marschner/Peyerl*, EStG, 12th ed. (2019), section 30 para. 17.
35. *Cf.* section 1.1.4(b), *infra*.
36. *Cf.* section 8(4) of the Austrian Income Tax Act.
37. *Cf.* sections 6(1) and 6(2)(a) of the Austrian Income Tax Act. Such write-downs are not mandatory. Note that taxpayers subject to the additional accounting rules of the Austrian Companies Act (*Unternehmensgesetzbuch*) are obliged to make a write-down in case of fixed assets which are presumably permanently impaired as well as in case of current assets.
38. *Schmidt,* Kryptowährungen und Blockchains (2019), 140; section 36(2)(1) of the Austrian Reorganization Tax Act (*Umgründungssteuergesetz*); section 4(2) of the Austrian Regulation on Corporate Actions (*Kapitalmaßnahmen-VO*).
39. This is for example relevant in order to determine whether capital gains realized in case of a later sale of crypto assets qualifying as non-business assets are taxable as income from speculative transactions section 1.1.2(b), *supra*.
40. *Cf. Steinhauser,* ÖStZ 2018, 602 et seq. A different view is held by *Brameshuber,* ecolex 2018, 693, who assumes that both the receipt of the new asset and its sale are tax-free.

(j) *What are the income/capital gains tax consequences of airdrops of crypto assets and are the tax consequences different if the airdropped tokens are unwanted?*

The tax consequences of airdrops, meaning cases where crypto assets are given free of charge (mostly for marketing reasons), depend on whether the crypto assets are received within or outside of an active trade or business:[41]

- Crypto assets received within an active trade or business lead to taxable income equal to the amount which the taxpayer would have had to pay in order to receive the assets.[42]
- Crypto assets received outside of an active trade or business qualify as non-taxable gifts.[43]

From a tax perspective, it is of no relevance whether the airdropped tokens are wanted or unwanted. If the airdropped crypto assets were received as consideration for a service performed (*e.g.*, positive postings on forums and social media sites regarding the project), then irrespective of other circumstances the airdrop would result in taxable income outside of an active trade or business.[44]

(k) *What are the income/capital gains tax consequences of (solo, pool, and cloud) mining?*

In the view of the Austrian Ministry of Finance, mining always leads to taxable income from an active trade or business.[45] While this is normally true,[46] it is not necessarily always the case:

- A miner who takes out loans, rents premises and has employees is certainly carrying out an active trade or business. On the other hand, a miner who buys an ASIC (*i.e.*, a piece of mining hardware), attaches it to the internet and to power, enters his crypto address in the web interface of the hardware and otherwise only regularly checks how much income he has earned, likely does not fulfil the requirements of an active trade or business. The economic activity of such a taxpayer is similar to that of a landlord renting out an apartment on the basis of a long-term rent agreement. As a consequence, such a miner should not earn income from an active trade or business, but rather the so-called other income (*sonstige Einkünfte*).[47] This income is tax-free up to an exemption limit of EUR 220 per year.

41. *Schmidt*, Kryptowährungen und Blockchains (2019), 141.
42. *Cf.* section 6(1)(9)(b) of the Austrian Income Tax Act.
43. As mentioned in s. 1.1.2(b) the recipient would, in case of an on-sale, need to know the donor's acquisition date and acquisition cost in order to determine his or her tax liability.
44. *Cf.* section 29(3) of the Austrian Income Tax Act.
45. *Schmidt*, Kryptowährungen und Blockchains (2019), 135.
46. *Cf. Inreiter/Marschner*, taxlex 2018, 19.
47. *Cf.* section 29(3) of the Austrian Income Tax Act.

- Also, it is important to note that for tax purposes a source of income can only be assumed if profits can be achieved in the long term. Otherwise, neither active nor passive income of such hobby activity (*Liebhaberei*) is to be taken into consideration. Mining is a very competitive business today. Taking into account electricity costs and depreciation expenses, amateur miners often do not break even. In such a situation (positive or negative) income would not be relevant for tax purposes.[48]

In case mining does lead to taxable income, any crypto assets received by the miner (*i.e.*, block reward and transaction fees) are taxable at the point in time they are received by the miner. This income can then be offset by expenses such as electricity costs, rent regarding the premises and depreciation charges regarding the technical equipment. These statements regarding solo mining equally apply to pool mining (where many smaller miners join together to form a mining pool, which in turn distributes computing tasks among the individual pool members) and cloud mining (where a miner does not have to worry about hardware and software, but instead rents hash power from the operator of a data centre, with the crypto assets earned by the use of the computing power belonging to the customer).[49]

(l) *What are the income/capital gains tax consequences of staking crypto assets?*

Proof of stake is a consensus mechanism (an alternative to proof of work) whereby transactions are validated by persons who have substantial holdings in a particular crypto asset and would therefore suffer the greatest damage from a blockchain with incorrect entries. Staking is like mining, but with hardly any use of resources and much more passive in appearance; it therefore even less fulfils the criteria of an active trade or business. Thus, any income earned from staking should be taxable as so-called other income.[50]

(m) *What are the income/capital gains tax consequences of an indirect investment in crypto assets?*

Investors seeking exposure to crypto assets but not wishing to hold them directly have various possibilities of an indirect investment:[51]

- One example is bonds which are issued at nominal value, which may or may not pay interest and which are repaid at maturity in an amount based on the performance of one specific crypto asset, of a basket of several crypto assets or

48. *Cf. Aigner/Bräumann/Kofler/Tumpel* in *Felten/Kofler/Mayrhofer/Perner/Tumpel*, Digitale Transformation im Wirtschafts- & Steuerrecht (2019), 335.
49. *Schmidt*, Kryptowährungen und Blockchains (2019), 137.
50. *Cf.* section 29(3) of the Austrian Income Tax Act.
51. *Schmidt*, Kryptowährungen und Blockchains (2019), 139.

of a crypto asset index: From a tax perspective, any income earned at redemption (*i.e.*, repayment amount minus purchase price) from this product would qualify as income from investments (*Einkünfte aus Kapitalvermögen*)[52] and would normally be taxable at a flat rate of 27.5 %. In case of an investment horizon of more than one year, investing in such a product is disadvantageous compared with a direct investment since crypto assets can normally be sold tax-free after expiry of the one-year speculation period.[53]

- Another possibility would be to purchase units in an investment fund, which in turn invests in crypto assets.[54] In this case, 30 % of income from the sale of the fund's crypto assets would be deemed to constitute income from speculative transactions,[55] the rest being tax-free.[56] Again, if the investor has an investment horizon of more than one year, the investment through such fund product is disadvantageous compared to a direct investment in the crypto assets.

(n) *How is income from crypto assets to be treated under double tax treaty law?*

The Austrian tax authorities have not issued any general statements regarding the treatment of crypto assets under double tax treaty law. At any rate, income earned in connection with crypto assets can fall under various allocation rules of the OECD Model Convention:

- Pursuant to Article 7 of the OECD Model Convention, profits of an enterprise of a contracting state are taxable only in that state; if the enterprise, however, carries on business in the other contracting state through a permanent establishment situated therein, then the profits that are attributable to this permanent establishment may be taxed in that other state. Thus, for example, profits of a crypto mining enterprise carried on by a resident of Austria may only be taxed in Austria. However, if the crypto mining enterprise, however, carried on business in Iceland (a popular mining location) through a permanent establishment situated in Iceland, then the profits that are attributable to this permanent establishment may be taxed in Iceland.
- Pursuant to Article 13(5) of the OECD Model Convention, gains from the alienation of any property, other than that referred to in certain other paragraphs, are taxable only in the contracting state of which the alienator is resident. Thus, for example, an investor resident in Austria selling bitcoins

52. *Cf.* section 27(4) of the Austrian Income Tax Act.
53. *Cf.* *Polivanova-Rosenauer*, taxlex 2017, 381.
54. Such fund would normally qualify as a so-called Alternative Investment Fund (AIF).
55. *Cf.* section 1.1.2(b), *supra*.
56. *Cf.* section 186(5) of the Austrian Investment Funds Act (*Investmentfondsgesetz 2011*). It should be noted that this simplification rule does not apply if the units in the fund are held by at most fifty unitholders.

through a crypto exchange located in the United Kingdom may only be taxed in Austria.

It is interesting to note that the Austrian Ministry of Finance has issued a ruling dealing with the question of whether a cloud mining contract may lead to a permanent establishment within the meaning of Article 5(1) of the OECD Model Convention.[57] In this ruling, the following two cases are differentiated:

- If mining hardware is purchased or rented by a taxpayer and if such hardware is operated on the taxpayer's own premises or on the premises of a third-party data centre (so-called housing), then the taxpayer disposes over a fixed place of business, which therefore results in the taxpayer having a permanent establishment pursuant to Article 5(1) of the OECD Model Convention. As a consequence of having a foreign permanent establishment, the application of a double tax treaty can lead either to the exclusion of the foreign income from the domestic Austrian tax base (if the exemption method is applicable) or to the crediting of the foreign tax due on the foreign income against the Austrian domestic tax (if the credit method is applicable).
- The situation is different, however, if the taxpayer merely rents computing capacity (*i.e.*, a certain hash rate over a certain period of time) from a cloud mining company without being provided with specific hardware (which is what usually happens in practice). In this case, according to the Austrian Ministry of Finance the existence of a permanent establishment would have to be denied, because the taxpayer does not have at its disposal a fixed place of business. This form of mining is no different from other services offered in the cloud.

(o) *What are the income/capital gains tax consequences of selling crypto assets in an ICO/STO/IEO?*

The few sales of tokens launched in Austria to date (whether through an ICO, STO, or IEO) have been carried out by corporations as issuers (rather than by individuals). Such sales of tokens result in the following tax consequences:[58]

- Any tokens generated are to be capitalized at their cost of manufacturing; they should be reported as current assets. Tokens that are not intended for a sale qualify as fixed assets and must not be capitalized.[59]
- The exchange of the tokens against the purchase price (for example, ether) leads to the capitalization of the purchase price received, the closing out of the

57. Austrian Ministry of Finance, EAS Ruling of 30 Apr. 2018, BMF-010221/0042-IV/8/2018.
58. *Schmidt*, Kryptowährungen und Blockchains (2019), 142.
59. *Cf.* section 4(1) of the Austrian Income Tax Act.

capitalized tokens and in principle (but see immediately below) to the realization of taxable profits.[60]

- In case of so-called utility tokens, where the issuer has the legal obligation to provide a certain service in the future to the investor (similar to the buyer of a voucher), it may be possible for the issuer to post a liability and thus suppress the realization of a taxable profit (later on, a profit might be realized when the utility tokens are redeemed).
- The so-called security tokens may, depending on their structure, be accounted for as equity capital (if subordination, profit-related remuneration, participation in losses up to the full amount and no maturity exist) or as debt capital (in all other cases), thus also avoiding a taxable profit.[61]

1.1.3 Other Taxes

(a) What are the value added tax/sales tax consequences of selling crypto assets?

The ECJ had to deal with bitcoins in 2015.[62] In the case at hand, a certain Mr Hedqvist operated a website where one could buy bitcoins from him or sell bitcoins to him (the consideration being Swedish fiat currency). The question, which was referred to the ECJ for a preliminary ruling, was whether his activity was subject to value added tax. The ECJ held that, first, no supply of bitcoins was to be assumed, but rather a service of exchange. Second, the court stated that transactions in crypto assets fall within the scope of the exemption provided for in the EU's value added tax directive[63] (which covers transactions relating to foreign exchange, banknotes and coins), insofar as these crypto assets have been accepted by the parties concerned as an alternative means of payment to legal tender and insofar as they do not serve any purpose other than use as a means of payment.

The Austrian Ministry of Finance follows the opinion of the ECJ.[64] As a consequence, the following applies:[65]

- An entrepreneur selling bitcoins in its own name through a website (*i.e.*, having the same business model as Mr Hedqvist) carries out a service. If the customer is an entrepreneur, then such service is performed at the place from which the customer runs his business;[66] otherwise, the service is performed at the place where the recipient has his residence, registered office, or habitual

60. *Cf.* section 6(14)(a) of the Austrian Income Tax Act.
61. *Cf.* section 8(1) of the Austrian Corporate Income Tax Act.
62. ECJ 22 Oct. 2015, C-264/14, *Hedqvist*.
63. *Cf.* Article 135(1)(e) of Council Directive 2006/112/EC of 28 Nov. 2006 on the common system of value added tax, as amended.
64. Austrian Ministry of Finance, Austrian Value Added Tax Guidelines, para. 759.
65. *Schmidt*, Kryptowährungen und Blockchains (2019), 146 *et seq*.
66. *Cf.* section 3a(6) of the Austrian Value Added Tax Act.

abode.[67] Should the place of performance of the service be in Austria, then it should be tax-exempt.[68] As a result of the applicability of the tax exemption, the entrepreneur selling the bitcoins should normally not be entitled to a deduction of input tax.[69]

- An entrepreneur selling bitcoins in its own name through a crypto ATM similarly carries out a service, namely at the physical location of such crypto ATM.[70] Again, the service should be tax-exempt,[71] with no possibility for the entrepreneur to recover input tax (*e.g.*, on the purchase price of the crypto ATM).
- An entrepreneur who operates an exchange and acts as an intermediary between sellers and buyers of bitcoins for a fee is to be seen from a value added tax perspective as providing either an agency service (*Vermittlungsleistung*) or a procurement service (*Besorgungsleistung*). Both types of services are tax-free,[72] so that crypto exchanges having Austrian customers (whether entrepreneurs or not) should not become subject to value added tax in Austria.

The statements just made for bitcoins should apply analogously to other crypto assets, provided that they have been accepted by the parties concerned as an alternative means of payment to legal tender and insofar as they do not serve any purpose other than use as means of payment. Whether this is the case will depend on the concrete facts and circumstances. One important caveat applies to the sale of utility tokens by an entrepreneur: These can be subject to value added tax if they constitute so-called single-purpose vouchers (*i.e.*, if at the time of their issuance it is clear where and how the supply of goods or services to be purchased with the voucher will be subject to value added tax).

(b) Are payments in crypto assets subject to withholding taxes?

For purposes of the applicability of withholding taxes, payments made by a debtor through the transfer of crypto assets are to be treated in the same manner as payments made in cash. For example, dividends paid by a corporation with its legal seat and/or place of management in Austria to an individual are subject to a withholding tax of 27.5%.[73] If the shareholders of a limited liability company (*Gesellschaft mit beschränkter Haftung*) with its legal seat and its place of management in Austria were to resolve upon a dividend distribution in kind so that the company were to pay out a dividend of,

67. *Cf.* section 3a(13) of the Austrian Value Added Tax Act.
68. *Cf.* section 6(1)(8)(b) of the Austrian Value Added Tax Act. Note that this provision will have to be amended by the Austrian legislator in order to comply with the ECJ's interpretation. In the meantime, taxpayers may directly invoke higher-ranking EU law.
69. *Cf.* section 12(3) of the Austrian Value Added Tax Act.
70. *Cf.* Article 24a of the Council Implementing Regulation (EU) No. 282/2011 of 15 Mar. 2011 laying down implementing measures for Directive 2006/112/EC on the common system of value added tax, as amended.
71. *Cf.* section 6(1)(8)(b) of the Austrian Value Added Tax Act.
72. *Cf.* section 6(1)(8)(b) of the Austrian Value Added Tax Act.
73. *Cf.* section 93(1) of the Austrian Income Tax Act.

for example, 100 bitcoins, then the distributing entity would have to calculate the 27.5% withholding tax and remit it to the competent tax office. In order to do this, the crypto assets distributed would have to be converted into fiat currency (at the exchange rate prevailing on the day of the dividend distribution),[74] with the withholding tax payable to be calculated based on the grossed-up amount. Similarly, an employer paying out wages or salaries through transfer of crypto assets will normally have to calculate and remit the wage withholding tax.

(c) *Does payment of compensation in crypto assets give rise to payroll tax consequences?*

Compensation in crypto assets such as bitcoins does not give rise to any special payroll tax consequences and thus is to be treated as any payment in kind. Normally, the employer will have to calculate and remit wage withholding tax and various social security contributions.[75]

(d) *Do transactions with crypto assets trigger any transfer taxes?*

Under Austrian tax law, assignments made against consideration trigger a stamp duty (*Rechtsgeschäftsgebühr*).[76] In addition to assignments of debt claims, assignments of other rights are also covered (*i.e.*, intangible assets that grant rights vis-à-vis a specific person or the public at large). Crypto assets such as bitcoins which do not grant debt claims, but which are basically records in a digital ledger (i.e., the blockchain) and which do not grant any (absolute or relative) rights do thus not trigger stamp duty on assignments. There are, however, also other crypto assets – such as the tokens issued in the course of an ICO/STO/IEO, which often do confer rights vis-à-vis the issuer (e.g., a right to profit sharing). In this case, stamp duty of 0.8% of the consideration could actually be triggered (although in practice the other prerequisites for stamp duty to apply – written document regarding the assignment and a nexus to Austria – will often be lacking).

(e) *Are firms operating in the crypto space subject to digital service taxes?*

While Austria has – as of 1 January 2020 – introduced a digital tax,[77] the scope of this charge is not comprehensive and actually only covers online advertising services.

74. *Cf.* section 1.1.2(e) *supra* regarding the exchange rate to be used.
75. *Cf.* sections 47 and 81 of the Austrian Income Tax Act.
76. *Cf.* section 33(21) of the Austrian Stamp Duty Act (*Gebührengesetz*); *Schmidt*, Kryptowährungen und Blockchains (2019), 144.
77. *Cf.* section 1 of the Austrian Digital Tax Act (*Digitalsteuergesetz 2020*).

Thus, for example cross-border services provided by non-resident crypto asset exchanges or by non-resident crypto asset custodians to customers resident in Austria would not be covered by such tax.[78]

(f) *Are crypto assets subject to gift, inheritance, estate, or wealth taxes?*

Austria does not have any gift, inheritance, estate, or wealth taxes.

However, in the case of gifts, a specific notification obligation must be observed.[79] This notification obligation applies to gifts of money, receivables, shares in corporations, participations in partnerships, businesses, movable tangible assets, and intangibles. Thus, gifts of crypto assets – these being intangible assets[80] – are also covered.[81] The notification obligation applies if the donor and/or the donee have a domicile (*Wohnsitz*), the habitual abode (*gewöhnlicher Aufenthalt*), the legal seat (*Sitz*) or the place of management (*Ort der Geschäftsleitung*) in Austria.[82] Both the donor and the donee are obliged to effect the gift notification. The notification has to be done electronically and within three months from the date of the gift. Intentional violation of the notification obligation may lead to the levying of fines of up to 10% of the fair market value of the assets transferred.[83] Not all gifts are covered by the notification obligation: In case of gifts to certain related parties,[84] a threshold of EUR 50,000 per year applies; in all other cases, a notification is obligatory if the value of gifts made exceeds an amount of EUR 15,000 during a period of five years. An exception from the notification obligation also applies for transactions falling under the Austrian Foundation Transfer Tax Act.[85]

Pursuant to the just mentioned statute, gratuitous transfers of assets to (Austrian or foreign) private law foundations and comparable legal estates are subject to foundation transfer tax (*Stiftungseingangssteuer*). This tax is only triggered if there is a certain territorial nexus to Austria. This is the case if either the transferor (*i.e.*, typically the settlor/founder) or the transferee (*i.e.*, the private law foundation or comparable

---

78. Such services would normally be rendered without the necessity of having a permanent establishment in Austria (*i.e.*, the jurisdiction of the customer). Thus, Austria would – under domestic tax law – not be in a position to tax the income earned from such activities; *cf.* section 98(1)(3) of the Austrian Income Tax Act.
79. *Cf.* section 121a of the Austrian Federal Fiscal Procedures Act.
80. *Cf.* section 1.1.2(a), *supra*.
81. *Schmidt*, Kryptowährungen und Blockchains (2019), 142.
82. A domicile for tax purposes is maintained where a taxpayer has a dwelling place under circumstances which permit the conclusion that the taxpayer intends to keep and use it; *cf.* section 26(1) of the Austrian Federal Fiscal Procedures Act. A habitual abode for tax purposes is maintained where a taxpayer stays under circumstances which permit the conclusion that the taxpayer intends to dwell there not only temporarily; *cf.* section 26(2) of the Austrian Federal Fiscal Procedures Act. A corporation's legal seat is the place designated as such in its constitutional documents (e.g., articles of association, memorandum, trust deed) or in the applicable statute; *cf.* section 27(1) of the Austrian Federal Fiscal Procedures Act. A corporation's place of management is the place where a corporation has its centre of management; *cf.* section 27(2) of the Austrian Federal Fiscal Procedures Act.
83. *Cf.* section 49a of the Austrian Fiscal Criminal Act (*Finanzstrafgesetz*).
84. *Cf.* section 25 of the Austrian Federal Fiscal Procedures Act.
85. *Stiftungseingangssteuergesetz*, as amended.

legal estate), at the point in time of the transfer, have a domicile, the habitual abode, the legal seat and/or the place of management in Austria.

The tax basis is the fair market value of the assets transferred minus any debts; the tax rate generally is 2.5% (but 25% in certain cases). Thus, settling crypto assets into a trust may trigger foundation transfer tax.

(g) Are crypto assets subject to exit tax?

Austrian law provides for an exit tax:[86] In case circumstances occur which lead to a restriction of Austria's right to tax certain assets in relation to other jurisdictions, a sale is deemed to have happened and income tax falls due. A restriction of Austria's taxing right can follow from the rules of Austrian domestic law or can be the consequence of an applicable double tax treaty. Typical cases where exit tax is triggered involve the relocation of a taxpayer abroad, gifts by a taxpayer of assets to non-residents and the death of a taxpayer with non-resident heirs. Inversely, where Austria's right to tax comes into existence in relation to other jurisdictions, the assets concerned are to be valued at fair market value (*i.e.*, a step-up in basis is granted).[87] Not all types of assets are covered by the exit tax provision, but only assets within the meaning of section 27(3) of the Austrian Income Tax Act and derivatives within the meaning of section 27(4) of the Austrian Income Tax Act. The main cases of assets subject to exit tax are shares, bonds, options, futures, swaps and units in investment funds. Crypto assets such as bitcoins are not covered by the two above-mentioned provisions,[88] thus exit tax should not apply.[89] A taxpayer who acquires crypto assets and leaves Austria a few months later, at a time when they have increased in value, will thus not be taxable. Conversely, if a taxpayer holding crypto assets becomes an Austrian tax resident (so that these assets enter the Austrian tax jurisdiction for the first time), no step-up in basis can be claimed for these assets.

(h) Can mining trigger gambling tax?

It has been argued in Austrian scholarly literature that a bitcoin miner – similar to a treasure hunter with a metal detector – participates in a game of chance. As a consequence, in case of success such miner should not be subject to income tax on the block reward received (*i.e.*, currently 6.25 bitcoins), but should rather be subject to

86. *Cf.* section 27(6)(1) of the Austrian Income Tax Act regarding non-business assets. A similar provision exists in section 6(6)(b) of the Austrian Income Tax Act regarding business assets. Note that the statute does not use the German equivalent of the term 'exit tax' (*Wegzugsbesteuerung*), this is only used colloquially.
87. *Cf.* section 27(6)(1)(e) of the Austrian Income Tax Act.
88. *Beiser*, ÖStZ 2018, 3, is of a different view and considers bitcoins as derivatives.
89. *Schmidt*, Kryptowährungen und Blockchains (2019), 142. Note that the Austrian tax authorities are of the view that crypto assets can in certain cases qualify as assets pursuant to section 27(3) of the Austrian Income Tax Act; *cf.* section 1.1.2(a), *supra*.

gambling tax (*Glücksspielabgabe*).[90] This view appears problematic,[91] especially since in a game of chance the aleatory element would have to dominate in comparison to other elements, which is not the case with mining:[92] While none of the players participating in a lottery provides an economically valuable service (in other words, lottery players only pick numbers), each individual miner provides a relevant service. It is often overlooked that this is especially true for the unsuccessful miners: Every single miner strengthens the security of the whole system with his (successfully or unsuccessfully utilized) hashing power. In every field of economic activity (*e.g.*, that of a lawyer), success depends in part on chance, but this does not immediately make it a game of chance. Thus, no gambling tax should be triggered through crypto mining activities.

1.1.4 Compliance and Documentation Obligations

(a) What documentation requirements exist for taxpayers regarding crypto assets and are there best practices in recordkeeping to support representations made in tax returns?

In Austria, there are no specific documentation requirements for taxpayers holding crypto assets. Thus, such taxpayers must comply with the general documentation requirements. The law, for example, contains the obligation of taxpayers (not already subject to the requirements of double entry bookkeeping) to record revenues and expenses.[93] Intentional violation of this obligation is punishable with a fine of up to EUR 5,000.[94] Taxpayers trading crypto assets on exchanges should therefore download and store their transaction histories in order to be prepared for a tax audit.[95]

(b) What is the evidentiary burden of supporting tax positions when a digital wallet address is lost or shared with other persons?

Under Austrian tax law, the authorities must investigate and determine ex officio the factual and legal circumstances which are essential for the levying of taxes; they have to take into account any information provided to them, even if it is for the benefit of the taxpayer.[96] This official duty of investigation is limited in certain cases: If unusual circumstances exist which only the taxpayer can clarify, then the taxpayer has an increased duty of cooperation (*erhöhte Mitwirkungspflicht*) to help in clarifying the facts of the case.[97] This does, however, not mean that the taxpayer has the burden of

90. *Cf. Varro*, taxlex 2017, 401. The relevant provisions are section 12a and 58(3) of the Austrian Gambling Act (*Glücksspielgesetz*).
91. *Schmidt*, Kryptowährungen und Blockchains (2019), 136.
92. *Cf. Gorzala/Hanzl*, ÖJZ 2018, 849.
93. *Cf.* section 126 of the Austrian Federal Fiscal Procedures Act.
94. *Cf.* section 51(1)(c) of the Austrian Fiscal Criminal Act.
95. *Schmidt*, Kryptowährungen und Blockchains (2019), 149.
96. *Cf.* section 115 of the Austrian Federal Fiscal Procedures Act.
97. *Ritz*, Bundesabgabenordnung, 6th ed. (2017), section 115 para. 13.

proof; rather, the tax authorities have to freely assess the evidence. Thus, a taxpayer who has lost private keys and cannot anymore dispose over certain crypto assets will have the duty to explain to the tax office what his or her usual key management practice is and what went wrong in the concrete case at hand. The tax office will then have to consider whether the statement made by the taxpayer seems truthful or not.

(c) Are crypto asset exchanges and wallet providers subject to reporting obligations?

Under Austrian domestic tax law, crypto asset exchanges and wallet providers are not subject to any periodic reporting obligations vis-à-vis the tax authorities regarding their customers. However, the tax authorities do have powers to compel a person to provide information which is relevant for taxation of a third party.[98]

(d) Are taxpayers holding crypto assets subject to reporting obligations apart from the filing of income tax/capital gains tax returns?

Under Austrian domestic tax law, taxpayers holding crypto assets are not subject to any reporting obligations vis-à-vis the tax authorities apart from the filing of income tax/capital gains tax returns. Thus, in particular a taxpayer who is holding crypto assets and who has not realized taxable income in connection therewith does not have to disclose to the tax authorities his or her crypto investments.[99]

(e) Are crypto asset exchanges and wallet providers subject to CRS/FATCA reporting?

The tax authorities have not issued any guidance on the question of whether operators of crypto exchanges or providers of crypto wallets must annually report their customers' data under CRS/FATCA. In this context, it may be argued that the term 'financial asset' as currently defined under CRS[100] essentially only covers traditional financial assets and does not include crypto assets.[101] A crypto asset exchange or wallet provider would thus only be classified as a financial institution (meaning that it becomes subject to reporting) if it – in addition to crypto assets – also allows deposits of fiat currency.[102]

98. *Cf.* section 1.1.5(a).
99. This is not specific to crypto assets but applies to all other types of assets as well. Austria does not have rules such as exist in the United States regarding the reporting of Foreign Bank and Financial Accounts (FBAR).
100. OECD, Standard for Automatic Exchange of Financial Account Information in Tax Matters, 2nd ed., 45.
101. *Cf. Polivanova-Rosenauer*, taxlex 2017, 380.
102. *Schmidt*, Kryptowährungen und Blockchains (2019), 150.

1.1.5 *Civil and Criminal Tax Enforcement*

(a) *What powers do the tax authorities have to compel the disclosure of information by third parties, such as exchanges or wallet providers, and have these been used in the past?*

Under Austrian law, the tax authorities have the right to request the supply of information, which is relevant for the enforcement of taxes, from a person, even if it does not concern that person's own taxability.[103] Such requests have to be complied with, and the information is to be provided truthfully to the best of the person's knowledge and belief. The obligation to provide information includes the obligation to submit, or to allow the inspection, of written documents which are relevant for the determination of tax claims. There exist certain limits to questions that may be asked: For example, nobody is obliged to make enquiries with third parties or procure documents from third parties in order to answer a request. Also, requests have to be necessary, proportionate, reasonable and appropriate.[104] Close relatives and persons subject to a statutory obligation of confidentiality have the right to refuse to respond. Thus, the Austrian tax authorities could indeed compel an Austrian crypto asset exchange or wallet provider to hand over information regarding Austrian customers. Whether this has happened in the past is not in the public domain. According to a statement of the Austrian Ministry of Finance made in 2018, there were no agreements in place with trading platforms for crypto assets regarding the transmission of data to verify taxable actions.[105]

(b) *What measures have the tax authorities undertaken in the past to ensure crypto tax compliance?*

It is not known what measures the Austrian tax authorities have undertaken in the past to ensure crypto tax compliance, apart from publishing guidance regarding the application of the existing laws to transactions with crypto assets.[106]

(c) *Are the tax authorities cooperating with tax authorities in other jurisdictions on enforcement?*

In order to ensure compliance by taxpayers holding crypto assets, the Austrian tax authorities have several tools at their disposal for obtaining information from abroad (e.g., from crypto asset exchanges located outside of Austria): All of Austria's (currently 88) double taxation treaties contain articles on the exchange of information

103. *Cf.* section 143 of the Austrian Federal Fiscal Procedures Act.
104. *Ritz*, Bundesabgabenordnung, 6th ed. (2017), section 143 para. 8.
105. Austrian Ministry of Finance, Parlamentarische Anfragebeantwortung 382/AB vom 27.4.2018 zu 382/J, 26. GP.
106. *Cf.* section 1.1.1(a), *supra*.

between competent authorities.[107] Austria has also concluded seven tax information exchange agreements with certain no-tax jurisdictions. Furthermore, Austria can, based on EU law, request information from other EU Member States that is foreseeably relevant to the administration and enforcement of its domestic laws.[108] Finally, Austria has also ratified the OECD/Council of Europe Convention on Mutual Administrative Assistance in Tax Matters, which similarly gives the Austrian tax authorities access to information held abroad. It is currently not public knowledge whether the Austrian tax authorities are cooperating with tax authorities in other jurisdictions on enforcement and whether they have made use of the various instruments mentioned above in respect of crypto asset holdings of taxpayers.

107. *Cf.* Article 26 of the OECD Model Convention.
108. *Cf.* Council Directive 2011/16/EU of 15 Feb. 2011 on administrative cooperation in the field of taxation and repealing Directive 77/799/EEC, as amended.

Belgium

Gerd D. Goyvaerts & Stephanie Gabriel

1. COUNTRY GUIDES

1.1 Belgium

1.1.1 Applicable Tax Law, Guidance, and Case Law

(a) Which laws, regulations, and other administrative guidance exist dealing with crypto assets?

Belgium has not developed or implemented any specific tax[1] or accounting regulations on crypto assets. Neither the Belgian tax authorities nor the Commission for Accounting Standards[2] published any comments or advice with respect to crypto assets to date (22 April 2020). Because of the lack of specific rules on 'crypto assets,' we have to rely on the existing general tax and accounting principles.[3] The answers on the below questions will make clear that it is not possible to provide a 'one-size-fits-all' answer with respect to the tax treatment of transactions with crypto assets, but that a case-by-case approach will always be necessary.[4]

It is to be noted that as to the tax on stock exchange transactions[5] and the specific tax on securities accounts (the latter however has been annulled by the

1. Nor does the Belgian Income Tax Code or the Belgian Code on VAT contain any provision related to crypto assets in general or to bitcoins in particular.
2. In Dutch: *Commissie voor Boekhoudkundige Normen*.
3. This also has been confirmed in Decision No. 2018.0249 of the Ruling Commission of 7 Sep. 2018, No. 12.
4. K. Hellinckx, A. Bergmans and K. Van Ende, 'The Fiscal Fate of Crypto Coins', *AFT* 2019/5, p. 7 (hereinafter 'Fiscal Fate'), stating this as a general preliminary remark.
5. Crypto assets do not fall within scope of the tax on stock exchange transactions as been confirmed by the Ruling Commission in several decisions, e.g., Decision No. 2019.0771 of 16 Jan. 2020, at

Constitutional Court in its judgment of 17 October 2019), there are no specific rules for crypto assets.[6]

In absence of a legal framework and a regulatory body controlling crypto assets, it is generally accepted that, at least as concerns Belgium,[7] crypto assets are not accepted as legal currency.[8] There is, however, a decision of the European Court of Justice (ECJ) in 2015 dealing with value added tax (VAT) in relation to bitcoins providing that the buying and selling of bitcoins is exempt from VAT (*see* discussion in section 1.1.3(a) below).[9]

The only guidance we have so far is a couple of advance clearance decisions (rulings) of the Ruling Commission addressing gains realized upon the sale of crypto assets.[10] Moreover, the scope of these clearance decisions is limited to the specific case of the applicant only. The Ruling Commission also has published a questionnaire that can be used as a guideline in order to assess the tax treatment thereof in a specific case.[11]

Finally, the Royal Decree of 3 April 2014 should be mentioned, providing for a ban for private individuals that are non-professionals on the commercialization of certain financial products, including financial products of which the investment return is directly or indirectly linked to 'virtual money'.[12]

---

11 and Decision No. 2018.0688 of 17 Dec. 2018, at 6. Despite the annulment of the tax on securities accounts on 17 Oct. 2019, the consequences thereof will only apply for the future, i.e., from 30 Sep. 2019.

6. A. Henkes, General Lawyer with the Court of Cassation described the Belgian regulations on bitcoins and other crypto assets as 'the remarkable limbo in the Belgian legal order in which bitcoins and other crypto assets evolve' in 'About Cross-Border Taxation and the Contribution of the Supreme Court, the Brussels International Business Court and Bitcoins', *RW* 2018-19, 16, p. 602 (hereinafter 'Cross-Border Taxation').
7. Several central banks and supervisory authorities warned about risks associated with bitcoin and/or virtual currency schemes in general. For example, the German Federal Financial Supervisory Authority (BaFin), the Banque de France and the Dutch and Belgian Central Banks and supervisor have published warnings about the possible use of bitcoin in money laundering and financing terrorism, the lack of supervision, price fluctuations and security risks. European Central Bank, Virtual Currency Schemes, A Further Analysis, Feb. 2015, p. 30, https://www.ecb.europa.eu/pub/pdf/other/virtualcurrencyschemesen.pdf.
8. Question No. 762 C. Gennez, 7 Feb. 2014, Q&A. Chamber 2013-14, No. 152, 248 and question No. 2016, Calomne, 4 Feb. 2018, Q&A. Chamber, 146, 339-342. S. Reynders, 'Bitcoin: To VAT or not to VAT?', *Fisc. Act.* 2015, 36, 5-6 (hereinafter 'To VAT or not to VAT'); Fiscal Fate, *supra* n. 4, at 13-14. Crypto assets can be qualified as a contractual currency, yet.
9. Article 135, section 1, e), of VAT-Directive 2006/112/EG. This decision only applies as to bitcoins. With respect to other types of crypto assets, it is not clear whether the decision of the ECJ would apply.
10. Decision No. 2017.852 of 5 Dec. 2017; Decision No. 2018.0688 of 25 Sep. 2018; Decisions No. 2018.0709 and No. 2018.0710 both of 16 Oct. 2018; Decision No. 2019.0771 of 24 Sep. 2019; Decision No. 2019.0826 of 8 Oct. 2019. As to investments in crypto assets for company tax law, reference can be made to Decision No. 2018.310 of 8 May 2018. There is also a Decision No. 2018.0249 of 7 Sep. 2018 dealing with the tax treatment of a company providing for investments in crypto assets to private individuals.
11. Ruling Commission annual report 2017, No. 6.1.9, p. 36, https://www.ruling.be/sites/default/files/content/download/files/jaarverslag_dvb_2017_nl.pdf. See also Ruling Commission, published on 7 Jun. 2018, https://www.ruling.be/sites/default/files/content/download/files/vragenlijst_cryptomunten_0.pdf.
12. In 2014, the Belgian Financial Services and Markets Authority (FSMA) issued a Regulation to prohibit the distribution of a financial product where the return depends, directly or indirectly,

(b) *Which court cases exist dealing with crypto assets?*

At present, there exists no case law of the Belgian Tax Courts[13] or the Belgian Administrative Courts dealing with crypto assets. There is, however, a 2015 decision of the ECJ dealing with VAT in relation to bitcoins (*see* discussion in section 1.1.3(a), below).[10]

1.1.2 *Income and Capital Gains Taxes*

(a) *How are crypto assets classified for income and capital gains tax purposes?*

For corporate income tax purposes, the legal qualification of crypto assets is far from clear. As a general rule, taxable profits will be determined in accordance with the accounting principles, unless explicit deviations are provided by tax law.[14] We therefore have to rely on Belgian accounting rules in the first place.

When examining the tax consequences of 'mining' of crypto assets, this could be considered as a service to the crypto assets network, but the mined crypto assets also could be qualified as a self-produced asset, e.g., issued stock.[15] The difference in classification will determine the moment at which the value of the mined crypto assets will be included in taxable income. When crypto assets are classified as 'stock', mining itself will not lead to a taxable event. When mining is considered as the rendering of a service to the crypto assets network, it can be argued that mining itself would lead to taxable income, although this is debatable (*see* discussion in section 1.1.2(k) below).

Once a company has acquired crypto assets through mining, as payment in kind for providing services or goods or through a sale, the distinction in qualification of crypto assets can be made between monetary assets or non-monetary assets.[16] Characteristic to monetary assets is that it entitles the holder to a certain amount of

on virtual money, to non-professional clients. This prohibition can be found in the FSMA Regulation of 3 Apr. 2014. A royal decree of 24 Apr. 2014 (Article 2.2°), which entered into force on 1 Jul. 2014, has approved the regulation. This ban only applies to commercialisation at a national level. The ban does not apply to the commercialisation of virtual money, but only to the distribution of financial products the return on which depends on crypto assets. The regulation does not regulate crypto assets themselves or other services that would be provided in relation to crypto assets.

13. In Belgium, such tax disputes fall within the exclusive jurisdiction of the Court of First Instance.
14. This principle is also referred to in Dutch as 'De primauteit van het boekhoudrecht' and has been confirmed by the Court of Cassation, 20 Feb. 1997, Pas. 1997, I, 259. *See also* report to the King on Royal Decree of 8 Oct. 1976, Official Gazette 19 Oct. 1976, 13463).
15. *See* Fiscal Fate, *supra* n. 4.
16. For a detailed explanation, reference can be made to Fiscal Fate, *supra* n. 4, at 21-25. Note that monetary and non-monetary assets are sub-categories of movable assets, discussed immediately below.

cash.[17] To the contrary, any other assets are non-monetary items, e.g., certain financial assets, stock or cash investments. There are strong arguments in favour of the qualification of crypto assets as non-monetary assets for (Belgian) accounting purposes. In particular, bitcoins, altcoins, etc. are not currently legal currency and do not directly entitle the holder to a certain amount of money.[18]

For personal income taxes, income from crypto assets could be taxed either as professional income or as miscellaneous income.

- Professional income: the qualification as professional income depends on an underlying professional activity.
- Miscellaneous income: miscellaneous income is a residuary type of taxable income.[19] As a general rule, any income received from any performance, transaction or service that does not qualify as professional income, movable income[20] or immovable income,[21] qualifies as miscellaneous income, albeit an exception applies when this income arises from the normal management of privately held portfolio values and/or movable assets (the 'Exception').[22]

  Income from crypto assets that do not qualify as professional income and that fall within the Exception, i.e., the income arises from the normal management of privately held portfolio values and/or movable assets, is tax exempt. In this respect, it should be noted that it is up to the tax authorities to prove that a transaction does not fall within scope of the normal management of such privately held assets.[23] The Exception however only applies to income of privately held portfolio values and/or movable assets.
- Movable assets, being 'objects or chattels', are defined as 'material' assets, which exclude 'intangible' assets such as 'virtual claims' or 'non-secured claims'. Although it is possible to create a physical carrier (to the key of) crypto assets, crypto assets are not 'physical' by their nature and thus considered as intangible assets.[24]
- The so-called portfolio values (or widely tradeable values) are defined as 'movable values' that can be bought or sold, both on short term (cash) and

17. Fiscal Fate, *supra* n. 4, at 22 with reference to P. COOSEMANS en P. DRIJKONINGEN, 'The Tax of Exchange Rate Results and Translation Differences. Or How the Observation Instruments Influence the Observation', AFT 2010, 2, 5-66 (hereinafter 'Tax Exchange Rate').
18. Fiscal Fate, *supra* n. 4, at 25.
19. When the income is qualified as professional income, capital gains can no longer be taxed as miscellaneous income. *Cf.* Court of Cassation, 14 Dec. 2007.
20. Immovable income is defined by Article 7 Belgian Income Tax Code ('BITC') containing any income received from real estate, for example, rental income from the rent of an apartment, etc.
21. Movable income is defined by Article 17 BITC including any income received from capital and movable assets such as interest income, dividends, rental income, lease and concession of movable assets, (life) annuities and concession of royalties.
22. Article 90, 1° BITC; *see also* Constitutional Court, 15 Jun. 2017, No. 74/2017.
23. Com. BITC 1992, No. 90/5.3.
24. T. Spaas, 'Bitcoin and the Blockchain in Direct Taxation', *Fisc. Act.* 2015, 36 (hereinafter 'Direct Taxation'), with reference to Cass. 24 Oct. 1975, Cass. 1976, 244, concl. Krings; Bull. Bel. 1977, 1299 and *Fisc. Act.* 2007, 27/1, 2010, 35/5 and 2012, 37/14.

long term.[25] The concept of 'movable value' is however not defined. For the qualification as a 'portfolio value', a financial product is required by a minimum standard to be a tradable value, such as currency.[26] This condition is, at least with respect to bitcoins, fulfilled, as a seller can go to several exchanges.[27] Usually an evolutionary interpretation is given to the concept of portfolio values.[28] It is therefore generally accepted that the tax treatment of crypto assets should be similar to that of portfolio values and therefore that the income from crypto assets will be tax exempt subject to the condition that the income does not qualify as professional income and that the condition of the normal management of the privately held assets is fulfilled.[29]

(b) *What are the income/capital gains tax consequences of selling crypto assets against fiat currency?*

The tax treatment of capital gains and losses on the sale of crypto assets against fiat currency will be different depending on whether the seller is an individual (i.e., personal income tax) or a company (i.e., corporate income tax).

In the case of crypto assets held by a private individual, the assessment should be made whether, based on the transaction, the income/capital gain realized upon the sale can be qualified as professional income and if not, whether the underlying sales transaction can be considered as part of the normal management of privately held assets (in order for the Exception to apply).

- The income/capital gain qualifying as professional income will result in a taxation at the progressive tax rates for personal income tax of 25% up to 50% (to be increased by communal (local) taxes and social contributions). Professional income is taxable on a net basis, meaning that the professional costs are deductible. The taxpayer has the choice between the deduction of the actual cost, e.g., the electricity and electronic device, including any other related costs subject to proof, or the deduction of a flat rate. Losses of a professional activity also can be offset against profits of another professional activity, including any available carried forward losses.
- When income/capital gains are not realized in the course of a professional activity, such income/capital gains are, in principle, taxable as miscellaneous

25. *Cf.* Commentary to the Belgian Income Tax Code. *See* Fiscal Fate, *supra* n. 4, at 32 with reference to 'Report Commission of Finance', H. van HOUTE and L. DESMET, period 1961-62, No. 366, 148.
26. In Dutch: *ruim verhandelbare waarde.*
27. Direct Taxation, *supra* n. 24, with reference to H. Vanhulle, 'The Normal Management of Private Assets in 2005: the Tax Authorities Evolve with it?', *Actualia vermogensrecht*, 225.
28. Direct Taxation, *supra* n. 24 with reference to B. Colmant, Belgium Country Report, IFA Cahiers 1995, vol. 80b, 'Tax aspects of derivative financial instruments'.
29. Decision No. 2019.0826 of 18 Jan. 2020, al 16; *see also* Fiscal Fate, *supra* n. 4, at 32 with reference to Decision No. 2018.0688 of 24 Sep. 2018, Direct Taxation, *supra* n. 24, at 6; D. Mussche and H. Putman, 'Capital Gains on Bitcoins, a Tax Dime on Three Sides?', *Fisc. Act.* 18/2, 1-5 (hereinafter 'Capital Gains').

income at a flat tax rate of 33%, unless the income/capital gains are realized within the scope of the normal management of privately held assets. As explained in section 1.1.2(a) above, the latter income/capital gains are tax exempt.[30] Costs that have been incurred in order to receive or retain such income are tax deductible.[31] Losses realized in the application of Article 90,1° BITC (i.e., the provision providing for the taxation of miscellaneous income) only can be offset against other income qualifying as miscellaneous income under that provision.[32] These losses cannot be offset against other types of income, e.g., professional income. Furthermore, no social contributions are due on miscellaneous income.

The examination on income/capital gains falling in scope of the normal management of privately held assets is to be made on a case-by-case basis. The Ruling Commission has published several advance clearance decisions on income realized on the sale of bitcoins and the tax treatment thereof for personal income tax. As part of these assessments, the Ruling Commission compiled a questionnaire containing various criteria that may indicate the speculative nature as well as the professional nature of the income. In a (first) preliminary decision of 5 December 2017,[33] the Ruling Commission concluded that the capital gains realized on the sale of bitcoins should not be considered professional income, instead, given the speculative nature of the transactions – at least in the opinion of the Commission – the capital gains were taxable as miscellaneous income at the 33% tax rate. This decision related to the specific situation where an IT student had developed an application for the automatic purchase and sale of bitcoins (day trading) and realized a profit through this online bitcoin trading platform.

It must be emphasized that the qualification as miscellaneous income was not dictated by the fact that it concerned capital gains on crypto assets, but rather by the very specific way in which the capital gains were realized. Indeed, Belgian tax rules depend on the type of transaction rather than on the type of asset. Had the student in question developed the same methodology for listed securities, the outcome of the ruling would (most likely) have been similar. Generalizations are therefore not appropriate. It is also to be noted that large fluctuations in value are not only typical for crypto assets but also for other assets such as shares. Moreover, the investment in crypto assets also can be motivated by diversifying the investment portfolio.[34] In a second decision, mentioned by the Ruling Commission in its annual report for 2017,[35] it once again was decided that the proposed transactions could not be considered as 'the normal management of privately held assets', since at the moment of acquisition

30. Article 171 BITC.
31. Article 97 BITC.
32. Article 103, §1 BITC.
33. Decision No. 2017.852.
34. Fiscal Fate, *supra* n. 4, at 35; Capital Gains, *supra* n. 29.
35. Annual Report 2017 - https://www.ruling.be/nl/downloads/jaarverslag-2017.

there was a risk of losses.[36] Other factors affecting the Ruling Commission's conclusion were the anticipation of rapid increases in value within a short period of time and the amounts and frequency of sales.

In more recent decisions, however, the Ruling Commission reached a different conclusion and decided that, given the underlying facts, the sales transactions could be regarded as falling in scope of the normal management of privately held assets.[37]

As to the calculation of the capital gains, it could be argued that the taxpayer himself can choose an identification method (FIFO or LIFO, weighted average, etc.). However, he will have to prove the dates of acquisition and disposal and consistently apply the chosen method in the absence of specific guidelines.[38]

For corporate income tax purposes, e.g., in case crypto assets are held by a corporation, there is no difference when income/profits/capital gains are realized on crypto assets compared to other types of assets. For companies subject to corporate income tax, selling crypto assets against fiat currency, the income/capital gains generated from such transaction will be taxable under the standard corporate income tax rules,[39] i.e., a tax rate of 25%[40] will apply, to be lowered to 20% subject to certain conditions. Losses can, as a general rule, be fully offset against other income and may also be carried forward. However, beginning in tax year 2019, there are limitations to certain tax losses carried forward, which results in a minimum taxable income.[41] Expenses that cannot be deducted due to this minimum taxable income limitation can be carried forward to the following years.

(c) *What are the income/capital gains tax consequences of exchanging crypto assets against other crypto assets?*

The exchange of crypto assets against other crypto assets is considered as a taxable event. The income/capital gains tax consequences of exchanging crypto assets are similar as described in section 1.1.2(b) above, when realizing capital gains on the sale of crypto assets against fiat currency.

The taxation of income/capital gains realized upon the exchange of crypto assets has been questioned by A. Henkens, General Lawyer with the Court of Cassation, as it only leads to 'virtual' income, particularly when considering the high volatility of

36. Thereby referring to the media and warning of the National Bank of Belgium (NBB), Financial Services and Markets Authority (FSMA) and European Bankers Alliance (EBA) on the risks related on trading in crypto assets.
37. Decision No. 2019.0771, No. 13.
38. Direct Taxation, *supra* n. 24, at 6.
39. At present, there are not any specific accounting rules with respect to crypto assets. *See also* Ruling No. 2018.049, al. 10.
40. Beginning from tax year 2021. *See* Law of 25 Dec. 2017.
41. Taxable income exceeding the threshold of 1 million. EUR will lead to a minimum taxation of 30% of the taxable basis exceeding this 1 million. Threshold. Article 207, al 5 BITC.

virtual coins.[42] These lawyers believe that the capital gain should only be taxed upon the exchange of the crypto asset against fiat currency.[43]

(d) If a distinction is made between business assets and non-business assets, when does trading in crypto assets lead to a trade or business?

In essence, under Belgian tax rules, reference can be made to the so-called 'affectation to a business', albeit that this 'category' is not defined as such in tax law. Such 'affectation' will have to be determined on a case-by-case basis and is never defined by the nature of the crypto assets as such.[44]

The income realized upon trading in crypto assets can qualify as professional income, i.e., income 'affected to a business"[45] which is to be assessed case by case.

In the administrative comments to the Belgian Income Tax Code, a profitable business is defined as '*a set of actions/transfers which are sufficiently numerous and interlinked to constitute a regular and continuous activity and which, outside the scope of the normal management of the private estate, are of a professional nature.*'[46] In case law and doctrine, several criteria such as the organization of the activity, the infrastructure, the frequency of the transactions, the funding of the activities via external debt financing, the fact that the activity relates to the (main) professional activity of the tax payer and so on are put forward.[47] Similar criteria are also reflected in the questionnaire of the Ruling Commission, which appears to be ultimately intended to determine whether the sale of crypto assets could lead to taxable capital gains. As explained in section 1.1.2(b) above, it will be decisive whether the capital gain is realized in scope of the normal management of privately held assets. This questionnaire can however also serve to determine whether income realized on a transaction with crypto assets could qualify as professional income. Several criteria referred to by the questionnaire are for determining the assessment of the nature of the realized income, i.e., professional or miscellaneous income. These criteria should enable the taxpayer to determine whether the transactions are carried out with a profit-making intention, which is essential to decide whether there is a professional activity and

---

42. Cross-Border Taxation, *supra* n. 6, quoting M. Delanote and P. Smeyers, 'Taxation of Crypto Coins: the Ruling Service is Attempting to Provide More Clarity', *Fisc. Act.* 20 (hereinafter 'Taxation of Crypto Coins').
43. Cross-Border Taxation, *supra* n. 6, at 628.
44. Gent, 28 Sep. 2000, Gerd D. Goyvaerts, *TFR* 2001, 211, 1088-1089; Goyvaerts, G.D., 'Rents Insurance Portfolio Lead to Movable Income' *TFR* 2001, 193? 23-28.
45. As explained in section 1.1.2(b), above, for personal income tax purposes, the income/capital gains realized on transactions with crypto assets can be qualified either as professional income or as miscellaneous income.
46. Commentaries on BITC No. 23/35 with reference to Cass., 6.5.1969, Grazia and de Mesmay, Bull. 475, p. 1067; id., 24.9.1968, Petit, Bull. 466, p. 1345.
47. C. Coudron and T. De Meyer, 'Tiberghien – Handbook for Tax Law 2019-2020', Mechelen, Wolters Kluwer, No. 1096 with reference to *Fisc. Act.* 2006, 34, p. 13 and 2005, 27, p. 9 (hereinafter 'Handbook 2019-2020').

professional income.[48] The fact that a profit or gain has been realized is, in itself, not sufficient to qualify as professional income. The questionnaire of the Ruling Commission focuses among other things on the following criteria, whereby one element or criteria is not more decisive than the others:

- the way the crypto assets are acquired (gift, inheritance, mining, etc.);
- the amount of the investment in crypto assets;
- the frequency of the purchase and sale transactions with crypto assets;
- the investment strategy (e.g., buy and hold, trending, active trading/day trading, scalping, arbitrage, and so on);
- the holding period of the crypto assets;
- the sale through an automatically data process or software; and
- the professional background, education, etc. of the taxpayers.

The Ruling Commission remains unclear with respect to the importance that can be given to each of these criteria. In specific cases, the Ruling Commission seems to give particular attention to the number of transactions and the amount invested in relation to the total movable assets of the taxpayer.[49]

Moreover, the Ruling Commission confirmed in this respect that the receipt of crypto assets by solving a 'one-off' internet puzzle (i.e., mining) would, in any event, not lead to professional income.[50] Yet, income received from a subsequent sale of these initially mined crypto assets still could be taxable as professional or miscellaneous income.

(e) What are the income/capital gains tax consequences for an employee receiving wages or salaries in crypto assets?

Today, there is no case law known, nor has the Ruling Commission issued any ruling or comment about the taxation of wages or salaries paid in crypto assets. In the absence of any specific rules, it can be concluded that there is no difference in the tax treatment of the payment of wages or salaries in crypto assets compared to the standard ways of payment. The income will be taxed on a net basis at the progressive tax rates for personal income tax of 25% up to 50% (to be increased by communal (local) taxes and social contributions).[51] It seems consistent that the taxable income will then have to be

48. Questionnaire Cryption Coins, https://www.ruling.be/sites/default/files/content/download/files/vragenlijst_cryptomunten_0.pdf. This questionnaire is, however, mainly focused on the sale and the transfer or exchange of crypto assets and not on the 'mining' thereof. Fiscal Fate, *supra* n. 4, at 28.
49. Taxation of Crypto Coins, *supra* n. 42.
50. In Decision No. 2019.0826 of 18 Jan. 2020, al 2, the Ruling Commission states clearly that 'receiving crypto assets by solving a 'one-off' internet puzzle can, under no circumstances, lead to immovable, movable or professional income. It should be further assessed whether the (free) receiving of crypto assets falls in scope of Article 90, 1° BITC and would be taxable as miscellaneous income.
51. Article 31 BITC provides for a very broad definition of professional income.

determined based on the amount in Euro equivalent at the time the remuneration is received.[52]

Importantly, the Salary Protection Act of 12 April 1965 requires that wages and salaries are paid out in a currency which is legally customary or accepted in Belgium when the employee carries out his activities in Belgium, i.e., in Euro.[53] If an employee exercises his activities abroad, then his salary must be paid, fully or partly, either in the currency legally accepted in Belgium (in Euro) or in the currency legally accepted in the country where the employee exercises his activities, at the election of the employee. As cryptocurrencies such as bitcoin are not officially accepted currencies, either in Belgium or in any other European country, an employee's salary simply cannot be paid out in such cryptocurrency. As to granting crypto assets as an 'additional benefit in kind' on top of the normal salary, the Belgian Federal Ministry of Employment takes a very rigid position, arguing that such additional payment would qualify as a 'payment in kind' and that only the benefits enumerated in an exhaustive list included in Article 6 of the Salary Protection Act can be paid 'in kind'. This statement has been subject to criticism, though.[54]

Besides possible criminal penalties on the basis of the Social Penal Code, salaries and wages paid out in violation of the Salary Protection Act[55] will be regarded as 'not paid-out'. Consequently, the employer risks having to pay such salary twice. The situation will be different when working with self-employed persons. Indeed, since the Salary Protection Act only applies to employees and not to the self-employed, the latter could (partly) be paid out in a cryptocurrency.[56]

(f) What are the income/capital gains tax consequences for a merchant receiving payment in crypto assets?

The income and capital gain tax consequences of a merchant receiving payment in crypto assets will have to be examined in accordance with the general principles that are applicable to any other compensation or payment received for similar assets or services. For example, when the payment in crypto assets relates to services or goods provided by the merchant in the scope of his professional activities, the payment will be treated as professional income. On the other hand, the merchant receiving payments in the form of crypto assets on a private investment, e.g., by selling pieces of art assuming that he is not an art dealer, could be subject to capital gains tax when the sale is not considered as a transaction falling in scope of the normal management of the privately held estate.

The taxable income can be determined based on the amount of the crypto assets received in Euro equivalent at the time of the payment, as there are no contrary

52. Fiscal Fate, *supra* n. 4, at 33.
53. Article 4 of the Salary Protection Act of 12 Apr. 1965.
54. Esther Soetens, 'Your Salary in Bitcoin: Reality or Sci-Fi?' (25 Jan. 2019), https://www.altius.com/blog/424/your-salary-in-bitcoin-reality-or-sci-fi (hereinafter 'Salary').
55. Article 47 of the Salary Protection Act.
56. Salary, *supra* n. 54.

provisions or administrative guidelines in this respect.[57] When the crypto assets received are subsequently converted into fiat currency, the conversion is, as a general rule, also considered as a taxable transaction, i.e., taxable as professional income. Yet, when the crypto assets are no longer used in a sustainable way as business assets, they can lose their status as such and become part of the private estate ('desaffectation'). Since crypto assets become part of the private estate, the tax treatment of the conversion of the crypto assets into fiat currency is then to be examined from a privately held assets income tax perspective, i.e., taxation as miscellaneous income when the conversion is not considered as the normal management of the privately held assets (*see* section 1.1.2(a) above) or tax exempt if the conversion falls in the scope of the normal management of privately held assets.

(g) What are the income/capital gains tax consequences of a loss of crypto assets?

There are no specific rules or administrative guidelines/decisions dealing with the tax treatment of crypto assets in case of a loss, such as the loss of the private key associated with an address at which crypto assets are stored.

Capital gains on privately held crypto assets are taxable as miscellaneous income when not realized in scope of the normal management of privately held assets. The loss of privately held crypto assets is therefore only relevant when such loss can be offset against miscellaneous income. Such loss can be carried forward for seven years.

As for business assets, professional losses suffered in respect of any professional activity can be deducted from the income from other professional activities. However, there is a legal exception to this rule in case of partnership losses,[58] where the law does not provide for a definition of losses as such. In general, the tax authorities accept that the loss of an asset as a result of theft, damage to or destruction due to any harmful event such as storm, flood, lightning, fire and so on are tax deductible as professional expenses.[59] These losses are, however, required to be certain and of a fixed nature and have to be accounted for accordingly.[60] In this respect, it should be acknowledged that the risk of direct loss of digital currencies is higher than the risk of loss of electronic deposits. For example, a lost password to an online bank account is recoverable or can be reset by the bank. On the other hand, if the private key granting access to the cryptocurrency wallet is lost, then it would be unrecoverable as there is no central server to provide a reset. So it all relates to the facts.

---

57. Fiscal Fate, *supra* n. 4, at 33.
58. Article 80 BITC.
59. Handbook 2019-2020, *supra* n. 47, at 358, No. 1281. *See also* Commentaries BITC 52/214 and 52/189 with reference to Cass., 25.4.1950, Mary, Pas. I, 1950, 587 and commentaries BITC 49/6-49/10.
60. When the loss of the crypto assets has been insured by an insurance policy, the loss is to be determined on the amount of the damage that has not been covered by the insurance policy. Com. BITC 49/6.

(h) *What are the income/capital gains tax consequences of a loss in value of crypto assets?*

The loss in value of crypto assets, which has not been realized, e.g., through a sale transaction, is irrelevant if crypto assets are privately held. However, the loss may be relevant if and to the extent such loss could be qualified as a miscellaneous loss. Such loss can be carried forward for seven years.

On corporate tax level, the tax consequences of a loss in value of crypto assets is in the first place to be examined by the general accounting principles and the qualification that is given to crypto assets according to Belgian accounting rules.[61] As explained in section 1.1.2(a) above, with respect to the legal classification of crypto assets for corporate income tax purposes, different approaches can be followed but the classification as non-monetary assets seems to be most likely.

Assuming that crypto assets are classified as non-monetary assets, fluctuations in exchange rates at year end, e.g., closing of the financial year, will not be reflected in the financial statements. Since tax law does not provide any deviating tax rules in this respect, such fluctuations in exchange rates will not have any tax impact.[62]

When crypto assets should be qualified as monetary assets, negative fluctuations in exchange rates will have to be reflected in the financial statement at closing and as a consequence thereof would result in a tax deductible loss.[63]

(i) *What are the income/capital gains tax consequences of forks of crypto assets?*

Simply put, a fork of crypto assets occurs when a single crypto blockchain breaks into two separate chains. This chain-split has no obvious analogy for personal or corporate income tax purposes. The result is, however, that the owner of crypto assets after the split is entitled to an equal number of crypto assets on each chain.[64] Yet there is no exchange of crypto assets against the forked crypto assets and the receipt of the forked crypto asset is a consequence of holding the crypto assets in the first place.[65] Two different approaches can be followed.[66] In the first approach, the owner of the crypto asset realizes ordinary income to the extent of the value of the forked crypto asset. This income will thus be taxable either as professional income, or as miscellaneous income unless it can be demonstrated that the transaction is in the scope of the normal

61. Fiscal Fate, *supra* n. 4, at 22 with reference to Circ. nr. CI.RH. 421/494.543, 8 Oct. 1997; Tax Exchange Rate, *supra* n. 17.
62. Fiscal Fate, *supra* n. 4, at 22.
63. Tax Exchange Rate, *supra* n. 17.
64. J. Calvin, 'Adequately Identifying Bitcoin Dispositions For Federal Income Tax Purposes', Bloomberg BNA, Tax Management Memorandum, Vol. 58, 18, p. 363, 09/04/2017, p. 2, https://coincenter.org/pdf/BitcoinTaxesCalvin.pdf (hereinafter 'Identifying Bitcoin Disposition s').
65. Identifying Bitcoin Dispositions, *supra* n. 64, at 3.
66. Identifying Bitcoin Dispositions, *supra* n. 64, at 3.

management of privately held assets.[67] In the second approach, the chain-split is considered as a property division. The tax treatment of such a property division is however not clear, but if part of privately held assets, it is likely not taxable.

(j) *What are the income/capital gains tax consequences of airdrops of crypto assets and are the tax consequences different if the airdropped tokens are unwanted?*

An airdrop occurs when someone receives an allocation of tokens or other crypto assets, for instance as part of a marketing or advertising campaign. Airdrops also could involve tokens being provided automatically due to other tokens being held. The airdropped token typically has its own infrastructure that operates independently of the infrastructure of the existing crypto asset. The Belgian tax authorities have not issued any guidelines related to the tax consequences of such 'airdrops', and therefore we have to fall back once again on the general personal and corporate income tax rules.

Airdropped crypto assets can be provided either gratuitously or in return for or in expectation of a service (i.e., a transaction for valuable consideration). Airdropped tokens can be received within or outside of an active trade or business. It is of no relevance whether the airdropped tokens are wanted or unwanted.

- The Belgian Income Tax Code defines professional income in a broad sense encompassing any income that directly or indirectly is related to any professional activity of any kind.[68] According to this provision, airdropped crypto assets received in the scope of a professional activity will qualify as professional income and are to be valued in Euro equivalent. Assets received without consideration will be accounted at acquisition value or historic cost, which is (close to) nil. Hence, airdropped crypto assets that are granted for free will most likely not result in a taxable event upon receipt.[69]
- Airdropped crypto assets received outside the scope of a professional activity could qualify either as non-taxable gifts or miscellaneous income when received as consideration for a service performed (e.g., positive postings on forums and social media sites regarding the project).[70]

67. It should be clear that this exemption does not apply to professional income.
68. Article 23, §1 BITC.
69. The debate on accounting assets received without consideration was finally decided by the ECJ, 3 Oct. 2013, C-322/12, Gimle and ECJ 6 Mar. 2014, C-5 10/12, Bloomsbury NV. *See also* advice No. 126/17 of the Commission of Accounting Standards; Handbook 2019-2020, *supra* n. 47, at 162, 115, 25.
70. Article 90, 1° BITC.

(k) *What are the income/capital gains tax consequences of (solo, pool, and cloud) mining?*

An important preliminary remark is that mining does not necessarily result in receiving crypto assets. Miners are in competition with each other. However, there will always have to be a performance in the form of computing power in order to be able to 'mine' crypto assets. It therefore could be questioned whether mining should result in taxable income. Under case law of the Court of Cassation, it could be argued that the taxability only occurs when the miner actually converts the crypto assets, e.g., by selling them to other crypto assets or fiat currency and thus not at the time the crypto assets are mined. Thus, it is assumed that at the moment of mining, the miner receives a certain and fixed claim, albeit this claim only will be collected when converted into currency or by selling it.[71] Some authors also state that crypto assets or tokens do not represent a claim on the issuer.[72] In particular, when crypto assets are received by mining, some believe that the miner himself should be considered to be the issuer, and therefore will not result in any taxable income.[73]

Assuming that mining would give rise to taxable income, it is again to be examined, based on the underlying facts, whether the mining activity involves a professional activity resulting in professional income, and if not, whether the mining activity involves speculation or at least cannot be considered as the normal management of privately held assets, which then results in a taxation as miscellaneous income. Expenses can be offset against professional, as well as miscellaneous income, e.g., the purchase and depreciation cost of device, electricity costs and so on, when being made with the purpose to generate income.

In general, as miners do not act in anticipation of the market price and the expected price increases of crypto assets, mining is not considered to be 'speculative'. Mining activities are usually not that risky as the only costs are rather limited, mainly including electricity and equipment. Yet, as mining is becoming increasingly energy intensive and more expensive in recent years, the question is whether this reasoning still can be upheld for the future. Also, other elements, e.g., the fact that miners are able through software applications to determine at which point in time the crypto assets should be mined, taking into consideration the expected price increases, will be relevant. When the mined crypto assets are kept for a longer period of time, this could

71. Fiscal Fate, *supra* n. 4, at 33 with reference to Cass. 1 Feb. 1999, *FJF* No. 2002/40, Cass. 19 Apr. 1999, *FJF* No. 2002/41 and Cass, 5 May 2017, *F* 15.0171, N. *Fisc. Koer*. 2017, 11, 703-705. The Belgian tax authorities have confirmed that indeed a bitcoin is considered to be a claim and is not to be seen as a currency. To VAT or not to VAT?, *supra* n. 8, at 5-6.
72. *See* the Second E-Money Directive, Directive 2009/110/EC, (18), states that the issuer of electronic money should at any time be able to redeem the electronic money at par value without any possibility to agree a minimum threshold for redemption. This requirement is, for most types of crypto assets, not fulfilled and the only possibility to convert the crypto assets is by selling them, which is because of the volatility in value of most crypto assets not at purchase value. N. VANDEZANDE, 'Virtual Currencies: A Legal Framework', Cambridge, Intersentia, 2018, 212.
73. *Contra* J. GOOSSENS, K. VERSLYPE, 'Blockchain and Smart Contracts', Brussels, Larcier, 65.

be an indication of speculation.[74] Yet, according to some authors, it is difficult to argue that the bitcoins obtained from mining should be considered as normal management of privately held assets, as performance will always be needed to mine bitcoins.[75] The only fact that the underlying assets of the mining activity concern crypto assets is however not a reason to consider the activity as 'exotic' or abnormal.[76]

It is also unclear how to determine the taxable basis, i.e., on the value of the crypto assets at the date of mining or on the date on which the mined crypto assets are converted into fiat currency and whether losses between those two moments can be deducted.[77]

When crypto assets are being mined by a company subject to corporate tax, it is unclear whether the mined crypto assets are to be considered as self-produced assets (e.g., stock) or rather as a payment in kind for the services the company rendered to the network.[78] This distinction is relevant as in the first scenario, where the mined crypto assets are classified as 'stock', they will be accounted at historic value and not at market value. Hence, mining itself will not lead to a taxable event.[79] When the mined crypto assets are subsequently sold against fiat currency or will be used for the payments of other goods or services, the capital gains will become taxable. If the mined crypto assets are considered as a payment in kind for services or goods, the tax authorities could argue, although this is debatable, that the crypto assets should be valued at fair market value on the date of mining and therefore would lead to taxable income.[80]

(l) What are the income/capital gains tax consequences of staking crypto assets?

Proof of Stake concept states that a person can mine or validate block transactions according to how many coins he holds. In contrast, the algorithm of Proof-of-Work-based cryptocurrencies such as bitcoin uses mining; that is, the solving of computationally intensive puzzles to validate transactions and create new blocks.[81] Proof of Stake will make the entire mining process virtual and replace miners with validators. Proof of Stake is also seen as less risky in terms of the potential for miners/validators to attack the network, as it structures compensation in a way that makes an attack less advantageous for the validator.[82]

74. Fiscal Fate, *supra* n. 4, at 31.
75. J. Horemans, K. Verhoeven, D. Lemaire Cryptomunten, 'The Sky Seems the Limit, But What About (Income) Tax', *VIP* 2018/1, p. 6 (hereinafter 'Sky Seems the Limit'), with reference to B. Springael, 'Bitcoins: The Virtual Gold?', *TFR* 2014, 468, 759.
76. Capital Gains, *supra* n. 29.
77. Fiscal Fate, *supra* n. 4, at 30.
78. Fiscal Fate, *supra* n. 4, at 15.
79. Fiscal Fate, *supra* n. 4, at 17.
80. Fiscal Fate, *supra* n. 4, at 20.
81. Proof of Stake, Wikipedia, https://en.wikipedia.org/wiki/Proof_of_stake.
82. Proof of Stake, Binance Academy, https://www.binance.vision/nl/blockchain/proof-of-stake-explained.

Since Proof of Stake can result in receiving passive income and is essentially a lighter and more energy-efficient and safe alternative to Proof of Work (mining), it could be argued that it even less fulfils the criteria of a professional activity or a speculative activity.[83] As a general conclusion, for personal income taxes, any income generated through Proof of Stake will less likely qualify as professional income or miscellaneous income, compared to any income received by Proof of Work. A case-by-case analysis is however still to be made.

(m) What are the income/capital gains tax consequences of an indirect investment in crypto assets?

Movable income resulting from the indirect investment in crypto assets (e.g., investments via securities, exchange-traded notes and funds, futures and so on), will not be treated different than if the movable income was received in traditional currency.[84] The relevant provisions in the Belgian Income Tax Code do not make any distinction according to the method of payment or execution.[85] When two private parties agree to take out a loan in bitcoins for instance via a platform providing peer-to peer loans, such as 'Bitbond' and 'BTC POP' or 'magnr',[86] with interest payment in bitcoins as well, that interest income will be taxable as movable income at a tax rate of 30%[87] and thus according to the value at the time of payment or attribution as converted in Euro.[88] In addition, when the investor subsequently exchanges the crypto assets received into fiat currency, another taxable transaction will occur.[89]

As to indirect investments in companies trading and investing in crypto assets, the Ruling Commission already took a position on the tax treatment of the investment return on the level of the company.[90] The taxpayer, a Belgian company, offers indirect investments in crypto assets in the form of a loan to private individuals. With these funds, the company performs direct day trading via the exchange in various types of crypto assets and virtual currencies on exchange markets in China, Korea, and the US. The Ruling Commission confirmed that the loan should be regarded as a debt claim within the meaning of Article 19, § 1, 1° WIB 92 and, consequently, that the payments made to the private investors within the meaning of this provision qualify as interest

83. Ameer Rosic, 'Proof of Work vs Proof of Stake: Basic Mining Guide', Blockgeeks, https://blockgeeks.com/guides/proof-of-work-vs-proof-of-stake/; Peter Kent, Tyler Bain, 'Cryptocurrency Mining and Proof of Stake Algorithms', Dummies, https://www.dummies.com/education/finance/cryptocurrency-mining-and-proof-of-stake-algorithms/.
84. Direct Taxation, *supra* n. 24.
85. A dividend is defined as all advantages granted by a company to shares and profit-sharing certificates, by whatever name, for whatever reason and by whatever means (Article 18 1° ITC 92). Interest includes interest, premiums and all other income from loans (Article 19 1°), without making a distinction according to the manner in which the income is obtained.
86. Sky Seems the Limit, *supra* n. 75, at 8.
87. The applicable rate for tax year 2020.
88. Article 17, §2 BITC and Article 20 *bis* BITC; Direct Taxation, *supra* n. 24; Vandelanotte, Tax Implications of Crypto Coins, https://www.vandelanotte.be/data/documents/pagebuilders/fiscale-implicaties.pdf.
89. Fiscal Fate, *supra* n. 4, at 33.
90. Decision 2018.0249 of 7 Sep. 2019, No. 17.

income. Hence, obligations such as the company remitting withholding tax to the tax authorities on the interest income must also be complied with. As far as the company is concerned, this interest is deductible as a professional expense provided that all the relevant conditions are met.[91]

(n) *How is income from crypto assets to be treated under double tax treaty law?*

The Belgian tax authorities have not issued any general statements or comments regarding the treatment of crypto assets under the Belgian double tax treaties. Income earned in connection with crypto assets can fall under various allocation rules of the OECD Model Convention:

- Pursuant to Article 7 of the OECD Model Convention, profits of an enterprise of a contracting state are taxable only in that state. If the enterprise, however, carries on business in the other contracting state through a permanent establishment situated therein, then the profits that are attributable to this permanent establishment (PE) may be taxed in that other state. Thus, for example, profits of a crypto mining enterprise carried on by a resident of Belgium may only be taxed in Belgium. If the crypto mining enterprise, however, carried on business outside Belgium through a PE, then the profits that are attributable to this PE may be taxed according to the tax laws of that country where the PE is located.
- As to indirect investments in crypto assets, among others by tokens, Article 10(1) (dividends) and art. 11(1) (interest) may also be relevant. Given the broad definition of dividend and interest income in the OECD Model Convention, movable income resulting from indirect investment in crypto assets may fall within scope of these provisions.[92] According to the OECD Model Convention, dividend and interest income is taxable in the state of residence of the beneficial owner of that income. For example, the return of a Belgian resident on his loan in bitcoins granted to a non-resident company, e.g., through a peer-to-peer lending platform such as Bitbond, will have to be declared in his Belgian personal income as taxable interest income.
- Article 13(5) of the OECD Model Convention may be relevant, dealing with capital gains from the alienation of any property, other than referred to in the prior paragraphs of this provision, that are taxable only in the state of residence of the alienator. Thus, for example, an investor resident in Belgium selling bitcoins through a crypto exchange located in the United Kingdom may only be taxed in Belgium (Article 13(4) of the Belgo-UK DTT).

91. Decision 2018.0249 of 7 Sep. 2019, No. 18.
92. K. PAUWELS and A. SNYERS, 'The Wonderful World of Initial Token Offerings', *RGF&C* 2018, 9, 18-19 (hereinafter 'Wonderful World').

(o) *What are the income/capital gains tax consequences of selling crypto assets in an ICO/STO/IEO?*

Tokens are often not (only) intended as a means of payment or exchange, but have another specific functionality, e.g., they can be used for the financing and the start-up of innovative business models by means of crowdfunding.[93] Thereby a distinction can be made between 'utility tokens' and 'investment tokens'. Utility tokens represent a right on a future service or good, e.g., WePower issuing tokens representing a certain amount of 'green' energy. Investment tokens represent a claim or right on the issuing company in exchange for financial investment.[94] As tokens can take a variety of forms[95] and ICOs can be structured in different ways, the taxation regime will be different. However, there are no specific accounting or tax rules,[96] so the general rules will apply. For instance, on the level of the issuing company, when the ICO is structured for the purpose of fundraising and can be compared to a bond issue or to a public offering of shares, it is unlikely that the transfer of crypto assets pursuant to the ICO would give rise to corporate income tax. On the other hand, when utility tokens are issued representing the payment of a future good or service, it is likely that realized profits in the ICO will be subject to corporate income tax. Depending on the valuation method used, the revenue could be taken into account and taxed either at the time of delivery of the utility tokens, at the time of delivery of the product or service or pro rata to the completion of the platform.[97]

The Ruling Commission issued one advance clearance decision[98] on the tax treatment of income deriving from investments by a company in crypto assets through an ICO,[99] stating in the first place that these investments are not similar to investments in shares.[100] Any capital gains realized by the company on the investments are therefore taxable as profits[101] to which losses can be offset as deductible costs when certain conditions are met.[102]

Importantly, the Ruling Commission stated that investments in crypto assets in an ICO are not considered as a tax abuse under the general anti-abuse provision of Article 344, §1 BITC.

With respect to the investors (private individuals) in tokens, the tax consequences are to be examined in view of the nature of the tokens. Income received from

93. J. BAUKEMA, 'Initial Coin Offerings (ICOs): Crowdfunding 2.0?, *TFR* (NL) 2018, p. 113.
94. Fiscal Fate, *supra* n. 4, at 11; WePower, WPR Token, https://wepower.network/wpr-token.
95. Wonderful World, supra n. 92, at 9, 10-11.
96. Wonderful World, *supra* n. 92, at 9, 17.
97. Wonderful World, *supra* n. 92, at 9, 17.
98. Decision No. 2018.0310 of 8 May 2018.
99. An ICO is often used as a form of crowdfunding, however a private ICO, which does not seek public investment, is also possible. In an ICO, a quantity of crypto asset is sold in the form of 'tokens' ('coins') to speculators or investors in exchange for legal tender or other crypto assets (generally established and more stable) cryptocurrencies such as bitcoin or ether. Initial Coin Offering, Wikipedia, https://en.wikipedia.org/wiki/Initial_coin_offering.
100. This in view of the (non-)application of Article 198, §1, 7° BITC provides for the non-deductibility of depreciations on shares.
101. *Cf.* Article 24 BITC.
102. *Cf.* Article 49 BITC.

investment tokens could qualify as dividend income, debt tokens could lead to interest income, etc. In the majority of the cases, investment tokens will lead to Belgium source income. For foreign investors investing in tokens in Belgium, it therefore will be important to review the applicable double tax treaty provisions.[103]

1.1.3 Other Taxes

(a) What are the value added tax/sales tax consequences of selling crypto assets?

As a general rule, Belgium does not accept bitcoin and other crypto assets as a legal currency.[104] According to the tax authorities, bitcoins must be considered as a debt claim and are therefore also exempt from VAT.[105]

The ECJ case in 2015 (*Hedqvist*) whereby the ECJ had to deal with the VAT tax treatment of services provided through an exchange platform facilitating the purchase, sale and conversion of bitcoins into traditional currency, is also relevant for Belgium.[106]

In line with *Hedqvist*, buying and selling of bitcoins as well as the conversion of bitcoins into traditional currency, e.g., Euro or US Dollar and vice versa whereby a gain is realized, are transactions that are exempt of VAT.[107] Yet, the tax authorities indicated that this statement is temporary and still could be subject to change in view of new European case law.[108] It is important to note that the Hedqvist case only deals with services carried out through an exchange platform with respect to bitcoins. It therefore does not provide a comprehensive framework for the VAT treatment of all types of crypto assets and other crypto asset-related activities, such as mining.[109]

The tax authorities remark that intermediary services provided by an online exchange platform, which are limited to making specific software available for consideration in order to give bitcoin users access to a digital interface, cannot be regarded as an exempted mediation service within the meaning of Articles 44, §3, 90 of the VAT Code. The service provided by such a platform in no way exhibits the essential characteristics of an intermediary service as defined by the Court of Justice of the European Union.[110]

103. Wonderful World, *supra* n. 92, at 9, 18.
104. Q&A 762 C. Gennez, 7 Feb. 2014, Chamber 2013-14, No. 152, 248.
105. Cf. Article 44, §3, 7° of the Belgian VAT Code. *See also* J. Van Overtveldt, Minister of Finance on Question 7021 of 17 Nov. 2015, report, Com 267, p. 9-10.
106. CJEU 22 Oct. 2015, C-264/14, *David Hedqvist*.
107. Handbook 2019-2020, *supra* n. 47, at 1947, 5658, Fiscal Fate, *supra* n. 4, at 37.
108. To VAT or not to VAT?, *supra* n. 8, at 5-6.
109. Fiscal Fate, *supra* n. 4, at 37.
110. VAT comments, 2, 'Bitcoins and Other Contractual Means of Payment', 23 Jul. 2018 with reference to Court of Justice of the European Union, Judgment of *Commissioners of Customs and Excise v. CSC Financial Services Ltd*, Case C-235/00, 13.12.2001, paras 39 et seq., also stating that the taxable basis (*maatstaf van heffing*) will be determined. *Cf.* Article 27, §2, section 2 VAT code.

(b) *Are payments in crypto assets subject to withholding taxes?*

For withholding taxes, payments made in crypto assets will not be treated different than payments made in traditional currency. Dividend payments made by means of crypto assets by a company with its legal seat and/or its place of management in Belgium[111] will be subject to a withholding tax of 30%[112] which will be remitted to the Belgian tax authorities. The crypto assets distributed will have to be converted into fiat currency and valued upon date of attribution or granting, with the withholding tax payable to be calculated based on the grossed-up amount. That is similar to the procedure applied when a dividend in kind is distributed.[113] The value of the crypto assets at the date of payment (when different from the date of attribution or granting) is irrelevant.[114]

Any Belgian withholding tax – if due – will in principle be creditable to the income tax due of the recipient and the excess is refundable, if the income qualifies as professional or miscellaneous income. If the income is movable income from privately held assets, then the withholding tax can be recovered.

(c) *Does payment of compensation in crypto assets give rise to payroll tax consequences?*

Under the Salary Protection Act, it is forbidden for employers to pay salary in crypto assets. As to the payment of crypto assets as a benefit in kind on top of the salary, different positions can be taken, albeit that the Federal Ministry of Employment stated that this would be an infringement on the Salary Protection Act.[115] Since the Salary Protection Act only applies to employees and not to the self-employed, the latter could (partly) be paid out in crypto assets.

Compensation in crypto assets such as bitcoins does not give rise to any special payroll tax consequences and thus is to be treated as any payment in kind. Yet, professional withholding tax (*bedrijfsvoorheffing*) is to be withheld on remuneration paid to company directors. When remuneration to company directors is made by means of crypto assets, the company will have to withhold professional withholding tax (payroll taxes), and remit this tax on a monthly or quarterly basis to the tax

111. Articles 261 and 262 BITC.
112. Applicable rate for tax year 2020.
113. Article 267, section 1 and Article 269, §1, 1° BITC; Handbook 2019-2020, *supra* n. 47, at 868-869, 1639.
114. Handbook 2019-2020, *supra* n. 47, at 868-869, 1639. (It states the following: 'The law explicitly defines the taxable amount when movable income is granted in kind. In the case of allocation or payment of movable income in the form of goods in kind, the amount of taxable income is the market value of the goods on the date of their grant or payment, even if the actual transfer of the goods takes place later' referring to Article 267 BITC: 'In particular, the following is considered to be an award: the entry of an income into an account opened for the benefit of the transferee, even if that account is unavailable, provided that the unavailability is the result of an express or tacit agreement with the transferee.')
115. Article 6 of the Salary Protection Act provides for an exhaustive list of benefits in kind, and crypto assets are not included.

authorities, file withholding tax returns (forms 274), and prepare an individual annual tax slip (form 281) that is sent to the director and tax authorities. The professional withholding tax is to be calculated based on fixed scales.[116]

(d) *Do transactions with crypto assets trigger any transfer taxes?*

Since crypto assets do not qualify as financial products or as public funds, the tax on stock exchanges does not apply to the trading of crypto assets through a specialized exchange market.[117] This is, however, different for indirect investments (exclusively) investing in crypto assets or other structured products linked to value fluctuations in crypto assets.[118] Investment tokens or certain utility tokens therefore could fall in scope of the tax on stock exchanges.[119]

(e) *Are firms operating in the crypto space subject to digital service taxes?*

The OECD, as well as the European Union acknowledges that the international taxation environment is no longer adapted to the reality of the digital economy.

As an OECD member, Belgium contributes to the discussions held at the Inclusive Framework level with respect to proposals to address the challenges of the digitalized economy - better known as Pillar 1 and Pillar 2 proposals.

On a national level, on 23 January 2019, two proposals, i.e., the Digital Services Tax proposals and the draft Bill aiming at the introduction of a digital services PE, were submitted in the Chamber of Representatives. Both draft Bills were rejected on 28 March 2019. These bills have subsequently been reintroduced. Under the current political environment, it is less likely that Belgium will take any individual initiative to implement a digital tax. It is rather expected that Belgium will follow the EU law initiative in this respect.

(f) *Are crypto assets subject to gift, inheritance, estate, or wealth taxes?*

As a general remark, the mere holding of crypto assets, will not automatically lead to the increase of the amount of crypto assets or to any other revenue.[120] The mere holding of crypto assets will thus not lead to any taxable movable income. Latent capital gains are for privately held crypto assets not taxable, and under the present legislation, Belgium does not have a wealth tax in the strict sense.

Regarding gift and inheritance tax, the federal government, as well as each of the three Regions (the Flemish, Brussels Capital, and Walloon region) apply their own

116. Annex III of Royal Decree on the Belgian Income Tax Code.
117. *See also* Decision No. 2018.0688, 25 Sep. 2018.
118. It should be noted that it is prohibited in Belgium to trade in a professional context for a non-professional customer a financial product of which the investment return is directly or indirectly related to crypto assets.
119. Wonderful World, *supra* n. 92, at 9, 22.
120. Direct Taxation, *supra* n. 24.

rules.[121] All three regions apply different categories of gift and inheritance tax rates depending on the degree of kinship, the amount, and the nature (i.e., movable or immovable property) of the gift/inheritance. Within the scope of this article, only the Flemish rules will be briefly discussed, albeit that Brussels' and Walloon regulations are similar.

In principle, movable assets, including crypto assets, can be donated at a flat rate of 3% (Flanders & Brussels) or 3,3% (Wallonia) for donations in the direct line (i.e. between (grand-) parents and (grand-)children, between spouses and cohabiting persons and at a flat rate of 7% (Flanders & Brussels) or 5,5% (Wallonia) for donations to other persons.[122] As a general rule, gift tax will be due by the beneficiary, albeit that the donor can decide differently without it being a second gift of the gift taxes due. A gift of movable assets, when not being registered for a Belgian notary, is exempt from gift tax subject to the condition that the donor survives a period of three years after the donation, at least according to the present legislation in the Flanders Region.[123] When not surviving this three-year waiting period, the donated crypto assets will become subject to inheritance tax. Inheritance taxes, ranging between 3% and 27% in direct line (Flanders Region), are applicable on a Flanders tax resident's worldwide estate, after deduction of certain debts and costs. The rules in Brussels and Wallonia are similar but the rates in direct line vary between 3% and 30%. As a general rule, the assets of the inheritance are to be valued at the sales price at the date of death.[124] Yet, the question rises, what if the 'key' to provide access to the wallet of the inheritor is lost or has not been passed on to the heirs? In such case, the crypto assets can no longer be used and it is therefore arguable to state that the sales price of the crypto assets is nil. When selling these 'lost' crypto assets to a third party, the sales value will also be zero.[125]

(g) *Are crypto assets subject to exit tax?*

This topic refers to an exit tax over the change of location of the crypto assets from Belgium to any other place outside Belgium such as upon change of the seat of management of a company holding the crypto assets.

Belgium is entitled to tax the hidden gains and tax-exempt retained earnings that exist at the time of the transfer or 'exit' of assets to another member state of the

121. For inheritance taxes, tax residency is determined by the place where the deceased had his habitual abode or seat of fortune at the moment of his death. When qualifying as a Belgian tax resident, the place of residence of the deceased will be important to determine whether the legislation of the Flemish, Brussels Capital or Walloon Region is applicable. In order to prevent persons moving from one region to another within a short period prior to their death, an anti-abuse measure was introduced by means of which the tax regime of the region where the deceased lived the longest during the five years prior to his death applies.
122. Article 2.8.4.1.1., §2 Fl. TC.
123. The Flemish Government has announced that it will prolong this waiting period from three years up to four years. Agreement of the Flemish Government 2019-2024, 30 Sep. 2019, https://www.vlaanderen.be/publicaties/regeerakkoord-van-de-vlaamse-regering-2019-2024.
124. Article 2.7.3.3.1. of the Flemish Inheritance Tax Code.
125. Fiscal Fate, *supra* n. 4, at. 42.

European Economic Area (EEA) in view of a restructuring of the company such as outbound mergers or demergers, transfer of the seat of management or transfer of a Belgian PE to its foreign head office.[126] Hidden gains are defined as the positive difference between the fair market value of an asset and its acquisition or investment value reduced by accepted write-offs and depreciations.

For instance, a company that acquired crypto assets through mining activities and accounted for the mined crypto assets at historic value, which moves the seat of management to Luxembourg, will be subject to exit taxation on the positive difference between the fair market value of the crypto assets in euro equivalent on the date of transfer and the historic value of the crypto assets.

For transactions carried out since 8 December 2016, companies subject to corporate tax can elect between immediate payment and deferred payments over a period of five years.[127]

(h) Can mining trigger gambling tax?

From a technical point of view, mining could be considered as a lottery or a game of chance whereby the chance on profit will increase in terms of the capacity of processing and computing power that is engaged. Mining is a process of trial and error whereby the miner always has a chance to win or to lose.

Belgian taxation on gambling not only envisages gambling in public, but also gambling in private. No distinction is made between lawful and unlawful gambling. The concept of gambling, in Dutch 'spelen en weddenschappen' is however not defined by law. However, the gambling tax generally applies to 'aleatory contracts' (*kanscontract*)[128] which encompass a mutual agreement whereby the consequences related to profit or loss for all parties or at least one of them is conditional and subject to an uncertain event. As mining cannot be considered as a mutual agreement between two parties, it seems unlikely that it would fall in scope of gambling tax.

1.1.4 Compliance and Documentation Obligations

(a) What documentation requirements exist for taxpayers regarding crypto assets and are there best practices in recordkeeping to support representations made in tax returns?

In Belgium, there are no specific documentation requirements for taxpayers holding crypto assets. Holders of crypto assets must comply with the general documentation requirements. In the context of a tax investigation, a taxpayer is, however, subject to an obligation to cooperate. Any person subject to personal income tax, corporate income

126. Article 413/1 – without these assets being attributed to a PE in Belgium.
127. Law of 1 Dec. 2016, published 8 Dec. 2016. This in view of European case law: HvJ 29 Nov. 2011, *National Grid Indus*, C-137-10; HvJ 23 Jan. 2014, DMC, C-164/12) and the European Anti-abuse Directive of 12 Jul. 2016.
128. Article 1964 BITC. *See also* Handbook 2019-2020, *supra* n. 47, at 1257, 1855.

tax, tax on legal entities or tax for non-residents is required to submit to the tax authorities, upon their request, all books and records necessary to determine the amount of its taxable income.[129] This requirement applies not only to bookkeeping, but also to other documents, e.g., worksheets, order and delivery notes, shareholders registers, etc. Taxpayers are required to keep these documents for a period of seven (accounting) years following to the taxable period. When using a computerized system, the carriers and the data placed on them must be kept.

Violation of this requirement can be punished by administrative penalties ranging between 50 EUR up to 1.250 EUR and even criminal penalties. The tax authorities could also assess a tax ex officio ('*Aanslag van ambtswege*') when a certain document cannot be submitted as further explained in section 1.1.4(b) below.

Assuming that a crypto wallet could be considered a foreign bank account (*see* section 1.1.4(d) below), this would not result in the taxpayer being able to invoke his right to remain silent.[130] A taxpayer only can refuse to answer a request for information made by the tax authorities to the extent that based on this information he could be confronted with criminal law incriminations. A taxpayer is however obliged to answer the question whether he holds foreign accounts and whether he received on these accounts (professional) income as such questions relate to information that any taxpayer is required to mention in his tax return.[131]

Taxpayers trading crypto assets on exchanges should therefore download and store their transaction histories in order to be prepared for a tax audit.

(b) *What is the evidentiary burden of supporting tax positions when a digital wallet address is lost or shared with other persons?*

In the context of a tax investigation, a taxpayer is, in principle, subject to an obligation to cooperate. A taxpayer must submit all books and documents necessary to determine the amount of his taxable income, and must provide all information required of him for the purpose of examining his tax position.[132] When the taxpayer did not file a regular tax return or did not timely provide the necessary justification documents or required information to the tax authorities, the tax authorities could assess a tax ex officio, based on the information at their disposal or can assume, for instance, information that can be deducted (e.g., the gross turnover) from the VAT returns or published balance sheets, but also an interest can be assumed on sums received by the taxpayer in view of an inheritance, etc.[133] The burden of proof will then be shifted to the taxpayer.

When the tax authorities have the suspicion that a taxpayer's expenses are higher than the declared income, the so-called indicia' taxation[134] can be imposed whereby it is presumed that all of these expenses derive from taxable income. The burden of proof

129. Article 315 BITC.
130. Handbook 2019-2020, *supra* n. 47, at 976, 1704 with reference to Court of First Instance Brussels, 29 Jun. 2017, 03/4738/A; Article 315, section 2 BITC.
131. Tribunal of first instance Brussels, nr. 03/4738/A, 29 Jun. 2017.
132. Handbook 2019-2020, *supra* n. 47, at 987, 1709,50.
133. Article 351 BITC.
134. Article 341 BITC.

will thus be shifted to the taxpayer who will have to prove that the expenses were not covered by taxable income. For example, a person investing in crypto assets and buying a Tesla will be presumed to have purchased the Tesla with the capital gains realized on his successful investment, and will have to demonstrate where the funds came from if these capital gains have not been reported (when taxable) in his personal income tax return.

When the tax authorities suspect that the taxpayer did not declare all taxable income related to the crypto assets he owns, a tax *ex officio* can be assessed. The taxpayer will have then the burden of proof that he lost his private keys to the crypto wallet (which is unrecoverable as there is no central server to provide a reset) and that he can no longer dispose of these assets. Such proof may, however, be impossible to deliver since it clearly is a 'negative' proof.

(c) *Are crypto asset exchanges and wallet providers subject to reporting obligations?*

Belgian financial institutions are required to report account numbers and certain types of contracts related to Belgian accounts to the Central Point of Contact (CPC) of both resident and non-resident individuals or legal persons. The CPC is a databank comprising of a register of the bank account numbers and all types of contracts held at financial institutions in Belgium by both resident and non-resident natural or legal persons,[135] as well as of a register of numbers and identification record of foreign bank accounts of Belgian tax residents.[136] As to centralized crypto exchanges located in Belgium, it could be argued that they fall in scope of this reporting obligation, albeit that this is not stated by the CPC in the publicly available information.[137] There is currently no firm position of the tax authorities on this subject. The tax authorities are empowered to consult the CPC in order to obtain banking information on persons/entities subject to taxation when there are indications of tax fraud, or where taxes need to be recovered.

(d) *Are taxpayers holding crypto assets subject to reporting obligations apart from the filing of income tax/capital gains tax returns?*

Belgian tax residents are required to disclose the existence of any foreign bank account of which they, their spouse, legal cohabitating partner or minor child are the accountholders with the CPC.[138] The fact that this reporting duty has been fulfilled must

135. National Bank of Belgium, Central Point of Contact, https://www.nbb.be/en/central-credit-register/central-point-contact.
136. Article 307, § 1/1 BITC (amended by Article 94 of the bill of 25 Dec. 2017).
137. Article 322, §3 BITC and Com BITC No. 322/16, https://financien.belgium.be/nl/experten_partners/banken/centraal_aanspreekpunt; I. Rivière and K. Pauwels, 'Foreign Account Declaration: A Bitcoin Account Also Falls Under the Declaration Obligation?', *AFT* 2019/5, p. 48 (hereinafter 'Foreign Account Declaration').
138. Article 307, §1/1, a) BITC.

be once more confirmed in the annual personal income tax return. The non-disclosure of a foreign account can be punished with a fine of 50 EUR up to 1.250 EUR.[139]

The concept of a reportable account is defined by the CPC in a very broad sense.[140]

If a wallet were to consist of an exchange or platform through which crypto assets or tokens can be traded against other crypto assets or currency and vice versa, there are strong similarities between the wallets held by such exchanges/platforms and an ordinary securities account with an online broker.[141] This would mean that the wallets on crypto exchanges licensed abroad would have to be reported to the CPC, as well as reported in the personal income tax return.[142] When there is however no interaction with a crypto asset exchange, wallets do not to fall under this reporting obligation.[143] A wallet holder will thus not have to identify himself to a national supervisor or financial institution (e.g., the Financial Services and Market Authority) when the wallet is privately held, i.e., not via a crypto assets exchange.[144]

When the wallet is held on a third-party server, the country in which the server is located will determine whether a CPC reporting should be made.[145] It is not clear how this reporting obligation with the CPC in practice is to be done. Most likely it would be appropriate to report the public key to the CPC when the wallet is held with a central entity acting as a crypto asset exchange.[146]

(e) Are crypto asset exchanges and wallet providers subject to CRS/FATCA reporting?

On 23 April 2014, Belgium signed the intergovernmental agreement with the US on the mutual automatic exchange of financial information, i.e., the Foreign Account Tax Compliance Act, better known as 'FATCA'. On 29 October 2014, Belgium also signed the model of automatic exchange of information on a mutual basis, based on the 'Common Reporting Standard' (CRS). Like other jurisdictions, Belgium committed to

139. Article 445, §1 BITC.
140. Form for Communication of Accounts Abroad at the Central Contact Point, Explanatory Note, https://www.nbb.be/doc/cr/cap/2019%20-%20verklarende%20nota%20mededeling.pdf. The concept of account is understood by the CPC as 'any account of any kind which, even during a very short period of time, has existed at any time with a bank, foreign exchange, credit or savings institution established abroad.' It concerns 'accounts of any kind' and is thus understood to mean current accounts, savings accounts, term accounts, securities accounts, accounts linked to a mortgage loan or to any other form of credit, etc. *See also* Article 1 Royal Decree of 3 Apr. 2015.
141. The CPC however does not give any guidance in this respect, nor any reference to licensed crypto asset exchanges is mentioned in view of these reporting obligations.
142. Foreign Account Declaration, *supra* n. 137, at 47, 10.
143. Foreign Account Declaration, *supra* n. 137, at 47, 10.
144. Fiscal Fate, *supra* n. 4, at 11, footnote 31.
145. Foreign Account Declaration, *supra* n. 137, at 47.
146. Foreign Account Declaration, *supra* n. 137, at 47.

exchange information under CRS as of 2017.[147] Financial institutions are therefore obliged to provide the Federal Tax Authorities with the financial information required by law, which will then be sent by Belgium to the partner countries.

The Belgian tax authorities have not issued any guidance on the question whether operators of crypto exchanges or providers of crypto wallets must annually report their customers' data under CRS/FATCA.

The first question we have to ask ourselves is whether crypto assets do fall in scope of FATCA or CRS. Most likely crypto assets are like any other currency to be considered as financial assets and thus will be subject to FATCA and CRS disclosure practice.[148] It should be noted, however, that no intermediation of financial intermediaries is required – for example, crypto assets may not held by financial institutions and wallets can be held by the wallet owner himself.

1.1.5 Civil and Criminal Tax Enforcement

(a) What powers do the tax authorities have to compel the disclosure of information by third parties, such as exchanges or wallet providers, and have these been used in the past?

The tax authorities can for the purpose of verification of the correctness of the tax return, require any written certificates and oral or written information to be submitted by third parties of any identified taxpayer.[149] Third parties also can be heard and be the subject of an investigation. Questions of the tax authorities should, however, be fiscally relevant. The so-called 'fishing expeditions' are forbidden.

In addition, the administration has the possibility to obtain information from any individual or legal entity (e.g., certain fintech service providers where it is possible to convert crypto assets into traditional currency and financial institutions) regarding a taxpayer or group of persons who are not identified and with whom the third party has been in direct or indirect contact by virtue of its activities or transactions.[150]

To the investigation rights of the tax authorities in relation to third parties, there are two important exceptions, i.e., professional secrecy and banking secrecy.

Third parties that are subject to professional secrecy (e.g., accountants, lawyers) can under certain conditions invoke their professional secrecy when certain information is requested by the tax authorities in view of a taxation of a person who is protected

147. As concerns the exchange of information with other EU Member States and eighteen other CRS jurisdictions. The automatic exchange of information has been implemented in national law by law of 16 Dec. 2015.
148. Several analyses have been made on the (lack) of regulatory framework on crypto assets in international context. *See* 'Reporting Taxation: Analysing Loopholes in the EU's Automatic Exchange of Information and How to Close Them', p. 16 stating that 'it is not clear if all entities trading, issuing or exchanging crypto-currencies are covered by the CRS' with the suggestion of EU countries should establish regulations making it explicit that entities issuing, trading, or exchanging cryptocurrencies are covered by the CRS (p. 3), http://extranet.greens-efa-service.eu/public/media/file/1/5729.
149. Article 322, §1 BITC.
150. Article 323 BITC.

by this professional secrecy. As soon as this professional secrecy has been invoked, the tax administration should address the competent disciplinary authority to intervene. This disciplinary authority must decide whether, and if so to what extent, the request for information or the submission of documents can be reconciled with respect for the professional secrecy.[151]

With regard to banking secrecy, the administration is in principle not authorized to collect information from a bank, exchange, credit or savings institution in regard of taxing its customers.[152] This applies *a fortiori* to an investigation on third parties connected with these customers. Financial institutions include all financial institutions in general as referred to in normal language, for example, also leasing companies.[153]

Although this matter has not been fully crystalized by case law, banking secrecy could also be invoked by the bank's system operators, e.g., Atos Wordline.[154] It is not clear whether banking secrecy can also apply to wallet providers. Using a wallet has many similarities with internet banking, but the underlying operation is different.[155] The wallet does not serve to store the crypto assets itself. In the wallets, only the private keys (which can be compared to the PIN code or password of a bank account) are stored that give access to manage or control the crypto assets in the blockchain.[156] Case law seems to give a rather broad application to fiscal banking secrecy. It is therefore likely, or at least it could be argued, that wallet providers could invoke bank secrecy.

There are also several exceptions to banking secrecy. For instance, when a tax investigation would reveal elements indicating tax evasion or when the tax authorities intend to impose an ex officio tax assessment based on general information of which the authorities already have at their disposition (*indiciaire taxatie*),[157] the administration can only do this after it has first requested the taxpayer to provide the necessary information himself.[158]

Breach of banking secrecy is also possible in certain cases when information is requested by a foreign state.[159] In the context of an international request for information, an authorisation to conduct a bank investigation is automatically granted.

At present, we have no information on the Belgian tax authorities compelling Belgian crypto assets exchanges or wallet providers to disclose information on their clients.

151. Handbook 2019-2020, *supra* n. 47, at 988, 1709,70 and 993, 1711,30, 1711,40.
152. Handbook 2019-2020, *supra* n. 47, at 994, 1711,40 with reference to M. VAN DEN BOSSCHE, 'Tax Banking Secrecy in Belgium. Looking for Consistency in the Case Law in 2007', *TFR* 2007, 321, 335-361; Brussels 13 Sep. 2017, *RABG* 2017,19, 1467.
153. Handbook 2019-2020, *supra* n. 47, at 994, 1711,40 with reference to Cass. 16 March 2007, FJF, No. 2007/225 and Fisc.Act. 2007, afl. 27, 4; Luik 5 March 2014, FJF, No. 2014/261
154. Handbook 2019-2020, *supra* n. 47, at 995, 1711,40 with reference to Brussel 14 Oct. 2010, *TFR* 2011, 395, 97, T. AFSCHRIFT and P. VAN HISSENHOVEN and *AFT* 2011, 5, 17.
155. J.S., 'Dash Wallet - Everything You Need to Know About Keeping Dash', https://blockk.nl/dash-wallet/.
156. Foreign Account Declaration, *supra* n. 137, at 46.
157. For instance, an exception on bank secrecy applies when the tax authorities are investigating a taxpayer's letter of objection (Article 374 BITC). *See also* Article 318, section 2 BITC.
158. Article 322, §2; §5 BITC.
159. Article 322, §4 BITC.

(b) What measures have the tax authorities undertaken in the past to ensure crypto tax compliance?

It is not known what measures the Belgian tax authorities have undertaken in the past to ensure crypto tax compliance. The Belgian tax authorities have not yet provided any guidance regarding the application of the existing laws on the taxation of crypto assets.

(c) Are the tax authorities cooperating with tax authorities in other jurisdictions on enforcement?

Whether the Belgian tax authorities are cooperating with the tax authorities in other jurisdictions on enforcement in relation to crypto assets is not in the public domain. However, ongoing investigations by the Special Tax Inspection whereby the Belgian tax authorities received information on Belgian investors in a Finish broker account have been reported in the media in March 2018.[160]

In general, the Belgian tax authorities have several international instruments at their disposal allowing them to call upon the assistance of foreign authorities. Such assistance must always be channelled through the Central Tax Administration, as a tax assessment is based on data obtained in breach of this principle will be null and void.[161]

In addition to the exchange of information under the European directives,[162] Belgium concluded several double tax treaties providing for the possibility to exchange data, which provisions are inspired by Article 26 of the OECD Model Convention.[163] Also several administrative agreements have been concluded which allow for far-reaching administrative assistance, among other with the Netherlands, France, Italy, Latvia, Lithuania, Ukraine, the Czech Republic and the USA.[164]

Belgium has also ratified the OECD/Council of Europe Convention on Mutual Administrative Assistance in Tax Matters, which similarly gives the tax authorities access to information held abroad.[165]

160. Money Talks, Many Cryptocurrency Investors Have No Idea If and How Their Profits Are Taxed, 25 Apr. 2018, https://moneytalk.knack.be/geld-en-beurs/belastingen/veel-beleggers-in-cryptomunten-hebben-geen-idee-of-en-hoe-hun-winst-belast-wordt/article-opinion-1139595.html; Karsten Lemmens, Tax Searches for Bitcoin Investors, The Standard, 3 Feb. 2018, https://www.standaard.be/cnt/dmf20180301_03384942.
161. Handbook 2019-2020, *supra* n. 47, at 1003; 1706,40 with reference to administrative guideline No. Ci.R.9.Div/460.792, 27 Nov. 1996.
162. Article 338 BITC.
163. Handbook 2019-2020, *supra* n. 47, at 1005; 1716,60.
164. An overview of this agreement can be consulted on www.fiscus.fgov.be.
165. This agreement has been in force since 2000. Administrative Guideline AFZ-2000/237, 20 Aug. 2001. This agreement on mutual administrative assistance in tax matters has been amended by Protocol of 27 May 2010, Official Gazette, 15 Jan. 2015, *see also* F. SMET, 'International Financial and Tax Transparency: Increasingly Reality', Fiscoloog Internationaal, 2015, 380, 4.

Brazil

Raquel Novais & Alina Miyake

1. COUNTRY GUIDES

1.1 Brazil

1.1.1 Applicable Tax Law, Guidance, and Case Law

(a) Which laws, regulations, and other administrative guidance exist dealing with crypto assets?

'Crypto asset' is not a synonym of 'cryptocurrency' for cryptocurrency is a king of the crypto assets gender. For the purposes of this work, they will be treated as equivalent. This means that 'crypto asset' will be considered as a kind of token which main function is to be used as mean of payment, or conversion into other cryptocurrencies or into legal tender. Whenever other kinds of token be analysed, they will be specifically named.

There are no statutory provisions dealing with crypto assets and its tax treatment in Brazil.

The Brazilian tax administration has issued some manifestations with respect to crypto assets, more focused on cryptocurrencies.[1]

Normative Ruling issued by the Brazilian Revenue Service (RFB) No. 1,888/2019 introduced reporting obligations for: (i) Brazilian exchanges; and (ii) Brazilian individuals and legal entities carrying out transactions involving crypto assets. Such Ruling also established some definitions applicable to crypto asset's environment.

Under Normative Ruling RFB No. 1,888/2019 'crypto assets' are the ones that have the following characteristics:

1. The tax administration has not focused on other kinds of crypto assets, such as investment tokens or utility tokens.

- They are digital representations of value denominated in their own accounting unit.
- Their price can be converted into legal tender.
- They are traded electronically with the utilization of cryptography or distributed ledger technology (DLT).
- They can be used as form of investment, transfer of value, or access to services and which are not qualified as legal tender.

This rule also qualified 'exchange of crypto assets', as a legal entity, financial institution or not, that offers services related to crypto asset transactions, including intermediation, negotiation, and custody and accepts any payment means, including other crypto assets.

The tax administration also stated that crypto assets are similar to financial assets for the purposes of being reported in the individual's annual tax return, based on their respective value in Brazilian currency *Reais* (BRL).[2]

The Central Bank of Brazil (BACEN) has not issued any administrative rules in relation to crypto assets or its related activities. A few communiques were issued by BACEN: (i) alerting the sudden changes in price of crypto assets as well as the potential use of crypto assets for unlawful activities;[3] (ii) clarifying that exchanges are not regulated, authorized, or supervised by BACEN for cryptocurrencies are not qualified as legal tenders or electronic currencies for regulatory purposes.[45]

The Brazilian Securities Exchange Commission (CVM) has not issued any guidance regulating crypto assets activities within the context of capital markets activities as well.

The CVM issued some statements warning on the speculative nature of certain crypto assets, expressing the opinion that certain crypto assets may be qualified as financial assets. For such qualification purposes, there must be both a public offering of the assets and a right to participation, partnership, or remuneration deriving from the crypto assets negotiated. CVM emphasized its prerogative of analysing the matter on a case-by-case basis.[6]

In addition, the CVM issued a rule prohibiting the Brazilian investment funds to invest in crypto assets once they are not qualified as permitted investments. In this sense, CVM reiterated its understanding that most of the crypto assets are not qualified as financial assets, for the purposes of meeting the investment funds portfolio requirements.[7]

2. *See* Receita Federal do Brasil, *Imposto sobre a Renda da Pessoa Física: Perguntas e Respostas IRPF – 2020*, Ministério da Economia (2020), http://receita.economia.gov.br/interface/cidadao/irpf/2020/perguntao/p-r-irpf-2020-v-1-0-2020-02-19.pdf.
3. BACEN Communiques Nos 25,306/2014 and 31,379/2017.
4. Electronic currencies are further regulated by sections 6 and 7 of Law No. 12,865/2013.
5. BACEN Communique No. 31,379/2017.
6. Published in CVM website on 1 Mar. 2018, 16 Nov. 2017 and 11 Oct. 2017.
7. CVM Circular Ordinance No. 1/2018.

We may expect new statutory developments resulting from certain bills of law under discussion in the Brazilian House of Representatives,[8] which, if approved, may affect virtual currency transactions, exchanges, and e-wallets.[9]

(b) Which court cases exist dealing with crypto assets?

There are no relevant judicial or administrative tax court cases dealing with crypto assets.

The CVM has issued some administrative decisions on the qualification or not of certain crypto assets as financial assets.

One notorious case is the *'Niobium'*,[10] in which CVM dealt with the non-qualification of Niobium as a financial asset. In this case, CVM has refused the place of competent authority to rule or supervise Niobium ICO.[11]

1.1.2 Income and Capital Gains Taxes

(a) How are crypto assets classified for income and capital gains tax purposes?

Except for the non-binding qualification of crypto assets as similar to financial assets for individual annual tax reporting purposes, there is no other specific guidance on the crypto asset nature in the Brazilian law.

The assessment of the crypto assets' classification will rely on interpretation of the law, vis-à-vis certain aspects of the assets, the respective holder nature and activity as well as the use of those assets.

The identification of the legal nature of the crypto assets has been a challenging task in many jurisdictions, and in Brazil, it is not different. There are attempts to qualify the crypto assets as financial investments, virtual form of legal tender, commodities, or intangible assets, etc.

8. The main Bill of Laws being discussed before the House of Representatives are the following: (i) Bill of Law No. 2,303/2015, which initially proposed for the inclusion of virtual currencies and mileage programs as 'payment arrangements' within the Brazilian payment/electronic currency regulations; (ii) Bill of Law No. 2,060/2019, which expressly excludes crypto assets such as virtual currencies and utility tokens from regulation related to securities, which are mainly issued by the CVM. Also, this Bill authorizes the free issuing of crypto assets by any legal persons, as long as it relates to their activity or market; and (iii) Bill of Law No. 3,825/2019, which places virtual currency exchanges under BACEN supervision, creating a series of rules and principles for their activity and protects user resources in the event of exchange bankruptcy.
9. E-wallet or virtual wallets are kinds of software which store crypto assets and allow transfers of crypto assets ownership (*see* Raquel Novais & Alina Miyake, *Criptomoedas, um Novo Paraíso fiscal? Uma análise do Desenvolvimento do Mercado de Criptomoedas na era da Conformidade Tributaria à Luz da Legislação Brasileira,* Estudos de Tributação Internacional, edição especial, 259-289 (Ana Paula Saunders et al. ed., Lumen Juris, 2019)).
10. CVM Proceeding No. 19957.010938/2017-13.
11. *Initial Coin Offering* – Means by which the issuer receives *fiat* or other crypto assets for the development of a new blockchain project. In exchange, the developer issues a digital token to the parties that subscribed the ICO.

Although the qualification of such assets is not free from controversy, the most suitable legal qualification applicable to crypto assets under the Brazilian law is of movable property.[12] Such classification is in general enough to be compatible with sub-classifications whenever the other elements are present (holder nature and activity as well as the holding purpose and use).

The option for movable property qualification excludes the qualifications of: (i) 'virtual form of legal tender', given the position of Brazilian regulatory bodies; and (ii) 'financial investment', once there is no underlying contractual instrument supporting the crypto assets.

Such position is relevant, once the qualification as financial instruments or virtual form of legal tender would lead to tax consequences different than the ones analysed in this chapter. With respect to the qualification of certain crypto assets as financial instruments, it should be noted that CVM has already stated that some of them may receive such qualification. However, at this stage none of the crypto assets received such qualification, reason why its tax consequences are not mentioned in this work.

(b) What are the income/capital gains tax consequences of selling crypto assets against fiat currency?

On the basis that crypto assets shall be considered as movable property, for individual income tax purposes (*Imposto sobre a Renda da Pessoa Física* – IRPF), the capital gains taxation regime should apply. Therefore, the difference between the sales price (amount received in fiat currency upon sale) and the acquisition cost (amount initially paid in fiat currency upon acquisition) would be subject to IRPF at progressive rates from 15% to 22.5%, depending on the amount of the gain.[13]

There is no clear guidance for the definition of the acquisition cost in a scenario that: (i) a certain amount of crypto assets of the same kind has been acquired in several portions, at different acquisition costs; and (ii) only a portion of these crypto assets is then sold. A reasonable approach for this situation would be to consider the average cost of all acquisitions, once a similar criterion is valid for the assessment of the capital gain on the sale of shares.

If the crypto asset is derived from mining activity or has been received with no compensation, the acquisition cost shall be considered as zero. In this scenario, as

12. *See* Raquel Novais & Alina Miyake, *Criptomoedas, um Novo Paraíso fiscal? Uma análise do Desenvolvimento do Mercado de Criptomoedas na era da Conformidade Tributaria à Luz da Legislação Brasileira,* Estudos de Tributação Internacional, edição especial, 259-289 (Ana Paula Saunders et al. ed., Lumen Juris, 2019).
13. According to section 21 of Law No. 8,981/1995 (as amended by Law No. 13,259/2016), capital gains obtained by Brazilian resident individuals are subject to the IRPF at progressive rates from 15% rate up to 22.5%, under the following criteria: (i) 15% on the portion of the capital gains that do not exceed BRL 5 million; (ii) 17.5% on the portion of the capital gains that exceed BRL 5 million but is equal to or lower than BRL 10 million; (iii) 20% on the portion of the capital gains that exceed BRL 10 million but is equal to or lower than BRL 30 million; and (iv) 22.5% on the portion of the capital gains that exceeds BRL 30 million.

there are no deductibility rules applicable for Brazilian tax resident individuals, this approach may lead to a double taxation.[14]

For Corporate Income Taxes (CIT)[15] purposes, the tax treatment would depend on the accounting classification of the crypto asset (i.e., whether it is booked as asset or inventories as well as current or non-current assets), the corporate purpose of the legal entity (i.e. whether the trading of crypto assets is part of the corporate purpose), and the tax regime adopted by the company exchanging crypto assets into fiat currency. Those are the elements which reflect the holder's nature and activity as well as the holder purpose and use of the crypto assets.

Brazilian accounting standards generally follow the International Financial Reporting Standards (IFRS). Although a relevant set of tax rules are guided by the underlying accounting treatment, in most cases the relevant feature for the definition of the applicable tax treatment is the legal nature of the transaction and the general tax principles (in the case of IRPF/CIT, the availability of income is the guiding principle).

The IFRS Interpretations Committee (IFRIC) concluded that cryptocurrency qualifies as intangible asset as defined by paragraph 8 of International Accounting Standards (IAS)[16] 38, except if crypto asset is held for trading where it shall be accounted as 'inventories'.[17] There is no complementary guidance as to deal with the peculiarities of the matter.[18]

---

14. The set of deductions available for Brazilian tax resident individuals is very narrow, and this situation is common. No specific guidance in relation to this situation (or similar ones) is made by RFB.
15. Under Brazilian legislation there are two taxers imposed on the corporate profits: (i) Corporate Income Tax (*Imposto sobre a Renda da Pessoa Jurídica* – IRPJ) and (ii) Social Contribution on Net Profits (*Contribuição Social sobre o Lucro Líquido* – CSLL), jointly named CIT.
16. The IRIC met on Jun. 2019.
17. 'In June 2019, the IFRS IC published its agenda decision on "Holdings of Cryptocurrencies", and it considered a subset of cryptographic assets with the following characteristics: a. a digital or virtual currency recorded on a distributed ledger that uses cryptography for security; b. not issued by a jurisdictional authority or other party; and c. does not give rise to a contract between the holder and another party.

    The IFRS IC concluded that IAS 2, "Inventories", applies to such assets where they are held for sale in the ordinary course of business. If IAS 2 is not applicable, an entity applies IAS 38, "Intangible Assets", to holdings of cryptocurrencies.

    There are many judgemental areas that will require further investigation as entities determine the applicable accounting treatment and as the technologies and markets continue to develop. For some topics, no uniform or definitive answers currently exist.' (*See* PwC, *In depth, a look at current financial reporting issues: Cryptographic assets and related transactions: accounting considerations under IFRS*, 2019-05, https://www.pwc.com/gx/en/audit-services/ifrs/publications/ifrs-16/cryptographic-assets-related-transactions-accounting-considerations-ifrs-pwc-in-depth.pdf.)
18. 'IFRS does not include specific guidance on the accounting for cryptographic assets and there is no clear industry practice, so the accounting for cryptographic assets could fall into a variety of different standards, but not 'Property, Plant and Equipment', once it is not qualified as a tangible asset. Consideration should also be given to the entity's purpose for holding the cryptographic assets to determine the accounting model. We explore below the accounting standards and other considerations that might be relevant to the subsets of cryptographic assets. Financial asset – other than cash Holding a unit of a cryptocurrency typically does not give the holder a contractual right to receive cash or another financial asset, nor does the cryptocurrency come into existence as a result of a contractual relationship. Moreover, crypto assets do not provide

The crypto asset not held for trading may receive the treatment of either current or non-current assets, depending on whether they are being held for long or short term.

Brazilian CIT regulations applicable to medium to large-sized legal entities allow the election of one among the two main alternative tax regimes methods according to the tax position of the taxpayer and the respective compliance with the conditions for election: real profit method regime and presumed profit method regime. Micro- and small-sized legal entities may elect a simplified tax regime that encompasses a variety of taxes which are assessed on a jointly basis.[19]

The CIT rate is a combination of CIT at 15% plus 10% additional rate, and social contribution on profit, at 9%. The combined CIT rate is 34% on the real profit (margin) or on the presumed profit (presumed margin) according to the taxpayers' election.

If the seller adopts the real profit regime,[20] upon realization of the crypto assets:

- If the crypto assets are booked as current assets, the acquisition cost and the sales price of the crypto asset would be considered for the purposes of CIT assessment (margin).

---

the holder with a residual interest in the assets of an entity after deducting all of its liabilities. Therefore, crypto assets that we have seen so far (November 2019) do not meet the definition of a financial asset.

Equipment', because they are not tangible items. (...)

Property, plant and equipment

Cryptocurrencies do not fall into the scope of IAS 16, 'Property, Plant and Equipment', because they are not tangible items.

Inventory

IAS 2 does not require inventories to be in a physical form, but inventory should consist of assets that are held for sale in the ordinary course of business. Inventory accounting might be appropriate if an entity holds cryptocurrencies for sale in the ordinary course of business. An entity that actively trades the cryptocurrencies, purchasing them with a view to their resale in the near future and generating a profit from fluctuations in the price or traders' margin, might consider whether the guidance in IAS 2 for commodity broker-traders should be applied.

However, if the entity holds cryptocurrencies for investment purposes (that is capital appreciation) over extended periods of time, it would likely not meet the definition of inventory.' (*See* PwC, *In depth, a look at current financial reporting issues: Cryptographic assets and related transactions: accounting considerations under IFRS*, 2019-05, https://www.pwc.com/gx/en/audit-services/ifrs/publications/ifrs-16/cryptographic-assets-related-transactions-accounting-considerations-ifrs-pwc-in-depth.pdf.)

19. The so-called 'SIMPLES Nacional' approved by Complementary Law no. 123/2006. For being able to enjoy the simplified regime, the companies' annual revenue shall not exceed BRL 4,800,000.00.

20. Under the real profit regime method (*regime do lucro real*), companies calculate their CIT liability annually or quarterly, at their discretion, based on an option performed at the beginning of the year) on the accounting net profits for the taxable period, calculated on the basis of generally accepted accounting principles, adjusted by additions and exclusions provided by tax law. The taxable event occurs when the income becomes economically or legally available to the recipient. Accrual regime generally applies to the recognition of revenues. Only necessary and usual expenses and costs incurred by companies are deductible. Thus, the net profit, adjusted by tax additions and exclusions provided by law, is subject to CIT at 34% aggregate rate.

Legal entities adopting the real profit regime for CIT purposes are subject to Contribution to the Employee's Profits Participation Program (*Contribuição para o Programa de Integração Social* – PIS) and Contribution to the Financing of Social Security (*Contribuição para Financiamento da Seguridade Social* – COFINS) under the non-cumulative regime (at a 9.25% aggregate rate on the gross revenues, with deduction of credits).

- If the crypto assets are booked as non-current assets, CIT rates on the capital gains derived by the legal entity would be imposed.

Depreciation or amortization does not apply given the non-amortizable legal nature of the crypto asset.

Adjustments to reflect fair market value that may result in impairment and revaluation of the crypto assets along the period they are held (including potential mark-to-market adjustments required for accounting purposes) should not have any effect for CIT purposes until the realization.

There is no explicit accounting guidance to market-to-market adjustments to reflect the fluctuations of crypto assets. A fair interpretation of tax principles leads not to give potential adjustments of this nature any tax effect until realization.

If the seller adopts the presumed profit regime,[21] the following tax effects would be verified upon the realization of the crypto assets:

- If the crypto assets are booked as current assets and the trading of crypto assets is part of the legal entity's corporate purpose, the presumed profit calculation method will apply, except if crypto assets are treated as financial investments which is not the basic assumption of this chapter. The presumed profit method requires the identification of a percentage to be multiplied by the total gross revenue derived by the trading activity,[22] over this amount the 34% CIT rate applies. The percentages vary from 8% to 32% depending of the business-related income nature.
- If the crypto assets are booked as non-current assets, CIT rates on the capital gains derived by the legal entity will apply.

21. Presumed profit regime is a simplified tax method under which the legal entity calculates its taxable base by applying a percentage to its total gross revenue earned during the quarter or the year (presumed profit) depending on taxpayer's election. Gross revenue is the amount derived from: (i) the sale of products; (ii) the rendering of services; and (iii) other revenues derived from the main activity developed by the company. The presumed profit percentages vary depending on the business activity developed by the company. For the sale of goods, the presumed percentages of profit are 8% for IRPJ and 12% for CSLL. For the provision of services, the presumed percentages of profit are 32% for IRPJ and for CSLL.

    Legal entities adopting the presumed profit regime for CIT purposes are subject to PIS and COFINS under the cumulative regime (at a 3.65% aggregate rate on the gross revenues, with no deduction of credits).

22. There is a controversy whether the presumed percentages of profit are: (i) 8% and 12% for IRPJ and CSLL; and (ii) 32% for both, IRPJ and CSLL. The treatment mentioned in (i) tends to be the most adequate, once it deals with the sale of assets. However, the tax administration tends to take the position that the treatment mentioned in (ii) is the most suitable, once it refers to the assignment of rights. This understanding is similar to the one supported by the tax administration in relation to the sale of real estate property. In this case, they have construed that the sale of such property by a real estate company should be qualified as assignment of rights and, consequently, the 32% presumed percentage of profit applies.

(c) What are the income/capital gains tax consequences of exchanging crypto assets against other crypto assets?

The exchange of crypto assets against other crypto assets would be qualified as an asset barter.

As general rule, an asset barter does not imply realization of any gain or income. This is because, the exchange of crypto assets against other crypto assets would have as consequence the new crypto assets acquired replacing the book value of the one given in exchange. Thus, no capital gain or loss would derive by an asset barter transaction.

Although this is a fair interpretation of the tax effects of an asset barter, the tax administration might challenge it under the grounds that the non-taxable barter regime only applies to exchange of immovable assets (real estate). This line of interpretation supports that other sort of asset barters (not involving real estate property) should be perceived as two distinct and respective purchase and sale transactions, each of them subject to CIT.

In this scenario, the tax administration may require the use of the market value of each crypto asset subject to the transaction on the exchange date to assess the capital gains.

(d) If a distinction is made between business assets and non-business assets, when does trading in crypto assets lead to a trade or business?

For tax purposes, there is no distinction in Brazil regarding the effects of transactions with business assets and non-business assets. The different tax implications arise from the qualification as current or non-current assets for accounting purposes and of whether the trading activity is within the corporate purpose of the entity.

As an immediate consequence of a trading activity involving crypto assets (i.e., holding crypto assets for trading and actually performing of a trading activity), losses with the crypto asset trading activity might be considered deductible for CIT purposes. If a non-trading business activity involving crypto assets is to be characterized as pure speculative, the tax administration may deny the deductibility of the losses under the grounds that such losses are neither necessary nor usual for the ongoing taxpayer business and income generation. A similar approach is adopted for transactions involving derivatives: if they have hedge purposes, the losses are deductible; if they are characterized as speculative, tax authorities may deny their deductibility.

(e) What are the income/capital gains tax consequences for an employee receiving wages or salaries in crypto assets?

If an employee receives his or her salary in crypto assets, such payment would be considered as payment *in natura*, being subject to payroll taxes and social security contributions (due by both the employee[23] and the employer[24]) as well as the withholding income tax. Such taxes are due by the time the crypto asset is received.

Withholding income tax and social security contribution should be calculated by the employer on a gross-up basis and paid by the employer in favour of the tax administration. There is no specific guidance in relation to the valuation of the crypto assets in this situation. A fair interpretation would be to take the market value of the crypto asset in Brazilian currency *Reais*, on the payment date, for calculation of the respective taxes as well as for recording the value by the individual, in order to guide capital gain assessment on future sale.[25]

Any reliable public quotation could be used. If there is no official or reliable public data available to help the fair market assessment, the taxpayer shall gather the most reliable documentation as possible to support the adopted value.

(f) What are the income/capital gains tax consequences of a loss of crypto assets?

If a crypto asset is lost by a Brazilian tax resident individual, we understand that no tax effects would arise. The individual should only inform the loss of the crypto asset in the income tax return.

There is no guidance in relation to the treatment applicable to the situation in which a legal entity loses a crypto asset. Depending on the circumstances of the concrete case, one possible approach is to treat this situation as embezzlement, misappropriation, or theft. In this case, if the legal entity assesses CIT under real profit regime, such loss would be deductible provided that the legal entity initiates an investigation under the terms of the labour or criminal law (depending on who was responsible for the loss if this circumstance can be assessed).[26]

In other cases, no deductibility rule is available.

(g) What are the income/capital gains tax consequences for a merchant receiving payment in crypto assets?

A merchant of goods and services receiving its compensation through crypto assets should be subject to the same tax treatment applicable to the payment in fiat currency.

23. At rates varying from 7.5% up to 14%, depending on the remuneration value, as follows: (i) 7.5% for remunerations up to BRL 1,045.00; (ii) 9% for remunerations between BRL 1,045.01 and BRL 2,089.60; (iii) 12% for remunerations between BRL 2,089.61 and BRL 3,134.40; and (iv) 14% for remunerations between BRL 3,134.41 and BRL 6,101.06. If the remuneration exceeds BRL 6,101.06, the exceeding amount is not subject to Social Security Contribution due by the employee.
24. As general rule, the applicable rate is 20%.
25. A similar approach has been adopted by the tax administration and the administrative tax court when dealing with the valuation of shares received by employees within stock option programmes.
26. Under the terms of section 376 of the Income Tax Regulations.

Thus, for income tax purposes, the fair market value of the goods or services constitute the merchant's taxable income.

Upon the merchant exchanging the crypto assets received into fiat currency, another taxable transaction might occur, if the value of the crypto asset increases in value from the moment it is received in payment of goods or services and the moment they are exchanged for fiat currency.

The fair market value of the crypto asset is a key procedure for compliance purposes. In the absence of a public quotation, the taxpayer shall gather the most reliable documentation as possible to support the respective valuation.

(h) What are the income/capital gains tax consequences of forks of crypto assets?

There is no guidance on the matter. A reasonable interpretation to be followed by individuals as well as legal entities would be to split the crypto asset acquisition cost/book value proportionally into two crypto assets resulting of the fork.[27]

The fork should not be considered a crypto asset realization transaction for taxation purposes. The potential gains would stay unrealized in the book value of the split asset and taxed upon future sale or exchange.

(i) What are the income/capital gains tax consequences of airdrops of crypto assets and are the tax consequences different if the airdropped tokens are unwanted?

Individuals should not suffer any tax consequences of airdrops. Crypto assets received as airdrops should be reported in the income tax return with zero value.

In relation to legal entities, if the airdrops are given for free and if their respective value is easily assessed, they might represent income for the recipient legal entity, irrespective of being unwanted. The way the airdrops are accounted for by the legal entity may also be an important element to determine the actual tax treatment (i.e., if they are accounted for as a positive entry in the P&L, it may be harder to sustain that there is no taxable income in practice).

(j) What are the income/capital gains tax consequences of (solo, pool, and cloud) mining?

There is no specific regulation of mining activities in the Brazilian law.

27. A similar approach has been adopted by the tax administration in relation to share splits, as there is express manifestation in the sense that, upon a share split, the same acquisition cost previously held for the original shares should be maintained for the new overall number of shares. Therefore, in practice, it would have the effect of a simple split of the acquisition cost among the old and new shares.

If the mining activity is developed under a contract, the miner is rendering service in favour of the contractor. In the capacity of an individual the miner will be subject to report crypto assets received in consideration of the blockchain validation. Tax on services (ISS) may also be imposed at a maximum 5% rate on the price of the service.

If the miner is a legal entity and acts as an entrepreneur and not as a contracted entity, crypto asset resulting from the mining activity should be booked at mining cost value and taxation should occur upon sale on an ICO, IEO, or conversion into *fiat* or exchange into other crypto asset for the market value the crypto asset was traded.

If the miner is an individual, no deductibility of mining costs such as energy will be allowed. If the miner is a legal entity, deduction of costs will depend on the CIT regime the miner has elected: Presumed Profit or Simples Nacional do not allow deduction of operational costs as opposed to Real Profit Regime which allows the deductibility of costs and expenses.

(k) What are the income/capital gains tax consequences of staking crypto assets?

Proof of Stake is a consensus mechanism (an alternative to proof of work) whereby transactions are validated by users of the blockchain. The main interest involved is to keep the integrity of the blockchain by the users.

Any potential remuneration derived by Proof of Stake will be qualified under income and not capital gain and will be taxed according to the recipient nature, if individual or legal entity, as well as the tax regime adopted by the recipient taxpayer as follows.

Individuals will be subject to taxation at rates which vary from 7.5% to 27.7%, depending on the income level.

Legal entities will be subject to taxation according to what was clarified in section 1.1.2(b) above.

(l) What are the income/capital gains tax consequences of an indirect investment in crypto assets?

Due to regulatory constraints currently in force, Brazilian investment funds are not allowed to directly invest in crypto assets.

The only indirect investment in crypto assets available in Brazil are those made via Brazilian investment funds which invest in foreign investment funds holding portfolio investments in crypto assets.

The taxation of such type of investment does not differ from the taxation on investment funds in general.

Capital gains derived from investment funds are subject to withholding income tax at rates which range from 15% to 22.5%, depending on whether the fund qualifies as long term or short term, as well as on the period the investor keeps the investment in the investment fund. Income tax on capital gains is withheld from the fund equity attributed to each investor on a semi-annual basis, in case of open-ended funds. In case of close-ended funds, in general, taxation occurs on distributions made to the investors.

Tax on financial transaction (IOF) at 1% rate may be imposed if the investment period in the fund is lower than thirty days.

(m) How is income from crypto assets to be treated under double tax treaty law?

Cross-border transactions involving crypto assets have not been regulated. The tax administration has not issued any guidance on the matter as well.

Any form of revenue derived by crypto asset cross-border transactions can fall under various allocation rules of the OECD Model Convention, depending on the income nature, to be assessed on a case-by-case basis.

As reviewed in this work, there are two kinds of income derived from crypto assets under Brazilian domestic legislation: (1) capital gains, whenever the holder disposes from the crypto assets or income in connection with crypto assets is made available to the holder under the form of ordinary income; and (2) earnings, whenever someone receives compensation for mining. As general rule, the double tax treaties executed by Brazil allow the taxation of capital gains in both jurisdiction (except for the one executed with Japan, which allows the taxation only in the residency state).

Brazil is not a popular jurisdiction for mining activities due to the high cost of energy in the country as compared to other jurisdictions where cheaper energy is available. As a result, if the mining activity is exercised in a jurisdiction with which Brazil has a tax treaty and such mining activity derives revenues, the revenues will be qualified under Article 7 of the OECD Model Convention (Business Profits). The adoption of Article 7 for the rendering of services is a matter of controversy in Brazil, once tax authorities adopt the approach that this item of income should fall into the scope of Article 12 (Royalties).[28] The most recent tax treaties concluded with Singapore and Switzerland[29] have a specific article concerning technical services, which allows the source taxation in Brazil.[30]

(o) What are the income/capital gains tax consequences of selling crypto assets in an ICO/STO/IEO?

The tax effect of the ICO, from the developer's perspective, depends on whether the offering involves coins or rights to coins to be still developed. If coins are sold the income will be treated as ordinary income and will be taxed accordingly (please *see* section 1.1.2(a), (b) and (c)). If the offering involves right to receive cryptocurrency to be developed, the taxation is deferred up to the moment the cryptocurrency is actually delivered, when the funds initially raised will be recognized as income to the

28. Exception is made to the tax treaties executed Austria, France, Finland, Japan and Sweden.
29. These treaties have not been approved by the National Congress yet.
30. In line with the UN Model Convention.

developer. From the perspective of the investor, no tax effect is derived from the ICO. The crypto asset acquired will be recorded by the investor and such value will be taken into consideration for tax effects upon future realization (please *see* section 1.1.2(a), (b) and (c) above).

The tax effect of an IEO should be the same of an ICO, for both the developer and the investor. From the perspective of the exchange, the service fee received either in *fiat* currency of in crypto asset should be taxed as ordinary service income.

At this stage, no STO took place in Brazil. The STOs should be subject to an assessment on a case-by-case basis, examining the nature of the offered security. Depending on the features of the offering, an STO could qualify as a process to be taken within the capital markets regulatory environment and could be subject to CVM supervision. Theoretically speaking an STO may involve the offering of equity participation or any type of tokenized debt instrument. Having this as an assumption from the issuer perspective, there should be no tax effect. In the first case, the issuer would receive fiat or other crypto asset in consideration of a tokenized equity interest; in the second case, the issuer would receive fiat or other cryptocurrency in consideration of a tokenized debt instrument (bonds). None of this situation should trigger tax effects in Brazil, provided that it is properly accounted for (i.e., equity or debt entry in the financial statements). From the perspective of the investor, no tax effect should take place as well.

The only potential tax effect could be the STO being subject to Tax on Financial Transactions (IOF), for which further and more specific regulations would be required to clearly define both the tax event and the tax rate.

1.1.3 Other Taxes

(a) What are the value added tax/sales tax consequences of selling crypto assets?

Crypto assets have not been specifically targeted by federal or State value added taxes (VAT). However, since federal VATs (PIS and COFINS) are imposed on gross revenues, the result of selling crypto assets would be to have the received amounts comprising the legal entity's gross revenue, therefore being subject to federal VATs.

The federal VAT regime would depend on: (i) the kind of activity developed by the legal entity;[31] (ii) how the crypto assets are booked for accounting purposes; and (iii) the CIT calculation regime adopted, as follows:

- For the legal entities assessing CIT under the real profit regime, federal VATs would be imposed at a 9.25% aggregate rate on the total sales value of crypto assets booked as current assets. Such tax is imposed on a non-cumulative basis

31. Certain legal entities are obliged to assess federal VATs under the cumulative regime (with no credit deductions or special deductions). This is the case of financial institutions, insurance companies, among others. For the purpose of this chapter, only the general rules are being analysed.

(with credit deductions). If the crypto assets are booked as non-current assets, no federal VATs would be imposed on this transaction.
- For legal entities assessing CIT under presumed profit regime, federal VATs would be imposed at a 3.65 % aggregate rate on the total sales value of crypto assets booked as current assets. If the crypto assets are booked as non-current assets, no federal VATs would be imposed on this transaction.

State VAT (ICMS)[32] is imposed on the circulation of merchandise. Given the unregulated nature of crypto assets, until now such assets have not been targeted by State VAT. The possibility of the States claiming the imposition of VAT on crypto assets cannot be excluded, if the position in the sense that crypto assets are qualified as merchandise prevails.[33]

(b) Are payments in crypto assets subject to withholding taxes?

As mentioned in section 1.1.2(e) above, employees receiving salaries or remuneration for work in crypto assets will be subject to withholding income tax.

If crypto assets are exchanged for the provision of certain types of services, withholding income tax would be imposed at 1.5 % rate, as anticipation of the IRPJ due. In addition, for certain types of service provision, CSLL would be withheld at 1 % rate, PIS at 0.65 % rate, and COFINS at 3 % rate.

(c) Does payment of compensation in crypto assets give rise to payroll tax consequences?

As clarified in section 1.1.2(e) above, if a taxpayer is remunerated under an employment relationship, the compensation in crypto assets would be considered as payment *in natura*, being subject to payroll taxes and Social Security Contributions (due by the employee and the employer) at the moment it is received. There is no guidance in relation to the valuation of the crypto assets in this situation. Employer and employee should endeavour the best efforts to keep reliable documentation supporting the payment values.

32. *Imposto sobre Operações relativas à Circulação de Mercadorias e Prestação de Serviços de Transporte Interestadual e Intermunicipal e de Comunicação.*
33. In should be noted that a similar discussion occurred in the past in relation to the imposition of state VAT on the sale of real estate property. In this case, the prevailing position was in the sense that the sale of real estate property is not equated to the circulation of merchandise. Thus, no state VAT should be imposed in this case. The same type of debate occurred as regards software licence transfers. In this case the nature of the software is relevant for the ICMS imposition. If the software is of shelf type it is considered merchandise and the ICMS is imposed. On the other hand, if it is of a customized nature the merchandise nature is not characterized thus ISS (tax on service) is imposed.

(d) Do transactions with crypto assets trigger any transfer taxes?

There is no transfer tax applicable to crypto assets transactions in Brazil.

(e) Are firms operating in the crypto space subject to digital service taxes?

There are no digital service taxes in Brazil.

However, firms operating in the crypto environment that charge an intermediation fee per transaction or services providers receiving compensation in crypto assets may be subject to Tax on Services (*Imposto sobre Serviços de Qualquer Natureza* – ISS).

As a Municipal tax, each Municipality is entitled to enact its own rules on ISS and to define the rates applicable to each specific service, in compliance with Federal Complementary Law No. 116/2003. The rates may range from a minimum 2% rate to a maximum 5% rate, depending on the nature of the service. The ISS taxable basis is the service fee.

There is no clear guidance in connection with the conversion criteria for ISS purposes.

(f) Are crypto assets subject to gift, inheritance, estate, or wealth taxes?

The Brazilian legislation only provides a State Gift and Inheritance Tax (*Imposto sobre Transmissão Causa Mortis e Doação* – ITCMD). There are no wealth taxes in Brazil.

With respect to ITCMD, the State legislations do not make any difference between which assets are subject to ITCMD. In this sense, any transfer of crypto assets under a donation or inheritance should be subject to ITCMD.

The legislation of each State of Brazil (with differences between them) regulates the imposition of ITCMD, through applicable specific laws. Notwithstanding, the general taxation guidance imposed by the Federal Constitution (*Constituição Federal* – CF/1988) and the National Tax Code (*Código Tributário Nacional* – CTN)[34] shall be observed.

ITCMD rates vary in accordance with the laws of the relevant State, though a maximum limit of 8% shall be observed. In the State of São Paulo, the applicable rate is 4%. Currently, transfers involving less than BRL 62,000, corresponding to approximately USD 12,000 are exempt.

CF/1988 provided for a *situs* principle that shall govern the imposition of ITCMD on gifts or bequests involving real estate. With respect to movable property, the ability to charge is attributed to: (i) the State where the probate is processed, in relation to inheritances; and (ii) the State where the donor is domiciled, in case of donations.

As the crypto assets may be stored with foreign exchanges, it may be qualified as an asset located outside of Brazil. In this scenario, there is a controversy whether ITCMD would be imposed, once the CF/1988 provided that a Federal complementary law should be enacted to regulate the imposition of the tax in relation to foreign

34. Law No. 5,172/1966.

assets.[35] Despite the fact that no such complementary law was enacted, several Brazilian States introduced the imposition of ITCMD on donations/inheritances involving foreign *situs* assets. This is a controversial matter, which will be ruled by the Federal Supreme Court (STF) with binding effects to all taxpayers and tax authorities (*repercussão geral*).[36]

Brazil has not executed any treaty to avoid double taxation on gift and estate taxes, this being the reason why the States of the Brazilian Federation are not restricted by any treaty in relation to the imposition of ITCMD.

(g) Are crypto assets subject to exit tax?

There is no exit tax in Brazil.

(h) Can mining trigger gambling tax?

There is no gambling tax in Brazil.

1.1.4 *Compliance and Documentation Obligations*

(a) What documentation requirements exist for taxpayers regarding crypto assets and are there best practices in recordkeeping to support representations made in tax returns?

There is no statutory rule defining which documentation should be kept by taxpayers. For the purposes of filling in the individual's annual tax return, RFB issued a ruling stating that the individual must demonstrate the exchange rate (fiat/crypto asset) adopted in the statement by a good standing documentation.[37]

If transactions are carried out on exchanges, the taxpayer must keep its transaction records to support the reported transactions.[38]

35. Under section 155, paragraph 3, item III, of the CF/1988, the imposition of ITCMD, if the donor is domiciled outside of Brazil, shall be expressly and previously allowed by a Federal complementary law, in the following situations: (i) donations performed by non-resident donors to Brazilian resident individuals; (ii) inheritances involving (a) deceased persons resident outside of Brazil; (b) Brazilian resident deceased persons with respect to assets located outside of Brazil; or (c) Brazilian resident deceased persons when the probate is processed in a foreign jurisdiction.
36. Extraordinary Appeal No. 851,108/SP, reporting judge Minister Dias Toffoli.
37. *See* Receita Federal do Brasil, *Imposto sobre a Renda da Pessoa Física: Perguntas e Respostas IRPF – 2020*, Ministério da Economia (2020), http://receita.economia.gov.br/interface/cidadao/irpf/2020/perguntao/p-r-irpf-2020-v-1-0-2020-02-19.pdf.
38. Sections 6 and 7 of Normative Ruling RFB No. 1,888/2019.

(b) *What is the evidentiary burden of supporting tax positions when a digital wallet address is lost or shared with other persons?*

Under Brazilian law, the authorities may investigate and determine ex officio the factual and legal circumstances which are essential for the levying of taxes; they must take into account any information provided to them, whether or not it is for the benefit of the taxpayer.

The taxpayer is bound by the duty of cooperation and has to act in good faith in providing information to the tax authorities in an audit procedure. Brazilian law provides for stronger penalties for situations where the taxpayer refuses to provide proper and diligent information than the general penalties (112.5% and 225% as opposed to 75% and 150% general penalties).

As a normal rule, the burden of proof is on the tax authorities. If the taxpayer does not cooperate and the tax authorities have little information they would probably extract conclusion of what they could obtain and transfer the burden of proof to the taxpayer to deconstruct the conclusions taken in those specific circumstances. There is no guidance in relation to situations in which the holders loses the access to digital wallet, and there is no mechanism to obtain the relevant data.

(c) *Are crypto asset exchanges and wallet providers subject to reporting obligations?*

Yes, under Normative Ruling RFB No. 1,888/2019, exchanges domiciled in Brazil are obligated to report to the RFB, on a monthly basis, any transaction related to crypto assets (Transaction Report) and yearly balance information related to its users (Balance Report).

The Transaction Report must include the following information for each transaction carried out through the exchange: (a) date of the transaction; (b) the type of transaction (whether purchase and sale, exchange, donation, transfer of crypto assets to an exchange, withdrawal of crypto assets from an exchange, temporary assignment (borrowing), payment in kind, issuance, or other transaction that results in transfer of crypto assets); (c) the parties involved in the transaction (identified by their names, addresses, tax domiciles, tax identification numbers in the RFB, and other registration information); (d) the type of crypto assets involved in the transaction; (e) the number of crypto assets traded, in units, to the tenth decimal place; (f) the total amount of the transaction, in Brazilian *Reais*, excluding the service fees charged for the execution of the transaction, if any; and (f) the amount of the service fees charged for the execution of the transaction, if any.

The Balance Report must include the following information with respect to each user, considering the preceding year: (a) the balance of fiat money, in Brazilian *Reais*; (b) the balance of each type of crypto asset, in its respective units; and (c) the cost, in Brazilian *Reais*, for the purchase of each type of crypto asset, declared by the user of its services, if any.

If the exchange does not comply with the above-mentioned reporting obligations, up to 3% penalty would be imposed on the value corresponding to the omitted, inaccurate, or incomplete pieces of information.

(d) *Are taxpayers holding crypto assets subject to reporting obligations apart from the filing of income tax/capital gains tax returns?*

Under Normative Ruling RFB No. 1,888/2019, Brazilian taxpayers (either individuals or legal entities) are obliged to fill in a Transaction Report regarding transactions carried out through exchanges domiciled outside of Brazil and transactions made without the intermediation of exchanges.

The information to be disclosed in the Transaction Report is the same required for Brazilian exchanges: (a) date of the transaction; (b) the type of transaction (whether purchase and sale, exchange, donation, transfer of crypto assets to an exchange, withdrawal of crypto assets from an exchange, temporarily assignment (borrowing), payment in kind, issuance, or other transactions that result in transfer of crypto assets); (c) the parties involved in the transaction (identified by their names, addresses, tax domiciles, tax identification numbers in the RFB, and other registration information); (d) the type of crypto assets involved in the transaction; (e) the number of crypto assets traded, in units, to the tenth decimal place; (f) the total amount of the transaction, in Brazilian *Reais*, excluding the service fees charged for the execution of the transaction, if any; and (f) the amount of the service fees charged for the execution of the transaction, if any.

If the taxpayer does not comply with the abovementioned reporting obligations, up to 3% penalty would be imposed on the value corresponding to the omitted, inaccurate, or incomplete pieces of information.

(e) *Are crypto asset exchanges and wallet providers subject to CRS/FATCA reporting?*

Not in Brazil.

1.1.5 Civil and Criminal Tax Enforcement

(a) *What powers do the tax authorities have to compel the disclosure of information by third parties, such as exchanges or wallet providers, and have these been used in the past?*

Under Brazilian law, the tax authorities have the right to request the supply of information, which is relevant for the enforcement of taxes, from a person, even if it does not concern that person's own tax situation. Such requests have to be complied with and the information is to be provided truthfully to the best of knowledge and belief. The obligation to provide information includes the obligation to submit, or to allow the inspection of, written documents which are relevant for the determination of tax claims. The request must be addressed to specific facts or circumstances.

In the past there was a controversy on whether the tax authorities could request information from third parties, like financial institutions, for instance, without judicial authorization, if related to a specific matter under investigation. The Supreme Court (STF)[39] decided on the matter in the sense that a motivated request is enforceable before third parties and shall be complied with by third parties.

(b) What measures have the tax authorities undertaken in the past to ensure crypto tax compliance?

It is unknown what measures the Brazilian tax authorities have undertaken in the past to ensure crypto tax compliance, apart from publishing the Normative Ruling RFB No. 1,888/2019, which provided for the reporting obligations as clarified in section 1.1.4(c) and section 1.1.4(d) above.

(c) Are the tax authorities cooperating with tax authorities in other jurisdictions on enforcement?

Brazil is party to various Tax Information Exchange Agreements (TIEAs).[40] The TIEAs have supported the cooperation in other situations, such as Federal Police investigations.

Brazil is also a party to the Convention on Mutual Administrative Assistance in Tax Matters as well as to thirty-three double tax treaties. These agreements can be used as legal basis for exchange of information upon request or simultaneous tax inspections.

At this stage, there is no public information on whether Brazil is involved in any specific international cooperative action specifically targeting the holding crypto assets.

39. STF has decided under Lawsuits Nos 2,859, 2,390, 2,397 and 2,386 (*Ação Direta de Inconstitucionalidade* – ADIN) and Special Appeal (*Recurso Especial*) No. 601,314 that tax authorities have the power to obtain information from a financial institution provided that access is in line with banking secrecy laws and is made in the context of an administrative proceeding in course against the taxpayer. Access of information shall not require the granting of a judicial order.
40. United States of America (2007), United Kingdom (2012), Uruguay (2012), Bermuda (2012), Cayman (2013), Guernsey (2013), Jersey (2013) and Switzerland (2015). The TIEAs concluded with the United States, Switzerland, United Kingdom, and Jersey had been internalized by the National Congress (Decrees Nos 8,003/2013, 9,814/2019, 9,815/2019 and 9,969/2019).

Canada

Saam Nainifard & Angelo Gentile

1. COUNTRY GUIDES

1.1 Canada

1.1.1 Applicable Tax Law, Guidance, and Case Law

(a) Which laws, regulations, and other administrative guidance exist dealing with crypto assets?

The federal *Income Tax Act* (the '**Canadian Tax Act**'), the *Income Tax Regulations*, and the respective taxing statutes of Canada's provinces and territories contain the income tax rules that apply to transactions involving crypto assets. The federal *Excise Tax Act* (the '**Canadian Excise Tax Act**') - Canada's federal goods and services tax / harmonized sales tax (GST/HST) legislation - may also apply to such transactions.

At the time of publication, the Canadian Tax Act and provincial and territorial tax legislation do not include rules that specifically apply to transactions involving crypto assets. However, Canada's federal tax authority, the Canada Revenue Agency (CRA), has issued some administrative guidance on the subject.

With respect to Canada's VAT (i.e., the GST/HST) Canada's Department of Finance has drafted proposed legislation governing certain crypto assets at the time of writing. Such draft legislation is described below.

(b) Which court cases exist dealing with crypto assets?

At the time of publication, there are no reported federal or provincial tax cases that deal with the taxation of crypto assets.

In the experience of the authors, the CRA is aggressively auditing transactions involving crypto assets. The CRA has established internal policy guidelines with the goal of identifying and targeting crypto asset transactions. The authors expect tax disputes involving crypto assets will make their way to the Tax Court of Canada in the near future.

1.1.2 *Income and Capital Gains Taxes*

(a) How are crypto assets classified for income and capital gains tax purposes?

The classification of crypto assets as currency, securities, commodities, or some other property has been the subject of much debate among tax practitioners in Canada.[1] Although a consensus has not been reached on this particular question, the CRA has opined that crypto assets can be bought and sold like a commodity;[2] therefore, any resulting gain or loss on its disposition by a taxpayer could be realized on:

(a) income account as a sale of inventory of a business or an adventure or concern in the nature of trade carried on by the taxpayer; or
(b) capital account (taxable capital gains) from the disposition of a capital property of the taxpayer.

See section 1.1.2(d) below for a discussion on when crypto assets are held as inventory or capital property by a taxpayer.

A gain on income account is included in the computation of the taxpayer's profit[3] and fully taxable in the hands of the taxpayer. A business for Canadian income tax purposes includes an adventure or concern in the nature of trade;[4] therefore, even a single transaction in crypto assets may be considered a business for purpose of Canadian federal income taxation, depending on the facts.

Currently, capital gains are taxable at half the rates of ordinary income.[5] Due to the preferential tax treatment of capital gains, investors in crypto assets are generally inclined to characterize the gains they realize on the disposition of crypto assets as capital gains.[6] The authors expect this will be the subject of much litigation in the future.

---

1. For example, *see* Olivier Fournier and John J. Lennard, 'Rebooting Money: The Canadian Tax Treatment of Bitcoin and Other Cryptocurrencies,' in Report of Proceedings of the Sixty-Sixth Tax Conference, 2014 Conference Report (Toronto: Canadian Tax Foundation, 2015), 11:1-27.
2. CRA Document No. 2015-03-17.
3. Subsection 9 of the Canadian Tax Act. Profit is determined under well-accepted principles of business (or accounting) or 'well accepted principles of commercial trading' (*Symes*, [1994] 1 C.T.C. 40 (SCC), paragraph 43). These are usually but not always the same as generally accepted accounting principles (GAAP). The determination of profit is a question of law, not accounting, and must present an accurate picture of the taxpayer's income for a given year (*Candarel Ltd.*, [1998] 2 C.T.C. 35 (SCC)).
4. Canadian Tax Act, subsection 248(1), definition of 'business'.
5. Paragraph 38(a) and subsection 39(1) of the Canadian Tax Act.
6. The issue of whether gains are taxable on income or capital account is the most litigated subject in Canadian income tax. The authors expect that the CRA will challenge many reported capital gains realized on the sale of crypto assets as being gains that are taxable on income account.

(b) What are the income/capital gains tax consequences of selling crypto assets against fiat currency?

The tax treatment of a sale of crypto assets for fiat currency is treated in the same manner as a disposition of property for cash and ultimately depends on whether the crypto asset is held on income or capital account (*see* section 1.1.2(d) below for a discussion on when crypto assets are held on income or capital account).

A sale of crypto assets that are inventory (i.e., assets that are held on account of income) for fiat currency will give rise to income or a loss[7] computed as the difference between the value of the fiat currency, expressed in Canadian Dollars, and the taxpayer's cost in the crypto assets.

For purposes of computing a taxpayer's income for a taxation year from a business that is not an adventure or concern in the nature of trade,[8] crypto assets that are inventory must be valued at the end of the year at:

- the cost at which the taxpayer acquired the crypto assets or its fair market value at the end of the year, whichever is lower; or
- its fair market value at the end of the year.[9]

Accordingly, a taxpayer carrying on a business that is not an adventure or concern in the nature of trade may choose to write its crypto asset inventory up or down, thereby affecting the profit calculation for unrealized changes in value of the crypto assets.

If the business of the taxpayer is an adventure or concern in the nature of trade, the crypto assets must be valued at the cost at which the taxpayer acquired them.[10] Consequently, a taxpayer engaging in an adventure or concern in the nature of trade cannot write down crypto assets to affect the calculation of the taxpayer's profit when the value of the crypto assets decline.

A sale of crypto assets that are capital property (i.e., assets that are held on account of capital) of a taxpayer for fiat currency will give rise to a capital gain (half of which is taxable) or loss (half of which is allowable).[11] Where a taxpayer holds two or

7. The loss (non-capital loss) realized in a taxation year may be carried back three years or forward for the next twenty years to be applied against income in those years (paragraph 111(1)(a) of the Canadian Tax Act).
8. Generally, a person carries out an adventure or concern in the nature of trade when the person habitually does a thing that is capable of producing a profit notwithstanding that these activities may be quite separate and apart from the person's ordinary occupation (business). An example is that of a dentist who habitually buys and sells real estate. For more, *see* IT-459 – *Adventure or Concern in the Nature of Trade.*
9. Subsection 10(1) of the Canadian Tax Act and section 1801 of the *Income Tax Regulations.*
10. Subsection 10(1.01) of the Canadian Tax Act.
11. Generally, a capital gain on the sale of crypto assets would be the amount by which the value of the fiat currency, expressed in Canadian Dollars, exceeds the taxpayer's adjusted cost base in the crypto assets (i.e., the taxpayer's cost in the crypto asset that is adjusted up or down in accordance with subsections 53(1) and (2) of the Canadian Tax Act) and any outlays and expenses to the extent they are made or incurred by the taxpayer for the purpose of making the sale (paragraph 40(1) of the Canadian Tax Act). The taxpayer's taxable capital gain is half of the taxpayer's capital gain (paragraph 38(a) of the Canadian Tax Act).

more crypto assets of the same type, the crypto assets are treated as identical properties and the adjusted cost base is computed by taking the average of such adjusted cost bases.[12]

(c) *What are the income/capital gains tax consequences of exchanging crypto assets against other crypto assets?*

An exchange of one crypto asset for another is regarded as a barter exchange for Canadian federal income tax purposes.[13] In a barter exchange involving crypto assets, the fair market value of the crypto asset disposed of by a taxpayer, expressed in Canadian Dollars, is included in the computation of the taxpayer's income from a business if the crypto asset is inventory or the taxpayer is engaging in an adventure or concern in the nature of trade.[14] If the crypto asset is capital property of the taxpayer, the fair market value of the crypto asset forms the taxpayer's proceeds of disposition for purposes of computing the taxpayer's capital gain or loss.[15] In either case, the fair market value of the disposed crypto asset forms the taxpayer's cost in the consideration received.

(d) *If a distinction is made between business assets and non-business assets, when does trading in crypto assets lead to a trade or business?*

If a taxpayer is trading crypto assets with a subjective intention to profit and there is evidence of businesslike behaviour that supports the taxpayer's profit-motive (e.g., large volumes of purchase and sale transactions), then the taxpayer's trading activities should be considered a business.[16] In this case, gains realized on the sale of crypto assets will be taxed on account of income as a sale of inventory.

As mentioned, even a single speculative transaction may be considered an adventure or concern in the nature of trade, and therefore, a business for Canadian

Generally, the taxpayer's capital loss would be the amount by which the taxpayer's adjusted cost base in the crypto assets immediately before the sale and any outlays and expenses incurred by the taxpayer for the purpose of making the sale exceeds the amount of the fiat currency received by the taxpayer, expressed in Canadian Dollars (paragraph 40(1)(b) of the Canadian Tax Act). The amount of the taxpayer's allowable capital loss would be equal to half of the taxpayer's capital loss (paragraph 38(b) of the Canadian Tax Act). Any net capital losses (the amount of allowable capital losses that exceed the taxpayer's taxable capital gains in the year) may be carried back three years or forward indefinitely to be applied against capital gains in those years (paragraph 111(1)(b) of the Canadian Tax Act).

12. Subsection 47(1) of the Canadian Tax Act.
13. CRA Document Number 2014-0525191E5.
14. *Ibid.*
15. The volatility of crypto assets produces significant intra-day price swings. The price at the time a transaction occurs seems to be the most appropriate method of computing the tax result of the transaction. However, given the volatility, consider whether the average intra-day price of the crypto assets should be used.
16. *Stewart v. The Queen*, 2002 SCC 46. In this case, the court distinguished a business activity from a hobby, stating that 'in order for an activity to be classified as commercial in nature, the taxpayer must have the subjective intention to profit' and there must be evidence of 'business-like behaviour' that supports that intention.

income tax purposes. Due to the preferential tax treatment of capital gains under Canadian income tax law, taxpayers are motivated to characterize the gains they realize as being on account of capital. The courts have often grappled with the distinction between taxing gains on income account or capital account and a large body of case law has developed as a result. The key test from the jurisprudence to determine whether a taxpayer's dealings is on capital or income account is the taxpayer's subjective intention at the time of acquisition of the property in question,[17] including any secondary intention.[18] Other factors simply serve to either contradict or add credibility to the stated taxpayer's intentions with respect to the acquisition of property.[19] Accordingly, crypto assets that are acquired by a taxpayer for the purpose of resale are inventory of the taxpayer or held by the taxpayer in an adventure or concern in the nature of trade. Any resulting gains are taxed on account of income either as a disposition of inventory or as an adventure or concern in the nature of trade.[20] On the other hand, crypto assets that are acquired for investment purposes (i.e., to buy and hold) are capital property. Any resulting gains are taxed as capital gains.

The CRA has referred to paragraphs 9–32 of Interpretation Bulletin IT-479R, *Transactions in Securities*, as a tool in determining whether transactions are on income or capital account.[21] In particular, paragraph 11 provides CRA's view on some factors that suggest a taxpayer's course of conduct indicates the carrying on of a business, including an adventure or concern in the nature of trade:

(i) frequency of transactions: a history of extensive buying and selling crypto assets or of a quick turnover of crypto assets;
(ii) period of ownership: crypto assets are usually owned only for a short period of time;

17. *See Friesen (J.) v. Canada* (1995 3 SCR 103) at paragraph 44 where Major J. of the Supreme Court of Canada stated that in determining whether the gains from a sale of real estate are income or capital, particular emphasis is placed on the taxpayer's intention at the time of the initial purchase of the real estate. *See also Canada Safeway Ltd. v. R* (2008 2 CTC 149) at paragraph 43 where the Federal Court of Appeal stated the taxpayer's intention at the time of acquiring the property is the most determinative factor to determine whether a transaction constitutes an adventure in the nature of trade or a capital transaction.
18. *See* the leading case of *Regal Heights v. MNR* (1960 CTC 384), which was the first case in Canada to consider the doctrine of secondary intention. Put simply, the doctrine of secondary intention provides that if an asset is acquired with the intention of holding it as a long-term investment but a secondary intention exists at the time of purchase to sell the asset for a profit, the profit realized on a future sale of the asset will be considered income from an adventure or concern in the nature of trade if the secondary intention formed an operating motivation for the acquisition.
19. *See Happy Valley Farms Ltd. v. Minister of National Revenue* (1986 2 CTC 259) at paragraph 14 where the Federal Court of Canada (Trial Division) listed the following factors used by the courts in determining whether a gain is of an income or capital nature: (1) the nature of the property sold; (2) the length of period of ownership; (3) the frequency or number of other similar transactions taken by the taxpayer; (4) work expended on or in connection with the property realized; (5) the circumstances that were responsible for the sale of the property; and (6) motive. At paragraph 15, the Federal Court of Canada stated that while all these factors have been considered by the courts, it is the last one (i.e., motive or the taxpayer's intention in acquiring the property) that generally influences the finding of the court.
20. *Friesen, supra* n. 17 at paragraph 44.
21. Document Number 2015-03-17.

(iii) knowledge of crypto markets: the taxpayer has some knowledge of or experience in the crypto markets;
(iv) crypto transactions form a part of a taxpayer's ordinary business;
(v) time spent: a substantial part of the taxpayer's time is spent studying crypto markets and investigating potential purchases;
(vi) financing: crypto asset purchases are financed primarily on margin or by some other form of debt; and
(vii) advertising: the taxpayer advertises or makes it known that he is willing to purchase crypto assets.

There is a presumption that the purchase and sale of crypto assets by a corporation is made in the course of a business. The Federal Court of Appeal in *Weaver v. The Queen*[22] and *Ollenberger v. R.*[23] made reference to a corporation only requiring a minimum degree of activity to be considered to be carrying on a business. In *Ollenberger*, the Court used this reference to conclude that most, if not all, corporations are carrying on a business.

(e) *What are the income/capital gains tax consequences for an employee receiving wages or salaries in crypto assets?*

An employee's employment income for a taxation year is the salary, wages, and other remuneration, including gratuities, received by the employee in the year.[24] If an employee receives crypto assets from his/her employer as payment for salary, wages, or a bonus, the fair market value of the crypto assets at the time of receipt must be included in the employee's income.[25] The amount must be computed in Canadian Dollars. The employee will be subject to tax on the amount based on federal and applicable provincial or territorial marginal income tax rates.[26]

In addition, the value of any benefit of any kind whatever that is received or enjoyed by the employee or a person not dealing at arm's length with the employee in the year in respect of, in the course of, or by virtue of the employee's employment is included in the computation of the employee's income from an employment.[27] Thus, an employee who receives, for example, crypto assets from his employer at a discount would receive a taxable employment benefit.

22. 2008 FCA 238.
23. 2013 FCA 74.
24. Subsection 5(1) of the Canadian Tax Act.
25. CRA Document Number 2015-03-17.
26. The federal and provincial or territories governments each assess income tax on amounts earned or realized. Generally, personal tax rates on employment income will depend on the amount of income earned and the province in which the individual was resident on 31 Dec. of each year. The top combined federal and provincial tax rate on salary income for an individual resident in Ontario at the end of the year is 53.53%.
27. Subsection 6(1) of the Canadian Tax Act.

(f) What are the income/capital gains tax consequences for a merchant receiving payment in crypto assets?

A barter transaction occurs when two parties agree to exchange goods or services and carry out that exchange without using legal tender.[28] As crypto assets are not legal tender, it follows that when crypto assets are used to pay for, or is received as payment for, goods or services, the transaction is treated as a barter transaction.[29]

In a barter transaction between persons who are dealing with each other at arm's length, it is a fundamental principle in income tax law that each of those persons considers that the value of whatever is received is at least equal to the value of whatever is given up. In the view of the CRA, where an amount must be brought into income, that amount is the price that the taxpayer would normally have charged an arm's length person for the good or service provided.[30] Accordingly, a merchant that receives payment in crypto assets for goods or services is required to include in its income from a business the amount that the merchant would normally have charged an arm's length person. For Canadian tax purposes, the amount must be stated in Canadian Dollars.

Every payor, including a non-resident payor, who makes a payment of fees, commissions, or other amounts paid or allocated to a non-resident person in respect of services provided in Canada must withhold and remit 15% of the gross amount to the CRA.[31] The payor is required to withhold the amount even if the non-resident is not subject to tax in Canada under the terms of an applicable income tax treaty. A non-resident may avoid or reduce the amount of withholding on the payment by obtaining a waiver from the CRA.[32] Accordingly, a person who pays a non-resident merchant crypto assets for services provided in Canada is required to withhold and remit 15% of the fair market value of the payment to the CRA. The CRA will not accept a remittance of tax in crypto assets. Therefore, it is incumbent on the payer to withhold such number of crypto assets that would satisfy the withholding tax liability, liquidate the tokens on the market (which itself is a taxable event) and remit the proceeds to the CRA. The ability to liquidate the crypto assets and value the crypto assets to quantify the withholding tax amount is something the payor should consider before paying crypto to a non-resident service provider.

28. CRA Document Number 2018-0776611I7.
29. CRA Document Number 2013-0514701I7.
30. *Ibid.*
31. Section 105 of the *Income Tax Regulations*.
32. An application for a waiver from withholding under Regulation 105 must be submitted using Form R105.

(g) *What are the income/capital gains tax consequences of a loss of crypto assets?*

Lost or stolen crypto assets should give rise to a disposition of the crypto assets on the date the loss was discovered.[33] In situations where no compensation is received for the loss or theft of crypto assets, a loss is normally created for income tax purposes. Whether the loss is treated as a non-capital (business) loss or a capital loss depends on whether the crypto assets are inventory or capital property of a taxpayer, or whether the taxpayer carries on an adventure or concern in the nature of trade.

The CRA's published position is that a loss of trading assets, such as inventory, through theft or embezzlement, is normally deductible in computing income from a business if such losses are an inherent risk for carrying-on the business and the loss is reasonably incidental to the normal income-earning activities of the business.[34] The amount of the taxpayer's loss would normally be determined by reference to the cost of the inventory to the taxpayer less the amount of compensation received (e.g., insurance), if any.[35] In the experience of the authors, the CRA does not always follow this position, instead choosing to disallow the loss altogether.

(h) *What are the income/capital gains tax consequences of a loss in value of crypto assets?*

Generally, accrued losses on property do not give rise to a loss for income tax purposes. It is only when the loss is realized on a disposition of the asset that a loss is recognized for Canadian income tax purposes. However, inventory of a business carried on by a taxpayer that is not an adventure or concern in the nature of trade must be valued at the end of the year at the cost at which the taxpayer acquired the crypto assets or its fair market value at the end of the year, whichever is lower,[36] or its fair market value at the end of the year. Therefore, a taxpayer carrying on a business that is not an adventure or concern in the nature of trade[37] is afforded the unique ability to write down its crypto asset inventory to account for depressed crypto asset values when determining the profit of the business at the end of a fiscal period.

---

33. CRA Document Number 2014-0525191E5 states that the comments in IT-185R - Losses from Theft, Defalcation or Embezzlement are applicable to lost or stolen crypto assets. Paragraph 6 of IT-185R states that a loss will usually be deductible in computing income of the year in which the loss is discovered.
34. IT-185R (Consolidated), *Losses from Theft, Defalcation, or Embezzlement*.
35. CRA Document Number 2014-0525191E5.
36. Subsection 10(1) of the Canadian Tax Act.
37. If the business of the taxpayer is an adventure or concern in the nature of trade, the crypto assets must be valued at the cost at which the taxpayer acquired the property. The implication of this rule is that a taxpayer engaging in an adventure or concern in the nature of trade cannot write down crypto assets to affect its profit calculation when the value of the crypto assets declines.

(i) What are the income/capital gains tax consequences of forks of crypto assets?

A fork of crypto assets is a very new phenomenon which the Canadian Tax Act does not specifically contemplate through a tailored rule set that neatly applies to such transactions. There is also an absence of case law applicable to crypto asset forks, and the CRA's guidance on this point is similarly lacking at the time of writing.

Notwithstanding, it appears that a taxpayer who receives forked crypto assets in the course of a business or an adventure or concern in the nature of trade may be taxable on account of income. The amount that would be included in the income of the taxpayer would be the fair market value of the forked crypto assets at the time of receipt, expressed in Canadian Dollars. The cost in the new crypto assets would be the amount included in the income of the taxpayer from the fork. Practically, the value of the forked crypto assets may be hard to determine or it may even be worthless. It would be prudent for the taxpayer to support whatever valuation is used.

It is useful to analogize when considering novel transactions. To this end, crypto assets received from a fork where the taxpayer holds the original crypto assets as capital property may be analogous to the yield received on securities (e.g., interest on a bond) and therefore taxable as income from property.

Some non-Canadian commentators have suggested that forked crypto assets may be akin to a stock split, in which case there may not be significant tax consequences due to certain automatic rules that deem the transaction to be tax-deferred. However, given that crypto assets are not shares of a corporation, a split of the crypto asset would not be treated the same as a stock split for Canadian income tax purposes.

Without more guidance from the CRA or the courts, there is some ambiguity in the tax treatment of these types of transactions.

(j) What are the income/capital gains tax consequences of airdrops of crypto assets and are the tax consequences different if the airdropped tokens are unwanted?

In an airdrop, the administrators of a blockchain deliver a specified number of newly created crypto assets to persons already holding existing crypto assets that are or will be compatible with the blockchain, or to persons who meet specified criteria (e.g., persons holding more than a specified number of crypto assets). Generally, airdrops are delivered for free and are commonly used for marketing campaigns to create awareness for the new blockchain project. The creation of the crypto assets in an airdrop occurs the same way as in an ICO (except in an ICO the users pay for the crypto assets): the founder simply creates the crypto assets on the blockchain and then issues them to digital wallets meeting the specified criteria.[38]

38. Ron Dueck and Blake Allan, 'Taxation of the Token Economy: Cryptocurrency and DLT Tokens,' 2018 British Columbia Tax Conference (Toronto: Canadian Tax Foundation, 2018), 4:1-74.

If a taxpayer is employed or carries on a business for income tax purposes (including an adventure or concern in the nature of trade) and receives airdropped crypto assets in the course of the taxpayer's employment or business, the taxpayer must include the fair market value of the airdropped tokens, expressed in Canadian Dollars, in computing the income of the taxpayer from the employment[39] or business,[40] as the case may be. Practically, there is often difficulty in valuing airdropped tokens at the time of receipt, and in many instances airdropped crypto assets are worthless.

Airdropped crypto assets may be analogous to the yield received on investment assets. Accordingly, a receipt of airdropped crypto assets other than in the course of a business or by virtue of the taxpayer's employment may be taxable as income from property[41] if the crypto assets that prompt the airdrop are capital property of the taxpayer. In this case, the fair market value of the airdropped tokens would be included in computing the income of the taxpayer. The cost to the taxpayer in the airdropped crypto assets would be equal to the amount included in the taxpayer's income.

It does not matter if a taxpayer wishes to avoid receipt of airdropped crypto assets - - if the taxpayer receives value, he will be taxed.

(k) What are the income/capital gains tax consequences of (solo, pool, and cloud) mining?

Crypto assets received by a miner to validate transactions are consideration for services provided by the miner. Crypto miners are taxed depending on whether their mining activities constitute a personal activity (or hobby) or a business. If the mining activities are a hobby, the crypto assets received are not from a source of income for Canadian tax purposes and are therefore not taxable. The relevant test in distinguishing between a personal activity and a business was established by the Supreme Court of Canada in *Stewart v. Canada*.[42] Significant capital is required to mine crypto assets on an efficient basis; therefore, the CRA and Courts would be inclined to consider a taxpayer's mining activities as a business for Canadian income tax purposes. In this case, the value of mined crypto assets is to be included in the taxpayer's income at the time it is earned. The amount must be expressed in Canadian Dollars.

The CRA takes the position that where a taxpayer carries on a crypto mining business and is in receipt of crypto assets as a result, they must bring into income the value of the services rendered or the value of the crypto asset received, whichever is more readily valued.[43] The CRA says that in most cases it expects the value of the

39. Subsection 5(1) of the Canadian Tax Act.
40. The GAAP would include the amount of airdropped crypto assets in the computation of the taxpayer's profit from the business under section 9 of the Canadian Tax Act.
41. Computed on the basis of the taxpayer's profit pursuant to section 9 of the Canadian Tax Act.
42. 2002 SCC 46. In this case, the court distinguished a business activity from a hobby, stating that 'in order for an activity to be classified as commercial in nature, the taxpayer must have the subjective intention to profit' and there must be evidence of 'businesslike behaviour' that supports that intention.
43. 2018-0776661I7.

bitcoins received to be more readily valued than that of the services rendered, and accordingly, this is the amount to be brought into income.[44]

Every person who pays, in crypto or fiat, a non-resident miner fees, commissions, or other amounts in respect of mining services provided in Canada must withhold and remit 15% of the gross amount to the CRA.[45] The payor is required to withhold the amount even if the non-resident is not subject to tax in Canada under the terms of an applicable income tax treaty. The non-resident miner may avoid the amount of withholding on the payment by obtaining a waiver[46] from the CRA if its income from Canadian tax would be exempt pursuant to an applicable income tax treaty.[47] If the non-resident is not resident in a treaty jurisdiction or would be refused a waiver because the income is not exempt under the terms of am applicable treaty, then it can reduce the amount of the withhold if it can establish that its estimated Canadian tax payable is lower than the 15% withholding based on its estimated income and expenses from its Canadian operation.

(l) *What are the income/capital gains tax consequences of staking crypto assets?*

Proof of Work rewards a miner for solving complex equations. In Proof of Stake, the individual that creates the next block is randomly rewarded based on the amount of crypto assets a person 'stakes'.[48] Those who contribute to the Proof of Stake process may be regarded as earning crypto assets as a transaction fee, and the profit therefrom may be taxable as income from a business or property. Whether the taxpayer carries on a business or earns income from property depends on the degree of activity undertaken by the taxpayer in the process. The Federal Court of Appeal in both *Weaver v. The Queen*[49] and *Ollenberger v. The Queen*[50] made reference to a corporation only requiring a minimum degree of activity to be considered to be carrying on a business. In *Ollenberger*, the Court used this reference to conclude that most, if not all, corporations are carrying on a business. One may argue that the low threshold required to be carrying on a business includes all Proof of Stake activities.

On the other hand, the concept of earning income from property involves the ownership of a particular asset by a person and utilized by another person in exchange for an asset of monetary value. This is present in the Proof of Work and Proof of Stake

44. *Ibid.*
45. Section 105 of the *Income Tax Regulations.*
46. An application for a waiver from withholding under Regulation 105 must be submitted using Form R105.
47. Business profits would typically be exempt from taxation in Canada under Article 7 of an applicable income tax treaty on the basis that the business is not carried on through a permanent establishment in Canada.
48. For example, an individual decides to stake coins to earn some Proof of Stake rewards. The blockchain has a total of 1,000 coins in circulation. The individual purchases and stakes 100 coins. This means the individual has staked 10% of the total coins in circulation. The individual now has a 10% chance of winning every reward.
49. *Weaver v. The Queen*, 2008 FCA 238.
50. *Ollenberger v. The Queen*, 2013 FCA 74.

models. But when compared to the Proof of Work model, the Proof of Stake concept involves much less activity, requiring only the staking of crypto assets and the reward based on the stake by random chance. It is arguable that the receipt of crypto assets in staking is analogous to the yield on investment assets, which is regarded as income from property for Canadian income tax purposes. In this case, a payment of crypto assets by a Canadian person to a non-resident for crypto assets staked by the non-resident may be subject to withholding tax.[51]

(m) *What are the income/capital gains tax consequences of an indirect investment in crypto assets?*

An investment in an entity (e.g., a corporation, partnership, or trust) that holds crypto assets is treated as an investment in the entity itself, not in the underlying crypto assets. For example, an investor that acquires shares in a corporation that holds crypto assets would be regarded as a shareholder and subject to shareholder level tax on dividends received from the corporation or capital gains and losses on a disposition of the shares.

A taxpayer's investment in a foreign fund may be subject to the offshore investment property fund rules in section 94.1 of the Canadian Tax Act if one of the main reasons for the taxpayer acquiring, holding, or having the offshore investment property fund interest is to defer or reduce Canadian income tax.[52]

(n) *How is income from crypto assets to be treated under double tax treaty law?*

There are no special rules for the treatment of income earned or realized by a taxpayer from crypto assets under any of Canada's income tax treaties. Standard rules of treaty interpretation and application apply. For example, crypto assets received by a US resident in the course of mining bitcoin in Canada would be subject to tax in Canada based on the value of the bitcoins received to the extent that the mining activities are carried on through a permanent establishment in Canada.

Canada's income tax treaties also have a gains article, which states that gains derived by a contracting state of which the alienator is resident, other than gains

51. Under section 212 of the Canadian Tax Act, perhaps as a 'rent, royalty or similar payment' (paragraph 212(1)(d) of the Canadian Tax Act), including a payment 'for the use of or for the right to use in Canada any property, invention, ... plan, secret formula, process, or other thing whatever' (subparagraph 212(1)(d)(i) of the Canadian Tax Act).
52. Like traditional hedge funds, many crypto funds are domiciled in tax havens, with the Cayman Islands being the most popular location. Section 94.1 is an anti-avoidance rule aimed at Canadian residents who, motivated by tax considerations, invest in portfolio investments through a foreign entity (other than a controlled foreign affiliate). Where section 94.1 applies, the taxpayer is required to include in income a percentage (currently equal to the prescribed rate plus 2%) of the designated cost (generally the taxpayer's cost) of its investments on an annual basis, to the extent that this amount exceeds the taxpayer's income from the offshore investment property rules. The section 94.1 income inclusion increases the taxpayer's cost basis in the investment fund (e.g., shares or a partnership interest in the offshore fund), thereby reducing the taxpayer's gain otherwise arising on the disposition of the interest in the fund.

described in certain paragraphs, are taxable only in the contracting state of which the alienator is resident. The most common types of gains that Canada asserts taxing rights to are gains realized on the disposition of Canadian real estate and shares of a corporation or an interest in a partnership or trust that derives the majority of its value from Canadian real estate. Canada's tax treaties specify that any other gain is taxable only in the jurisdiction in which the alienator is resident. Accordingly, gains on crypto assets realized by a non-resident would not fall into the category of specific gains that Canada would assert taxing rights over.

(o) What are the income/capital gains tax consequences of selling crypto assets in an ICO/STO/IEO?

In a token offering through an ICO/STO/IEO, the founders will create tokens and sell them to investors for consideration to provide the founders with capital to develop their business in which the tokens will be used. The process of creating tokens will not result in any immediate tax consequence to the founder.

The Act does not expressly contemplate the economic reality of this situation, which is fundamentally a capital raise by an ICO. However, where an issuer conducts an ICO for an application that is functional at the time of issuance, the sale may constitute a sale of either a licence or a sale of a service, depending on the access terms of the token.[53] In either case, the proceeds of sale would be characterized as business income to the vendor. In this model, the acquisition cost to the token purchasers would generally constitute the tax cost of inventory if the token was purchased for the purpose of resale, or the cost of a Class 14 depreciable property if the token was purchased to use the licence for an income-earning purpose.[54] If the investor acquires the token outside the scope of business and does not intend to use it for the purpose of earning income or resale, then the token would be a capital asset to the investor[55] and the amount paid to acquire the token would form the investor's adjusted cost base in the token.

53. Ron Dueck and Blake Allan, 'Taxation of the Token Economy: Cryptocurrency and DLT Tokens,' 2018 British Columbia Tax Conference (Toronto: Canadian Tax Foundation, 2018), 4:1-74.
54. Section 1102(1)(c) of the *Income Tax Regulations* states that depreciable property does not include property that was not acquired by the taxpayer for the purpose of gaining or producing income.

    The cost to the purchaser of a Class 14 depreciable property is apportioned over the life of the asset, and such amount as is apportioned for the year may be deducted in computing the income of the purchaser from the business each year (paragraph 1100(1(c) of the *Income Tax Regulations*).
55. Depreciable property must be acquired for the purpose of earning income from a business or property.

1.1.3 Other Taxes

(a) What are the value added tax/sales tax consequences of selling crypto assets?

All crypto assets are unique. Depending on the attributes of the crypto asset, the GST/HST treatment of that asset may change.

The Canadian Excise Tax Act does not, at present, include any provisions that specifically address crypto asset transactions. Nevertheless, the Canadian Department of Finance announced draft legislation in May 2019 to amend the *Excise Tax Act*.[56] If enacted, the legislation will have a significant impact on the GST/HST treatment of crypto assets.

Under the law currently in force, the CRA considers crypto assets to be commodities rather than 'money'.[57] As a consequence, GST/HST registrants who sell crypto assets must collect and remit GST/HST on the fair market value of the crypto assets sold, and persons who purchase other goods or services with crypto assets are considered to have made a barter transaction and must collect and remit GST/HST on the fair market value of the crypto assets used to purchase such goods or services.[58] Moreover, non-registrants who acquire crypto assets to spend as money will generally experience double-tax when acquiring crypto assets from Canadian providers (i.e., unrecoverable GST/HST arises on the acquisition of the crypto asset, and again when the crypto asset is spent to acquire property or services). This may create an incentive to source crypto assets from non-residents of Canada, as non-residents who are not registered for GST/HST and are not carrying on business in Canada for GST/HST purposes are not required to charge or collect any GST/HST on crypto asset sales.

If the draft legislation is enacted, a new definition will be added to the *Excise Tax Act* for 'virtual payment instruments' (VPIs). All VPIs would be included in the definition of 'financial instrument', and not in the definition of 'money'. This means that transactions for the purchase of, or concluded by the use of, such VPIs would be exempt from any GST/HST. The proposed definition of 'virtual payment instrument' is:

---

56. *See Draft Legislation Relating to the Excise Tax Act and Explanatory Notes*, Department of Finance Canada, May 2019, retrieved on 6 Apr. 2020, https://fin.canada.ca/drleg-apl/2019/gst-hst-tps-tvh-eng.html.
57. *See CRA Views, Interpretation – internal, 2013-0514701I7 – Bitcoins*, 23 Dec. 2013. *See Guide for cryptocurrency users and tax officials*, Canada Revenue Agency, June 2019, retrieved on 6 Apr. 2020, https://www.canada.ca/en/revenue-agency/programs/about-canada-revenue-agency-cra/compliance/digital-currency/cryptocurrency-guide.html. The definition of 'money' in subsection 123(1) of the *Excise Tax Act* reads as follows: '*money* includes any currency, cheque, promissory note, letter of credit, draft, traveller's cheque, bill of exchange, postal note, money order, postal remittance and other similar instrument, whether Canadian or foreign, but does not include currency the fair market value of which exceeds its stated value as legal tender in the country of issuance or currency that is supplied or held for its numismatic value.'
58. *See* archived IT-490 *Barter Transactions*, Canada Revenue Agency, 5 Jul. 1982, retrieved on 6 Apr. 2020, https://www.canada.ca/en/revenue-agency/services/forms-publications/publications/it490/archived-barter-transactions.html.

virtual payment instrument means property that is a digital representation of value, that functions as a medium of exchange and that only exists at a digital address of a publicly distributed ledger, other than property that:

(a) confers a right, whether immediate or future and whether absolute or contingent, to be exchanged or redeemed for money or specific property or services or to be converted into money or specific property or services;
(b) is primarily for use within, or as part of, a gaming platform, an affinity or rewards program or a similar platform or program; or
(c) is prescribed property.

Many crypto assets will fall within this proposed definition, particularly those that rely on blockchain technology. However, not all crypto assets will meet this definition, and it is possible that some cryptocurrencies will not meet every requirement. For example, if the crypto asset relies on a private ledger and not a publicly distributed ledger, it will not be a 'VPI' under the proposed definition.

Although 'utility tokens' (a crypto asset that can be exchanged for various goods and services), cryptocurrencies backed by hard assets or money, and digital gaming 'coins' are not covered by the proposed amendments, such cryptocurrencies may be subject to the existing GST/HST rules respecting gift certificates, reward programs, or coupons.

By transforming certain cryptocurrencies into financial instruments, the proposed amendments make the sale in Canada of qualifying cryptocurrencies into an exempt supply of financial services. Following enactment, input tax credits would no longer be available for GST/HST paid in selling qualifying cryptocurrencies, and anyone who is a dealer in these assets will become a listed financial institution under subsection 149(1) of the ETA if their 'principal business is as a trader or dealer in, or as a broker or salesperson of' VPIs. If such a listed financial institution operates in multiple provinces, it will also be a 'selected listed financial institution' (SLFI) and have to start using the complicated 'special attribution method' (SAM) calculations to determine its net tax.

The proposed amendments do not specifically contemplate the activities of crypto asset 'miners' who verify transactions in a blockchain. If the miner's supplies are characterized as the service of 'endorsement' of or 'processing' a financial instrument (i.e., the VPI), then the miner's supplies would be exempt, and the GST/HST paid by the miner in respect of crypto mining activities would be unrecoverable. CPA Canada has suggested that miner activity is best compared with mining precious metals, and so legislation should be enacted to treat their supplies similarly (i.e., both as zero-rated supplies). No such draft legislation has yet been proposed. Notably, under the existing rules, the activities of a crypto miner would constitute 'commercial activity' rather than 'exempt activity', and the crypto miner should be entitled to fully recover all GST/HST paid on expenses/inputs in conducting such mining activities.

The GST/HST treatment of non-VPI crypto assets would depend on the attributes of the crypto asset in question. If the crypto asset entitles the holder to dividends or interest, such crypto asset might be considered a financial instrument on account of being a debt security or equity security. In that case, the sales of the crypto asset might nevertheless be exempt supplies of financial services.

Importantly, the proposed legislative amendments have not yet been enacted into law, and further changes to the definition may be proposed in the interim. Accordingly, it is necessary to consult with a Canadian GST/HST advisor if contemplating future transactions involving crypto assets in Canada.

As a final note, it should be noted that the Province of Quebec has its own separate value added tax (the Quebec Sales Tax, or QST) that largely mirrors the application of the federal GST/HST. Accordingly, with the exception of the proposed legislative amendments to the federal *Excise Tax Act* (which would not apply to QST), the same rules that apply with respect to GST/HST would also apply to QST in Quebec.

(b) Are payments in crypto assets subject to withholding taxes?

Generally, the Canadian Tax Act imposes a flat tax of 25% (subject to reduction pursuant to the terms of an applicable income tax treaty) on a non-resident person on every amount that a person resident in Canada pays or credits to the non-resident person for certain items, including management fees, certain interest payments, estate or trust income, rents, royalties, and dividends.[59] A non-resident that receives a payment of crypto assets from a person resident in Canada on account of such items would be subject to the 25% flat tax (subject to reduction under the terms of an applicable income tax treaty).

The Canadian Tax Act imposes an obligation on the person paying the foregoing amount to the non-resident to deduct and withhold from the payment the amount of tax that is applicable and remit the amount to the CRA on the fifteenth day of the month following the month in which the payment occurs.[60] If the Canadian-resident does not remit the full amount of tax, he is liable to pay the amount owing.[61] This is known as 'withholding tax'.

The CRA will not accept a remittance of withholding tax in crypto assets. Therefore, it is incumbent on the Canadian-resident payer to withhold such number of crypto assets that would satisfy the withholding tax liability, liquidate the tokens on the market (which itself is a taxable event) and remit the proceeds to the CRA. The ability to liquidate the crypto assets and value the crypto assets to quantify the withholding tax amount is something a Canadian-resident payor should consider before paying an amount to a non-resident in crypto assets.

59. Subsection 212(1) of the Canadian Tax Act.
60. Subsection 215(1) of the Canadian Tax Act.
61. Subsection 215(6) of the Canadian Tax Act.

(c) *Does payment of compensation in crypto assets give rise to payroll tax consequences?*

Every person that pays salary, wages or other remunerations at any time in a taxation year to an employee must deduct and withhold from the payment the appropriate amount of income tax,[62] Canada Pension Plan, and employment insurance contributions. Section 102 of the *Income Tax Regulations* provides rules in determining the amount of income tax that must be withheld. If an employee is remunerated with crypto assets, the employer should deduct and withhold from the payment such number of crypto assets with a value equal to the amount that must be withheld and deducted.

The CRA will not accept a remittance of payroll source deductions in crypto assets. Therefore, it is incumbent on the employer to withhold such number of crypto assets that would satisfy the employer's liability for income tax payroll deductions, liquidate the tokens on the market (which itself is a taxable event) and remit the proceeds to the CRA. The ability to liquidate the crypto assets and value the crypto assets paid to the employee to quantify the amount to be remitted is something the employer should consider before paying remuneration to the employee in the form of crypto assets.

(d) *Do transactions with crypto assets trigger any transfer taxes?*

Canada does not assess transfer taxes separate and apart from the GST/HST (and QST in Quebec). No other federal legislation governs the taxation of crypto assets. The Canadian provinces of British Columbia, Saskatchewan, and Manitoba have separate standalone provincial sales tax statutes that govern the taxation of tangible personal property and certain services in those provinces, but none of them would apply to crypto assets, which would almost certainly be regarded as intangible personal property.

(e) *Are firms operating in the crypto space subject to digital service taxes?*

Canada does not have a digital services tax at the time of publication. However, Prime Minister Justin Trudeau's Government promised during Canada's recent national election campaign in 2019 to impose a 3 % digital services tax on digital companies with worldwide revenues of at least CAD 1 billion and Canadian revenues of more than CAD 40 million. It is unlikely that any one firm operating in the crypto space would be subject to such a Canadian digital services tax given the high revenue thresholds.

62. Paragraph 153(1)(a) of the Canadian Tax Act and section 102 of the *Income Tax Regulations*.

(f) *Are crypto assets subject to gift, inheritance, estate, or wealth taxes?*

Canada does not levy a gift, inheritance, estate, or wealth tax. However, a person who gifts crypto assets would be deemed to receive proceeds equal to the fair market value of the property, thereby realizing any accrued gains on the gifted crypto assets.[63] Moreover, the Canadian Tax Act generally deems an individual to dispose of all of his capital property immediately before death.[64] Crypto assets that are capital property of an individual would be subject to this rule immediately before the individual's death. As a result, any accrued gains on the crypto assets would be realized and tax would be payable by the deceased for the year. The estate trustee of the deceased should determine the adjusted cost base and value if the crypto assets at the time of the individual's death to quantify the capital gain realized in the year of death.

If a taxpayer's estate includes crypto assets and the administration of a deceased individual's estate requires the granting of probate, probate fees may be payable on the value of the crypto assets owned by the deceased individual at the time of death based on applicable provincial rates.

(g) *Are crypto assets subject to exit tax?*

Generally, individuals (including trusts) and corporations are deemed to dispose of all of their assets at fair market value immediately before ceasing to be resident in Canada.[65] The taxpayer is deemed to reacquire the assets immediately after such time at such cost.[66] This rule would operate to realize and tax any gains accruing on crypto assets during the time an individual (including a trust) or corporation is resident in Canada.

A corporation which emigrates from Canada is generally subject to an additional tax under section 219.1 equal to 25% of the difference between the fair market value of all the property of the corporation and the paid-up capital of the shares of the corporation. The rate of tax may be reduced from 25% under certain circumstances.

(h) *Can mining trigger gambling tax?*

Canada does not assess income tax or specialized taxes on windfalls from gambling earnings.

63. Section 69(1)(b) of the Canadian Tax Act. The recipient of the gift would be deemed to receive the crypto assets equal to such fair market value, which results in a stepped up cost in the property.
64. A similar rule applies for depreciable property in subsection 104(5) of the Canadian Tax Act.
65. Paragraph 128.1(4)(b) of the Canadian Tax Act. The volatility of crypto assets produces significant intra-day price swings. The price at the time of the taxpayer's departure seems to be the most appropriate method of computing the tax result on ceasing to be resident in Canada. However, given the volatility, consider whether the average intra-day price of the crypto assets should be used.
66. Paragraph 128.1(4)(c) of the Canadian Tax Act.

It may be difficult for a taxpayer to argue that mined crypto assets are received as a non-taxable windfall from gambling. If gambling activities are undertaken with a degree of professionalism or commerciality, the gambling activities may constitute a business for income tax purposes and the gambling earnings will be subject to tax based on the profits earned therefrom.

1.1.4 Compliance and Documentation Obligations

(a) What documentation requirements exist for taxpayers regarding crypto assets and are there best practices in recordkeeping to support representations made in tax returns?

The rules governing documentation and recordkeeping requirements in respect of taxpayers trading in (or utilizing) crypto assets are no different than the rules that apply with respect to all businesses or taxpayers operating in Canada. Every business or taxpayer must maintain sufficient books and records to enable the Canadian taxation authorities to verify all amounts reported or reportable in the required income tax or GST/HST returns. Such records must generally be kept for at least six years after the end of the taxation year to which the records relate, and such records may constitute a combination of paper and digital records, paper records alone, or digital records alone.

The Canadian taxation authorities have the power to request any document from a taxpayer that will enable them to determine amounts that were or ought to have been reported. They also have the power to send out questionnaires to persons they suspect have traded in crypto assets, for purposes of determining if a full-blown audit is required.

In the case of businesses engaged in trading crypto assets, certainly the digital wallet constitutes a key piece of evidence. However, it is also prudent to maintain back-ups or contemporaneous manual (paper or digital) transcriptions of crypto asset transactions in the event the digital wallet is lost or is no longer accessible.

(b) What is the evidentiary burden of supporting tax positions when a digital wallet address is lost or shared with other persons?

If a digital wallet is lost, and the taxpayer has other evidences to support its tax filing positions (e.g., daily, monthly, or yearly manual transcriptions of all crypto asset transactions), the taxpayer may rely on such indirect evidence in the event of an audit or review. Practical issues arise where the taxpayer has not maintained *any* other evidence of crypto asset transactions, since Canadian tax authorities are entitled to make assumptions when proposing and issuing assessments, and it is generally up to the taxpayer to disprove the assumption (unless the assumption relates to the decision to re-open statute-barred taxation years, in which case the evidentiary burden is on the Canadian tax authorities). Auditors may then have regard to secondary audit techniques, such as net worth audits or bank account deposit/withdrawal analyses, to try to determine any unreported income or tax. In the absence of any evidence supporting the crypto asset transactions, it is often challenging to disprove assumptions underpinning such assessments.

If a digital wallet is shared between persons, it is the responsibility of each person to maintain records of his or her own crypto asset transactions. Otherwise, the Canadian tax authorities may make the initial assumption that all transactions in a shared wallet belong to only one of the persons who use it.

(c) Are crypto asset exchanges and wallet providers subject to reporting obligations?

Crypto asset exchanges and wallet providers are not subject to special tax reporting obligations over and above the usual Canadian tax reporting obligations (if any) of any person conducting business in Canada or selling to Canadians. However, crypto asset exchanges or wallet providers may receive formal 'requirements' to provide information pursuant to section 231.2 of the Canadian Tax Act or section 289 of the Canadian Excise Tax Act. Such powers are described below, under section 1.1.5(a).

(d) Are taxpayers holding crypto assets subject to reporting obligations apart from the filing of income tax/capital gains tax returns?

Canadian taxpayers that hold crypto assets directly or through funds should consider their filing obligations under the foreign property reporting rules in section 233.3 of the Canadian Tax Act if the crypto assets are situated, deposited, or held outside of Canada. The CRA considers that crypto assets are funds or intangible property and therefore 'specified foreign property'.[67] Further, the CRA is of the view that the interest in a foreign partnership that invests in crypto assets (to the extent the partnership is not a 'specified Canadian entity')[68] is also a 'specified foreign property'.[69] Therefore, where the cost amount of such crypto assets exceed CAD 100,000 at any time in the year and the crypto asset is not used or held exclusively in the course of carrying on an active business, the taxpayer must file Form T1135 with the CRA to report the property. These reporting obligations must be carefully considered given the CRA's automatic application of the late filing penalty of CAD 2,500 in subsection 162(7) of the Canadian Tax Act (after 100 days) and the six-year normal reassessment period under paragraph 152(4)(b.2) of the Canadian Tax Act.[70]

67. CRA Views 2014-0561061E5, 'Specified Foreign Property' (16 Apr. 2015). Query what the CRA means by funds given its position that crypto assets do not constitute currency. Further, this position seems questionable given the central location of crypto assets remains ambiguous.
68. A partnership is a specified Canadian entity if, pursuant to paragraph (b) of the definition of 'specified Canadian entity' in subsection 233.3(1) of the Act, the total of all non-resident members' shares of the income or loss of the partnership for the fiscal period is less than 90% of the total income or loss of the partnership for the period.
69. CRA Views 2014-0561061E5.
70. CRA Views 2015-0588971C6. The CRA indicated that this position still applies, APFF Financial Strategies and Instruments Roundtable, Q. 14 (6 Oct. 2017).

(e) Are crypto asset exchanges and wallet providers subject to CRS/FATCA reporting?

Many assume that crypto assets are invisible to tax authorities. However, FATCA and CRS may frustrate this ideal and require crypto asset exchanges and digital wallet service providers to disclose information about its customers to the US (in the case of FATCA) and foreign tax authorities (in the case of CRS). The question, however, is far from clear, and the CRA has not issued any guidance on this point.

Among other things, FATCA and CRS obligations apply to institutions that hold deposits or financial assets on behalf of customers. Crypto assets may be treated as financial assets insofar as their value is derived from a contractual claim, and they are bought and sold on public exchanges, similar to securities, which are financial assets. Crypto assets may also be currency for FATCA and CRS purposes. Accordingly, crypto asset exchanges and digital wallet service providers may fall within the purview of the FATCA and CRS regimes. At the time of publication, there is no public information about the approach Canadian crypto asset exchanges and wallet providers have taken to meet their potential FATCA and CRS obligations.

1.1.5 *Civil and Criminal Tax Enforcement*

(a) What powers do the tax authorities have to compel the disclosure of information by third parties, such as exchanges or wallet providers, and have these been used in the past?

Canadian tax authorities have the power to issue formal 'requirements' to exchanges or wallet providers, in an effort to gain information regarding named or unnamed persons (if seeking information on unnamed persons, the Canadian tax authorities need to obtain prior judicial authorization to do so, although such authorization is often granted). A third party who receives a 'requirement' letter is well advised to seek Canadian legal advice immediately, as such letters typically provide thirty days to respond and a failure to respond may result in the Canadian tax authorities seeking a compliance order in Federal Court. Of course, the practical implications of such remedies will vary depending on whether the exchange or wallet provider is Canadian-based or foreign-based.

(b) What measures have the tax authorities undertaken in the past to ensure crypto tax compliance?

The CRA has established internal policy guidelines with the goal of identifying and targeting crypto asset transactions.

In the 2019 Canadian Federal Budget, the Department of Finance stated that it would provide the CRA with approximately CAD 317 million of additional funding over five years to support various initiatives, including CAD 150.8 million to fund new initiatives and extend existing programmes aimed at tax evasion and aggressive tax avoidance, including programmes aimed at crypto asset transactions and the digital economy.

(c) *Are the tax authorities cooperating with tax authorities in other jurisdictions on enforcement?*

Leaders of tax enforcement authorities from Australia, Canada, the Netherlands, the United Kingdom, and the United States have established a joint operational group – the Joint Chiefs of Global Tax Enforcement (J5) – to increase collaboration in the fight against international and transnational tax crime and money laundering. At a press conference in 2019, Joanne Charbonneau, the Director General of the Canada Revenue Agency, said:

> The formation of the J5 demonstrates the serious commitment of governments around the globe in enhancing international cooperation in fighting serious international tax and financial crimes, money laundering, and cybercrime through the use of cryptocurrencies. The J5 complements the important international work of the OECD through operational collaboration. Our collative efforts and experience will be shared to jointly identify an address the increasingly sophisticated and global schemes and the professional enablers that facilitate such schemes.

The authors expect that as crypto asset transactions increase, so will domestic and multilateral enforcement measures.

Cayman Islands

Bradley Kruger & Michael Robinson

1. COUNTRY GUIDES

1.1 Cayman Islands

1.1.1 Applicable Tax Law, Guidance, and Case Law

(a) Which laws, regulations, and other administrative guidance exist dealing with crypto assets?

On 20 May 2020, the Cayman Islands Government enacted the Virtual Assets (Service Providers) Law, 2020 (the **VASP Law**), which will come into force upon issue of a commencement order. The VASP Law provides a framework for the regulation of 'virtual asset services'. These services include the issuance of virtual assets and the business of providing one or more of the following services for or on behalf of a third party: (a) exchange between virtual assets and fiat currencies; (b) exchange between one or more other forms of convertible virtual assets; (c) transfer of virtual assets; (d) virtual asset custody service; or (e) participation in, and provision of, financial services related to a virtual asset issuance or the sale of a virtual asset.

With the exception of virtual asset issuances, the VASP Law will only affect persons that carry out virtual asset services as a business or in the course of a business for or on behalf of other persons. It does not appear to affect persons that carry out those functions for and on behalf of themselves. With regard to virtual asset issuances, this distinction does not apply. This means that most issuers of virtual assets for their own benefit will be subject to the VASP Law.

It should also be noted that a 'virtual asset' is defined as a digital representation of value that can be digitally traded or transferred and can be used for payment or investment purposes but does not include a digital representation of fiat currencies.

While this wide definition likely captures all cryptocurrencies, security tokens, utility tokens or other digital assets, it excludes tokens that are not tradeable or transferable.

Businesses providing custodial services for virtual assets and businesses that operate or intend to operate a virtual asset transfer platform will require a licence. All other persons carrying on or intending to carry on virtual asset services will require registration.

In addition to the VASP Law, the Government has also amended a number of existing laws to contemplate virtual assets. These include the Mutual Funds Law (Revised) (**MF Law**) and the Securities Investment Business Law (Revised) (**SIB Law**). These amendments are expected to come into force at the same time as the VASP Law. Under the MF Law, the result of the amendments now means that mutual funds issuing redeemable tokens instead of shares or other equity interests will be caught by the MF Law and will need to be registered or licensed under that law. Under the SIB Law, persons dealing in, arranging deals in, managing or advising on virtual assets that are securities will also be required to register or be licensed under the SIB Law. Certain significant exemptions (e.g., for issuers that issue their own security tokens) apply in each case.

Finally, the Proceeds of Crime Law (2020 Revision) (**PCL**) and the Anti-Money Laundering Regulations (2020 Revision) also contemplate virtual assets. The PCL was the first law in the Cayman Islands to contemplate virtual assets and the definitions used therein differ slightly to those used in the VASP Law. CIMA has issued specific anti-money laundering related guidance to virtual asset service providers and the standards of compliance it expects for businesses carrying on virtual asset services. Furthermore, under the most recent amendments, new regulatory requirements will be put in place to ensure sufficient information is obtained relating to transfers of virtual assets by intermediaries.

(b) Which court cases exist dealing with crypto assets?

There have been no court cases in the Cayman Islands dealing with crypto assets. However, English common law is often applied in the absence of any case law in the Cayman Islands. The recent English High Court case of *AA v. Persons Unknown*, which found that crypto assets such as Bitcoin are 'property' and therefore capable of being the subject of a proprietary injunction or freezing order, will likely apply.

1.1.2 Income and Capital Gains Taxes

(a) How are crypto assets classified for income and capital gains tax purposes?

The Cayman Islands currently levies no taxes on individuals or corporations based upon profits, income, gains, or appreciation. Therefore, there is no resultant classification of crypto assets for these purposes.

Under Cayman law, crypto assets are not regarded as securities unless the crypto asset represents a security (as such term is defined in the SIB Law). The definition of securities under the SIB Law is narrow and so most crypto assets would not be regarded as securities. Crypto assets are not regarded as currencies.

(b) *What are the income/capital gains tax consequences of selling crypto assets against fiat currency?*

The Cayman Islands currently levies no taxes on individuals or corporations based upon profits, income, gains, or appreciation. Therefore, there are no tax consequences of selling crypto assets against fiat currency. However, where a person seeks to sell crypto assets against fiat currency for and on behalf of a third party, such person will be required to register under the VASP Law (and will require a licence where such services include any custodial services).

(c) *What are the income/capital gains tax consequences of exchanging crypto assets against other crypto assets?*

The Cayman Islands currently levies no taxes on individuals or corporations based upon profits, income, gains, or appreciation. Therefore, there are no tax consequences of exchanging crypto assets against other crypto assets. However, where a person seeks to exchange crypto assets against other crypto assets for and on behalf of a third party, such person will be required to register under the VASP Law (and will require a licence where such services include any custodial services).

(d) *If a distinction is made between business assets and non-business assets, when does trading in crypto assets lead to a trade or business?*

No distinction is made between business assets and non-business assets in the Cayman Islands.

(e) *What are the income/capital gains tax consequences for an employee receiving wages or salaries in crypto assets?*

The Cayman Islands currently levies no taxes on individuals or corporations based upon profits, income, gains, or appreciation. Therefore, there are no tax consequences for an employee receiving wages or salaries in crypto assets.

There are no restrictions in the Cayman Islands for paying employees in crypto assets. Businesses should be mindful of the VASP Law when issuing newly minted crypto assets to their employees in the form of wages or salaries to ensure that it is not a 'virtual asset issuance'.

(f) What are the income/capital gains tax consequences for a merchant receiving payment in crypto assets?

The Cayman Islands currently levies no taxes on individuals or corporations based upon profits, income, gains, or appreciation. Therefore, there are no tax consequences for a merchant receiving payment in crypto assets.

There are no restrictions in the Cayman Islands for merchants receiving crypto assets as payment provided that payment is not for or on behalf of a third party (in which case, the merchant may be required to comply with the VASP Law).

(g) What are the income/capital gains tax consequences of a loss of crypto assets?

The Cayman Islands currently levies no taxes on individuals or corporations based upon profits, income, gains, or appreciation. Therefore, there are no tax consequences for a loss of crypto assets.

(h) What are the income/capital gains tax consequences of a loss in value of crypto assets?

The Cayman Islands currently levies no taxes on individuals or corporations based upon profits, income, gains, or appreciation. Therefore, there are no tax consequences for a loss in value of crypto assets.

(i) What are the income/capital gains tax consequences of forks of crypto assets?

The Cayman Islands currently levies no taxes on individuals or corporations based upon profits, income, gains, or appreciation. Therefore, there are no tax consequences for forks of crypto assets.

(j) What are the income/capital gains tax consequences of airdrops of crypto assets and are the tax consequences different if the airdropped tokens are unwanted?

The Cayman Islands currently levies no taxes on individuals or corporations based upon profits, income, gains, or appreciation. Therefore, there are no tax consequences for airdrops of crypto assets or if the airdropped tokens are unwanted.

An airdrop of crypto assets by a token issuer will not be considered a 'virtual asset issuance' under the VASP Law so long as the token issuer receives no consideration for the airdrop.

(k) *What are the income/capital gains tax consequences of (solo, pool, and cloud) mining?*

The Cayman Islands currently levies no taxes on individuals or corporations based upon profits, income, gains, or appreciation. Therefore, there are no tax consequences of (solo, pool, and cloud) mining.

(l) *What are the income/capital gains tax consequences of staking crypto assets?*

The Cayman Islands currently levies no taxes on individuals or corporations based upon profits, income, gains, or appreciation. Therefore, there are no tax consequences for staking crypto assets.

Provided that crypto assets are staked for a person's own benefit, the staking of tokens will not trigger the VASP Law. However, where tokens are staked for and on behalf of another person, the VASP Law may become relevant. Where a business wishes to operate a staking business or staking pool, this activity may engage with the VASP Law.

(m) *What are the income/capital gains tax consequences of an indirect investment in crypto assets?*

The Cayman Islands currently levies no taxes on individuals or corporations based upon profits, income, gains, or appreciation. Therefore, there are no tax consequences of an indirect investment in crypto assets.

The VASP would not affect any person seeking to invest in crypto assets directly or indirectly, so long as the investment was made by that person for his/her own benefit.

(n) *How is income from crypto assets to be treated under double tax treaty law?*

Double tax treaty law is not relevant in the Cayman Islands, because no income taxes are imposed on individuals or corporations in the Cayman Islands.

(o) *What are the income/capital gains tax consequences of selling crypto assets in an ICO/STO/IEO?*

The Cayman Islands currently levies no taxes on individuals or corporations based upon profits, income, gains, or appreciation. Therefore, there are no tax consequences of selling crypto assets in an ICO/STO/IEO.

Most ICOs, STOs, and IEOs are likely to be 'virtual asset issuances' under the VASP Law where: (a) the crypto asset is exchanged for some form of consideration and (b) the crypto asset is tradeable, exchangeable, or transferable.

A 'virtual asset issuance' means the sale of newly created virtual assets to the public in or from within the Cayman Islands in exchange for fiat currency, other virtual assets or other considerations but does not include the sale of virtual service tokens.

The term 'newly created virtual assets' means virtual assets which have never been sold, offered, or distributed to the public. Accordingly, the resale of tokens that have already been issued would not be a virtual asset issuance.

The term 'public' is not defined and therefore should be interpreted with caution and given a broad meaning. However, limited private sales to owners, affiliates, and employees will likely not be within scope of the meaning of a virtual asset issuance. Furthermore, as the definition is limited to sales for consideration, airdrops and bonus issues should also be excluded.

The definition of 'virtual service tokens' is narrow and means a digital representation of value which is not transferrable or exchangeable with a third party at any time and includes digital tokens whose sole function is to provide access to an application or service or to provide a service or function directly to its owner.

Persons wishing to issue virtual assets from or within the Cayman Islands must first register with the Cayman Islands Monetary Authority (**CIMA**). Once registered, and prior to issuance, they must then submit a request to CIMA for the approval of a virtual asset issuance and the issuance must not exceed a prescribed threshold that will be an amount in fiat currency that can be raised by an issuer within a given timeframe. Such threshold has not yet been announced. Issuers that intend to raise funds over the prescribed threshold will be required to conduct the sale in the fashion of an 'IEO' through a licensed virtual asset trading platform.

1.1.3 Other Taxes

(a) What are the value added tax/sales tax consequences of selling crypto assets?

The Cayman Islands currently levies no value added taxes, and therefore there are no value added tax consequences of selling crypto assets.

(b) Are payments in crypto assets subject to withholding taxes?

Payments in crypto assets are not subject to withholding taxes in the Cayman Islands.

(c) Does payment of compensation in crypto assets give rise to payroll tax consequences?

No.

(d) *Do transactions with crypto assets trigger any transfer taxes?*

The Cayman Islands currently levies no transfer taxes.

(e) *Are firms operating in the crypto space subject to digital service taxes?*

No.

(f) *Are crypto assets subject to gift, inheritance, estate, or wealth taxes?*

The Cayman Islands currently levies no gift, inheritance, estate, or wealth taxes.

(g) *Are crypto assets subject to exit tax?*

No.

(h) *Can mining trigger gambling tax?*

The Cayman Islands currently does not have gambling taxes.

1.1.4 Compliance and Documentation Obligations

(a) *What documentation requirements exist for taxpayers regarding crypto assets and are there best practices in recordkeeping to support representations made in tax returns?*

Individuals and corporations in the Cayman Islands do not currently file tax returns or submit any other taxpayer documentation.

(b) *What is the evidentiary burden of supporting tax positions when a digital wallet address is lost or shared with other persons?*

The Cayman Islands currently levies no relevant taxes, and therefore, there is no evidentiary burden.

(c) *Are crypto asset exchanges and wallet providers subject to reporting obligations?*

Crypto asset exchanges (or 'virtual asset trading platforms') and wallet providers that involve a custody service are required to be licensed under the VASP Law. Persons licensed under the VASP Law will be subject to ongoing reporting requirements. For all licensees, these include: (a) undertaking audits of their anti-money laundering (**AML**) systems and procedures at the request of CIMA; (b) preparing audited accounts and submitting those to CIMA annually; (c) obtaining prior approval from CIMA to appoint senior officers or AML compliance officers; (d) providing certain notices to CIMA confirming their compliance with the AML regulations and data protection laws and ensuring that all communications relating to the virtual asset service are accurate; and (e) obtaining prior approval from CIMA before issuing or transferring shares or other equity interests totalling 10% or more of the licensee's ownership. Virtual asset trading platforms must also apply to CIMA for each virtual asset issuance over a prescribed threshold (yet to be determined).

In addition to the above, virtual asset trading platforms and custody providers must promptly report suspicions of money laundering or terrorist financing, including those involving or relating to virtual assets and/or providers that are suspicious.

(d) Are taxpayers holding crypto assets subject to reporting obligations apart from the filing of income tax/capital gains tax returns?

No.

(e) Are crypto asset exchanges and wallet providers subject to CRS/FATCA reporting?

Legislation has been passed to give effect to the registration, due diligence and reporting requirements of CRS/FATCA in the Cayman Islands. Therefore, where the crypto asset exchanges or wallet providers provide investment, custodial or depository services, such exchanges and wallet providers would be considered relevant financial institutions and are obliged to report on their account holders to the Tax Information Authority (**TIA**) of the Cayman Islands.

Subject to certain exceptions, each reporting financial institution must report the following information with respect to each of its reportable accounts: (i) the name, address, jurisdiction(s) of residence, TIN(s) and date and place of birth (in the case of an individual) of each reportable person; (ii) the account number (or functional equivalent in the absence of an account number); (iii) the name, GIIN (if applicable) and other identifying number (if any) of the reporting financial institution; (iv) the account balance or value as of the end of the relevant calendar year or other appropriate reporting period or, if the account was closed during such year or period, the closure of the account; and (v) the total gross amount paid or credited to the account holder with respect to the account during the calendar year or other appropriate reporting period with respect to which the reporting financial institution is the obligor or debtor, including the aggregate amount of any redemption payments made to the account holder during the calendar year or other appropriate reporting period.

1.1.5 *Civil and Criminal Tax Enforcement*

(a) What powers do the tax authorities have to compel the disclosure of information by third parties, such as exchanges or wallet providers, and have these been used in the past?

There are no tax authorities in the Cayman Islands other than the TIA. With the permission of the courts of the Cayman Islands, the TIA may search the premises of RFIs or any other person obliged to report to the TIA where the TIA considers it necessary to do so. It may also seize any relevant information. The TIA has the power to fine or imprison RFIs or any other person obliged to report to the TIA where they fail to do so or if they alter, destroy, mutilate, deface, hide or remove any information.

(b) What measures have the tax authorities undertaken in the past to ensure crypto tax compliance?

No such measures have been taken to date.

(c) Are the tax authorities cooperating with tax authorities in other jurisdictions on enforcement?

The TIA of the Cayman Islands cooperates with tax authorities in other participating jurisdictions in disclosing information on account holders for CRS/FATCA purposes.

China

David Dingfa Liu

1. COUNTRY GUIDES

1.1 China

The People's Republic of China consists of thirty-one provinces/provincial-level municipalities, Hong Kong Special Administrative Region ('**Hong Kong SAR**') and Macau Special Administrative Region ('**Macau SAR**'). However, for purposes of this chapter, 'China' refers only to Mainland China, since Taiwan is a de facto separate jurisdiction, and Hong Kong SAR and Macau SAR have their own independent judicial and tax systems.

1.1.1 Applicable Tax Law, Guidance, and Case Law

(a) Which laws, regulations, and other administrative guidance exist dealing with crypto assets?

There are no specific laws or administrative guidance dealing with crypto assets. Thus, the general rules would be applied, which are as follows: The *Enterprise Income Tax Law of the People's Republic of China* ('**EIT Law**'), the *Implementing Regulations for the Enterprise Income Tax Law of the People's Republic of China* ('**EIT Implementing Regulations**') (EIT Law and EIT Implementing Regulations are, hereinafter, collectively referred to as '**EIT Law and Regs**'), the *Individual Income Tax Law of the People's Republic of China* ('**IIT Law**'), the *Implementing Regulations for Individual Income Tax Law of the People's Republic of China* ('**IIT Implementing Regulations**') (IIT Law and IIT Implementing Regulations are, hereinafter, collectively referred to as '**IIT Law and Regs**'), the *Interim Regulations of the State Council on Value Added Tax* ('**VAT Regulations**'), various statutes dealing with stamp duty and other transfer taxes ('**Transfer Tax Statutes**'), and tax circulars or announcements issued by the State

Council, the Ministry of Finance and/or the State Administration of Taxation (collectively, '**Tax Circulars**').

EIT Law and Regs, IIT Law and Regs, VAT Regulations, Transfer Tax Statutes and Tax Circulars will, hereinafter, be collectively referred to as '**Chinese Tax Law**'.

(b) Which court cases exist dealing with crypto assets?

Given that crypto assets are still a new creature in China, only a few court cases exist. Some civil or criminal cases were heard and adjudicated by trial courts at the provincial level.[1] One of the main issues dealt with by the courts concerned the nature of crypto assets, i.e., whether the crypto assets in question (bitcoin) were intangible property, personal private computer data, or if crypto assets should be protected by Chinese law as property rights of the owner of the crypto assets. There are no reported court cases dealing with taxation of crypto assets.

1.1.2 Income and Capital Gains Taxes

(a) How are crypto assets classified for income and capital gains tax purposes?

Crypto assets are not specifically listed as a distinct item of income under the EIT Law and Regs, nor under the IIT Law and Regs. However, in a response to the Beijing Municipal Tax Bureau's ruling dated 29 October 2008, the State Administration of Taxation (**SAT**) stated that gains from disposing of online crypto coin issued by online gaming companies would be treated as capital gains.[2] Thus, given the nature of crypto assets and SAT's characterization of the crypto coin for purposes of taxation, gains realized and losses suffered from selling crypto assets would most likely be treated as capital gains or losses.

Under the EIT Law and Regs, capital gains realized by corporate taxpayers are taxed at the same rate (i.e., 25%) as that applicable to their ordinary income. However, under the IIT Law and Regs, the tax rate for capital gains tax (i.e., 20%) is in most situations lower than the progressive tax rates (ranging from 5% to 45%) applicable to salaries/wages earned by individual taxpayers.

(b) What are the income/capital gains tax consequences of selling crypto assets against fiat currency?

Under Chinese Tax Law, income/capital gains realized from selling crypto assets against fiat currency would be treated as capital gains and taxed at 25% rate in the

1. China is a civil code jurisdiction. No cases decided by courts would be officially published. The cases which the author found over the Internet are unofficial summaries of those cases.
2. Response of the State Administration of Taxation on the Imposing Individual Income tax on Income Generated from Individuals' Online Trading of Crypto Coins, Guoshuihan [2008] No. 818.

hands of corporate taxpayers or 20% rate where the taxpayer realizing the capital gains are individuals, regardless of the use of the crypto assets.

(c) What are the income/capital gains tax consequences of exchanging crypto assets against other crypto assets?

Under the EIT Law and Regs as well as the IIT Law and Regs, the tax authorities have discretionary authority to deem income/capital gains to have been realized by the taxpayers in cases whereby taxpayers exchange one asset for another (in-kind transactions). The tax would be based on the difference between (i) the value of crypto assets given away and (ii) the value of crypto assets received in exchange for the crypto assets given away. However, there are no specific guidelines from Chinese tax authorities on the tax consequences of exchanging crypto assets for other crypto assets.

(d) If a distinction is made between business assets and non-business assets, when does trading in crypto assets lead to a trade or business?

For Chinese income tax purposes, there is not a distinction between business assets and non-business assets.

(e) What are the income/capital gains tax consequences for an employee receiving wages or salaries in crypto assets?

If an employee were to receive wages or salary in crypto assets, the employee would be required to report such income as wage or salary income and, most likely, would be required to pay personal income tax at the progressive rates of 5% to 45% on the fair market value of such crypto assets at the time the crypto assets were received. Chinese Tax Law does not specifically address the valuation issue concerning a taxpayer's receipt of crypto assets in return for services or in exchange for other crypto assets. At the end of the day, under Chinese law, payment in China in fiat and cryptocurrencies, other than Chinese legal currency (Renminbi), is illegal.

(f) What are the income/capital gains tax consequences for a merchant receiving payment in crypto assets?

Crypto assets received by a merchant would most likely be treated as payment for goods sold and, as a result, the merchant would be required to pay VAT at applicable VAT rate (16% or lower rate, depending on the type of goods sold), and income tax on the fair market value of the crypto assets. Again, at present, it is illegal to make payments in China in fiat or cryptocurrencies other than Renminbi; and there are not clear valuation guidelines for valuing crypto assets for tax purposes.

(g) *What are the income/capital gains tax consequences of a loss of crypto assets?*

If a taxpayer is taxed on gains from disposing of his/her crypto assets, the taxpayer would be able to offset his/her losses reasonably related to the acquisition, holding and disposing of crypto assets in disposing of crypto assets in the current tax year. If his/her losses are greater than gains from disposing other crypto assets, the taxpayer should be able to carry forward such losses within the statutory loss carry-forward period (i.e., five years for corporate taxpayers).

(h) *What are the income/capital gains tax consequences of a loss in value of crypto assets?*

Chinese Tax Law does not specifically address the tax treatment of buying, holding, and disposing of crypto assets. Thus, the tax treatment of the gains realized and losses suffered as a result of buying, holding and disposing of crypto assets is highly dependent, in practice, on how the Chinese tax authorities would deal with this new creature.

If any clarification of the tax consequences of a loss in value of crypto assets is made, the State Administration of Taxation would, in consultation with the Ministry of Finance, formulate and publish a tax circular, outlining the tax treatment of taxpayers buying, holding and disposing of crypto assets. Before the publication of such a circular, we can only speculate that if the gains from disposing crypto assets are treated as capital gains, then losses suffered in disposing crypto assets should be allowed as an offset (an outright deduction or amortization over a period of time) against current and/or future gains from disposition of other crypto assets.

(i) *What are the income/capital gains tax consequences of forks of crypto assets?*

The income/capital gains tax consequences of forks of crypto assets would be identical to the tax consequences of crypto assets. Crypto assets and forks of crypto assets are still brand new concepts for Chinese regulators and taxing authorities. Hence, no specific taxation rules have been formulated to deal with the tax consequences of forks of crypto assets.

(j) *What are the income/capital gains tax consequences of airdrops of crypto assets and are the tax consequences different if the airdropped tokens are unwanted?*

Based on the general taxation principles in China, airdrops could be viewed as incidental income, which would be subject to a 25% income tax in the hands of corporations or a 20% income tax in the hands of individuals who received airdropped tokens. In the case of unwanted airdropped tokens, the recipient would be subject to income tax, so long as he/she takes possession and becomes owner of the airdropped tokens.

(k) What are the income/capital gains tax consequences of (solo, pool, and cloud) mining?

Based on the general taxation principles in China, mining itself, irrespective of whether it is solo mining, pool mining or cloud mining, would not be treated as a taxable event. However, if the miner is paid transaction fees and/or other monetary rewards or subsequently disposes of crypto assets resulting from the mining, activities would be subject to an income tax at 25% in the hands of corporations or 20% in the hands of miners who are individuals.

(l) What are the income/capital gains tax consequences of staking crypto assets?

Staking crypto assets is the process of holding funds in a cryptocurrency wallet to support the operations of a blockchain network. Essentially, it consists of locking cryptocurrencies to receive rewards. As such, the act of staking crypto assets would not trigger any tax consequences. However, if an individual or corporate taxpayer receives rewards in fiat currency or crypto assets, the taxpayer would be deemed to have received income from provision of service of staking crypto assets. Subsequent disposition of crypto assets resulting in gains would also trigger income tax.

(m) What are the income/capital gains tax consequences of an indirect investment in crypto assets?

Gains and losses realized from an indirect investment in crypto assets would be viewed as gains and losses from an indirect investment (investment products derived from crypto assets), whereby gains would be subject to a 25% income tax in the hands of the corporations or 20% income tax in the hands of individual investors; and losses of corporations can be carried forward for five years. However, at present, it is unclear if and how individual investors would be allowed to offset/carry forward these capital losses.

If gains or losses were realized by a pass-through entity such as a partnership, the pass-through entity itself would not be subject to income tax. Instead, each member of the pass-through would be required to report its capital gains or losses based on its own taxpayer status (i.e., corporate income taxpayer or individual income taxpayer).

(n) *How is income from crypto assets to be treated under double tax treaty law?*

The Chinese tax authorities have not dealt with the potential double tax treaty implications of income from crypto assets involving two contracting parties (e.g., source of income, permanent establishment and other issues).

(o) *What are the income/capital gains tax consequences of selling crypto assets in an ICO/STO/IEO?*

The Chinese tax authorities have not dealt with the potential tax implications of an ICO/STO/IEO, which transactions are prohibited by Chinese law[3].

Assuming that ICO/STO/IEO were permissible under Chinese law, selling crypto assets in an ICO/STO/IEO, and thereby realizing gains, would trigger income/capital gains tax in the hands of the sellers.

1.1.3 *Other Taxes*

(a) *What are the value added tax/sales tax consequences of selling crypto assets?*

The VAT Regulations have not specified if selling crypto assets would be subject to VAT. If crypto assets are treated as intangible assets for purposes of VAT, selling crypto assets would be subject to a 6% VAT in the hands of general VAT taxpayers (who can offset their input VAT against their output VAT) or a 3% gross receipts VAT in the hands of small-scale VAT taxpayers (who are subject to VAT on gross sales, without the benefit of offsetting input VAT against the output VAT).

In China, VAT taxpayers must register with the competent tax authority and be granted a general VAT taxpayer status or small-scale VAT taxpayer status before they can pay VAT in the capacity of a general VAT taxpayer or small-scale VAT taxpayer. It remains to be seen how the Chinese tax authorities would enforce VAT collection in respect of sale of crypto assets by holders of crypto assets, most of whom are individual investors and have not gone through VAT registrations.

(b) *Are payments in crypto assets subject to withholding taxes?*

In China, only non-residents are subject to withholding (income) taxes if they derived passive income, such as capital gains, from selling their property situated in China. In the case of crypto assets, it would extremely difficult to determine the situs of crypto assets. Presumably, non-residents for Chinese tax purposes would not be living in

3. Announcement of the People's Bank of China, the Office of the Central Leading Group for Cyberspace Affairs, the Ministry of Industry and Information Technology and Other Departments on Preventing the Financing Risks of Initial Coin Offerings, published on 4 Sept. 2017.

China, and thus the situs of their crypto assets acquired, or disposed of, from their computers or pool/cloud mining platform in territories outside China would logically not be deemed to be in China.

Also, as a general rule, a non-resident would be subject to a 10% withholding tax if the taxpayer receives payment of interest, dividends and other passive income, other than capital gains, from a source within China. However, given that outbound payments in currency other than fiat currency (Renminbi or one of the hard currencies) is illegal, payments in cryptocurrency would not be made through any Chinese banks. Therefore, the Chinese tax authorities would not be able to monitor and enforce withholding tax vis-à-vis outbound payments, if any, made in cryptocurrency.

(c) Does payment of compensation in crypto assets give rise to payroll tax consequences?

Yes, even though it is illegal for employers in China to pay their employees compensation in crypto assets.

(d) Do transactions with crypto assets trigger any transfer taxes?

No. Crypto assets are not specifically listed as taxable items under Chinese tax law.

(e) Are firms operating in the crypto space subject to digital service taxes?

No. China does not impose any digital service taxes.

(f) Are crypto assets subject to gift, inheritance, estate, or wealth taxes?

No. China currently does not impose any gift, inheritance, estate, or wealth taxes, although the fair market value of certain gifts received by a taxpayer must be included in the recipient's taxable income for income tax purposes.

(g) Are crypto assets subject to exit tax?

No. China does not impose any exit tax.

(h) Can mining trigger gambling tax?

No. China does not impose gaming tax.

1.1.4 *Compliance and Documentation Obligations*

(a) *What documentation requirements exist for taxpayers regarding crypto assets and are there best practices in recordkeeping to support representations made in tax returns?*

Generally, all taxpayers, corporate entities in particular, are required to maintain complete and accurate business records. However, there are no specific documentation requirements tailored to taxpayers regarding crypto assets, nor are there any best practices in recordkeeping to support representations made in tax returns vis-à-vis crypto assets. The best practice is to maintain complete digital records to prove the acquisition cost and sales/exchange price of crypto assets acquired and sold.

(b) *What is the evidentiary burden of supporting tax positions when a digital wallet address is lost or shared with other persons?*

Taxation of crypto assets in China is still in a nascent stage. No evidentiary burden has been specified by the Chinese tax authorities. As a general rule, however, taxpayers bear the burden of proving that certain expenditures or losses warrant pre-tax deduction in calculating taxable income.

(c) *Are crypto asset exchanges and wallet providers subject to reporting obligations?*

Crypto asset exchanges are prohibited by Chinese law, and no wallet providers legally exist in China. So, the Chinese Tax Law does address this issue.

(d) *Are taxpayers holding crypto assets subject to reporting obligations apart from the filing of income tax/capital gains tax returns?*

No.

(e) *Are crypto asset exchanges and wallet providers subject to CRS/FATCA reporting?*

In the eyes of Chinese law, these exchanges and providers do not exist. Thus, CRS reporting is a moot issue.

1.1.5 *Civil and Criminal Tax Enforcement*

(a) *What powers do the tax authorities have to compel the disclosure of information by third parties, such as exchanges or wallet providers, and have these been used in the past?*

Neither Chinese Tax Law nor tax practice exists vis-à-vis compelling the disclosure of information by third parties, such as exchanges or wallet providers.

(b) *What measures have the tax authorities undertaken in the past to ensure crypto tax compliance?*

There are no reported cases where tax authorities undertook to ensure crypto tax compliance.

(c) *Are the tax authorities cooperating with tax authorities in other jurisdictions on enforcement?*

No public information is available describing enforcement cooperation of Chinese tax authorities with tax authorities in other jurisdictions.

Colombia

Monica Reyes Rodriguez

1. COUNTRY GUIDES

1.1 Colombia

1.1.1 Applicable Tax Law, Guidance, and Case Law

(a) Which laws, regulations, and other administrative guidance exist dealing with crypto assets?

The Colombian Congress has not yet issued any specific regulations on crypto assets.

The National Government, however, has been required to identify the Financial, Accounting, Exchange Control, Tax and Money Laundering regulations that apply to any transactions on crypto assets:

- Circular 29 of 26 March 2014, issued by the Financial Superintendence in Colombia, identified the risks relating to the use and negotiation of crypto assets arising from the fact that related transactions are not subject to the surveillance of any governmental authority. The Superintendence also confirmed that users are entitled to acquire, trade, and invest in crypto assets, at their own risk.
- Statement 4637 of 1 April 2019 issued by the Colombian Central Bank reiterated a position held since 2014 in the sense that bitcoins do not qualify as legal tender in Colombia or abroad and that consequently, bitcoins do not qualify as a means to extinguish liabilities.

  In consequence, related transactions may not be channelled through the official Exchange Control market and may not be used to pay any obligations with third parties abroad.
- The National Council for Accounting Rules has established that bit coins represent valuable intangible assets and that as such, independent of the fact

that the International Financial Reporting Standards (IFRS) do not contemplate a specific account to represent crypto assets, a separate Account Unit must be registered to report transactions on the mentioned assets. (Statement 10-00906-2018. Consultation 1-2018-009713 dated 16 July 2018).

- The Group for International Financial Action (*Grupo de Acción Financiera Internacional, GAFI*) defined crypto assets in 2014, as the digital representation of value that is traded digitally and used as a means for exchange, a unity of account and value deposit. Although crypto assets do not qualify as legal tender in any jurisdiction and are not supported by any Central Bank or monetary authority, these qualify as digital exchange means that are valued at the price assigned by the market and are used to acquire goods and services.

(b) *Which court cases exist dealing with crypto assets?*

There is no jurisprudence on crypto assets in Colombia, to date.

1.1.2 *Income and Capital Gains Tax*

(a) *How are crypto assets classified for income and capital gains tax purposes?*

Crypto assets must be recorded at purchase price and classified as intangible assets, and as fixed assets or inventories in accordance with accounting standards.

Under Colombian rules, any accounting provisions that have not been expressly excluded by the Tax Statute must be applied for tax purposes.

(b) *What are the income/capital gains tax consequences of selling crypto assets against fiat currency?*

The income/capital gains tax consequences of selling crypto assets against fiat currency depend on the qualification of the crypto assets under income and complimentary taxes.

If the crypto assets have been classified as inventories or if held by an individual, these assets have not remained in possession of the individual for more than two years, the profit arising from the sale is subject to income tax.

Doctrine by the Colombian tax administration[1] established that notwithstanding that crypto assets do not qualify as a legal tender in Colombia, inasmuch as virtual currency is exchanged for services and/or goods, related transactions are subject to income and capital gains taxes.

1. Ruling No. 20419 dated 4 Aug. 2019 issued by the Colombian Tax Administration (*Dirección de Impuestos y Aduanas Nacionales – DIAN*).

If the taxpayers holding the assets are required to keep accounting books, the profit from the sale of the assets will be equivalent to the difference between the costs of the crypto assets and the price of sale, on the date of accrual.

If the assets are held by individuals and other taxpayers who are not required to keep accounting books, and the crypto assets have not been purchased, but have been 'formed', i.e., the profit will be assessed on the difference between the price of sale on the date of payment and a deemed cost equalling 50% of the price of sale.

The fiscal cost of intangible assets pertaining to industrial, literary, artistic, and scientific activities, such as invention patents, trademarks, author rights and other intangibles, formed by taxpayers who are not required to keep accounting books, is deemed equal to 50% of the price of sale, under current provisions.[2]

Corporate income tax applies at a corporate tax rate of 32% for 2020, 31% for 2021, and 30% as of 2022. Individuals are subject to progressive income tax rates applied in accordance with the level of income, up to a 39% rate.

If, on the other hand, crypto assets have remained in possession of the taxpayer, a legal entity or an individual, for more than two years, and qualify under IFRS as a fixed asset, the profit arising from the sale will be subject to Capital Gains Tax (*Impuesto a las Ganancias Ocasionales*) at a 10% rate.

(c) What are the income/capital gains tax consequences of exchanging crypto assets against crypto assets?

A barter or exchange is a contract under which the parties accept to transfer an asset in kind for another.[3]

The Colombian Civil Code[4] establishes that regulations on the sale of goods will be applicable to the barter in everything that is not contrary to the nature of the contract: each party will be deemed the seller of the good and the value of the mentioned good will be deemed to be the price paid for the good received in exchange.

The value of payments in kind that qualifies as income for the beneficiary is determined by the market value of the species on the date of delivery. The same rule[5] applies to payments in kind that represent a cost for the payor.

The mentioned rules imply that if the crypto assets being exchanged have different market values, the party receiving the more valuable asset will be deemed to have made a profit equalling the difference between the market price of the crypto asset paid in exchange for the asset received.

The party receiving a crypto asset with a price lower than the price of the asset transferred is entitled to support a tax deduction for the loss arising from the transfer.

2. Section 75 of the Colombian Tax Code.
3. Section 1955 of the Colombian Civil Code.
4. Section 1958 of the Colombian Civil Code.
5. Section 29 of the Colombian Tax Code.

(d) *If a distinction is made between business assets and non-business assets, when does trading in crypto assets lead to a trade or business?*

Under Colombian tax and commercial law, the distinction between business assets and non-business assets depends on the qualification of the activities by the holder.

In 2018, a draft law[6] was filed before the Colombian Congress with the purposes of regulating all types of transactions in crypto assets.

Under the draft, traders are defined as individuals with the knowledge and expertise required to perform trading activities on their own behalf or under a crypto asset management contract.

Section 4 of the draft referred to legal entities trading in crypto assets, as those legal entities acting as traders for profit, with commercial establishments registered before the respective Chamber of Commerce, whose social purpose is the commercialization, administration or trading of crypto assets, and which are duly authorized by the Information Technology and Communications Ministry.

The Colombian Congress did not enact the draft law. As of today, the definition of traders and trading activities is supported on the main principles of commercial law,[7] which qualify as traders, all legal entities, and/or individuals executing the following activities, among others:

- acquisition of goods for profit with the purpose of transferring the goods under the same title and the corresponding transfer;
- brokerage activities, business agencies, and the representation of national and foreign firms;
- any enterprise for the production, transformation, manufacture, and circulation of goods;
- any enterprises promoting business and those purchasing, selling, managing, keeping custody, or circulating all types of goods.

Given that the Colombian Code of Commerce does not differentiate between tangible and intangible goods, and that the crypto assets qualify as intangible assets irrespective of any other characteristics, it is necessary to conclude that taxpayers trading with the mentioned assets in any of the forms described by the Code of Commerce, are required to keep accounting books and to report any inventories held and any profits deriving from the trade, for accounting and tax purposes.

(e) *What are the income/capital gains tax consequences for an employee receiving wages or salaries in crypto assets?*

Wages or salaries in crypto assets qualify as salary in kind and the crypto assets are valuated at market price. Wages in kind are restricted to 50% of the salary under current labour regulations.

6. Proyecto de Ley 28, 2018.
7. Section 20 of the Colombian Code of Commerce.

As explained above, under section 29 of the Colombian Tax Code, the value of payments in kind that qualifies as income for the beneficiary is determined by the market value of the species on the date of delivery.

The same rule applies to payments in kind that represent a cost for the payor, which means that when the employee sells the crypto assets, the price of sale will only be subject to taxes on the difference between the value for which the crypto assets were received and the value for which they are sold.

Under Colombian tax and labour regulations in force at present, payments to employees will be subject to social security contributions and pay roll taxes and income tax withholding. The employer will be required to pay approximately 70% of the social security contributions and pay roll taxes and to withhold the remaining percentage from the payment to the employee.

Income tax withholding, on the other hand, is exclusively borne by the employee who is subject to withholding taxes at progressive rates on the value of the monthly payment, or alternatively, at a fixed rate computed on the average salary received in the last twelve months.

Only if withholding taxes, social security contributions and pay roll taxes are paid, the payments to employees in cryptocurrencies will be deductible from income tax for the employer.[8]

(f) What are the income/capital gains tax consequences for a merchant receiving payment in crypto assets?

The payment in crypto assets to a merchant should be characterized as the payment in kind under section 29 of the Colombian Tax Code above, or as a barter under section 1958 of the Colombian Civil Code.

The latter provision was construed for tax purposes, under a literal interpretation for many years. In consequence, the cost of the good delivered under the barter would be deemed equal to the market price of the good received.

Doctrine by the Colombian tax authorities, however, has restricted this interpretation to the rules in section 90 of the Colombian Tax Code, and establishes that the exchange of assets will generate a profit equal to the difference between the price for which the asset is delivered and its acquisition cost.

The mentioned doctrine also determines that the merchant selling goods for crypto assets will be deemed to have received the crypto assets for at least 85% of their market price on the date of sale, irrespective of the price agreed by the parties.

8. Sections 126-1, 207, 383 and 387 of the Colombian Tax Code.

(g) What are the income/capital gains tax consequences of a loss of crypto assets?

Section 148 of the Colombian Tax Code establishes that losses incurred in goods are deductible if the good is used in the production of income and only when the cause of the loss qualifies as force majeure.

This means that only the deduction for loss applies when the crypto assets qualify as inventories or when these render a capital yield. In that case, the cause for the loss must be duly supported to prove that it was generated by a force majeure event.

Under section 64 of the Colombian Civil Code, force majeure is defined as an unforeseeable event that is impossible to resist, like a shipwreck, an earthquake, an order from a legal authority and so on.

The value of the loss is deemed equal to the cost of purchase of the asset plus any improvements (where applicable), less any prior allowed deductions for amortizations or losses.

(h) What are the income/capital gains tax consequences of a loss in value of crypto assets?

Under rules enforceable from 2017, a loss in the value of crypto assets does not generate any income/capital gains tax consequence until it is realized. This means that except that the crypto assets are sold for a price lower than the acquisition cost, the loss in value does not have tax consequences.

(i) What are the income/capital gains tax consequences of forks of crypto assets?

A fork of crypto assets is the case when a software upgrade brings new technical features to a blockchain and the cryptocurrency platform's existing code is changed so that an old version of the blockchain remains on the network while a new version of the blockchain is created.

If both blockchains subsist, it is necessary to differentiate between costs assignable to the first development and those incurred in the development of the new version of the blockchain.

Costs of hard forks would probably be assigned chronologically, so that the costs of the original blockchain would be all those incurred before the update, and the costs of the new blockchain would be those attributable to the update.

In case a loss arises from the sale of the original blockchain, such loss may be compensated with any earnings arising from the sale of the newest.

(j) What are the income/capital gains tax consequences of airdrops of crypto assets and are the tax consequences different if the airdropped tokens are unwanted?

An airdrop for a crypto asset is defined as the marketing strategy consisting of distributing new tokens/coins by awarding them to existing holders of a particular blockchain currency, in determined proportions.

As any other marketing expenses, the cost for the distributor should be deductible from taxable income for miners and developers, in as long as the expense has a direct relationship with the production of earnings and the expense is proportionate to the earnings produced and necessary for the generation of income.

If the airdrop procedure takes place before the crypto assets are traded, the cost of the airdrop must be capitalized and treated as an amortizable expense against future income.

The issue to take into account regarding this deduction is that under section 122 of the Colombian Tax Code, deductions for expenses abroad for the generation of income within the country may not exceed 15% of the net earnings of the taxpayer before the expenses.

On the other hand, the beneficiaries of airdrops will be taxable on the value of the coins received at a 10% tax rate applying on occasional gains, irrespective of whether the air dropped tokens are unwanted.

Tax would not apply if the air dropped tokens are transferred back.

(k) What are the income/capital gains tax consequences of (solo, pool, and cloud) mining?

Solo mining is the scenario where the miner individually carries out the mining procedures. In a solo mining venture, blocks are mined and produced exclusively by the miner.

The miner will be able to depreciate the computer equipment he uses while generating the crypto assets at a general 20% rate, and to deduct electricity expenses and any payroll taxes applied on his income as an independent professional, as applicable, as well as any other related expenses and will be required to declare the value of the crypto assets he produces in any taxable year.

Pool mining represents a common fund with various miners' resources. The miners share the processing capacity of the equipment in the fund and the income arising from the joint venture.

In that case, the crypto assets received from the fund will be subject to income tax as income from a trade or business. The pool will probably be characterized as a Joint Venture Agreement under current tax regulations. In Colombia, the Joint Venture would be required to keep separate accounting books and to distribute the earnings in proportion to the contribution by each miner, irrespective of the difficulty to define the amount of contribution in cases of pools where hundreds of miners participate.

Cloud mining processes require that miners exercise the mining activities remotely by accessing a data centre in the cloud that they hire from the company managing the data centre. The miners are rewarded by the system and the users. The remuneration for the miners is income from the trade, and the deductions they can apply for include depreciation of any equipment they use to access the data centre, the fee to the company hiring the equipment in the cloud, payments for electricity and rentals, social security costs paid as independent professionals or salaries and payroll taxes in case they have employees, among other related expenses.

(l) *What are the income/capital gains tax consequences of staking crypto assets?*

Staking consists of setting aside a specific number of coins to participate through a consensus mechanism in a process within a cryptocurrency network, namely, the Proof of Stake (PoS), whereby transactions are validated.

The network participants hold an amount of the native cryptocurrency in a specific wallet for a certain period of time.

Although staking does not require expensive investments or massive amounts of processing, it would, in our opinion, be subject to income tax as earnings from any other mining activities, for miners, or as a capital yield, for investors.

(m) *What are the income/capital gains tax consequences of an indirect investment in crypto assets?*

Currently, investors who prefer to buy stocks instead of digital assets can choose between blue-chip tech stocks of companies involved in blockchain development, stocks of financial services companies who are venturing into crypto asset investments, small and medium-cap blockchain entities, and funds that invest in digital assets.

The income/capital gains tax consequences of an indirect investment in crypto assets will depend on the structure of the entity receiving the funds and the type of investment.

In the event that the investment is made through a legal entity, profits from the investment will be treated as dividends subject to withholding taxes at rates of 0%, 7.5% or 10% depending on the qualification of the beneficiary, on profits that have been taxed at the company level.

Dividends from profits that have not been taxed at the company level will be subject to withholdings at a basic 32%, 31% or 30% rate for years 2020–2021 or 2022 onward, plus a marginal rate of 0%, 5% or 10%.

Stocks and shares must be sold at a minimum price for tax purposes, which may not be less than 130% of the book value of the company issuing the shares, except that these are listed in a recognized Stock Exchange Market.[9]

9. Section 90 of the Colombian Tax Code.

Private Investment Funds and Foreign Capital Investment Funds do not qualify as taxpayers in Colombia. In consequence, any contributions to investment funds dealing with digital assets will be deemed to be held directly by the investor.[10] Income earned by the private capital fund less any expenses and less the remuneration to the administrator will be distributed to the participants at the same title at which the income was earned by the fund and will be subject to withholding taxes on the same concept.

The remuneration to the entity administering the fund will be subject to income tax and to income tax withholding.

Recent legislation[11] consecrated rules against the deferral of income through investment funds not listed in a stock exchange, in cases where the fund is held in more than 50% by the same effective beneficiary or by a group of economically related investors or where one of the effective beneficiaries of the fund exercises control on the distributions. These funds will be required to distribute profits on the year the profit accrues or on the subsequent year.

Funds with the exclusive purpose of developing new innovative projects, and to collect risk capital for the same, will not be subject to the rule that allows for deferral of income for one year at the most.

Investments in financial instruments, where the underlying assets are crypto assets, are subject to income tax on financial yield, and to withholding taxes applying at a general rate of 7%. If the financial yield is paid to foreign entities or individuals, withholding taxes will apply at 20%.

Income tax and income tax withholding on interest and dividends may also be reduced in accordance with any applicable Double Taxation Treaties.

(n) How is income from crypto assets to be treated under double tax treaty law?

The majority of the Double Taxation Treaties executed by the Colombian Government, with the specific exception of the Andean Pact (*El Acuerdo de Cartagena*) which is still in force with Peru, Ecuador, and Bolivia, follow the OECD Model Convention.

Under the OECD Model Convention, income from crypto assets may be characterized as profits of an Enterprise of a contracting state or as capital or income gains from investments in or sales of intangible assets.

Profits of an enterprise of a contracting state are only taxable in the place of incorporation of the company or of location of the business, except that the enterprise is deemed to hold a permanent establishment in another jurisdiction under Article 5(1) of the OECD Model Convention.

The Colombian Tax Administration has not yet referred to the characterization under current legislation or under Double Taxation Treaties, of permanent establishments arising from the execution of mining activities abroad.

10. Section 23-1 of the Colombian Tax Code.
11. Section 68, Law 2010 of 2019.

Capital gains or losses, on the other hand, refer to the increase or decrease in the value of a capital asset upon sale or other types of transfer. The purchase price of a capital asset plus the value of any additions will generate a profit for the investor if the price of sale/transfer is higher, or a loss if it is lower. Capital gains will be taxable in the country of residence of the seller of the asset.

(o) What are the income/capital gains tax consequences of selling crypto assets in an ICO/STO/IEO?

The Initial Exchange Offer (IEO) in our opinion does not qualify as a sale because the investor will only be acquiring a right to future profits or may not acquire anything. The fact that the investor's rights are represented in tokens does not necessarily imply that the investor is buying the token, as the token does not have any value in itself.

The trader, on the other hand, will be receiving a commission for any funds deposited in the project which may or may not be profitable, as it may or may not cover the costs of the Platform, etc.

Developers are only offering a profit in the event that the project is implemented and provided the project is successful. In strict sense, the money they receive from the IEO, is not income and does not generate a profit from the sale as it is represented in the rights granted to the investor on the capital of the enterprise.

Except in the case that the developers receive a developers' fee at closing, these would not be subject to income tax in Colombia. In the event they do, they would be subject to income tax on the amount of the fee.

Initial Coin Offerings (ICOs) represent blockchain crowdfunding. ICOs are not subject to any legal restrictions or investor protection measures.

Decrees 2555, 2010 and 1357, 2018 are the first set of regulations on collaborative financing activities in Colombia. Under the regulations in force, the maximum amount to collect through crowdfunding is 10,000 minimum monthly salaries (USD 1,200,000 approx., at the current exchange rate) and the maximum investment authorized for the contributor is 20% of yearly income/net assets.

Recent articles on crowdfunding[12] share our opinion in the sense that even though investment by the contributor may be paid through credit cards, the value of the contribution should not be subject to the 1.5% withholding on income from sales.

Security Token Offers (STO) refer to the trade of tokens held by the new investors in exchange for dividends or vote rights or any other rights deriving from other types of valuables.

In this case, investors will be taxable at a progressive income tax rate on the difference between the capitalization cost of the token and the value at which the tokens are traded.

The brokers in STOs receive brokerage commissions at lower percentages, which will also be subject to income tax.

12. *An Approximation to Income Tax*, Nicolás Jaramillo Pineda. Revista 79 Instituto Colombiano de Derecho Tributario 79. Nov. 2018.

1.1.3 *Other Taxes*

(a) What are the Value Added Tax/Sales Tax consequences of selling crypto assets?

Under Colombian law, the sale of crypto assets is not subject to Value Added Tax, because VAT in Colombia only applies on sales and imports of tangible assets and on services.

The above, however, is not true, with regard to services rendered by traders and payable with commissions, or by the owners of processing centres who lease equipment or to cloud computing centres or warehouses charging technical services fees or royalties. All services related to crypto assets will be subject to Colombian Value Added Tax (*Impuesto al Valor Agregado*, IVA), when paid by a user located within Colombian territory. The general rate is 19%.

For VAT purposes, services rendered and intangibles licensed or purchased from abroad, will be deemed to be rendered, licensed or purchased within Colombian territory and will be subject to tax when the direct user or recipient qualifies as a Colombian tax resident, or holds domicile or a permanent establishment, or the principal place of business within Colombian territory.[13]

(b) Are payments in crypto assets subject to withholding taxes?

Any payments in kind are subject to withholding taxes in as long as the payment generates taxable income for the beneficiary.[14]

The withholding tax rate will vary in accordance with the nature of the transaction.

(c) Does payment of compensation in crypto assets give rise to payroll tax consequences?

As explained in section 1.1.2(e) above, under Colombian tax and labour regulations, in force at present, payments to employees in crypto assets will be subject to social security contributions and pay roll taxes and to income tax withholding.

The employer will be required to pay approximately 70% of the social security contributions and 100% of the pay roll taxes and to withhold the remaining portion from the payment to the employee.

Income tax withholding, on the other hand, will be exclusively borne by the employee who will be subject to progressive rates in accordance with the value of the monthly salary or to the average compensation received in the last twelve months.

13. Section 420 of the Colombian Tax Code.
14. Section 24 of the Colombian Tax Code.

Payments to employees in crypto assets will be tax deductible for the employer, provided that withholding taxes, social security contributions and pay roll taxes are duly paid.[15]

(d) Do transactions with crypto assets trigger any transfer taxes?

Transfer taxes are not applicable in Colombia.

(e) Are firms operating in the crypto space subject to digital service taxes?

Under current Colombian tax rules, only VAT applies to firms operating in the crypto space which renders services to users located within the country. No specific tax has been imposed on digital services.

(f) Are crypto assets subject to gift, inheritance, estate, or wealth taxes?

The transfer of crypto assets by way of gift or inheritance is subject to Occasional Gains Tax on inheritances or donations at a 10% rate.[16]

The valuation of the crypto assets that will be taken into account to apply the aforementioned tax will be the market price estimated for the mentioned assets on 31 December of the year prior to the liquidation of the succession or to the completion of the donation or to any other free transaction *inter vivos*.

If the crypto asset quote is in foreign currency, the exchange rate applying will be that in force on the last working day of the year prior to the liquidation of the succession or to the completion of the donation or of any other gift.14

Crypto assets also trigger Wealth Tax.

Wealth Tax is not a permanent tax in Colombia, although it has been repeatedly imposed by the different Administrations throughout the last thirty years.

The last time that the Wealth Tax was imposed was with Law 2010, 2019 in force as of 1 January 2020, with reference to individuals holding net assets valued for COP 5,000,000,000 (USD 1,500,000 approximately), or more.

The basis to assess the Wealth Tax for years 2020 and 2021 is the value of gross assets held on 1 January 2020 less liabilities in charge on the same date, less the value of the house of abode up to COP 480,695,000 (USD 128,000 approximately) and less 50% of the value of any assets reported for the first time under normalization rules and which have been repatriated into the country under Laws 1943, 2018 or 1020, 2019.

The regulations in force do not apply to assets acquired in subsequent years, if not held by 1 January 2020.

15. Sections 126-1, 207, 383 and 387 of the Colombian Tax Code.
16. Section 302 of the Colombian Tax Code.

(g) Are crypto assets subject to exit tax?

There is no exit tax in Colombia.

(h) Can mining trigger gambling tax?

Under Law 643, 2001 Gambling Tax in Colombia applies on:

> all mechanisms-actions based on the different combinations of calculation and chance or coincidence, that give place to a recreative game where one wins or loses, which is played for entertainment or amusement and/or with the purpose of winning money or goods.[17]

In our opinion, the definition of gambling in force at present in Colombia does not cover mining activities, which should not trigger Gambling Tax. Other transactions with crypto assets may be subject to Gambling Tax provided that these fall under the scope of the definition above.

Promotion campaigns, for example, that is, crypto air drops, may trigger Gambling Tax in certain cases.

1.1.4. Compliance and Documentation Obligations

(a) What documentation requirements exist for taxpayers regarding crypto assets and are there best practices in recordkeeping to support representations made in tax returns?

Doctrine by the Colombian Tax Administration[18] has concluded that in the case that the taxpayers dealing with crypto assets are not liable for Value Added Tax and given that under current rules[19] taxpayers that are not liable for VAT are not required to issue invoices[20], the seller or the buyer in the transaction, either one, is authorized to issue a document equivalent to an invoice describing the date, the value, the name of the parties in the transaction and the good being transferred, in this case, the type of crypto asset or token.

In the case of traders and other intermediaries rendering services to users in Colombia, the Tax Administration is clear that a numbered invoice, complying with all the requisites established for Colombian taxpayers, is required.

17. Section 75 of Decree 400, 1999.
18. Ruling No. 1324 dated 29 May 2019 by the Colombian Tax Administration.
19. Section 616-2 of the Colombian Tax Code.
20. As per sections 771-2 of the Colombian Tax Code and 16.1.4.44 and 1.61.4.10 of Decree 1625, 2016.

(b) *What is the evidentiary burden of supporting tax positions when a digital wallet address is lost or shared with other persons?*

The evidentiary burden will depend on whether the taxpayer is obligated or not obligated by law to keep accounting books. In the first case, the accounting books together with all support documentation and evidence must be kept for at least five years and supplied to the tax authorities as required.[21]

In case the taxpayer is not required to keep accounting books, the evidentiary burden regarding a lost or shared digital wallet address is not restricted, so that the taxpayer is allowed to prove the existence of the digital wallet and of any transactions on crypto assets with any available evidence, and the tax authorities are required to valuate any means of proof.

(c) *Are crypto asset exchanges and wallet providers subject to reporting obligations?*

Crypto exchange operators and/or wallet providers will be subject to the same income, Value Added, Industry and Commerce and Wealth Tax reporting obligations applying to any other taxpayers receiving earnings from service, industrial and commercial activities or holding assets that are subject to Wealth Tax.

Under Colombian tax rules, tax returns must be duly supported with the documents and evidence that prove the different factors in the assessment of taxes. This evidence must be filed upon request by the tax authorities.

In addition, the Colombian tax authorities issue a yearly Resolution whereby they designate the taxpayers that are required to file additional reports regarding transactions with third parties in the prior year, the identification of the parties from whom payments were received or to whom payments were made, the value of the transaction and the corresponding tax withholdings.[22]

The inclusion of a taxpayer in the mentioned Resolution depends, as a general rule, on the amount of earnings and the volume of the transactions with third parties. The nature of the transactions or of the assets, that are being dealt with, are exceptionally considered.

(d) *Are taxpayers holding crypto assets subject to reporting obligations apart from the filing of income tax/capital gains tax reports?*

As explained above, Colombian tax regulations do not include specific reporting obligations for taxpayers holding crypto assets.

The mentioned taxpayers will be required to file reports on Value Added Tax, on Industry and Commerce Tax, on net wealth and/or on assets held abroad, if they qualify under the specific regulations.

---

21. Section 634 of the Colombian Tax Code.
22. Section 633 of the Colombian Tax Code.

(e) *Are crypto exchanges and wallet providers subject to CRS/FATCA reporting?*

In as long as traders do not qualify as financial entities under the treaties, it is our opinion that crypto exchanges are not subject to CRS/FATCA. If the traders also qualify as financial entities under the definitions included in the mentioned Agreements, the transactions on crypto assets will be subject to reporting.

Investment funds for example, or the operators of Bitcoin ATM's, together with other financial services companies that are involved in the cryptocurrency sector, are required to report their clients under CRS/FATCA.

Under the mentioned Agreements, the Colombian Tax Authorities would be collaborating with other countries for enforcement.

1.1.5. *Civil and Criminal Tax Enforcement*

(a) *What powers do the tax authorities have to compel the disclosure of information by third parties, such as exchanges or wallet providers, and have these been used in the past?*

Colombian tax authorities have ample inspection and investigation faculties to ensure compliance of substantive dispositions. For such purposes, they may request taxpayers or third parties to file reports or answer interrogations under oath, or exhibit accounting ledgers, or grant testimonies, and in general, are free to carry any investigation to ensure the correct assessment of taxes.[23]

We are not aware of any precedents regarding audits against exchanges or wallet providers.

(b) *What measures have tax authorities undertaken in the past to ensure crypto tax compliance?*

We do not know of any precedents regarding audits by tax authorities or jurisprudence on claims dealing with crypto tax compliance.

Doctrine by the Colombian Tax Administration, however, has been clear that crypto assets transactions generate income and complimentary taxes such as Capital Gains and Wealth Tax.

23. Section 684 of the Colombian Tax Code.

(c) Are the tax authorities cooperating with tax authorities in other jurisdictions on enforcement?

Colombian tax authorities are always keen to cooperate with tax authorities in other jurisdictions under the OECD Convention, Double Taxation Treaties and the Andean Pact Agreement.

We do not know of any joint efforts to enforce tax compliance on the crypto asset sector.

Cyprus

Elias Neocleous

1. COUNTRY GUIDES

1.1 Cyprus

1.1.1 Applicable Tax Law, Guidance, and Case Law

(a) Which laws, regulations, and other administrative guidance exist dealing with crypto assets?

In Cyprus there is currently no special legal or regulatory framework in force concerning crypto assets. The Cyprus tax laws, as well as the tax regulations issued on their basis, do not explicitly mention crypto assets, either in general, or, in particular. Additionally, when approached by the author for guidance on this topic the Tax Department would not commit itself. However, the Central Bank of Cyprus (CBC)[1] and the Cyprus Securities Commission (CySEC) have taken the initiative to issue circulars including warnings to potential crypto asset investors and to investment firms (CIFs) having an interest in crypto businesses. CySEC is also pressing for the transposition of the European Union 5th Anti Money Laundering Directive (AMLD 5) into Cyprus law which would bring the regulation of crypto asset trading under its supervision as regards anti-money laundering (AML) procedures.

On 15 May 2018, CySEC issued Circular C.268 (hereinafter the 'Circular'), entitled *Introduction of New Rules Governing Derivatives on Virtual Currencies*. The Circular affirmed the lack of any regulation on behalf of CySEC on any direct activity relating to cryptocurrencies. However, the Circular mentions that persons wishing to

1. On 7 Feb. 2014, the CBC issued an announcement entitled *Attention to the Risks Associated with Virtual Currencies*.

provide investment services in relation to derivatives on virtual currencies will need to be specifically authorized by CySEC, depending on their specific characteristics and use.

It should also be noted that Cyprus adheres to *International Financial Reporting Standards* (IFRS), therefore, the conclusions of the June 2019 IFRS Interpretation Committee (IFRSIC) as regards the application of IFRS to holdings of cryptocurrencies may also be viewed as relevant[2] guidance. The Committee observed that a holding of cryptocurrency meets the definition of an intangible asset.

(b) Which court cases exist dealing with crypto assets?

No cases currently exist of the courts of Cyprus dealing with crypto assets. There is, however, a decision of the European Court of Justice (ECJ) dealing with value added tax (VAT) in relation to bitcoins.[3] Since Cyprus is a member of the EU and abides by rulings of the ECJ, this case can be deemed to be relevant.

1.1.2 Income and Capital Gains Taxes

(a) How are crypto assets classified for income and capital gains tax purposes?

The Tax Department has not issued any specific guidance on this point. IFRSIC concluded that where crypto assets are held for sale in the normal course of business, they should be classified as inventory. In other circumstances, they should be dealt with as an intangible asset.

(b) What are the income/capital gains tax consequences of selling crypto assets against fiat currency?

There is no specific tax guidance available on this matter. The basic and existing principles of Cyprus tax should apply.

If the crypto assets sold form part of inventory, gains should be subject to income tax. If the crypto assets sold form part of a capital asset (intangible asset), then no Cyprus tax should apply whatsoever. There would be an exemption from income tax due to the non-trade, non-business nature of the sale. There would be an exemption from capital gains tax as Cyprus capital gains tax applies only on the direct or indirect sale of Cyprus immovable property.

2. https://www.ifrs.org/projects/2019/holdings-of-cryptocurrencies.
3. ECJ, 22 Oct. 2015, C-264/14, *Hedqvist*; cf. section 1.1.3(a).

(c) *What are the income/capital gains tax consequences of exchanging crypto assets against other crypto assets?*

The same responses as in section 1.1.2(b), above, apply (i.e., it depends as to whether the exchange forms part of a trading transaction – if classified as inventory – or whether the exchange forms part of a capital transaction – if classified as intangible).

(d) *If a distinction is made between business assets and non-business assets, when does trading in crypto assets lead to a trade or business?*

The Tax Department has no rules specific to the trading of crypto assets. In determining whether a transaction in crypto assets constitutes carrying out a trade or business, the Tax Department will, as with all other non-crypto asset transactions, have regard to ten factors generally known as Badges of Trade. These are as follows:

(1) Subject matter of transaction – transactions akin to those of an existing trade may be regarded as trading.
(2) Length of ownership – assets held for a short period of time with the intention of resale will support an assumption of trading.
(3) Frequency of similar transactions – systematic and repeated transactions will support an assumption of trading.
(4) Supplementary work – modification of an asset to make it more saleable will support an assumption of trading.
(5) Circumstances responsible for the transaction – was the asset sold in a manner of a trading organization or, e.g., did it have to be sold to raise cash in an emergency? The former will support an assumption of trading.
(6) Motive for transaction – evidence that the asset was purchased with the sole intention of resale at a profit will support an assumption of trading.
(7) Method of financing the cost – was the transaction financed out of own funds or was use made of bank loans, company funds, etc.? The latter will support an assumption of trading.
(8) Knowledge of the owner – is there a history of being engaged in trading? If the answer is yes, this will support an assumption of trading.
(9) Method of acquisition – were the assets originally purchased by or gifted to the seller? The former might be regarded as supporting an assumption of trading.
(10) What happens to the transaction proceeds – e.g., are they used to fund further stock or transactions? If the answer is yes, this will support an assumption of trading.

It is not necessary for all the 'Badges' to be present for the Tax Department to decide that trading is taking place. It will have regard to the overall picture of any transaction.

(e) What are the income/capital gains tax consequences for an employee receiving wages or salaries in crypto assets?

Crypto assets provided to employees as wages will be treated as normal employment income and will be subject to income tax. Crypto assets provided to employees as any other form of employment income (bonus, benefits, etc.) will again be treated as normal employment income and will be subject to income tax.

In either of these instances, the Tax Department will determine the value of the crypto assets to be:

- in the case of a transfer of an 'in house' asset (i.e., one generated by the employer), the normal selling price of the asset minus the 'price' at which the asset was transferred to the employee; or
- in the case of a transfer of an 'external' asset, the higher of the original cost to the employer or the market value of the asset minus the price at which the asset was transferred to the employee.

In either of these events, the costs associated with the transfer of the asset to the employee will also be assessed as a 'benefit in kind'.

Subsequent disposal of the crypto assets by the employees should constitute a non-trading event (capital in nature) in which case no taxation will apply.

(f) What are the income/capital gains tax consequences for a merchant receiving payment in crypto assets?

There is no specific guidance available on this; however, it is reasonable to assume that the Tax Department will regard receipts of crypto assets as a manner of payments for the sale of inventory as normal taxable proceeds subject to income tax. The value attributed to the crypto assets would be equivalent to their fair market value at the time of receipt.

(g) What are the income/capital gains tax consequences of a loss of crypto assets?

Crypto assets may be effectively lost as a result of:

- the theft of, or unauthorized access to, a private key which then results in the theft of the asset;
- the loss or corruption of a private key in which case although the asset still exists the owner will be unable to access it; or
- poor internal controls allowing a mistaken transfer of assets to an incorrect address.

The Tax Department has no specific guidance relating to any of these circumstances. However, it is reasonable to assume that where the crypto assets are held as a non-trading asset there should be no tax implication since crypto assets are not currently subject to capital gains tax.

Conversely, where the crypto assets are traded in the normal course of business, such a loss might be expected, in most circumstances, to create an income tax deduction. The situation is less clear where the crypto asset loss is due to personal key loss or corruption since the actual crypto asset still exists and is unlikely to be claimed by any other party. Such instances are likely to be looked at on a case-by-case basis.

(h) What are the income/capital gains tax consequences of a loss in value of crypto assets?

There are no capital gains implications. In general, there are no income tax consequences in cases of fluctuations/changes in values until trading gains or losses are realized.

(i) What are the income/capital gains tax consequences of forks of crypto assets?

The Tax Department has issued no specific guidance regarding a fork in a blockchain. It could be argued that as with a demerger the cost of the original blockchain asset should be split and allocated on a pro rata basis between it and the new blockchain asset. The actual fork should thus not give rise to any immediate tax consequences. Tax consequences would only arise upon the sale of the crypto assets in the old or the new blockchain.

(j) What are the income/capital gains tax consequences of airdrops of crypto assets and are the tax consequences different if the airdropped tokens are unwanted?

Again, there is no specific guidance from the Tax Department on this. As previously stated, crypto assets are not subject to capital gains tax. It is reasonable to assume that:

- If the crypto assets are received within an active trade or business, they will be treated as taxable revenue of an amount equal to the normal purchase cost of the crypto assets.
- If they are received outside of the above, and are not consideration for a service performed, they would be regarded as a tax-exempt gift.

(k) What are the income/capital gains tax consequences of (solo, pool, and cloud) mining?

Again, there is no specific guidance from the Tax Department on this. It is reasonable to suggest that in each case (solo, pool, or cloud), the Tax Department would have regard to the Badges of Trade, as outlined in section 1.1.2(d), above, when determining whether or not an active business exists. If it determines that an active business does exist, then normal corporation or income tax rules will apply and the revenue, less allowable deductions, would be subject to taxation.

Where the mining is of a non-business nature – to the extent that the miner receives any crypto assets or fiat income – this would be classed as 'Other Income', and related expenses could be deducted from it.

There are no capital gains consequences.

(l) What are the income/capital gains tax consequences of staking crypto assets?

There are unlikely to be income tax consequences for staking (validating) crypto assets. Staking would not normally be expected to be classed as a business activity. To the extent that any income is received as the result of staking, it would be deemed to be 'Other Income' and taxable as such.

There are no capital gains consequences.

(m) What are the income/capital gains tax consequences of an indirect investment in crypto assets?

In Cyprus, indirect investments in crypto assets are possible via an Alternative Investment Fund (AIF). The taxation regime for holdings in AIFs is benign. Foreign investors suffer no withholding tax on dividends, no taxation on redemption of units, and there are no deemed distribution restrictions.

Non-domiciled resident investors are exempt from withholding tax on dividends, there is no taxation on redemption of units, and company investors suffer no withholding tax.

Domiciled residents pay 17% withholding tax on dividends, there is no taxation on the redemption of units, and company investors suffer no withholding tax.

(n) How is income from crypto assets to be treated under double tax treaty law?

The Tax Department has not issued any guidance on the treatment of crypto assets under double tax treaty law. Cyprus is a party to more than sixty-four such treaties all of which generally follow the OECD Model Convention. A potential taxpayer should, therefore, have regard to Article 7 of the OECD model concerning business profits. Specifically:

- The profits of an enterprise of a Contracting State shall be taxable only in that State unless the enterprise carries on business in the other Contracting State through a permanent establishment situated therein. If the enterprise carries on business as aforesaid, the profits of the enterprise may be taxed in the other

State but only so much of them as is attributable to that permanent establishment.
- In general, where an enterprise of a Contracting State carries on business in the other Contracting State through a permanent establishment therein, the profit shall in each Contracting State be attributed to that permanent establishment which it might be expected to make if it were a distinct and separate enterprise engaged in the same or similar activities under the same or similar conditions and dealing wholly independently with the enterprise of which it is a permanent establishment.

Given the virtual nature of crypto assets, the issue is to determine where the income from the crypto assets is earned in order to determine how much tax is payable in each Contracting State. The determination of that issue is a difficult and much debated matter.

Tax residency issues and degree of substance will also need to be carefully reviewed along with the anti-abuse rules introduced by the OECD/BEPS project.

(o) What are the income/capital gains tax consequences of selling crypto assets in an ICO/STO/IEO?

There is no official guidance from the Tax Department available on this topic. It is reasonable to assume that ICO proceeds from the sale of tokens would constitute taxable income (income tax) in Cyprus for the issuing company if the tokens are linked to the provision of an asset or service by the issuer towards the subscriber.

STOs in Cyprus are governed under already existing securities laws and regulations. The most popular two ways to launch an STO in Cyprus are to either incorporate a company or establish a Cyprus investment fund. Both would be subject to a maximum corporate tax rate on net profits of 12.5%.

The most feasible road to an IEO in Cyprus is to incorporate a Cyprus limited liability company that will launch the project. Again, such companies would be liable for a maximum corporate tax rate of 12.5% on net profits.

There would be no capital gains tax implications for the purchaser of such assets if they were to be held as an investment and sold at a profit as a later date since, as stated in section 1.1.2(b), Cyprus capital gains tax applies only on the direct or indirect sale of Cyprus immovable property. If, however, the purchaser regularly traded in such assets, then any profit or loss made would form part of the purchaser's annual trading profit or loss, and the purchaser would be subject to income tax, or corporation tax, as appropriate.

1.1.3 *Other Taxes*

(a) *What are the value added tax/sales tax consequences of selling crypto assets?*

Minimal guidance in relation to the VAT treatment of crypto assets is currently available. In *Hedqvist*,[4] the Court found that exchange services, where the supplier bought and sold bitcoins acting as a principal, were exempt from VAT under Article 135(1)(e). Since Cyprus usually follows ECJ rulings, it is probable that where crypto assets are sold in the normal course of business, these will also be judged by the Tax Department to be exempt from VAT. It follows that no input tax may be reclaimed by the vendor.

(b) *Are payments in crypto assets subject to withholding taxes?*

No, payments in crypto assets are not subject to withholding taxes, and this is a situation that appears unlikely to change. Cyprus only levies a withholding tax on very limited category of payments made to non-residents of Cyprus. These include royalties earned on rights used within Cyprus and on certain types of individual income.

(c) *Does payment of compensation in crypto assets give rise to payroll tax consequences?*

Yes, the comments made in section 1.1.2(d), above, apply.

(d) *Do transactions with crypto assets trigger any transfer taxes?*

Transactions with crypto assets do not currently trigger any transfer taxes in Cyprus.

(e) *Are firms operating in the crypto space subject to digital service taxes?*

No, Cyprus has not yet introduced a digital service tax.

(f) *Are crypto assets subject to gift, inheritance, estate, or wealth taxes?*

No, Cyprus does not levy any gift, inheritance, estate, or wealth taxes. This situation is unlikely to change.

4. ECJ, 22 Oct. 2015, C-264/14, *Hedqvist*.

(g) Are crypto assets subject to exit tax?

Cyprus has introduced an exit tax – applicable from 1 January 2020 – when a taxpayer moves assets or its tax residence out of the country. The tax to be paid is based on a sum to be equal to the market value minus the value for tax purposes of assets to be transferred outside of the net of Cyprus tax legislation while remaining under the same ownership, i.e., the asset is treated as having been 'sold' and subject to capital gains tax. However, since no capital gains tax currently applies to crypto assets, it seems unlikely that the Tax Department will seek to impose an exit tax on them.

(h) Can mining trigger gambling tax?

Gambling in Cyprus is regulated under the *Betting Law 2012* which introduced a licensing regime for specific categories of gambling. This was supplemented by the *Casino Law 2015*. Every licensed premise in Cyprus pays a betting (gambling) tax of up to 10% of its net revenue and 3% of its net revenue to the State Gaming Board. However, currently, 'mining' is not an activity which falls within the scope of the Betting Law 2012 and, therefore, it cannot trigger gambling tax.

1.1.4 Compliance and Documentation Obligations

(a) What documentation requirements exist for taxpayers regarding crypto assets and are there best practices in recordkeeping to support representations made in tax returns?

There are no specific documentation requirements for taxpayers regarding crypto assets. They should comply with general documentation requirements as regards the recording of purchases, sales, and expenses relating to their crypto asset activities.

(b) What is the evidentiary burden of supporting tax positions when a digital wallet address is lost or shared with other persons?

There is no specific guidance available on this topic. In general, however, it might be expected that the Tax Department would require the taxpayer to furnish it with evidence that the address has been genuinely lost, and hence any subsequent income found to be accruing as a result of use of that address should not be attributed to that taxpayer. If the address is shared, one might expect that the Tax Department would wish to see evidence of the arrangements governing the sharing arrangement.

(c) *Are crypto asset exchanges and wallet providers subject to reporting obligations?*

Crypto asset exchanges and wallet providers are not subject to special reporting obligations to the Tax Department. As stated in section 1.1.1(a), above, however, CySEC is pushing for the transposition of AMLD 5 into Cyprus domestic law. If this happens, such activities will be subject to CySEC regulatory oversight which will include specific AML reporting obligations.

(d) *Are taxpayers holding crypto assets subject to reporting obligations apart from the filing of income tax/capital gains tax returns?*

No, currently, under Cyprus law, they are only obliged to file standard income tax/capital gains returns.

(e) *Are crypto asset exchanges and wallet providers subject to CRS/FATCA reporting?*

Cyprus has enacted legislation to implement a *FATCA Model 1 IGA* with the United States. It has also adopted CRS. All local financial institutions need to comply with FATCA and CRS regulatory requirements. Accounts held by them which fall within the scope of a Reportable Account under FATCA and CRS are subject to reporting on an annual basis. For US taxpayers living in Cyprus, it is not yet clear whether digital assets held in 'wallets' in foreign exchanges need to be reported on the United States Internal Revenue Service (IRS) Form 8938, Statement of Specified Foreign Financial Assets. However, it would be prudent to declare them, since recent unofficial pronouncements from the IRS suggest that it intends to turn its attention to the taxation of crypto assets.[5] The Tax Department has published guidance regarding automatic exchange of financial account information and other information relating to the CRS. However, the definition of 'financial asset' currently used in CRS would not appear to include crypto assets. Organizations operating a crypto asset exchange or acting as a wallet provider would therefore seem to fall outside of CRS reporting requirements.

1.1.5 Civil and Criminal Tax Enforcement

(a) *What powers do the tax authorities have to compel the disclosure of information by third parties, such as exchanges or wallet providers, and have these been used in the past?*

There are no powers in place which are specific to crypto asset linked activities such as exchanges or wallet providers. The Tax Department does have a general right to

5. https://www.jdsupra.com/legalnews/irs-hints-at-form-8938-requirements-for-21273.

request the disclosure of information from a third party which it regards as relevant for the enforcement of taxes of another person. Information as to whether or not this right has been used in respect of exchanges or wallet providers is not in the public domain.

(b) What measures have the tax authorities undertaken in the past to ensure crypto tax compliance?

There have been no measures publicized which relate specifically to crypto tax compliance.

(c) Are the tax authorities cooperating with tax authorities in other jurisdictions on enforcement?

While there are no guidelines or legislation specific to the taxation of, or the exchange of information relating to, crypto assets it should be noted that Cyprus complies fully with all information exchange standards. Specifically:

- Cyprus has ratified the Convention on Mutual Administrative Assistance in Tax Matters.
- It is a signatory to the Multilateral Competent Authority Agreement on the Automatic Exchange of Financial Account Information.
- It has implemented the *Common Reporting Standard* (CRS) from the beginning of 2016 and as of 2017 has started exchanging information with other countries.
- It is bound by *Directive 2014/107/EU* (DAC2) on mandatory automatic exchange of information in the field of taxation.

The *Assessment and Collection of Taxes Law* does, however, contain strong safeguards against inappropriate disclosure of taxpayer information and requires requests for disclosure to conform to strict requirements, thus ruling out so-called fishing expeditions.

Denmark

Anders Oreby Hansen

1. COUNTRY GUIDES

1.1 Denmark

1.1.1 Applicable Tax Law, Guidance, and Case Law

(a) Which laws, regulations, and other administrative guidance exist dealing with crypto assets?

As of May 2020, Denmark has not introduced legislation that specifically deals with crypto assets. Denmark generally treats crypto assets as capital property for tax purposes, taxing gains and allowing for deductions of losses against gains on similar crypto assets.[1] The general rule is that losses may not be deducted as a business expense against ordinary business income when the value of crypto assets that have been received as payment for goods or services has decreased.

The Danish Financial Supervisory Authority (DFSA) has issued various statements explaining that Danish laws may apply depending on the nature of the crypto asset and how it is used.[2] A crypto asset transaction may fall under Danish regulatory authority, depending on whether the crypto asset is considered a form of payment (currency), capital asset (investment), or financial service. The DFSA has rejected the position that crypto assets that were construed like bitcoins or similar cryptocurrencies

1. Juridisk vejledning C.C.2.1.3.3.3 (2020) published by the Danish Tax Authorities.
2. Press Release, Finanstilsynet, 'Orientering om ICO'er' (Information on ICOs) (13 Nov. 2017), https://finanstilsynet.dk/da/Nyheder-og-Presse/Sektornyt/2017/Orientering-om-ICO, archived at https://perma.cc/3A5Y-W4PS.

can be classified as a currency and stated that it would not regulate the use of such assets.[3]

The DFSA has stated that the use of cryptocurrencies as payment is generally not regulated by the Authority, but the applicability of Danish securities law will depend on the specifics of the initial coin offering (ICO). ICOs that are similar to initial public offerings (IPOs) are subject to securities law, and the issuing corporation must publish a prospectus in connection with the ICO. The DFSA has found that cryptocurrencies such as bitcoins and other crypto assets do not fall under any of the financial services categories, including the issuing of electronic money, payment for services, currency exchanges, or the issuing of mortgages. Cryptocurrency/asset activity is thus not covered under current financial regulations.[4]

(b) Which court cases exist dealing with crypto assets?

As of March 2020, only relatively few rulings have been published. The generally most interesting are the following.

In a ruling from 2014, the Danish Tax Council issued a ruling stating that an invoice amount cannot be issued in cryptocurrencies but must be issued in Danish Kroner or another recognized currency. The Council found that any losses in the value of bitcoins cannot be deducted as a cost of doing business when bitcoins are used as a means of payment.[5] Losses on cryptocurrencies can consequently be set off against gains on cryptocurrencies but not against other kind of income/gains.

In a ruling from 2017, the Danish Tax Council found that gains and losses on bookcoins should be taxed according to the rules on financial contracts, as bookcoins should be classified as a structured product covered by the capital gains tax act (section 29.3). Furthermore, the Danish Tax Council found that bookcoin is not a currency.[6]

In a ruling from 2018, the Danish National Tax Council found that income from bitcoin speculation is taxable income (as opposed to income from gains realized on, for example, an individual's one-off sale of a painting, a watch, silverware). Depending on the circumstances, expenses that can be documented and allocated may be deducted according to specific rules in (other) cryptocurrency income.[7]

In another ruling from 2018, the Danish Tax Council found that gains and losses on bitcoins and ether should be included in the taxable income in situations where the transactions had been made for speculation purposes, which from a practical perspective, means that it must always be included in income. The Council also found that it

3. Press Release, Finanstilsynet, Advarsel mod virtuelle valutaer (bitcoin m.fl.) (Warnings Regarding Digital Currencies (Bitcoins etc.)) (17 Dec. 2013), https://www.finanstilsynet.dk/da/Nyheder-og-Presse/Pressemeddelelser/Arkiv/Presse-2013/Advarsel-mod-virtuelle-valutaer-bitcom-mfl-2013, archived at https://perma.cc/UZ2E-G7S7.
4. Cf. 2.
5. SKM2014.226.SR.
6. SKM2017.520.SR.
7. SKM2018.104.

was not possible to deduct any other expenses than those paid directly in connection with the transactions.[8]

In a third ruling from 2018, the Danish Tax Council stated that the main rule is that gains/losses are computed according to a 'bitcoin-for-bitcoin' principle (which correspond to an asset-for-asset principle) and not a first-in first-out (FIFO) principle. However, it is conditional on it being possible to identify each individual asset. If this is not possible a FIFO principle shall be applied. The Danish Tax Council specifically stated that if a method can be established where it is possible to identify each individual bitcoin and Ethereum a bitcoin-for bitcoin principle could be applied.[9]

In a fourth ruling from 2018, the Danish Tax Council confirmed that losses when disposing of bitcoins could be deducted according to specific rules and that direct costs, commissions, and mining fees could be added to the acquisition price and deducted from the sales price.[10]

In a ruling from 2019, the Danish Tax Council confirmed its 2018 position[11] stating that the main rule is that an asset-for-asset principle is applied when computing the taxable income, and as an exception the FIFO principle shall be applied when a partial sale is made of an asset which cannot be identified individually. The Danish Tax Council found it could not discharge the possibility that it is possible to identify which bitcoins and Ethereum that leaves the portfolio but placed the burden of proof in this respect on the taxpayer.[12]

As illustrated by the difference in classification of bitcoins[13] and bookcoins,[14] the case law emphasizes the importance of assessing each specific crypto asset on a stand-alone basis.

1.1.2 Income and Capital Gains Taxes

(a) How are crypto assets classified for income and capital gains tax purposes?

As outlined above under section 1.1.1, Denmark has not introduced legislation that specifically deals with crypto assets. The classification of cryptocurrencies consequently poses challenges and uncertainty for tax purposes due to the lack of a regulatory framework, the absence of common definitions and the diverse technical structure of tokens and coins. The classification for Danish tax law purposes should therefore always be based on a case-by-case assessment of the specific cryptocurrency. That being said, there is no doubt that any crypto asset is considered a taxable asset as

8. SKM2018.130.SR.
9. SKM2018.288.SR.
10. SKM2018.458.
11. From SKM2018.288.SR.
12. SKM2019.67.SR.
13. SKM2014.226.SR.
14. SKM2017.520.SR.

it falls under Denmark's 1903 Tax Act.[15] Consequently, all cryptocurrencies traders are obligated to report their losses and earnings.

The Danish Tax Council has issued rulings on the tax treatment of gains on bitcoins and other crypto assets, cf. section 1.1.1 above, where the Council found that crypto assets should generally be regarded as acquired with a purpose of speculation. The consequence is that gains and losses are included when computing the taxable income. Gains and losses are included in the taxable income (no labour market contributions are triggered on gains in this respect).[16] Investors are taxed on notional gains.[17] Losses can only be carried forward against similar gains according to specific rules. The difference between a classification as 'speculation' compared to a classification as 'business', 'trade' or similar is that the possibilities of deducting losses against other income groups are quite limited. If you, for example, run a leasing business which generates a profit, losses on crypto assets cannot be deducted against that profit. If you run a hotel, which is profitable, and a restaurant, which is loss-making, you can deduct the losses of the restaurant against the profits of the hotel. If you realize a gain on crypto assets that gain is taxable, and you cannot deduct the losses of the restaurant against this profit. If you realize a loss on crypto assets, that loss cannot be deducted against the profits of the hotel, but only carried forward against future gains on similar crypto assets.

No rulings have been published as of May 2020 which deals with security and utility tokens. It is likely that also they will be regarded as acquired with a purpose of speculation and for tax purposes treated as outlined above.

For individuals, gains on speculation are taxed as personal income, whereas losses on speculation only will have a limited deduction value.[18] In round numbers, the tax on profits is approx. 53%, while the losses are deducted by about 28%, as the deduction that can be achieved is only a tax allowance.

For companies, profits and losses are taxed as corporate income at 22% (2020). Partnerships are from a Danish tax perspective tax transparent.

15. Gevinst og tab ved handel med bitcoins og ether, SKAT (3 Apr. 2018), https://skat.dk/skat.aspx?oid= 2271473, archived at https://perma.cc/B9AZ-GZRL.
16. SKM2018.104.SR, SKM2018.130.SR, SKM2018.288.SR, SKM2018.458.SR.
17. The exercise of timely calculation of profit is known as notional gains (or profit). Since there are often a lot of fluctuations, if the profit calculation is done after completion, the profit in respect of each contract in progress is transferred to the profit and loss account of the year by calculating the notional profit. The portion of notional profit to be transferred to the profit and loss account depends on the stage of completion of the individual contract. The notional profit can be the total value of a position, how much value a position controls or an agreed-upon amount in a contract. This term is also used when describing derivative contracts in the options, futures, and currency markets.
18. Personal Income Tax Act paragraph 3, section 2 per contra.

(b) *What are the income/capital gains tax consequences of selling crypto assets against fiat currency?*

From a Danish tax perspective, selling crypto assets against fiat currency is simply a disposal. The gain/loss will have to be computed and included in the taxable income, cf. section 1.1.2(a), above.

(c) *What are the income/capital gains tax consequences of exchanging crypto assets against other crypto assets?*

The exchange of one crypto asset against another crypto asset is regarded as a taxable exchange. A taxpayer exchanging for example bitcoins into another crypto asset and then exchanging such crypto asset back into fiat currency thus triggers two potentially taxable exchanges (rather than only one on the second transaction). From a tax point of view, the exchange of assets involves both an acquisition and a disposal. The sales price of the asset given away and the acquisition cost of the asset acquired is the fair market value of the asset given away. Establishing the fair market value may in itself present a challenge.

(d) *If a distinction is made between business assets and non-business assets, when does trading in crypto assets lead to a trade or business?*

Generally speaking, no published ruling deals with traders in cryptocurrencies. It can be argued that if you are a trader in cryptocurrency, then you will still be taxable on the income, but the tax value of losses and cost may increase. The 'tax value' of a loss is the amount of payable tax 'saved' when a taxpayer can deduct a loss. Example: If a company has a loss of 100 and the corporate tax rate is 22, the tax value would be 22.

The following indicia would suggest that a taxpayer engaged in crypto asset trading is carrying out a business and thus earning income from an active trade or business, rather than having non-business income:

- exercising the trading activity as the taxpayer's main occupation;
- maintaining a separate office or an organization to carry out the transactions;
- exploiting market opportunities by using relevant professional securities trading experience;
- concluding transactions also on behalf of third parties;
- a high number of purchases and sales carried out (e.g., through the use of trading bots); and
- debt financing of transactions.

The difference between a classification as earning income from an active trade or business rather than earning non-business income is exactly the same as described above under section 1.1.2.(a) regarding a classification of income as 'speculation' compared to a classification as 'business', 'trade' or similar. The possibilities of deducting losses against other income groups are quite limited. If you, for example, run a leasing business which generates a profit, losses on crypto assets cannot be deducted against that profit. If you run a hotel, which is profitable, and a restaurant, which is loss-making, you can deduct the losses of the restaurant against the profits of the hotel. If you realize a gain on crypto assets that gain is taxable, and you cannot deduct the losses of the restaurant against this profit. If you realize a loss on crypto assets, that loss cannot be deducted against the profits of the hotel, but only carried forward against future gains on similar crypto assets.

If a taxpayer is successful in demonstrating that he/she in fact from a Danish tax perspective has been carrying out a business in relation to crypto assets, then the ordinary rules will apply. The burden of proof rests with the taxpayer. It must be expected that the threshold for lifting this burden of proof will be rather high.

(e) What are the income/capital gains tax consequences for an employee receiving wages or salaries in crypto assets?

If a taxpayer (e.g., a developer) is remunerated for work carried out under an employment agreement and if such remuneration consist of crypto assets, then taxable income from employment arises at the point in time when the crypto assets are received (thus, not only at the point in time of the exchange of such crypto assets into fiat currency). Depending on the nature of the employment, a withholding obligation resting on the employer may be triggered and the withholding tax (and income tax) will be computed based on the fair market value of the currency in question at the time of receipt. Should the taxpayer at a later point in time sell the crypto assets received as wages or salaries, then the acquisition cost of the crypto assets should be equal to the value used for purposes of calculating the income from employment (i.e., no double taxation).

(f) What are the income/capital gains tax consequences for a merchant receiving payment in crypto assets?

The supplies by a merchant of goods and services, which are remunerated through crypto assets, are to be treated in the exact same way as supplies whose remuneration consists in fiat currency. Thus, for income tax purposes, the fair market value of the cryptocurrency at the time of delivery constitutes the merchant's taxable income. Once the merchant exchanges the crypto assets received into fiat currency, another taxable transaction will occur.

(g) What are the income/capital gains tax consequences of a loss of crypto assets?

The loss of crypto assets – meaning the loss of the private key associated with an address at which crypto assets are stored – is not relevant if the crypto asset is a non-business asset. In particular such circumstances do not lead to negative income from speculative transactions, the reason being that the total extinction or destruction of an asset is not seen as a sale. In contrast, it can be argued that the loss of crypto assets qualifying as business assets may lead to a tax-deductible expense, provided it can be proved what crypto assets were lost. However, it should be stressed that no rulings or guidelines have been published on this topic as of May 2020.

In relation to the difference between business assets and speculative/non-business assets reference is made to the descriptions above under sections 1.1.2(a) and 1.1.2(d).

(h) What are the income/capital gains tax consequences of a loss in value of crypto assets?

The loss in value of crypto assets, which has not been realized through a sales transaction, is normally not relevant if the crypto assets qualify as non-business/speculative assets, cf. above under sections 1.1.2(a) and 1.1.2(d).

(i) What are the income/capital gains tax consequences of forks of crypto assets?

There are no rulings or statements by the Danish tax authorities on blockchain forks, in which a blockchain splits into two blockchains, so that a taxpayer holding crypto assets on the original blockchain now additionally holds the same number of crypto assets on the new blockchain.

It can be argued that forks are to be treated in a similar manner as cases where a listed corporation spins off assets into a separate entity by way of a demerger. Thus, the acquisition costs of the original (forked) crypto asset are to be allocated to the original crypto asset and to the newly received crypto asset, pursuant to the ratio of the fair market values of these two assets at the time of the fork. Additionally, the date of acquisition of the original crypto asset is also the date of acquisition for the newly received crypto asset. This applies equally to crypto assets held within and outside of an active trade or business. Consequently, the fork itself should not yet have any tax consequences: these would only occur when the newly received crypto assets were sold. Determining the fair market value of the newly received crypto asset at the time of the fork can be difficult, and in extreme cases its fair market value can be zero.

An alternative to this approach is to regard the fork as a sale with a subsequent acquisition, in which case taxable income may crystalize, cf. also above under section 1.1.2(a)-(c).

(j) What are the income/capital gains tax consequences of airdrops of crypto assets and are the tax consequences different if the airdropped tokens are unwanted?

An airdrop is a case where crypto assets are given free of charge (mostly for marketing reasons).

A gift of this kind would most likely be classified as personal income and taxed as such at rates up to 56%. An alternative is taxation as a gift, in which case the taxation will depend on the relationship between the donor and the recipient. If it is a gift from parents to children, children to parents, the gift tax will be 15%. Gifts to/from grandparents are also subject to the 15% rate. If a gift is given from a corporation to an individual, or from anyone but the parents/grandparents/children, the gift will be treated as ordinary income and taxed accordingly at rates up to 56%.

It is of no relevance whether the airdropped tokens are wanted or unwanted.

(k) *What are the income/capital gains tax consequences of (solo, pool, and cloud) mining?*

Mining is a proof of work consensus mechanism that always leads to taxable income.[19] In the case of solo mining, any crypto assets received by the miner (i.e., block reward and transaction fees) should be taxable at the point in time they are received by the miner. This income can then be offset by documented expenses such as electricity costs, rent regarding the premises and depreciation charges regarding the technical equipment. These statements regarding solo mining should equally apply to pool mining (where many smaller miners join to form a mining pool, which in turn distributes computing tasks among the individual pool members) and to cloud mining (where a miner does not have to worry about hardware and software, but instead rents hash power from the operator of a data centre, with the crypto assets earned using the computing power belonging to the customer). No rulings or guidelines had been published as of March 2020 which directly address this topic.

(l) *What are the income/capital gains tax consequences of staking crypto assets?*

Proof of stake is a consensus mechanism (an alternative to proof of work) whereby transactions are validated by persons who have high holdings of this respective crypto asset and would, therefore, suffer the greatest damage from a blockchain with incorrect entries. Staking is like mining, but with hardly any use of resources and much more passive in appearance. Thus, any income earned, including staking rewards, should be taxable as income.

(m) *What are the income/capital gains tax consequences of an indirect investment in crypto assets?*

Investors seeking exposure to crypto assets but not wishing to hold these themselves, have various possibilities of an indirect investment through bonds, investment funds of various kinds, etc. In these cases, the taxation depends on the specific nature of the

19. SKM2018.104.SR, SKM2018.130.SR, SKM2018.288.SR, SKM2018.458.SR.

investment vehicle. Danish and foreign equity-based investment funds are as of 2020 allowed to elect a tax classification as equity-based investment companies. Consequently, individual investors may be taxed on any distributions, gains, and losses in the equity income basket, i.e., the same income type as if the investments were made directly in the underlying shares or in an 'Investeringsinsitut med minimumsbeskatning' (IMB) with equity fund status. Taxation in the equity income basket will typically be more beneficial than taxation in the capital income basket. Moreover, for individual investors the 2020 rules may be beneficial when it comes to utilizing any losses on the units. Individual investors can utilize any losses on the units in equity-based investment companies in the equity income while losses on units in equity-based IMBs can only be set off against dividends and gains derived from shares listed on a regulated market and units in equity-based IMBs/investment companies. However, according to the 2020 rules individual investors in equity-based investment companies are still taxed annually according to a mark-to-market principle on any realized dividends as well as unrealized losses and gains and not according to the realization principle. Taxation according to a mark-to-market principle is often considered less beneficial than taxation according to a realization principle as it advances the timing of taxation of gains. The rules are rather extensive and detailed and will not be described further here.

As mentioned in section 1.1.1(b) above, in 2017 the Tax Council found that other cryptocurrencies (bookcoins in that case) that are tied to another value, in the specific case silver, are more similar to structured debt (trade in commodities), and therefore subject to financial contracts taxation. Thus, any income derived from the increase in value of these types of cryptocurrencies is subject to gains tax and loss deductions under the same conditions as financial contracts.[20]

(n) *How is income from crypto assets to be treated under double tax treaty law?*

The Danish tax authorities have not issued any general statements regarding the treatment of crypto assets under double tax treaty law. At any rate, income earned in connection with crypto assets can fall under various allocation rules of the OECD Model Convention:

- Pursuant to Article 7 of the OECD Model Convention, profits of an enterprise of a contracting state are taxable only in that state; if the enterprise, however, carries on business in the other contracting state through a permanent establishment situated therein, then the profits that are attributable to this permanent establishment may be taxed in that other state. Thus, for example, profits of a crypto mining enterprise carried on by a resident of Denmark may only be taxed in Denmark. If the crypto mining enterprise, however, carried on business in

20. SKM2017.520.SR. *See also* 'Digital valuta anset for struktureret fordring' SKAT (31 Aug. 2017), https://skat.dk/skat.aspx?oid=2251503, archived at https://perma.cc/TU75-Y8ZE;Kursgevins tloven (Capital Gains Act) (LBK nr 1283 af 25/10/2016), https://www.retsinformation.dk/Forms/r0710.aspx?id=183750, archived at https://perma.cc/2SC5-3XHR.

Iceland (a popular mining location) through a permanent establishment situated in Iceland, then the profits that are attributable to this permanent establishment may be taxed in Iceland.
- Pursuant to Article 13(5) of the OECD Model Convention, gains from the alienation of any property, other than that referred to in certain other paragraphs, are taxable only in the contracting state of which the alienator is resident. Thus, for example, an investor resident in Denmark selling bitcoins through a crypto exchange located in the United Kingdom may only be taxed in Denmark.

(o) What are the income/capital gains tax consequences of selling crypto assets in an ICO/STO/IEO?

As outlined above crypto assets are not regulated by the DFSA and the Danish Securities legislation and the Capital Markets Act. As an exception certain ICOs may qualify as securities if they, because of their specific nature, are in effect similar to initial public offerings (IPOs), and they may in specific cases fall under the general definition of 'financial instruments' in the Act on Capital Markets.[21] Consequently, they should most likely be taxed as capital income under the Capital Gains Tax Act, Chapter 6. However, an individual assessment must be made in each case.[22] If the ICOs/STOs/IEOs are construed in a manner which mean that they can be classified as a 'financial instrument' gains and losses will generally be taxed or deductible according to the mark-to-market principle.

No rulings have been published as of May 2020 which deals with security and utility tokens in relation to ICOs.

1.1.3 Other Taxes

(a) What are the value added tax/sales tax consequences of selling crypto assets?

The European Court of Justice dealt with value added tax (VAT) aspects of bitcoins in 2015.[23] In the case at hand, Mr Hedqvist operated a website where one could buy bitcoins from him or sell bitcoins to him (the consideration being Swedish fiat currency). The question, which was referred to the ECJ for a preliminary ruling, was

21. Lov om kapitalmarknader (Act on Capital Markets) (LBK nr 12 af 08/01/2018), https://www.rets information.dk/Forms/r0710.aspx?id = 196949, archived at https://perma.cc/74FA-F3PJ; Erhvervsministeriet, Bekendtgørelse om hændelsesrapportering for operatører af væsentlige tjenester (Regulation on Trade Reporting Requirements for Providers of Substantial Services) (BEK nr 457 af 09/05/2018), https://www. finanstilsynet.dk/ ~ /media/Lovgivning/Lovsamlin g/2018/457-090518-pdf.pdf, archived at https://perma.cc/F3XE-FUJP.
22. Finanstilsynet tager stilling til konkret ICO (The Financial Supervisory Authority Considers a Concrete ICO), Finanstilsynet (3 Oct. 2018), https://www.finanstilsynet.dk/Nyheder-og-Press e/Sektornyt/2018/FT-tagerstilling-ICO, archived at https://perma.cc/79Z2-94Q5.
23. ECJ 22 Oct. 2015, C-264/14, *Hedqvist*.

whether his activity was subject to VAT. The ECJ held that, first, no supply of bitcoins was to be assumed in relation to Mr Hedqvist operating the website, but rather a service of exchange. Second, the Court stated that transactions in crypto assets, insofar as they have been accepted by the parties concerned as an alternative means of payment to legal tender and insofar as they do not serve any purpose other than use as means of payment, fall within the scope of the exemption provided for in the EU's VAT Directive for transactions relating to foreign exchange, banknotes, and coins.

In 2016 the Danish Tax Council considered how to classify cryptocurrencies in relation to VAT and found that cryptocurrencies are exempt from VAT.[24] The classification is consistent with the preliminary ruling in the *Hedqvist* case. As of May 2020 no rulings have been published on security and utility tokens in relation to VAT.

The Danish Tax Council has also decided on how the mining of bitcoins should be treated from a VAT perspective.[25] The matter involved a Danish individual who wanted to sell hashing capacity (data capacity) on the electrical grid to foreign customers, an activity that was subject to VAT and the EU reverse charge rules. In its comments to the question, the Council remarked that bitcoin can only be paid if the miner manages to find the correct algorithm – the element of chance could be compared to the situation were the taxpayer wins in a lottery, which also fall outside the Danish VAT regime. Consequently, the Council did not classify the remuneration as a 'remuneration for a service'. The Tax Council also confirmed that income realized from bitcoin mining would not be subject to VAT (but still subject to income tax), and that the taxpayer could receive a refund of electricity duties according to specific rules.

(b) Are payments in crypto assets subject to withholding taxes?

For purposes of the applicability of withholding taxes, payments made by a debtor through the transfer of crypto assets is to be treated in the same manner as payments made in cash. For example, dividends paid out by a corporation with its legal seat and/or its place of management in Denmark to an individual are subject to a withholding tax of 27% (may be reduced/refunded according to an EU directive or tax treaty). If the shareholders of a limited liability company (A/S or ApS) with its legal seat and its place of management in Denmark were to resolve upon a dividend distribution in kind so that the company were to pay out a dividend of, for example, 100 bitcoins, then the distributing entity would have to calculate the 27%/applicable withholding tax and remit it to the competent tax office. In order to do this, the crypto assets distributed would have to be converted into fiat currency, with the withholding tax payable to be calculated based on the grossed-up amount. A conversion is for Danish tax purposes a tax event, and the conversion date would be defined as the day on which

24. SKM2016.83.SR. Momsfritagelse og lønsumsafgift - Køb og salg af Bitcoins (VAT Exemption and Payroll Taxes – Purchase and Sale of Bitcoins), SKAT (26 Jan. 2016), http://skat.dk/skat.aspx?oid=2225268, archived at https://perma.cc/XZG2-WB6J.
25. SKM2017.453.SR. Bitcoin mining og tilrådighedsstillelse af datakapacitet - moms og godtgørelse af elafgifter (Bitcoin Mining and Supply of Data Capacity – VAT and Payment of Electricity Fees), SKAT (27 Jun. 2017), https://skat.dk/skat.aspx?oid=2249418, archived at https://perma.cc/N772-UTZQ.

the conversion is a legal reality. The settlement day may – depending on the specific agreement – differ from the conversion day in this respect. Similarly, an employer paying out wages or salaries through transfer of crypto assets will normally have to calculate and remit the wage withholding tax on the value of the crypto asset, cf. section 1.1.2(e) above.

(c) Does payment of compensation in crypto assets give rise to payroll tax consequences?

Compensation in crypto assets such as bitcoins does not give rise to any special payroll tax consequences and is thus to be treated as any payment in kind. Normally, the employer will have to calculate and remit wage withholding tax and various social security contributions.

(d) Do transactions with crypto assets trigger any transfer taxes?

No stamp duties or similar levies would be applicable under Danish law.

(e) Are firms operating in the crypto space subject to digital service taxes?

As of March 2020, Denmark has not introduced a digital tax.

(f) Are crypto assets subject to gift, inheritance, estate, or wealth taxes?

Transfers of crypto assets between family members are subject to the ordinary rules on gift, inheritance, and estate taxes.

Denmark does not have a wealth tax. However, individuals must still fill out asset declarations.

Inheritance left by a Danish resident is, in general, subject to Danish estate tax regardless of the country of residence of the beneficiary. Inheritance received by a Danish resident from an individual who was not resident in Denmark prior to death is not subject to Danish estate tax except if the inheritance consists of property located in Denmark or of assets related to a permanent establishment in Denmark. However, if an estate is settled before a Danish court, the entire inheritance will become taxable in Denmark, regardless of the country of residence of the deceased and the heirs. The Estate tax is, as the name indicates, a tax on the estate and amounts to 15% and is levied on the part of the assets that falls to the deceased's children and descendants, stepchildren and their descendants, parents, or cohabitant during the last two years of one's life. Inheritance and insurance payments that fall to the deceased's spouse are exempt from estate tax. Inheritance received by any other relatives than the above-mentioned is subject to a supplementary estate tax of 25% of the value of the asset after deduction of the first 15%. The taxes are not levied on the first DKK 301,900 (in 2020) of the estate. All assets of the deceased is valuated on January 1 in the year of death.

Any income, gains, losses, etc. realized prior to that date is taxed according to the ordinary rules. Any net gains on fluctuations, income, etc. realized between 1 January in the year of death and the distribution of assets to the heirs from the estate is subject to a 50% estate tax. Income from gains on shares and dividends are taxed with up to 42%.

Gifts and donations not exceeding DKK 67,100 (in 2020) to the donor's descendants are tax exempt. Gifts to the descendant's spouses may not exceed DKK 23,500 (in 2020) in order to be tax exempt. Gifts and donations to the donor's offspring and their descendants in excess of DKK 67,100 are levied with a gift tax amounting to 15%, and gifts to the donor's stepparents and grand stepparents are levied with a gift tax of 36.25%.

Gifts or inheritance between unrelated individuals are taxable as ordinary income with up to 56% if the recipient is subject to tax in Denmark. A gift is not deductible for the donor.

(g) *Are crypto assets subject to exit tax?*

Denmark has a general exit tax on assets with a latent gain. In short, if you have assets (real estate, shares, speculative assets, business assets, etc.), where there is a latent gain upon relocation, you will be taxed on this gain on departure from Denmark. The latent gain will be computed based on the assets' market value at the time of immigration. The rules on share gains taxation and capital gains tax includes rules in which the exit tax will only be applied if you have been subject to tax in Denmark for 7 of the last 10 years. If you are subject to tax in Denmark for less than 7 years in the last 10 years, you are generally exempt from exit tax with respect to these assets. It is possible to apply for a deferral of any taxes triggered. Often the Danish Tax Authorities will request some kind of security/collateral for giving such extension.

(h) *Can mining trigger gambling tax?*

The situation has not been specifically decided by the Danish Tax Authorities. However, so far income from mining has been classified as taxable income, cf. section 1.1.2(k) above, not gambling income.[26]

26. SKM2018.104.SR, SKM2018.130.SR, SKM2018.288.SR, SKM2018.458.SR.

1.1.4 Compliance and Documentation Obligations

(a) What documentation requirements exist for taxpayers regarding crypto assets and are there best practices in recordkeeping to support representations made in tax returns?

Denmark has no specific documentation requirements for taxpayers holding crypto assets.

Thus, such taxpayers must comply with the general documentation requirements. The law, for example, contains the obligation of taxpayers (not already subject to the requirements of double entry bookkeeping) to record revenues and expenses. Intentional violation of this obligation may be punished. Taxpayers trading crypto assets on exchanges should therefore download and store their transaction histories in order to be prepared for a tax audit.

(b) What is the evidentiary burden of supporting tax positions when a digital wallet address is lost or shared with other persons?

Formally, under Danish tax law, the authorities must investigate and determine ex officio the factual and legal circumstances which are essential for the levying of taxes; they have to take into account any information provided to them, even if it is for the benefit of the taxpayer. However, under Danish law the burden of proof lies on the taxpayer. This burden is not always easy to carry, but the result remains the same.

(c) Are crypto asset exchanges and wallet providers subject to reporting obligations?

Under Danish law all individuals, corporations, businesses, and any kind of non-transparent entity are subject to an obligation to declare all assets on a yearly basis (together with the tax return). Non-compliance may be a criminal offence.

(d) Are taxpayers holding crypto assets subject to reporting obligations apart from the filing of income tax/capital gains tax returns?

As mentioned above under (c) you are under Danish law subject to an obligation to declare all your assets on a yearly basis (together with the tax return). Non-compliance may be a criminal offence.

(e) Are crypto asset exchanges and wallet providers subject to CRS/FATCA reporting?

The Danish tax authorities have not issued any guidance on the question whether operators of crypto exchanges or providers of crypto wallets must annually report their customers' data under CRS/FATCA. In this context, it may be argued that the term 'financial asset' as currently defined under CRS[27] essentially only covers traditional financial assets and does not comprise crypto assets. A crypto asset exchange or wallet provider would thus only be classified as a financial institution (meaning that it becomes subject to reporting) if it – in addition to crypto assets – also allows deposits of fiat currency. The topic is, however, currently undecided.

1.1.5 Civil and Criminal Tax Enforcement

(a) What powers do the tax authorities have to compel the disclosure of information by third parties, such as exchanges or wallet providers, and have these been used in the past?

The Danish Tax Authorities have rather extensive legislative power to request and obtain information and can request such information on specific individuals/enterprises. Thus, the Danish tax authorities could indeed compel a Danish crypto asset exchange or wallet provider to hand over information regarding Danish customers. Whether this has happened in the past is not in the public domain.

(b) What measures have the tax authorities undertaken in the past to ensure crypto tax compliance?

It is not known what measures the Danish tax authorities have undertaken in the past to ensure crypto tax compliance, apart from publishing guidance regarding the application of the existing laws to transactions with crypto assets.

(c) Are the tax authorities cooperating with tax authorities in other jurisdictions on enforcement?

In order to ensure compliance by taxpayers holding crypto assets, the Danish tax authorities have several tools at their disposal for obtaining information from abroad (e.g., from crypto asset exchanges located outside of Denmark): All of Denmark's (currently approximately seventy-five) double taxation treaties contain articles on the exchange of information between competent authorities.[28] Denmark has also concluded seven tax information exchange agreements with certain no-tax jurisdictions.

Furthermore, Denmark can – based on EU law – request information from other EU Member States that is foreseeably relevant to the administration and enforcement of its domestic laws.[29] Finally, Denmark has also ratified the OECD/Council of Europe

27. OECD, Standard for Automatic Exchange of Financial Account Information in Tax Matters, 2nd ed., 45.
28. Cf. Article 26 of the OECD Model Convention.
29. Cf. Council Directive 2011/16/EU of 15 Feb. 2011 on administrative cooperation in the field of taxation and repealing Directive 77/799/EEC, as amended.

Convention on Mutual Administrative Assistance in Tax Matters, which similarly gives the Danish tax authorities access to information held abroad.

It is currently not public knowledge whether and to what extent the Danish tax authorities are cooperating with tax authorities in other jurisdictions on enforcement and whether they have made use of the various instruments mentioned above in respect of crypto asset holdings of taxpayers.

Finland

Antti Lehtimaja

1. COUNTRY GUIDES

1.1 Finland

1.1.1 Applicable Tax Law, Guidance, and Case Law

(a) Which laws, regulations, and other administrative guidance exist dealing with crypto assets?

Finnish tax laws do not mention crypto assets. However, in 2013, the Finnish Tax Administration published on its website[1] specific guidance ('the Guidance') dealing with certain tax issues relating to crypto assets. The Guidance has been renewed a few times, with the most recent update being issued in January 2020.[2]

(b) Which court cases exist dealing with crypto assets?

A decision of the Supreme Administrative Court[3] dealt with the income tax treatment of capital gains from the sale of the ether cryptocurrency. Also, a decision of the Administrative Court of Helsinki[4] dealt with the income tax treatment of the exchange of cryptocurrency into another cryptocurrency. In addition, a decision of the Central Tax Board[5] dealt with the VAT treatment of the exchange provision charged for the sale

1. www.vero.fi.
2. Virtuaalivaluuttojen verotus 22 Jan. 2020 (VH/5083/00.01.00/2019).
3. *Korkein hallinto-oikeus*, KHO 2019:42.
4. *Helsingin hallinto-oikeus*, 6 Jul. 2018 (18/0426/3).
5. *Keskusverolautakunta*, KVL 2014/34.

and purchase of cryptocurrencies. Finally, a decision of the European Court of Justice (ECJ)[6] dealt with the VAT treatment of a bitcoin exchange service.

1.1.2 *Income and Capital Gains Taxes*

(a) *How are crypto assets classified for income and capital gains tax purposes?*

In accordance with the Guidance, for taxpayers who are taxed in accordance with the Finnish Income Tax Act,[7] crypto assets are classified as property (*omaisuus*) and are therefore subject to tax rules relating to capital gains from the alienation of property. The classification is based on the above-mentioned decision of the Supreme Administrative Court (KHO 2019:42). In that case, the tax ruling applicant had invested in the ether cryptocurrency and intended to sell these tokens for profit for either euros or dollars. As ether had 'monetary value', the court deemed it to be property and the sale of it was subject to capital gains taxation rules.

However, crypto assets are not treated as securities (*arvopaperi*), currencies (*valuutta*) or other means of payment for the purposes of the Finnish Income Tax Act. For those taxpayers who are taxed in accordance with the Finnish Business Income Tax Act,[8] crypto assets are treated either as liquid assets (*rahoitusomaisuus*), inventories (*vaihto-omaisuus*), investment assets (*sijoitusomaisuus*), fixed assets (*käyttöomaisuus*) or other assets (*muu omaisuus*), depending on the circumstances.

(b) *What are the income/capital gains tax consequences of selling crypto assets against fiat currency?*

In accordance with the Guidance, any gain or loss when selling crypto assets against fiat currency is either taxable income or a deductible loss. The calculation of the gain or loss and the applicable tax rate depends generally on whether the assets are business assets or non-business assets and whether or not the seller is a natural person or a corporate entity.

For natural persons who hold their crypto assets as non-business assets, any capital gain is taxed as capital income (*pääomatulo*). In accordance with the Income Tax Act, capital income is subject to a flat 30% tax rate, but to the extent the annual total amount of the capital income of the taxpayer exceeds EUR 30,000, the tax rate increases to 34%. The capital gain is calculated by deducting from the sales price the sales and acquisition costs. Unless the taxpayer can prove otherwise, a FIFO (first in first out) principle is applied when deciding which assets have been sold. Where the capital gain amount is substantial, the taxpayer is entitled to use in the calculation of the capital gain a presumptive acquisition cost (*hankintameno-olettama*), which is

6. ECJ 22 Oct. 2015, C-264/14, *Hedqvist*.
7. *Tuloverolaki*, 1992, as amended.
8. *Laki elinkeinotulon verottamisesta*, 1968, as amended.

20% of the sales price, or 40% of the sales price if the crypto assets have been held for ten years prior to the sale. In case a presumptive acquisition cost is used, no sales costs can be deducted from the sales price. A capital loss can be carried forward for five years to be deducted from capital income. To the extent the total annual sales price of property (including crypto assets) sold by a natural person does not exceed EUR 1,000, any gain is exempted and any loss is not deductible.[9]

For natural persons who hold their crypto assets as business assets, any sales price of the assets is business income and any acquisition cost is deductible therefrom. In accordance with the Finnish Income Tax Act, business income is taxed so that an amount up to 20% (or 10% if the person requests so) of the assets relating to the business activity at the end of the tax year is taxed as capital income and the remaining amount is taxed as earned income (*ansiotulo*). Earned income is taxed on a progressive tax rate rising from 0% to approximately 56%. Losses of the business income source can be carried forward for ten years to be deducted from business income.[10]

For corporate entities, any sales price of the assets is income and any acquisition cost is deductible. A gain is taxed at a rate of 20%. Losses can be carried forward for five years to be deducted from capital gains in case the crypto assets belong to non-business assets of the entity. In case crypto assets belong to the business assets of the entity, losses can be carried forward for ten years to be deducted from the business income. For partnerships, the taxation of the gain (after deducting any losses of the partnership) takes place at the level of the partners. Certain corporate entities are exempted.[11]

(c) What are the income/capital gains tax consequences of exchanging crypto assets against other crypto assets?

In accordance with the Guidance, the exchange of crypto assets against other crypto assets is a taxable event for income tax purposes and thus creates a capital gain or a deductible loss. The position taken in the Guidance is based on the above-mentioned Administrative Court of Helsinki decision of 6 July 2018. The rules regarding capital gains and losses described above in section 1.1.2(b) apply to these situations. The values used for income tax purposes in the exchange transaction are the fair market values of the different crypto assets denominated in euros. In case a market value cannot be reliably denominated for either of the crypto assets, the acquisition cost is used (i.e., the exchange does not lead to a realization event).

9. Sections 45-48, 50 and 124 of the Finnish Income Tax Act.
10. Sections 38 and 118 of the Finnish Income Tax Act, section 1 of the Finnish Act on the Income Tax Scale in 2020 (*Vuoden 2020 tuloveroasteikkolaki*), List of the income Tax Percentages of Finnish Municipalities and Congregations in 2020 (*Luettelo kuntien ja seurakuntien tulovero-prosenteista vuonna 2020*).
11. Sections 16, 20-23, 119 and 124 of the Finnish Income Tax Act, section 8a of the Finnish Business Income Tax Act.

(d) *If a distinction is made between business assets and non-business assets, when does trading in crypto assets lead to a trade or business?*

In accordance with the Guidance, trading in crypto assets is generally deemed as business activity if it is continuous, systematic, active, based on economic risk and strives to produce profits. The activity is evaluated as a whole when determining whether or not these characteristics are fulfilled. If an entity carries on business activity and, in addition to that invests into crypto assets, such crypto assets are generally deemed to belong to the business assets of the entity. If such activity is carried on by a natural person, it is generally not deemed to constitute business activity, unless the above-mentioned characteristics apply and the capital amount invested in the activity is substantial.

(e) *What are the income/capital gains tax consequences for an employee receiving wages or salaries in crypto assets?*

The Guidance does not address this scenario. Pursuant to basic taxation principles, the fair market value of the crypto assets at the time of receipt of the crypto assets should be regarded as earned income of the employee. If the employee also receives a monetary salary (euros), the tax must be withheld from this salary by the employer and paid to the Tax Administration monthly. In case no monetary salary is paid, the tax is assessed directly to the employee as 'back taxes' after the taxation for the tax year in question has been processed. Any realized increase or decrease in value after receiving the crypto assets is taxed as capital income or loss as described above in section 1.1.2(b).

(f) *What are the income/capital gains tax consequences for a merchant receiving payment in crypto assets?*

In accordance with the Guidance, the supply by a merchant of goods or services remunerated through crypto assets is to be treated in the exact same way as supplies whose remuneration consists in fiat currency. Thus, for income tax purposes, the fair market value of the crypto assets received constitutes the merchant's taxable income. Once the merchant exchanges the crypto assets received into fiat currency, another taxable transaction will occur.

(g) *What are the income/capital gains tax consequences of a loss of crypto assets?*

In accordance with the Guidance, a loss of crypto assets that belong to the business assets of the taxpayer results in the acquisition cost being tax deductible. In case the crypto assets are non-business assets, a tax deduction will not be allowed.

(h) *What are the income/capital gains tax consequences of a loss in value of crypto assets?*

In accordance with the Guidance, to the extent the crypto assets belong to the non-business assets, liquid assets, fixed assets, or other assets of the taxpayer, the non-realized loss in value of the crypto assets are not deductible for income tax purposes. However, a non-realized loss in value at the end of the fiscal year of crypto assets belonging to the inventories or investment assets of a taxpayer is deductible for income tax purposes (and decrease the acquisition cost of the assets correspondingly).

(i) *What are the income/capital gains tax consequences of forks of crypto assets?*

In accordance with the Guidance, when a blockchain splits into two blockchains so that a taxpayer holding crypto assets on the original blockchain holds thereafter the same number of crypto assets also on the new blockchain, the acquisition cost of the new crypto assets is deemed to be zero for income tax purposes. The Guidance does not, however, state what the holding time of the new crypto assets (from the date of the acquisition of the original crypto assets or from the date of the fork) should be at the sale of these assets as the holding time is relevant for calculating the amount of the capital gain in the case of non-business assets of an natural person (as explained above in section 1.1.2(b)).

(j) *What are the income/capital gains tax consequences of airdrops of crypto assets and are the tax consequences different if the airdropped tokens are unwanted?*

There are no specific rules regarding airdrops in the Guidance. However, on the basis of general taxation principles, it is likely that crypto assets granted free of charge would be subject to gift taxation in the hands of the recipient if the fair market value of the gift exceeds EUR 5,000. In case such crypto assets are sold, the acquisition cost would be the fair market value of the assets when receiving such assets. If the airdropped crypto assets are received as consideration for a supply of service, the party granting the crypto assets should then be taxed on the realized value increase, whereas the fair market value of the crypto assets should be deemed as taxable income (either business income or earned income) for the party receiving the crypto assets.

(k) *What are the income/capital gains tax consequences of (solo, pool, and cloud) mining?*

In accordance with the Guidance, for a natural person not engaged in a business activity, the fair market value at the time of receipt of any crypto assets received from mining activities is treated as earned income. The Guidance does not, however, distinguish whether it is a question of solo, pool or cloud mining. Should the activity be deemed to constitute a business activity (*see* the requirements above in section 1.1.2(d)), the fair market value of the crypto assets would be deemed as business income. Similarly, the fair market value of any crypto assets received from mining activities received by a corporate entity is treated as taxable income of such a corporate entity. Any cost relating to mining activity, such as electricity and depreciation from the acquisition cost of equipment, is deductible. When selling the crypto assets received from mining activities, the acquisition cost of such assets is deemed to be the fair market value of the assets at the time of receipt.

(l) *What are the income/capital gains tax consequences of staking crypto assets?*

In accordance with the Guidance, for a natural person not engaged in a business activity, the fair market value at the time of the receipt of any crypto assets received from staking operations are taxed as capital income. Should the activity be deemed as a business activity, the fair market value of the crypto assets would be deemed as business income. Similarly, the fair market value of any crypto assets received from staking activities received by a corporate entity is treated as taxable income of such a corporate entity. When selling the crypto assets received from staking activities, the acquisition cost of such assets is deemed to be the fair market value of the assets at the time of receipt.

(m) *What are the income/capital gains tax consequences of an indirect investment in crypto assets?*

The Guidance does not address any indirect investment issues. On the basis of general taxation principles, the same capital gain and loss rules apply to direct and indirect investments in crypto assets. Normal dividend/interest taxation rules apply to dividends/interests received from entities investing in crypto assets.

(n) *How is income from crypto assets to be treated under double tax treaty law?*

The tax treaties concluded by Finland do not mention anything about the treatment of crypto assets. Nor does the Guidance mention anything about the matter. Therefore, the general rules are followed, which means that a Finnish resident's income and capital gains relating to crypto assets is taxed in Finland unless the Finnish resident has a permanent establishment in a tax treaty state and the income pertains to that permanent establishment. It also not clear to what extent mining operations in Finland would create a permanent establishment to a non-resident taxpayer.

(o) What are the income/capital gains tax consequences of selling crypto assets in an ICO/STO/IEO?

The Guidance does mention generally the tax treatment of Initial Coin Offerings (ICOs), stating that if an investor acquires crypto assets from a company in an ICO, the investor will realize a taxable capital gain or deductible loss later when selling these crypto assets. It is stated, however, that the terms of ICOs are different in each case and, therefore, the tax consequences will be determined on the basis of the true nature of the investment to be made. So far, there has been at least one ICO in Finland and the Tax Administration has issued non-public advance rulings on a few more cases.[12] The Guidance does not mention Security Token Offerings (STOs) or Initial Exchange Offerings (IEOs), but the above-mentioned statement about the determination of the true nature of the investments in those transactions and basing the taxation on that should also apply.

1.1.3 *Other Taxes*

(a) What are the value added tax/sales tax consequences of selling crypto assets?

According to the Guidance, following the direction offered by the ECJ in the C-264/14 (*Hedqvist*) case, the sale of crypto assets is generally deemed to be a VAT exempt financial service. However, in case of utility tokens, the sale could be deemed as a supply of goods or services and thus be subject to VAT. Finland does not levy any sales tax.

A decision of the Central Tax Board (KVL 2014/34) dealt with the VAT treatment of exchange provision charged for the sale and purchase of cryptocurrencies. The applicant company offered a technical platform for purchasing and selling bitcoins. It charged a provision from purchasers and sellers that was a certain percentage of the sales or purchase price. The Central Tax Board considered that bitcoins were 'payment instruments' for VAT purposes and thus the provision was a reward for supplying a financial service as meant by section 42 of the Finnish VAT Act and Article 135.1(d) of the EU Directive (2006/112/EC). The provision received by the applicant company was exempted from VAT.

(b) Are payments in crypto assets subject to withholding taxes?

The Guidance does not address withholding tax treatment of crypto assets. However, as the Tax Administration does not accept payment of tax in crypto assets, any payments made in the form of crypto assets should be treated for withholding tax purposes in the same way as any payments made in kind. In case the payment of a

12. *Stellato*, Is Finland the Next Crypto Tax Super Power?, Kluwer international Tax Blog, 21 Jun. 2019.

dividend, interest, royalty or a salary is subject to withholding tax and there is not an attached cash payment from which the withholding of the tax could be made, the payer is not obligated to make the withholding and the obligation to pay the tax shifts to the non-resident recipient of the payment.

(c) Does the payment of compensation in crypto assets give rise to payroll tax consequences?

The Guidance does not address any payroll tax situations relating to crypto assets. However, in case crypto assets are received by an employee as compensation for work, the employer would need to pay the same social security contributions and statutory employment-related insurance contributions as in the case of a cash salary. The amount of these contributions would be based on the fair market value of the crypto assets at the receipt of the compensation.

(d) Do transactions with crypto assets trigger any transfer taxes?

The Guidance does not address the transfer tax consequences relating to transactions with crypto assets. Finnish transfer tax is levied only in the case of transfers of securities (shares) or real property. In case crypto assets are used as a means of payment when purchasing securities or real property, transfer taxes would be due. Security tokens that entitle their holder to subscribe for shares in a Finnish company could be deemed as 'securities' for Finnish transfer tax purposes. Therefore, transactions with such tokens could be subject to Finnish transfer tax.

(e) Are firms operating in the crypto space subject to digital service taxes?

Finland does not levy a digital services tax.

(f) Are crypto assets subject to gift, inheritance, estate, or wealth taxes?

The Guidance mentions the possibility of receiving crypto assets without acquisition cost, but does not elaborate on the related gift or inheritance taxation. However, on the basis of general taxation principles, any crypto assets that are donated or that pass from a deceased person to a beneficiary are subject to gift tax or inheritance tax at progressive rates (up to 33 %) that depend on the relationship of the donor/deceased and the recipient. Donations up to EUR 5,000 and inheritances up to EUR 20,000 are generally exempted.

Finland does not levy any wealth tax (other than real estate tax).

(g) *Are crypto assets subject to exit tax?*

Finland has implemented the EU's ATAD 1 exit tax provisions in the Finnish Business Income Tax Act. On the basis of those rules, an exit tax is levied on corporate entities on the accrued value of certain assets until the exit date. Taxation is effectuated in specifically defined situations where the assets or the residence of the owner of the assets is transferred out of Finland thereby making it so that Finland no longer has a taxation right to those assets. The rules do not specify whether the 'assets' should also include crypto assets and the Guidance is also silent on this issue, but crypto assets should be within the scope of these rules. Currently, no exit tax rules apply to natural persons holding crypto assets.

(h) *Can mining trigger gambling tax?*

Finland does not levy any gambling tax. Finland does levy a lottery tax but, even though the Guidance does not address this matter, the scope of the lottery tax should not cover mining activities.

1.1.4 *Compliance and Documentation Obligations*

(a) *What documentation requirements exist for taxpayers regarding crypto assets and are there best practices in recordkeeping to support representations made in tax returns?*

The Guidance states that the taxpayer should voluntarily disclose all the income received from a crypto asset transaction (as this information is, for example, in case of natural persons not included in their pre-filled tax return forms since the Tax Administration cannot acquire this information beforehand). It is recommended to save all the documentation and keep sufficient calculations of the assets and transactions for at least six years for possible tax audits.

(b) *What is the evidentiary burden of supporting tax positions when a digital wallet address is lost or shared with other persons?*

In accordance with the Finnish tax laws, after the taxpayer has completed its tax reporting obligations, both the taxpayer and the Tax Administration must participate in the investigation of the matter. Primarily, the party who has better access to the information must present evidence. In the case of the loss of the crypto assets due to the loss of the digital wallet address, this question is not relevant as, according to the Guidance, the loss of the crypto assets other than by realizing the decrease of the value is not tax deductible. For natural persons engaged in business activity or corporate entities, such losses could be deductible (if also deducted in accounting).

(c) *Are crypto asset exchanges and wallet providers subject to reporting obligations?*

Registered crypto assets exchanges and wallet providers are required to report the identification information of their clients to the banking and payment account register held by Finnish Customs. The Finnish Tax Administration does not have access to the information recorded in the banking and payment account register as it is held only for terrorism financing and money laundering monitoring purposes.

(d) *Are taxpayers holding crypto assets subject to reporting obligations apart from the filing of income tax/capital gains tax returns?*

No.

(e) *Are crypto asset exchanges and wallet providers subject to CRS/FATCA reporting?*

The Guidance does not state whether crypto assets exchanges and wallet providers should be deemed subject to reporting obligations under CRS/FATCA.

1.1.5 Civil and Criminal Tax Enforcement

(a) *What powers do the tax authorities have to compel the disclosure of information by third parties, such as exchanges or wallet providers, and have these been used in the past?*

Under the Finnish tax law any third party is required to provide information to the Finnish Tax Administration if such information is necessary for determining another party's taxation. The information request of the Tax Administration must be, however, specific and not general in its nature.[13]

(b) *What measures have the tax authorities undertaken in the past to ensure crypto tax compliance?*

As noted in section 1.1.1(a), the Finnish Tax Administration has published the Guidance relating to the taxation of crypto assets. In addition, by managing to obtain certain information from crypto asset exchanges and wallet providers, the Finnish Tax

13. Section 19 of the Finnish Act on Tax Assessment procedure (*Laki verotusmenettelystä 1995, as amended*).

Administration has been successful in assessing taxes for some taxpayers who have failed to disclose their profits from crypto asset trades in their tax returns.[14]

(c) Are the tax authorities cooperating with tax authorities in other jurisdictions on enforcement?

Although the exchange of such information through cooperation is allowed by the articles in Finnish tax treaties, agreements on the exchange of information in tax matters with non-tax treaty countries, the EU Assistance Directive on administrative cooperation in the field of taxation and the (OECD/Council of Europe) Multilateral Convention on Mutual Administrative Assistance in Tax Matters, there is no evidence of this kind of cooperation to date.

14. In an interview with the Finnish National Broadcasting company published in Nov. 2017, the Finnish Tax Administration informed that it had analysed the transaction information of over 10,000 wallets which resulted in back taxes in more than 500 cases.

France

Michel Collet & Matthieu Sabonnadiere

1. COUNTRY GUIDES

1.1 France

1.1.1 Applicable Tax Law, Guidance, and Case Law

(a) Which laws, regulations, and other administrative guidance exist dealing with crypto assets?

For tax purposes, most of the treatment of crypto assets relies on standard tax provisions.

However, the Finance Act for 2019[1] introduced a specific provision in the French tax code[2] dealing with the taxation of gains derived by individuals from the occasional sale of crypto assets. It was later completed by a decree[3] which introduced filing obligations. The new obligations are now included in the French tax code.[4]

Additionally, the French tax authorities published guidance on crypto assets:

- transactions realized by individuals on an occasional basis;[5]
- transactions realized by individuals and businesses on a regular basis;[6]
- mining operations;[7] and
- inheritance and gifts of crypto assets.[8]

1. Law n°2018-1317 of 28 Dec. 2018.
2. Article 150 VH *bis* of the French Tax Code.
3. Decree n°2019-656 of 27 Jun. 2019 regarding tax filing obligations for resident individuals as they derive gains from the sale of digital assets
4. Article 1649 *bis* C of the French Tax Code.
5. BOI-RPPM-PVBMC-30.
6. BOI-BIC-CHAMP-60-50 n°730.
7. BOI-BNC-CHAMP-10-10-20-40 n°1080.
8. BOI-ENR-DMTG-10-10-20-10 n°10.

(b) Which court cases exist dealing with crypto assets?

A landmark Tax Supreme Court's decision of the *Conseil d'Etat*[9] determined that:

- Occasional sales of cryptocurrencies by individuals are subject to capital gains tax ('CGT') on movable assets. However, this holding was later overridden by the Finance Act for 2019.
- Trading business in cryptocurrencies, by individuals or companies, is subject to income tax as business income. The French tax authorities' guidance is line with this ruling.[10]
- Earnings derived from crypto mining, by individual or companies, are subject to income tax as non-business income in accordance with the French tax authorities' guidance.[11]

The European Court of Justice (ECJ) ruled that the exchange of crypto assets for fiat currency is VAT-exempt.[12]

From a civil law perspective, a French commercial court (*Tribunal de Commerce*) ruled that crypto assets are fungible and consumable items (*fongibles et consomptibles*).

1.1.2 Income and Capital Gains Taxes

(a) How are crypto assets classified for income and capital gains tax purposes?

The tax treatment depends on whether transactions are regarded an occasional trading or constitute a business due to the conditions of trading and their volume.

- Individual/Non-Business Treatment

The Individual/Non-Business regime applies to:

- Tokens (for example, received through an ICO) that do not have the features of securities; and
- Any **digital representation of value** which is not issued by a central bank or public authority but is accepted as a medium of exchange and can be transferred, stored or traded electronically[13] (practically speaking, currency tokens, bitcoins, ether, etc.).

9. Tax Supreme Court (Conseil d'Etat) 26 Apr. 2018, n° 417809.
10. BOI-BIC-CHAMP-60-50 n°730.
11. BOI-BNC-CHAMP-10-10-20-40 n°1080.
12. ECJ 22 Oct. 2015, C-264/14, *Hedqvist*.
13. Article L. 54-10-1 of the French 'Code monétaire et financier'.

However, should the trading activity of the individual be regarded as meeting the conditions of business activity, the tax treatment would be different as described in section 1.1.3(b) below.

The Individual/Business regime does not apply to crypto assets that have the features of securities, futures contracts, or savings bonds.[14] The tax treatment of those crypto assets is not defined in the guidelines, but should be applicable to the comparable existing securities.

- Business Treatment for Individuals and Companies

The tax treatment of transactions in crypto assets essentially depends on their accounting classification:[15]

- **Utility tokens** are classified as **intangibles,**[16] if the owner intends to use the services or goods attached to the token over several tax years. These assets may be amortized and depreciated under standard accounting principles.
- **Security tokens** that have the features of **securities, futures contract or savings bonds** receive the same accounting treatment as these financial instruments.
- **Currency tokens** and other tokens are treated as **cash instruments.**[17] Potential exchange variations are booked in specific transitory accounts[18] but are disregarded for tax purposes. However, unrealized losses may be addressed through a tax-deductible provision for losses.[19]

(b) *What are the income/capital gains tax consequences of selling crypto assets against fiat currency?*

- Individual/Non-Business

Capital gains derived from the occasional trading of crypto assets by individuals[20] are taxable at a flat 30% rate (including 12.8% personal income tax rate and 17.2% social taxes) unless the sales proceeds are lower than € 305. Losses may be offset against gains on other crypto assets derived in the same tax year. Losses may not be carried forward.

Gross capital gain formula: Sales price - (Tax cost of the portfolio * Sales Price / Portfolio value)

14. BOI-RPPM-PVBMC-30-10 n° 50 and 60.
15. Article 619-1 of the French Accounting Code (PCG).
16. Article 619-11 of the PCG.
17. Account 5202 'jetons détenus'.
18. Accounts 478602 and 478702.
19. Article 619-12 of the PCG.
20. Article 150 VH *bis* of the French Tax Code.

- Sales price: consideration received for the sale of crypto assets (cash, assets, services, etc.). Transaction fees are deductible from the sales price, but not from the ratio Sales Price / Portfolio value.
- Tax cost is portfolio's purchase price (not only assets being sold) with adjustment in case of previous sales or exchanges. The tax cost of inherited crypto assets is their fair market value upon death (or the value reported to the tax authorities).

The tax value of the existing crypto assets is not itemized. The tax cost of the sold assets is defined in proportion of the aggregate value of the portfolio.

Example:[21]

In January, Judy purchases € 1,000 in crypto assets.

In March, the fair market value of her portfolio is € 1,200. She sells some assets for € 450. The gain is: 450 (sales price) – (1,000 (acquisition cost) x 450 (sale price) / 1,200 (portfolio value)) = 450 – 375 = € 75.

In August, the value of the portfolio increases to € 1,300. She decides to sell all her crypto assets. For the computation of the gain, the fraction of capital registered in the first sale (€ 375) must be deducted. The taxable gain is calculated as follows: 1,300 (sale price) – [(1,000 (acquisition cost) – 375 (initial capital) x 1,300 (sale price) /1,300 (portfolio value)] = 1,300 – 625 = € 675

Ultimately, Judy received € 1,300 + €450 = € 1,750 for a € 1,000 initial investment. The taxable gain is € 750 (75 + 675).

– Individuals/Business and Companies

Profits derived from regular/recurring trading of crypto assets by individuals[22] are treated as business income and subject to standard progressive income tax.

The tax treatment of transactions should depend on the accounting classification of the crypto assets:

- Transfer of utility tokens booked as intangibles should entail a capital gain or a loss depending on the book value. For companies, standard corporate income ('CIT') tax rate should apply (28% or 31%).
- Transfer of security tokens which have the same features as securities, future contracts or saving bonds should be subject to the tax regime applicable to those financial instruments[23] (CIT and personal income tax for individuals).

21. All examples are based on the French tax authorities' guidelines registered as BOI-RPPM-PVBMC-30-20.
22. Article L. 110-1 of the French Commercial Code, Article 34 of the French tax Code, and BOI-BIC-CHAMP-60-50 n°730.
23. Position from the paper on taxation of crypto assets issued by Paris Europlace, Apr. 2019 (*Rapport du groupe de travail de Paris Europlace sur la fiscalité des actifs numériques*), and by the reference book of accounting (Memento Comptable 2020, §37085, Editions Francis Lefebvre).

- Transfer of currency tokens and other tokens should be treated as ordinary income or loss.[24]

For the purpose of the calculation of the taxable income or gain (or loss), the First-In First-Out method of determining which crypto asset has been sold should apply.

(c) *What are the income/capital gains tax consequences of exchanging crypto assets against other crypto assets?*

The consequences are:

- One-off transactions by individuals/non-businesses: gains derived from the exchange should be tax neutral with the tax value of the original assets to be carried over. However, exchanges of crypto assets for cash (or other kind of consideration) are taxable events.[25]
- Business treatment: neither the statute nor guidance addresses that kind of transaction. Therefore, the exchange should be regarded as a taxable event (even though there has been a lobbying effort for roll-over relief).[26]

(d) *If a distinction is made between business assets and non-business assets, when does trading in crypto assets lead to a trade or business?*

The line between personal and business assets is drawn by the trading pattern and the search for profits.[27]

According to administrative guidance, the distinction between regular and occasional trading of crypto assets is based on a case-by-case analysis which relies on facts and circumstances. Distinction is made generally made based on the following criteria[28]: frequency of the transactions, duration of the holding periods, number, and value of the transactions or conditions of purchase.

(e) *What are the income/capital gains tax consequences for an employee receiving wages or salaries in crypto assets?*

Because of a lack of specific tax provisions addressing the payment of wages or salaries in crypto assets, the standard provisions should apply with the following effects:

- payments would be subject to both employer and employee social taxes under standard conditions, and

24. Article 619-15 of the PCG.
25. Article 150 VH *bis*, II, A of the French tax Code.
26. Rapport sur la fiscalité des actifs numériques, Paris Europlace, Apr. 2019.
27. Article L110-1 of the French Commercial Code.
28. BOI-BIC-CHAMP-60-50 n°730.

- the employee would be taxable at standard personal income tax rate[29] on the value of the assets, even if no cash was received.

(f) What are the income/capital gains tax consequences for a merchant receiving payment in crypto assets?

There are no specific tax provisions existing for payments received in crypto assets in exchange for the sale of goods or services. Under general tax provisions, such payments should be treated as business profits for income tax purposes equal to their fair market value at the time the exchange is completed.

(g) What are the income/capital gains tax consequences of a loss of crypto assets?

There are no specific provisions governing the loss of crypto assets (theft, etc.). General principles should therefore apply:

- Loss of crypto assets held by an individual/non-business: general rules do not provide any tax deductibility in case of theft or destruction of other assets (furniture, art, car, etc.). Moreover, the applicable tax regime only concerns the disposal of crypto assets. Therefore, in the absence of tax guidance, individuals should not get any tax relief from the loss of crypto assets.
- Loss of assets held as business investments (by companies or individuals): general rules provide that thefts and uncollectible debts are tax deductible losses.[30] Such regime could apply to crypto assets but the matter remains to be addressed by administrative guidance.

(h) What are the income/capital gains tax consequences of a loss in value of crypto assets?

The unrealized loss in value does not entail any tax consequences.

However, businesses can book and deduct provisions for depreciation (on utility tokens and currency tokens) or provisions for losses (on currency tokens) under general rules.[31]

29. Article 82 of the French Tax Code.
30. BOI-BIC-CHG-60-20-10 n° 40.
31. Article 39,1 5° of the French Tax Code.

(i) What are the income/capital gains tax consequences of forks of crypto assets?

A fork can be defined as the split of a cryptocurrency into two different chains. This event is not addressed by law or administrative guidelines.

Applying general tax principles, assets received by businesses (including individuals trading crypto assets on regular basis) or in consideration for services may be treated as business income.

Assets received by individuals/non-business should not be a tax event. However, potential capital gains on the future disposal of these assets would be based on a nil tax cost.

These solutions remain to be confirmed by law or guidance.

(j) What are the income/capital gains tax consequences of airdrops of crypto assets and are the tax consequences different if the airdropped tokens are unwanted?

There are no specific provisions considering airdrops of crypto assets as taxable events.

Applying general tax principles, assets received by businesses (including individuals trading crypto assets on regular basis) or in consideration for services may be treated as business income (such as a subsidy).

On the other hand, assets received by individuals not involved in trading or without any consideration may not entail any tax consequences upon payment. However, potential capital gains on the future disposal of these assets would be based on a nil tax cost.

These solutions remain to be confirmed by law or guidance.

(k) What are the income/capital gains tax consequences of (solo, pool, and cloud) mining?

For individuals, revenues from solo, pool, and cloud mining are subject to income tax as non-business income, in application of administrative guidance and the aforementioned Supreme Tax Court ruling in section 1.1.1(b), above.[32] These provisions do not draw a distinction between occasional mining and regular mining activities.

For businesses, revenues derived from mining activities should be taxable to corporate income tax under standard conditions.

(l) What are the income/capital gains tax consequences of staking crypto assets?

Staking is not addressed by law or guidance.

32. BOI-BNC-CHAMP-10-10-20-40 n°1080.

However, guidance states that non-business income applies to 'crypto assets purchased either free of charge in return for taking part in the process of the system, or for consideration on Internet platforms meant for trading crypto assets against currencies.' Since staking contributes to the process of the blockchain, it may fall within the scope of non-business profits in the same way as gains from mining.

Yet, this solution needs to be confirmed.

(m) What are the income/capital gains tax consequences of an indirect investment in crypto assets?

Personal investments made by individuals in flow-through entities (partnership, funds) which hold a portfolio are eligible for the tax regime described in section 1.1.3(b), above – i.e., 30% flat tax on gains and income.[33]

Investments held in (i) incorporated taxable entities or (ii) flow-through entities carrying out an activity other than portfolio holding are treated as business operations and taxable as business income of the company in the accounts of which the crypto assets are booked. They are subject to either 28% corporate income in 2020 for companies or standard income tax brackets for flow-through entities held by individuals.

(n) How is income from crypto assets to be treated under double tax treaty law?

The French tax authorities have not yet taken take any formal position on the status of crypto assets under double tax treaties.

France may rely on the legal nature of the crypto asset and the type of transaction to determine the tax treatment on a domestic level before applying the relevant article of the tax treaty such as business income, capital gains, or other income.

France generally follows OECD Guidelines for the interpretation of the tax treaties. Based on commentaries on the OECD Model Convention, it can reasonably be assumed that:

- Pursuant to Article 13(5) of the OECD Model Convention, gains from the alienation of any property, except as otherwise provided, are taxable only in the contracting state of which the alienator is resident. Thus, gains realized by an investor on the sale of crypto assets held abroad may only be taxed in the state of residence of the investor.
- According to Article 7 of the OECD Model Convention, profits of an enterprise of a contracting state are taxable only in this state, except if the enterprise carries out a business in the other contracting state through a permanent establishment. As such, businesses related to crypto assets (trading, mining,

33. BOI-RPPM-PVBMC-30-10 n° 20.

etc.) operating in France should be taxable in France except for the operations carried out through a permanent establishment located abroad.

More generally, the Commentary on the OECD Model Convention regarding the digital economy may be used to determine whether mining constitutes a permanent establishment within the meaning of Article. 5 of the Model Convention:[34]

- If the enterprise which carries on an electronic business (for instance, a mining business or a cryptocurrency trader) has the server at its own disposal – i.e., it owns or leases and operates its own server – then the place where that server is located could constitute a permanent establishment of the enterprise.
- However, if the enterprise carries on an electronic business under a hosting arrangement with a service provider, it has no physical presence at the location of the server and cannot be considered to have a place of business there.

(o) *What are the income/capital gains tax consequences of selling crypto assets in an ICO/STO/IEO?*

There are no specific tax provisions governing ICOs; thus, the tax treatment of ICOs should be based on the guidelines issued by the French Accounting Standards Authority (*Autorité des normes comptables*).[35] The structuring of the tax and accounting norms is clarified by a paper issued by Paris Europlace, the lobbying organization which worked with experts and practitioners to provide informal guidance on crypto assets and proposals to the authorities.[36]

- Tax treatment of the issuer

The tax treatment of issuance for corporate income tax purposes should depend on the accounting classification of the tokens:

- Issuance of security tokens with the features of securities, future contracts or saving bonds would not entail any tax consequences.
- Issuance of utility tokens booked as:
  - debt would not entail any tax consequences;
  - advance payments (from the obligation to provide goods or services in the future) would be taxable at the same time as the effective delivery of goods or services; or
  - payment, i.e., the service or good is treated as provided or delivered at the time of issuance and taxable immediately.

34. Commentary under Article 5 of the OECD Model Tax Convention on Income and Capital §122 and following.
35. Règlement ANC N°2018-07 of 10 Dec. 2018 introducing Articles 619-1 and et seq. in the Accounting Code.
36. Rapport sur la fiscalité des actifs numériques, Paris Europlace, Apr. 2019.

- Tax treatment of the beneficiary

We assume in the below analysis that tokens are purchased as opposed to be acquired for free.

For individual beneficiaries:

The acquisition of tokens is tax neutral for individuals/non-businesses unless it was made through an exchange against other crypto asset. The exchange or contribution would be treated as taxable disposal (*see* rules described in section 1.1.2(b), above).

Later gains and losses on the transfer of tokens acquired through an ICO observe the same rules as discussed in section 1.1.2(b), above.

For corporate beneficiaries:

The same principles mentioned in section 1.1.2(a) and (b) apply. In short:

- The purchase of security tokens should be tax neutral. Future gains or losses on the disposal of the tokens should be in line with the tax treatment of the financial instruments to which they may be assimilated (securities, futures contracts or savings bonds).
- The acquisition of utility tokens should be tax neutral. If the investor intends to use the services over several fiscal years, the tokens will be booked as fixed assets and amortized over the estimated period of use. The amortization charges will be tax deductible.
- Tokens that do not fulfil these conditions are booked in a specific account and are not amortizable. Potential unrealized losses should be deductible through the booking of provisions for losses.

1.1.3 Other Taxes

(a) What are the value added tax/sales tax consequences of selling crypto assets?

The ECJ ruled that the sale of crypto assets against fiat currency is VAT-exempt.[37] The question was whether a bitcoin exchange service falls within the scope of VAT. The ECJ determined that transactions in crypto assets are exempt as supply of services on currency (of exchanges of traditional currencies for bitcoins and vice versa)[38]

The French tax authorities have issued a specific ruling on ICOs:[39]

37. ECJ 22.10.2015, Case 264/14 *Statteverket c/ H.*
38. Article 135(1)(e) of European Council Directive 2006/112/EC of 28 Nov. 2006, as amended.
39. 7 Aug. 2019 ruling BOI-RES-000054-20190807.

- On the day of the ICO, the amounts received by the issuer are not subject to VAT. However, the issuer may still deduct for VAT purposes the expenses related to the ICO.[40]
- After the ICO, the use of utility tokens to obtain services or goods is subject to VAT on the value of the consideration received on the day of the ICO, regardless of the variations that may have affected this value between the issuance and the use of the tokens. VAT would generally be due on the day the tokens are traded for services and goods.[41] An exception concerns the situation where the date of delivery of goods or services is already known at the day of the issuance; in such a situation, VAT is due upon issuance.
- After the ICO, the use of security tokens to receive dividends or take part in the decision process is not subject to VAT.
- After the ICO, exchange transactions – for fiat currencies or other crypto assets – are VAT-exempt.[42]

(b) *Are payments in crypto assets subject to withholding taxes?*

There is no provision dealing specifically with withholding taxes on payments made in crypto assets.

However, payments in crypto assets made to non-residents should be subject to withholding taxes depending on the nature of the operation (dividends, interests, remunerations for a professional activity carried out in France by a non-resident, etc.). The rates provided for by domestic tax law should be reduced by applicable double tax treaties.

(c) *Does payment of compensation in crypto assets give rise to payroll tax consequences?*

Compensation in crypto assets as such is subject to no specific provision regarding payroll tax and should be in keeping with general rules except where payment in crypto assets may be regarded as (even indirect) compensation derived from an employment contract.

(d) *Do transactions with crypto assets trigger any transfer taxes?*

Transactions with crypto assets do not trigger any specific registration duties. Duties may still apply if eligible assets (shares, real estate assets, going concerns) are bought with crypto assets.

---

40. Reference is made to ECJ 8 Feb. 2007, C#435/05, *Investrand*, and ECJ 29 Oct. 2009, C#29/08, *SKF*.
41. Reference is made to EU Directive 2006/112 and ECJ 24 Oct. 1996, C-288/94, *Argos*.
42. ECJ 22 Oct. 2015, Case C-264/14, *Hedqvist*.

(e) *Are firms operating in the crypto space subject to digital services taxes?*

France introduced a digital services tax in July 2019.[43] Liable companies are those who profit from: (i) a digital interface that allows users to interact with other users (social networks, sales platforms, etc.) or (ii) online advertisement services and have a gross revenue which exceeds € 750 million (including at least € 25 million in France). In the current wording, the tax does not apply to services that provide users with digital content, payment services, interfaces to manage interbank settlements systems or transactions involving financial assets.[44] As a result, firms operating in the crypto space should not be liable for this tax. However, this tax has been amended several times and its application should be reviewed on a case-by-case basis.

(f) *Are crypto assets subject to gift, inheritance, estate, or wealth taxes?*

The beneficiary of the gift or inheritance may be liable for tax under general tax rules, but there are no specific rules for crypto assets.[45]

Concerning wealth tax, the French wealth tax (*Impôt sur la fortune*) became a tax on real estate wealth (*Impôt sur la fortune immobilière*) on 1 January 2018.[46] As a result, crypto assets, which do not qualify as real estate assets, are excluded from the scope of wealth tax.

(g) *Are crypto assets subject to exit tax?*

The French exit tax applies to taxpayers upon the transfer of their tax residence outside France. Basically, the unrealized capital gain resulting from the holding of corporate rights and securities of a total value exceeding € 800,000 or 50% of the profits of a company is taxable upon residence transfer.[47]

As a result, no exit tax should apply on most crypto assets as they do not qualify as corporate rights or securities.

(h) *Can mining trigger gambling tax?*

There is no gambling tax applicable to gains derived from the mining of crypto assets.

43. Article 299 of the French Tax Code introduced by Law n°2019-759.
44. Article 299, II(a) and (b) of the French Tax Code.
45. BOI-ENR-DMTG-10-10-20-10 §10.
46. Article 964 of the French Tax Code.
47. Article 167 *bis* of the French Tax Code.

1.1.4 *Compliance and Documentation Obligations*

(a) What documentation requirements exist for taxpayers regarding crypto assets and are there best practices in recordkeeping to support representations made in tax returns?

It is recommended to keep documentation pertaining to the acquisition price of the assets. In absence of justification of the price, the tax authorities may consider that the assets were acquired for nil.[48]

(b) What is the evidentiary burden of supporting tax positions when a digital wallet address is lost or shared with other persons?

The law does not specifically address this situation.

(c) Are crypto asset exchanges and wallet providers subject to reporting obligations?

There are several reporting obligations that exist for online platforms.[49] However, these obligations concern platforms which connect people for the sale or exchange of goods and services. The drafting of the law and the intention of the lawmakers (regulating marketplaces, online renting services, etc.) suggest that it does not apply in other cases. However, it should be reviewed with respect to the business of each company.

Even in the absence of reporting obligations, the French tax authorities may always require a third party to communicate information needed to assess a taxpayer's taxable base.[50] Failure to comply with such a requirement may give rise to a € 10,000 penalty.[51]

(d) Are taxpayers holding crypto assets subject to reporting obligations apart from the filing of income tax/capital gains tax returns?

Crypto assets are subject to two types of filing obligations:

(1) Filing of the yearly personal income tax return (for individuals)[52] and corporate income tax return (for businesses) with the gains and losses realized during the year. Additionally, individuals eligible for the 30% flat tax regime on occasional gains must file an appendix which reports the details of the sales (sales price, tax cost, balance payment in cash, global value of the

48. BOI-RPPM-PVBMC-30-20 §90.
49. Article 242 *bis* of the French Tax code, and Article 1649 *quater* A *bis* of the French Tax Code.
50. Article L81 of the Tax Procedural Code.
51. Article 1734 of the French Tax Code.
52. Article 170 of the French Tax Code, form n°2042-C.

portfolio, etc.).[53] Another appendix is required to report the details of sales realized through tax flow-through entities.[54]

(2) Resident individuals, associations and companies must also disclose their offshore wallets including digital assets opened, held or closed during the fiscal year.[55] A € 750 penalty will apply for each undisclosed wallet, or € 125 for each omission or misstatement, within a total limit of € 10,000 a year. Penalties are doubled when the value of the wallets exceeds € 50,000.

(e) Are crypto asset exchanges and wallet providers subject to CRS/FATCA reporting?

There is no existing provision related to the obligations of crypto assets exchanges and wallet providers under CRS/FATCA reporting.

1.1.5 Civil and Criminal Tax Enforcement

(a) What powers do the tax authorities have to compel the disclosure of information by third parties, such as exchanges or wallet providers, and have these been used in the past?

Apart from the tax audit itself, the tax authorities may get information in two different ways:

(1) They may request information from a taxpayer to review the consistency of his tax returns (*demande de justification et d'éclaircissements*). Since 1 January 2020, the scope of binding information requests from the tax authorities has been explicitly extended to gains on the disposal of digital assets.[56] Failure to answer or an inadequate answer from the taxpayer allows the tax authorities to assess such gains on a non-adversarial basis.

(2) They may also require a third party to disclose the information needed to assess a taxpayer's taxable income or to ensure his tax compliance.[57] This also includes the obligation to communicate, or make available, any written document that could help reviewing one's tax compliance.

53. Article 41 *duovicies* J, appendix III, of the French Tax Code.
54. Article 41 *duovicies* K, appendix III, of the French Tax Code.
55. Article 1649 *bis* C of the French Tax Code.
56. Article L16 of the Tax Procedural Code as amended by Article 176 of Finance Act for 2020.
57. Article L81 of the Tax Procedural Code.

(b) What measures have the tax authorities undertaken in the past to ensure crypto tax compliance?

The Minister of Finance stated during a press conference held in 2017 that he had instructed the tax authorities to secure crypto tax compliance.[58]

The recent reinforcement of audit instruments and disclosing obligations prove that the tax authorities are fully aware of the development of the crypto economy and intend to enforce the taxation of related gains. However, the results of this approach have not been made public yet.

(c) Are the tax authorities cooperating with tax authorities in other jurisdictions on enforcement?

The French tax authorities actively cooperate with foreign authorities. France signed many tax treaties including an exchange of information clause (about 118). Since 2009, France has been developing its own network of bilateral agreements which specifically aim at promoting communication between tax authorities (about 28). Finally, this cooperation between tax authorities is enhanced within the EU under EU Directive on Administrative Cooperation in the Field of Taxation.[59]

58. Statement reported at a press conference held at the Ministry of Economy and Finance on 12 Dec. 2017.
59. Council Directive 2011/16/EU of 15 Feb. 2015 on administrative cooperation in the field of taxation and repealing Directive 77/799/EEC.

Germany

Stefan Richter

1. COUNTRY GUIDE

1.1 Germany

1.1.1 Applicable Tax Law, Guidance, and Case Law

(a) Which laws, regulations, and other administrative guidance exist dealing with crypto assets?

There are no tax laws which specifically deal with crypto assets in Germany. Rather, the general rules apply, in particular those of the German Income Tax Act (GITA),[1] the German Corporate Income Tax Act (GCITA),[2] the German Trade Tax Act (GTTA),[3] the German Value Added Tax Act (GVATA),[4] and the German General Fiscal Code (GGFC).[5] Accounting standards are derived from the German Commercial Code,[6] which are to a great extent authoritative for tax accounting.[7] Some specific rules pertaining to crypto assets exist in legislation regarding financial market supervision – namely, the German Banking Act[8] includes crypto assets as financial instruments.[9] However, this has no direct consequence for tax purposes.

There are some administrative guidelines and statements regarding the tax treatment of crypto assets, which have been issued by different authorities. They

1. *Einkommensteuergesetz.*
2. *Körperschaftsteuergesetz.*
3. *Gewerbesteuergesetz.*
4. *Umsatzsteuergesetz.*
5. *Abgabenordnung.*
6. *Handelsgesetzbuch.*
7. *Cf.* section 5(1) GITA.
8. *Gesetz über das Kreditwesen.*
9. Section 1(11) sentence 1 no. 10 of the German Banking Act.

concern the taxability of private crypto sales,[10] the use of crypto assets as a means of payment,[11] the taxability of profits from mining,[12] the valuation of crypto assets,[13] and certain questions of value added tax treatment.[14]

The German Federal Ministry of Finance is currently working on an administrative guideline which shall deal with questions for private crypto sales. Yet, it is not to be expected that the administrative guideline will deviate strongly from the current prevailing views in literature as laid out in this chapter.

(b) *Which court cases exist dealing with crypto assets?*

So far, there are only few preliminary[15] court rulings concerning the income tax implications of crypto assets, which have not yielded comprehensive insights.[16] For value added tax purposes, the *Hedqvist* decision of the European Court of Justice (ECJ) should be noted, *see infra* 1.1.3(a).

1.1.2 Income and Capital Gains Taxes

(a) *How are crypto assets classified for income and capital gains tax purposes?*

The classification of crypto assets depends on their specific characteristics. There is no uniform standard. Nonetheless, some guidance can be drawn from the German Federal Financial Supervisory Authority, which differentiates between three kinds of (archetypal) crypto assets.[17] Based on its work, crypto assets can be classified using the following categories:

- Currency[18] tokens serve as a means of payment (without being a legal tender) and do not have an intrinsic value.

10. Financial Authority Hamburg, 11 Dec. 2017, document S 2256-2017/003-52; Regional Financial Authority Nordrhein-Westfalen, 20 Apr. 2018, Kurzinfo ESt No. 04/2018; Bundestag, 21 Jun. 2013, document 17/14062, 25.
11. Financial Authority Hamburg, 11 Dec. 2017, document S 2256-2017/003-52; Bundestag, 21 Jun. 2013, document 17/14062, 25.
12. Regional Financial Authority Nordrhein-Westfalen, 20 Apr. 2018, Kurzinfo ESt No. 04/2018; Bundestag, 5 Jan. 2018, document 19/370, 21 f.
13. State Tax Authority Bayern, 14 Jan. 2019, document S 3812b.1.1-16/12 St 34 FMNR02a130019; Ministry of Finance Brandenburg, 6 May 2019, document 36 – S 3812b – 2018#005.
14. German Federal Ministry of Finance, 27 Feb. 2018, document III C 3 – S 7160-b/1310001 – DOK 2018/0163969.
15. The decisions concerned the interlocutory suspension of the enforcement of tax debts. In such cases, the courts only conduct a cursory examination of the merits.
16. Fiscal Court Berlin-Brandenburg, 20 Jun. 2019, Case 13 V 13100/19; Fiscal Court Nürnberg, 20 Apr. 2020, Case 3 V 1239/19.
17. German Federal Financial Supervisory Authority, *Blockchain Technologie – Gedanken zur Regulierung*, 1 Aug. 2018.
18. The German Federal Financial Supervisory Authority refers to these tokens as payment tokens.

- Security[19] tokens provide their holders with a specific claim or right against the issuer. They can be subdivided into equity, debt, or asset-backed tokens providing the owner of the token with rights comparable to a shareholder, lender, or owner of an asset.
- Utility tokens can be used for acquiring or receiving goods or services.

This general classification would help to apply tax rules.

Another important preliminary question concerning the classification of crypto assets is whether they constitute an asset in the sense of German income tax law. An asset in that sense is an object, right, concrete perspective, or effective condition which is expected to be useful for several years, is transferable, and has an objective value for an external merchant.[20] It is widely acknowledged that this is at least the case for prominent crypto assets which are traded regularly on crypto exchanges.[21] However, for low-profile crypto assets which are not traded, a careful case-by-case assessment is needed.[22]

Furthermore, for German income tax purposes, one needs to distinguish between income from a business (*Gewerbebetrieb*)[23] and such derived from other sources[24] (*see* for this distinction *infra* (d)). This means that a crypto asset can be held by an individual as a private or as a business asset. It can also be held by a partnership, which is taxed transparently for income tax purposes.[25] A partnership is not necessarily qualified as a business but can also merely be engaged in private asset management. Corporations, on the other hand, are taxed opaquely and only have business assets.

(i) Private

For private individuals, crypto assets qualify as 'other assets',[26] which can lead to the taxation of private sales (*see infra* (b)).

19. The German Federal Financial Supervisory Authority refers to these tokens as equity and other investment tokens.
20. *Cf.* Oliver Christian Schroen, *Sind 'Bitcoin und Co.' Wirtschaftsgüter gemäß der gefestigten BFH-Rechtsprechung?*, 57 DStR 1369, 1371 (2019).
21. For example, Fiscal Court Berlin-Brandenburg, 20 Jun. 2019, Case 13 V 13100/19; Stefan Richter & Katharina Schlücke, *Zur steuerbilanziellen Erfassung von Token im Betriebsvermögen*, 101 FR 407, 408 (2019); Lutz Richter & Christian Augel, *Die bilanzielle und ertragsteuerliche Behandlung von virtuellen Währungen anhand des Bitcoins*, 99 FR 937, 940 (2017); Ingo Heuel & Isabell Matthey, *Im Betriebsvermögen gehaltene Kryptowährungen – Steuer- und handelsrechtliche Einordnung*, 20 EStB 342, 343 (2018). However, a different position is maintained by Oliver Christian Schroen, *Sind 'Bitcoin und Co.' Wirtschaftsgüter gemäß der gefestigten BFH-Rechtsprechung?*, 57 DStR 1369, 1375 (2019).
22. *Cf.* Fiscal Court Nürnberg, 20 Apr. 2020, case 3 V 1239/19.
23. Section 15 GITA.
24. Sections 22 and 23 GITA.
25. Note that a partnership might constitute a trade business, which is taxed non-transparently for trade tax purposes.
26. Section 23(1) no. 2 GITA.

(ii) Business

Businesses have to classify crypto assets for the purpose of accounting. The classification depends on the characteristics and can only be determined through a case-by-case analysis. However, the following general guidelines will apply:

- Crypto assets, especially currency tokens, are usually intangible assets.
- The classification as fixed assets (*Anlagevermögen*) or as current assets (*Umlaufvermögen*) depends on whether the assets are intended to serve the business permanently. Currency tokens will often qualify as current assets.[27] Self-created intangible assets must not be capitalized for tax purposes (*see infra* (k)).
- In most cases, crypto assets are not subject to wear and tear (*nicht abnutzbar*) (i.e., there is no depreciation over time for the purpose of accounting). However, this might be different for tokens held as fixed assets which grant a right of use over a limited time.[28]

(b) What are the income/capital gains tax consequences of selling crypto assets against fiat currency?

(i) Private

Profits (and losses) from the sale of crypto assets which are held as private assets are taxable if the period between acquisition and sale has been one year or less; if the holding period has been more than one year profits and losses are not taxable.[29] The profit is calculated by subtracting the acquisition costs and other incidental costs, such as fees from trading platforms or transaction fees, from the selling price.[30] If the profits derived from the sale of crypto assets and other private sales (*private Veräußerungsgeschäfte*[31]) cumulate to less than EUR 600 for a year, the profits are not taxable.[32] If the profits cumulate to EUR 600 or more, the full amount is taxable.

27. Stefan Richter & Katharina Schlücke, *Zur steuerbilanziellen Erfassung von Token im Betriebsvermögen*, 101 FR 407, 408 (2019).
28. Stefan Richter & Katharina Schlücke, *Zur steuerbilanziellen Erfassung von Token im Betriebsvermögen*, 101 FR 407, 409 (2019).
29. *Cf.* section 23(1) no. 2 GITA; Andreas Kortendick & Felix Rettenmaier, *Besteuerung von Token-Transaktionen im Privatvermögen – Ausgewählte Einzelfragen und Erklärungspflichten*, 101 FR 412, 413 (2019). The taxation of private sales of crypto assets is briefly noted in an obiter dictum of a lower fiscal court in a decision which dealt with the private sale of expensive football tickets. The Court considered the taxation of the specific sale to be unconstitutional due to a structurally prevailing lack of tax enforcement in this context and noted that the situation may be similar for crypto assets, Fiscal Court Baden-Württemberg, 2 Mar. 2018, case 5 K 2508/17. However, this argument was dismissed by the Federal Fiscal Court in second instance, German Federal Fiscal Court, 29 Oct. 2019, Case IX R 10/18.
30. Section 23(3) sentence 1 GITA.
31. Section 23 GITA. Taxable private sales notably include the sale of real estate if the time period between purchase and sale is ten years or less.
32. Section 23(3) sentence 5 GITA.

There is a debate on whether lending or staking crypto assets trigger a regulation which would extend the holding period of one to ten years.[33] This regulation applies if the taxpayer has used the asset in question as a source of income and has actually obtained income from it in at least one calendar year. Lending and staking crypto assets are therefore covered by the wording of the regulation. However, most authors nonetheless reject its application to lending and staking for teleological reasons: The regulation has a very broad wording but was only introduced to fight certain tax savings schemes. It should therefore be interpreted restrictively. Some authors want to apply the regulation only for improper tax saving schemes, i.e., not for regular lending and staking.[34] Others want to apply the regulation only if the assets were acquired with the specific intention to use them to generate income.[35] Additionally, it can be argued that income from lending and staking is comparable to interest derived from the holding of foreign currency. For such income, some authorities have specifically stated that the respective regulation does not apply.[36] It is expected that the above-mentioned guideline of the German Federal Ministry of Finance will clarify question.

For the purpose of determining the acquisition costs and adherence to the holding period for privately held crypto assets, the prevailing view in the literature is to apply the 'first in, first out' method, at least as a default.[37] This view is shared by the tax authorities.[38] Nonetheless, a taxpayer should be allowed to use an average cost approach or even an asset-by-asset approach if he can prove the acquisition costs for every specific asset sold individually.[39] In any case, if different wallets are used the respective token transactions should be treated separately.

---

33. *Cf.* section 23(1) no. 2 sentence 4 GITA.
34. Andreas Kortendick & Felix Rettenmaier, *Besteuerung von Token-Transaktionen im Privatvermögen – Ausgewählte Einzelfragen und Erklärungspflichten*, 101 FR 412, 416 f. (2019); Ingo Heuel & Isabell Matthey, *Im Privatvermögen gehaltene Kryptowährungen (II) – Spezialfälle und Abgrenzungskriterien zur Gewerblichkeit*, 20 EStB 300, 303 (2018); Oliver Lohmar & Juien Jeuckens, *Besteuerung von Kryptowährungen im Privatvermögen: Bestandsaufnahme und Ausblick*, 101 FR 110, 115 (2019); *cf.* Fabian Krüger, *Kryptowährungen: Gewinne aus Token-Verkäufen als Einkünfte aus privaten Veräußerungsgeschäften*, 73 BB 1887, 1891 (2018).
35. Christian Reiter & Dirk Nolte, *Bitcoin und Krypto-Assets – ein Überblick zur steuerlichen Behandlung beim Privatanleger und im Unternehmen*, 73 BB 1179, 1182 (2018); Thomas Kanders et al., *Geschäfte mit Kryptowährungen – Abgrenzung zwischen Gewerbebetrieb und privater Vermögensverwaltung und weitere Problemstellungen aus Anlegerperspektive*, ErbStB 145, 150 (2018).
36. State Tax Authority Bayern, 10 Mar. 2016, document S 2256.1.1-6/6 St 32.
37. *Cf.* e.g. Ingo Heuel & Isabell Matthey, *Im Privatvermögen gehaltene Kryptowährungen – Ertragsteuerliche Beleuchtung von Verkauf, Tausch und Schürfen von virtuellen Währungen*, 20 EStB 263, 267 (2018); Wilfried Kraus & Daniel Blöchle, *Einkommensteuerliche Behandlung von direkten und indirekten Investments in Kryptowährungen*, 56 DStR 1210, 1212 (2018).
38. Financial Authority Hamburg, 11 Dec. 2017, document S 2256-2017/003-52; Regional Financial Authority Nordrhein-Westfalen, 20 Apr. 2018, Kurzinfo ESt 03/2018.
39. Andreas Kortendick & Felix Rettenmaier, *Besteuerung von Token-Transaktionen im Privatvermögen – Ausgewählte Einzelfragen und Erklärungspflichten*, 101 FR 412, 417 (2019); Wilfried Kraus & Daniel Blöchle, *Einkommensteuerliche Behandlung von direkten und indirekten Investments in Kryptowährungen*, 56 DStR 1210, 1212 (2018). It should be noted that section 23(1) sentence 1, no. 2 sentence 3 of the German Income Tax Act, which prescribes the 'first in, first out' method, is not applicable here, because it only applies to trading in fiat currencies.

(ii) Business

Crypto assets held as business assets are generally capitalized with their acquisition costs. This includes incidental costs.[40] Hence, the purchase of a crypto asset will be profit neutral for a taxpayer applying accrual-based accounting. Selling these assets will in turn realize respective profits or losses.

For business assets, neither the 'first in, first out' method may be used, nor the 'last in, first out' method.[41] Rather, the attribution of acquisition costs to specific assets has to be based on an asset-by-asset approach, which should normally be technologically feasible considering the nature of the distributed ledger technology. If determining the specific acquisition costs for an asset is not possible, which might be the case for assets held on an exchange, it has to be based on the average acquisition costs of all respective assets.

The situation differs for taxpayers using cash-based accounting (*Einnahmen-Überschuss-Rechner*[42]). In this case, the purchase costs for crypto assets qualifying for current assets generally are fully tax-deductible at the time of the purchase, whereas the selling price is fully taxable at the time of sale.

This full tax deductibility of purchase costs of current assets has been used in the past for tax structuring (so-called 'Goldfinger' model): Taxpayers would acquire large amounts of assets (typically gold or securities) to offset high income in one year and sell the assets in a year with low or negative income. This would flatten the tax burden and would have advantageous effects for the progressive income tax rate. Germany has introduced certain safeguards to prevent this procedure.[43] Whether these rules apply for crypto assets is questionable.[44] It therefore seems at least possible that the 'Goldfinger' model can be used in crypto trading under certain conditions. Yet, it would involve a higher risk than trading in gold or securities due to value fluctuations.

40. *Cf.* section 255(2) of the German Commercial Code; Ingo Heuel & Isabell Matthey, *Im Betriebsvermögen gehaltene Kryptowährungen – Steuer- und handelsrechtliche Einordnung*, 20 EStB 342, 344 (2018).
41. This is because section 6(1) no. 2a GITA only allows for the "last in, first out" method to be used on inventory (*Vorratsvermögen*). Crypto assets do not constitute inventory, *cf.* Stefan Richter & Katharina Schlücke, *Zur steuerbilanziellen Erfassung von Token im Betriebsvermögen*, 101 FR 407, 411 (2019).
42. Section 4(3) GITA.
43. Specifically section 4(3) sentence 4 GITA concerning fixed assets which grant a security-like claim or right against a third party, section 15b(3a) GITA concerning current assets which are transferred without a physical handover and section 32b(1) sentence 3 and (2) no. 3 lit. c) GITA concerning effects in tax progression for cross-border income.
44. Ingo Heuel & Isabell Matthey, *Im Betriebsvermögen gehaltene Kryptowährungen – Steuer- und Handelsrechtliche Einordnung*, 20 EStB 342, 345 ff. (2018).

(c) What are the income/capital gains tax consequences of exchanging crypto assets against other crypto assets?

(i) Private

An exchange of crypto assets for other crypto assets is treated as a sale of the transferred assets for the fair market value of the assets received expressed in EUR.[45]

(ii) Business

Trading crypto assets for other crypto assets is an exchange (*Tausch*[46]) for the purpose of German tax accounting law, having the following consequences.

A taxpayer using accrual-based accounting has to capitalize the received assets with the fair market value of the transferred assets. This means that the taxpayer will uncover any hidden reserves[47] of the assets given away or realize losses in value.

For taxpayers using cash-based accounting, the effects are similar: The exchange is treated as a sale of the transferred assets at their fair market value and a purchase of the assets received at the same price.[48]

(d) If a distinction is made between business assets and non-business assets, when does trading in crypto assets lead to a trade or business?

A business is an independent and sustained operation, which is conducted with the intention to realize profits and which participates in the general economic market.[49] These prerequisites might be met by trading in crypto assets. However, it is established under jurisprudence that an activity is only deemed a business if it is not to be classified as mere private asset management (*private Vermögensverwaltung*).[50]

The distinction between private asset management and a business is whether the prevailing view in the relevant market would consider the activity to be a business (*Verkehrsanschauung*). Such assessment can only be made on a case-by-case basis. Since generally accepted specific criteria for trading in crypto assets are yet to be established, guidance can be drawn from the jurisprudence governing securities

45. Andreas Kortendick & Felix Rettenmaier, *Besteuerung von Token-Transaktionen im Privatvermögen – Ausgewählte Einzelfragen und Erklärungspflichten*, 101 FR 412, 413 (2019); Ingo Heuel & Isabell Matthey, *Im Privatvermögen gehaltene Kryptowährungen – Ertragsteuerliche Beleuchtung von Verkauf, Tausch und Schürfen von virtuellen Währungen*, 20 EStB 263, 269 (2018).
46. *Cf.* section 6(6) GITA.
47. Fair market values exceeding the book values.
48. *Cf. Hans-Joachim Kanzler*, in: Herrmann/Heuer/Raupach, 296. Ed. 02/2020, § 4 EStG margin no. 581.
49. Section 15 (2) GITA.
50. German Federal Fiscal Court, 11 Jul. 1968, Case IV 139/63, *cf.* also section 14 GGFC.

trading.[51] Hence, the assessment should be based on the following circumstances, which respectively indicate a business rather than private asset management:[52]

- trading for third-party account;
- using debt capital;
- offering transactions to a broad public;
- exploiting market opportunities by using relevant occupational experience;
- exercising the activity full time by utilizing special software ('day-trading'); and/or
- maintaining an office and/or organization.

Within this assessment, it should be noted that the threshold for considering an activity to be a business will be comparatively high. Investing a substantial amount of capital or recomposing one's portfolio regularly is generally not sufficient to establish a business.

(e) What are the income/capital gains tax consequences for an employee receiving wages or salaries in crypto assets?

Wages or salaries paid in crypto assets are payments in kind. An employee realizes taxable income when he receives the assets.[53] The taxation is based on the value of the assets at the time of payment, being the moment at which the employee acquires the economic ownership (i.e. the economic power of disposal).

If an employee is granted options for tokens as a remuneration, taxable income should only be realized when the options are exercised and the employee has received the underlying assets.[54] In this case as well, taxation is based on the value of the assets at the moment of transfer, not on the value at the moment the options were granted.[55] If the employee sells his assets at a later point in time, the value of the assets at the time he received them constitutes his acquisition costs for the purpose of possible further taxation of private sales.[56]

Wages paid in crypto assets constitute tax-deductible costs of employment for the employer.

51. German Federal Fiscal Court, 20 Dec. 2000, Case X R 1/97; 24 Aug. 2011, Case I R 46/10; Julian Albrecht & David John, *Die einkommensteuerliche Abgrenzung zwischen Gewerbebetrieb und Vermögensverwaltung bei Investitionen in Kryptotoken*, 101 FR 393, 399 (2019).
52. Julian Albrecht & David John, *Die einkommensteuerliche Abgrenzung zwischen Gewerbebetrieb und Vermögensverwaltung bei Investitionen in Kryptotoken*, 101 FR 393, 400 ff. (2019).
53. *Cf.* sections 8(1) and 11(1) GITA.
54. *Cf.* for stock options German Federal Fiscal Court, 20 Nov. 2008, Case VI R 25/5.
55. *Cf. ibid.*
56. *Cf.* for stock options Regional Financial Authority Frankfurt, 14 Dec. 2001, document S 2256 A - 22 - St II 27.

(f) What are the income/capital gains tax consequences for a merchant receiving payment in crypto assets?

If a merchant using accrual-based accounting receives a payment in crypto assets for selling goods (assets) or to balance receivables, the received crypto assets are booked with the fair market value of the asset sold.[57] This means that the profit impact when selling assets can differ from a sale against fiat currency: If the taxpayer sells assets for fiat currency at prices above fair market value, the difference between carrying value and price constitutes an immediate taxable profit. If the payment is made in cryptocurrency, only the difference between carrying value and fair market value is realized. Any additional payments are not taxed before the received crypto assets are sold again.

For merchants using cash-based accounting,[58] the consequences are principally the same.

(g) What are the income/capital gains tax consequences of a loss of crypto assets?

(i) Private

If a taxpayer loses a crypto asset completely (i.e., loses the private key associated to a crypto asset), no income tax consequences follow. For lack of a sale, the loss of a crypto asset is not tax-deductible, regardless of whether the speculation period is over.

(ii) Business

For taxpayers using accrual-based accounting, losing the private key for a crypto asset leads to a loss. For taxpayers using cash-based accounting, this has no effect.

(h) What are the income/capital gains tax consequences of a loss in value of crypto assets?

(i) Private

A loss in value has no direct impact for taxpayers holding crypto assets as private assets. If the assets are sold within the speculation period of one year (ten years), realized losses are deductible from profits derived from other private sales. However, such losses cannot be offset with income from other sources (e.g. income from employment).[59]

57. *Cf.* section 6(6) sentence 1 GITA.
58. Even though a merchant will normally be obligated to use accrual-based accounting (*cf.* section 238 of the German Commercial Code, section 140 GGFC, and section 5(1) GITA), cash-based accounting can be used for merchants running small enterprises (section 241a of the German Commercial Code).
59. Section 23(3) sentence 7 GITA.

(ii) Business

A taxpayer using accrual-based accounting has to revalue current assets according to market values at year end leading to a loss if there was a decrease in value. Any increases in value in excess of the acquisition costs are not capitalized. Fixed assets may only be subject to a write-off if there was a presumably permanent reduction of their fair market value.[60] For losses of value due to value fluctuations, there are no established criteria yet. However, it seems reasonable to apply the jurisprudence covering securities trading,[61] which allows for write-offs if the value of the security has fallen by more than 5% from the time of purchase. It should be noted that a taxpayer who has exercised this option will have to raise the value of the asset on his balance sheet again if the market value rises, resulting in taxable income.[62]

For taxpayers who determine their income by cash-based accounting, the loss in value has no direct effect on their taxable income before the asset is sold.

(i) What are the income/capital gains tax consequences of forks of crypto assets?

(i) Private

For taxpayers holding crypto assets as private assets, the hard fork itself should have no consequences for income tax purposes.[63] However, if the taxpayer sells assets received from a fork, the impact thereof is not clear. The question is whether an act of acquisition (*Anschaffungsvorgang*) can be attributed to the assets, which is a prerequisite for taxation as a private sale. Some authors take the view that assets derived from a fork lack an act of acquisition, since they appear automatically and without assistance from the taxpayer in his wallet.[64] The opposing view would attribute the new assets received from the fork to the acquisition of the old assets.[65] This would lead to the

60. *Cf.* section 6(1) no. 1 sentence 2, no. 2 sentence 2 GITA.
61. German Federal Fiscal Court, 21 Sep. 2011, Cases I R 7/11 and I R 89/10. Arguing for such application: Ingo Heuel & Isabell Matthey, *Im Betriebsvermögen gehaltene Kryptowährungen – Steuer- und handelsrechtliche Einordnung*, 20 EStB 342, 344 (2018); Stefan Richter & Katharina Schlücke, *Zur steuerbilanziellen Erfassung von Token im Betriebsvermögen*, 101 FR 407, 410 (2019).
62. *Cf.* section 6 (1) no. 1 sentence 4, no. 2 sentence 3 GITA.
63. Especially, the fork does not qualify as income from services in the sense of section 22 no. 3 of the German Income Tax Act, *cf.* Andreas Kortendick & Felix Rettenmaier, *Besteuerung von Token-Transaktionen im Privatvermögen – Ausgewählte Einzelfragen und Erklärungspflichten*, 101 FR 412, 414 (2019); Anka Hakert & Benjamin Kirschbaum, *Ether Classic und Bitcoin Cash: Bilanzierung und Besteuerung von Kryptowährungen aus einer Hard Fork*, 56 DStR 881, 882 (2018).
64. Lutz Richter & Christian Augel, *Die Spaltung des Bitcoins: Entstehung steuerfreier Veräußerungsgewinne?*, 99 FR 1131, 1132 (2017); Ingo Heuel & Elisabeth Matthey, *Im Privatvermögen gehaltene Kryptowährungen (II) – Spezialfälle und Abgrenzungskriterien zur Gewerblichkeit*, 20 EStB 300, 301 (2018).
65. Andreas Kortendick & Felix Rettenmaier, *Besteuerung von Token-Transaktionen im Privatvermögen – Ausgewählte Einzelfragen und Erklärungspflichten*, 101 FR 412, 414 (2019); Anka Hakert & Benjamin Kirschbaum, *Ether Classic und Bitcoin Cash: Bilanzierung und Besteuerung*

taxation of profits from the sale of assets received through a fork if the speculation period of one year since the acquisition of the original assets has not elapsed.[66]

(ii) Business

For taxpayers who hold crypto assets as business assets, the consequences of a hard fork are uncertain as well. However, if a hard fork is to be understood as the split-up of the original crypto asset into two, the original acquisition costs should be divided among the new assets for accounting purposes as well.[67] This would mean that the hard fork itself would not lead to taxable income until the sale of the assets at a later point in time.

(j) What are the income/capital gains tax consequences of airdrops of crypto assets and are the tax consequences different if the airdropped tokens are unwanted?

(i) Private

For crypto assets received from an airdrop outside of a business, the airdrop itself should not lead to taxable income.[68] If the taxpayer sells these assets, the profits should not be taxable as well due to a lack of an act of acquisition.[69] Even though the acquisition of the distributor might be attributed to the taxpayer because the transaction was unpaid,[70] the distributor usually has not acquired the assets in the sense of German income tax law either, since he is the original creator.[71]

(ii) Business

If a taxpayer receives crypto assets from an airdrop in the course of his business, the tax accounting consequences have not been comprehensively discussed yet. However, the

---

von Kryptowährungen aus einer Hard Fork, 56 DStR 881, 885 (2018); Wilfried Kraus & Daniel Blöchle, *Einkommensteuerliche Behandlung von direkten und indirekten Investments in Kryptowährungen*, 56 DStR 1210, 1212 (2018).

66. *See supra* 1.1.2(b).
67. Stefan Richter & Katharina Schlücke, *Zur steuerbilanziellen Erfassung von Token im Betriebsvermögen*, 101 FR 407, 410 (2019); Anka Hakert & Benjamin Kirschbaum, *Ether Classic und Bitcoin Cash: Bilanzierung und Besteuerung von Kryptowährungen aus einer Hard Fork*, 56 DStR 881, 886 (2018).
68. Andreas Kortendick & Felix Rettenmaier, *Besteuerung von Token-Transaktionen im Privatvermögen – Ausgewählte Einzelfragen und Erklärungspflichten*, 101 FR 412, 415 (2019); Ingo Heuel & Elisabeth Matthey, *Im Privatvermögen gehaltene Kryptowährungen (II) – Spezialfälle und Abgrenzungskriterien zur Gewerblichkeit*, 20 EStB 300, 302 (2018).
69. *Cf.* for this requirement *supra* 1.1.2(i).
70. Section 23(1) sentence 3 GITA.
71. Andreas Kortendick & Felix Rettenmaier, *Besteuerung von Token-Transaktionen im Privatvermögen – Ausgewählte Einzelfragen und Erklärungspflichten*, 101 FR 412, 415 (2019); Ingo Heuel & Elisabeth Matthey, *Im Privatvermögen gehaltene Kryptowährungen (II) – Spezialfälle und Abgrenzungskriterien zur Gewerblichkeit*, 20 EStB 300, 302 f. (2018).

guidelines of the German Federal Ministry of Finance for the free distribution of bonus shares[72] could apply analogously.[73] This would mean that crypto assets received in airdrops would lead to taxable income in the amount of their fair market value. If a market value cannot be established, which would be presumed for international matters, the value would be set to EUR 0. Selling the assets received from the airdrop would then lead to taxable income.

The tax consequences should not differ if receiving the crypto assets by an airdrop is not wanted.

(k) What are the income/capital gains tax consequences of (solo, pool, and cloud) mining?

The income tax consequences of mining depend on whether the mining operation constitutes a business or is to be qualified as a private activity.[74] Because of the intense usage of resources required for successful mining (e.g. computing hardware, power supply, etc.), a mining operation should usually constitute a business.[75] However, the German Federal Ministry of Finance has stated that 'occasional' mining can qualify as a non-business (i.e., private) activity.[76] Mining may however even be considered an entirely non-taxable hobby activity (*Liebhaberei*) if conducted in an objectively non-profitable manner. In this case, losses derived from the mining operation are not tax-deductible.

(i) Private

If the taxpayer is mining crypto assets outside of a business (but not as a hobby activity), profits derived from the sale of the mined assets are not taxable as private sales. This is because mining involves no act of acquisition from the perspective of German income tax law.[77] However, according to the German Federal Ministry of Finance,[78] profits derived from private mining can be taxed as income from other

72. German Federal Ministry of Finance, 18 Jan. 2016, document IV C 1 – S 2252/08/10004:017, margin no. 111 f.
73. Christian Reiter & Dirk Nolte, *Bitcoin und Krypto-Assets – ein Überblick zur steuerlichen Behandlung beim Privatanleger und im Unternehmen*, 73 BB 1179, 1182 (2018).
74. *See supra* 1.1.2(d).
75. Regional Financial Authority Nordrhein-Westfalen, 20 Apr. 2018, Kurzinfo ESt 03/2018.
76. Bundestag, 5 Jan. 2018, document 19/370, 21 f.
77. This is the case both for assets received as block-rewards and assets received as transaction fees, *cf.* Marco Brinkmann & Marius Meseck, *Besteuerung von Kryptowährungen im Privatvermögen in Deutschland*, 8 RdF 231, 234 (2018); Andreas Kortendick & Felix Rettenmaier, *Besteuerung von Token-Transaktionen im Privatvermögen – Ausgewählte Einzelfragen und Erklärungspflichten*, 101 FR 412, 413 (2019).
78. Bundestag, 5 Jan. 2018, document 19/370, 21 f. Some voices in literature disagree and want to differentiate between block-rewards and transaction fees, *cf.* Marco Brinkmann & Marius Meseck, *Besteuerung von Kryptowährungen im Privatvermögen in Deutschland*, 8 RdF 231, 234 f. (2018).

services.[79] In this case, the profits are fully taxed if they cumulate to EUR 256 or more per year.[80] If this threshold is not met, they are not taxed.

(ii) Business

For taxpayers who use cash-based accounting, mining will lead to taxable income only when the received (current) crypto assets are sold, while the costs of the operation are deductible at the time they occur. Taxpayers applying accrual-based accounting must capitalize mined assets with their development costs, which means that the difference between development costs and selling price is taxable income at the time of sale. An exception should apply for mined assets held as fixed assets since they should qualify as self-manufactured intangible assets: In this case, capitalization is prohibited for the purpose of tax accounting,[81] leading to tax consequences similar to the situation in cash-based accounting. The latter would not apply to the extent the mining operation is rewarded by transaction fees paid with already existing crypto assets.

(l) What are the income/capital gains tax consequences of staking crypto assets?

Contrary to mining crypto assets, staking does not require substantial resources other than the asset itself (e.g., no specific computing hardware, power supply, etc.). This means that staking is considerably less likely to constitute a business than mining.[82]

Based upon the determination of whether the staking operation constitutes a business or not, the income tax consequences are the same as for mining crypto assets.

(m) What are the income/capital gains tax consequences of an indirect investment in crypto assets?

The tax consequences of an indirect investment in crypto assets strongly depend on the intermediary mechanism used and the exact nature of the crypto assets. There are various options for an indirect investment. The following constellations are possible examples:[83]

- An investor might invest in a partnership which in turn invests in crypto assets. Since the partnership is taxed transparently for income tax purposes and the income of the partnership is attributed to the partners, the income tax effects are similar to a direct investment. The consequences will therefore

79. Section 22 no. 3 GITA.
80. Section 22 no. 3 sentence 2 GITA.
81. *Cf.* section 5(2) GITA.
82. *Cf.* Julian Albrecht & David John, *Die einkommensteuerliche Abgrenzung zwischen Gewerbebetrieb und Vermögensverwaltung bei Investitionen in Kryptotoken*, 101 FR 393, 406 (2019).
83. *See* for a detailed analysis of different indirect investments in crypto assets under German tax law Wilfried Kraus & Daniel Blöchle, *Einkommensteuerliche Behandlung von direkten und indirekten Investments in Kryptowährungen*, 56 DStR 1210 (2018).

mainly depend on whether the activity of the partnership constitutes a business or not.

- An investor might acquire call options or other derivatives on the purchase of crypto assets. If the call options were held as business assets, they would be capitalized with their acquisition costs in accrual-based accounting. Exercising an option, the acquisition costs for the option and the exercise price will determine the acquisition costs of the crypto asset.[84] Therefore, exercising the option itself is profit neutral. For privately held assets, profits from options and other derivatives will normally be taxed as capital gains.[85] For options granted as wages or salaries, *see supra* (e).
- An investor might grant a profit participating loan to a company owning crypto assets, which entitles him to a share of the company's revenues or profits (*partiarisches Darlehen*). If the investor does so in the course of a business, the income is taxed at his normal income tax rate. If it is a private investment, it is subject to the preferential flat tax rate on capital income. If the investor is a corporation, the income is taxed as part of the profits. It should be noted that participation rights under further circumstances might qualify for a taxation as a trading partnership.
- Indirect investments might also be conducted by investment in a crypto fund which trades in or holds crypto assets. The taxation of the fund depends on its structure and classification. For a closed-end alternative investment fund which is structured as a partnership, the fund itself is typically not subject to income taxation. Rather, any profits achieved are directly attributed to the investors and taxed on their level, regardless of whether profits are retained or not. If the activity of the fund amounts to a business (as opposed to mere asset management), the fund may be subject to trade tax. An open alternative investment fund structured as a corporation is only subject to corporate income taxation if its activity amounts to a business.[86] Private investors in such fund pay capital gains tax on retained profits,[87] income from distributions[88] or the sale of fund shares.[89] Investors who hold their fund shares as business assets are taxed with their normal (corporate) income tax rate.[90]

84. *Cf.* for options on shares German Federal Fiscal Court, 22 May 2019, case XI R 44/17.
85. *Cf.* section 20(2) sentence 1 no. 3 GITA.
86. *Cf.* section 6 of the German Investment Tax Act that defines which income of a fund is subject to corporate income taxation. The section does not include a provision that would cover income from crypto trading if it does not amount to a business. If the fund is not exercising significant active economic activity, it will also not be subject to trade tax, *cf.* section 15(2) of the German Investment Tax Act. *See* Wilfried Kraus & Daniel Blöchle, *Einkommensteuerliche Behandlung von direkten und indirekten Investments in Kryptowährungen*, 56 DStR 1210, 1214 (2018).
87. Sections 18, 16 of the German Investment Tax Act and section 20(1) no. 3 GITA
88. Section 16 of the German Investment Tax Act and section 20(1) no. 3 GITA.
89. Sections 19, 16 of the German Investment Tax Act and section 20(1) no. 3 GITA.
90. Note that the tax exemptions which normally apply for shares held as business assets do not apply, *cf.* section 16(3) of the German Investment Tax Act.

(n) *How is income from crypto assets to be treated under double tax treaty law?*

The double tax treaties of Germany are based on the OECD Model Convention on Income and on Capital (OECD-MC), which means that income has to be qualified under the Convention. There is no guidance of the tax authorities specifying the application to crypto assets. Due to a lack of specific rules within the tax treaties the application should be based according to Art. 3(2) OECD-MC upon the German tax law as outlined before; taxation rights are allocated as follows:

- Income from a business is normally allocated to the state the business is located. It is however allocated to the other state if the business has a permanent establishment in this state. The location of hardware (e.g., for mining) in a specific jurisdiction may constitute a permanent establishment.
- Dividend or interest income derived from indirect investments into crypto assets is allocated to the state of the creditor.[91] Yet, the state in which the dividends or interests are paid is allowed to tax the income up to a certain extent.[92]
- Private sales of crypto assets are allocated to the state the seller is resident.[93]

(o) *What are the income/capital gains tax consequences of selling crypto assets in an ICO/STO/IEO?*

(i) Generating and selling crypto assets in an ICO/STO/IEO

Taxpayers who generate and sell tokens will usually do so within the framework of a business, which means that the effects of an ICO have to be classified for accounting purposes. The exact classification varies.

If the generated tokens are held as current assets, which will normally be the case, they are to be capitalized with their development costs.[94] If they are classified as fixed assets, capitalization is not permitted for tax purposes.[95]

From selling the tokens, the taxpayer will generate revenue, which involves the risk of high taxable profits if a corresponding expense, equity, or liability cannot be accounted for.[96] This depends on the kind of tokens generated:

- If the generated tokens are mere currency tokens, meaning that no obligations or use cases apart from the use as a currency are attached to them, no expense,

91. Articles 10(1) and 11(1) OECD-MC.
92. Articles 10(2) and 11(2) OECD-MC.
93. Article 13(5) OECD-MC.
94. *Cf.* section 6(1) no. 2 GITA.
95. Section 5(2) GITA.
96. Dirk Niedling & Florian Merkel, *Initial Coin Offerings (ICO) – Steuerliche Rahmenbedingungen einer neuen Finanzierungsform*, 8 RdF 141, 145 (2018).

equity, or liability can be accounted for. The issuer will realize a taxable profit from the collected funds (fiat or other crypto assets).

- For security tokens, the situation depends on whether the issued and/or sold tokens are equity, debt, or asset-backed tokens. If they are equity tokens and grant participation rights which are strong enough to qualify as equity in the sense of German tax law, the collected capital will be profit neutral. This is because it would be treated as a contribution and be accounted for as equity. If the security tokens qualify as debt tokens and grant a claim against the issuer, the income from the token sale will be neutralized by a corresponding liability. However, a liability may not be booked if the claim derived from the security token is conditional on future revenue or profits.[97] If the token were asset-backed this might lead to a realization as if the underlying assets were sold by the issuer of the tokens.
- In the case of utility tokens, the situation depends on whether the tokens grant an enforceable claim against the issuer. If this is the case, an accrual for future liabilities could be booked, (partly) balancing the received funds until the point in time when the tokens are actually used.[98] If no such claim exists, the collected funds lead to taxable income.[99]

(ii) Acquiring crypto assets in an ICO (STO/IEO)

If an ICO includes the distribution of tokens to an employee, the assets are qualified as income in kind and are taxable for the employee.[100] The taxation will depend on the fair market value of the crypto assets when received by the employee. For crypto assets which already have a significant market value, granting token options might be preferable in certain cases to avoid immediate dry income taxation and give the employee control over the timing of the tax burden.[101] Alternatively, the tokens can be transferred early by letting the employee purchase them financed by an employer loan, which is offset by a bonus payment after a vesting period. Hereby, only the bonus payment would be subject to income taxation, unaffected by changes in value of the tokens.

97. Section 5(2a) GITA.
98. Fabian Krüger & Michael Lampert, *Augen auf bei der Token-Wahl – privatrechtliche und steuerliche Herausforderungen im Rahmen eines Initial Coin Offering*, 73 BB 1154, 1160 (2018).
99. One could consider justifying an accrual for future liabilities based on the jurisprudence of the German Federal Fiscal Court concerning non-profitable services offered by a merchant out of goodwill. If such services are accepted on a regular basis to advertise for the business, a goodwill accrual for future liabilities (*Kulanzrückstellung*) may be booked. Prerequisite for this is that the merchant may believe that the respective losses cannot be avoided from a commercial or moral (*sittlichen*) point of view, *cf.* German Federal Fiscal Court, 20 Nov. 1962, case I 242/61 U; German Federal Ministry of Finance, EStR 2012, 5.7 para. 12. Whether this applies for the issuance of tokens is at least questionable. While such treatment may be possible for commercial accounting purposes, it is very likely that the approach would not be accepted in tax accounting.
100. *See supra* 1.1.2(e).
101. Fabian Krüger & Michael Lampert, *Augen auf bei der Token-Wahl – privatrechtliche und steuerliche Herausforderungen im Rahmen eines Initial Coin Offering*, 73 BB 1154, 1157 (2018).

For other taxpayers, the acquisition of tokens through an ICO has no different effects than other trade in crypto assets.

1.1.3 Other Taxes

(a) What are the value added tax/sales tax consequences of selling crypto assets?

Pursuant to the determinations made by the European Court of Justice in *Hedqvist* decision,[102] the German Federal Ministry of Finance has released an administrative guideline to implement the decision for the German tax administration.[103] The guideline specifies that selling cryptocurrencies for fiat currency and vice versa constitutes a taxable service under section 1(1) no. 1 GVATA, but is tax-exempt under section 4 no. 8 lit. b GVATA when interpreted in conformity with the Value Added Tax Directive (VATD)[104]. Yet, this only applies for currency tokens which are accepted by the parties to a transaction as an alternative means of payment and which do not serve another purpose than the use as such.[105]

The German Federal Ministry of Finance also outlines its view on related issues:

- It considers the acquisition of tokens from mining (irrespective whether from a block-reward or from a transaction fee) not to be a taxable service under the GVATA.
- An entrepreneur who is providing wallets against payment carries out a taxable service under the GVATA. No tax-exemption applies.

The treatment of other tokens (i.e., utility and security tokens) is not discussed by the administrative guideline.

Nevertheless, utility tokens which grant the right to receive goods or services can be qualified as vouchers in the sense of the VATD.[106] Article 30a VATD differentiates between single-purpose and multi-purpose vouchers. A single-purpose voucher is a voucher 'where the place of supply of the goods or services to which the voucher relates, and the VAT due on those goods or services, are known at the time of issue of the voucher'.[107] If a utility token qualifies as a single-purpose voucher, the transfer of the token is regarded as the supply of the good or service and is therefore taxable. The actual handover of the good or the actual provision of the service will in this case not be considered as an independent transaction (i.e., it will not be taxable). However, utility tokens might not meet the criteria and will therefore qualify as multi-purpose

102. European Court of Justice, 22 Oct. 2015, C-264/14, *Hedqvist*.
103. German Federal Ministry of Finance, 27 Feb. 2018, document III C 3 - S 7160-b/1310001 – DOK 2018/0163969.
104. Council Directive 2006/112/EC of 28 Nov. 2008, as amended.
105. *Ibid.*
106. Christian Joisten, *Umsatzsteuerliche Behandlung von Token-Transaktionen – Gelöste und ungelöste Fragen*, 101 FR 421, 424 (2019).
107. Article 30a(2) VATD.

vouchers. In this case, not the transfer of the token, but the actual handover of the good or actual provision of the service is taxable.[108]

The VAT treatment of security tokens depends on whether they are to be qualified as equity, debt, or asset-backed tokens.[109] Pursuant to the *KapHag* decision of the ECJ,[110] in which the court stated that the inclusion of a shareholder against cash distributions is no taxable service, the acquisition of equity tokens should not be taxable either.[111] The acquisition of debt tokens equates to granting a loan, which is not entrepreneurial in nature, but merely private asset management for VAT purposes. Therefore, it is normally not a taxable activity under the VATD. The acquisition may be taxable however if it is the necessary extension of a market activity. In this case, it should be tax-exempt under section 4 no. 8 lit. a GVATA.[112] For asset-backed tokens the common VAT rules for selling (tangible) assets could become applicable.

(b) Are payments in crypto assets subject to withholding taxes?

There are no specific withholding taxes tailored to payments in crypto assets. Whether withholding taxes apply will depend on the nature and context of the payment. Notable withholding taxes in Germany are the payroll tax (*supra* (c)) as well as the withholding tax on income from capital such as dividends and interest (*Kapitalertragsteuer*[113]). These are not autonomous taxes, but a method to collect the income tax. In all cases, the debtor is liable for the amounts to be withheld. This can become problematic for payments which are made completely in crypto assets, because the tax must be paid in fiat currency. It may force the debtor to sell a portion of the crypto assets to be able to discharge the tax debt.

(c) Does payment of compensation in crypto assets give rise to payroll tax consequences?

The income tax on income from employment is levied by a payroll tax (*Lohnsteuer*) which is withheld by the employer.[114] The amount of payroll tax to be withheld is calculated on the basis of the salary of the employee, including the fair market value of any remuneration in kind, which includes crypto assets.[115] The value is determined by the fair market value of the crypto assets at the moment the employee receives them.[116]

The payroll tax must be paid in fiat currency and cannot be discharged with crypto assets. If the wage of the employee does not include a sufficient amount of fiat

108. Article 30b VATD.
109. *See supra* 1.1.2(a).
110. European Court of Justice, 26 Jun. 2003, case C-442/01 – *KapHag*.
111. Christian Joisten, *Umsatzsteuerliche Behandlung von Token-Transaktionen – Gelöste und ungelöste Fragen*, 101 FR 421, 425 (2019).
112. *Ibid.*, 426.
113. Section 44 GITA.
114. Sections 38 ff. GITA.
115. *Cf.* section 38a(2) GITA.
116. *See supra* 1.1.2(e).

currency to be withheld, the employee will have to pay for the missing amount.[117] The employer can be secondarily liable for any outstanding amount which cannot be collected from the employee.[118]

(d) *Do transactions with crypto assets trigger any transfer taxes?*

Germany has not introduced a financial transfer tax yet, even though the introduction of such tax has been on the political agenda for a long time. The current proposal of the German Federal Ministry of Finance[119] only includes taxation of the purchase of shares of certain companies (i.e., no taxation of crypto transactions).

The only transfer tax that could potentially apply to crypto transactions is the German real estate transfer tax. This is because the tax is not only triggered by the actual transfer of legal ownership of real estate (which is not possible by the transfer of crypto assets for lack of a notarial certification); it is also due on the transfer of at least 95 % of the membership interest or shares in a company which owns real estate.[120] The transfer of equity tokens which represent membership interest or shares in such company can therefore be a taxable transaction.

(e) *Are firms operating in the crypto space subject to digital service taxes?*

To date, Germany has not introduced a digital service tax.

(f) *Are crypto assets subject to gift, inheritance, estate, or wealth taxes?*

Gift and inheritance taxes apply to transactions with crypto assets under the standard rules of the German Inheritance and Gift Tax Act (*Erbschaftsteuer- und Schenkungsteuergesetz*). The tax is normally based on the fair market value of the transferred assets at the moment they are received by the donee or successor.[121] However, complex provisions and tax exemptions apply if the subject of donation or inheritance is a business. The tax rate ranges between 7 % and 50 %, depending on the relationship of the donee/successor to the donor/testator,[122] which also determines tax-exempt amounts.[123]

117. Section 38(4) GITA.
118. Section 42d(1) GITA. The employer will however not be liable if he fulfils certain reporting requirements towards the competent authority, section 42d(2) GITA.
119. German Federal Ministry of Finance (10 Dec. 2019), https://www.bundesfinanzministerium.de/Content/DE/Standardartikel/Themen/Schlaglichter/Steuergerechtigkeit/2019-12-10-Gesetzesvorschlag-Finanztransaktionsteuer.html.
120. Section 1(2a) and (3) of the German Real Estate Transfer Tax Act.
121. *Cf.* section 12(1) of the German Inheritance and Gift Tax Act and section 9(1) of the German Valuation Act; State Tax Authority Bayern, 14 Jan. 2019, document S 3812b.1.1-16/12 St 34 FMNR02a130019.
122. Section 19 of the German Inheritance and Gift Tax Act.
123. Section 16 of the German Inheritance and Gift Tax Act.

Since the tax-exempt amount per donee is at least EUR 20,000 for ten years, airdrops will not trigger gift taxes in most cases.

Formally, Germany has a wealth tax with the relevant act still being in force.[124] However, due to a decision of the German Federal Constitutional Court in 1995,[125] the legislature would have needed to reform the tax to be able to further levy it. Instead, it was decided to cease its collection, which means that effectively, there is no wealth tax in Germany.

Germany also does not have an estate tax. However, family estates are subject to inheritance tax every thirty years.[126]

(g) *Are crypto assets subject to exit tax?*

Germany has exit taxation rules.[127] These apply to individuals who have been subject to unlimited income taxation[128] for the last ten years and relocate outside of Germany. However, it only relates to hidden reserves of corporate shares when certain thresholds are met. This means that crypto assets held by an individual as private assets are not subject to exit taxation if not qualifying as equity tokens.

If a corporation relocates[129] or transfers a business or assets to a permanent establishment outside of Germany,[130] hidden reserves are generally taxed. There exist no specific provisions concerning crypto assets.

Individuals who relocate outside of Germany who have been subject to unlimited income taxation for five years within the last ten years can also be subject to so-called extended limited income taxation.[131] This is the case if they have substantial economic interests inside of Germany and relocate to a low-tax territory. In this case, they are treated as if they are still subject to unlimited income taxation, except for foreign income in the sense of section 34d GITA.

(h) *Can mining trigger gambling tax?*

Germany has a gambling tax on race bets and lotteries (*Rennwett- und Lotteriesteuer*[132]). The person liable to pay the gambling tax is the organizer of the lottery.[133] There is however no reason to consider mining to be a lottery or the miner to be the organizer of such lottery. For this reason, the application of the lottery tax to mining is

124. German Wealth Tax Act of 1974.
125. German Federal Constitutional Court, 22 Jun. 1995, Case 2 BvL 37/91.
126. Section 1(1) no. 4 of the German Inheritance and Gift Tax Act.
127. Section 6 of the German Foreign Tax Act. Note that it is planned to modify the regulations by an Act to implement the Anti-Tax-Avoidance-Directive (*ATAD-Umsetzungsgesetz*). The Act has not been enacted yet (Apr. 2020).
128. Section 1 GITA.
129. Section 12(3) GCITA.
130. Section 4(1) sentences 3 and 4 GITA.
131. *Cf.* section 2 of the German Foreign Tax Act.
132. *Cf.* the German Race Bet and Lottery Act.
133. Section 19(1) of the German Race Bet and Lottery Act.

not being discussed. Germany also has a casino tax (*Spielbankabgabe*) for public casinos, which is clearly not applicable to mining crypto assets.

1.1.4 *Compliance and Documentation Obligations*

(a) What documentation requirements exist for taxpayers regarding crypto assets and are there best practices in recordkeeping to support representations made in tax returns?

No specific documentation obligations exist for crypto assets, but only the general requirements. This means that businesses must comply with specific accounting obligations,[134] while private individuals are subject to an obligation to cooperate with the tax authorities in determining the facts of the case.[135] To comply with this obligation, taxpayers should keep records of their trade in and other activities with crypto assets. Noncompliance can lead to determinations of the tax base by estimate,[136] which is typically detrimental to the taxpayer. A taxpayer who does not include profits from crypto assets in his tax returns can incur an administrative fine for reckless understatement of taxes of up to EUR 50,000[137] or be criminally liable for tax evasion.[138]

If a taxpayer wants to prevent the application of the 'first in, first out' method for private trades in crypto assets, it is advisable to separate the assets into different wallets which serve different purposes, e.g., one wallet for long-term investments and one wallet for day-trading.[139] Even though the tax authorities may not accept such separation in every case, separate wallets will make it more likely.

(b) What is the evidentiary burden of supporting tax positions when a digital wallet address is lost or shared with other persons?

German tax authorities must investigate and clarify the facts relevant for taxation ex officio,[140] which means that in principle there is no burden of proof for the taxpayer to fulfil. However, within their duty of cooperation, taxpayers must support the authorities by naming relevant facts and evidence. Hence, a taxpayer who has lost or shared a digital wallet address will have to lay out to the authorities the specificities of his situation to be able to convince them that his statement is truthful.

---

134. Sections 140 ff. GGFC.
135. Section 90 GGFC.
136. Section 162 GGFC.
137. Section 378 GGFC.
138. Section 370 GGFC.
139. *Cf.* Andreas Kortendick & Felix Rettenmaier, *Besteuerung von Token-Transaktionen im Privatvermögen – Ausgewählte Einzelfragen und Erklärungspflichten*, 101 FR 412, 417 (2019).
140. Section 88 GGFC.

(c) *Are crypto asset exchanges and wallet providers subject to reporting obligations?*

Crypto asset exchanges and wallet providers are subject to the general reporting requirements under German tax law (e.g., the obligation to file tax returns). There are however no specific obligations tailored to crypto activities. As any other person, they can be compelled by the authorities to provide relevant information for the taxation of third parties, *see infra* 1.1.5(a).

The question of specific tax reporting requirements for exchanges and wallet providers is mainly theoretical because the main impediment for such enterprises are the regulatory requirements in the field of financial market supervision, requiring them to file for a banking licence.

(d) *Are taxpayers holding crypto assets subject to reporting obligations apart from the filing of income tax/capital gains tax returns?*

There are no crypto-specific additional reporting obligations.

(e) *Are crypto asset exchanges and wallet providers subject to CRS/FATCA reporting?*

Germany has ratified and transformed into domestic law both its Intergovernmental Agreement (IGA) with the US concerning the FATCA requirements[141] and the Multilateral Competent Authority Agreement of 29 October 2014.[142]

There exists however no guidance from the German tax authorities on whether they consider crypto asset exchanges or wallet providers to be subject to these regimes. It could be argued that crypto exchanges and wallet providers are no financial institutions under the provisions of the relevant German law,[143] because crypto assets are not financial assets in a traditional sense.[144] That would mean that they would not be subject to CRS/FATCA and other exchange of information requirements.

141. Law of 31 May 2013, BGBl. II 2013, 1362.
142. Law of 21 Dec. 2015, BGBl. II 2015, 1630.
143. *Gesetz zum automatischen Austausch von Informationen über Finanzkonten in Steuersachen* (FKAustG).
144. Section 19 no. 7 FKAustG provides a list of instruments considered financial assets which does not include crypto assets. The handling of financial assets is a requirement for storage institutions to be considered financial institutions, section 19 no. 3 and no. 4 FKAustG.

1.1.5 *Civil and Criminal Tax Enforcement*

(a) What power do the tax authorities have to compel the disclosure of information by third parties, such as exchanges or wallet providers, and have these tools been used in the past?

Tax authorities may request information from third parties if clarification of the matter by the taxpayer does not or is not likely to produce any results.[145] They may also issue group information requests to third parties regarding facts concerning yet to be identified taxpayers.[146] This power could be used to compel information from exchanges or wallet providers.

Information requests from tax authorities must be complied with. In case of non-compliance, the authorities may apply coercive measures (i.e., coercive fines, substitutive execution, or direct enforcement).[147] However, close relatives and certain professionals such as lawyers or tax consultants may refuse to surrender information under certain conditions.[148]

Whether these tools have been used in the past against exchanges or wallet providers is not in the public domain.

(b) What measures have tax authorities undertaken in the past to ensure crypto tax compliance?

German tax authorities have issued above-mentioned guidelines and statements regarding the application of tax law to crypto assets. Other measures are not known.

(c) Is the tax authority cooperating with tax authorities in other jurisdictions on enforcement?

Cooperation with other tax authorities is based on exchange of information and assistance in enforcement.

There are different options for German tax authorities to obtain information from other jurisdictions and to provide them with information vice versa.[149] For states with which Germany has concluded a double tax treaty or tax information exchange agreement, competent authorities can exchange information under the relevant treaty provisions. Under European Union law, authorities can request information from other

145. Section 93(1) sentence 3 GGFC.
146. Section 93(1a) GGFC.
147. Section 328 GGFC.
148. Sections 101 ff. GGFC.
149. *Cf.* for the procedure sections 117 ff. GGFC.

Member States for the administration and enforcement of domestic laws.[150] Furthermore, Germany has ratified and transformed into domestic law the OECD/Council of Europe Convention on Mutual Administrative Assistance in Tax Matters.[151]

For the purpose of assistance in enforcement, Germany is subject to EU Council Directive 2010/24/EU,[152] which requires Member States to enforce tax debts owed to Member States upon request.

150. *Cf.* Council Directive 2011/16/EU of 15 Feb. 2011, as amended.
151. Law of 23 Jul. 2015, BGBl. II 2015, 966.
152. Council Directive 2010/24/EU of 16 Mar. 2010.

Gibraltar

Vikram Nagrani

1. COUNTRY GUIDES

1.1 Gibraltar

1.1.1 Applicable Tax Law, Guidance, and Case Law

(a) Which laws, regulations, and other administrative guidance exist dealing with crypto assets?

Gibraltar taxation law makes no special provision for crypto assets. They are, therefore, to be taxed in accordance with the general underlying principles of Gibraltar tax as contained in the Income Tax Act 2010. This means that when answering any question as to the treatment of crypto assets for taxation purposes one should merely consider the treatment of any similar asset. The fact that an asset is a 'crypto' asset has no influence on its tax treatment.

In terms of applicable regulations, the Financial Services Act[1] governed the introduction of an outcome-focused, principle-based regulatory framework[2] to regulate DLT providers who, by way of business in or from Gibraltar, store or transmit value (including crypto assets) belonging to others. The Financial Services (Distributed Ledger Technology Providers) Regulations (the 'DLT Regulations') do not seek to regulate crypto assets themselves, nor do they deal with the taxation of crypto assets.

1. Financial Services Act 2019.
2. Financial Services (Distributed Ledger Technology Providers) Regulations 2020.

(b) *Which court cases exist dealing with crypto assets?*

The Gibraltar Courts have not yet dealt with any cases regarding the taxation of crypto assets.[3]

1.1.2 *Income and Capital Gains Taxes*

(a) *How are crypto assets classified for income and capital gains tax purposes?*

There is no classification of crypto assets for tax purposes under Gibraltar law. As a result, a crypto asset is taxed in accordance with the general principles of Gibraltar tax law. No formal guidance has been issued by the Commissioner of Income Tax in respect of crypto assets though we understand he has commented on specific cases as they have arisen. Such comments confirm the position that the general principles apply to crypto assets as they would to any other 'real world' assets which exhibit similar characteristics.

Under the general principles of Gibraltar taxation law relating to the profits or gains arising from the disposal of any asset, the relevant matter is the nature of the activity which gives rise to the profit or gain, not the nature of the assets in themselves. If the disposal giving rise to the profit or gain is by way of trade then such profit or gain will be taxable as income; if the profit or gain is not generated by a disposal by way of trade then the profit or gain will be treated as a capital gain. It is pertinent to point out that no capital gains tax is levied under Gibraltar law. It is also worthy of note that income generated by a company which is not accrued in or derived from Gibraltar is not subject to tax in Gibraltar.

As such, the tax treatment of gains and losses from the sale of crypto assets against fiat currency depends on whether the sale of such crypto assets comprises a business, trade, profession, or vocation in the nature of a trade.

Under Gibraltar's existing tax legislation and common law principles, any profits or gains received from a business, trade, profession or vocation are subject to income tax.[4] English law is persuasive in Gibraltar and as such, the Gibraltar Courts as well as the Commissioner of Income Tax would normally consider the badges of trade[5] as interpreted by Her Majesty's Revenue and Customs.

Her Majesty's Revenue and Customs considers the following nine badges of trade:

(1) profit-seeking motive;
(2) number of transactions;
(3) nature of the asset;
(4) existence of similar trading transactions or interests;

3. Gibraltar Courts Service.
4. Table A, Schedule 1, Income Tax Act 2010.
5. https://www.gov.uk/hmrc-internal-manuals/business-income-manual/bim20205.

(5) changes to the asset;
(6) way the sale was carried out;
(7) source of finance;
(8) interval of time between purchase and sale; and
(9) method of acquisition.

Profit-Seeking Motive

As stated above, the intention to make a profit can indicate a trading activity, but this intention by itself is not enough.[6] The English case of *Salt v. Chamberlain*[7] concluded that share trading by a private individual can never have the badges of trade pinned to them, and that such transactions are subject to capital gains tax in England and Wales. However, the English case of *Rutledge v. CIR*[8] demonstrated that the single purchase and resale in a very large quantity of a single item was 'an adventure in the nature of trade' because of the fact that the purchase was not made for own use or investment purposes.

Number of Transactions

As stated above, a single transaction can amount to a trading activity, but the Courts and taxation authorities are more likely to deem an activity as being in the nature of a trade if there is an indication of repeated and systematic transactions.[9] The English case of *Pickford v. Quirke* demonstrated that the asset-stripping of a number of mills and the sale of those stripped assets on a piecemeal basis to make profits were trading profits and taxable as such.

Nature of the Asset

This badge looks at when assets are bought either as:

- an investment that has the ability to generate income;
- personal assets; or
- some assets used by a trade such as plant and machinery.

The Courts and taxation authorities will generally look at the specifics to determine whether the transaction involving a particular asset of a taxpayer and the nature of that asset, including how the acquisition of that asset was funded. If the asset is far removed from the taxpayer's normal business activity so as to comprise an investment it may not be considered a trading profit,[10] but if the asset is acquired on a

6. *Salt v. Chamberlain* - Ch D 1979, 53 TC 143; [1979] STC 750.
7. *Salt v. Chamberlain* [1979] 53 TC 143.
8. *Rutledge v. CIR* - CS 1929, 14 TC 490.
9. *Pickford v. Quirke* - CA 1927, 13 TC 251.
10. *Marson v. Morton* - Ch D 1986, 59 TC 381; [1986] STC 463; [1986] 1 WLR 1343.

short-term basis and financed by a loan then it may be considered as an adventure in the nature of a trade and therefore a trading profit.[11]

Existence of similar trading transactions or interests

This badge may be exemplified by the English case of *CIR v. Fraser*[12] in which the taxpayer (a woodcutter) bought a consignment of whisky on bond and subsequently sold the whisky through an agent at a profit. The taxpayer was considered to be 'an adventurer in a transaction in the nature of a trade' because he was thought to be a 'purchaser of a large quantity of a commodity like whisky, greatly in excess of what could be used by himself, his family and friends, [and] a commodity which yields no pride of possession.'

Changes to the asset

Where an asset is changed or modified by a taxpayer to make that asset more marketable, that may make a transaction involving such an asset to comprise a trade or business which is assessable as a trading profit.[13]

Way the sale was carried out

In the English case of *CIR v. Livingston and Others*,[14] it was held that in determining whether a transaction is in the nature of a trade, one must consider whether 'the operations involved in it are of the same kind, and carried on in the same way, as those which are characteristic of ordinary trading in the line of business in which the venture was made.' If that is the case, then it is likely that the transaction will be assessable as a trading profit.

Source of finance

The assumption of finance to purchase an asset may indicate that in order to repay the debt, the asset would have to be sold at a profit. The source and terms of the financing may indicate whether the acquisition and sale of an asset comprises a transaction that is assessed as a trading profit.[15]

Interval of time between purchase and sale

The length of time an asset is held is an important indicator of trade. The longer the period of ownership, the greater the chance it will be seen as an investment rather than a trade, but the intention of the taxpayer is also an important consideration here.[16]

11. *Wisdom v. Chamberlain* - CA 1968, 45 TC 92; [1969] 1 WLR 275; [1969] 1 All ER 332.
12. *CIR v. Fraser* [1942] 24 TC 498.
13. *Cape Brandy Syndicate v. CIR* - CA 1921, 12 TC 358; [1921] 2 KB 403.
14. *CIR v. Livingston and Others* 11TC538.
15. *Wisdom v. Chamberlain* - CA 1968, 45 TC 92; [1969] 1 WLR 275; [1969] 1 All ER 332.
16. *Wisdom v. Chamberlain* - CA 1968, 45 TC 92; [1969] 1 WLR 275; [1969] 1 All ER 332 and *Marson v. Morton* - Ch D 1986, 59 TC 381; [1986] STC 463; [1986] 1 WLR 1343.

Method of acquisition

It is also important to look at how an asset is acquired. If it is inherited or gifted, it is a good indication that a trade is not being carried on, although this is not always the case. An asset acquired at a market could indicate that it has either been purchased for a trade or an investment.[17]

The above comprise only a summary of the badges of trade and the principal English tax law cases, all of which are of persuasive authority in Gibraltar. When determining whether any transaction is undertaken in an adventure of a trade or business, it will always be necessary to determine that transaction on the basis of the facts surrounding the transaction as well as the circumstances and intention of the taxpayer, and judging all of these individually and collectively on their own merits.

(b) *What are the income/capital gains tax consequences of selling crypto assets against fiat currency?*

Following on from the previous section, where a person acquires an asset with a view to resell at a profit without any intention of holding it as an investment, this is usually an indication that a trade is being carried on. However, a profit-seeking motive is of itself not determinative of the existence of a business, trade, profession, or vocation as there are other badges of trade that need to be considered. Some assets are more likely to be held as investments than others, and this could be argued to be true of crypto assets. As stated above, the English case of *Salt v. Chamberlain*[18] held that the buying and selling of quoted securities with the intention of making a profit were to be considered speculative dealings, and as such the transactions were not a trade despite other badges of trade being present.

In the English courts, the standard position under *Salt v. Chamberlain* applies to private individuals and not companies. This is based on the position that there is a rebuttable presumption that a standard limited company (as opposed to a company limited by guarantee) carries out its activities by way of business; it is not impossible for a company to gamble but it is less likely. The Commissioner of Income Tax interprets *Salt v. Chamberlain* in line with the general principles of Gibraltar law and treats both companies and individuals alike on the basis that there should be no materially worse underlying tax treatment of a profit or gain merely because a limited company has been inserted between an individual and a taxable transaction. While other relevant persuasive English case laws exist,[19] there has been no Gibraltar litigation or decision binding on the Commissioner of Income Tax which directly applies this other case law.

In the absence of any legislation specific to crypto assets and there being no formal guidance on the taxation of crypto assets, the general principles of taxation on

17. *Taylor v. Good* – CA 1974, 49 TC 277; [1974] STC 148; [1974] 1 WLR 556; [1974] 1 All ER 1137.
18. *Salt v. Chamberlain* [1979] 53TC143.
19. *A Ali v. HMRC* [2016] UKFTT 8.

the disposal of any asset apply. As stated above, the test is whether or not the disposal arises from an adventure in the nature of a trade.

When disposing of any asset, the test for taxability in the case of a company is:

(i) Is the disposal by way of trade?
(ii) If the disposal has been by way of trade, then was the income from that trade accrued in or derived from Gibraltar?

If the answer to any of the above questions is 'no', then no taxable event arises in Gibraltar. If the income following a disposal of an asset by way of trade accrues in or derives from Gibraltar, then there is a taxable event. Losses may be rolled forward to be set off against following year profits. Note that capital gains are not subject to tax.

In the case of an individual, worldwide income is taxable, but the same rules apply as to the taxability of capital or income to both companies and individuals.

A key point to note in this regard is that while individuals in Gibraltar are subject to taxation on their worldwide income, a territorial basis of taxation applies to companies – that is to say: (i) individuals who are tax resident in Gibraltar will be subject to taxation on their income accrued in or derived from any part of the world; and (ii) companies will be subject to taxation only on income that is accrued in or derived from Gibraltar.[20] 'Accrued in and derived from' is given meaning within the Income Tax Act[21] and, generally, is defined by reference to the location of the activities which give rise to the profits. However, in the case of licensable or regulated activities, the income generated by a business whose underlying business activity is licensable or regulated in Gibraltar will be deemed to accrue and derive its income from Gibraltar and as a result such income will be taxable in Gibraltar. As a consequence, businesses such as crypto asset exchanges or crypto asset custodians which are licensed under Gibraltar's DLT Regulations[22] are deemed to undertake their business activity in Gibraltar and therefore are subject to tax in Gibraltar on that income.

Companies are subject to taxation at the rate of 10%, while individuals are subject to tax either on an allowance-based system on tax brackets which range from 14% to 39% or on a gross income-based system at a blended effective rate of approximately 25%. Individuals may elect whichever of the allowance-based or gross income-based systems are most beneficial giving a maximum effective rate of 25% of gross income.

By way of example, in the case of crypto assets acquired free of charge which are subsequently sold in a one-off transaction, these would not be subject to taxation as it would not be deemed to be a disposal in the nature of a trade.

Similarly, if crypto assets have been acquired in several tranches at different acquisition costs and if a part of these crypto assets is subsequently sold, then again one needs to consider if the disposals have been in the nature of a trade and if so, one then needs to consider which of the various tranches have been sold. Subject to the

20. Section 11(i), Income Tax Act 2010.
21. Section 74, Income Tax Act 2010.
22. Gibraltar Financial Services Commission, Distributed Ledger Technology Regulatory Framework.

sales being determined as having been carried on in the nature of a trade, the taxpayer would normally determine which tranche was sold. This may lead to a taxable event.

(c) *What are the income/capital gains tax consequences of exchanging crypto assets against other crypto assets?*

In accordance with general principles of Gibraltar law, exchanging one asset at market value for another asset does not of itself give rise to a taxable event. As such, exchanging crypto assets into other crypto assets will not be regarded as triggering tax.

(d) *If a distinction is made between business assets and non-business assets, when does trading in crypto assets lead to a trade or business?*

There is no distinction made under Gibraltar law between business assets and non-business assets for tax purposes. Please refer to section 1.1.2(a) above and the badges of trade as an indication of when trading in crypto assets may lead to the determination that a trade or business has been undertaken.

(e) *What are the income/capital gains tax consequences for an employee receiving wages or salaries in crypto assets?*

As with other situations relating to crypto assets, the general principles of Gibraltar tax law apply. Where an employment contract provides that an employee receives remuneration denominated in fiat currency and will receive crypto assets by way of bonus, that payment of crypto assets would amount to a benefit in kind and would be taxable in accordance with Schedule 7 of the Income Tax Act 2010 at the normal marginal rate for that taxpayer. Where an employment contract provides that: (i) an employee's remuneration is to be paid exclusively in crypto assets, or (ii) the employer or the employee may elect to pay in crypto assets all or part of the remuneration denominated in fiat currency, then legal advice should be sought as the particular circumstances as well as the terms and conditions of the employment contract will determine the tax treatment of the remuneration, how the tax is calculated and when the tax is payable.

(f) *What are the income/capital gains tax consequences for a merchant receiving payment in crypto assets?*

The supply of goods and services by a merchant in the nature of a business, trade, profession, or vocation, where the goods or services supplied are paid for in crypto assets, would be treated for tax purposes in the same way as if payment for those goods or services were made in fiat currency. In calculating the assessable income, the Commissioner of Income Tax would generally take into account the fair market value of the goods or services supplied, less any allowable expenses and deductions.

Should the merchant delay in converting the crypto consideration into fiat then any gain attributable to the increase in the value of the crypto consideration compared to its market value at the point of supply of the goods or services would be subject to the normal rules of taxation for the income profits or capital gains as applicable and would be considered separately from the consideration for the goods or services.

(g) What are the income/capital gains tax consequences of a loss of crypto assets?

Where the sale of crypto assets in the nature of a trade gives rise to a trading loss, that loss would normally be an allowable loss for tax purposes.

However, in the event of a loss of access passphrases or private keys relating to the ability to transfer crypto assets (thereby resulting in the loss of ownership of crypto assets), this would not have any impact on taxation under Gibraltar law as no transaction will have taken place.

(h) What are the income/capital gains tax consequences of a loss in value of crypto assets?

The mere loss in the market value of crypto assets, which has not been realized as a consequence of a sales transaction in the nature of a trade or business, would not be relevant for tax purposes.

Where a Gibraltar business actively undertakes a trade or business in crypto assets (such as a crypto asset exchange), it may be possible for such a business to write down assets to the fair market value.

(i) What are the income/capital gains tax consequences of forks of crypto assets?

In the absence of any legislation of guidance on the matter, crypto assets created from a hard fork will very likely be treated as assets that have been acquired for nil value (i.e., assets which have been received as a gift or as inheritance). These will likely therefore not be subject to taxation.

(j) What are the income/capital gains tax consequences of airdrops of crypto assets and are the tax consequences different if the airdropped tokens are unwanted?

Income tax will not apply to an airdrop of crypto assets provided:

- they are received by the recipient without the recipient having to do anything to receive them; or
- they are not received as part of a trade or business involving crypto assets.

If the airdrop is provided in return for a service, the crypto assets will likely be part of either miscellaneous income or trading profits (if the taxpayer is a business). In either of those cases, the airdropped crypto assets would be subject to income tax at their market value on the date of receipt. Any increase in the valuation of the airdropped crypto assets would be added to trading profits and be subjected to income tax when sold.

(k) What are the income/capital gains tax consequences of (solo, pool, and cloud) mining?

Mining of crypto assets could either be considered as a hobby or as a business. This will depend on several factors such as:

- degree of activity;
- organization;
- risk; and
- commerciality.

In the event of mining being a hobby, it is likely that the taxpayer in question would be an individual. If a taxpayer's mining activity is classified as a hobby, then any income from mining would be required to be declared and would be subject to taxation. The income in this case would be the fair market value of the crypto assets at the time they are received by the taxpayer. Appropriate expenses would be capable of being deducted. Rewards received in exchange for mining activity would also be considered as income subject to tax.

If mining is classified as a business based on the criteria mentioned above, then the mining income would be added to trading profits and be subject to income tax. Similarly, fees or rewards received in exchange of any mining activity would also be added to taxable income. Appropriate expenses would of course be deductible.

When disposing of such cryptocurrency, any increase in value from the time of acquisition would be added to the trading profits.

(l) What are the income/capital gains tax consequences of staking crypto assets?

See section 1.1.2(k). The same considerations for mining crypto assets apply to the staking of crypto assets.

(m) What are the income/capital gains tax consequences of an indirect investment in crypto assets?

Investors seeking exposure to crypto assets, but not wishing to hold these directly, may obtain such exposure by investing in funds that may be listed or unlisted. If a fund is listed on a recognized exchange, then all dividends, interest, or other receipts will be exempted from tax. Any increase in the value of the fund units will not be subject to tax as these will comprise a capital gain which is not subject to tax in Gibraltar. If a fund is not listed, then dividends and interest received for participation shares or units in the fund will be subject to tax, but any gain in the value of the share or participation unit of the fund would be a capital gain and would not be subject to tax.

(n) How is income from crypto assets to be treated under double tax treaty law?

The only double tax agreement currently in force in Gibraltar is that between Gibraltar and the United Kingdom. This agreement follows the OECD Model Convention as follows:

- Pursuant to Article 7 of the OECD Model Convention, profits of an enterprise of a contracting state are taxable only in that state; if the enterprise, however, carries on business in the other contracting state through a permanent establishment situated therein, then the profits that are attributable to the permanent establishment may be taxed in that other state. Thus, for example, profits of a crypto asset exchange carried on by a resident of Gibraltar may only be taxed in Gibraltar. If the crypto asset exchange, however, carried on business in the United Kingdom through a permanent establishment situated in the United Kingdom, then the profits that are attributable to the permanent establishment may be taxed in the United Kingdom.
- Pursuant to Article 13(5) of the OECD Model Convention, gains from the alienation of any property, other than that referred to in certain other paragraphs, are taxable only in the contracting state of which the alienator is resident. Thus, for example, an investor resident in Gibraltar selling bitcoins through a crypto exchange located in the United Kingdom may only be taxed in Gibraltar.

(o) What are the income/capital gains tax consequences of selling crypto assets in an ICO/STO/IEO?

The Commissioner of Income Tax has taken the view in respect of ICOs and IEOs undertaken by Gibraltar companies that these have been undertaken in the nature of a trade and as such, those profits have been subject to tax at the corporate rate of 10%.

In the case of utility tokens, where the issuer has the legal obligation to provide certain services in the future to the investor (similar to the buyer of a voucher), it may be possible for the issuer to post a liability and thus defer the realisation of a taxable profit.

In the event that security tokens are issued and comprise equity, no taxable event would arise.

1.1.3 *Other Taxes*

(a) What are the value added tax/sales tax consequences of selling crypto assets?

There are no value added taxes or sales taxes in Gibraltar.

(b) Are payments in crypto assets subject to withholding taxes?

There are no withholding taxes in Gibraltar, except in the following cases:

- Payments to subcontractors in the construction industry. Unless the subcontractor is in possession of an exemption certificate, tax is withheld at the rate of 25% of the amount that relates to the labour and profit element of the contract.
- Payments to employees under the PAYE (Pay As You Earn) system. Under the PAYE regulations, employers are obligated to deduct an amount of tax in accordance with the employee's tax code (under Gibraltar tax law, taxpayers have different tax codes depending on their allowances; the tax codes allow employers to deduct the correct amount of tax and social insurance from the employee's wages).

Payments in crypto assets in the above circumstances would be subject to the stated withholding.

(c) Does payment of compensation in crypto assets give rise to payroll tax consequences?

Compensation in crypto assets does not give rise to any special payroll tax consequences and thus is to be treated as any payment in kind. Normally, the employer will have to calculate and remit PAYE and social insurance contributions (social insurance contributions are payments that go towards contributory benefits such as maternity benefits, old age pension, death grant, survivor's benefits, unemployment benefit, and healthcare).

(d) Do transactions with crypto assets trigger any transfer taxes?

There are no transfer taxes in Gibraltar.

(e) Are firms operating in the crypto space subject to digital service taxes?

There are no digital service taxes in Gibraltar.

(f) Are crypto assets subject to gift, inheritance, estate, or wealth taxes?

There are no gift, inheritance, estate, or wealth taxes in Gibraltar.

(g) Are crypto assets subject to exit tax?

On 30 January 2020, the Gibraltar Government published new Income Tax Regulations to implement the remaining part of Council Directive (EU) 2016/1164 (the Anti-Tax Avoidance Directive or ATAD), which introduces an exit tax.

The exit tax applies to any of the following circumstances:

- An entity transfers assets from its head office in Gibraltar to its permanent establishment (PE) outside Gibraltar, and Gibraltar no longer has the right to tax the transferred assets as a consequence of the transfer.
- An entity transfers assets from its PE in Gibraltar to its head office or another PE outside Gibraltar, and Gibraltar no longer has the right to tax the transferred assets as a consequence of the transfer.
- A taxpayer takes steps to relocate its tax residence from Gibraltar to another jurisdiction, except for those assets which remain effectively connected with a PE in Gibraltar.
- A taxpayer transfers the business carried on by its PE in Gibraltar to another jurisdiction and Gibraltar, as the Member State of the PE, no longer has the right to tax the transferred assets as a consequence of the transfer.

A 'transfer of business' is defined as being the undertaking of those actions which result in an entity ceasing to have a taxable presence in Gibraltar and acquiring a taxable presence in another jurisdiction, without becoming tax resident in that other jurisdiction.

A 'transfer of assets' is defined as being the undertaking of those actions which result in Gibraltar losing the right to tax the transferred assets, while the assets remain under the ownership of the same taxpayer.

In the above scenarios, tax would be applied at the applicable corporate rate (currently 10%) on the difference between the market value of the transferred assets less their value for tax purposes.

The legislation applies to accounting periods commencing on or after 1 January 2020.

(h) Can mining trigger gambling tax?

Under Gibraltar's Gambling Act 2005, the term 'gaming' is defined as playing a game of chance for a prize.

Mining activities would technically come within the scope of the Gambling Act 2005 of Gibraltar, and this would ordinarily trigger the payment of gambling duty. However, following discussion with the Gambling Commissioner of Gibraltar, he has advised that the Gambling Act 2005 never intended to capture the activity of mining of crypto assets and as such, the provisions of the Gambling Act 2005 would not be triggered. The matter remains under review by the Government of Gibraltar, and it is possible that the position changes in the future if the amount of mining activity being undertaken from Gibraltar increases.

1.1.4 Compliance and Documentation Obligations

(a) What documentation requirements exist for taxpayers regarding crypto assets and are there best practices in recordkeeping to support representations made in tax returns?

Taxpayers holding or trading in crypto assets by way of business are not subject to any specific or additional requirements in terms of tax filings. Such taxpayers would simply comply with the normal requirements for filing and providing supporting documentation. Corporate entities and self-employed individuals are required to file returns and calculate their tax liability for the assessable year.[23] They must submit their tax return, estimated liability and payment of the tax owed to the Income Tax Office within nine months of the end of the relevant tax year.[24]

(b) What is the evidentiary burden of supporting tax positions when a digital wallet address is lost or shared with other persons?

A taxpayer who has lost his/her private keys thereby depriving him/her of the ability to transfer his/her crypto assets would ordinarily explain the situation to the Income Tax Office. It would be expected by the Income Tax Office that the taxpayer would provide some evidence of his/her usual private key management practice and how the loss or private keys arose. The Income Tax Office would then have to consider the merits of the case and act accordingly.

The Income Tax Act 2010 of Gibraltar confers several administrative powers and powers of investigation on the Commissioner of Income Tax. In addition, taxpayers are required to cooperate with the Commissioner of Income Tax in the process of any tax investigation.

(c) Are crypto asset exchanges and wallet providers subject to reporting obligations?

There are no additional tax reporting obligations under the Income Tax Act 2010 of Gibraltar for crypto asset exchanges or crypto asset custodians.

However, under Gibraltar law, crypto asset exchanges and crypto asset custodians are required to be licensed in accordance with the provisions of the Financial Services Act 2019 and the DLT Regulations. The terms of the licences granted to crypto

23. Section 29, Income Tax Act 2010.
24. Section 31(1)(b), Income Tax Act 2010.

asset exchanges and crypto asset custodians will contain several reporting obligations of those entities to the Gibraltar Financial Services Commission, but it would be very unusual for any of those reporting obligations to be related to any tax matter. The reporting obligations imposed by the Gibraltar Financial Services Commission in the licences that it issues to crypto asset exchanges and crypto asset custodians would normally relate to regulatory, governance, operational, financial, and security matters.

(d) Are taxpayers holding crypto assets subject to reporting obligations apart from the filing of income tax/capital gains tax returns?

No, taxpayers holding crypto assets are not subject to any additional tax reporting obligations apart from the filing of income tax returns.

(e) Are crypto asset exchanges and wallet providers subject to CRS/FATCA reporting?

The Commissioner of Income Tax has not issued any guidance on the question whether operators of crypto asset exchanges or providers of crypto asset wallets must annually report their customers' data under CRS/FATCA. In this regard, it may be argued that the term 'financial asset' as currently defined under CRS only covers traditional financial assets and does not comprise crypto assets. A crypto asset exchange or crypto asset wallet provider may accordingly only be classified as a financial institution (meaning that it becomes subject to reporting) if it allows deposits of fiat currency by its customers.

1.1.5 Civil and Criminal Tax Enforcement

(a) What powers do the tax authorities have to compel the disclosure of information by third parties, such as exchanges or wallet providers, and have these been used in the past?

Under the provisions of the Income Tax Act 2010 of Gibraltar,[25] the Income Tax Tribunal has the right to request the supply of information, which is relevant for the enforcement of taxes prior to the enforcement of a tax appeal, from any person even if it does not concern that person's own taxability. Such requests have to be complied with, and the information is to be provided truthfully to the best of knowledge and belief. The obligation to provide information includes the obligation to submit, or to allow the inspection, of written documents which are relevant for the determination of tax claims.

As such, the Income Tax Tribunal could compel a Gibraltar-based crypto asset exchange or wallet provider to provide information regarding its customers. Details of

25. Income Tax Act 2010, Schedule 2, paragraph 11.

such information requests are not made public, and as such it is not possible to state whether such powers have been exercised in the manner enquired.

(b) What measures have the tax authorities undertaken in the past to ensure crypto tax compliance?

The measures (if any) which the Commissioner of Income Tax may have undertaken in the past to ensure tax compliance by crypto asset businesses or traders in Gibraltar has not been made public. In addition, there is no Gibraltar case law regarding any tax proceedings involving crypto asset businesses or traders in Gibraltar.

(c) Are the tax authorities cooperating with tax authorities in other jurisdictions on enforcement?

Gibraltar has also concluded twenty-seven tax information exchange agreements with certain jurisdictions. Furthermore, Gibraltar can request information from other EU Member States that is foreseeably relevant to the administration and enforcement of its domestic laws (and vice versa).[26] Gibraltar has also transposed into local law the OECD/Council of Europe Convention on Mutual Administrative Assistance in Tax Matters, which similarly gives the Gibraltar tax authorities access to information held abroad (and vice versa). The Gibraltar Income Tax Office has indicated that it has fully cooperated on a number of occasions with a number of EU Member States and non-EU jurisdictions in respect of tax information requests.

26. Cf. Council Directive 2011/16/EU of 15 Feb. 2011 on administrative cooperation in the field of taxation and repealing Directive 77/799/EEC, as amended.

Greece

Theodoros Skouzos

1. COUNTRY GUIDES

1.1 Greece

1.1.1 Applicable Tax Law, Guidance, and Case Law

(a) Which laws, regulations, and other administrative guidance exist dealing with crypto assets?

The Greek legal theory which has dealt with the nature of crypto assets is very limited and only deals with cryptocurrency; it primarily sets the question on whether these may be classified as money or as means of enrichment like other financial instruments. There is no reference of crypto assets in statutes or secondary legislation.[1] Thus, our study on the Greek taxation aspects of crypto assets will, unavoidably, be based on certain assessments, presumptions, and analogous application of existing rules. Such approach is risky, because one of the fundamental principles of Greek tax law is the principle of legality of tax. The principle of the legality of tax is laid down in the current

1. At the time of publishing, a draft law for the Amendment of Law 4557/2018 for the prevention of the use of the financial system for the purposes of money laundering or terrorist financing (implementation under Greek law of Article 3 of Directive 2019/2177 (L334)) is discussed in Parliament. By virtue of Article 1 paragraph 4, new paragraphs 24 and 25 are added in Law 4557/2018 which read as follows:

   24. Virtual currencies: The digital presentation of value which is not issued by a central bank or a public authority and does not enjoy their guarantee, does not necessarily correspond to a legally circulating currency and does not enjoy the legal status of a currency or money, but is accepted by individuals or legal persons as a medium for transactions and may be transferred, stored or moved with electronic means.
   25. Provider of custody services for portfolios of virtual currencies: The legal entity which provides services for the safeguarding of private cryptographic keys on behalf of its clients, with the purpose of custody, storage, and transfer of virtual currencies.

Greek Constitution of 1975/1986/2001 in Article 78(1) and (4). In particular, paragraph 1 states that: 'No tax shall be levied without a statute enacted by Parliament, specifying the subject of taxation and the income, the type of property, the expenses and the transactions or categories thereof to which the tax pertains.' Moreover, paragraph 4 supplements that by saying, 'The object of taxation, the tax rate, the tax abatements and exemptions and the granting of pensions may not be subject to legislative delegation.'

(b) *Which court cases exist dealing with crypto assets?*

The only references to crypto assets, and in particular to bitcoin, are to be found in two judgments of the Council of State. These judgments do not provide a legal characterization of the cryptocurrencies nor do they interpret their tax status; they simply refer to bitcoin in an incidental manner.

The first[2] can be characterized as being of historical importance because it relates to the application to annul filed by the notorious Alexander Vinnik, also known as Mr Bitcoin, who was being held in Greece against the decision of the Minister of Justice to extradite him to France, the USA and to Russia, whereas he wanted to be extradited first to Russia. The senior judges first ruled that his application to the Council of State was not lawful, since the decision of the Minister of Justice did not 'constitute a governmental act nor is it an act related to the administration of justice', since it is a decision to determine the order in which those countries which had simultaneously requested the extradition of a citizen were to be put. However, in addition to that, citing the domestic legal order and the rules applicable in the European Union on citizen extradition and the safeguarding of human rights, the Court ruled that the Minister's decision did not violate the said rules and consequently rejected the Vinnik application on its merits, thereby paving the way for him to be extradited to France and then to the USA, while Russia, which was his country of origin, was listed last.

The second judgment[3] relates to the application submitted by the Thessaloniki Medical Association to annul a Joint Ministerial Decision of the Ministers of Economy Development and Finance[4] to the extent that they enacted an obligation for medical practitioners to accept card-based payment instruments and mandatory placement of POS terminals at their surgeries. Among other things, the reasoning behind the application was that the economic freedom of doctors, medical confidentiality, and sensitive personal health data under Article 5(1) of the Greek Constitution were infringed. Among other arguments, the applicant Medical Association argued that mandatory acceptance of a card as a means of payment is not an appropriate solution for combating tax evasion, because it overlooks the fact that tax evasion by freelance professionals presupposes a relationship of prior acquaintance and trust between the payer and the professional, and that all those who want to evade tax will not seek payment using 'plastic money'' but will prefer payment in cash or even using

2. Council of State Judgment No. 110/2020.
3. Council of State Judgment No. 2461/2018.
4. No. 45231/2017.

ever-expanding cryptocurrencies (bitcoin, etc.), or gold, or other anonymous payment methods.

1.1.2 *Income and Capital Gains Taxes*

(a) How are crypto assets classified for income and capital gains tax purposes?

Under the Greek accounting and tax system, all financial resources owned by an individual or an undertaking and having monetary value, whose exploitation is expected to generate economic and other benefits, are classified as assets. So, crypto assets would be classified as such. Undertakings employ resources to produce and distribute products or to provide services. In other words, in a company's balance sheet, assets refer to all assets held by it, usually at cost, as well as all claims against third-party debtors. For a financial resource to be part of the assets:

- it should be owned by the undertaking or be in the undertaking's control as if it were owned by it;
- its cost or value should be objectively measurable according to the monetary unit (Euro); and
- measurable economic benefits should be expected by the undertaking from its use or exploitation.

Cash, investments, stocks, machinery, land, buildings, vehicles, deposits, merchandise, accounts receivable, etc., are considered to be assets.

Based on accounting rules and depending on their liquidity, assets are distinguished into:

(a) current assets;
(b) non-current assets;
(c) current assets include any asset which:
  - is intended to be realized, sold, or consumed within the undertaking's normal operating cycle;
  - is intended to be realized or sold within twelve months following the end of the current financial year; and
  - is cash or may be converted into cash.

Current asset items include: stocks, claims, debt securities, post-dated cheques, prepaid expenses, blocked deposits, cash, sight deposits.

The totality of current assets is called working capital.

Non-current assets include all items not included in current assets. These are items that are intended to be realized, sold, or used within a period of time that exceeds the duration of the normal operating cycle or goes beyond the end of the following financial year.

For example, stocks cannot be considered non-current assets, since they are purchased with the intention of either being immediately sold or being used as intermediary goods for manufacturing the final product.

(b) *What are the income/capital gains tax consequences of selling crypto assets against fiat currency?*

Undertakings are taxed on the profit resulting from earnings minus expenditure, for all their activities, which are classified as business profit. So the profit or loss from the sale of crypto assets against fiat currency would also be taken into account for income tax. On the contrary, in the case of individuals, if the transactions lack periodicity and of a permanent source of origin, they will not be considered as taxable income. For example, if an individual buys a number of bitcoins at certain price and sells them after some time at a higher price, this profit will not be subject to tax. But if transactions are entered into systematically to generate profit (when a transaction is repeated at least three times during the six-month period) then this is a business transaction subject to income tax.

(c) *What are the income/capital gains tax consequences of exchanging crypto assets against other crypto assets?*

According to Article 573 of the Greek Civil Code, the provisions relating to sale apply *mutatis mutandis* to exchange. Each of the contracting parties is deemed to be a seller for the performance which is incumbent on him and as a purchaser for the performance which he claims. Like the sale, an exchange is a contractual, promissory, onerous, bilateral and – in principle – informal arrangement, in the context of which the parties are obliged to mutually exchange things, assets (e.g., claims) or rights. So each party, depending on the actual gain or loss he realises upon the exchange is subject to the income tax or capital gains tax consequences.

(d) *If a distinction is made between business assets and non-business assets, when does trading in crypto assets lead to a trade or business?*

Whether a person carries out a business is a question of fact. If they do, they must register as a businessperson (sole trader) by declaring the 'initiation of taxable activities' before the competent tax office and keep accounting books for the recordation of their transactions. These rules would apply to transactions in crypto assets as they apply to transaction in any other assets.

An individual who is not a registered businessperson acquires extraordinary profits from a sale

One characteristic feature of extraordinary profits is the lack of periodicity and of a permanent source of origin. These amounts are not considered as income.[5] They must be declared in the annual tax return for information purposes only, but can be used to cover the cost of living presumption (taxation of deemed income) and the acquisition of assets presumption.[6]

If the transactions are entered into systematically to generate profit, and when a transaction is repeated at least three times during the six-month period, the individual would have to register as a business person, and this will be classified as a business transaction.

An individual who is already a registered businessperson will be taxed for any profit derived even from a single transaction.

Income from such transactions is considered as profit from business activity and is taxed at the following rates:[7]

Income (Salaries, Pensions, Business Activities) in EUR	*Tax Rate (%)*
0–10,000	9%
10,001–20,000	22%
20,001–30,000	28%
30,001–40,000	36%
40,001–	44%

A tax advance of 100% of the corresponding tax is also calculated (Article 69 of Law 4172/2013). The advance payment is only calculated as a percentage of the tax amount due for the current year. If there are circumstances that indicate that the tax due for the next year will be significantly lower, the taxpayer can apply to the tax office for the reassessment of the advance payment.[8]

(e) *What are the income/capital gains tax consequences for an employee receiving wages or salaries in crypto assets?*

Under the current legal framework, payments to employees using cryptocurrencies and other crypto assets must be treated as benefits in kind. According to the Greek Income Tax Code,[9] any benefits in kind received by an employee[10] or relative thereof shall be taken into account in taxable income at market value, provided the total value of benefits in kind exceeds the sum of EUR 300 per tax year. Evaluation is made as of the date when the payment is due.

5. And are therefore also excluded from the 'extraordinary solidarity levy'.
6. Article 34 of Law 4172/2013 Income Tax Code.
7. Same scale as for salaried employees but without reductions for salaried employees – Article 15 of Law 4172/2013.
8. The government already considers the lowering of the tax advance for 2021 to 50% but this has not been legislated yet.
9. Article 13 of Law 4172/2013.
10. As defined in Articles 12 et seq. of the Greek Income Tax Code.

(f) What are the income/capital gains tax consequences for a merchant receiving payment in crypto assets?

The supply by a merchant of goods and services, which are remunerated through crypto assets, are to be treated in the exact same way as supplies whose remuneration consists in fiat currency: The merchant's taxable income will be the value of the crypto asset at the time when the consideration was due to be paid to him. Once the merchant exchanges the crypto assets received into fiat currency, another taxable transaction will occur.

(g) What are the income/capital gains tax consequences of a loss of crypto assets?

The loss of crypto assets qualifying as business assets can lead to a tax-deductible expense. More specifically, it may qualify as 'loss of capital' which is deducted from the taxable earnings of the business, under the condition that the asset has been registered in its accounting books and that there is no entitlement of compensation, e.g., from an insurance policy.

(h) What are the income/capital gains tax consequences of a loss in value of crypto assets?

An individual who is not a registered businessperson may not claim tax relief for the loss in value of crypto assets. However, in calculating the taxable profit in a portfolio of crypto assets, the aggregate value will be taken into account. In relation to registered businesspersons and undertakings, according to Article 19 of Law 4308/2014 on the Greek Accounting Standards all financial assets are initially evaluated at the acquisition value. Subsequently they are evaluated at the acquisition value minus losses due to an evaluation at a lower value. Financial assets are audited for possible de-evaluation when there are indications to that effect. Such indications exist when: (a) there are obvious, serious financial circumstances for their issuer or the person liable to pay them; (b) when the value appearing in the accounting books is significantly higher than their fair market value; (c) when significant negative circumstances in the local, national, or global market raise the chances that obligations relating to these financial assets are not going to be fulfilled. If, according to the above, the accounting value of the assets is less than the market value of the assets, an accounting/taxable loss is taking place.

(i) What are the income/capital gains tax consequences of forks of crypto assets?

The definition of blockchain forks is totally unknown to Greek legislation. A comparable situation may be the splitting of shares listed in the Stock Exchange, which – from a tax point of view – does not affect the acquisition value of the shares. Consequently, the fork itself should not yet have any tax consequences; these would only occur when the newly received crypto assets were transferred for consideration. The cost basis will remain with the original crypto asset and the new crypto asset would be taxed as capital gain.

(j) What are the income/capital gains tax consequences of airdrops of crypto assets and are the tax consequences different if the airdropped tokens are unwanted?

It depends on whether the crypto assets are received within or outside of an active business or undertaking.

- Crypto assets received within an active trade or business lead to taxable income equal to the amount which the taxpayer would have had to pay to receive the assets.
- Crypto assets received outside of an active trade or business would qualify as gifts and be subject to gift tax.

It is of no relevance whether the airdropped tokens are wanted or unwanted. If the airdropped crypto assets were received as consideration for a service (e.g., perform a certain task such as posting about the currency on a social media forum, connecting with a particular member of the blockchain project, or writing a blog post), then the airdrop could be subject to tax from business activity, if this is performed systematically.

(k) What are the income/capital gains tax consequences of (solo, pool, and cloud) mining?

There is no law or administrative guidance on the tax treatment of crypto mining.

Assuming that such activity will be undertaken by an active trade or business (see section 1.1.2(d), the taxable profit will be the result of income resulted from the disposal of the crypto asset minus the expenses of the activity. There is no difference provided by law between solo, pool, and cloud mining activities. There are no legal grounds to treat pool mining as a partnership.

(l) What are the income/capital gains tax consequences of staking crypto assets?

The staking process is similar to the average bank savings account. But, unless and until this is legislated, tokens issued through staking could only be taxed as capital gain.

(m) What are the income/capital gains tax consequences of an indirect investment in crypto assets?

An indirect investment in crypto assets, i.e., investment through stocks, shares, mutual funds, etc., would fall under the classification of a financial instrument, the capital gains of which are taxable at a rate of 15%.

(n) How is income from crypto assets to be treated under double tax treaty law?

Greek tax authorities have not issued any administrative guidelines about the treatment of crypto assets in double tax treaties. What is peculiar in relation to crypto assets is that although there is no central depository or central issuing agent, or any authority governing their circulation (so that issues of geographical locality could be resolved), their creation (mining) is in fact an activity which requires the existence of a fixed place of business for the placement of the mining processors. Such fixed place of business would fall under the definition of a permanent establishment under the OECD model tax treaties, and the resulting profits would be taxed in Greece. On the other hand, mining through rented third-party data centres would not create a permanent establishment for the mining enterprise.

(o) What are the income/capital gains tax consequences of selling crypto assets in an ICO/STO/IEO?

The matter is not regulated. Presumably, if the ICO/STO/IEO is launched as part of a business activity, the tokens generated are to be capitalized at manufacturing cost and they should be reported as current assets. Tokens that are not intended for a sale qualify as fixed assets and must not be capitalized. Money raised through an ICO may be taxed as income from business activity, unless it is raised with the use of a corporate entity in which case the amount raised will be treated as capital. In an IEO the exchange would be regarded as two independent sales.

1.1.3 Other Taxes

(a) What are the value added tax/sales tax consequences of selling crypto assets?

The Court of Justice of the European Union (ECJ) decision in the Swedish case of *Skatteverket v. David Hedqvist*[11] concluded that no VAT is due on the exchange of a fiat currency into 'bitcoin' (and vice versa). The Court was asked to consider how an exchange which sold bitcoin for traditional currencies would be taxed. It held that,

11. Case C-264/14.

although services providing for the exchange of traditional currency with bitcoin constitute a supply of services for consideration, these services are exempt from VAT under the EU VAT Directive provision that requires Member States to grant a VAT exemption for financial transactions involving 'currency, bank notes, and coins used as legal tender'. This very significant case is binding for the Greek legislator and tax administration as to the VAT treatment of cryptocurrencies.

(b) Are payments in crypto assets subject to withholding taxes?

For purposes of the applicability of withholding taxes (e.g., on dividends, interest, or payroll taxes), payments made by a debtor through the transfer of crypto assets would be treated in the same manner as payments made in cash. The crypto assets payable would have to be converted into euros with the withholding tax payable to be calculated on the euro amount. Because crypto assets are not classified by law as money, payments in crypto assets are acceptable to the same extent as payments in kind.

(c) Does payment of compensation in crypto assets give rise to payroll tax consequences?

Given that it is difficult to calculate the value of benefits in kind under Article 13 of Law 4172/2013 at the time they are granted, no withholding tax on those benefits is applied; instead, the tax owed is calculated when the tax return is being finalised, given that their value (taxable if above EUR 300 per year and only fort the amount in excess thereof) increases the income of beneficiaries from salaried work. In the cases where withholding tax has already been withheld for these benefits,[12] that tax will be offset when the tax return is finalized.[13] Moreover, the case law has accepted that pay on which social security contributions are calculated means all manner of benefits in cash or in kind provided by the employer to the employee, even if those benefits are not given as consideration for the work offered by the latter, but are provided to him by the employer voluntarily and at his discretion, and all events in relation to the employment relationship binds them. Only extraordinary social benefits which are restrictively enumerated in the law are excluded, such as wedding gifts to the employee, the birth of the employee's children and allowances to the family of a deceased. In addition to the aforementioned exceptions, any benefit provided by the employer in cash or in kind to the employee in respect of the employment relationship falls within the concept of salary, on which social security contributions are due.

12. For example, Council of State Judgment No. 1089/2009.
13. Circular No. ΠΟΛ 1072/31.3.2015.

(d) *Do transactions with crypto assets trigger any transfer taxes?*

Under Greek tax law, assignments[14] (of claims, of contractual rights, etc.) made against consideration trigger a stamp duty of either 2.4% or 3.6%. In addition to assignments of debt claims, assignments of other rights are also covered, i.e., intangible assets that grant rights vis-à-vis a specific person or the public at large. Crypto assets that incorporate rights vis-à-vis the issuer (e.g., a right to profit sharing could, in theory, trigger a stamp duty obligation. However, there are certain formal conditions for defining whether an assignment agreement is or is not subject to stamp duty, such as the nationality of the parties (if Greek or not), the place of signature of the contract, the place of execution of the obligations assigned. Prima facie, it seems that the formal conditions for the imposition of Greek stamp duty on crypto transactions would not be met.

(e) *Are firms operating in the crypto space subject to digital service taxes?*

Greece has not introduced digital service tax.

(f) *Are crypto assets subject to gift, inheritance, estate, or wealth taxes?*

Yes. Article 13 of Law 2961/2001[15] regulates the definition of the taxable value of movable inheritance assets. More specifically, the value of the movable assets included in the inheritance is calculated based on each evidence. Not only tangible assets fall within the meaning of movable assets but also non-tangible assets (such as name, trademarks etc.): blogs, e-mails, websites, domain names and in general any other digital goods (we consider that within this definition we should include any type of crypto assets and blockchain applications). The value of these non-tangible goods may be assessed by Accredited/Certified Evaluators of Law 4152/2013.[16]

(g) *Are crypto assets subject to exit tax?*

Exit tax has been incorporated in the Greek legal order very recently by virtue of Articles 58-60 of Law 4714/2020 implementing Article 5 of EU Directive laying down rules against tax avoidance practices.[17] By virtue of this provision, Article 66A is added to the Income Tax Code dealing with exit taxation. According to this article, assets subject to exit taxation are defined 'any assets upon which the taxpayer exercises control and from which he envisages future financial profits'. As 'transfer of assets' is defined an act by which a Member State loses its right to tax the assets transferred, even though they remain under the control of the same taxpayer. Such transfer will be

14. Articles 455-470 of the Civil Code.
15. *Code on Taxation of Inheritance, Donations,* and *Parental Grants.*
16. Paragraph C, sub-paragraph C5.
17. ATAD 2016/1164/EU and 2017/952/EU.

taxable with the corporate income tax rate which is currently 24%. The definition of assets is so wide that one can support the view that crypto assets will definitely fall within the reach of this provision when it starts being applied.

(h) Can mining trigger gambling tax?

It is hard to say, because this matter is not resolved. However, to the extent that luck is an inherent factor in crypto mining, it does seem to fall within the definition of gambling, which is defined as follows under Greek law:[18]

(a) the influence of luck, wholly or partially, in the result of the game;
(b) that there is an economic risk (wager or bet), i.e., the choice by a player to take the risk of investing money or other property of any value, with intent to acquire directly or indirectly an economic gain from the result.

However, gambling tax is only imposed on specific games of chance that are listed by law, so there is no scope for taxation of crypto mining under the current legal framework.

1.1.4 Compliance and Documentation Obligations

(a) What documentation requirements exist for taxpayers regarding crypto assets and are there best practices in recordkeeping to support representations made in tax returns?

The Greek Tax Procedures Code[19] states that all persons with income from business activities are obliged to keep a reliable accounting system and suitable accounting records in accordance with the accounting standards specified in Greek law in order to prepare financial statements and other information in accordance with the tax laws. The accounting system and accounting records are examined as a whole, and not individual parts thereof, in terms of their reliability and suitability. 'Accounting records, electronic tax registers, tax memories and files generated by electronic tax registers' must be retained for at least:

(a) a period of five years 'from the end of the relevant tax year within which there is an obligation to submit a tax return'; or
(b) where the conditions in Article 36(2) of the Code are met, until the tax administration's right to issue a decision levying tax in accordance with the provisions of this paragraph becomes statute-barred; or
(c) until the tax administration's claim arising from a tax audit becomes final or until the claim is fully extinguished due to settlement in full.

18. Article 25 of Law 4002/2011.
19. Article 13 of Law 4174/2013.

Under Article 24 of that Code ('Access to accounting books and records'), the tax administration is entitled to obtain copies of the books and records and other documents, and the taxpayer must declare that they represent true copies. Where the taxpayer refuses to make the said declaration, the employee appointed by the tax administration makes a note on the documents. The designated employee may also require that the taxpayer or his tax agent attend the place where the tax audit is carried out and answer questions posed to him to make it easier for a tax audit to be carried out. If the books and records are kept in electronic format, the tax administration is entitled to access any related files. More specifically, the taxpayer is obliged to provide all information needed to ensure uninterrupted access to the tax administration's designated employee, irrespective of the place where the data are stored and the format of that data. All third parties who provide digital services to the taxpayer relating to the storage and processing of digital data have the same obligation, where that is requested by the tax administration. The tax administration is entitled to receive the electronic files in readable electronic format or hard copy. The employee designated by the tax administration may seize books and records kept or held in accordance with the tax laws and any other unofficial books, documents, files or records, if considered necessary to safeguard them as evidence.

Taxpayers with no income from business activities are only required to safeguard the documentation which constitutes evidence related to their income tax return.

(b) What is the evidentiary burden of supporting tax positions when a digital wallet address is lost or shared with other persons?

Combating tax evasion, by establishing the relevant infringements and imposing, through the administration, payment of the avoided tax, as well as the administrative sanctions provided by the law, is, according to the Constitution,[20] an overriding objective relating to the public interest. According to the fundamental principles of respect of human dignity,[21] rule of law,[22] proportionality,[23] and the presumption of innocence, guaranteed by Article 6(2) ECHR also applicable to administrative proceedings attributing infringements and imposing the relevant sanctions,[24] the burden of proof regarding the facts constituting the tax infringement attributed to a certain person, which entails imposing on such person payment of the avoided tax and the relevant sanctions, is borne, in principle, by the State, i.e., the tax authority[25]

The taxpayer bears the burden to prove the information included in his income tax return which he is (presumed to be) aware of or should be aware of. He is also required, in principle, to produce to the tax authority any supporting evidence, and the relevant information which is capable of being verified as to its accuracy and adequacy,

20. Article 4(5) and Article 106 (1) and (2).
21. Article 2(1) of the Constitution.
22. Article 25(1) first sub-paragraph of the Constitution.
23. Article 25(1) fourth sub-paragraph of the Constitution.
24. Cf. ECJ 21.1.2016, C-74/14 *Eturas*, ECLI:EU:C:2016:42, paragraph 38, and ECJ 23.12.2009, C-45/08, *Spector Photo Group*.
25. Cf. Council of State 4049/2014, 2442/2013, 886/2005.

assuming otherwise the risk that conclusions may be drawn against him about commission of a tax infringement. Equally, all supporting documentation relating to transactions in crypto assets must be kept to be shown in a tax audit.

(c) Are crypto asset exchanges and wallet providers subject to reporting obligations?

Under Greek domestic tax law, crypto asset exchanges and wallet providers are not subject to any periodic obligations vis-à-vis the tax authorities regarding their customers. However, the tax authorities do have powers to compel a person to provide information which is relevant for a taxation of a third party.[26]

(d) Are taxpayers holding crypto assets subject to reporting obligations apart from the filing of income tax/capital gains tax returns?

No, under Greek domestic tax law, taxpayers holding crypto assets are not subject to any reporting obligations apart from the filing of income tax/capital gains (or inheritance/gift) tax returns. Thus, a taxpayer who is holding crypto assets and who has not realized taxable income in connection therewith does not have a specific disclosure obligation to the tax authorities for his or her crypto investments.

(e) Are crypto asset exchanges and wallet providers subject to CRS/FATCA reporting?

Greek tax authorities have not issued any guidance on whether operators of crypto exchanges or providers of crypto wallets must annually report their customers' data under CRS/FATCA. The term 'financial asset' as currently defined under CRS seems to cover only traditional financial assets and does not comprise crypto assets. The otherwise wide definitions contained in both CRS and FATCA create a reasonable expectation that reposting on crypto assets will also be encompassed once they are recognized and defined by law.

1.1.5 Civil and Criminal Tax Enforcement

(a) What powers do the tax authorities have to compel the disclosure of information by third parties, such as exchanges or wallet providers, and have these been used in the past?

Article 15 of Law 4174/2013 on tax procedures and other provisions[27] states that following a written or electronic request from the Secretary General for Public

26. *See* answer on section 1.1.4(a) above.
27. Government Gazette 170/A/26.7.2013.

Revenues, public services and all other General Government agencies, including judicial and prosecuting authorities and all public organizations, bodies and companies in which the State participates or over which it exercises supervision, and independent authorities, are obliged to provide the tax administration with all available information and to present – without transferring them off the premises – all original documents, registers, and data in their possession. The Secretary General shall be entitled to request information or documents from other third parties, such as financial institutions, collective investment undertakings, chambers, notaries public, land registrars, heads of cadastral offices, economic or social or professional bodies or organizations, to determine the tax liability arising from cross-checks of data and collection of tax debts. In order to give effect to the foregoing indent, the tax administration may send a question, in hard copy or electronic format, which the third party must respond to within ten days of receiving it. In exceptionally complex cases, the deadline may be extended for twenty additional days. Moreover, the tax administration may request, by written or electronic request, from any digital platform operator operating in the sharing economy, regardless of whether it has a permanent establishment in Greece in accordance with the provisions of Article 6 of Law 4172/2013 or the provisions of double taxation treaties concluded by Greece, any information or data relating to persons using the platform as vendors for whom tax obligations arise in Greece. The information or data requested above shall be provided or sent by the digital platform operator to the Independent Authority for Public Revenue by the last day of the month after the month in which the request was received. The deadline referred to in the previous indent may be extended by one month, depending on the volume of information or data requested, where a request to that effect is submitted by the digital platform operator. Internet Service Providers (ISPs) and any other person, whether a natural or legal person or legal entity or authority, shall send the Tax Administration, upon a request from it which sets out the time and mode of transmission, any information in their possession relating to the persons who own, use, and/or are responsible for the operation and/or management of the websites/domain names of the above digital platforms. 'Digital platform' means any software, including a website or part thereof, and applications, including mobile applications, where two or more users or groups of users communicate via the internet with the intermediation of the platform operator in order to facilitate a transaction between them, allowing vendors to connect to other persons for the provision of related services and goods to them in return for a fee. The Secretary General may issue a decision designating certain categories of persons who are obliged to automatically provide information about their financial transactions with taxpayers. Third parties bound by professional secrecy are obliged to provide information which relates to their financial transactions with the taxpayer. Other information protected by professional secrecy shall require written permission from the competent Public Prosecutor. The tax administration may not take cognizance of information or documents relating to criminal cases pending before the competent prosecuting authorities or criminal courts without the prior written consent of the competent Public Prosecutor.

(b) *What measures have the tax authorities undertaken in the past to ensure crypto tax compliance?*

It is not known what measures the Greek tax authorities have undertaken in the past to ensure crypto tax compliance.

(c) *Are the tax authorities cooperating with tax authorities in other jurisdictions on enforcement?*

To ensure compliance by taxpayers holding crypto assets, Greek tax authorities have several tools at their disposal for obtaining information from abroad. Most of the double taxation treaties[28] that Greece has signed with other countries contain articles on the cooperation between tax authorities. Greece has ratified the OECD/Council of Europe Convention on Mutual Administrative Assistance in Tax Matters, which similarly gives the tax authorities access to information held abroad. It is not public knowledge whether the Greek tax authorities are cooperating with tax authorities in other jurisdictions on enforcement and whether they have made use of the various instruments mentioned above in respect of crypto asset holdings of taxpayers.

Law 3943/2011 on Combating tax evasion, staffing audit services, and other provisions relating to the competence of the Ministry of Finance provided in its Article 7 for the enhancement of international administrative cooperation in matters of direct taxation. More specifically, it established within the Directorate for International Financial Relationships of the Ministry of Finance a 'Service of International Administrative Cooperation in matters of direct taxation' with very extended responsibilities in relation to exchange of information, enhancement of mutual administrative assistance between the competent authorities of European Union Member States, the implementation of international agreements entered into with other countries on the exchange of information in matters of direct taxation, etc.

28. Fifty-seven at the time of writing.

Hong Kong

Vivien Chan

1. COUNTRY GUIDES

1.1 Hong Kong

1.1.1 Applicable Tax Law, Guidance, and Case Law

(a) Which laws, regulations, and other administrative guidance exist dealing with crypto assets?

There are currently no laws or regulations that specifically govern activities relating to crypto assets. That said, the Securities and Futures Commission (the SFC), the watchdog for securities and futures markets in Hong Kong, has issued the Proforma Terms and Conditions for Licensed Corporations which Manage Portfolios that Invest in Virtual Assets (the 'Proforma Terms') in October 2019 and subsequently a Position Paper on the Regulation of virtual asset trading platforms (the 'Position Paper').

Other than the Proforma Terms, activities relating to virtual/crypto assets may be regulated under the existing laws relating to the trading of goods and securities, for example, the Sales of Goods Ordinance, the Trade Descriptions Ordinance and the Securities and Futures Ordinance, depending on the type of assets.

(b) Which court cases exist dealing with crypto assets?

There has not been any landmark case that sheds light on the classification, regulation or recognition of crypto assets in Hong Kong.

1.1.2 *Income and Capital Gains Taxes*

(a) How are crypto assets classified for income and capital gains tax purposes?

While there is no legal classification of virtual/crypto assets as to the type of legally recognized assets, the general notion, as supported by the Position Paper and designations used by the relevant authorities, is that crypto assets, specifically cryptocurrencies, can be differentiated into 'virtual commodities' and 'security tokens'. The former is not considered as a form of legal tender. The latter refers to digital representations of ownership of assets or economic rights utilizing the blockchain technology and would thus constitute a type of security that would come under the regulations of the SFC.

The Hong Kong Inland Revenue Department (IRD) published a revised Departmental Interpretation and Practice Notes No. 39 ('DIPN 39') in March 2020, which shed light on the IRD's position on digital assets, such as cryptocurrencies. In the DIPN 39, the IRD classified digital tokens into three categories, namely payment tokens, security tokens and utility tokens. That said, the IRD has indicated explicitly in the DIPN 39 that tax treatment of digital tokens would depend on their nature and use instead of the above-mentioned classification.

Hong Kong does not impose any capital gains tax. Income tax can be classified into salaries tax (for individuals) and profits tax (mainly for corporations though this also applies to individuals). Generally, salaries tax is charged on every person in respect of his or her income arising in or derived from Hong Kong from any office or employment of profit. In the context of crypto assets, if a person is remunerated for services rendered by him or her in Hong Kong in the form of crypto assets, such remuneration should be subject to salaries tax based on the market value of the cryptocurrency at the time of accrual of such remuneration represented in fiat currency (i.e., Hong Kong dollars).

On the other hand, corporations or persons carrying on any trade, profession business in Hong Kong are chargeable to tax on all profits (excluding profits arising from the sale of capital assets) arising in or derived from Hong Kong from such trade or business. Whether certain profits arose in or derived from Hong Kong is a question of fact and degree upon a consideration of all the circumstances. In the context of crypto assets, it would mainly depend on the geographical location where such business activity takes place. Generally, if a company engages in the business of trading cryptocurrencies for others in Hong Kong and profit through a fixed or variable commission rate, it would be chargeable to tax on such profits.

(b) What are the income/capital gains tax consequences of selling crypto assets against fiat currency?

Hong Kong does not impose any capital gains tax. If an employee receives cryptocurrencies or any form of digital assets as remuneration for his or her services, the market value of the cryptocurrencies or digital assets at the time of accrual of such remuneration will be reported as the employee's income and chargeable to salaries tax. Any subsequent gains or losses as a result of selling such assets against fiat currency would not affect the assessable income.

If a company trades or invests in cryptocurrencies, whether the gains arising therefrom are assessable for tax purpose would depend on whether the gains are capital or revenue in nature. Whether an asset is of capital or revenue nature is a question of fact and degree and all relevant circumstances, including the purpose of investment, accounting treatment, degree and frequency of the trading activity, level of system or organization (i.e., business-like manner), and the general 'badges of trade' principle. As a general rule, where an asset is acquired or incurred principally for the purpose of selling or repurchasing or where there is a pattern of short-term profit-taking, it would be classified as trading, and the gains would prima facie be taxable.

For trading gains from a sale of crypto assets, the gains against fiat currency relative to the value of the crypto assets in that fiat currency at the time of each transaction generating the revenue should be accounted as part of the profits in the relevant financial year. Where the crypto assets are not profits of a business (e.g., business of trading cryptocurrencies for others in consideration of an amount in fiat currency), any gains from a sale of such crypto assets against fiat currency would not give rise to any tax consequences as such assets are not assessable for tax purpose.

(c) What are the income/capital gains tax consequences of exchanging crypto assets against other crypto assets?

Hong Kong does not impose any capital gains tax. In Hong Kong, cryptocurrencies such as bitcoins are not recognized as a form of legal tender. That said, gains or losses arising from the exchange of crypto assets against other crypto assets would be assessable as profits tax only if such assets are revenue in nature based on all relevant facts and circumstances. Such gains and losses should be calculated based on the difference of the market value of the respective crypto assets in fiat currency at the time of the exchange. Where the crypto assets are revenue in nature, the gains or losses may be taxable or deductible.

(d) If a distinction is made between business assets and non-business assets, when does trading in crypto assets lead to a trade or business?

Any profits made by any entity conducting a business of trading crypto assets in Hong Kong are subject to profits tax in the same way as any other company acquiring profits by any legitimate means. Where an entity makes gains by investing in cryptocurrencies in a capital nature, such gains may be treated as capital gains, as opposed to profits, and is not taxable in Hong Kong.

(e) *What are the income/capital gains tax consequences for an employee receiving wages or salaries in crypto assets?*

An employee receiving wages or salaries in any form, including crypto assets, would be subject to salaries tax. The assessable value of the wages would be calculated based on the market value of the cryptocurrency at the time of accrual of such remuneration represented in fiat currency (i.e., Hong Kong Dollars).

(f) *What are the income/capital gains tax consequences for a merchant receiving payment in crypto assets?*

If a business provides goods or services in return for crypto assets as consideration, such assets would be treated as revenue of the business and would thus be assessable as profits for tax purposes. According to DIPN 39, the market value of the cryptocurrency, and by reasonable extension any other crypto assets, accrued at the date of transaction should reflect the amount of the sale and purchase. As such, the value of any revenue in the form of crypto assets should be calculated based on the market value of such asset at the time of the transaction for tax and accounting purposes.

(g) *What are the income/capital gains tax consequences of a loss of crypto assets?*

In the absence of any guidance from official statements or laws, the loss of crypto assets is treated in the same way as the loss of any other assets of the business. Where the crypto assets are taxable assets of a revenue nature, according to the general accounting principles in Hong Kong, losses made are to be set-off against future profits. In the context of salaries tax, where an employee is remunerated by his/her employer in the form of cryptocurrencies, provided that the transfer of the remuneration has occurred and completed, any loss of such remuneration on the part of the employee would not affect his/her tax position as salaries tax would be chargeable as long as payment was received and calculated based on the market value of the crypto asset at the time of accrual of the remuneration.

(h) *What are the income/capital gains tax consequences of a loss in value of crypto assets?*

In the case where the crypto assets are received in the ordinary course of business of an entity as a form of payment for its services or is otherwise revenue in nature and has not been exchanged for fiat currency after receipt, the loss in value may affect the amount of assessable profits of the company during the relevant financial year subject to the auditor's accounting treatment on such assets (i.e., whether capital or revenue in nature).

Any unrealized losses in the value of crypto assets at the year end of that financial year should be reflected as part of the profit and loss of the business. Such gains or losses should be calculated relative to the value of the crypto assets in that fiat currency at the time of each transaction generating the revenue or incurring the loss. That said, only where the crypto assets are determined to be revenue in nature would the assessable tax be deductible as a result of the loss in value. If the crypto assets are capital in nature, a loss in value would not have any tax consequence, as it will be excluded from the charge of profits tax.

(i) *What are the income/capital gains tax consequences of forks of crypto assets?*

While various jurisdictions treat forks and/or airdrops as taxation events, there is no established position by the IRD or the court on the tax or accounting treatment of forks. Forks of crypto assets may be analogous to the demerger or a shareholding restructure of a listed company. Based on the current tax principles, no additional tax will be incurred or affected in a fork event other than the profits tax relating to the resulting change in total assets. Whether the change of total value in the crypto assets can affect one's tax position would depend on whether the assets are capital or revenue in nature. Any gains or losses in the total value, including receipt of additional assets, would only be taxable if the original invested assets are revenue in nature.

(j) *What are the income/capital gains tax consequences of airdrops of crypto assets and are the tax consequences different if the airdropped tokens are unwanted?*

While DIPN 39 does not explicitly provide guidance on the treatment of airdrops, it refers to airdrops and blockchain forks collectively as events that may give rise to new cryptocurrencies. DIPN 39 further indicates that if new cryptocurrencies are received in the course of a cryptocurrency business, the new cryptocurrencies are to be regarded as receipts of the business. By applying existing accounting principles not specifically designed for crypto assets, such additional assets obtained by way of airdrop may be treated analogously to interests or dividends from any other form of investments. As such, the ultimate issue for determining tax consequences is whether the crypto assets are capital or revenue in nature. Whether the airdropped tokens are wanted or unwanted is irrelevant as long as the same is received by the taxpayer.

(k) *What are the income/capital gains tax consequences of (solo, pool, and cloud) mining?*

If a party carries out the business of mining cryptocurrencies, such as by hiring employees and renting premises for such activity, any profits made from mining would likely be subject to profits tax and any expenses relating thereto, such as the purchasing of hardware and electricity fees, should be deductible from the assessable profits. Whereas if an individual conducts cryptocurrency as a hobby or investment, it will unlikely be considered as carrying out a business or trade and it depends on all relevant facts and circumstances. Where the mining of cryptocurrencies is organized as a joint effort of multiple parties, the tax consequences on individual miners or parties would depend on the distribution of the profit.

(l) What are the income/capital gains tax consequences of staking crypto assets?

Staking of crypto assets is generally regarded similarly as mining, and thus the tax consequences would be similar. However, given that staking is more passive in nature and requires direct contribution of capital, subject to other surrounding circumstances and the nature of funds contributed, it may more likely be treated as an investment and capital gains, which are not subject to tax in Hong Kong.

(m) What are the income/capital gains tax consequences of an indirect investment in crypto assets?

Whether an investment in crypto assets is direct or indirect has no effect on the relevant tax consequences. Investment in a financial instrument relating to crypto assets or the value of specific crypto assets would be treated as any other investment in financial instruments or securities for tax purpose in Hong Kong. As such, whether indirect investment in crypto assets would be subject to profits tax is also dependent on whether it is capital or revenue in nature.

(n) How is income from crypto assets to be treated under double tax treaty law?

There have not been any specific guidelines or laws governing the treatment of crypto assets in the context of double tax treaty law. As such, it will likely be treated in the same way as monetary salaries or profits. Where the crypto assets are taxable in Hong Kong and that the taxpayer is either a resident of Hong Kong or another jurisdiction which Hong Kong has entered into Double Taxation Agreements with, the tax positions may be affected by the agreements. The specific arrangements differ from jurisdiction to jurisdiction depending on the content of the specific agreement between Hong Kong and the other jurisdiction and the corresponding subsidiary legislation in Hong Kong.

(o) What are the income/capital gains tax consequences of selling crypto assets in an ICO/STO/IEO?

According to DIPN 39, the tax treatment of proceeds from a public offering of crypto assets is determined by the rights and obligations of the tokens offered. As ICOs may relate to digital assets of different natures, the Commissioner of the IRD would review the white paper or any other underlying documents of an ICO and examine what rights and benefits (e.g., equity interests or a right to access to a future service similar to a voucher) are attached to the digital tokens. If digital tokens offered represent equity or ownership interests in the issuer (i.e., in an STO), the proceeds of the STO would be capital in nature since the token holders would be given shareholders' rights (e.g., the right to receive dividend) and thus would not be subject to profits tax, which is consistent with the tax treatment of share issuance of a company.

If digital tokens offered in an ICO give the token holders a right to future benefits (i.e., utility tokens) without any equity or ownership interests, such tokens would require the issuer to supply goods to or perform a service for the token holder. The proceeds of the ICO would be viewed as a prepayment for future goods or services and thus likely subject to profits tax. The timing of revenue recognition would depend on the details of the issuer's performance obligations and should be determined in line with generally accepted accounting principles (i.e., market value of the proceeds at the time of accrual). Subject to any specific exemptions provided, profits arising in or derived from Hong Kong from the ICO can be charged to profits tax.

1.1.3 Other Taxes

(a) What are the value added tax/sales tax consequences of selling crypto assets?

Hong Kong does not impose any value added tax or sales tax.

(b) Are payments in crypto assets subject to withholding taxes?

Hong Kong does not impose any withholding tax.

(c) Does payment of compensation in crypto assets give rise to payroll tax consequences?

In Hong Kong, employers generally have the obligation to report the remuneration paid to its employees to the IRD on an annual basis. Under the existing framework, in addition to any monetary salaries, any allowance, perquisite or fringe benefit, any stock awards and gains realized therefrom and payable to employees shall be reported. That said, it is unclear how the IRD evaluates cryptocurrencies given its volatility and the lack of any specific guidelines.

(d) Do transactions with crypto assets trigger any transfer taxes?

Transfer of crypto assets is not currently chargeable to stamp duty in Hong Kong (this does not constitute a transfer of Hong Kong stock).

(e) Are firms operating in the crypto space subject to digital service taxes?

Hong Kong does not impose any digital service tax.

(f) Are crypto assets subject to gift, inheritance, estate, or wealth taxes?

No, Hong Kong does not impose any inheritance, estate, or wealth taxes. For transfer of crypto assets as a gift, stamp duty should not be chargeable.

(g) Are crypto assets subject to exit tax?

Hong Kong does not impose any exit tax.

(h) Can mining trigger gambling tax?

Under the Gambling Ordinance (Cap. 148 of the laws of Hong Kong), gambling, including gaming, betting and bookkeeping, is generally unlawful unless authorized by the relevant authorities. 'Game' in this context is defined as a game of chance and a game of chance and skill combined and a pretended game of chance or chance and skill combined, and also means any game whatever in which: (a) a bank is kept by one or more of the players exclusively of the others; or (b) the chances of the game are not equally favourable to all the players, including among the players, the banker or other person by whom the game is managed or against whom the players stake, play or bet.

Further, pursuant to the Betting Duty Ordinance (Cap. 108 of the laws of Hong Kong), betting duty is generally charged on companies authorized to carry out betting activities relating to horse races, cash-sweeps, lotteries and football matches.

As such, mining of cryptocurrencies by individuals would not fall under the definition of gambling and or be subject to betting duty in Hong Kong as miners generally do not 'bet' but rather invests on the hardware for a potential return, and that betting duty only applies to specific activities as aforementioned.

1.1.4 Compliance and Documentation Obligations

(a) What documentation requirements exist for taxpayers regarding crypto assets and are there best practices in recordkeeping to support representations made in tax returns?

There are no specific documentation requirements regarding crypto assets. In Hong Kong, taxpayers are generally not required to provide document in support of their representations made in the tax returns subject that the IRD may request for further information to be provided subsequently.

(b) *What is the evidentiary burden of supporting tax positions when a digital wallet address is lost or shared with other persons?*

The IRD has not indicated its position nor is there any case on the consequences of loss or sharing of digital wallet address relating to one's tax position. Where the address of a digital wallet storing cryptocurrencies that are assessable profits of a business is lost, it should be treated in the same way as the loss of any other assets of the business.

According to the generally accounting principles in Hong Kong, losses made are to be set off against future profits. In Hong Kong, a company's tax position is generally based on its tax return as supported by an auditor's report produced by a third-party auditor. In the case of a loss of digital wallet address, such loss should be endorsed in writing by the management of the company and confirmed in writing by the wallet service provider to the satisfaction of the auditor.

In the context of salaries tax where an individual is remunerated by his/her employer in the form of cryptocurrencies, provided that the transfer of the remuneration has occurred and completed, loss or sharing of the digital wallet address on the part of that individual would not affect his/her tax position as salaries tax would be chargeable as long as payment was received and calculated based on the market value at the time of accrual of the remuneration.

(c) *Are crypto asset exchanges and wallet providers subject to reporting obligations?*

The SFC has expressly indicated that platforms that only provide a direct peer-to-peer marketplace for transactions by investors who typically retain control over their own assets will not fall under the scope of the current regulatory framework under the Securities and Futures Ordinance (Cap. 571 of the laws of Hong Kong) which governs the securities and futures industry and activities as administered by the SFC. Thus, crypto assets exchanges do not have special reporting obligations to the SFC. However, the Position Paper has established an opt-in mechanism for virtual asset trading platforms to apply to be licensed by the SFC. Once licensed, the platform would have to, *inter alia*, provide monthly reports to the SFC on its activities in a prescribed form.

As to the reporting obligations of crypto asset wallet providers, the legal position is unclear. If the wallet is 'deposit-taking' by nature, it may constitute a financial institution that would come under robust regulation of various regulatory bodies, such as the SFC, IRD and the Monetary Authority and various legislations, including the Securities and Futures Ordinance and the Banking Ordinance (Cap. 155 of the laws of Hong Kong). Whereas if the wallet provider merely safekeeps the keys relating to crypto assets analogous to password managing service providers, they will unlikely be considered as a financial institution and be subject to those entailing reporting obligations. The usual company reporting obligations must also be observed, which include the filing of annual return with the Companies Registry and annual tax return with the IRD.

(d) *Are taxpayers holding crypto assets subject to reporting obligations apart from the filing of income tax/capital gains tax returns?*

There is no requirement to report any possession or transactions of crypto assets in Hong Kong. Income gained by way of salary or profits, whether in the form of crypto asset or fiat currency, would be subject to tax (for details, please refer to our response to section 1.1.2(a)).

(e) *Are crypto asset exchanges and wallet providers subject to CRS/FATCA reporting?*

There has not been any guideline on CRS/FATCA reporting for crypto asset exchanges and wallet providers. The Inland Revenue (Amendment) (No. 3) Ordinance 2016 has introduced the relevant provisions to the Inland Revenue Ordinance, incorporating the CRS developed by the OECD. Whereas the Agreement between the Government of the Hong Kong Special Administrative Region of the People's Republic of China and the Government of the United States of America for the Exchange of Information Relating to Taxes (TIEA) entered into in 2014 gave effect to FATCA in Hong Kong. In general, both types of reporting obligations are mandated on 'financial institutions'.

Under the relevant legislations and the TIEA, financial institutions generally cover any deposit-taking companies. As per the above analysis, whether crypto asset exchanges and wallet providers constitute financial institutions depend on various factors such as the type of crypto assets handled and their exact scope of business. Where the service provider has some degree of control over their own assets as part of their services, they will likely be treated as a financial institution with CRS/FATCA reporting obligations.

1.1.5 Civil and Criminal Tax Enforcement

(a) *What powers do the tax authorities have to compel the disclosure of information by third parties, such as exchanges or wallet providers, and have these been used in the past?*

Generally, if the Commissioner of the IRD has reasonable grounds for suspecting that a person has made an incorrect return or supplied false information, he may apply to the magistrate for a search warrant to take possession of any books, records, accounts, or documents of that person or that person's spouse. While there is no general guideline for accessing exchanges or wallets in relation to crypto assets, the above general power should also apply to any exchanges or wallet providers situated in Hong Kong.

(b) What measures have the tax authorities undertaken in the past to ensure crypto tax compliance?

The IRD has indicated in a reply to Legislative Council Questions in April 2019 that they do not maintain statistics specifically on tax payable by persons carrying on virtual (crypto) asset-related activities and relevant investigation cases. There has also not been any report on significant cases where the IRD has taken special measures enforcing tax liabilities specifically relating to crypto assets.

(c) Are the tax authorities cooperating with tax authorities in other jurisdictions on enforcement?

The IRD has indicated in a reply to Legislative Council Questions in April 2019 that they will seek relevant information from other tax authorities through the exchange of information mechanism under tax treaties so as to enhance its capability of detecting tax avoidance and evasion. No further relevant guidelines or cases have been published since then.

Hungary

Pál Jalsovszky & Ákos Baráti

1. COUNTRY GUIDES

1.1 Hungary

1.1.1 Applicable Tax Law, Guidance, and Case Law

(a) Which laws, regulations, and other administrative guidance exist dealing with crypto assets?

There are no specific rules regarding crypto assets; thus, the general tax rules apply to crypto assets - particularly, the Hungarian Income Tax Act, the Corporate Income Tax Act and the Value Added Tax Act - and their complementary regulations. Apart from some interpretation published in professional journals, no official guideline is available on the subject.

In the absence of specific tax rules and official guidance, the currently known tax practice is summarized below, which could be subject to change anytime.

(b) Which court cases exist dealing with crypto assets?

Apart from the value added tax related decision of the European Court of Justice (ECJ), explained in section 1.1.3(a), below, no specific cases relating to crypto assets have been published in Hungary.

1.1.2 Income and Capital Gains Taxes

(a) How are crypto assets classified for income and capital gains tax purposes?

There are no special rules for crypto assets under Hungarian law. According to the current interpretation of the law, crypto assets are generally treated as short-term receivables (regardless of the investment period) for legal entities. Crypto assets, as short-term receivables, are considered as movable property for gift tax and inheritance tax purposes.

(b) What are the income/capital gains tax consequences of selling crypto assets against fiat currency?

Selling crypto assets against fiat currency is considered realization. Transactions should be evaluated one-by-one to determine the result of the transaction (selling price less acquisition value).

The positive difference between the selling price and the acquisition value (gain) is subject to tax.

As for private individuals, in the absence of special rules, the income arising from selling crypto assets is considered as so-called other income. Such income is subject to 15% personal income tax and 17.5% social contribution (the tax base is 85% of the income). Losses are not deductible from the tax base in case of private individuals. This may result in extreme tax burden for actively trading individuals.

In the case of legal entities selling crypto assets, profit will be considered as financial income and will be a part of the general accounting profit (subject to 9% corporate income tax rate). Losses incurred on crypto transactions are deductible from the tax base for legal entities.

(c) What are the income/capital gains tax consequences of exchanging crypto assets against other crypto assets?

There are no specific rules; thus, exchanging crypto assets is subject to the same tax treatment as if the exchange was against fiat currency (as detailed above). The tax base is the fair market value of the crypto assets to be acquired less the tax book value (acquisition value, which could be subject to adjustment) of the crypto asset to be sold.

(d) If a distinction is made between business assets and non-business assets, when does trading in crypto assets lead to a trade or business?

No distinction is made between business and non-business assets. The tax treatment is the same regardless if trading in crypto assets is carried out on commercial scale or on a non-business basis.

(e) What are the income/capital gains tax consequences for an employee receiving wages or salaries in crypto assets?

There is no restriction for paying salary in crypto assets. In such a case, the fair market value of the asset will be considered as salary when received by the employee and such value will be taxed the same way as salary. Exchanging the crypto assets into fiat currency could generate further tax obligations (as explained in section 1.1.2(b)).

(f) What are the income/capital gains tax consequences for a merchant receiving payment in crypto assets?

Due to the lack of specific Hungarian legislation for crypto assets, the supply of goods and services by a merchant, if remunerated through crypto assets, is to be treated the same way as if they were remunerated through fiat currency. The fair market value of the crypto asset at the time of the transaction is considered as revenue.

(g) What are the income/capital gains tax consequences of a loss of crypto assets?

The loss of the private key associated with a crypto asset storing address leads to derecognition of a crypto asset. Loss of crypto assets is not recognized for private individuals for tax purposes. Practically the same applies for legal entities, as the crypto asset (being recorded as a receivable) would be subject to impairment, which is not tax deductible in case of a loss.

(h) What are the income/capital gains tax consequences of a loss in value of crypto assets?

Non-realized losses do not have a tax consequence for private individuals. Tax is only incurred if the asset is sold (or otherwise transferred), in which case a loss-making transaction is not subject to tax, and the loss cannot be utilized against other (profitable) transactions.

For legal entities, non-realized losses could have relevance if the fair market value of the crypto asset is significantly lower than its book value (acquisitions value) for more than one year. In such a case, the legal entity would have to impair the crypto asset, which is not tax deductible. Losses realized during crypto asset transactions are tax deductible.

(i) What are the income/capital gains tax consequences of forks of crypto assets?

Forks are not recognized for tax purposes, i.e., forks do not trigger taxation. There are no exact rules for the determination of the cost base. Most likely, the original acquisition value (book value) should be split based on the fair market value of the new and forked crypto assets at the time of the fork.

(j) What are the income/capital gains tax consequences of airdrops of crypto assets and are the tax consequences different if the airdropped tokens are unwanted?

In cases where crypto assets are given for free (for promotional or marketing reasons), the tax consequences are the following:

- Private individuals receiving assets for free are subject to gift tax with the rate of 18%, payable on the fair market value of the assets received, provided that the value is above HUF 150,000 (approximately EUR 430) and that the assets are received in Hungary (this has to be reviewed on a case-by-case basis). Special rules may apply for airdrops made by Hungarian tax resident entities.
- Legal entities realize other financial income when receiving airdrops of crypto assets, which is subject to 9% corporate income tax with a tax base of the fair market value of the asset.

(k) What are the income/capital gains tax consequences of (solo, pool, and cloud) mining?

Income from self-employment activities, such as the mining of crypto assets, is part of the private individual's consolidated tax base. The income from such activity can be decreased by qualifying expenses, such as electricity costs and the cost of the technical equipment (itemized expenses), or by 10% of the income (lump sum deduction), at the election of the individual. Fifteen per cent personal income tax and 17.5% social contribution are levied on the tax base. Note that the individual must determine the income and expenses of each activity separately.

Crypto assets realized from mining activity are subject to 9% corporate income tax. Under the current interpretation of the law, the corporate entity has to defer the income from the time of acquisition (when the coin is received) until the asset is actually exchanged or traded, meaning that tax obligation only arises when the crypto asset is sold (or transferred in another way).

(l) What are the income/capital gains tax consequences of staking crypto assets?

The income (the fair market value of the consideration) received for the staking is subject to the same tax consequences as in the case of mining.

(m) What are the income/capital gains tax consequences of an indirect investment in crypto assets?

Indirect investments are taxed based on the type of the intermediate instrument. For instance, most of the financial instruments (including bonds, investments units of public investment funds, or indices linked to the exchange rate of crypto assets) are subject to only 15% personal income tax and a capped amount of social security contribution. However, income from tax transparent intermediate vehicles/instruments may be treated as 'other income', which is subject to a higher effective tax burden (approximately 28%). In the absence of specific tax regulations, this has to be reviewed on a case-by-case basis. For instance, EU investment funds are generally not considered tax transparent for Hungarian tax purposes.

(n) How is income from crypto assets to be treated under double tax treaty law?

The Hungarian tax authority or Ministry of Finance has not yet issued any general statement or ruling regarding the treatment of crypto assets under double tax treaty law. Thus, the only available guidance is the OECD Model Convention. Income in connection with crypto assets is more than likely to fall under the rules of Article 7 or 13, depending on the personal status of the receiver.

Pursuant to Article 7 of the Convention, profits of a legal entity (enterprise) of a contracting state are generally taxable only in that state, however, if the enterprise carries on business in another contracting state through a permanent establishment, profit attributable to the permanent establishment may be taxed in that other contracting state.

Pursuant to Article 13(5) of the Convention, gains from the alienation of any property, other than that specifically referred to in previous paragraphs, are taxable only in the contracting state of which the alienator is a resident. Thus, an investor resident in a contracting state selling crypto assets through a crypto exchange in another contracting state may only be taxed in the state of residence.

(o) What are the income/capital gains tax consequences of selling crypto assets in an ICO/STO/IEO?

The Hungarian regulatory environment for ICO/STO/IEOs is yet to be developed. Due to the lack of regulation and any official ruling from either the Ministry of Finance or the National Bank of Hungary (MNB), only assumptions can be made on how such activities might be treated - based on the similarities between crowdfunding and ICO/STO/IEO mechanisms, the general opinion tends towards the regulation of investment-based crowdfunding. The MNB has stated that collecting funds from the public (similar to crowdfunding) with a fixed repayment obligation is an activity strictly reserved for financial institutions.

Provision of investment services is a strictly regulated, licensed activity with the financial authority of both the Ministry of Finance and the MNB; however, ICO/STO/IEO activities do not fall under the scope of the securities provided by the regulation and the authorities. The MNB has issued multiple press releases warning potential investors of the risks of ICO/STO/IEOs, stating that these investments are not under governmental control, have no financial security behind them and involve the risk of losing most of, or even all invested funds.

From a tax point of view, ICO/STO/IEOs are not subject to taxation.

1.1.3 Other Taxes

(a) What are the value added tax/sales tax consequences of selling crypto assets?

Based on the ECJ Case No. C-264/14, VAT consequences of crypto and fiat currency exchanges are the same as the exchange of regular, fiat currencies, meaning that it falls within the scope of the exemption for transactions related to foreign exchange, bank notes and coins.

(b) Are payments in crypto assets subject to withholding taxes?

Payments made by the transfer of crypto assets are subject to the withholding taxes if the underlying transactions have been subject to withholding taxes if paid in fiat currency.

(c) Does payment of compensation in crypto assets give rise to payroll tax consequences?

The compensation will trigger the general tax consequences, but the value of the compensation will be determined based on the fair market value of the crypto asset transferred.

(d) Do transactions with crypto assets trigger any transfer taxes?

The Hungarian Transfer Tax Act includes gift, inheritance and transfer taxes as well as stamp duties. All these taxes are applicable to crypto assets under the general rules, as crypto assets would be treated as movable property. For instance, receiving crypto asset without consideration from a sibling would be subject to the same 18 % gift tax on the donee, as if cash were gifted.

(e) Are firms operating in the crypto space subject to digital service taxes?

No special digital tax rules are in force in Hungary.

(f) Are crypto assets subject to gift, inheritance, estate, or wealth taxes?

Gift and inheritance taxes are applicable under the general rules (at the rate of 18 %, but numerous exemptions could apply, for instance, in case of direct line of descent or ancestry). No estate or wealth tax is imposed in Hungary.

(g) Are crypto assets subject to exit tax?

An exit tax was introduced on 1 January 2020 in Hungary, with the incorporation in the Hungarian Corporate Income Tax Act. If circumstances lead to the restriction of Hungary's right to tax certain assets, the Act levies income tax as if a sale of the assets has occurred. The tax base is the fair market value less the book value of the assets transferred, with a tax rate of 9 %. However, if the destination of the transfer is another EU Member State, the legislation provides for an option to pay the tax in five separate instalments over the following four years.

Individuals are not subject to exit tax.

(h) Can mining trigger gambling tax?

Under the current interpretation of the law, mining should not trigger gambling tax, as gambling tax is levied strictly on 'classic' gambling activities (e.g., online casinos, card rooms, and lottery).

1.1.4 Compliance and Documentation Obligations

(a) What documentation requirements exist for taxpayers regarding crypto assets and are there best practices in recordkeeping to support representations made in tax returns?

Hungarian taxpayers are not subject to any specific documentation obligations with regard to holding or trading with crypto assets; thus, taxpayers only have to comply with the general documentation requirements.

(b) What is the evidentiary burden of supporting tax positions when a digital wallet address is lost or shared with other persons?

Losing a wallet has no tax implications, thus, no supporting documentation is required.

(c) Are crypto asset exchanges and wallet providers subject to reporting obligations?

Due to the lack of regulation regarding crypto assets, exchange and wallet providers are not subject to specific reporting obligations apart from the general requirements.

(d) *Are taxpayers holding crypto assets subject to reporting obligations apart from the filing of income tax/capital gains tax returns?*

No special rules apply. Apart from the filing of income tax or personal income tax return annually, the holder of a crypto asset is not subject to any specific reporting obligation.

(e) *Are crypto asset exchanges and wallet providers subject to CRS/FATCA reporting?*

Hungarian tax authorities have not yet issued any guidance on whether providers of crypto exchange and crypto wallet services must report their customer's data under CRS/FATCA Regulation. At this point, it is ambiguous whether the CRS definition of 'financial assets' includes crypto assets or whether it only covers traditional financial assets. Due to the nature of crypto asset exchanges and wallet providers, we expect that reporting obligations will prevail for these service providers as well.

1.1.5 Civil and Criminal Tax Enforcement

(a) *What powers do the tax authorities have to compel the disclosure of information by third parties, such as exchanges or wallet providers, and have these been used in the past?*

Under Hungarian law, the tax authorities have the right to request information from third parties as a part of a tax audit of a taxpayer. Third parties have an obligation to respond to the best of their knowledge and even provide information or documents based on such inquiries, though certain limits exist to the depth of questioning. The statutory obligation of confidentiality applies in tax procedures as well, meaning that close relatives have the right to refuse to respond.

In conclusion, Hungarian tax authorities are in a position to compel the disclosure of information by exchange or wallet providers, however, information about such inquiries is not public.

(b) *What measures have the tax authorities undertaken in the past to ensure crypto tax compliance?*

Apart from press releases made by the MNB, warning investors of the probable risks of governmentally uncontrolled investments, Hungarian authorities have not made any official guidance in the topic of crypto assets yet.

(c) *Are the tax authorities cooperating with tax authorities in other jurisdictions on enforcement?*

The Hungarian tax authority is generally cooperative to all requests received from other counties' tax offices, especially within the EU. Moreover, Hungary is one of the 136 jurisdictions currently participating in the Convention on Mutual Administrative Assistance in Tax Matters, developed by the OECD and the Council of Europe. The Convention is a comprehensive multilateral agreement available to tackle tax evasion and avoidance. It provides for all possible forms of administrative cooperation between contracting states in the collection of taxes. The tools provided by the Convention range from exchange of information to the recovery of foreign tax claims. Hungary has also concluded more than eighty double taxation treaties that contain articles on the exchange of information, providing further tools for the tax authorities to obtain information about taxpayers.

India

Aseem Chawla, Suvrat Mehta & Tapasi Sharma

1. COUNTRY GUIDES

1.1 India

1.1.1 Applicable Tax Law, Guidance, and Case Law

(a) Which laws, regulations, and other administrative guidance exist dealing with crypto assets?

Under the Indian law, taxation of 'income' and 'capital gains' is primarily governed under the Income Tax Act, 1961 (ITA), and the Income Tax Rules. However, 'crypto assets' as such are not explicitly defined or included within its scope.

Further, it is relevant here to mention that, India proposes to pass a law entitled **Banning of Crypto Asset and Regulation of Digital Currency Bill, 2019** ('the Cryptocurrency Bill'), *inter alia*; *first*, mining, buying, holding, selling, dealing in, issuance, disposal or use of crypto asset would be punishable with imprisonment up to ten years;[1] *second*, any advertising, soliciting, assisting or inducing participation in the use of crypto asset would be punishable with imprisonment up to seven years.[2] *Lastly*, acquisition, storage, or disposal of crypto asset to use it for non-commercial purposes would be punishable with fine.[3]

In 2017, an Inter-Ministerial Committee was set up by the Government of India to examine the policy and legal framework for the regulation of virtual currencies. In its

1. Section 3(1)(a) read with section 8(1) of the Cryptocurrency Bill, 2019.
2. Section 8(3) of the Cryptocurrency Bill, 2019.
3. Section 8(4) of the Cryptocurrency Bill, 2019.

report, which was released on 22 July 2019,[4] it highlighted following facets/challenges concerning a crypto asset: (1) cryptocurrencies are subjected to market fluctuations; (2) cryptocurrencies are decentralized making them difficult to regulate; (3) they are vulnerable to risk of phishing cyber-attacks and Ponzi schemes; (4) the need for ample storage and processing power would impact country's energy resources; and (5) they are vulnerable to money laundering and terrorist funding activities because of the anonymity involved therein.

Therefore, the proposed legislation should ensure that any kind of crypto asset will be prohibited from being: (a) used as a medium of exchange, store of value or unit of account;[5] and (b) used as a payment system, providing registration services, trading, selling or clearing of crypto asset, trading with other currencies, issuing any financial products related to it, using it as a basis of credit, using it for raising funds or using it as means of investments.[6]

However, at present, there is no relevant per se law, a specific regulatory framework that recognizes 'crypto asset' and applies to it as such. The following legislations in the absence of a particular statute would therefore, in general, require consideration:

- Income Tax Act, 1961 (**ITA**);
- Central Goods and Services Tax Act, 2017 (**GST Act**);
- Foreign Exchange Management Act, 1999 **(FEMA)**; and
- Securities Contracts (Regulation) Act, 1956 (**SCRA**).

Section 2(h) of FEMA defining 'currency' would be relevant for crypto asset, even and can as 'foreign currency' under section 2(m) of FEMA. A crypto asset may be classified as a 'capital asset' for income tax purposes under section 2(14) of the ITA and/or as a 'securities' under section 2(h) of the SCRA depending upon the nature and parties to the transaction. The details of the applicability of the provisions of ITA are discussed under various parts hereunder. Further, the following laws and regulations made thereunder would also be relevant:

*- Information Technology Act, 2000 (**IT**)*

The blockchain mechanism on which cryptocurrency relies on and various other players may fall within the definition(s) provisions of IT Act, such as section 2(za) originator, section 2(b) addressee, section 2(o) data, section 2(v) information, section 2(w) intermediary and so on.

- Consumer Protection Act, 1986

4. Report of the Committee to propose specific actions to be taken in relation to virtual currencies; available at https://dea.gov.in/sites/default/files/Approved%20and%20Signed%20Report%20and%20Bill%20of%20IMC%20on%20VCs%2028%20Feb%202019.pdf.
5. Section 6 of the Cyrptocurrency Bill, 2019.
6. Section 7 of the Cyrptocurrency Bill, 2019.

The participants are also likely to qualify within the definition of 'consumer' under section 2(d) and 'services' under section 2(o), which means services of any description made available to potential users.

Existing laws in India such as the Indian Penal Code, Payment and Settlement Systems Act, Prevention of Money Laundering Act, Prize Chits and Money Circulation Schemes (Banning) Act, deposits-related laws, securities laws and tax laws would have enforcement, in aspects relatable to crypto-asset business activity, as the above-stated laws already cover a host of these transactions and events. The applicability of some of these laws may also be further clarified or fine-tuned concerning crypto assets.

(b) Which court cases exist dealing with crypto assets?

Purely, in terms of volume or numbers, there have not been a lot of litigation concerning crypto assets in India. However, there have been media reports regarding raids by the Enforcement Directorate, on a couple of Ahmedabad based firms namely rBitco.in and buysellbitco.in[7] engaged in trading of bitcoins. This raid was reportedly a first of its kind on a crypto assets trading firm. Further, during December 2017 and July 2019, the Income Tax Department reportedly issued notices under section 131 of the ITA to several investors, investing in crypto assets seeking the details of investment and sales of bitcoins and other cryptocurrencies.[8]

However, a significant legal development recently has been the landmark decision of Hon'ble Supreme Court of India in *Internet and Mobile Association of India v. Reserve Bank of India*,[9] whereby the Hon'ble Apex Court vide its verdict dated 4 March 2020, has lifted the ban on cryptocurrencies/crypto assets earlier notified by the Reserve Bank of India (RBI) through its circular dated 6 April 2018.

As per the RBI Circular,[10] entities regulated by RBI were directed: (i) not to deal in virtual currencies nor to provide services for facilitating any person or entity in dealing with or settling virtual currencies; and (ii) to exit the relationship with such persons or entities, if they were already providing such services to them.

As per the verdict, it was held that the RBI's Circular violated the rights of virtual currency exchanges guaranteed under Article 19(1)(g) of the Constitution of India and that the prohibition measure was not proportionate to the threat. The Apex Court observed that the central bank had not substantiated the risk with empirical data or credibly examined alternative means. Further, the Court also held that the RBI Circular infringing Article 19(1)(g) does not pass the four-pronged test summed up in the

7. 'ED officials raided two bitcoin trading firm in Ahmedabad' available at https://economictimes.indiatimes.com/news/economy/finance/ed-officials-raided-two-bitcoin-trading-firm-in-ahmedabad/articleshow/28006859.cms?from = mdr (last visited 20 Mar. 2020).
8. 'Bitcoin: Income tax department in tough spot as investors go all tech', available at https://economictimes.indiatimes.com/news/economy/policy/bitcoin-income-tax-department-in-tough-spot-as-investors-goes-all-tech/articleshow/62302684.cms?from = mdr (last visited 20 Mar. 2020).
9. Writ Petition (Civil) Nos 373 and 528 of 2018 dated 4 Mar. 2020.
10. Reserve Bank of India, Prohibition on dealing in Virtual Currencies (VCs), Circular dated 6 Apr. 2020 available at https://www.rbi.org.in/Scripts/BS_CircularIndexDisplay.aspx?Id = 11243 (last visited 20 Mar. 2020).

opinion of the majority in *Modern Dental College and Research Centre v. State of Madhya Pradesh* (2016) 7 SCC 353. These four tests are used to evaluate that:

(1) the measure is designated for a proper purpose;
(2) the standards are rationally connected to the fulfilment of the purpose;
(3) there are no alternative less invasive measures; and
(4) there is a proper relation between the importance of achieving the aim and the importance of limiting the right.

The court in the crypto assets case stated that a mere ritualistic incantation of 'money laundering' or 'black money' does not satisfy the first test and that alternative methods should be explored. As a result, the Hon'ble Apex Court lifted the ban, allowing banking facilities to crypto-asset exchanges.

The lifting of the ban will attract investments and transactions of crypto assets in India that are likely to have various income tax implications as well. The Central Board of Direct Taxes (CBDT) would have to come up with a comprehensive set of regulations regarding the tax treatment of various transactions involving crypto assets, which, till now, have been based only on logic and assumptions.

1.1.2 *Income and Capital Gains Taxes*

(a) *How are crypto assets classified for income and capital gains tax purposes?*

The exact identity and characterization of crypto assets eludes precision in India and globally too. Some call it an exchange of value; some refer it a stock, and some call it a good/commodity.

However, as per the only available guidance in India, '**Crypto Asset**'[11] has been understood to be any information, code, number or token, generated through crypto-graphic means or otherwise, which has a digital representation of value and which is exchanged with or without consideration, with the promise or representation of having inherent value in any business activity which may involve risk of loss or an expectation of profits or income, or functions as a store of value or a unit of account and includes its use in any financial transaction or investment, but not limited to, investment schemes.

Therefore, if crypto assets were to be regarded as '**currency**', as something carrying a value, they would not be liable to be taxed under ITA. This is because, under the direct tax regime in India, the tax incidence is on the 'transaction' and not on the 'currency' or 'medium'. Though the definition of '**income**' is an inclusive one and comprises of items mentioned under section 2(24) of the ITA,[12] neither under its

11. Under section 2(1)(a) of the Crypto Asset Bill, 2019.
12. *CIT/CWT v. P.R.S. Oberoi* (1990) 183 ITR 103 (Cal.) ('The word "includes" is often used in interpretation clauses in order to enlarge the meaning of the words or phrases occurring in the body of the statute.'). *See also Dooars Tea Co. Ltd. v. CAIT* (1962) 44 ITR 6 (SC) ('The word

natural meaning nor under its items, it includes 'money' or 'currency' per se as 'income', although it includes 'monetary payment'.

The word 'currency' is defined in section 2(h) of FEMA to include *'all currency notes, postal notes, postal orders, money orders, cheques, drafts, travelers' cheques, letters of credit, bills of exchange and promissory notes, credit cards* ***or such other similar instruments as may be notified by the Reserve Bank.'*** However, as on date, the RBI has not recognized and notified any crypto asset as a 'currency' as under section 2(h) of the FEMA.

The GST Act defines '**money**' under section 2(75) to mean 'the Indian legal tender or any foreign currency, cheque, promissory note, bill of exchange, letter of credit, draft, pay order, traveller cheque, money order, postal or electronic remittance or any other instrument recognized by RBI, when used as a consideration to settle an obligation or exchange with Indian legal tender of another denomination but shall not include any currency that is held for its numismatic value.'

The Hon'ble Supreme Court of India interpreted the term 'money' as used under section 41(2) of the ITA in *CIT v. Kasturi Lal & Sons Ltd*,[13] wherein it was held that it would mean only actual money or cash and not as any other thing or benefit which could be evaluated in terms of money.

The very concept of '**money**' or '**currency**' has changed over the years, and different jurisdictions and different statutes have adopted different definitions of '**money**' and '**currency**', depending upon the issue sought to be addressed.

On the other hand, the Sale of Goods Act, 1930 defines the word 'goods' to specifically exclude 'money' or 'currency' meaning, and thereby, section 2(14) of the ITA defines 'capital asset' to mean 'property' of any kind held by the assesse, and the expression 'property' includes every conceivable thing, right or interest or liability as was held by Hon'ble Kerala High Court in *Syndicate Bank Ltd. v. Addl. CIT* [1985] 155 ITR 681.

The Central Goods and Services Tax Act, 2017 (CGST Act) defines the term 'goods' under section 2(52), which means every kind of movable property other than money and securities but includes actionable claim, growing crops, grass and things attached to or forming part of the land which are agreed to be severed before supply or under a contract of supply.

Further, the term 'services' is defined under section 2(102) which means anything other than goods, money and securities but includes activities relating to the use of money or its conversion by cash or any other mode, from one form, currency or denomination, to another form, currency or denomination for which a separate consideration is charged.

In this regard, an important question arises whether crypto assets can be recognized as money/currency. While many developed economies recognize crypto assets as legal tender, there are many countries where crypto assets are not explicitly legal or illegal, but where a ban on them is in place. The taxability of crypto assets can

"income" is formidably wide and vague and its extent and sweep are not controlled or limited by the use of the words "profits and gains".').

13. (1999) 3 SCC 346.

be assessed once the RBI has notified such recognition of India. It has been widely speculated that The Central Board of Indirect Taxes and Customs (CBIC) is mulling over a proposal that will further be put before the GST Council on the taxability of crypto assets.

Hence, if crypto assets are considered as goods/property, then a transaction in them would be either fall within the provisions of **'Profit and Gains from Business and Profession'**[14] (in case of goods) or **'Income from Capital Gains'**[15] (property), depending upon whether it has been held for business/profession or not.

Herein it must be noted that the ambit of the word **'income'** is not restricted to the words '**profits**' and **'gains'**, and anything which can appropriately be designated as **'income'** is liable to be taxed under the ITA, unless expressly exempted.[16]

(b) What are the income/capital gains tax consequences of selling crypto assets against fiat currency?

It would depend as to on whether the crypto assets bought against the fiat currency are held as stock-in-trade or as an investment. In this aspect, the guidance available vide a Circular No. 4 of 2007[17] dated 15 June 2007, issued by the CBDT, the Apex direct tax administration body in India, would apply to the crypto assets as well.

In case if crypto assets are held as an investment, which are capital assets, being transferred in exchange for fiat currency, then the appreciation in value would give rise to long-term capital gain (**LTCG**) or a short-term capital gain (**STCG**) depending on the period of holding the Crypto Assets. If the period of holding is more than thirty-six months, it would be long-term capital asset taxable at such rates as prescribed under the ITA on such LTCGs.[18] In all other cases, the tax would be determined as per the provisions relating to STCGs.[19]

Further, in case the crypto assets are held as **'stock-in-trade'** and are transferred in exchange of fiat currency, this would give rise to income from business and accordingly, the profits arising out of such business would be subject to tax as per the applicable rates.

As per section 2(13) of ITA, the definition of '**business**' is inclusive, and comprises of 'trade, commerce or manufacture or any adventure or concern of such nature'. Therefore, a continuous activity in the nature of trade in crypto assets would

14. Section 28 of the Income Tax Act, 1961.
15. *Ibid.*, section 45(1).
16. *Maharajkumar Gopal Saran Narain Singh v. CIT* (1935) 3 ITR 23.
17. Government of India, Income Tax Department, Circular No. 4 of 2007, available at https://www.incometaxindia.gov.in/_layouts/15/dit/Pages/viewer.aspx?path=https://www.incometaxindia.gov.in/communications/circular/910110000000000316.htm&grp=&searchFilter=&k=Circular%20No.%204%20of%202007&IsDlg=0 (last visited 20 Mar. 2020).
18. *See* the Income Tax Act, 1961, section 112 (the rate of tax for LTCGs is 20%).
19. In case of non-equity capital assets held for short term, STCGs on such funds are taxed as per the slab rates of individual investor.

classify within the definition of **'business'** and profits realized are taxable thereunder, chargeable to tax as per section 28 of the ITA.[20]

(c) What are the income/capital gains tax consequences of exchanging crypto assets against other crypto assets?

The expression 'exchange of asset' is nowhere defined in the ITA. But the term 'exchange' is included in the definition of the term 'transfer' defined in section 2(47) of the ITA. Therefore, an exchange of asset would attract capital gains tax under the Indian law. One of the benchmarks for 'exchange' is that the asset continues to exist, and it is understood to be different from 'extinguishment' in which the right on the asset is given up either voluntarily or situations beyond the control of the taxpayer.

An example of exchange could be, when an old asset is exchanged for new asset with better workmanship/model/version, there could be some extra cost involved in the exchange. The value of old asset based on the wear and tear fixed by the merchant and the sale price of new asset will have to be compared. The capital gain implication for the old asset will be with reference to its cost of acquisition and the price fixed for exchange by the crypto asset merchant. The cost of acquisition of new crypto asset will be the price fixed for old crypto asset for exchange vis-à-vis any payment made or received besides the value of new crypto asset acquired.

While the methodology of the quantification of capital gain is understandable, the timing, i.e., the previous year in which such capital gain would be chargeable to tax in the hands of the owner may result in controversy. The sale consideration whether it must be with reference to the date of agreement of exchange or the actual cost of new crypto asset incurred by the merchant or the fair market value on the date of completion of any development may lead to multiple interpretations and consequent litigations.

(d) If a distinction is made between business assets and non-business assets, when does trading in crypto assets lead to a trade or business?

India is a country where exchange and capital controls do still subsist, and therefore, flows of foreign exchange into and outside the country are regulated under FEMA. The Foreign Direct Investment Policy and TISPRO, made under FEMA, regulate FDI in Indian entities. Most business models facilitating the buying and selling of virtual currencies can be characterized as e-commerce marketplaces, in which foreign investment is permitted up to 100% of the capital, without government approval.

Trading in crypto assets held as business stock-in-trade could be seen as yielding business income. However, when trading is conducted not in the regular course of a business, but only as a matter of past time or incidental as an isolated activity, the

20. The Income Tax Act, 1961, section 28 (Charging Provision provides a list of incomes that are chargeable to tax under the head 'Profits and Gains from Business and Profession').

income therefrom is likely to qualify as 'income from other sources',[21] meaning thereby, that trading in such crypto assets would not be considered as business assets yet it shall be taxable.

(e) *What are the income/capital gains tax consequences for an employee receiving wages or salaries in crypto assets?*

Under section 2(14) of the ITA, the total income of a person includes income from salaries. The term '**salaries**' has been defined under section 17(1) to include '**wages**' under clause (i) and **'perquisites'** and '**profits in lieu of salaries or wages**' under sub-clause (iv). However, it is pertinent to note that the genesis behind a 'perquisite' has been enumerated in the residuary part of Explanation 3 to sub-clause (iv) of section 17(3) to mean '***any monetary payment by whatever name called*** ... .' Hence, upon a combined and comprehensive reading of the section 17, a position may be taken that the idea behind the taxation of a receipt as a '**salary**' is to bring to tax any monetary payment by whatever name called. Still, it must not include something which has only a monetary value/equivalent or a property.

However, given that the definition has been considered to be of a very wide importance,[22] the income tax authorities are likely to bring the same to tax as '**salaries**' under section 15 of the ITA. Therefore, this possibility cannot be ruled out.

An alternative to this premise, can be found within section 17 sub-section (2) clause(iii) sub-clause (c) which provides that perquisite shall also include the value of any benefit or amenity provided for by the employer free of cost or at concessional rate in any non-monetary form, but only when the value of these exceeds INR 50,000. Thus, viewed in this sense, crypto assets being benefit provided for by the employer in a non-monetary form may also be considered as a prerequisite and hence considered as 'salary'.

In similar terms, the value of any benefit or perquisite, whether convertible into money or not, arising from the business or the exercise of a profession are also chargeable as profits and gains from business and profession under section 28 clause (iv) of the ITA. However, under an employment contract, since the receipt of crypto assets would be as a consideration for the rendering of services as between employer and employee, provision of section 28(iv) would not be applicable, and the income in the hands of employee (being the value of crypto assets) would be taxable as salaries.

21. Income from other sources is one of the heads of income chargeable to tax under the Income Tax Act, 1961. Any income that is not covered in the other four heads of income is taxable under income from other sources, because of this, it is known as residuary head of income. All the incomes excluded from salary, capital gains, house property or business and profession (PGBP) are included in IFOS, except those which are exempt under the ITA.
22. *CIT v. Gopal Krishna Suri* (2000) 113 Taxmann 707 (Bom).

(f) *What are the income/capital gains tax consequences for a merchant receiving payment in crypto assets?*

In the case of a merchant receiving payments in crypto assets, as consideration of the sale of goods/services, the crypto assets received can be treated at par with receiving money or fiat currency. Such sale of goods/services would ordinarily be taxed as income from business/profession by taking the fair market value of the goods and services provided by the merchant as its income. Any further exchange or transfer of the crypto assets by the merchant would give rise to another taxable event that would depend on the nature of the transaction.

(g) *What are the income/capital gains tax consequences of a loss of crypto assets?*

Under the ITA, a '**transfer**'[23] concerning a capital asset is understood to include the relinquishment of the asset itself or the extinguishment of the rights therein. Further, the Explanation 2 to section 2(47) clarifies that even an indirect or involuntary transfer in the absence of any agreement would also be considered as '**transfer of capital asset**'. Hence, if we proceed with the understanding that crypto asset may be considered as '**capital assets**', then the loss of the asset thereof could be treated as an extinguishment of rights therein, thus resulting in a transfer for no consideration and the capital gains would be required to be computed as envisaged under the provisions of section 48 of the ITA.

(h) *What are the income/capital gains tax consequences of a loss in value of crypto assets?*

A loss in value of crypto assets necessarily assumes the referencing to the value carried by the crypto assets at a time prior to its transfer or redemption in fiat currency, as the case may be. While it is certain that the provisions of computation of capital gains would apply in such a case, however, there may be certain difficulties in the process. For instance, it may be practically difficult to compute the conversion of each and every crypto asset into currency, in the absence of a specific guidance or prescription (current position of law).

23. Section 2(47) of the Indian Income Tax Act reads:

> A transfer in relation to a capital asset includes –
> (i) The sale, exchange or relinquishment of the asset; or,
> (ii) The extinguishment of any rights therein.

(i) *What are the income/capital gains tax consequences of forks of crypto assets?*

The activity of forking, by itself, may have no tax consequences, it only when such forking of a blockchain gives rise to a crypto asset that there comes into existence an asset carrying certain value. Hence, there is no income/capital gains tax implication at that time when the fork takes place.

It is only, when the crypto asset, which has come into existence from a fork, is transferred for a consideration that capital gains arise therefrom, and then after computation of its 'cost of acquisition' (which may be determined in reference to original crypto asset) and 'cost of improvement' (which may be determined in reference to the activity of forking), the computation of capital gains, maybe concluded as provided for under section 55 of the ITA read with sections 48 and 49 of the ITA.

(j) *What are the income/capital gains tax consequences of airdrops of crypto assets, and are the tax consequences different if the airdropped tokens are unwanted?*

Commonly, on receipt of a property being a capital asset for no consideration or for a considerably lesser than the fair market value of such capital asset on the date of receipt, the provisions of section 56 of the ITA get attracted, and the fair market value of such asset, or the difference in the value of such fair market value and consideration paid for it, is considered as income in the hands of the recipient. However, the term 'property' as used in Explanation (d) to section 56(2)(viib) of the ITA makes a reference to a selective list of items, one of them being shares and securities. The term 'securities' not being defined under the ITA, as understood in reference to the provision of section 2(a) of the SCRA. Therefore, unless, the crypto assets are notified as '**securities**' as such, the airdrops of crypto assets, even when the same are unwanted, would not be taxable as per the existing provisions of ITA.

(k) *What are the income/capital gains tax consequences of (solo, pool, and cloud) mining?*

The term 'mining' as defined under section 2(j) of the Crypto Asset Bill, 2019, means an activity aimed at the creation of crypto asset and/or validating a transaction of crypto asset between a buyer and seller of crypto asset.

A '**business income**' is chargeable to tax under section 28 of the ITA and the term, '**business**' as defined under section 2(13) of the ITA, includes ***'any trade, commerce or manufacture or any adventure or concern in the nature of trade, commerce or manufacture'***. The definition is wide enough to include within itself the business of mining (solo, pool, or cloud), and therefore, the income therefrom may well be chargeable to tax in the hands of the miners as business income.

There may be two kinds of receipts in the business of mining: one in the form of a 'fee' received by the owner of a digital platform, as a consideration for providing such platform to users for undertaking the activity of mining; and second, in the form of generation of fresh/new cryptocurrency resulting from the activity of mining and accruing or arising to the owner of such digital platform. In respect of the first kind of receipts, the fee paid to the owner of the digital platform may even be considered as a 'Royalty' as defined under Explanation 5 to section 9(1)(vi) of the ITA, which includes a payment made as a consideration for the transfer of rights in relation to use of a computer software, irrespective of the medium through which such right is transferred.

However, when the activity of mining is conducted infrequently and irregularly, more in the fashion of a hobby, the income therefrom would most likely be taxable under income from other sources under section 56 of the ITA.

(l) *What are the income/capital gains tax consequences of staking crypto assets?*

Income from staking of crypto assets would most likely be taxable as 'income from other sources' under section 56 of the ITA. However, if staking is undertaken as a regular business activity or part of the profession, it may also be taxed as income from business and profession. However, it is only a conceptual view, based on the similarity between the activity of staking and activity of earning interest income from fixed deposits in banks, and there is no finality of view on tax consequences of staking supported either by an express provision of the ITA or under any judicial precedent as of today.

(m) *What are the income/capital gains tax consequences of an indirect investment in crypto assets?*

Indirect investments made in crypto assets, through entities like portfolio management funds operating in the crypto assets industry, are likely to be treated in the same manner as the indirect investments in shares of companies through portfolio managers. In this regard, the principle usually followed by income tax authorities is that unless the investment is made for profit enhancement, and on a regular basis, the same shall be treated as capital gains. The principle purpose test adopted by tax authorities suggests that when the purpose behind making an investment is simply to maximize wealth and not profit, then income from such indirect investments is to be treated as capital gains.

(n) *How is income from crypto assets to be treated under double tax treaty law?*

As in the case of determining the taxability of the crypto assets under the ITA, the nature and character of crypto assets would determine its taxability under the Double Taxation Avoidance Agreements (DTAA) as well. India has entered into DTAA with around eighty-nine countries so far. Section 90 of the ITA gives the Central Government of India an authority to enter into an agreement with any country for the avoidance of double taxation under the ITA as well as under the respective income tax law of that country.

By virtue of the operation of subsection (2) of section 90 of ITA, when a particular income is taxable under both the ITA and the DTAA, then the provision which is more beneficial to the assessee would apply. Generally, the benefit is in terms of a lower rate of tax deducted at source, which is contemplated under the DTAA, as compared to that under the Act.

Certainly the treaty allocates the tax rights and does not include taxation per se. For example,[24] the provisions of domestic tax laws in subsection (2) of section 90 of ITA, do clarify that if the treatment invasion under the tax treaty is favourable vis-à-vis domestic tax law prescription, the taxpayer is entitled to claim benefits under the tax law.

From the discussion under the response to section 1.1.2(a), if the crypto assets are treated capital asset under section 2(14) of the ITA which is a property, then their transfer under section 2(47) of the ITA would be chargeable to tax as capital gains under section 45 of the ITA. However, under Article 13 of most of the DTAAs entered into by India, capital gains from transfer of a property being a capital asset situated in India are subjected to tax as per the provision of ITA only. However, each case would have to be dealt with on the basis of its own facts.

Further, from the discussion under the response to section 1.1.2 (k), if the crypto assets are treated as a medium of exchange, i.e., carrying a value, whether expressible in terms of money or not, then the same would come to be classified as business income of the non-resident. However, under Article 7 of most of the DTAAs entered into by India, business income of a non-resident is liable to be taxed, under the respective law of the country of residence, except when such non-resident is found to constitute a permanent establishment (PE) in the other country and the income is attributable to the activities of the PE. In such cases, so much of income of the non-resident as is attributable to the activities of the PE shall be taxable in India, and the rest would be taxable in the country of residence of the non-resident.

The following are the most common classes of income, in respect of which an assessee, being covered by the DTAA can avail the benefit of a lower rate of tax:

– *Royalties*

Under the ITA, section 9(1)(vi) an income by way of royalty is deemed to accrue or arise in India when it is payable by a non-resident in respect of any right, property or information used or services utilized for the purposes of a business or profession carried on by such non-resident in India or for the purposes of making or earning any income from any source in India.

Explanation 2(iv) enumerates that royalty means a consideration paid for imparting of any information concerning technical, industrial, commercial or scientific knowledge, experience or skill or the rendering of any services in connection with it (excluding any consideration which would be the income of the recipient chargeable

24. Circular No. 333 (F. No. 506/42/81-FTD) dated 2 Apr. 1982.

under the head 'capital gains'). This definition is mostly replicated under Article 12 of most of the DTAAs entered into by India with various countries.

Therefore, if the definition under the Crypto Asset Bill is adopted, i.e., if the crypto asset is understood to mean any information or code or number or token generated through cryptographic means or otherwise, then it may be understood to be consideration paid for imparting of information concerning a technical skill and services in connection with it and hence 'Royalty'.

However, under the DTAAs, the scope and ambit of the term 'Royalty' may be the same as under the ITA and, therefore, whether crypto assets would be considered as Royalty under the DTAAs would be considered on case-by-case basis.

– Fee for Technical Services/Included Services

Under the ITA, section 9(1)(vii) an income by way of fees for technical services is deemed to accrue or arise in India, when it is payable by a non-resident in respect of ***services utilized*** for the purposes of a business or profession carried on by such non-resident in India or for the purposes of making or earning any income from any source in India.

Explanation 2 enumerates that FTS means consideration for the rendering of any managerial, technical or consultancy services (including the provision of services of technical or other personnel) but does not include consideration which would be income of the recipient chargeable under the head 'Salaries'. This definition resembles the definition of FTA under Article 12 of most of the DTAAs entered into by India with various countries.

For an activity to constitute FTS, as has been held by the Hon'ble Supreme Court of India in the decision *of DIT v. AP Moller Maersk AS* reported in 392 Income Tax Reporter 186, that, for provision of technical services, human intervention is a sine qua non and that results generated through automated systems would not be enough to constitute FTS. Therefore, given that the generation of crypto assets is a result of the user-to-user validation during mining which is conducted using the technical expertise of miners, a possibility of crypto asset qualifying the definition of FTS cannot be ruled out.

(o) What are the income/capital gains tax consequences of selling crypto assets in an ICO/STO/IEO?

Generally, a sale of capital asset would attract capital gains under the ITA as enumerated at section 1.1.2(b) above; however, with an aim to curb evasion of capital gains on sale purchase of capital asunder the ITA, a Securities Transaction Tax (STT) was introduced by Finance Act, 2004. An STT is a direct tax levied on sale purchase of securities that are listed on recognized stock exchanges in India.

Even though in India, a sale of a crypto asset on or through ICO/STO/IEO is at present not regulated by any law and would generally have capital gains consequences only; however, in the event the Central Government exercises it is right under section 2(h)(iia) of the Securities Contracts (Regulation) Act, 1956 (SCRA) and declares crypto assets as '**Securities**', the purchase and sale of the crypto assets, on the floor of a recognized stock exchange would be considered as a 'taxable securities transaction' as under section 97(13) and be leviable to STT as defined under section 98. Under the Indian law, the entities shall issue tokens minting to securities. It must adhere to the relevant obligations under the Companies Act.

As far as the utility tokens are concerned, tokens shall be issued in exchange for money or other tokens which solely undertake as an advance against future services are applicable and are also further subject to cross-border issuances. And the RBI shall ensure that the taxes are appropriately levied on utility tokens in such circumstances.[25]

1.1.3 *Other taxes*

(a) What are the value added tax/sales tax consequences of selling crypto assets?

Indian Government implemented the Central Goods and Services Tax Act, 2017, from July 2017, and it subsumes most of the indirect taxes. The treatment of crypto assets as goods or property would mean that supply of crypto assets and hence subject to Goods and Service Tax (GST).

(b) Are payments in crypto assets subject to withholding taxes?

The obligation of withholding taxes on payments of sum made under various types of transactions is imposed on the payer under Chapter XVII of the ITA[26] and is coupled with penalties and interests obligations for delays and or complete failure.

Although withholding tax provisions do not specify that the payment is required to be made by any particular mode, only the phrase used under most of the provision is ***'in cash or by the issue of a cheque or by draft or by any other mode'***. The term 'any other mode' has been understood to mean even when the payment is 'made in kind'.[27]

However, there is a specific provision[28] which is applicable when a payment is made by way of cash, the payer therein (being a bank or post office or a cooperative society) is required to deduct tax 2% when aggregate payment is above INR 1 crore. Hence, if crypto assets are used as a medium of exchange, i.e., as currency, the

25. Michael S. Sackheim and Nathan A. Howell eds, *The Virtual Currency Regulation Review* (Nov. 2018).
26. Chapter XVII is titled as 'Collection and Recovery of Taxes' that ranges from sections 190 to 234F. It imposes withholding tax obligations on payments such as salaries (section 192), dividend (section 194), fees for professional or technical service (section 194J), provides for credit of taxes deducted (section 199), penalty payable when tax in default (section 221) and interest for defaults in furnishing of returns (section 234A).
27. *Kanchanganga Sea Foods Ltd v. ITO* (1995) 54 ITD 38; *High Sea Foods Ltd v. ACIT* (200) 113 Taxmann 117.
28. Section 194N requires every banking company to withhold 2% as tax, while making a cash payment of more than INR 1 crore to any person from any account maintained by it. The same was introduced vide Finance Act, 2019 with an aim to limit the use of cash for bigger transactions.

provision of this section will require to be amended accordingly, or a similar section will need to be introduced.

(c) *Does payment of compensation in crypto assets give rise to payroll tax consequences?*

This may be understood in light of the discussion in under section 1.1.2(e) above. Further, it is to be noted that, other than Income Tax, which includes 'Income from Salaries', there is no separate payroll tax in India.

(d) *Do transactions with crypto assets trigger any transfer taxes?*

There is no transfer tax which is triggered on the transfer of crypto asset per se. However, the Indian Stamp Act, 1899 is a fiscal statute, which deals with a tax on transactions under certain instruments which create, transfer, extend, limit of record, a right or liability. It is leviable on transfer of property, shares, debentures, bills of exchange, on conveyance deeds, promissory notes, increase in authorized share capital of companies, lease/rent agreements, sale deed, partnership deeds, gift deeds, etc. A 'stamp duty' is levied on the basis of place/location and type of transaction. Thus, when a crypto asset would be understood to be a digital representation of value and which is exchanged with or without consideration, with the promise or representation, it may attract a Stamp Duty (however, it would depend upon the valuation of such asset).

(e) *Are firms operating in the crypto space subject to digital service taxes?*

The digital taxation regime was introduced in India in 2016 as an equalization levy. However, the same is applicable only on specified services, which are primarily such services that are connected with the online advertisement or digital platforms serving as advertisement spaces. Even though the Finance Bill, 2020, has proposed to expand the definition of specified services, the same includes only e-commerce supplies or services. Therefore, by its very nature, the transaction in crypto space, prima facie do not attract the equalization levy, unless they also provide services in connection with digital advertising space or understood as sale purchase of goods on a transaction.

However, as envisaged under Explanation 2A to section 9(1) of the ITA, if the operations carried on by the miners (being non-residents) are being considered to be a *transaction in goods, services or property in India* or could be seen as *systematic and continuous interaction or engagement with users in India,* this could constitute a significant economic presence of such non-resident in India and there by a business connection of such non-resident in India. Consequently, any income accruing or attributable to such business connection is taxable in India.

(f) Are crypto assets subject to gift, inheritance, estate, or wealth taxes?

It is required to be noted that under the Direct Tax regime in India, a wealth tax law was abolished in India from 2017 onwards, and at present, there is no Estate Tax or Inheritance Tax in India.

Therefore, when a crypto asset is understood as a 'capital asset' under section 2(14) of the ITA, it would attract capital gains tax under section 45 of the ITA. Further section 47 of the ITA specifically excludes transfer of any capital asset under a will or gift from the purview of capital gains tax. With respect to gift taxation, the *concept* finds place the head of 'income from other sources' under section 56 of the ITA, however, since this section adopts the very restricted definition of 'property' under Explanation (d) to section 56(2)(vii)[29] the crypto assets, even though otherwise considered as capital assets, do not fall within the definition of 'property' under section 56 of the ITA and do not attract gift taxation.

(g) Are crypto assets subject to exit tax?

Under the laws of India, there is no exit tax per se. The only provisions, which deal with a circumstance of 'exit', are Chapter XII-EB of ITA, which were inserted through the Finance Act, 2016. They impose a tax on 'accreted income' of charitable trusts registered under section 12AA or institutions registered under section 10(23C), when such trust or institution loses its 'charitable' nature (as envisaged under section 12AA and section 10(23C)), due to a merger or a dissolution or conversion. An 'exit tax' has been understood in that limited sense. Such tax liability is imposed on an accreted income, which means the difference between the fair market value of its assets and the liabilities, as on a specified date when such 'exit' happens. Assets of a trust or charitable institution are understood as under section 2(14) 'Capital asset' to mean property of any kind held by an assessee, whether connected with business or not.

Hence, only if crypto assets form part of the capital asset of a registered charitable trust or institution, which has undergone 'exit' in the sense of Chapter XII-EB and section 115TD of ITA, then they may be subjected to a tax.

Further, in 2018, the CBDT, which advises the finance ministry on income tax policies, had constituted a body to come up with a set of rules to make people pay for migrating out of India. The Government wished to initiate such a step as these exits could have a direct impact on the Government's tax revenues, and the CBDT panel may look at how to stop the erosion of the tax base and deter people from exiting the country.

Further, as reported publicly, the Government's worry has come to fore, because with the surfacing of scams worth crores, a surge in the use of unregulated virtual cryptocurrencies, investment opportunities overseas for the ultra-rich, etc., and thus

29. *Ibid.*, p. 13.

the tax aspects surrounding the ultra-rich have drawn attention.[30] Therefore, although there is no 'exit tax' in India, there is a likelihood of some development on that idea in the coming future.

(h) Can mining trigger gambling tax?

Due to the outdated nature of online gambling laws in India, there is no specific mention of online gambling and the online payments received through gambling. However, under the GST system, there does exist a provision for 'all other services not specified elsewhere', and any such activity that falls within this category is subject to an 18% rate.

1.1.4 Compliance and Documentation Obligation

(a) What documentation requirements exist for taxpayers regarding crypto assets and are there best practices in recordkeeping to support representations made in tax returns?

There are no documentation requirements prescribed specifically for crypto assets as such. However, the ITA requires people engaged in legal, medical, accountancy, architectural and other profession or business as mentioned under section 44AA, to maintain books of accounts, if the sale/turnover/gross receipts from such business or profession is above a specified threshold and also have the same audited by an independent accountant under section 44AB.

The general best practice is to keep maintain cash books, journals, ledgers, copies of bills or receipts, etc., and a failure to do so attracts penalty as well as adjustments in total income up to a certain percentage of the value of transactions as well.

Further, provisions of Companies Act also require the head office of a company to maintain, cash flow statement, records of sales and purchases, records of assets and liabilities, items of cost and deeds, vouchers, writing, documents, minutes, and registers whether in physical or electronic mode.

(b) What is the evidentiary burden of supporting tax positions when a digital wallet address is lost or shared with other persons?

Even though the Act does not specify a threshold, however, the jurisprudence requires a taxpayer to bear the burden of proving the genuineness of a transaction. Such evidentiary burden may be discharged with the support of disclosure of documents and information in possession of the taxpayer, such as the unique Permanent Account Number (PAN).

30. 'India wants to use an "exit tax" to stop its millionaires from fleeing', available at https://qz.com/india/1246023/india-plans-an-exit-tax-to-stop-millionaires-from-fleeing/ (last visited on 19 May 2020).

(c) *Are crypto asset exchanges and wallet providers subject to reporting obligations?*

Due to the dicey status of the crypto assets in India and crypto-asset exchanges and wallet providers, there are no particular reporting obligations as such.

In 2017, the Income Tax Department sent notices to some crypto asset investors. The department asked for details on the last three years of their income tax returns, credit and debit card transactions, as well as their investment in bitcoin or other cryptocurrencies. The department asked a total of twenty-six questions, and twenty-one of these were related to crypto investment, transacting on crypto-asset exchanges, using paid services via cryptocurrencies, using crypto wallets and other topics related to crypto. These were some of the questions:[31]

- Please state whether you are buying/selling bitcoins or other cryptocurrencies from LocalBitcoins.com via cash or via peer-to-peer transactions.
- Are you involved in mining by investing in your own physical setup or via cloud mining?
- Have you received any bitcoin/cryptocurrencies for any sale made/service rendered? Have you declared any such income in previous income tax returns?

The book that was issued by the Income Tax Department for training the officials states that if officials discover irregular activity with any offline or online wallet linked to an investor, they should issue a prohibitory order under section 132(3). If the investigation proves that the source is unexplained or represents unaccounted income, an intermediary can be directed to convert crypto into Indian Rupees, which can be seized.

If this is an on-chain or online wallet:

- If a private key is found, the person can be asked to convert crypto into rupees, which can be seized.
- If a private key is not found and the person is not cooperative, an authorized officer should place a prohibitory order on the person. Alternatively, suppose you own 10 bitcoin and are not cooperative, the department can convert that 10 bitcoin into rupees and can seize other assets equivalent to that value.[32]

(d) *Are taxpayers holding crypto assets subject to reporting obligations apart from the filing of income tax/capital gains tax returns?*

As per the Indian Tax Laws, there is no obligation whereby taxpayers holding crypto assets are subjected to the report that they are holding crypto assets apart from filing the income tax return.

31. 'India's Income Tax Department Is Secretly Training Its Officials to Investigate Cryptocurrencies', available at https://cointelegraph.com/news/indias-income-tax-department-is-secretly-training-its-officials-to-investigate-cryptocurrencies (last visited on 20 Mar. 2020).
32. *Ibid.*

But there have been cases during December 2017, and in July 2019, whereby the Income Tax Department had issued notices under section 131 of the ITA to many individuals who have invested in crypto assets for sharing details of investment and sales of bitcoins and other cryptocurrencies. This was the first time the Income Tax Department asked so many details. This was based on the presumption that nothing has been disclosed (in case of bitcoins).[33]

(e) Are crypto asset exchanges and wallet providers subject to CRS/FATCA reporting?

The tax authorities of India have not issued any guidance on the question of whether operators of crypto exchanges or providers of crypto wallets must annually report their customers' data under CRS/FATCA. The RBI, on 6 April 2018,[34] through a circular had directed the entities governed by them to: (i) not to deal in virtual currencies nor to provide services for facilitating any person or entity in dealing with or settling virtual currencies and (ii) exit the relationship with such persons or entities, if they were already providing such services to them.

Further, in the recent judgment of 4 March 2020, by the Hon'ble Supreme Court of India in the matter *Internet and Mobile Association of India v. Reserve Bank of India*[35] whereby the Hon'ble Apex Court has set aside the Circular of RBI dated 6 April 2018.

1.1.5 Civil and Criminal Tax Enforcement

(a) What powers do the tax authorities have to compel the disclosure of information by third parties, such as exchanges or wallet providers, and have these been used in the past?

The new global standards on automatic exchange of information, also known as Common Reporting Standards (CRS) oblige treaty partners to exchange a wide range of financial information after collecting the same from financial institutions in their country/jurisdictions including information about the ultimate controlling persons and beneficial owners of entities. As per this mechanism, identification, account and financial information is exchanged between countries, including name, address, state of residence and tax identification number, as well information concerning the reporting financial institution, account balance and capital income. The exchanged information allows tax authorities to verify whether taxpayers have correctly declared their financial accounts abroad in their tax returns.

---

33. 'Bitcoin: Income tax department in tough spot as investors go all tech' available at https://economictimes.indiatimes.com/news/economy/policy/bitcoin-income-tax-department-in-tough-spot-as-investors-goes-all-tech/articleshow/62302684.cms?from=mdr (last visited on 20 Mar. 2020).
34. Reserve Bank of India, Prohibition on dealing in Virtual Currencies (VCs), Circular dated 6 Apr. 2020, available at https://www.rbi.org.in/Scripts/BS_CircularIndexDisplay.aspx?Id=11243 (last visited 20 Mar. 2020).
35. Writ Petition (Civil) Nos 373 and 528 of 2018 dated 4 Mar. 2020.

For the implementation of these standards in India and to provide information to other countries, necessary legislative changes have been made through Finance (No. 2) Act, 2014, by amending section 285BA of the ITA. This section requires a person to furnish any detail concerning the following 'specified financial transaction' to any income tax authority when called upon to do so:

(a) transaction of purchase, sale or exchange of goods or property or right or interest in a property; or
(b) transaction for rendering any service; or
(c) transaction under a works contract; or
(d) transaction by way of an investment made or an expenditure incurred; or
(e) transaction for taking or accepting any loan or deposit.

In consultation with financial institutions, Rules 114E–114H of the Income Tax Rules have been suitably formulated to facilitate the reporting requirements. For example, as per the Rule 114E, a company is required to disclose the information concerning receipt from any person of an amount aggregating to INR 10 lakh or more in a financial year for acquiring shares (including share application money) issued by the company, and auditor is required to report receipt of cash payment exceeding INR 2 lakh for sale, by any person, of goods or services of any nature. These provisions are likely to be used by tax authorities to compel disclosure or information from third parties.

Further, in 2017 and 2018, the tax department sent notices to thousands of crypto investors and traders. The department also surveyed major crypto exchanges under section 133A of the ITA to collect the details of individual crypto traders and to ascertain if there was tax evasion.

(b) What measures have the tax authorities undertaken in the past to ensure crypto tax compliance?

It is not known what measures the income tax authorities of India have undertaken in the past to ensure crypto tax compliance.

But there have been news whereby it is stated that the Income Tax Department of India has been training officials to investigate crypto assets. Further, as stated earlier that during the period December 2017 and July 2019, it issued detailed notice to crypto assets investors. As per the notice, the Income Tax Department asked for details of the last three years income tax returns, credit and debit card transactions, and investment in crypto assets. It also had a questionnaire of twenty-six questions, out of which twenty-one were related to crypto-assets investment.

(c) Are the tax authorities cooperating with tax authorities in other jurisdictions on enforcement?

India has signed the OECD's Multilateral Competent Authority Agreement (MCAA) for the Automatic Exchange of Information (AEOI). This has enabled India to receive information from almost every country in the world and would be the key to prevent international tax evasion and avoidance and would be instrumental in getting information about assets of Indians held abroad, including through entities in which Indians are beneficial owners. However, the information about the state of cooperation between Indian income tax authorities and other jurisdictions is not in the public domain.

Ireland

Kevin Smith & Tomás Bailey

1. COUNTRY GUIDES

1.1 Ireland

1.1.1 Applicable Tax Law, Guidance, and Case Law

(a) Which laws, regulations, and other administrative guidance exist dealing with crypto assets?

Irish tax legislation does not have any specific rules relating to the tax treatment of crypto assets. Therefore, the general provisions of Irish tax law (including the Taxes Consolidation Act 1997 (TCA), the Value-Added Tax Consolidation Act 2010, the Capital Acquisitions Tax Consolidation Act 2003 and the Stamp Duties Consolidation Act 1999) are applicable.

The Irish Revenue Commissioners (the 'Irish Revenue') issued brief guidelines in May 2018 in relation to the taxation of cryptocurrency transactions (the 'Guidelines').[1] The Guidelines confirm that there are no special rules applicable to crypto assets and that the appropriate tax treatment in any given case should be determined by applying established tax principles based on the relevant facts and circumstances.[2]

(b) Which court cases exist dealing with crypto assets?

The taxation of crypto assets has not been considered by the Irish Tax Appeals Commission or by the Irish courts to date.

1. Irish Revenue, *Taxation of cryptocurrency transactions*.
2. Irish Revenue, *Taxation of cryptocurrency transactions* at paragraph 1.

The recent UK case *AA v. Persons unknown* acknowledged the proprietary nature of crypto assets.[3] The court held that a crypto asset – in this case, bitcoin – could be a form of property capable of being the subject of an interim proprietary injunction under English law because it was:

(i) definable;
(ii) identifiable by third parties;
(iii) capable in its nature of assumption by third parties; and
(iv) had some degree of permanence.

This judgment is not binding on the Irish Tax Appeals Commission or on Irish courts, though is of persuasive value and is likely to be followed in Ireland, so that crypto assets would be in the nature of property for Irish tax purposes.

The value added tax (VAT) treatment of bitcoin has been considered by the Court of Justice of the European Union (CJEU) in the *Hedqvist* case.[4] The CJEU held that the supply of bitcoin in exchange for fiat currency is an exempt supply related to currency for VAT purposes. The Guidelines confirm that the Irish Revenue agrees with this treatment in the context of currency exchange. The Guidance also notes that the Irish Revenue's view is that bitcoin and other cryptocurrencies should generally be treated as exempt negotiable instruments for Irish VAT purposes.[5]

1.1.2 Income and Capital Gains Taxes

(a) How are crypto assets classified for income and capital gains tax purposes?

There is no specific classification for crypto assets in Irish tax law, and they are generally treated like any other asset or commodity. The Guidelines indicate that crypto assets should not be treated as currency for Irish tax purposes.[6]

The designation of a crypto asset as capital or revenue (i.e., income) determines whether the relevant asset should be subject to Irish income tax rules or Irish capital gains tax (CGT) rules. This designation depends on a number of factors derived from case law, including the application of the asset (i.e., whether it constitutes fixed or floating capital), the manner in which it is dealt, the nature of the asset, the substance of the relevant transaction and the intention of the parties.

(b) What are the income/capital gains tax consequences of selling crypto assets against fiat currency?

The tax consequences of selling crypto assets will depend on whether the sale is completed in the course of a trade.

3. *AA v. Persons unknown*, [2020] 4 WLR 35.
4. C-264/14, *Skatteverket v. David Hedqvist*.
5. Irish Revenue, *Taxation of cryptocurrency transactions* at paragraph 2.
6. Irish Revenue, *Taxation of cryptocurrency transactions* at paragraphs 1.2 and 2.

If the sale is completed in the course of a trade (*see* section 1.1.2(d) below for further details on trading), the profits and losses of the relevant trade will be determined in accordance with income tax rules in the case of individuals and corporation tax rules in the case of companies. The profits of a trade carried on by an individual will be subject to income tax and social charges and contributions at the individual's marginal rate (up to 52%). The profits of a trade carried on by a company in Ireland will generally be subject to corporation tax at 12.5%. The taxation of any foreign exchange gains or losses arising on a trading transaction (i.e., where the crypto asset is sold for fiat currency which is not the taxpayer's functional currency) should follow generally accepted accounting principles.

The Guidelines confirm that where the sale of a crypto asset does not fall within the scope of the taxpayer's trade, it would generally be taxed under CGT rules.[7] Capital gains arising on the disposal of a crypto asset are computed for CGT purposes by reference to the Euro value of the asset on the date of acquisition and the date of disposal.

Capital gains are subject to CGT at a rate of 33%. For individuals, the first EUR 1,270 of total gains (after deducting losses) in a year are exempt. There is no similar exemption for companies.

(c) What are the income/capital gains tax consequences of exchanging crypto assets against other crypto assets?

There are no defined rules on this point in Ireland. In practice, we would expect that the exchange of a crypto asset for another crypto asset will be treated as a taxable exchange for Irish tax purposes and that gains and losses would be calculated by reference to the Euro values in each case.

Where the exchange is effected otherwise than in the course of a trade, the exchange should be treated as a disposal and acquisition of an asset for CGT purposes. Therefore, a gain arising on the disposal of the original asset (computed using the Euro value of the asset at acquisition and disposal) should be subject to CGT at 33%. The base cost in the asset acquired for CGT purposes should be the market value (in Euro) of the crypto asset acquired.

The Guidelines confirm that, in light of the fact that crypto assets may be traded on a number of exchanges at varying prices, the value of crypto assets should be determined for Irish tax purposes using an appropriate valuation for the transaction in question.[8] The Guidelines do not provide any insight into what an appropriate valuation might be but indicate that reasonable efforts should be made to ensure the valuation used is appropriate.

7. Irish Revenue, *Taxation of cryptocurrency transactions* at paragraph 1.3.
8. Irish Revenue, *Taxation of cryptocurrency transactions* at paragraph 4.

(d) If a distinction is made between business assets and non-business assets, when does trading in crypto assets lead to a trade or business?

The distinction between trading and non-trading transactions is an important feature of Irish income tax and corporation tax law. Disposals and acquisitions in the course of a trade are subject to income tax or corporation tax as trading income, whereas disposals and acquisitions which are not effected in the course of a trade are subject to Irish CGT rules.

The term 'trade' is not defined succinctly in Irish tax legislation. Section 3 TCA defines a 'trade' as including '*every trade, manufacture, adventure or concern in the nature of a trade*'. This definition contemplates that an isolated transaction can give rise to a trade but gives no guidance on when an adventure is '*in the nature of a trade*'.

The existence of a trade is determined on a case-by-case basis and largely depends on the activities of the taxpayer in question. In considering the existence or otherwise of a trade, the courts have been influenced by the view of the UK 1954 Royal Commission on the Taxation of Profits and Income, which established 'Badges of Trade', that is, factors that have importance in determining the question of trade.

These badges are:

(i) subject matter realized;
(ii) length of period of ownership;
(iii) frequency and number of transactions;
(iv) supplemental work done;
(v) circumstances giving rise to disposal; and
(vi) motive.

The badges of trade cannot, of course, produce conclusive answers in every situation but do provide guidance nonetheless. Some badges may not be relevant to a particular case. In order to establish that a company was trading in crypto assets it would be necessary to show a high level of activity. A higher level of activity and organization is likely to be required in the case of an individual acting on his/her own account compared to a company acting for itself and third parties. Such activity would need to involve the purchase and sale of crypto assets on a regular basis with related infrastructure and business planning. The mere passive holding and periodic acquisitions and sales of crypto assets would unlikely be enough to constitute a trade.

The Irish Revenue has indicated a willingness to give a view in advance on certain activities as to whether it would regard them as trading. The Irish Revenue has stated that the important factors from its perspective are whether:

(i) there is a commercial rationale for a transaction;
(ii) there is real value added in Ireland; and
(iii) there are employees in Ireland with a sufficient level of skill to indicate that a trade is being carried on in Ireland.

The Irish Revenue has consistently emphasized the presence of employees in Ireland that have the requisite skill, experience and knowledge to carry on the relevant business as a key indicator of the existence of a trade. In this regard where a company is engaged with a high volume of transactions involving crypto assets and employs people with the relevant skill set, these activities are likely to qualify as a trade for Irish tax purposes.

Although the Guidelines accept that a taxpayer may be trading in crypto assets, they do not provide any specific details on the level of activities required by a taxpayer in this context in order to meet the trading threshold. In contrast, the UK tax authority, HMRC, has published relatively detailed guidance on the taxation of crypto assets for business (the 'HMRC Guidance')[9] which indicate that a taxpayer may be engaged in a trade of crypto mining where the taxpayer has purchased a dedicated bank of computers to mine crypto assets for an expected net profit (taking into account the cost of equipment and electricity). Although not binding in Ireland, the HMRC Guidance may be persuasive in this context given that the rules on trading in Ireland are derived from UK case law and guidance.

(e) *What are the income/capital gains tax consequences for an employee receiving wages or salaries in crypto assets?*

The Guidelines confirm that where any wages, salaries, or other emoluments are paid to an employee in crypto assets, the employer is obliged to remit payroll taxes to the Irish Revenue in Euro calculated based on the Euro value of the relevant crypto assets at the time the payment is made to the employee.[10]

An employee will be subject to CGT on any gain arising on the subsequent disposal of the relevant crypto assets. The taxable gain in such circumstances will comprise any increase in the value of the relevant crypto asset calculated based on the Euro value of the assets at the time the crypto assets were paid to the employee by the employer and the Euro value of the crypto assets at the time of disposal by the employee.

(f) *What are the income/capital gains tax consequences for a merchant receiving payment in crypto assets?*

The Guidelines confirm that businesses which accept payment in crypto assets should be treated in the same way as if they had received payment in fiat currency for income tax and corporation tax purposes.[11] Therefore, the value of the cryptocurrency for tax purposes should generally be the value of the receipt expressed in fiat currency as recorded in the merchant's financial statements.

The taxation of a subsequent disposal of the crypto asset by the taxpayer will depend on whether the disposal may be treated as a trading transaction (in which case income tax or corporation tax rules will be applicable) or not (in which case CGT rules will be applicable).

9. HMRC, Cryptoassets: Tax for business.
10. Irish Revenue, *Taxation of cryptocurrency transactions* at paragraph 3.
11. Irish Revenue, *Taxation of cryptocurrency transactions* at paragraph 1.

(g) *What are the income/capital gains tax consequences of a loss of crypto assets?*

Where the crypto asset forms part of the trading inventory of a taxpayer, the taxpayer may be entitled to deduct the cost of the relevant asset as a trading expense when computing the taxpayer's taxable profits for income tax or corporation tax purposes.

The Guidelines do not comment on the tax implications of losing a crypto asset. Under CGT rules, the loss of a crypto asset may be treated as a disposal of the asset where the asset cannot be recovered. However, a taxable gain should not arise in such circumstances unless the taxpayer receives compensation for the lost asset. If no compensation is received by the taxpayer, an allowable loss should arise on the disposal. An allowable loss arising on the disposal of a crypto asset (including where the asset is lost) is computed in the same way as a chargeable gain for CGT purposes. Therefore, where no consideration is received in respect of the disposal of the asset, the allowable loss arising should be equal to the taxpayer's full base cost of the crypto asset.

(h) *What are the income/capital gains tax consequences of a loss in value of crypto assets?*

Where the crypto asset forms part of the trading stock of a taxpayer and the loss in value is realized, the loss will be a component of the taxpayer's trading profits or loss for the period, as the case may be. Although the Irish corporation tax rules make provision for the recognition of certain unrealized gains and losses arising from the fair market value recording of financial assets, the rules apply only where the relevant asset is a financial asset as defined for IFRS, which is unlikely to incorporate crypto assets.[12]

If the crypto asset is a capital asset in the hands of the taxpayer, any unrealized loss in value of crypto assets is generally disregarded for CGT purposes, unless the asset has become of negligible value. If the crypto asset has become of negligible value, the taxpayer is entitled to apply to the Irish Revenue to claim an allowable loss computed as if the asset has been disposed of for that value (notwithstanding that no disposal has in fact occurred).[13] The claim must be made within twelve months from the end of the taxable period for which relief is sought. The Irish Revenue guidance[14] indicates that a negligible value claim will not generally be accepted unless:

(i) the relevant asset is effectively worthless as a result of the fall in value (irrespective of how dramatic the fall in value may have been); and
(ii) there is no ready mechanism by which the taxpayer can in fact dispose of the asset (thereby realizing the loss).

12. Section 76B TCA.
13. Section 538 TCA.
14. Irish Revenue, *Tax and Duty Manual Part 19-01-09*, paragraph 9.6.

(i) What are the income/capital gains tax consequences of forks of crypto assets?

The Guidelines do not consider the Irish tax consequences of a blockchain fork (i.e., where a blockchain splits into two blockchains, so that a taxpayer holding crypto assets on the original blockchain now additionally holds the same number of crypto assets on the new blockchain).

Where the crypto asset constitutes a capital asset in the hands of the taxpayer, it is likely that the new crypto assets would be treated as being derived from the original crypto asset for CGT purposes. Therefore, when the taxpayer disposes of either the original or the new crypto asset, the consideration for the acquisition of the original crypto asset together with any enhancement expenditure incurred (the 'Base Cost') should be apportioned between the original and the new crypto asset in order to determine if any chargeable gain / allowable loss arises on the relevant disposal. The proportion of the Base Cost attributable to the asset being disposed of should be determined based on the market value of all the relevant assets at the time of the relevant disposal.

If the crypto assets form part of the taxpayer trading stock, any new crypto asset acquired by virtue of a fork is likely to be treated as a trading receipt.

(j) What are the income/capital gains tax consequences of airdrops of crypto assets and are the tax consequences different if the airdropped tokens are unwanted?

The Guidelines do not specifically consider the Irish tax consequences of airdrops (i.e., where crypto assets are received free of charge). The tax implications of an airdrop of crypto assets should largely depend on whether the crypto assets are received in relation to a taxpayer's trading activities or not:

- crypto assets received in relation to a taxpayer's trading activities (e.g., in return for an endorsement related to the trade) are likely to be treated as a trading receipt; and
- crypto assets received which are not treated as a trading receipt are likely to be treated as a taxable acquisition (i.e., gift taxable at the market value).

Where the crypto assets have been received by the taxpayer, the fact that they were unwanted is unlikely to impact on the tax implications above.

(k) What are the income/capital gains tax consequences of (solo, pool, and cloud) mining?

The Guidelines do not deal specifically with the income/corporation tax and CGT implications of mining. Therefore, the tax consequences of income generated from mining should be determined based on general principles and will largely depend on whether the mining activities form part of the taxpayer's trade or not.[15]

(l) What are the income/capital gains tax consequences of staking crypto assets?

The Guidelines do not deal specifically with the income/corporation tax and CGT implications of staking crypto assets. However, the income/corporation tax and CGT implications of staking should be the same as mining. In light of the fact that staking crypto assets is typically more passive than mining, it is perhaps less likely that a taxpayer's staking activities would be sufficiently active to constitute trading activities for Irish tax purposes. That said, each case should be determined on its own facts and circumstances.

(m) What are the income/capital gains tax consequences of an indirect investment in crypto assets?

There are no specific Irish tax rules dealing with indirect investments in crypto assets. Investors would be subject to Irish tax based on the direct investment they hold (e.g., as shareholders in a company or partners in a partnership holding crypto assets). The Irish tax consequences of an indirect investment in crypto assets should therefore be determined by reference to the direct investment in the asset holding vehicle, the nature of the relevant return on the investment and the taxpayer's circumstances.

(n) How is income from crypto assets to be treated under double tax treaty law?

The Guidelines do not refer to the appropriate treatment of income from crypto assets under Ireland's double tax treaties (DTTs). The allocation of taxing rights in respect of income from crypto assets should generally be determined under the business profits or other income articles of the relevant DTT.

(o) What are the income/capital gains tax consequences of selling crypto assets in an ICO/STO/IEO?

The Irish tax implications of selling crypto assets in an ICO/STO/IEO (an 'Offering') is not entirely clear and will largely depend on the relevant facts and circumstances. The Guidelines do not provide any guidance. Therefore, general Irish tax principles must be applied which may, in some cases, yield undesirable results notwithstanding the fact that the Offering is intended to serve the same economic function as an equity issuance.

15. *See* section 1.1.2(d) above for further details on the principles applicable to determine whether the taxpayer is engaged in a mining trade or not.

For corporation tax purposes, a company's trading profits are determined in accordance with generally accepted accounting practice (i.e., Irish GAAP or IFRS). Therefore, where the Offering constitutes a trading transaction and the terms of the Offering are such that it is accounted for as debt or equity with no revenue recognized for accounting purposes, it may be possible to complete the Offering without the proceeds being taxed as income for Irish corporation tax purposes. However, where such a result is achieved, there remains a risk that the disposal of crypto assets on an Offering would be subject to CGT at 33% (with no base cost in the crypto assets created).

In any event, in many cases the Offering is unlikely to constitute a trading transaction. In such circumstances, the proceeds of the Offering would likely be treated as taxable receipts which are subject to corporation tax at 25% (with limited cost and expense deductibility).

It is clear therefore that Irish taxpayers intending to undertake an Offering should proceed carefully.

1.1.3 Other Taxes

(a) *What are the value added tax/sales tax consequences of selling crypto assets?*

The CJEU held in the *Hedqvist* case that the supply of bitcoin in exchange for fiat currency is an exempt supply related to currency for VAT purposes.[16] The Guidelines confirm that the Irish Revenue agrees with this treatment in the context of currency exchange. The Guidelines also note that the Irish Revenue's view is that bitcoin and other cryptocurrencies should generally be treated as exempt negotiable instruments for Irish VAT purposes.[17]

The Guidelines also confirm that the Irish Revenue is of the view that income received from cryptocurrency mining activities will generally be outside the scope of VAT on the basis that the activity does not constitute an economic activity for VAT purposes.[18]

(b) *Are payments in crypto assets subject to withholding taxes?*

Irish tax law imposes withholding tax of 20% (except dividends which are subject to withholding tax at 25%) on certain payments, including dividends, annual interest and patent royalties ('Chargeable Payments'). Where the relevant Chargeable Payment is discharged by way of the transfer of a crypto asset, the transfer of the crypto asset will be treated in the same way as a payment of cash. Any withholding tax arising should

16. Case C-264/14, *Skatteverket v. David Hedqvist*.
17. Irish Revenue, *Taxation of cryptocurrency transactions* at paragraph 2.
18. Irish Revenue, *Taxation of cryptocurrency transactions* at paragraph 2.3.

be paid to the Irish Revenue in Euro. However, there are broad exemptions from withholding tax available under Irish law, including the following:

(i) dividends paid to a company which is under the direct or indirect control of persons who are tax resident in a jurisdiction with which Ireland has a DTT and is not under the direct or indirect control of persons who are not so resident;

(ii) interest paid by a company in the ordinary course of business to a company which is tax resident in a jurisdiction with which Ireland has a DTT and which imposes a tax that generally applies to interest received from abroad; and

(iii) patent royalties paid by a company in the course of business to a company which is tax resident in a jurisdiction with which Ireland has a DTT and which imposes a tax that generally applies to royalties received from abroad.

Where a Chargeable Payment is discharged by way of the transfer of a crypto asset and one of the relevant exemptions is applicable, no Irish withholding tax should arise on the payment.

(c) Does payment of compensation in crypto assets give rise to payroll tax consequences?

As noted, the Guidelines confirm that where any wages, salaries, or other emoluments are paid to an employee in crypto assets, the employer is obliged to remit the payroll taxes to the Irish Revenue in Euro calculated based on the Euro value of the relevant crypto assets at the time the payment is made to the employee.[19]

(d) Do transactions with crypto assets trigger any transfer taxes?

It is possible that a transfer of crypto assets may trigger a charge to Irish stamp duty where the transfer is effected by a written document which is signed in Ireland or which relates to property situated in Ireland or to something done or to be done in Ireland. Irish stamp duty should not arise where the transfer of crypto assets is effected digitally without any written document.

(e) Are firms operating in the crypto space subject to digital service taxes?

Irish tax law does not impose a digital services tax. Furthermore, Ireland is not expected to introduce any such tax in the absence of multilateral action at OECD level.

19. Irish Revenue, *Taxation of cryptocurrency transactions* at paragraph 3.

(f) Are crypto assets subject to gift, inheritance, estate, or wealth taxes?

Gifts and inheritances are generally subject to capital acquisitions tax (CAT) in Ireland. Although the Guidelines do not specifically deal with CAT, they do confirm that, for direct tax purposes, there are no special rules applicable to crypto assets. Therefore, crypto assets may be subject to CAT in the same way as other assets.

The charge to CAT in respect of a gift or inheritance of crypto assets is likely to arise where the person making the gift/inheritance or the beneficiary are resident or ordinarily resident in Ireland for tax purposes.

CAT is charged at 33% of the taxable value of the relevant crypto asset. The liability for CAT typically lies with the beneficiary of the relevant gift or inheritance. The taxable value of the crypto asset is determined by deducting certain liabilities, costs, and expenses incurred by the beneficiary in relation to the gift/inheritance from the market value of the crypto asset. The beneficiary may be entitled to some level of relief (up to certain lifetime thresholds depending on the relationship between the beneficiary and the person making the gift/inheritance).

A wealth tax is not imposed under Irish tax law.

(g) Are crypto assets subject to exit tax?

Crypto assets are treated like any other asset for the purpose of Ireland's exit tax, implementing the EU Anti-Tax Avoidance Directive. Therefore, where a company holding crypto assets triggers an exit event (i.e., where the asset remains in the company's ownership but ceases to be within the Irish tax net by virtue of the company ceasing to be Irish tax resident or transferring the asset to a permanent establishment or its head office outside Ireland), the company will be deemed to have disposed of the crypto assets for market value and immediately reacquired the crypto assets for Irish tax purposes.[20] A gain arising on the deemed disposal of the crypto assets (computed in accordance with CGT rules) is generally subject to tax at 12.5%. An anti-avoidance provision is included to ensure that a tax rate of 33% (rather than 12.5%) will apply if the exit forms part of a transaction to actually dispose of the asset and the purpose of the exit is to ensure that the gain is charged at the lower rate.

Individuals are not subject to exit tax on ceasing to be Irish tax resident under Irish tax law.

A taxpayer will not receive a step-up in the base cost of any crypto (or other) assets held upon becoming Irish tax resident.

(h) Can mining trigger gambling tax?

In Ireland, there is a betting duty of 2% for bets entered into by a bookmaker or remote bookmaker with persons in Ireland. Although the Guidelines do not refer to the betting tax implications of mining, betting tax should not generally be applicable where the

20. Section 627 TCA.

relevant taxpayer carrying on the mining activity does not have a licence to operate as a bookmaker in Ireland.

1.1.4 Compliance and Documentation Obligations

(a) What documentation requirements exist for taxpayers regarding crypto assets and are there best practices in recordkeeping to support representations made in tax returns?

In Ireland, there are no specific documentation requirements for taxpayers holding crypto assets. Therefore, such taxpayers must comply with general documentation requirements under Irish tax law. Taxpayers are obliged to retain and have available for inspection sufficient documentation and records as will enable true tax returns to be made by the taxpayer. The records must be kept on a continuous and consistent basis and must be prepared in a timely manner. The Guidelines confirm that in order to satisfy the general record keeping requirements, where a transaction involving crypto assets has an underlying tax event, a record of the transaction must be kept which includes a record in relation to the crypto asset.

There is no requirement for documentation to be kept in a standard form. A taxpayer is therefore entitled to choose the form in which the requisite information and the documentation are kept. In general, tax records must be prepared in written form in an official language of Ireland or by means of any electronic, photographic, or other process as permitted for accounting records. Records must be retained for a period of at least six years after the completion of the relevant transaction to which they relate.

(b) What is the evidentiary burden of supporting tax positions when a digital wallet address is lost or shared with other persons?

In Irish tax cases, the burden of proof depends on the particular section in the legislation that is subject to the dispute; however, generally, the burden rests with the taxpayer. The standard of proof in tax cases is on the balance of probabilities.

(c) Are crypto asset exchanges and wallet providers subject to reporting obligations?

Crypto asset exchanges and wallet providers are not subject to any specific obligations to report to the Irish Revenue in respect of their customers. The Irish Revenue has broad powers to compel the production of information or records from a taxpayer or third party in certain circumstances (*see* section 1.1.5(a) below).

(d) *Are taxpayers holding crypto assets subject to reporting obligations apart from the filing of income tax/capital gains tax returns?*

Taxpayers holding crypto assets are not subject to any specific tax reporting obligations in Ireland.

(e) *Are crypto asset exchanges and wallet providers subject to CRS/FATCA reporting?*

Ireland has signed up to both CRS and FATCA. However, the Irish Revenue has not issued any guidance on the question of whether operators of crypto exchanges or wallet providers are subject to CRS/FATCA reporting obligations in Ireland. Although it may be arguable that crypto assets are not within the scope of the reporting obligations (as they may not create financial accounts), the position remains unclear and as such should be considered on a case-by-case basis. It is worth noting in this context that there are other domestic tax reporting obligations which may arise where crypto assets are held in Ireland on behalf of third parties (i.e., obligations of trustees, agents and receivers).

1.1.5 Civil and Criminal Tax Enforcement

(a) *What powers do the tax authorities have to compel the disclosure of information by third parties, such as exchanges or wallet providers, and have these been used in the past?*

The Irish Revenue has powers to serve notice on third parties (including financial institutions) to make books, records or other documents available for inspection, if they contain information relating to a tax liability of a taxpayer, even if the taxpayer is not known to the officer but is identifiable by other means.[21] The Irish Revenue authorized officer must have reasonable grounds to believe that the relevant third party is likely to have information relating to this liability. The Irish Revenue is also entitled to apply to the High Court of Ireland for an order compelling the disclosure of information by third parties. The Irish Revenue's powers in this context are generally subject to legal privilege and client confidentiality.

The Irish Revenue's powers of inspection have been used in practice but, to the authors' knowledge, have not been used to compel disclosure of information by exchanges or wallet providers.

21. Chapter 4, Part 38 TCA.

(b) *What measures have the tax authorities undertaken in the past to ensure crypto tax compliance?*

Aside from the publication of the Guidelines, the authors are unaware of any measures taken by the Irish Revenue to ensure tax compliance in the context of crypto assets to date.

(c) *Are the tax authorities cooperating with tax authorities in other jurisdictions on enforcement?*

The Irish Revenue cooperates with multiple foreign tax authorities. Ireland has entered into DTTs and tax information exchange agreements with 100 jurisdictions worldwide. In addition, Ireland has signed up to the Multilateral Convention on Mutual Administrative Assistance in Tax Matters, which provides for information exchange to combat cross-border tax avoidance and evasion. Revenue also has information exchange obligations arising from Ireland's membership of the EU and the OECD, both of which involve automatic exchange of information in certain circumstances.

Israel

Miri Bickel & Doron Mutai

1. COUNTRY GUIDES

1.1 Israel

1.1.1 Applicable Tax Law, Guidance and Case Law

(a) Which laws, regulations, and other administrative guidance exist dealing with crypto assets?

Generally speaking, Israeli law relates to crypto assets as financial assets, rather than as 'currency' (as opposed to fiat currencies, which are defined as such under the law). In the last couple of years, there have been some changes in laws and publications of regulators that embrace this phenomenon and seek to formalize the activities in these assets from a legal perspective. The following are prominent examples of these law changes and promulgations.

The *Law for Supervision on Financial Service Providers, 2016* relates to 'virtual currencies' as some of the financial assets to which this law applies (similar to cash, cheques, etc.), and the *Law for Investment in Mutual Funds, 1994* has been recently changed to apply also to mutual investment in currencies. In this respect, there is a formal publication of the Israeli Securities Authority (ISA) that implies that this amendment would apply to crypto assets.[1]

The Israeli Ministry of Finance has recently published a *Draft Decree on Money Laundering (Identification Obligations, Reporting and Registration of Credit Service Providers, for Avoidance of Money Laundering and Terror Financing), 2018*. This Draft Decree includes the term 'virtual currency' in the definition of financial assets. The

1. *See*, Committee for Examination of Regulation of Issuance of Decartelized Cryptographic Coins to the Public – Final Report, Mar. 2019, at p. 33.

objective of this amendment is to allow supervision on the provision of financial services in these assets as well.

The Bank of Israel and the ISA have published announcements in the last three years in which they stated the potential risks in the use of crypto assets and investments in this industry. These announcements clarify the regulators' concerns from the risks, yet they do not discourage the use of such assets or investment in them. Moreover, the Bank of Israel published a comprehensive report of its team for the examination of a digital currency issued by central banks. Although this team recommended not to issue Digital Israeli Shekels in the near future, it seems that the reason for this recommendation is that this matter should be further analysed.

Several publications of the Israeli Tax Authority (ITA) are seeking to clarify the ITA's approach to this phenomenon, which is yet to receive a specific treatment by Israel's tax legislation. The ITA's Crypto Circular[2] related mainly to classification of crypto assets as 'assets' for tax purposes, rather than as 'currencies'. This approach was adopted by the District Court in a precedential case (*see* elaboration below). Another ITA circular[3] relates to the issuance of utility tokens and sets some guidelines for the taxation of employees and service providers under these very specific circumstances. As of September -2020, there is only one published ruling that was addressed to a taxpayer in this industry.[4] This ruling related to the method of writing down a receivable which is a decentralized token. Although this ruling is not binding on other taxpayers, it can provide guidelines on what should be the tax consequences in similar cases.

In summary, it appears that both the legislator and regulators seem to acknowledge the use of crypto assets and seek to formalize the activities of this industry. Yet, we are still working in a new legal era where all stakeholders are learning the material and are seeking compatible solutions for this rapidly evolving environment. Naturally, the prime legislation would be the last to adjust to this environment.

(b) Which court cases exist dealing with crypto assets?

Apparently, all relevant non-tax cases deal with companies' claims against banks that were reluctant to have them as clients, or to receive fiat derived from realization of crypto assets, while the only tax case related to the classification of crypto assets for tax purposes.

In the case of *Bits of Gold*,[5] a company had a business of conversion of crypto assets. The bank closed this company's account giving short notice and the company claimed that the bank breached its lawful obligation to provide banking services. The District Court held that the bank's decision to either maintain the company's account

2. ITA Circular 05/2018 Re: Taxation of Activity in a Decentralized Mean of Payment (AKA: 'Virtual Currencies'), dated 17 Jan. 2018 (hereinafter: the 'Crypto Circular').
3. ITA Circular 7/2018 Re: ICO – Issuance of Utility Tokens, dated 13 Mar. 2018 (hereinafter: the 'ICO Circular').
4. ITA Decision 0209/18. For an elaborated discussion, please refer to section 1.1.2(f) below.
5. 1992-06-15 (District Court of Tel-Aviv) *Bits of Gold v. Bank Leumi of Israel Ltd.*

or close it was reasonable. Hence, it did not rule against the bank. Nonetheless, the Supreme Court[6] held, in an intermediate decision, as part of the company's appeal, that it cannot be said that the chances of the appeal are nil. The parties eventually settled and the Supreme Court confirmed this settlement as a verdict.[7] It was agreed, without setting obligatory precedence to the bank in other cases, that the company would be able to maintain its account, while the bank would be able to monitor all the activities in this account. Hence, even though there is not a precedential ruling on this matter, it would be difficult for a bank to refuse to provide services to a company in the crypto industry, just because of the risks associated with this industry.

In the case of *Israminers Ltd.*,[8] the District Court held that the upfront approach of the bank that refused to open accounts to clients that deal in crypto assets was unreasonable. Moreover, the Court stated that the bank should have related to the variety of possible activities in crypto assets and to differentiate between them in terms of risk. The Court made a distinction between a client who mines bitcoin – and hence his bitcoins are brand new and have not gone through any digital wallet, a client who can provide evidence to the track the bitcoin made until he received it, and a client who cannot indicate such track (e.g., because he received it from a pool). The Court held that in the case of the latter client, the bank's concern of money laundering or terror financing cannot be dismissed. Based on this distinction, the Court held that the bank's decision to close the client's account was unreasonable. However, in case of money that the client received to this account from a pool, where he could not track its sources, the Court held that the bank's refusal to receive the money was reasonable.

The Attorney General has recently provided his approach on this matter to the District Court of Tel-Aviv. This approach relates to risk analysis, rather than to prevention of financial activity in crypto assets. Accordingly, the Attorney General related to a list of circumstances that seem to reduce the risk and should assist the bank in analysing the risk factor of a certain client. It should be noted, though, that this list relates solely to private clients, whereas no such list relates to business clients. Furthermore, it seems that the Supervision of Banks does not support this approach of the Attorney General.

The issue of classification of crypto assets for Israeli tax purposes was in the midst of a material debate in the Israeli market, where taxpayers took the position that it should be classified as a currency, and hence foreign exchange (FX) gains should not be taxable at the hands of Israeli individuals. The ITA's position, which was later published under the Crypto Circular, was that it should be classified as an asset, and then gains from disposal or exchange should give rise to capital gains tax.

On May 20, 2019, the District Court of the Central Area published its precedential ruling on the issue of *Kopel v. The Tax Assessing Officer of Rehovot*[9] and basically concluded the discussion on the classification of crypto assets for Israeli tax purposes.

6. Civil Appeal 6389/17-A *Bits of Gold v. Bank Leumi of Israel Ltd*, dated 25 Feb. 2018.
7. Civil Appeal 6389/17 *Bits of Gold v. Bank Leumi of Israel Ltd*, dated 3 Jun. 2019.
8. Civil Case (Tel-Aviv) 14643-04-18 *Israminers Ltd. v. Bank Egud, the Branch of the Industry Park of Herzlia 13079*.
9. Tax Appeal 11503-05-16.

The Court held that bitcoin is a 'currency' for legal or economical purposes. Moreover, it ruled that bitcoin could not be held as 'currency' for tax purposes, in the sense that gains from the disposal of bitcoins are tax exempt as FX gains.

Under Israeli jurisprudence, a District Court ruling is not formally binding other district courts and can be changed by the Supreme Court. Therefore, a taxpayer may take, in principle, an opposing position. Nonetheless, there were cases where courts reproached a party who took a position that contradicted a previous judicial ruling (ironically, in a prominent case the Supreme Court delivered a stinging rebuke to the ITA, who continued to take a certain position after losing in District Court). Hence, it appears that there should be very unique circumstances, under which a taxpayer should take a contradictive approach (i.e., that his crypto assets should be classified as currency for Israeli tax purposes).

1.1.2 Income and Capital Gains Taxes

(a) *How are crypto assets classified for income and capital gains tax purposes?*

As discussed above, the general approach regarding crypto assets is that these should be classified as 'assets' for Israeli tax purposes. Accordingly, gains from realization of these assets should be subject to capital gains. Nonetheless, if these gains are derived in the course of a business (e.g., by a person who maintains business activity of trading in crypto assets) then such gains would be classified as business income, rather than as capital gains.

Please refer to section 1.1.3(d) below for the tests for classification between business income and capital gains.

(b) *What are the income/capital gains tax consequences of selling crypto assets against fiat currency?*

If gains from sales of the crypto asset are treated as business income of an individual, it would be subject to tax at the marginal rate (up to approx. 50%).[10] Otherwise, it should be taxed as a capital gain, at the rate of 25%.[11]

If the gain is derived by an Israeli corporation, it would be subject to tax at the standard corporate income tax rate of 23%, regardless of its classification as capital gain or as business income.

Computation of the taxable gain would take into account the consideration, less indexation,[12] and less cost basis. Cost basis may include the acquisition costs, custody fees, and transaction costs.

---

10. In such case, VAT would apply as well. *See* discussion below.
11. Note, Israel applies surtax at the rate of 3% to an individual's income that exceeds a certain annual amount, regardless of the classification of such income.
12. Indexetion is calculated based on the Consumer Price Index, on the date of acquisition of the crypto assets and on the date of disposal of the crypto assets. There may be another method for

If crypto assets were acquired in several tranches at different acquisition costs and if part of these crypto assets is then sold, a question arises as to which of the various tranches was sold. There are no clear rules in this respect. Hence, it seems that the taxpayer may be able to determine which tranche was sold, provided that the holdings of crypto assets are completely documented in terms of acquisition dates and acquisition costs. If this is not the case, then the applicable approach may be learned from the regulations that relate to computation of traded securities,[13] which apply the first-in, first-out, or FIFO, method in cases where the taxpayer cannot demonstrate the dates and acquisition costs of identical securities that were acquired in different events. Accordingly, it seems that those tranches acquired first would be deemed to have been sold first. Nonetheless, given that there are no rules on this issue, the taxpayer may apply another method if he has solid grounds to justify his approach.

Current capital losses should be offset first against capital gains. Carried over capital losses can be offset only against capital gains. If the crypto asset is considered as a 'security' (which is not a typical approach), then current losses from disposal of such security could potentially be offset against income from interest or dividends, depending on the applicable tax rate on such interest or dividends.

Current losses from business activity could be offset against income from all other sources, including capital gains, whereas carried over business losses could be offset only against business losses and against a 'capital gain in a business'. This term typically relates to gain from the disposal of an asset that is used by the business.

(c) What are the income/capital gains tax consequences of exchanging crypto assets against other crypto assets?

Given the approach that crypto assets are indeed assets (rather than currencies), this transaction would be treated as an exchange of an asset against another one, which would give rise to a tax event for both parties. From each party's perspective, the sales price of the asset given away and the acquisition cost of the asset acquired is the fair market value (FMV) of the asset given away. Practically speaking, the gain should be computed based on the NIS value of each crypto asset, as if each party realized its crypto asset for cash (and realized a gain or a loss) and then used the cash for buying the other crypto asset.

The applicable tax rates would be as addressed in section 1.1.2(b) above.

calculating indexation, which is based on meeting some conditions. This approach is based on the position that cryptocurrency is a 'security' for Israeli tax purposes. In such case, and if (i) the crypto asset is held by an individual and (ii) the crypto asset is linked to a fiat currency other than the New Israeli Shekel (NIS), then indexation would be calculated based on the exchange rate between the NIS and the other fiat currency.

13. Regulation 5 of *Income Tax Regulations (Calculation of Capital Gain upon Sale of Traded Security, State Debenture, or Unit in a Mutual Fund), 2002*. Note, however that a crypto asset is not a 'traded security' for the purpose of these regulations. Therefore, these regulations are relevant only for interpretation purposes.

(d) *If a distinction is made between business assets and non-business assets, when does trading in crypto assets lead to a trade or business?*

Determination of whether an activity has reached a certain threshold that creates a business is based on case law. Basically, it includes several tests that aim at distinguishing between passive income (in this case, capital gains) and business income, where none of these tests is determinative.[14] Among these tests, the most relevant ones would be whether the volume of transactions is high? Are they frequent? Are the assets held for a long period or a short one? Does the level of knowledge and expertise of the person(s) involved in the activity is relatively high? Is it an organized and managed activity? Was external financing required for the activity?

Distinctly, these tests are rather qualitative than quantitative and require a certain degree of personal judgment. Moreover, there is no definite amount of tests that activity would have to meet in order to qualify as a business. Thus, it can be said that as long as the answers to some of the questions above would be positive, the ITA would tend to treat the activity as a business and to classify the income generated out of it as business income.

As can be seen from the discussion above, the differentiation between business income and capital gains, for Israeli tax purposes, is based on the actual activity rather than on the nature of the assets. Having stated that, the nature of the asset does matter in the context of capital gain in a business, that can be offset against carried over losses, as opposed to capital gains that are not 'in a business'.

(e) *What are the income/capital gains tax consequences for an employee receiving wages or salaries in crypto assets?*

Generally speaking, the provision of an asset as a substitute for cash entails the same tax consequences as if payment was made in cash in the first place. Hence, the employee would be subject to income tax at the marginal rate on his salary income, whereas the employer would be responsible for withholding the tax from this income upon payment and for paying all other payroll taxes (such as social security) out of this income (i.e., as a gross-up on the value of the crypto asset).

Practically speaking, the value of crypto assets paid as a salary would have to be converted into NIS, in order to calculate the actual tax liability, and grossed-up, to calculate the amount of tax liability. Should this taxpayer sell the crypto assets received as wages or salaries at a later point in time, then the acquisition costs of the crypto assets should be equal to the value used for purposes of calculating the income from employment (i.e., no double taxation). The gain from such sale should in principle be treated as a capital gain and be taxed accordingly (i.e., at a tax rate of 25%).

The ITA's ICO Circular relates to the issuance of utility tokens to employees (as well as service providers) and sets some guidelines for the taxation of employees under these very specific circumstances. In general, taxation of this benefit would be as a

14. *See*, for example, the ITA's Commentary on the Income Tax Ordinance (known as the HAVAK).

salary income for employees (and as business income for service providers) and would be subject to tax at the marginal rate upon disposal of the crypto asset. Calculation of the income would base on the value of the crypto asset on the date of disposal, less any exercise payment. Nonetheless, if the company opted that the tax event of the employees would be on the date of issuance, and notified the tax assessing officer at least sixty days in advance, the employee would be subject to tax on the date the crypto asset was issued to him. His taxable salary would then be the value of the crypto asset on that date, less any exercise payment. The employee's gain from the future realization of the crypto asset would be taxed as a capital gain (i.e., at 25%). The company's expenses associated with this salary expense should be deductible. The company would be responsible for withholding the tax.

Note, the value of crypto assets that were issued to the employee would be determined based on their average value in the next thirty days following the tax event. This event would be either the disposal of the crypto asset in the secondary market in the first alternative or receipt of the crypto asset in the ICO, in the second alternative.

(f) What are the income/capital gains tax consequences for a merchant receiving payment in crypto assets?

There are no clear rules on this issue under the law. However, the ITA related to this in its Crypto Circular. In general, the principle of the tax treatment in such cases should be similar to a barter transaction:

(1) The consideration amount should be equal for both parties. This amount would be either the FMV of the crypto assets or the value of the goods, to the extent they entail a certain value.
(2) The seller of the goods/provider of the service would recognize income at the time of the barter transaction. That would be the cost basis of the crypto assets he received as consideration. Hence, his gain from the disposal of the crypto assets would be the difference between such a cost basis and the FMV of the crypto assets upon disposal.
(3) The recipient of the goods/service that pays with crypto assets would be treated as a seller of the crypto assets on the one hand, and as a buyer of the service/goods on the other hand. Note, the gain of the seller of the crypto asset would be calculated with respect to the cost basis he has in that asset, which sometimes can be zero (e.g., if it was airdropped).

In ITA Decision 0209/18 that related to the method of writing down a receivable which is a decentralized token, it was determined that the merchant will write down the tokens upon receipt in its 'book of exchange transactions'. Moreover, as long as it realizes these tokens into fiat currency within two weeks from receipt, it will be able to issue an invoice on the actual amount it received on the date of realization; otherwise, the merchant will invoice based on the average exchange rate within this two-week period. In such a case, this amount will be treated as the cost basis in the tokens for calculation of the gain upon future realization of the token.

(g) *What are the income/capital gains tax consequences of a loss of crypto assets?*

The loss of crypto assets – meaning the loss of the private key associated with an address at which crypto assets are stored – should, in principle, give rise to the recognition of a capital loss. There are certain rules regarding the offsetting of capital losses. Please refer to section 1.1.2(b) above.

The above-mentioned ITA Decision 0209/18 related also to a situation where a merchant whose tokens were stolen within the time from receipt of the tokens and issuance of an invoice. It was held that in these circumstances the loss would be treated as an expense that is integral to the business and hence would be treated similarly to any other deductible expenses. If, however, the loss would occur after the issuance of an invoice, it would be treated as a capital loss. Moreover, it was held that in any event, the merchant would not be able to claim input VAT against such loss.

(h) *What are the income/capital gains tax consequences of a loss in value of crypto assets?*

Generally speaking, Israel does not levy tax based on appreciation/depreciation, with the exception of certain financial institutions (or instruments) that maintain their bookkeeping based on mark-to-market, and their tax accounting is following their books. Hence, gain or loss should be recognized only upon realization.

Offsetablity of such loss depends on the classification of whether it was an ongoing loss within the activity of the business, which as addressed above, entails more flexibility in offsetting; or whether it was a capital loss, which if not within a business, is much more limited in offsetting.

(i) *What are the income/capital gains tax consequences of forks of crypto assets?*

Neither the law nor the ITA's publications relate to cases where a blockchain splits into two blockchains so that a taxpayer holding crypto assets on the original blockchain now additionally holds the same number of crypto assets on the new blockchain. From a purely economic point of view, the total value of the two ancestor assets may have the same value of the predecessor one (otherwise, the holder would realize a gain or a loss). However, from a tax perspective, this may be treated as a 'sale' that gives rise to a capital gains tax event (note, there may be an opposing approach under which no capital gains tax event has occurred, as there was no asset that left the taxpayer's possession).

In order to achieve tax neutrality (if at all), the taxpayer may have to apply for a ruling that would confirm the deferral of tax event until actual realization. In addition, it would aim at determining the cost basis of each one of the two crypto assets and each one's date of acquisition, for a future calculation of the capital gain from the disposal of each one of them.

Note, such a ruling would be precedential in Israel as currently there are no formal publications (including any published ruling) on this matter. Moreover, determining the FMV of the newly received crypto asset at the time of the fork can be difficult, and in extreme cases, its FMV can be zero.

(j) *What are the income/capital gains tax consequences of airdrops of crypto assets and are the tax consequences different if the airdropped tokens are unwanted?*

Giving crypto assets free of charge is likely to trigger a taxable event to the recipient, as there are very limited situations of non-taxable gifts (e.g., within a family). Receipt of such crypto assets by an individual within a framework of a business (e.g., as a consideration for a service) would lead to tax liability at the marginal rate, calculated either on the amount which the taxpayer would have had to pay in order to receive the assets or at the value of the service. If the airdropped tokens are provided not as a return for goods or service, the recipient may be able to take a position that it should be treated as a capital asset without a cost basis, such that tax event would be deferred to actual realization, on the total amount of FMV (note, VAT considerations are discussed below).

If the token is received by a company, the tax rate would be 23%, regardless of the classification of the income as business income or capital gains. Again, if the capital asset approach that was addressed above is taken (and should be well evidenced), the tax event may be deferred to actual realization.

Apart from that, if the airdropped tokens are unwanted (i.e., that are not granted in return for goods or service) then the tax exposure may also lie with the giver, as the ITA may claim that he should recognize a deemed income or gain.

(k) *What are the income/capital gains tax consequences of (solo, pool, and cloud) mining?*

The ITA's approach, as was published in the Token Circular, is that income derived by a person from a token that he holds following mining activity would be classified as business income. Hence, it seems that the ITA considers any activity associated with mining as a business activity, with no distinction between solo mining, pool mining, and cloud mining.

A person whose business is mining of crypto assets would be registered as a dealer for VAT purposes and his transactions would be subject to VAT (17%) on the consideration he received. In cases of provision of services to a non-Israeli resident, VAT may apply at the rate of 0%.

(l) What are the income/capital gains tax consequences of staking crypto assets?

Income from staking, if derived by an individual, should be classified as ongoing income (either active or passive, depending on the tests mentioned above) and be taxed at the marginal tax rate (plus excess tax, if applicable).

If derived by a corporation, it would be subject to tax at the standard corporate income tax rate of 23%, regardless of its classification.

(m) What are the income/capital gains tax consequences of an indirect investment in crypto assets?

Analysis of the tax consequences that arise from indirect investment in crypto assets should relate to the actual vehicle that the investor invests in. If, for example, the investor acquires units in an investment fund, which invests in crypto assets, then the analysis would relate first to the structure of the fund (is it treated as a transparent entity for Israeli tax purposes, or as an opaque one) and then to the classification of distributions from the fund (dividends in case of an opaque entity, other classifications in a transparent one). An additional consideration would be whether any withholding tax obligations apply to the fund and whether it obtained a ruling from the relevant tax authorities.

Another example could be bonds that are issued at a nominal value, which may or may not pay interest and which are repaid at maturity in an amount based on the performance of one specific crypto asset, of a basket of several crypto assets or of a crypto asset index. From an Israeli tax perspective, income earned at redemption (i.e., repayment amount minus purchase price) could be classified as either interest or capital gain, depending on the nature of the bond; consideration upon disposal is likely to be classified as a capital gain.

Note, if the activity of the investor in any of these above-mentioned vehicles or instruments amounts to a business, based on the tests addressed above, income would be classified as business income and would be taxed accordingly.

Given the variety of instruments and the multiple classifications of income arising from them under the law, it is highly important to thoroughly analyse the specifications of the instrument in order to determine the relevant tax considerations.

(n) How is income from crypto assets to be treated under double tax treaty law?

The ITA has not issued any guidelines regarding the treatment of crypto assets under double tax treaties. Hence, it seems that the existing rules should apply, with any required modifications.

Under Israeli domestic law, and under most of Israel's tax treaties, a non-Israeli resident should be subject to Israeli tax on capital gains derived from the disposal of assets located in Israel. Hence, it would be crucial to analyse the location of the crypto asset which, based on the nature of this asset, may sometimes be a difficult task.[15] To the extent the crypto asset is not located in Israel and the gain is not allocated to a permanent establishment (PE) that the foreign resident has in Israel, then no Israeli tax should apply to such foreign resident's gain.

Clearly, the notion of a PE is based on the law of double tax treaties and should be analysed based on the determinants for the creation of a PE (i.e., the existence of a fixed place of business or of a dependent agent in Israel).

The ongoing income of a non-Israeli resident that is derived from a PE in Israel (either through mining, through trading in crypto assets, or through other activities) would be subject to Israeli tax, to the extent such income is allocated to the PE. Thus, for example, the profits of a crypto mining enterprise carried on by a non-Israeli resident in Israel would be subject to Israeli tax on the profits allocated to Israel. On the other hand, if an Israeli resident carries on a crypto mining enterprise located, in part or as a whole, outside Israel, then all his profits would be taxable in Israel, while the profits that are attributable to the other country may be taxed therein under the notion of a PE. In such a case, Israel should credit the foreign tax against the Israeli tax liability, even if no treaty exists with the other country.

(o) What are the income/capital gains tax consequences of selling crypto assets in an ICO/STO/IEO?

The ITA's ICO Circular sets some guidelines for cases of issuance of Utility Tokens:

- With respect to the issuing company, it provides the method of recognition of income:
  - The general rule is that if the issuing company is obliged to provide any service to the token holders it should register the proceeds from the ICO as deferred income (similar to advanced payments from clients).
  - If the issuing company provides goods or services in return for the tokens, then these advanced payments would be gradually recognized as income, in accordance with the provision of services or goods.
  - If the issuing company provides the token holder a continuous right to receive a service, it should recognize the whole amount of income on the day the service becomes available to the token holder.
  - If it provides the token holder a right to use a platform it should recognize the whole amount of income on the day the platform becomes available to the token holder.
  - If the company did not meet all of its obligations to the token holders under the whitepaper from any reason (liquidation, failure of the product, sale of activities), and did not repay the ICO proceeds, it should recognize the remaining part of the income that was deferred.

15. If the crypto asset qualifies as a *security* under domestic law, the foreign resident's gain may be exempt under domestic law.

  - If the issuing company is not obliged to provide any service to the token holders under the terms of the ICO, it should recognize income from the proceeds of the ICO on the day of the ICO.
- With respect to the token holders (either from the primary issuance or in the secondary market), it relates to situations where utility tokens should be treated as assets or as a return for service and the related tax treatment (e.g., deductibility of amounts paid for the tokens, or capitalization of these amounts to the cost basis of the token).
- Payment for tokens in other crypto assets would be treated by the ITA as barter transactions (*see* above).

1.1.3 Other Taxes

(a) What are the value added tax/sales tax consequences of selling crypto assets?

Israel does not apply sales tax, but VAT.

The Crypto Circular provides that crypto assets should be treated as intangibles for VAT purposes. Hence, it would not be treated as currency. Sale of a crypto asset by an investor whose activity does not amount to a business should not be subject to VAT.

Any person whose activity in crypto assets amounts to a business should register for VAT. Under the Crypto Circular, such activity entails financial characteristics and therefore the registration of such person may be of a financial institution for VAT purposes (similar to banks, insurance companies, etc.). In such a case, no VAT would apply to such person, but rather wage tax and profit tax; both would be calculated as a percentage of the profit.

The ICO Circular distinguishes between issuance of utility tokens that reflect an obligation to provide services and utility tokens that reflect an obligation for the sale of goods. Based on this distinction it provides the resulting VAT treatment, as well as the rules associated with the issuance of invoices for each case.

In case of a trader (as defined under VAT law) who receives payments in a crypto asset, VAT would apply to such payments. However, VAT would not apply to the realization of the crypto asset (unless that trader's activity, in conversion or sale of crypto assets, amounts to a business).

(b) Are payments in crypto assets subject to withholding taxes?

Israel applies a comprehensive withholding tax liability, such that any payer is obliged to withhold tax from any payments he makes, at the highest applicable withholding tax rate, unless the payee provides him with a withholding tax certificate that prescribes a reduced withholding tax rate (or an exemption from withholding).

There is no specific withholding tax exemption to payments in crypto assets.

(c) *Does payment of compensation in crypto assets give rise to payroll tax consequences?*

Please *see* above, in section 1.1.2(e).

(d) *Do transactions with crypto assets trigger any transfer taxes?*

Israel does not apply a transfer tax.

(e) *Are firms operating in the crypto space subject to digital service taxes?*

Israel does not apply a digital service tax.

(f) *Are crypto assets subject to gift, inheritance, estate, or wealth taxes?*

Israel does not apply gift, inheritance, estate, and wealth taxes. For the anticipated tax treatment of the giver of the gift, please *see* above, in section 1.1.2(j).

(g) *Are crypto assets subject to exit tax?*

The general rule regarding exit tax is that Israeli residents that cease to be residents of the country will be deemed to have sold their assets the day before their Israeli residency ceases. Under the law, payment of the tax associated with such deemed sale would defer until actual realization, unless the person asked not to defer the tax payment.

This issue gives rise to potential double taxation, as the actual realization may be taxable in the other country to which the person has relocated. Hence, this event should be planned ahead, as double taxation may be resolved through planning.

No specific rule applies to crypto assets in this regard.

(h) *Can mining trigger gambling tax?*

Israel does not apply a specific tax on gambling. Rather, it applies income tax on income from gambling, lottery, etc. (35% with no tax attributes).

However, given that this type of taxation would not apply to a business and given that mining activity seems to amount to a business, it seems that it would not apply to mining activity.

No specific rule applies to crypto assets in this regard.

1.1.4 *Compliance and Documentation Obligations*

(a) What documentation requirements exist for taxpayers regarding crypto assets and are there best practices in recordkeeping to support representations made in tax returns?

No specific rule applies to crypto assets in this regard. Having stated that, the ICO Circular mentions that any person who reports the sale of a token should keep the supporting documentation. This circular also provides that such a person should keep the ICO contract (whitepaper) as long as he held it, in order to present it to the tax assessing officer. The circular also implies that this document would be required in order to satisfy the tax assessing officer.

(b) What is the evidentiary burden of supporting tax positions when a digital wallet address is lost or shared with other persons?

No specific rule applies to crypto assets in this regard. Nonetheless, the ITA (as any other tax authority) seems to be very suspicious when it comes to crypto assets. Therefore, it is highly recommended to keep all documentation that can assist in supporting the taxpayer's position.

(c) Are crypto asset exchanges and wallet providers subject to reporting obligations?

No specific rule applies in this regards and the general rules should apply. Crypto asset exchanges and wallet providers may be subject to reporting obligations under the rules that were adopted by the Israeli tax law under FATCA and CRS (*see* discussion below at 1.1.5(e)).

An Israeli resident should report all his income on an annual basis and should pay monthly tax advances; while a non-Israeli resident should report his Israeli sourced income, unless he is exempt from such obligation under a tax treaty (i.e., because his activity in Israel does not meet the threshold of a PE), or because the tax was withheld from such income at source.

(d) Are taxpayers holding crypto assets subject to reporting obligations apart from the filing of income tax/capital gains tax returns?

Individuals are required to declare their capital – which would naturally include crypto assets, once they are approached by the ITA and are required to do so. Israel does not apply an annual reporting obligation on capital.

The annual tax return includes a certain box that relates to 'income from the realization of 'virtual currency' including exchange into other currencies'. Hence, it seems that the mere holding of crypto assets, rather than the actual exchange or sale may not be subject to a reporting obligation.

Apart from this annual reporting, it should be noted that given the general approach to crypto assets for Israeli tax purposes as 'assets', sale of such assets or any barter in them would trigger a reporting obligation within thirty days, similar to the sale of any other assets.

(e) Are crypto asset exchanges and wallet providers subject to CRS/FATCA reporting?

Israeli tax law and regulations adopted the provisions of the treaty between the governments of Israel and the United States in relation to FATCA. Other regulations adopted the CRS. Hence, both FATCA and CRS have been formally absorbed into Israeli law, with some minor modifications.

Nonetheless, the ITA has not yet formally addressed the question of whether operators of crypto exchanges or providers of crypto wallets must annually report their customers' data under CRS/FATCA. Hence, these players should operate based on the general rules of FATCA and CRS.

In this respect, a material question is whether the taxpayer (e.g., crypto asset exchanges or wallet providers) is treated as a 'financial institution' for the sake of this legislation. Accordingly, if it does not take deposits and it is not treated as a custodian, there may be some positions for escaping from the classification of a 'financial institution'. Alternatively, if it is considered as a 'financial institution' for the sake of this legislation, it may still be entitled to some relief, depending on the volume of its activity and the residency of its users/clients.

1.1.5 Civil and Criminal Tax Enforcement

(a) What powers do the tax authorities have to compel the disclosure of information by third parties, such as exchanges or wallet providers, and have these been used in the past?

There are no specific rules in these regards for the crypto industry. Having stated that, the ITA has a comprehensive authority to seek information on taxpayers. It has already happened in the past, that the ITA approached parties from the crypto industry that could potentially provide information on taxpayers. It is not clear what the legal basis for such an approach is, and whether the ITA is legally authorized to do that. Hence, if any player in this market is approached by the ITA, he should ask for legal advice in relation to the terms for the provision of such information to the ITA (if at all).

(b) What measures have the tax authorities undertaken in the past to ensure crypto tax compliance?

The ITA applies an 'intent disclosure procedure' from time to time, in which taxpayers are encouraged to report any unreported income they have in return for immunity from criminal procedures and sometimes for reduced tax. This procedure also applies to taxpayers who realized or exchanged crypto assets and did not report their income from these transactions.

By the end of 2019, the ITA completed its last round of 'intent disclosure procedures'. Hence, as of September 2020, there is no such procedure in place.

(c) Are the tax authorities cooperating with tax authorities in other jurisdictions on enforcement?

Israel's tax treaties include an exchange of information article, which is absorbed into domestic law. Apart from that, the ITA is authorized to disclose information under FATCA/CRS. The ITA tends to cooperate with other tax authorities. No formal publications exist as to actual discussions in relation to crypto assets.

Italy

Raul-Angelo Papotti & Gian Gualberto Morgigni

1. COUNTRY GUIDES

1.1 Italy

1.1.1 Applicable Tax Law, Guidance, and Case Law

(a) Which laws, regulations, and other administrative guidance exist dealing with crypto assets?

Italian tax laws – and in particular the Italian Tax Consolidated Act[1] (ITCA) and the Italian Value Added Tax Act[2] – do not explicitly mention crypto assets, or any of its different types (*i.e.*, bitcoin, ether, etc.). The Italian tax authority has published a number of answers to ruling requests addressing specific aspects of the taxation of crypto assets.[3] Although these are taxpayer-specific rulings and do not provide general guidance, they do indicate principles which may be useful in similar cases.

(b) Which court cases exist dealing with crypto assets?

Italian tax courts have not issued any relevant decisions concerning the qualification and taxation of crypto assets. To date, there is only one decision rendered by the Court of Justice of the European Union (ECJ) that clarified the value-added tax (VAT) treatment of bitcoins.[4]

1. Presidential Decree No. 917 of 22 Dec. 1986.
2. Presidential Decree No. 633 of 26 Oct. 1972.
3. Resolution No. 72/E issued on 22 Sep. 2016; Ruling No. 956-39/2018 issued on 22 Jan. 2018; Ruling No. 14 issued on 28 Sep. 2018.
4. ECJ, 22 Oct. 2015, Case C-264/14, *Skatteverket/Hedqvist*.

Furthermore, on 19 November 2019 the Regional Administrative Court of Lazio issued a decision[5] addressing certain tax monitoring obligations related to crypto assets held outside of Italy. Such decision confirmed the position upheld by the Italian tax authority in the above-mentioned rulings as described in section 1.1.4(d) below.

1.1.2 Income and Capital Gains Taxes

(a) *How are crypto assets classified for income and capital gains tax purposes?*

Although Italy still lacks an organic tax framework for crypto assets, the Italian tax authority maintained that crypto assets qualify as foreign currency and consequently the existing income and capital gains rules on taxation of foreign currencies apply also to crypto assets.

The Italian tax authority specified that a crypto asset has the nature of means of payment: crypto asset is a type of currency without legal tender, and it is characterized by the absence of materiality. This classification applies to payment tokens only, and no definition has been specifically issued by the Italian tax authority with respect to security or utility tokens.

(b) *What are the income/capital gains tax consequences of selling crypto assets against fiat currency?*

The taxation of exchanges of crypto assets to fiat currencies is different depending on whether crypto assets are held in connection to a business activity or not.

Capital gains arising from the exchange of cryptocurrencies to fiat currencies made by Italian tax resident individuals not carrying out a business activity are subject to the standard rules applicable to income arising from trades of foreign fiat currencies. In particular, capital gains realized upon the sale of foreign currency deriving from deposits and current accounts are subject to Italian personal income tax (IRPEF) provided that, during the tax period in which the sale occurs, the balance of such accounts exceeds EUR 51,645.69 for at least seven continuous working days. According to Italian tax law, the above-mentioned threshold – provided for foreign currency withdrawals – concerns all deposits and current accounts held by a taxpayer; thus, applying these standard rules to cryptocurrencies, the value of cryptocurrencies held – calculated on the basis of the exchange rate in force at the beginning of the tax period – must be aggregated with the equivalent value in Euro contained in wallets on other electronic portfolios and to the value of other traditional foreign currencies held by the taxpayer. In order to determine the capital gain, it is necessary to: (i) offset the value of the fiat currency against the acquisition cost of the cryptocurrency and (ii) consider the cryptocurrency acquired on the most recent date as being sold first (*i.e.*, Last In First Out method, or LIFO). The capital gain is then subject to a substitute tax at a 26% rate.

5. Judgment No. 01077/2020 issued by the Regional Administrative Court of Lazio on 19 Nov. 2019.

Capital gains realized by Italian tax resident individuals in the context of a business activity are deemed as business income and included in the taxable base subject to IRPEF at progressive rates (plus local surcharges up to 4%), as follows:

- up to EUR 15,000: 23%;
- over EUR 15,000 and up to EUR 28,000: 27%;
- over EUR 28,000 and up to EUR 55,000: 38%;
- over EUR 55,000 and up to EUR 75,000: 41%;
- over EUR 75,000: 43%.

Such capital gains may be relevant also for Italian regional income tax (IRAP), if the main business activity carried out by the entrepreneur consists of trading in cryptocurrencies.

Capital gains realized by Italian tax resident companies qualify as business income and should be subject to the Italian corporate income tax (IRES) at the ordinary 24% rate. The increase or decrease of the value of the cryptocurrencies held at the end of each tax period is included in income or deductible as a loss for IRES purposes. Further, such capital gains may be subject to IRAP at the ordinary 3.9% rate,[6] if the main business activity of the company consists of trading in cryptocurrency.

(c) *What are the income/capital gains tax consequences of exchanging crypto assets against other crypto assets?*

The exchange of crypto assets in consideration of other crypto assets may be subject to tax according to the rules set out under section 1.1.2(b) above.

Capital gains arising from such a transaction are subject to: (i) a flat 26% substitute tax in the hands of Italian tax resident individuals not carrying out a business activity; and (ii) IRPEF at progressive rates (up to 43%) and may be subject to IRAP at the ordinary 3.9% rate (depending on the specific business activity carried out) in the hands of individuals holding the cryptocurrencies in connection with a business activity. Furthermore, proceeds arising from speculative exchanges between cryptocurrencies are subject to IRES at the ordinary 24% rate and may be subject to IRAP (depending on the core business activity carried out) in the hands of Italian tax resident companies.

(d) *If a distinction is made between business assets and non-business assets, when does trading in crypto assets lead to a trade or business?*

Trading in crypto assets may be carried out within the context of a business activity or outside of a business activity. Italian tax laws do not provide specific rules to distinguish business from non-business activities. As a general rule, the Italian civil code provides a statutory definition[7] of the conduct of a business activity, which in

6. The competent Region may increase or decrease the applicable rate by 0.92%.
7. Article 2195 of the Italian civil code.

particular consists of carrying out the following activities: (i) industrial activities for the supply of goods or services; (ii) brokering for the transfer of goods; (iii) land, sea and air transport; (iv) banking and insurance activities; and (v) activities that are ancillary to the previous activities. In case the activity carried out falls in one of the activities comprised in such definition, it is automatically deemed as commercial activity.

In case a given taxpayer carries out activities which do not fall in the statutory definition of business activity, it is necessary to assess whether such activities are carried out by means of an organization in the form of an enterprise in order to determine their commercial nature.

According to the administrative guidance issued by the Italian tax authorities,[8] the following indicia would suggest that a taxpayer is carrying out a business activity (such criteria may be applicable also with respect to taxpayers engaged in crypto assets trading):

- arrangement of an organization of means and financial resources functional to the obtainment of an economic result;
- maintenance of an office to carry out the relevant transactions;
- existence of the necessary skills for the carrying out of the (trading) activity;
- provision of services and conclusion of transactions on behalf of third parties;
- existence of a relevant number of transactions; and
- characterization of the activity by the features of professionalism, systematic approach, and habituality.

In case crypto assets are held in the context of a business activity, any income deriving from crypto assets represent business income subject to IRPEF at proportional rate (up to 43%) and local surcharges.

(e) *What are the income/capital gains tax consequences for an employee receiving wages or salaries in crypto assets?*

According to ITCA, any compensation – either in cash or in kind – paid to an Italian resident employee in connection with its employment relationship, even if paid or granted by third parties (*i.e.*, by persons other than the employer), is treated as employment income subject to IRPEF at progressive rates ranging from 23% to 43% (plus certain local surcharges up to 4%), applicable on a cash basis principle. In case the employer is either an Italian resident company or an Italian branch of a foreign employer, income taxes shall be withheld and paid by the domestic employer.[9]

In case employees and directors are paid in crypto assets, these amounts constitute benefits in kind and are included in the computation of the comprehensive employment income. As a general rule, benefits in kind are taxable in the hands of the

8. Please *see, inter alia*, Resolution No. 286/E of 27 Sep. 2007, Resolution No. 148/E of 20 May 2002, Resolution No. 204/E of 20 Jun. 2002, Resolution No. 273/E of 7 Aug. 2002.
9. Article 23 of Presidential Decree No. 600/1973.

employee if their amount exceeds EUR 258.23 in a given tax period. The amount of benefits in kind is calculated according to their fair market value.[10]

Regarding the valuation of the crypto assets received, in order to determine the equivalent value in Euro of the crypto assets, it is necessary to evaluate them using the exchange rate in force at the date of receipt. Alternatively, should such exchange rate not be available, it is possible to refer to the average exchange rate of the official quotations on the online trading platforms.

If the employees/directors at a later stage sell the crypto assets, the capital gains will be subject to the 26% substitute tax, provided that, during the tax period in which the sale occurs, the balance of the deposits and current accounts held by the employees/directors exceeds EUR 51,645.69 for at least seven continuous working days. In such a scenario, the taxable basis of the capital gain will be equal to the difference between (i) the fair market value of crypto assets at the assignment date and (ii) the sale price.

(f) What are the income/capital gains tax consequences for a merchant receiving payment in crypto assets?

The fair market value of crypto assets received in exchange of supplies of goods or services is subject to income tax (both for IRPEF/IRES and IRAP purposes).

The subsequent sale of crypto assets will be subject to IRPEF or IRES.

(g) What are the income/capital gains tax consequences of a loss of crypto assets?

The Italian tax authority has not issued any guidance on the tax aspects of the loss of crypto assets. The loss of crypto assets should not be relevant for tax purposes if they are not held in the context of a business activity. In contrast, the loss of crypto assets held in the context of a business activity may constitute a tax-deductible cost.

(h) What are the income/capital gains tax consequences of a loss in value of crypto assets?

Losses in value of crypto assets (realized or not upon disposal of crypto assets) held in the context of a business activity are deductible from the aggregate taxable income.

In case the crypto assets are not held in connection with a business activity, losses in value are not relevant for tax purposes, if not effectively realized upon disposal.

10. Article 9 of ITCA.

(i) What are the income/capital gains tax consequences of forks of crypto assets?

The Italian tax authority has not issued any guidance on blockchain forks, meaning the split of a blockchain into two blockchains and the attribution to the taxpayer holding crypto assets on the original blockchain of crypto assets on the new blockchain.

However, it could be argued that the attribution to the taxpayer of the 'new crypto assets' derives from a withdrawal of crypto asset in the original blockchain. Consequently, according to this interpretation, the attribution to the taxpayer of a new crypto asset may be taxable if the conditions depicted in section 1.1.2(b) above are met (*i.e.*, capital gains realized by individuals not carrying out a business activity upon the sale of foreign currency deriving from deposits and current accounts are subject to IRPEF provided that, during the tax period in which the sale occurs, the balance of such accounts exceeds EUR 51,645.69 for at least seven continuous working days; capital gains realized by individuals or companies in the context of a business activity are in any case subject to IRPEF/IRES and IRAP).

(j) What are the income/capital gains tax consequences of airdrops of crypto assets and are the tax consequences different if the airdropped tokens are unwanted?

An airdrop is a distribution of a crypto asset, usually for free, to numerous wallet addresses. Airdrops may be used for marketing reasons (for example, as a way of gaining attention and new followers, resulting in a larger user-base and a wider disbursement of coins).

No specific guidance has been issued by the Italian tax authority on airdrops. Distributions of crypto assets to individuals not carrying out any business activity should not be taxable for IRPEF and gift tax purposes.

In the context of a business activity, the fair market value of crypto assets received free of charge is included in the taxable income, and it is subject to tax (IRPEF if received by an entrepreneur or IRES if received by a company) on a cash basis.

(k) What are the income/capital gains tax consequences of (solo, pool, and cloud) mining?

Even in the absence of any guidance, mining should lead to taxable income from an active trade or business falling in the category of business income and subject to IRPEF (up to 43%, plus local surcharges) if the miner is an individual engaged in a business activity and to IRES at 24% rate if the miner is a company.

However, if the mining activities are carried out by an Italian resident individual occasionally, income arising from such activities may fall into the category of miscellaneous income and would be subject to IRPEF up to 43% (plus local surcharges).

With respect to the crypto assets received by miners for the solving of the algorithms, such assets are taxable on a cash basis principle (*i.e.*, when received by the miner) on the basis of their fair market value. Such proceeds can be offset by the expenses incurred for the carrying out of the activity.

The above treatment applies to solo mining, pool mining (*i.e.*, the pooling of resources by miners, who share their processing power over a network, to split the reward equally, according to the amount of work they contributed to the probability of finding a block), and cloud mining (*i.e.*, the use of a remote data centre with rented processing power).

(l) *What are the income/capital gains tax consequences of staking crypto assets?*

Staking is the process of holding funds in a crypto assets wallet to support the operations of a blockchain network. Essentially, it consists of locking crypto assets to receive rewards. This is a passive activity, and any income arising from such activity should be qualified as miscellaneous income, as such subject to IRPEF in the hands of individuals not carrying out business activities. The proceeds arising from the staking of crypto assets received by companies and individuals in the context of a business activity are ordinarily subject to income taxes.

(m) *What are the income/capital gains tax consequences of an indirect investment in crypto assets?*

Italian resident investors may hold crypto asset indirectly, for instance by subscribing share/units of an investment fund or of exchange traded fund (ETF) which invests in crypto assets.

Under the currently applicable tax regime, a 26% final withholding tax applies to proceeds derived by Italian individuals from investments in: (i) funds/ETFs established in EU or white-listed European Economic Area Member States ('EEA Member States') in accordance with the Undertakings for Collective Investment in Transferable Securities Directive ('UCITS Directive') (*i.e.*, harmonized funds); and (ii) funds/ETFs established in EU or white-listed EEA Member States not in compliance with the UCITS Directive, the manager of which is an entity subject to regulation in accordance to Alternative Investment Fund Managers Directive ('AIFM Directive').

Conversely, proceeds derived by an Italian individual from an investment in non-harmonized ETFs are subject to IRPEF at the applicable progressive rates (up to 43%).

Proceeds from funds received by companies or individuals in connection with their business activity must be included in their business income and are subject to IRES or IRPEF.

(n) *How is income from crypto assets to be treated under double tax treaty law?*

The Italian tax authorities have not issued any guidance with respect to the treatment of crypto assets under double tax treaty law.

However, any income arising in connection with crypto assets may fall under the rules set out by the OECD Model Convention provided for business income. In particular, income realized by an enterprise (*i.e.*, an individual engaged in a business activity or a company) tax resident in a Contracting State is taxable only in that State. However, in case the enterprise carries on its business in the other Contracting State through a permanent establishment situated therein, then the quota of income attributable to this permanent establishment may be taxed in that other State.[11] This means, for example, that income realized by an Italian tax resident mining company is subject to tax in Italy, but if such company carries out its activity in Spain through a permanent establishment located therein, then the part of income attributable to that permanent establishment may be taxed in Spain.

Furthermore, as a general rule (but certain exceptions are provided) capital gains upon disposal of any property are taxable in the State in which the seller is tax resident.[12] As an example, an Italian tax resident investor who sells cryptocurrency deposited with an Estonian tax resident intermediary would be subject to tax in Italy only.

(o) *What are the income/capital gains tax consequences of selling crypto assets in an ICO/STO/IEO?*

The Italian tax authority released a response to a ruling regarding the tax treatment of the Initial Coin Offers (ICO).[13] The case at hand concerned a company that had issued utility tokens in an ICO; these tokens were to be transferred against payment with crypto assets or traditional currencies. For IRES purposes, the transfer of utility tokens is to be deemed as a mere financial transaction and as such not taxable. Also for IRAP purposes, the amounts collected upon transfer of tokens are not included in the taxable base.

Furthermore, for individuals' income purposes, the Italian tax authority clarified that transactions involving utility tokens – the ownership of which gives the right to purchase on a forward basis (*i.e.*, whenever available) certain goods or services agreed upon at the time of joining the ICO – may generate miscellaneous income and consequently is subject to the 26% substitute tax at the time of receipt in the hands of Italian tax resident individuals not holding the tokens in connection with a business activity.

11. Article 7 of the OECD Model Convention.
12. Article 13 of the OECD Model Convention.
13. Ruling No. 14 of 28 Sep. 2018.

1.1.3 *Other Taxes*

(a) What are the value added tax/sales tax consequences of selling crypto assets?

As mentioned in section 1.1.1(b) above, the ECJ issued a judgement on crypto assets in 2015. The case concerned Mr Hedqvist, owner of an exchange allowing the purchase and sale of bitcoin in exchange for currencies having legal tender (*i.e.*, Swedish fiat currency). The question brought to the attention of the ECJ concerned the applicability of VAT on the profits deriving from the difference – if positive – between the purchase and the sale prices applied. The ECJ stated that transactions such as the one in question can be regarded as supplies of services in exchange of a consideration. Furthermore, ECJ stated that transactions in crypto assets – the latter accepted by the parties as a means of payment other than legal tender currency – fall within the scope of the VAT exemption provided for in the EU VAT Directive for transaction relating to foreign exchange, banknotes, and coins.

The Italian tax authority agreed with the ECJ's conclusions confirming that the fees received by Italian exchangers are exempt services for Italian VAT purposes.

Furthermore, the Italian tax authority stated[14] that the transfer of utility tokens was out of the scope of VAT (as the transfer of utility tokens is similar to the transfer of vouchers).

Finally, in a recent response to a ruling request[15] concerning the sale for a consideration of utility tokens[16] by an Italian resident company to the members of an Italian resident consortium carrying out the activity of validation of certain blockchain transactions, the Italian tax authority has maintained that the sale of the utility tokens represents a supply of service subject to VAT at the ordinary 22% rate.

(b) Are payments in crypto assets subject to withholding taxes?

The distribution of crypto assets by an Italian resident company to its individual shareholders should be deemed as dividends in kind and subject to the 26% withholding tax. In order to apply the withholding tax, the crypto assets distributed to the shareholders have to be converted into fiat currency.

Furthermore, if an Italian resident employer pays its employees in crypto assets, it would have to withhold the income taxes due by the employees.

14. Ruling No. 14 of 28 Sep. 2018.
15. Ruling No. 110 of 20 Apr. 2020.
16. In the specific case, the ownership of the tokens did not give any right to participate in the Italian resident company or in the consortium.

(c) Does payment of compensation in crypto assets give rise to payroll tax consequences?

Payments of compensation in crypto assets should be deemed as benefits in kind and subject to withholding taxes.

In order to allow the employer to fulfil withholding tax obligations, it is common practice that the employee is required to provide the employer with the amount of the withholding tax due on the fair market value of crypto assets received.

(d) Do transactions with crypto assets trigger any transfer taxes?

In case of registration with the Italian tax authority of the agreements executed for the transfer of crypto assets – deemed as agreements for the sale of traditional currency – Italian registration tax should apply at the fixed amount of EUR 200. However, Italian tax law does not provide any obligation to register such agreements.

(e) Are firms operating in the crypto space subject to digital service taxes?

Article 1(678) of Law No. 160/2019, published in the Official Gazette No. 304 of 30 December 2019 (hereinafter the '**2020 Budget Law**'), has made significant changes to the provisions related to the digital services tax (hereinafter DST) in order to align the domestic rules to the part of the proposal for a Council Directive of the European Commission[17] aimed at implementing a common system of a digital services tax, and provided its application as of 1 January 2020, irrespective of the issuance of an implementing decree. It has been provided that the current domestic framework will be fully repealed when the international regulation on the digital economy taxation enters into force.

The DST applies – at a 3% rate – on the amount of revenues arising from the supply of certain digital services within Italy by companies exceeding certain financial thresholds.

In particular, the DST is due by entities carrying on business activities in the sector of digital services, if the following thresholds are jointly met in the hands of the single entity or of the group in the calendar year before the relevant year:

(i) the total amount of worldwide revenues reported exceeds EUR 750,000,000; and
(ii) the total amount of taxable revenues deriving from digital services relevant for DST purposes obtained within the Italian territory exceeds EUR 5,500,000.

The DST applies to revenues derived from the supply of the following digital services:

17. COM(2018) 148 final.

(a) the placing on a digital interface of advertising targeted at users of such interface;
(b) the making available to users of a multi-sided digital interface which allows users to be in contact and to interact with each other, also with the aim of facilitating the supply of goods or services, with the exception of the revenues received as consideration for the supply of goods or services representing, from an economic viewpoint, transactions independent from the use of the taxable service; or
(c) the transmission of data collected from users and generated from the users' activities of a digital interface.

The above-mentioned revenues must be considered net of VAT and other indirect taxes. Revenues arising from digital services provided to subsidiaries, parent companies or subsidiaries of the same controlling entity pursuant to Article 2359 of the Italian Civil Code are not subject to DST. For the sake of clarity, the deductibility of costs incurred is not permitted.

The Italian tax authority has not issued any guidance on whether firms operating in the crypto asset space are subject to DST. However, the activity carried out by crypto asset exchanges seems to fall within the scope of application of the DST.

(f) Are crypto assets subject to gift, inheritance, estate, or wealth taxes?

Crypto assets are not subject to wealth taxes. In this respect, the Italian tax authority clarified that individuals holding crypto assets abroad are not subject to wealth tax on assets held abroad.

Furthermore, transfer upon death and gifts of crypto assets are subject to Italian inheritance and gift tax (IHT). According to Italian tax law,[18] transfers of valuable assets as a result of death or gift (or other transfers for no consideration) to Italian tax resident individuals not engaged in a business activity are subject to IHT as follows:

(i) transfers in favour of spouse (or civil partner) and direct descendants or direct ancestors are subject to tax at the rate of 4%, on the value exceeding EUR 1,000,000;
(ii) transfers in favour of siblings are subject to tax at the rate of 6% on the value exceeding EUR 100,000;
(iii) transfers in favour of relatives up to the fourth degree or relatives-in-law up to the third degree are subject to tax at the rate of 6%; and
(iv) any other transfer is subject to tax at the rate of 8%.

The allowances provided apply to each beneficiary. The IHT is due by the heirs/donees.

Italian tax law provides for an exemption from IHT for gifts of 'non-relevant' value. In order to determine the 'non-relevant' value of the gift of crypto assets, the

18. Legislative Decree No. 346/1990.

value of the transferred assets must be compared with the value of the estates of the donor and the donee.

As regards the territorial scope of IHT, any transfer upon death or gift of assets and rights – wherever located – held by an Italian resident individual is subject to IHT. Conversely, transfers upon death or gift by a non-Italian resident individual are subject to IHT with respect to assets and rights located in Italy only. In brief, the residence of the deceased/donor in Italy triggers a worldwide tax liability; conversely, the residence abroad of the deceased/donor determines the applicability of IHT on a territorial basis.

In the absence of any specific guidance by the Italian tax authority, crypto assets are deemed to be held in the place where they are deposited (if the crypto assets are held with an Italian resident intermediary, the crypto assets are considered to be located in Italy).

(g) Are crypto assets subject to exit tax?

According to Italian tax law, an exit tax[19] applies where a resident company (i) transfers its tax residence abroad from Italy and no permanent establishment remains in Italy, (ii) transfers assets abroad from Italy to its foreign permanent establishment to which the foreign branch tax exemption applies, or (iii) transfers its tax residence or assets abroad from Italy as a result of cross-border reorganization transactions and no permanent establishment remains in Italy. In particular, the company is subject to tax on the deemed capital gain pertaining to the transferred assets, equal to the difference between their market value and their value recognized for tax purposes. Such provision applies to all the business assets held by the company, including crypto assets.

No exit tax regime is provided for Italian resident individuals. For example, if an Italian resident individual holding crypto assets leaves Italy, any accrued increase in the value of crypto assets is not subject to tax.

(h) Can mining trigger gambling tax?

No gambling tax should be triggered through crypto mining activities.

1.1.4 Compliance and Documentation Obligations

(a) What documentation requirements exist for taxpayers regarding crypto assets and are there best practices in recordkeeping to support representations made in tax returns?

In Italy there are no specific documentation requirements for taxpayers holding crypto assets. As a general rule, taking into account the fact that intermediaries are not entitled to apply the substitute taxes on capital gains related to crypto assets (taxpayers must

19. Article 166 of ITCA.

pay income tax on such capital gains and report the capital gains in a specific section of their yearly tax returns), it would be important to collect statements reporting the purchase valued of the crypto assets, as well statements reporting the sale price in case of disposal of crypto assets.

With respect to Italian resident companies holding crypto assets, they should apply the ordinary accounting rules (Italian GAAP or IAS/IFRS).

(b) What is the evidentiary burden of supporting tax positions when a digital wallet address is lost or shared with other persons?

In principle, it is up to the Italian tax authority to prove the facts on which the notices of assessment claiming for higher taxes issued to the taxpayers are based. Nevertheless, the burden of proof is on the taxpayers in case there are facts which trigger a reduction of the taxable base or the taxes due.

Accordingly, the burden of proof of a loss of digital wallet address or its co-ownership is on the taxpayer. The taxpayer who lost private keys and cannot anymore dispose over certain crypto assets should have the duty to explain to the Italian tax authority the usual management of the keys and what caused the loss. To this end, it may be useful that taxpayers keep a statement detailing the crypto assets held in their digital wallets and keep track of the usual management activities.

(c) Are crypto asset exchanges and wallet providers subject to reporting obligations?

Italian law provides for a public register in which the service providers relating to crypto assets will be registered for the purpose of tracing the owner of the crypto assets to intercept any possible money laundering operations.

The Italian resident exchangers are required to periodically report to the Italian tax authority the identity of the cryptocurrency holders, the value of their wallets and the transactions made in a given tax period.

(d) Are taxpayers holding crypto assets subject to reporting obligations apart from the filing of income tax/capital gains tax returns?

Transactions with crypto assets are relevant – apart from direct taxation purposes – also for tax monitoring purposes. According to the Italian tax monitoring obligations, taxpayers are required to indicate in a specific section (the 'RW' section) of the Italian tax return the amount of financial assets and immovable property held abroad in the tax period of reference. The Italian tax authority expressly stated[20] that the possession of crypto assets must be reported in the RW section under Code 14, 'Other Foreign Assets of a Financial Nature'.

20. *See* Ruling No. 956-39/2018 issued on 22 Jan. 2018.

In case of failure to file the RW section of the tax return, penalties apply from a minimum of 3% up to a maximum of 30% of the value of the unreported assets.

(e) Are crypto asset exchanges and wallet providers subject to CRS/FATCA reporting?

It is not clear whether crypto asset exchangers and wallet providers are subject to the international automatic exchange of information obligations.

Indeed, under the Italian legislation implementing the EU Directive on the mandatory automatic exchange of information in the tax area, any entity engaged in foreign currency trading as its principal business activity is subject to CRS obligations. Since crypto assets are deemed as foreign currencies for Italian tax purposes according to the Italian tax authority's position, it is reasonable to assume that crypto asset exchangers and wallet providers are subject to CRS/FATCA obligations.

Moreover, although crypto assets are still a rather uncharted territory in terms of CRS and FATCA, Italy has implemented adequate measures to increase the level of monitoring of crypto asset activity for tackling the misuse of crypto assets in illegal transactions (reference is made to the tax monitoring and anti-money laundering provisions[21]).

1.1.5 Civil and Criminal Tax Enforcement

(a) What powers do the tax authorities have to compel the disclosure of information by third parties, such as exchanges or wallet providers, and have these been used in the past?

According to Italian tax law, the Italian tax authority has the power to request the supply of information from the taxpayers or from third parties (*e.g.*, the Italian tax authority has the power to: (i) request the transmission of data and information; (ii) require the submission of certain written documents; and (iii) invite the taxpayers to appear in person to provide certain information or clarification). The requested information is to be provided truthfully to the best of knowledge and belief. As a general rule, the requests of the Italian tax authority have to be necessary, proportionate, and reasonable.

Requested information or documents which are not provided or submitted to the Italian tax authority cannot be taken into account in favour of the taxpayer for the purposes of any subsequent assessment procedure.

In principle, the Italian tax authority may ask the taxpayer (or third parties) to provide information or documentation with reference to transactions concerning crypto assets. However, there is no public evidence of such requests in the past.

21. Please *see*, respectively, Law Decree No. 167/1990 for tax monitoring provisions and Legislative Decree No. 231/2007 as modified by Legislative Decree No. 90/2017 for anti-money laundering provisions.

(b) *What measures have the tax authorities undertaken in the past to ensure crypto tax compliance?*

There is no public evidence of what measures the Italian tax authority has undertaken in the past in order to ensure crypto tax compliance, apart from publishing answers to ruling requests on certain tax aspects of transactions with crypto assets.

(c) *Are the tax authorities cooperating with tax authorities in other jurisdictions on enforcement?*

As regards the cooperation with tax authorities of other states, it is worth mentioning that Italy has implemented both the FATCA and the CRS. The Italian tax authorities can readily obtain financial information on investments and properties held in another jurisdiction that applies the CRS.

Furthermore, Italy is part of a diversified regional and international network of bilateral and multilateral information-based administrative cooperation. Italy has ratified the OECD Multilateral Convention on Mutual Administrative Assistance in Tax Matters. In addition, Italy is an EU Member State and has thus implemented EU secondary law in this area. Italy has an extensive network of tax treaties. In this regard, the exchange of information is channelled primarily through double tax treaties (providing for measures specifically addressing the avoidance of international double taxation, measures of administrative cooperation) and through tax information exchange agreements (TIEAs).

However, there is no public evidence of current cooperation of the Italian tax authority with tax authorities in other jurisdictions on enforcement and whether they have made use of the various instruments mentioned above in respect of crypto asset holdings of taxpayers.

Japan

Yushi Hegawa

1. COUNTRY GUIDES

1.1 Japan

1.1.1 Applicable Tax Law, Guidance, and Case Law

(a) Which laws, regulations, and other administrative guidance exist dealing with crypto assets?

Japanese taxation of crypto assets is governed by general tax statutes, along with all other income and gains. The Income Tax Act[1] deals with national taxation on individuals, and the Corporation Tax Act[2] deals with national taxation on corporations. Each of these Acts has subordinate rules as part of law (i.e., the Enforcement Cabinet Order[3] and the Enforcement Ministerial Ordinance).[4] As for local (i.e., prefectural and municipal) taxation, the Local Tax Act[5] as well as its subordinate Enforcement Cabinet Order[6] and Enforcement Ministerial Ordinance[7] governs local taxation on individuals and corporations; however, local taxation generally follows the consequences of national taxation insofar as taxation of crypto assets is concerned.

1. Act No. 33 of 1965, as amended.
2. Act No. 34 of 1965, as amended.
3. The Income Tax Act Enforcement Cabinet Order (Cabinet Order No. 96 of 1965, as amended) and the Corporation Tax Act Enforcement Cabinet Order (Cabinet Order No. 97 of 1965, as amended).
4. The Income Tax Act Enforcement Ministerial Ordinance (Ministry of Finance Ordinance No. 11 of 1965, as amended) and the Corporation Tax Act Enforcement Ministerial Ordinance (Ministry of Finance Ordinance No. 12 of 1965, as amended).
5. Act No. 226 of 1950, as amended.
6. Cabinet Order No. 245 of 1950, as amended.
7. Ministry of Internal Affairs and Communications Ordinance No. 23 of 1954, as amended.

In addition, while not law, the Income Tax Basic Circular[8] (for individuals) and the Corporation Tax Basic Circular[9] (for corporations) are important in practice, which provide an official interpretation of the foregoing tax statutes by the National Tax Agency (NTA), a governmental enforcement agency for tax law in Japan. Also, the NTA has published a document entitled '*Tax Treatment of Cryptocurrency (FAQ)*'[10] (the FAQ), to clarify more details on the tax treatment of various crypto assets transactions for the benefit of taxpayers. These do not bind taxpayers or courts as a technical legal matter; however, these are respected in tax practice as they provide for an official interpretation by the NTA.

(b) Which court cases exist dealing with crypto assets?

To the best of our research as of the date of this chapter, there are no published court decisions dealing with the taxation of crypto assets, nor are there published decisions of the National Tax Tribunal (a quasi-judicial administrative body for tax dispute resolution) dealing with the taxation of crypto assets.

However, many press reports indicate that the NTA is conducting vigorous tax audits on individuals and corporations who earned substantial income through crypto assets transactions but did not report that income by filing a tax return. One press article[11] reports that the NTA found that at least fifty individuals and thirty corporations underreported or failed to report income arising from crypto assets totalling around JPY 10 billion.

1.1.2 Income and Capital Gains Taxes

(a) How are crypto assets classified for income and capital gains tax purposes?

Crypto assets are not treated as assets giving rise to capital gains.[12] Income arising from various crypto assets transactions is, in principle, treated as 'miscellaneous income' for individuals.[13] This would apply to most taxpayers who carry out crypto assets transactions as an investment or asset management. However, only where crypto assets transactions are considered as reaching the level of business activity (e.g., where one makes his/her living through crypto assets transactions), the income could be treated as 'business income' for individuals.[14] The difference between miscellaneous income and business income is evident in the treatment of losses, as discussed in section 1.1.2(g) below.

---

8. National Tax Agency Circular No. 30 of 1970, as amended.
9. National Tax Agency Circular No. 25 of 1969, as amended.
10. Available at: https://www.nta.go.jp/publication/pamph/pdf/virtual_currency_faq.pdf (2019).
11. The Asahi Shimbun, dated 5 Jun. 2019.
12. FAQ, No. 8.
13. Article 35 of Income Tax Act.
14. Article 27 of Income Tax Act.

For corporations, there is no classification of income; so income arising from crypto assets is treated as taxable income in the same manner as all other income.[15]

(b) What are the income/capital gains tax consequences of selling crypto assets against fiat currency?

For individuals, the income is classified either as miscellaneous income or as business income, as discussed in section 1.1.2(a) above. In either case, taxable income arising from crypto assets transactions is calculated on the basis of gross receipts from the transaction less the acquisition cost of the crypto assets being disposed and other costs if any (e.g., commissions).[16] As to the acquisition cost of crypto assets, the taxpayer may elect to use 5% of the gross receipts as the acquisition cost as a convenience measure, instead of using the actual acquisition cost.[17] Then the taxable income is subject to the general aggregate taxation along with all other types of income being subject to the general aggregate taxation,[18] at progressive rates, where the marginal tax rate (national and local) is 55.945% as to the income bracket exceeding JPY 40 million.[19] It should be noted that income from crypto assets is taxed in a different manner[20] from other financial assets such as bonds, shares, and foreign exchange derivatives, all of which are taxed at a flat rate of 20.315% (national and local) separately from all other income being subject to the general aggregate taxation, and can enjoy a loss carry forward for the future three years. In that sense, taxation of income from crypto assets is not that favourable.

For corporations, the taxable income is calculated on the basis of gross receipts less the acquisition cost of the crypto assets being disposed and other costs if any (e.g., commissions).[21] The effective corporate income tax rate (national and local) is around 30% for corporations having stated capital of JPY 100 million or more, and otherwise around 33–34%.

In either case, the gross receipt is the fair market value of the fiat currency (if other than Japanese Yen).[22]

(c) What are the income/capital gains tax consequences of exchanging crypto assets against other crypto assets?

The taxation is the same as discussed in section 1.1.2(b) above. Here, the gross receipt is the fair market value of the other crypto assets.[23]

15. Article 22(2) of Corporation Tax Act.
16. FAQ, No. 9; Articles 35 and 27 of Income Tax Act.
17. FAQ, No. 13.
18. Article 22 of Income Tax Act.
19. Article 89 of Income Tax Act.
20. FAQ, No. 18.
21. FAQ, No. 20 and No. 21.
22. FAQ, No. 1.
23. FAQ, No. 3.

(d) *If a distinction is made between business assets and non-business assets, when does trading in crypto assets lead to a trade or business?*

For individuals, as discussed in section 1.1.2(a) above, income from crypto assets could be treated as business income, only where crypto assets transactions are considered as reaching the level of business activity. Whether or not a taxpayer's activity, including crypto assets transactions, reaches the level of business activity is determined by a well-established Supreme Court decision,[24] which held that the term 'business activity' means an activity that is conducted for the taxpayer's own account and at his/her own risk on an independent basis, is conducted for consideration and for profit, and establishes in an objective manner his/her intention and societal status to conduct the activity on a continuous and repeated basis. In practice, this criterion is generally understood to mean a situation where the principal source of income for the taxpayer to make his/her living is crypto assets transactions but not other means.[25]

For corporations, there is no such distinction, as discussed in section 1.1.2(a) above.

(e) *What are the income/capital gains tax consequences for an employee receiving wages or salaries in crypto assets?*

In this case, wages and salaries are treated as in-kind remuneration for income tax purposes and are treated as 'employment income,' in the same manner as remuneration and salary to be paid in cash.[26] The value of the crypto assets for the purpose of calculating the employment income is measured by the market rate as of the due date of the remuneration and salary.[27] In all other aspects, the tax treatment is the same as remuneration and salary to be paid in cash (e.g., withholding by the employer).

(f) *What are the income/capital gains tax consequences for a merchant receiving payment in crypto assets?*

The tax treatment is the same as where a merchant receives a payment in cash. That is, the total amount of the crypto assets received, which usually equals the fair market value of the goods sold or services performed, constitutes a gross receipt for income tax purposes of an individual and corporate merchant.[28]

In addition, because crypto assets are received in consideration of the goods sold or services performed in Japan, consumptions taxes (VAT) at 10% are also imposed, in the same manner as a sale for cash.[29] The individual and corporate merchant would receive crypto assets inclusive of the amount of such consumption taxes on top of the

24. Supreme Court decision dated 24 Apr. 1981.
25. FAQ, No. 8.
26. Article 28(1) of Income Tax Act.
27. Article 36(1) of Income Tax Act.
28. Article 36(1) of Income Tax Act; Article 22(1) of Corporation Tax Act.
29. Articles 4(1) and 6(1) of Consumption Tax Act (Act No. 108 of 1988, as amended).

value of the goods sold or services performed, and compute and report its consumption tax liability by filing a consumption tax return, together with all other taxable sales made for cash.

(g) *What are the income/capital gains tax consequences of a loss of crypto assets?*

For individuals, losses of crypto assets are in principle treated as losses incurred in the miscellaneous income classification, in the same manner as discussed in section 1.1.2(a) above. The losses can be offset against other miscellaneous income, including income from other crypto assets transactions, only to the extent of the positive amount of the total miscellaneous income being zero. In other words, the losses cannot be offset against income of other income classification, such as dividends, capital gains, employment income, and business income.[30]

If the losses arose due to a natural disaster, theft or embezzlement (e.g., by way of illegal hacking), there are discussions as to whether an individual taxpayer can take 'general loss deduction' as to the losses.[31] The 'general loss deduction' is one of general income deductions, not limited to the calculation of miscellaneous income mentioned above. The FAQ does not make this point clear; however, some practitioners argue that this should be available.[32] If this is available, an individual taxpayer can in general deduct, from the total taxable income being subject to the general aggregate taxation, the total amount of the losses less 10% of that total taxable income.[33]

On the other hand, where such losses are treated as losses incurred in the business income classification (*see* section 1.1.2(d) above), the losses can be offset against not only other business income but also income of all other income classification, such as dividends, capital gains, employment income, and miscellaneous income;[34] and further, if there still are losses that cannot be used up for the calendar year, the remaining losses can be carried forward for future three years, subject to certain filing requirements.[35]

For corporations, because there is no income classification, losses are deductible from and can be offset against all other income and gains.[36] If there still are losses that cannot be used up for the fiscal year, the remaining losses can be carried forward for future ten fiscal years, subject to certain filing requirements.[37]

30. FAQ, No. 17; Article 51(4) of Income Tax Act.
31. *See* Article 72 of Income Tax Act.
32. *See*, e.g., Shunta Nakao, Taxation of Crypto Assets (4), 63-1 Zeiri 150 (2020).
33. Article 72 of Income Tax Act.
34. Articles 27(2), 51(1) and (2) and Article 69(1) of Income Tax Act.
35. Article 70 of Income Tax Act.
36. Article 22(1) and (3) of Corporation Tax Act.
37. Article 57(1) of Corporation Tax Act.

(h) What are the income/capital gains tax consequences of a loss in value of crypto assets?

For individuals, a loss in value of crypto assets cannot be deducted or offset against any other income, unless such loss is realized by way of a sale or other disposition.[38]

The treatment is in principle the same for corporations;[39] however, a loss in value of certain crypto assets that are traded in an active and arm's length market is deductible as losses, by marking to market the crypto assets as of the close of the fiscal year.[40] Note that, in such case, not only a loss in value but also an appreciation in value must be marked to market as of the close of the fiscal year, and accordingly the corporation must recognize gains or losses for that fiscal year. Then, at the beginning of the following fiscal year, the gains or losses will be reversed, i.e., the corresponding amount of gains (if losses were recognised in the preceding fiscal year) or losses (if gains were recognised in the preceding fiscal year) will be recognized at the beginning of the following fiscal year.[41]

(i) What are the income/capital gains tax consequences of forks of crypto assets?

Forks of crypto assets do not give rise to any taxable income, because, according to the FAQ, newly generated crypto assets that arose from the forks do not have a market value at the time of the forks.[42] The acquisition cost of the new crypto assets that are acquired as a result of the fork is zero.[43] The FAQ is silent on the tax treatment where the newly generated crypto assets that arose from the forks did have a market value at the time of the forks; in that case, the fair market value of such newly generated crypto assets could constitute taxable income (as miscellaneous income or business income, as discussed in section 1.1.2(a) above).

(j) What are the income/capital gains tax consequences of airdrops of crypto assets and are the tax consequences different if the airdropped tokens are unwanted?

The tax treatment of airdrops of crypto assets is not made clear by the FAQ. However, the income, meaning the fair market value of the airdropped tokens, would most likely be treated in the same manner as other crypto assets transactions, as discussed in section 1.1.2(b). Even if the airdropped tokens are unwanted, it would be difficult to

38. *See* Article 37(1) of Income Tax Act.
39. *See* Article 33 of Corporation tax Act.
40. Article 61(2) of Corporation Tax Act.
41. *Id.*
42. FAQ, No. 5.
43. *Id.*

sustain a position that the receipt constitutes no income or that there should be some discount.[44]

(k) *What are the income/capital gains tax consequences of (solo, pool, and cloud) mining?*

Income from crypto assets acquired as a result of (solo, pool, and cloud) mining is treated in the same manner as income from other crypto assets transactions, as discussed in section 1.1.2(b). The income is calculated based upon the total fair market value of the acquired crypto assets less any costs and expenses required for the mining.[45]

(l) *What are the income/capital gains tax consequences of staking crypto assets?*

The tax treatment of staking crypto assets is not made clear by the FAQ. However, the income, meaning the reward earned from the staking, would most likely be treated in the same manner as income from other crypto asset transactions, as discussed in section 1.1.2(b).[46]

(m) *What are the income/capital gains tax consequences of an indirect investment in crypto assets?*

It depends upon the specific legal structure of the indirect investment. This is because the tax treatment generally follows the legal form.[47] For example, when an individual owns his/her asset management company and that company invests in crypto assets, the individual is taxed as he/she earns dividends and capital gains arising from the shares of the asset management company. The asset management company is taxed on the income arising from crypto assets as discussed in section 1.1.2(b).

(n) *How is income from crypto assets to be treated under double tax treaty law?*

The treatment of income arising from crypto assets under double tax treaties is not made clear by the FAQ. However, the income would most likely be dealt with by the 'other income' article (if the taxpayer's income would be classified as miscellaneous income under Japanese domestic tax law) or 'business profits' article (if the taxpayer's income would be classified as business income under Japanese domestic tax law) of

44. *See* Article 36(1) of Income Tax Act; Article 22(2) of Corporation Tax Act.
45. FAQ, No. 6.
46. Article 36(1) of Income Tax Act; Article 22(1) of Corporation Tax Act.
47. *See, e.g.*, Supreme Court decision dated 24 Jan. 2006.

double tax treaties.[48] Capital gains article would not be relevant because crypto assets are not assets giving rise to capital gains as discussed in section 1.1.2(a). Among the double tax treaties that Japan has entered into, some exempt Japanese taxation at source, while some preserve Japan's taxing power as a source country as to 'other income.' However, at the outset, there is no rule on how to determine the source of income from crypto assets.

(o) What are the income/capital gains tax consequences of selling crypto assets in an ICO/STO/IEO?

Japanese tax law provides for no special treatment for a sale of crypto assets in an ICO/STO/IEO, and the FAQ is silent on the tax treatment of an ICO/STO/IEO. Accordingly, the tax treatment is not clear, but would most likely follow the general principles of taxation of crypto assets as discussed in section 1.1.2(b). Because this is a sale or exchange of crypto assets, the income of the issuer would most likely be taxed at the time of the ICO/STO/IEO. Some industry groups argue for a need of a tax reform to defer the timing of income recognition to avoid immediate income taxation; however, this has not yet been legislated.

1.1.3 Other Taxes

(a) What are the value added tax/sales tax consequences of selling crypto assets?

A sale of crypto assets is non-taxable for Japanese consumption tax (or VAT) purposes, even if the sale is made within Japan.[49] Note that this deals with a sale of crypto assets themselves and should be distinguished from a situation where a merchant sells some goods or services and receives crypto assets as consideration in lieu of cash, as discussed in section 1.1.2(f) above.

(b) Are payments in crypto assets subject to withholding taxes?

A mere sale or exchange of crypto assets is not subject to withholding tax. As to payments in crypto assets, the withholding tax consequences depend upon what kind of payment is being made by using crypto assets. For example, a payment of a purchase price of goods is in general not subject to withholding tax. However, for example, if a company pays remuneration to its employee or pays interest on bonds or dividends on shares by using crypto assets, the payment is subject to withholding tax, in the same manner as a payment by cash.[50]

48. *See, e.g.*, Articles 7 and 21 of OECD Model Tax Convention.
49. FAQ, No. 29.
50. Articles 183 and 181 of Income Tax Act.

(c) Does payment of compensation in crypto assets give rise to payroll tax consequences?

Yes. When an employer makes a payment in Japan (e.g., where the employer is a Japanese resident individual or corporation) of compensation to its employee for services rendered in Japan, the employer must withhold applicable withholding tax pursuant to the schedules set forth in the Income Tax Act along with local tax and social security charges, in the same manner as a payment by cash.[51]

(d) Do transactions with crypto assets trigger any transfer taxes?

No. There is no applicable transfer tax as of the date of this article.

(e) Are firms operating in the crypto space subject to digital service taxes?

No. The applicable taxation is general income taxation only. There is no so-called digital service tax in Japan.

(f) Are crypto assets subject to gift, inheritance, estate or wealth taxes?

Yes. In the same manner as cash and other assets, the inheritance, bequest or gift of crypto assets is subject to inheritance tax or gift tax, on the side of the heir or donee who acquired the crypto assets from the deceased or donor who is an individual.[52] The tax rate of inheritance tax and gift tax is progressive, where the marginal rate is 55%.

In addition, on the side of the deceased who made the bequest or the donor who made the gift, by a special tax provision, he/she is deemed to have sold the crypto assets at the then fair market value by the bequest or the donation, and accordingly is subject to income tax, in the same manner as section 1.1.2(b).[53]

There is no wealth tax in Japan as of the date of this chapter.

(g) Are crypto assets subject to exit tax?

No. While Japan has introduced exit tax by the 2015 tax reform with respect to securities and derivatives, crypto assets are not included in the scope of the exit tax as at the date of this chapter.[54]

(h) Can mining trigger gambling tax?

No. Japan has no gambling tax as of the date of this chapter.

51. Article 183 of Income Tax Act.
52. FAQ, No. 26.
53. FAQ, No. 16.
54. *See* Article 60-2 of Income Tax Act.

1.1.4 *Compliance and Documentation Obligations*

(a) *What documentation requirements exist for taxpayers regarding crypto assets and are there best practices in recordkeeping to support representations made in tax returns?*

There is no documentation requirement that is particular to crypto assets. As a matter of practice, the FAQ states that the computation of taxable income arising from crypto assets should be made in accordance with the 'annual transaction report,' which is supposed to be delivered by the crypto assets dealer to the taxpayer who has an account with that dealer.[55] Also, the NTA has published a 'cryptocurrency calculation worksheet' in an excel spreadsheet format, together with an explanatory leaflet, in order to make it easier for taxpayers to calculate the taxable income, including the acquisition cost, of their crypto assets, based upon the 'annual transaction report.'[56]

The general recordkeeping obligation of the taxpayer of course applies to crypto assets transactions as well.

(b) *What is the evidentiary burden of supporting tax positions when a digital wallet address is lost or shared with other persons?*

As a general principle, the government has the burden of proof to justify a tax assessment, including the amount of the taxable income being assessed. The treatment in the case of the captioned situation is not made clear by the FAQ. However, if the records such as an 'annual transaction report' (*see* section 1.1.4(a) above) as obtained by the NTA through a tax audit indicate that the taxpayer has earned income from crypto assets, but where the taxpayer claims that he/she has lost the digital wallet address, it would most likely be difficult to sustain a position that he/she is not subject to tax only because of that fact. Also, where a taxpayer shares the digital wallet address with other persons and the NTA cannot establish the exact amount of the taxable income to be attributable to the taxpayer, the NTA should be entitled to invoke a provision enabling taxation by presumption as embedded in the applicable tax statute.[57] If this presumption taxation is invoked, the burden of proof is shifted to the taxpayer, so that the taxpayer has to rebut by proving the exact amount of the taxable income to be attributable to the taxpayer.

(c) *Are crypto asset exchanges and wallet providers subject to reporting obligations?*

Yes, if requested from the NTA. The 2019 tax reform has introduced a mechanism where the NTA can request crypto asset exchanges and wallet providers to provide

55. FAQ, No. 13 and No. 14.
56. Available at: https://www.nta.go.jp/information/release/kokuzeicho/2018/faq/index.htm.
57. Article 156 of Income Tax Act; Article 131 of Corporation Tax Act.

information pertaining to the customers and their transactions, for the purpose of tax audit.[58] The advantage of this mechanism is that this can be invoked without identifying the subject taxpayer that may be audited. On the other hand, if tax audit is already ongoing with respect to a particular identified taxpayer, the NTA can conduct a 'third-party audit,' to collect necessary information from a third party that has transactions with the taxpayer.[59]

(d) Are taxpayers holding crypto assets subject to reporting obligations apart from the filing of income tax/capital gains tax returns?

Yes. While this is not a reporting obligation that is particular to crypto assets, an individual resident taxpayer is required to file, together with an income tax return, a 'statement of assets and liabilities,' which shall include, among other information, the type/name and the amount of the crypto assets owned by the taxpayer as of the close of the immediately preceding calendar year.[60] This applies if the taxpayer exceeds certain thresholds in respect of income and assets. This does not apply to corporations.

(e) Are crypto asset exchanges and wallet providers subject to CRS/FATCA reporting?

No. As of the date of this chapter, crypto asset exchanges and wallet providers are not subject to CRS/FATCA reporting. While Japan has participated in the CRS framework, crypto assets are not included in its scope.[61] However, of course, the NTA can collect information from its treaty partners based upon the information exchange provision of an applicable tax treaty.

1.1.5 Civil and Criminal Tax Enforcement

(a) What powers do the tax authorities have to compel the disclosure of information by third parties, such as exchanges or wallet providers, and have these been used in the past?

The 2019 tax reform has introduced the reporting mechanism as discussed in section 1.1.4(c) above. Also, the NTA is entitled to conduct a third-party audit, as discussed in section 1.1.4(c) above. Refusal to unduly comply with these requests is subject to criminal penalty.[62] Information on the actual use of this mechanism in practice is not readily available to the public at large as the former mechanism is rather new;

58. Article 74-7-2 of Act on General Rules on National Taxation (Act No. 66 of 1962, as amended).
59. Article 74-2(1)(iii) and (2)(ii) of Act on General Rules on National Taxation.
60. FAQ, No. 30.
61. No. 37 of 'FAQ on Common Reporting Standard' published by the NTA (available at: https://www.nta.go.jp/taxes/shiraberu/kokusai/crs/pdf/04.pdf, 2019).
62. Article 128 of Act on General Rules on National Taxation.

however, for the future, it should be a powerful tool for the NTA to conduct tax audits and to properly assess tax.

(b) *What measures have the tax authorities undertaken in the past to ensure crypto tax compliance?*

The NTA has undertaken the following measures in particular:

(1) to publish the FAQ;
(2) to establish a practice for crypto assets dealers to deliver an 'annual transaction report' to the taxpayer who has an account with that dealer;
(3) to publish a 'cryptocurrency calculation worksheet' as well as an explanatory leaflet; and
(4) to conduct vigorous tax audits.

(c) *Are the tax authorities cooperating with tax authorities in other jurisdictions on enforcement?*

This is not clear from publicly available information as to crypto assets specifically. However, in general, the NTA is vigorous in cooperating with tax authorities in other jurisdictions, particularly through information exchanges.[63]

63. *See* 'Summary of Result of Information Exchanges through Tax Treaties for Business year 2018' published by the NTA (available at: https://www.nta.go.jp/information/release/kokuzeicho/2019/joho_kokan/pdf/joho_kokan.pdf, 2019).

Luxembourg

Johan Leonard & Roberto de Castro Mendonça

1. COUNTRY GUIDES

1.1 Luxembourg

1.1.1 Applicable Tax Law, Guidance, and Case Law

(a) Which laws, regulations, and other administrative guidance exist dealing with crypto assets?

Luxembourg has been one of the leading nations in attempting to regulate the cryptocurrency market.

In 2014, the Luxembourg Financial Sector Supervisory Commission (*Commission de Surveillance du Secteur Financier*, CSSF) issued an official *communiqué on virtual currencies,*[1] recalling the principle that the performance of activities in the Luxembourg financial sector is subject to the prior authorization of the Minister of Finance and to the CSSF's prudential supervision. From a Luxembourg tax standpoint, there is still no legal provision specifically mentioning or covering crypto assets in Luxembourg.

However, the Luxembourg tax authorities released the following two circulars aimed at clarifying the direct tax and VAT treatment applicable to crypto assets:

(i) Circular no. 14/5 - 99/3 - 99bis/3 of 26 July 2018, issued by the *Administration des Contributions Directes* (the 'Income Tax Circular on Virtual Currency').

The Income Tax Circular on Virtual Currency states that a cryptocurrency is not a currency, as its value is not monitored by any central bank. It is therefore an intangible

1. The Bitcoin *press release* is available on the official website of the CSSF: https://www.cssf.lu/fileadmin/files/Publications/Newsletter/Newsletter_2014/newsletter157eng.pdf.

asset for direct tax purposes, meaning that the Luxembourg tax authorities will not allow a company to draw up its financial statements or file its tax return in cryptocurrencies.[2] The Income Tax Circular on Virtual Currency further clarifies that if a cryptocurrency is used as a form of payment, this should not affect the nature of the income.[3]

(ii) Circular no. 787 dated 11 June 2018 issued by the *Administration de l'Enregistrement, des Domaines et de la TVA* (Luxembourg VAT authorities)[4] (the '**VAT Circular on Virtual Currencies**').

The VAT Circular on Virtual Currencies states that the VAT exemption under the VAT Directive,[5] which applies to transactions (including negotiation) concerning currency used as legal tender, is extended to virtual currencies to the extent that they are regarded as a method of payment and are accepted for this purpose by some operators. The VAT Circular on Virtual Currencies closely follows the judgment rendered by the Court of Justice of the European Union (CJEU) in *Skatteverket v. David Hedqvist*.[6]

(b) Which court cases exist dealing with crypto assets?

There is currently no known court case dealing with the taxation of crypto assets in Luxembourg.

1.1.2 Income and Capital Gains Taxes

(a) How are crypto assets classified for income and capital gains tax purposes?

The Luxembourg tax authorities consider that cryptocurrencies do not qualify as legal currencies in Luxembourg because their values are not monitored by a central bank. Therefore, they are treated as intangible assets for the purposes of income tax, business tax, and net wealth tax.[7]

It should be kept in mind that the potential evolution of the financial and legal status of crypto assets could ultimately affect the applicable tax framework.

2. Circular No. 14/5 – 99/3 – 99bis/3 dated 26 Jul. 2018, p. 1, paragraph 2. The Income Tax Circular on Virtual Currency is available at https://impotsdirects.public.lu/dam-assets/fr/legislation/legi18/circulaireLIR14-5-99-3-99bis-3du26072018.pdf.
3. Circular No. 14/5 – 99/3 – 99bis/3, dated 26 Jul. 2018, p. 2, paragraph 1.
4. Circular No. 787, dated 11 Jun. 2018, available at http://www.aed.public.lu/actualites/2018/06/Circulaire-787/Circulaires_787.pdf.
5. *Cf.* Council Directive 2006/112/EC of 28 Nov. 2006 on the common system of value added tax.
6. *Cf.* Case C-264/14, dated 22 Oct. 2015.
7. *Cf.* Circular No. 787, dated 11 Jun. 2018, p. 1.

(b) What are the income/capital gains tax consequences of selling crypto assets against fiat currency?

From a Luxembourg tax point of view, we should distinguish between transactions undertaken by a company and those performed by an individual.

Any gain realized on crypto assets by a Luxembourg company should be classified as commercial income and be subject to the usual corporate income tax scheme applicable.

For corporate taxpayers, Luxembourg corporate income tax and municipal business tax should be due on income derived from such crypto assets, after the deduction of related, deductible expenses. Net wealth tax would also apply on the value of the crypto assets held by a corporate taxpayer. In that context, the cryptocurrencies should be valued in accordance with the provisions of the *Bewertungsgesetz* (Luxembourg Evaluation Law), *i.e.*, at their fair market value.

Furthermore, general accounting principles apply to crypto assets with such assets being characterized as intangible assets. All products, income, operating costs, special costs, and exceptional costs expressed in crypto assets must be converted into Euro or another currency for which the European Central Bank publishes an exchange rate to the Euro. The conversion can be based on the daily rate published by an exchange platform approved by the Luxembourg CSSF, and the exchange rate that would be considered is the one applicable when the transactions or the events occur. Therefore, income should be converted at the rate published on the day when the income is put at the disposal of the taxpayer and at the costs based on the rate published on the day when they are incurred.

The gain should correspond to the positive difference between the sales price and the book value of the assets.

For individuals, commercial activities and those activities relating to the management of the individual's private wealth should always be distinguished on a case-by-case basis. The reason for this is that, for Luxembourg tax purposes, income derived by an individual from cryptocurrencies may constitute (i) commercial income or (ii) 'miscellaneous' income.

In that regard, Article 14 of the Luxembourg Income Tax Law provides that the income could be deemed as commercial income if the activity generating the income:

- is performed with a certain independence;
- is permanent;
- is carried out with the intent to realize profits; and
- involves participation in the general economic life.

As per the Income Tax Circular on Virtual Currency, the below additional criteria can be used to identify a business activity in the specific context of income generated in relation to crypto assets:[8]

8. Circular No. 14/5 – 99/3 – 99bis/3, dated 26 Jul. 2018, p. 2, paragraph 4.

- the business has dedicated premises or is an organization dedicated to virtual currency transactions;
- the business uses debt to finance its activities;
- the business involves a frequent rotation of virtual currency stock;
- the business involves the conducting of trading activities on behalf of third parties.

Commercial income is taxable on a net basis, which means that operational costs such as electricity consumed for mining the crypto assets or conversion costs on exchange platforms are deductible. Moreover, IT infrastructure can be amortized. Under Article 45 of the Luxembourg Income Tax Law, the condition for costs to be deductible is that they must be incurred exclusively to conduct the business activity.[9]

If the activities carried out fall under the scope of management of the individual's private wealth, the income derived from virtual currencies from such activities could fall under the miscellaneous income category (Article 99 of the Luxembourg Income Tax Law).[10]

In such a scenario, any gain or loss from the exchange of virtual currencies into other virtual or real currencies, or from the payment of a transaction (notably the purchase of goods or services), is considered a taxable capital gain or loss according to Article 99 of the Luxembourg Income Tax Law provided that the operation occurs within six months from the acquisition of the virtual currency. If the aggregate amount of these taxable gains is below EUR 500 during the tax year, they would not be subject to taxation.[11] Gains from currency sales occurring after more than six months from the acquisition should not be taxable either.

The burden of proof of the six-month holding period lies on the taxpayer. To meet that requirement, and in line with paragraph 171 of the Luxembourg General Tax Law,[12] the taxpayer must have coherent and uninterrupted documentation that evidences the date of acquisition or creation of the crypto asset and the costs relating to it.[13]

If the taxpayer cannot prove that it held the realized crypto asset for less than six months, the original acquisition price must be established. If the exact acquisition price of the realized crypto asset is difficult or impossible to prove due to specific circumstances, the acquisition price can be set using the weighted-average-price method. By contrast, the 'first-in, first-out' method and the 'last-in, first-out' method will not be accepted by the Luxembourg tax authorities.

Regardless of whether the income is characterized as commercial income or miscellaneous income, it should be determined using the exchange rates of the day during which the gain/expense occurred.

9. Circular No. 14/5 - 99/3 - 99bis/3, dated 26 Jul. 2018, p. 3, paragraph 3.
10. Circular No. 14/5 - 99/3 - 99bis/3, dated 26 Jul. 2018, p. 3, paragraph 4.
11. Circular No. 14/5 - 99/3 - 99bis/3, dated 26 Jul. 2018, p. 3, paragraph 6.
12. *Loi Générale des Impôts*, dated 22 May 1931, as amended.
13. Circular No. 14/5 - 99/3 - 99bis/3, dated 26 Jul. 2018, p. 4, paragraph 1.

(c) *What are the income/capital gains tax consequences of exchanging crypto assets against other crypto assets?*

As a rule, exchange of goods should be treated as a sale. Indeed, the Income Tax Circular on Virtual Currency states that exchanging a crypto asset for another should be regarded as a transfer at fair market value of the asset being transferred, followed by the acquisition of the asset received in exchange.

The related capital gain, to the extent taxable (*see* section 1.1.2(b) above), should thus be computed as being the difference between the estimated fair market value (*valeur estimée de réalisation*) of the crypto assets received and the book value (or, for an individual, the acquisition value) of the crypto assets being sold.

(d) *If a distinction is made between business assets and non-business assets, when does trading in crypto assets lead to a trade or business?*

As outlined above under section 1.1.2(b), income derived from the sale of crypto assets is taxable if it falls under the commercial income category or the miscellaneous income category.

Under Article 14 of the Luxembourg Income Tax Law, as a rule, income qualifies as commercial income if it is generated from an independent activity exercised permanently with a view to making profits and forming a participation in the general economic life.

The Income Tax Circular on Virtual Currency specifically states that these conditions are regularly met for cryptocurrency mining, the running of a cryptocurrencies exchange platform, or the running of a cryptocurrency ATM.[14]

As per the Income Tax Circular on Virtual Currency, the below additional criteria can be used to identify a business activity in the specific context of income generated in relation to crypto assets:[15]

- the business has dedicated premises or is an organization dedicated to virtual currency transactions;
- the business uses debt to finance its activities;
- the business involves a frequent rotation of virtual currency stock;
- the business involves the conducting of trading activities on behalf of third parties.

The Income Tax Circular on Virtual Currency further states that if the taxpayer takes the form of a collective entity such as a stock company, income generated by this entity should always qualify as commercial income.

14. Circular No. 14/5 – 99/3 – 99bis/3, dated 26 Jul. 2018, p. 1, paragraph 4.
15. Circular No. 14/5 – 99/3 – 99bis/3, dated 26 Jul. 2018, p. 2, paragraph 4.

(e) *What are the income/capital gains tax consequences for an employee receiving wages or salaries in crypto assets?*

Using a cryptocurrency to pay wages or salaries should have no consequence on the tax nature of the income, which will remain taxable as professional income. The income should be converted into euros at the time when the income is paid.

(f) *What are the income/capital gains tax consequences for a merchant receiving payment in crypto assets?*

Using a cryptocurrency to pay an invoice should have no consequence on the tax nature of the income, which will remain taxable as commercial income. The amount received should be converted into euros at the time when the income is paid.

(g) *What are the income/capital gains tax consequences of a loss of crypto assets?*

The loss of crypto assets should be accounted for as any loss on usual assets and thus deductible for the purposes of computation of profits in case of a commercial activity.

(h) *What are the income/capital gains tax consequences of a loss in value of crypto assets?*

Crypto assets are treated as intangible assets. A loss in value must therefore be reflected in the financial statements of the company provided that it is genuine and long lasting.

As for individuals, a loss in value of crypto assets should not have tax consequences until it is realized. The Circular on Virtual Currency confirms that losses realized within six months should enter the computation of the speculative income of a given year. Conversely, if the loss is realized after that six-month period, it should not be taken into account.

(i) *What are the income/capital gains tax consequences of forks of crypto assets?*

The Luxembourg tax authorities have not taken a specific position on blockchain forks, i.e., cases in which a blockchain splits into two blockchains. It would be reasonable to argue that the value of the new crypto assets derives from the crypto assets that were held initially.

Therefore, a crypto assets fork should not be considered a taxable event, and, in our view, the value of the initial asset should be reasonably split between the two new assets.

(j) What are the income/capital gains tax consequences of airdrops of crypto assets and are the tax consequences different if the airdropped tokens are unwanted?

Through the application of the general principles, we would consider that, if the beneficiary is a company, the asset received would be added to its balance sheet and thus represent a gain.

As for individuals, we understand that the typical airdrop should not trigger taxation for the individual, although, in our view, it would not be unreasonable to assume that a subsequent speculative gain on the asset could be subject to tax.

(k) What are the income/capital gains tax consequences of (solo, pool, and cloud) mining?

In the absence of specific guidance, no difference is to be made between solo, pool, or cloud mining. A case-by-case analysis based on the relevant facts and circumstances should be performed to determine whether the activity qualifies as a business activity within the meaning of Article 14 of the Luxembourg Income Tax Law. If it qualifies as a business activity, the related income would be subject to income taxation.

(l) What are the income/capital gains tax consequences of staking crypto assets?

We understand that proof of stake is a consensus mechanism (an alternative to proof of work) whereby transactions are validated by persons who have high holdings of this respective crypto asset and would therefore suffer the greatest damage from a blockchain with incorrect entries.

Considering that staking is deemed equivalent to mining, but with hardly any use of resources and much more passive in appearance, we consider that the general rules applicable to the taxation of mining activities should apply. There is no specific guidance given by the Luxembourg tax authorities on this.

(m) What are the income/capital gains tax consequences of an indirect investment in crypto assets?

As regards the tax treatment of an investment that a Luxembourg taxpayer has made into a vehicle holding crypto assets, this would depend on the intermediary vehicle itself and the status of the taxpayer.

For instance, a Luxembourg individual who holds shares in a Luxembourg taxable company that holds the crypto assets will be subject to the usual tax system that applies to individuals on dividends, liquidation proceeds, and capital gains in relation to its participation interest.

Should the crypto assets be held through a Luxembourg transparent entity, the taxpayer should be deemed to hold the underlying crypto assets directly and be subject to tax (as the case may be) on its portion of the underlying income.

(n) How is income from crypto assets to be treated under double tax treaty law?

The Luxembourg tax authorities have not given any guidance regarding the treatment of crypto assets under double tax treaties entered into by Luxembourg. Income derived from cryptocurrencies should therefore be analysed according to the allocation rules under the OECD Model Convention.

However, Article 13(5) of the OECD Model Convention (which Luxembourg follows closely) provides that gains from the alienation of any property, other than the properties referred to in other paragraphs, are taxable only in the state of residence of the beneficiary/recipient, meaning that Luxembourg may tax a resident investor that obtains income from the disposition of cryptocurrencies in another contracting jurisdiction.

(o) What are the income/capital gains tax consequences of selling crypto assets in an ICO/STO/IEO?

The Luxembourg tax system does not currently provide a clear delineation of the tax treatment of these operations. Additionally, unlike IPOs, ICOs are not subject to specific rules and regulations, so their tax treatment remains ambiguous. A case-by-case analysis is thus to be performed, depending on the underlying transaction and qualification of the cryptocurrency. For instance, for tokens, one should argue the tax implications depending on its nature, *i.e.*, depending on whether it is a utility token, debt token, or equity token.

1.1.3 Other Taxes

(a) What are the value added tax/sales tax consequences of selling crypto assets?

The Luxembourg tax authorities have followed the CJEU's position in the *Hedqvist*[16] case through the issuance of the VAT Circular on Virtual Currencies.[17]

The question, which was referred to the CJEU for a preliminary ruling, was whether the buying and selling of bitcoins for a traditional currency would be exempt from VAT under the currency exemption of Article 135(1)(e) of the VAT Directive.[18]

16. *Cf.* Case C-264/14, dated 22 Oct. 2015.
17. *Cf.* http://www.aed.public.lu/actualites/2018/06/Circulaire-787/Circulaires_787.pdf.
18. Article 135(1)(e) provides that 'transactions, including negotiation, concerning currency, bank notes and coins used as legal tender, with the exception of collectors' items, that is to say, gold,

The CJEU held that no supply of bitcoins was to be assumed, but rather a service of exchange. Furthermore, assuming that the crypto assets (i) have been accepted by the parties concerned as an alternative means of payment to legal tender and (ii) that they do not serve any purpose other than use as means of payment, the transaction falls within the scope of the exemption of Article 135(1)(e), of the VAT Directive 2006/112/EC, for transactions relating to foreign exchange, banknotes, and coins.

(b) Are payments in crypto assets subject to withholding taxes?

To answer this question, one should consider the nature of the underlying payment itself and not the means used to satisfy the payment (i.e., through the transfer of crypto assets). For instance, a payment of interest to a Luxembourg resident individual falling within the scope of the Luxembourg law of 21 June 2005, as amended, should be subject to withholding tax, regardless of whether the interest is actually paid using crypto assets.

(c) Does payment of compensation in crypto assets give rise to payroll tax consequences?

There is no specific guidance on this subject. Therefore, the general payroll tax framework applies.

As a rule, a Luxembourg employer is to withhold income tax and social security contributions from the salary paid to its employee and is responsible to make the related payments to the Luxembourg tax authorities and the Luxembourg social security organism (*Centre commun de la sécurité sociale*). The compensation received should be converted into Euro at the time when the compensation is paid.

(d) Do transactions with crypto assets trigger any transfer taxes?

In Luxembourg, some transactions may be subject to transfer taxes or registration duties at either a fixed rate or proportional rate, depending on the underlying transactions.

To the extent that the underlying transaction is subject to transfer taxes/registration duties, they will continue to be due, regardless of whether crypto assets were used for the payment.

In relation to the transfer of crypto assets, e.g., sale of crypto assets for fiat money, there is no specific provision that would impose transfer taxes or registration duties.

---

silver or other metal coins or bank notes which are not normally used as legal tender or coins of numismatic interest' may be VAT exempted by Member States. *Cf.* Council Directive 2006/112/EC of 28 Nov. 2006 on the common system of value added tax.

(e) Are firms operating in the crypto space subject to digital service taxes?

As of the time of writing, Luxembourg still has not implemented a digital service tax.

(f) Are crypto assets subject to gift, inheritance, estate, or wealth taxes?

Luxembourg inheritance and gift tax provisions do not mention crypto assets, and there are no official guidelines issued by any relevant Luxembourg authority on this specific topic.

However, there are arguments for substantiating that crypto assets should, in principle, be considered movable and intangible goods for purposes of inheritance and gift taxes.

Indirect taxes apply to inheritances and gifts and are levied by the *Administration de l'Enregistrement, des Domaines et de la TVA*.

Inheritance taxes are levied on the entire estate bequeathed by an inhabitant of the Grand-Duchy of Luxembourg at the time of his/her death, except real estate located abroad and movable goods located abroad, which are taxed based on the citizenship of the deceased. A person is considered a Luxembourg inhabitant, and thus liable for inheritance tax, if he/she has a domicile and the centre of their activities there. The residence of the heirs has no impact on inheritance taxes due in Luxembourg.

Regarding the inheritance tax rates, each beneficiary is taxed separately based on the value of the net share attributed to them, less personal allowances. It should be noted that the tax rates differ depending on the degree of the relationship between the heir and the deceased.

Tax is levied on gifts made during the individual's lifetime (i.e., *inter vivos* gifts). Gifts that are not required to be made in writing (e.g., movable assets transferred by hand delivery or *dons manuels*) are generally accepted without notarial deed and thus without registration. For these types of gifts, no tax is due except if the donor dies within the calendar year. If the latter occurs, the value of the gift is then reintegrated into the transferred estate for calculating the inheritance tax).

Luxembourg companies are subject to an annual net wealth tax calculated on their 'unitary value' (i.e., their net asset value as adjusted for net wealth tax purposes, which should include the crypto assets they hold).

(g) Are crypto assets subject to exit tax?

Luxembourg tax law provides for an exit tax, but there is no specific guidance on it in relation to crypto assets. The general provisions should therefore apply.

Following the implementation of the EU Anti-Tax Avoidance Directive 1 (ATAD 1) into Luxembourg legislation,[19] the scope of Article 38 of the Luxembourg Income

19. *Loi transposant la directive (UE) 2016/1164 du Conseil du 12 juillet 2016 établissant des règles pour lutter contre les pratiques d'évasion fiscale qui ont une incidence directe sur le fonctionnement du marché intérieur*, dated 21 Dec. 2018.

Tax Law relating to transfers out of Luxembourg has been extended to ensure that, in specific cases, taxpayers in Luxembourg are taxed on the transfer of assets (e.g. assets that are part of an enterprise or a permanent establishment, or isolated assets as part of the net-invested assets) from Luxembourg to any other jurisdiction in an amount equal to the fair market value of the transferred assets at the date of exit, less their tax value.

Furthermore, Article 127 of the General Tax Law provides that the payment of Luxembourg tax levied on a transfer of assets/residence outside the country may be made in instalments over five years, although it is limited to cases in which the transfer is made to a country within the EU or some countries of the European Economic Area. Luxembourg does not impose interest on the deferred payments or require a guarantee to benefit from the deferral.

(h) Can mining trigger gambling tax?

Mining activity should not trigger gambling tax in Luxembourg.[20]

1.1.4 Compliance and Documentation Obligations

(a) What documentation requirements exist for taxpayers regarding crypto assets and are there best practices in recordkeeping to support representations made in tax returns?

The Luxembourg tax authorities have mentioned on the Income Tax Circular on Virtual Currency the importance of keeping evidence of transaction records, holding periods and expenses/costs linked to crypto assets since the burden of proving virtual transactions remains the individual taxpayers' responsibility.[21]

Apart from these recommendations, there are no specific documentation requirements for taxpayers holding crypto assets. Therefore, taxpayers must comply with the general documentation requirements.

(b) What is the evidentiary burden of supporting tax positions when a digital wallet address is lost or shared with other persons?

We understand that a taxpayer who has lost private keys and can no longer dispose of certain crypto assets will have the duty to explain to the tax authorities what his or her usual key management practice is and what went wrong in the specific case at hand.

The tax authorities will then have to consider whether the statement made by the taxpayer seems truthful, and they may investigate such circumstances.

20. According to, *inter alia*, the *Loi relative à l'exploitation des jeux de hasard et des paris relatifs aux épreuves sportives*, dated 20 Apr. 1977.
21. Circular No. 14/5 - 99/3 - 99bis/3, dated 26 Jul. 2018, paragraph 1.

(c) Are crypto asset exchanges and wallet providers subject to reporting obligations?

Under Luxembourg domestic tax law, crypto asset exchanges and wallet providers are not subject to any periodic reporting obligations towards the tax authorities regarding their customers.

(d) Are taxpayers holding crypto assets subject to reporting obligations apart from the filing of income tax/capital gains tax returns?

Under Luxembourg domestic tax law, taxpayers holding crypto assets are not subject to any reporting obligations towards the tax authorities apart from the filing of income tax returns.

(e) Are crypto asset exchanges and wallet providers subject to CRS/FATCA reporting?

The Luxembourg tax authorities have not issued any guidance on whether operators of crypto exchanges or providers of crypto wallets must annually report their customers' data under CRS[22]/FATCA.[23]

The definition of 'financial asset' under FATCA and CRS[24] is broad and could possibly cover crypto assets. However, given there are no guidelines on this topic, the reporting remains subject to future instructions and rules on the subject.

---

22. *Loi concernant l'échange automatique de renseignements relatifs aux comptes financiers en matière fiscale et portant transposition de la directive 2014/107/UE du Conseil du 9 décembre 2014*, dated 18 Dec. 2015.
23. The FATCA relevant provisions were introduced in Luxembourg by the *Loi portant approbation de l'Accord entre le Gouvernement du Grand-Duché de Luxembourg et le Gouvernement des Etats-Unis d'Amérique en vue d'améliorer le respect des obligations fiscales à l'échelle internationale et relatif aux dispositions des Etats-Unis d'Amérique concernant l'échange d'informations communément appelées le Foreign Account Tax Compliance Act*, dated 24 Jul. 2014.
24. The CRS defines a financial asset to include a 'security (for example, a share of stock in a corporation; partnership or beneficial ownership interest in a widely held or publicly traded partnership or trust; note, bond, debenture, or other evidence of indebtedness), partnership interest, commodity, swap (for example, interest rate swaps, currency swaps, basis swaps, interest rate caps, interest rate floors, commodity swaps, equity swaps, equity index swaps, and similar agreements), Insurance Contract or Annuity Contract, or any interest (including a futures or forward contract or option) in a security, partnership interest, commodity, swap, Insurance Contract, or Annuity Contract.' The original text is available at https://eur-lex.europa.eu/legal-content/EN/TXT/PDF/?uri=CELEX:32014L0107&from=FRl (p. 17).

1.1.5 *Civil and Criminal Tax Enforcement*

(a) What powers do the tax authorities have to compel the disclosure of information by third parties, such as exchanges or wallet providers, and have these been used in the past?

The Luxembourg tax authorities may request any information that they consider to be relevant to enforcing tax compliance, even if it does not concern that person's own tax liability. Such requests have to be complied with, and the information provided must be truthful to the best of that person's knowledge and belief.

The obligation to provide information includes the obligation to submit, or to allow the inspection of, written documents that are relevant to determining tax claims.

(b) What measures have the tax authorities undertaken in the past to ensure crypto tax compliance?

Apart from the administrative guidance, there are no known measures that the Luxembourg tax authorities have specifically implemented in the past regarding the application of existing tax law provisions to cryptocurrencies.

(c) Are the tax authorities cooperating with tax authorities in other jurisdictions on enforcement?

The Luxembourg tax authorities have several agreements with other countries regarding the exchange of information, such as the provisions on the vast network of Luxembourg tax treaties (which have been consistently updated in order to accommodate the revamped provisions on the exchange of information), and there are also EU law provisions on the subject matter.

Luxembourg has also ratified the OECD/Council of Europe Convention on Mutual Administrative Assistance in Tax Matters,[25] which similarly gives the Luxembourg tax authorities access to information held abroad. It is currently not public knowledge whether the Luxembourg tax authorities are cooperating with tax authorities in other jurisdictions on enforcement and whether they have made use of the various instruments mentioned above in respect of crypto asset holdings of taxpayers.

In light of the above, and although we are not aware of any specific requests or procedures in cooperation with other tax authorities, we understand that there are several systems in place that provide for such mutual assistance also within the context of crypto assets.

25. The Convention on Mutual Administrative Assistance in Tax Matters was developed jointly by the OECD and the Council of Europe in 1988 and amended by Protocol in 2010. The Convention is the most comprehensive multilateral instrument available for all forms of tax cooperation to tackle tax evasion and avoidance. The original text is available at https://read.oecd-ilibrary.org/taxation/the-multilateral-convention-on-mutual-administrative-assistance-in-tax-matters_9789264115606-en#page1.

Malta

Nicholas Warren & Reuben Buttigieg

1. COUNTRY GUIDES

1.1 Malta

1.1.1 Applicable Tax Law, Guidance, and Case Law

As a general comment, please note that to date there are no court cases in relation to crypto assets and that no licence has been issued to a crypto operator in Malta.

(a) Which laws, regulations, and other administrative guidance exist dealing with crypto assets?

On 1 November 2018 the Maltese Government published and enacted the Virtual Financial Assets Act (VFA Act) (Chapter 590 to the Laws of Malta)[1] and the Innovative Technology Arrangements and Services Act (ITAS) (Chapter 592).[2] Subsequently, the Virtual Financial Assets (VFA) Regulations came into force through Subsidiary Legislation, Legal Notice 357 of 2018.

Following that the Maltese Commissioner for Revenue (CfR), issued its guidelines on the income tax, stamp duty, and VAT in relation to Distributed Ledger Transaction (DLT) assets.[3] These guidelines have been issued under Article 96(2) of the Income Tax Act.

The VFA Act seeks to provide regulation and investor protection through a variety of obligations, assurances, and guidelines. One particular part of the VFA Act pertains to Initial VFA Offerings, therefore covering *inter alia* Initial Coin Offerings

1. Act XXX of 2018.
2. Act XXXIII of 2018.
3. https://cfr.gov.mt/en/inlandrevenue/legal-technical/Documents/Guidelines%20-DLTs%20Income%20tax.pdf.

(ICOs) and other token offerings. Initial Exchange Offerings (IEOs) and Initial DEX Offerings may also be captured under the VFA Act, but one would also need to refer to traditional financial services legislation as may be necessary, based on the outcome of the financial instrument test. Under the new rules, companies operating in the sphere of virtual financial assets may be required to apply for a licence with the Malta Financial Services Authority, as well as adhere to a number of stipulations regarding their whitepaper, marketing materials, and civil liabilities. They are also required to implement fully compliant Know Your Customer (KYC)/Anti-Money Laundering (AML) checks that are applied to all parties deemed necessary by both local, and EU law.

Similarly, the ITAS Act is intended to be an extension to the Malta Digital Innovation Authority Act (MDIA) and the VFA Act. The ITAS act provides the definitions for 'Innovation Technology Arrangement' (UTA) and 'Innovative Technology Services' (ITS) which are subject to eligibility under the Malta Digital Innovation Authority rulings, which are not tax rulings.

(b) Which court cases exist dealing with crypto assets?

There are no court cases dealing with crypto assets. There is, however, a decision of the European Court of Justice (ECJ) dealing with value added tax in relation to bitcoins.[4]

1.1.2 Income and Capital Gains Taxes

(a) How are crypto assets classified for income and capital gains purposes?

The CfR has classified DLT assets into two categories. The first category is '**Coins**', whereby the CfR determined that coins refer to those DLT assets, that do not have the characteristics of a security and that have no connection with any project or equity in the issuer, and whose utility, value or application is in no way directly related to the redemption of goods or services. The CfR deems DLT assets as cryptocurrencies that are designed to be used as a means of payment or a medium of exchange, or else as a store of value. The CfR deems coins to functionally constitute the cryptographic equivalent of fiat currencies.

The second category is '**Tokens**' which are sub-categorized into two: ***Financial Tokens*** and ***Utility Tokens***.

In respect of Financial Tokens, the CfR deems such DLT assets as presenting qualities which are similar to those presented by equities, debentures, units in collective investment schemes, or derivatives including financial instruments which are referred to in the crypto world as security, asset, or asset-backed tokens. The CfR understands that such tokens would be analogous to equities, debentures, units in collective investment schemes, or derivatives including financial instruments, where such instruments would grant rights to dividends in a similar fashion or alternatively

4. ECJ, 22 Oct. 2015, C-264/14, *Hedqvist*; *cf.* section 1.1.3(a) below.

could grant rewards based on performance, voting rights, or represent ownership or rights in assets or a combination of both.

The CfR deems Utility Tokens as DLT assets, whose utility, value or application is restricted solely to the acquisition of goods or services either solely within the DLT platform or in relation to which they are issued with a limited network of DLT platforms. This definition reflects the understanding of the Malta Financial Services Authority. The CfR includes under the term Utility Token all other DLT assets that are tokens whose utility is restricted solely to the acquisition of goods or services, whether or not listed, may be transferred on a peer-to-peer basis or converted into another type of DLT asset, but only until such time as it is so converted.

The CfR also looks at hybrid tokens and states that the tax treatment should be dependent on the nature of the token at that particular moment in time. If the intention of such token is that of a Utility Token, then it needs to be treated as such. Nonetheless the CfR also leaves room for interpretation, wherein its guidelines state that the tax treatment of any type of DLT asset will ultimately by determined not by its categorization but on the purpose for, and the context in, which such DLT asset is used.

(b) *What are the income/capital gains tax consequences for selling crypto assets against fiat current?*

All transactions need to be analysed by reference to the nature of the activity, the status of the parties and the specific facts and circumstances of the particular case.

In the case of coins sold against fiat currency, the income tax treatment is the same as any other sale transaction between any other currencies. The determinative factor for tax purposes is not the categorization of the type of asset but the purpose and context in which it is used. In order to arrive at the value of income subject to tax, one needs to establish the market value of the crypto asset and convert it into fiat.

In the case of a transfer of Financial or Utility Tokens, one needs to analyse if the transfer is of a trading or capital nature. In the case of a trading transaction, tax will be charged as usual by adding the net proceeds (i.e., sales amounts less cost of acquisition of the tokens) from this transaction with all the trading profits for the year.

In the case of Financial Tokens which are of a non-trading nature, one needs to check if the transaction falls under the capital gains rules under Article 5 of the Income Tax Act. The analysis needs to consider whether the tokens meet the definition of securities. Transfers of tokens which do not fall within the definition of securities, fall outside the scope of the tax on capital gains and may not be taxed.

(c) *What are the income/capital gains tax consequences of exchanging crypto assets against other crypto assets?*

The tax consequences for the exchange of one asset to another depend on the market value of the assets in question and the capital gain made on such exchange. The decisive factor will depend on the market value of both assets. Taxable income will be derived on the difference on the gains made on the assets exchanged by both parties respectively. The Revenue in Malta will require the fair market value (FMV) of both transactions and then calculate the tax based on the difference between the two. Thus, by way of example, if Party A trades an item for EUR 100.00 when this was purchased for EUR 90.00, the taxable amount is based on the difference of EUR 10.00. If Party B is trading with Party A an item which cost EUR 80.00 and is traded at EUR 95.00 then the taxable amount is calculated on the EUR 15.00. The trading price is determined from the going market rate, i.e., the FMV.

One also needs to assess if this transaction falls under the provisions of the capital gains rules of Article 5 of the Income Tax Act. As an example, transfers of convertible tokens which would not be issued as a Financial Token at issue date do not fall under the capital gain rules unless they are converted into securities.

(d) If a distinction is made between business assets and non-business assets, when does trading in crypto assets lead to a trade or business?

In accordance with the Guidelines on the Income Tax Treatment of Transactions or arrangements involving DLT Assets ('Guidelines'),[5] an activity which is considered to be an ordinary course of business would lead to trading in crypto assets to be a business. The trading/non-trading nature of a transaction may not always be immediately evident. The badges of trade tests may need to be used for this purpose.

(e) What are the income/capital gains tax consequences for an employee receiving wages or salaries in crypto assets?

When a payment is made or received in a cryptocurrency, such payment is deemed to be treated as a payment in any other currency, and this would therefore mean that it is subject to income tax as any other income. Income tax is Malta is levied on a monthly basis, and the level of income tax levied in a particular month would be the fiat equivalent of the crypto assets received as payment in that particular month.

(f) What are the income/capital gains tax consequences for a merchant receiving payment in crypto assets?

When a merchant is accepting payment for goods or services in the form of cryptocurrencies, for Maltese Income Tax purposes, there is no difference to when the revenue is recognized or the manner in which taxable profits are calculated. The same principle as tax on salaries would apply.

5. Guidelines on the Income Tax Treatment of Transactions or arrangements involved DLT Assets.

(g) *What are the income/capital gains tax consequences of a loss of crypto assets?*

There are two ways of losing crypto assets. The first scenario is through theft which can happen from hacking of system through cyberattack. In such a case, if the blockchain does not manage to recoup the stolen bitcoins, a loss needs to be declared. The way the loss is treated will depend on the original recognition of such crypto asset. Reference to the badges of trade would be necessary, thus, if capital good, it is against capital losses, if trading nature then against trading profits.

In the second scenario, one can lose the key to access the system; therefore, although the bitcoins would still remain on the blockchain, without having access to these assets, one can never redeem them to realize a profit or loss. In such a case, one also needs to show a loss and write-off the tokens from assets. For Malta, a taxable person is treated equally the same being it an individual or company. The principles mentioned in the first scenario could also apply.

It must be noted that the loss is only deductible for Income Tax if one demonstrates that a reasonable effort was made to recoup such assets.

(h) *What are the income/capital gains tax consequences of a loss in value of crypto assets?*

In terms of Maltese Income Tax law, a distinction is made between realized and unrealized gains and/or losses. In relation to crypto assets such distinction does not exist and only realized losses are taken into consideration. A realized loss would apply when such crypto asset is either converted into fiat or sold.

(i) *What are the income/capital gains tax consequences of forks of crypto assets?*

A fork in a crypto asset occurs when parties within the DLT network are not in agreement, and this results in a split of such DLT network, creating alternative chains, such as with Ethereum, which when forked ended up with Ethereum and Ethereum Classic. Forks can form in two ways – a soft fork or a hard fork. A soft fork is a software update which would still be compatible with the previous version. A hard fork is when a software update is not backwards compatible, therefore all blocks need to follow the new rules to remain valid.

When a hard fork occurs, the person who held the original tokens has now given up such tokens in exchange for the new tokens. The event would need to be analysed to determine whether it is an event of a trading nature or not. The Maltese Income Tax guidelines are silent in this respect.

Upon the transfer to the new version of the blockchain, each crypto asset would be worth more or less, depending on the market value of the new tokens. Unless there is a transfer of ownership after the fork no income can be realized and therefore is not subject to tax.

The use of final withholding taxes in relation to crypto assets in terms of Maltese law is scarce and therefore tax is charged on capital gains from income derived from the trade.

If a profit is realized from the subsequent sale of the asset, then tax is to be paid as it would be similar to trading income. If tokens are held as an investment, then one needs to analyse if capital gains tax is triggered. In the event of a soft fork, this change does not create a new cryptocurrency, therefore no profit or loss would be realized. Apart from the trigger of direct taxation, stamp duty will also be triggered and the respective guidelines should be followed with respect to duty on transfer of assets.

(j) What are the income/capital gains tax consequences of airdrops of crypto assets and are the tax consequences different if the airdropped tokens are unwanted?

Airdrops are a distribution of a cryptocurrency for free with the intention of gaining attention and attracting new followers to widen the user base of such crypto asset. While the concept of airdrops is not mentioned in the guidelines issued by the CfR, by analogy an airdrop is somewhat similar to the issue of bonus shares, whereby an individual is given shares as a bonus. From a Maltese perspective, bonus shares are treated in the same manner as dividends. In terms of the Maltese Income Tax Act, since the entity would be distributing crypto assets to its users, upon allocating such, the entity should send to the token holder a statement showing the gross tokens, the tax paid on behalf of the token holder and the net amount involved in the allocation of the airdropped tokens. Malta applies the full imputation system, and the tax charged shall be settled by the entity performing the airdrop. The recipient will receive the net allocation.

(k) What are the income/capital gains tax consequences of (solo, pool, and cloud) mining?

For Income Tax purposes, the CfR guidelines mention that gains or profits from the mining of cryptocurrencies should be considered as income and subject to income tax. The local guidelines do not distinguish between the three different ways of mining. Solo mining occurs when an individual does all the mining work, without any help from anyone else.

Pool mining occurs when individuals pool resources together and compensation would be shared depending on the amount of work performed. Cloud mining is the process of bitcoin mining utilizing a remote data centre with shared processing power. Cloud mining enables users to mine bitcoins or alternative cryptocurrencies without managing the hardware. In this regard each partner is responsible for its tax self-assessment. Malta assesses income tax and capital gains within the same tax self-assessment form. Currently there is no guidance by the CfR in relation to income/capital gains in relation to cloud mining.

Although the CfR has not yet issued any guidelines in respect to pool mining, we believe that it should be treated like a partnership. Revenue will be received by the partnership for the mining work provided and then distributed to the partners with respect to the output given individually.

Individuals usually work as employees or self-employed entrepreneurs. Employers record and collect taxes on behalf of their employees. Individuals who work as independent entrepreneurs would need to declare their own taxes.

In relation to Value Added Tax (VAT) on mining activities the VAT guidelines provide for two instances. In the first instance, where mining constitutes a service, for which compensation arises in the form of newly minted coins, it would fall outside the scope of VAT. This is because there would be no direct link between the compensation received and the service rendered, and there would be no reciprocal performance between a supplier and receiver.

In the second instance, where miners receive other forms of payment, such is deemed to be a provision of services and such service would result in a chargeable event for VAT purposes. If the supply of the service would be in Malta, Maltese VAT would apply.

(l) What are the income/capital gains tax consequences of staking crypto assets?

In order to understand the tax consequences of staking crypto assets, one needs to better understand what staking means. Staking refers to a process through which a node on a DLT network sets aside a certain number of coins to participate in a validation process known as the Proof-of-Stake (PoS) consensus mechanism.

The Maltese CfR guidelines do not make a direct reference to staking; however, one should look at the purpose of such an activity. If the purpose of staking is seen as part of the ordinary course of business, any revenue or profits made would be deemed to be income and subject to income tax as per the ordinary rules as determined under the Maltese Income Tax Act. If on the other hand, the intention of staking would be to hold as a long-term investment, the resulting capital gain could fall outside the scope of the capital gains rules and thus may be subject to conventional tax treatments under the Income Tax Act. Capital gains may only arise if such tokens are deemed to be securities and clarity needs to be obtained on the nature of stake.

(m) What are the income/capital gains tax consequences of an indirect investment in crypto assets?

An indirect investment in crypto assets may constitute the investment in a company operating in the infrastructure of crypto assets. In this way, one would still be investing in crypto without actually buying any crypto assets. Since this type of investment will still be in fiat currency, the usual Maltese Income Tax rules would apply in the case of a dividend distribution to investors which is taxable at gross value. The company on the other hand will pay tax on any profits made in the operation of the company.

(n) *How is income from crypto assets to be treated under double tax treaty law?*

To date, there is no reference to crypto assets in the present double taxation treaties. Until guidelines are issued or a clause would be included in these treaties, one should assess the presented transaction and analyse how this would have been treated for taxation if transaction had been carried out in fiat currencies.

(o) *What are the income/capital gains tax consequences of selling crypto assets in an ICO/STO/IEO?*

For Maltese Income Tax purposes, the raising of finances through an ICO/STO/IEO would not be considered as an income-generating event and therefore would not be subject to either income or capital gains taxes, it would therefore show as a separate line item under other debts in the statement of financial position. Nonetheless the revenues generated through use of the proceeds of such an issuance in normal business operations would then be subject to Income Tax. The finance raised would be recorded as a debt irrespective of this being an ICO/STO/IEO.

1.1.3 Other Taxes

(a) *What are the value added tax/sales tax consequences of selling crypto assets?*

In the case of Financial Tokens which are of a non-trading nature, one needs to check if the transaction falls under the capital gains rules under Article 5 of the Income Tax Act. The analysis needs to consider whether the tokens meet the definition of securities. Transfers of tokens which do not fall within the definition of securities, fall outside the scope of the tax on capital gains and therefore are not taxed.

(b) *Are payments in crypto assets subject to withholding taxes?*

In Malta, withholding taxes will not be charged on payments in crypto assets.

(c) *Does payment of compensation in crypto assets give rise to payroll tax consequences?*

When a payment is made or received in a cryptocurrency, such payment is deemed to be treated as a payment in any other currency, and this would mean that it is subject to income tax as any other income. Income tax in Malta is levied on a monthly basis in accordance with the amount of income received. Therefore if payment in crypto is received with value Y then tax is calculated on that value. The market value of that crypto asset will be taken when determining the level of income tax due in a particular month.

(d) Do transactions with crypto assets trigger any transfer taxes?

Stamp duty treatment in relation to transactions involving crypto assets is assessed through the determination of whether such assets have the same characteristics of 'marketable securities' as defined in the Income Tax Act. If such definition is satisfied, then Stamp Duty must be paid in accordance with the provisions of Duty on Documents and Transfer Act.

(e) Are firms operating in the crypto space subject to digital service taxes?

Malta has to date not introduced a digital tax.

(f) Are crypto assets subject to gift, inheritance, estate, or wealth taxes?

There are no inheritance or wealth taxes in Malta. In some instances, donations are also exempt from tax. At the same time, tax is imposed on the transfer of certain capital assets such as immovable property and shares. The CfR has not yet issued any guidelines on taxation in relation to the transfer of crypto assets as in relation to inheritance, donations (as applicable) or wealth in Malta. At this stage, one should analyse carefully the tax liability upon the transfer of non-virtual assets and apply the same principles to crypto assets.

(g) Are crypto assets subject to exit tax?

The Anti-Tax Avoidance Directive (ATAD) rules have been implemented in Malta on 1 January 2019 with the exception of exit tax rules which were applicable from 1 January 2020. To date, the CfR has not issued any guidelines on exit tax treatment of crypto assets. One needs to analyse if these assets were being kept as a long-term investment or for trading purposes.

In the case of long-term investment assets, one needs to analyse the residence state of the crypto asset in question due to the decentralized blockchain system, and subsequently analyse tax consequences in the case that the same transaction was in fiat currency or any other asset held in Malta.

(h) Can mining trigger gambling tax?

Gaming tax in Malta is at a rate of 5% on gaming revenue for Malta based players. In mining, one is preparing and processing transactions or producing new bitcoins. Alternatively, mining is also necessary for miners to make the payment network trustworthy and secure by verifying its transaction information. Therefore, this process does not fall under gambling which is a mere dependence on luck unlike mining which is a service being provided to a blockchain companies and/or other relevant related entities/issuers.

1.1.4 Compliance and Documentation Obligations

(a) What documentation requirements exist for taxpayer regarding crypto assets and are there best practices in recordkeeping to support representation in tax returns?

Taxpayers are to maintain all necessary records and documentation as would be required if they were to receive income, gains, or profits from ordinary activities. In the CfR guidance note, the CfR states that *'Any obligation under the Income Tax Acts to keep proper records applies to transactions involving DLT assets. Values expressed in a cryptocurrency will need to be translated to the reporting currency in which the taxpayer presents its financial statements. Applicable sanctions in terms of the said Acts shall apply where proper records are not kept and where there is failure to report and pay any liability to tax.'*[6]

(b) What is the evidentiary burden of supporting tax positions when a digital wallet address is lost or shared with other persons?

In Malta, disputes are raised in the courts. Following a submission of a tax return, if the Commissioner for Revenue disagrees with the submission made, then a tax dispute will be brought to the courts. With respect to income tax, disputes are of a civil nature and the burden or onus of proof falls on the taxable person. Therefore, all considerable evidence which would have been used in the preparation of the tax computation shall be brought to the attention of the courts.

(c) Are crypto asset exchanges and wallet providers subject to reporting obligations?

Crypto Asset Exchanges and Wallet Providers are to be established as normal trading companies for income tax purposes and therefore are subject to the statutory reporting obligations in terms of the Income Tax Act and Value Added Tax Act (as applicable) in relation to their reporting obligations. Such entities also need to report to the financial services regulator, the Malta Financial Services Authority, since the service of a crypto exchange or a crypto wallet requires a licence by the Malta Financial Services Authority.

6. Guidelines on the Income Tax Treatment of Transactions or arrangements involved DLT Assets, p. 4.

(d) *Are taxpayers holding crypto assets subject to reporting obligations apart from the filing of income tax/capital gains tax returns?*

At the date of this chapter, there are no additional reporting obligations for those taxpayers holding crypto assets subject to the statutory reporting obligations in relation to the filing of income tax returns.

(e) *Are crypto asset exchanges and wallet providers subject to CRS/FATCA reporting?*

Due to the uncertainty in the respect to FATCA, US investors or clients of Maltese crypto exchanges should verify on a regular basis their US tax obligations, including FATCA.

1.1.5 *Civil & Criminal Tax Enforcement*

(a) *What powers do the tax authorities have to compel the disclosure of information by third parties, such as exchanges or wallet providers, and have these been used in the past?*

In terms of the Commissioner for Revenue Act, 'The Commissioner shall have the legal and judicial representation of the Government on all documents, judicial acts and actions relating to revenue collection and any other matter in which the revenue departments have an interest, unless such representation has been delegated in accordance with sub-article (4).'[7]

Moreover the Income Tax Act states that '*The Commissioner may, when and as often as he deems necessary, give notice in writing to any person to furnish him, within a reasonable time stated in such notice, not being less than thirty days, such information as may be necessary in order to provide information, including documents, to foreign tax authorities where arrangements between Malta and the respective State or its tax authorities exist for the reciprocal exchange of information for tax purposes.*'[8]

The Maltese Tax Authorities do not disclose to the industry at large the use of such powers.

(b) *What measures have the tax authorities undertaken in the past to ensure crypto tax compliance?*

The field of crypto tax compliance is a relatively new area, and the tax authorities are still developing their policies and procedures. Nonetheless the CfR has issued its

7. Article 3(5) – Commissioner for Revenue Act – Act XXII of 2011 as amended from time to time.
8. Article 10(A)(1) – Income Tax Management Act – Act XVIII of 1994 as amended from time to time.

guidance which is available to the general public in relation to its expectations for the treatment of income or gains from crypto assets.[9]

(c) Are the tax authorities cooperating with tax authorities in other jurisdictions on enforcement?

Most of Malta's signed and active double tax treaties have been amended in order to provide for the exchange of tax information. Malta has also concluded eight tax information exchange agreements with certain non-EU jurisdictions. Malta as an EU Member State can, based on EU law, request information from other EU Member States that is foreseeably relevant to the administration and enforcement of its domestic laws.[10]

Currently there is no public knowledge whether the Maltese tax authorities are cooperating with tax authorities in other jurisdictions on enforcement and whether they collaborated with such in relation to crypto asset holdings of taxpayers.

9. Guidelines on the Income Tax Treatment of Transactions or arrangements involved DLT Assets.
10. Council Directive 2011/16/EU of 15 Feb. 2011 on administrative cooperation in the field of taxation and repealing Directive 77/799/EEC, as amended.

Mexico

Ricardo Leon Santacruz & Jorge Lopez Lopez

1. COUNTRY GUIDES

1.1 Mexico

1.1.1 Applicable Tax Law, Guidance, and Case Law

(a) What laws, regulations, and other administrative guidance exist that deal with crypto assets?

On September 2018, the Mexican Congress enacted the Financial Technology Law (Fintech Law) with the purpose of regulating Financial Technology Institutions. This is the first Mexican normative framework that targets and regulates crypto assets. Nevertheless, instead of providing a general legal framework for crypto assets, the Fintech Law focuses mainly in regulating the use of crypto assets by Financial Technologies Institutions ('Fintech Institutions').

Fintech Law defines crypto assets as 'virtual assets' providing that a virtual asset is an electronic representation of value used as a medium of payment by the general public. In addition, crypto assets are clearly distinguished from foreign currency.[1]

Through General Regulations, the Mexican Central Bank has regulated the issuance and the transactions with crypto assets as follows:

(1) Authorized Fintech Institutions are allowed to use crypto assets only to conduct 'internal transactions'. Internal transactions are defined as any internal transaction carried out by the Fintech Institutions to conduct active,

1. Article 30 of the Fintech Law.

passive, and services activities with their clients. In addition, Fintech Institutions are not allowed to transfer, directly or indirectly, to its Clients any risk or exposure related to the internal transactions.

(2) Fintech Institutions are not allowed to exchange, transfer, or have the custody of crypto assets in transactions entered into with their clients.

(3) Subject to authorization, Fintech Institutions are allowed to make internal transactions with crypto assets that comply with the following characteristics:
   - They should be traceable units recorded in an electronic basis that does not represent the ownership of an underlying asset or, if they represent such ownership, the assets' value should be lower than the underlying assets.
   - They should have control protocols for asset issuance that can be subscribed by third parties.
   - They should control protocols that prevent the copy of the units that are available to be transferred at more than one time at the same moment.

(b) Which court cases exist dealing with crypto assets?

We do not know of any court cases dealing with crypto assets.

1.1.2 Income and Capital Gains Taxes

(a) How are crypto assets classified for income and capital gains tax purposes?

The Mexican Income Tax Law (MITL) does not provide special regulations for crypto assets. However, they cannot be considered as money or foreign currency, but crypto assets are treated as property. Hence, any transaction with cryptocurrency is governed by the applicable general income tax principles.

It is important to note that Monetary Law defines the Mexican peso as the official currency,[2] and although such law does not define 'foreign currency', the Fintech Law defines crypto assets as a virtual asset. In this regard, because no special rule for tax purposes is provided, crypto assets will be considered as assets, for tax purposes.

Since crypto assets are not treated as currency, no foreign currency gain or loss can result from dealing with such assets or from holding them.

Mexican tax law does not provide any characterization rule for securities referred to crypto assets or utility tokens. Therefore, to determine the character of such instruments, taxpayers should rely on general tax principles. Each instrument should be analysed in order to determine both the nature of the instrument and also the nature of its yields.

2. Article 1 of the Monetary Law.

In general terms, non-Mexican securities and utility tokens can be characterized as intangible property (if the instrument consists in contractual rights), shares (if the instrument consists of a participation in a vehicle that for Mexican purposes has legal personality), equity interest (if the instrument consists of a participation in a vehicle that for Mexican purposes lacks legal personality), or debt instruments (if the instrument consists of an unconditional obligation to repay).

The nature of the instrument will typically determine the nature of the yields. For example, if an instrument is characterized as a share, any yield will be treated as a dividend, but it if is characterized as a debt instrument, yields will be treated as interest.

(b) *What are the income/capital gains tax consequences of selling crypto assets against fiat currency?*

Mexican tax residents. For Mexican tax residents, selling crypto assets is a taxable event that can result in taxable gain or loss calculated on a net basis (i.e., sales price minus acquisition cost).[3] However, the treatment of the gain or loss is different for individuals and corporate taxpayers:

Individuals not engaged in a trade or business. The gain should be divided between the number of years that the taxpayer held the crypto asset, but not to exceed twenty years. The result of this operation should be accrued by the taxpayer as gross income in the fiscal year in which the sale takes place. The remaining gain, if any, is taxed at the election of the taxpayer, with the effective income tax rate of the taxpayer for the prior five fiscal years, or the effective tax rate of the year in which the sale took place.[4]

For example, if taxpayer A sells a crypto asset for Mexican pesos (MXP) 2,500 that she acquired five years ago for MXP 1,000.00, the tax burden for taxpayer A should be calculated as follows (for these purposes we are assuming an effective income tax rate of 25% for the last five years and an effective income tax rate of 35% for the year of the sale):

Net gain (Sale price – Acquisition cost)	MXP 1,500.00
Net gain taxed at a 35% income tax rate (Net gain per 5 years)	MXP 300
Income tax (1)	MXP 105
Net gain taxed at a 25% income tax rate (Net gain per 5 years)	MXP 1,200
Income tax (2)	MXP 300
Total income tax liability (1 + 2)	MXP **405**

Individual taxpayers are obliged to make advance income tax payments per each taxable transfer, be it a sale or exchange. Advance payments are calculated over a 20% income tax rate over the sales price in case of a sale, or the fair market value of the property received in case of a taxable exchange.

3. The acquisition cost should be adjusted for inflation.
4. Article 120 of the MITL.

It is important to note that the taxpayer is required to identify the acquisition cost of each crypto asset and to calculate the relevant gain upon each sale. If the taxpayer is selling only a fraction of the crypto asset, then the acquisition cost must be proportional to such fraction.

In case of loss, the taxpayer is not allowed to deduct it.

Corporate taxpayers and individuals engaged in a trade or business. All gain or loss derived from the sale of cryptocurrency accrues as taxable income. Corporate taxpayers must recognize such gain in the fiscal year of the sale, and individuals in the fiscal year in which the sales price is paid. Deduction of losses from dealing in crypto assets is allowed to the extent that the taxpayer can evidence that such dealings are ordinary and necessary for its business.

It is important to note that while corporate taxpayers can deduct the acquisition cost of the crypto assets only when such assets are sold,[5] individual taxpayers are required to deduct the acquisition cost in the fiscal year that the asset is purchased.

Finally, individual taxpayers are subject to a progressive tax rate of up to 35% and corporate taxpayers are subject to a flat rate of 30%.

FX gain and loss. It is important to note one of the main differences between crypto assets and foreign fiat currency. Mexican tax residents that hold foreign fiat currency are obliged to recognize the gain or loss from fluctuations in the FX exchange rate. However, holding a crypto asset is not subject FX rules and a gain or loss should not be recognized until a realization event occurs.

(c) *What are the income/capital gains tax consequences of exchanging crypto assets against other crypto assets?*

MITL treats the exchange of property as a taxable event, meaning that two different transfers are taking place. For this purpose, the taxpayer takes the fair market value of the property received, namely, the crypto asset,[6] as the price paid. For purposes of calculating the gain or loss, the same rules as in section (b) above are applicable.

For future transactions, the fair market value of the crypto asset received will be its acquisition cost.

(d) *If a distinction is made between business assets and non-business assets, when does trading in crypto assets imply a trade or business?*

For Mexican tax purposes there is no distinction between business and non-business assets. However, for individuals there is a distinction for persons engaged in a trade or business. An individual's dealings with crypto assets might fall into this category if, according to federal business law, the transaction has a business nature.

5. To identify the assets that are sold they can elect to use any of the following accounting method: (i) first-in, first-out (FIFO); (ii) identify the cost; (iii) average cost; and (iv) estimated costs.
6. Article 17 of the Federal Tax Code.

According to the Federal Tax Code, a taxpayer is engaged in a trade or business to the extent that it conducts certain listed activities (industrial, agricultural, fishing, livestock sectors) or if the activities that he/she conducts have a business nature according to Mexican business law. General principles of business law characterize a transaction as a business transaction under three different criteria:

(i) Entity criterion. All transactions executed by *per se* businesspersons or entities are deemed to be business transactions, unless the transaction has a *per se* civil nature (i.e., leasing of residential property). In this regard, Fintech Institutions are considered business entities.

(ii) Subjective criterion. An entity or an individual is deemed to be a businessperson or entity if he/she is engaged in transactions with a speculative purpose. In most cases it is not clear whether trading with securities or crypto assets for investment purposes should qualify as business activity. Nevertheless, it is important to note that although income deriving from capital gains, dividends, or interest might come from a speculative transaction, its tax treatment might fall under a specific tax regime (i.e., a specific tax regime per each type of income) different from the tax regime provided for business transactions. As of today there are no relevant precedents that distinguish when a transaction should be considered to be a business transaction for tax purposes or when it should be governed by the specific tax regime for such type of income.

(iii) Objective criteria. Transactions related to a per se business instrument (namely, an instrument governed by any business law) are deemed to be business transactions. For example, any transaction involving shares of a business entity is regarded as a business transaction.

Notably, in the case of individual taxpayers there is not a clear line between the treatment of income that is specially regulated by the MITL (i.e., dividends, interest, and capital gains), and the treatment of business income where the taxpayer derives the same items of income as part of its business activities.

(e) What are the income/capital gains tax consequences for an employee receiving wages or salaries in crypto assets?

The fair market value of the crypto asset received will be taxed as compensation for subordinated services or salary. It is important to note that the payor of wages is required to withhold the applicable income tax, so employers must transfer to employee the relevant cryptocurrency with a fair market value equivalent to the salary minus the applicable income tax.

(f) *What are the income/capital gains tax consequences for a merchant receiving payment in crypto assets?*

Since crypto assets are considered neither as money nor as a foreign currency, any trading that involves the use of crypto assets is treated as a taxable exchange, meaning that, for tax purposes, two properties are exchanged. Seller should consider the fair market value of the crypto asset received, as consideration received. Consequently, the seller taxpayer (individuals and corporations) will be allowed to deduct the cost of goods sold.

As pointed out in section (d), there is not a clear line between the business income and the other regimes applicable to special types of income (i.e., capital gains). Therefore, if the trading of an individual taxpayer is not construed as a business activity, instead of accruing the fair market value of the crypto asset received and deducting the cost of goods sold, such taxpayer should calculate a net gain as indicated in section (b) above.[7]

Individual taxpayers are obliged to make advance income tax payments per each taxable transfer, be it sale or exchange. Advance payments are calculated at a 20% income tax rate over the sale price, in case of a sale, or the fair market value of the property received, if a taxable exchange. The taxpayer cannot deduct any losses.

Finally, as previously pointed out, individual taxpayers are subject to a progressive tax rate of up to 35% and corporate taxpayers are subject to a flat rate of 30%.

(g) *What are the income/capital gains tax consequences of a loss of crypto assets?*

Only corporate taxpayers are allowed to deduct the loss of crypto assets to the extent that such crypto assets are used in their trade or business. If the crypto asset is part of the inventory (namely, the taxpayer holds the crypto assets for trading purposes), such taxpayer shall deduct the acquisition cost according to the rules applicable to the determination its COGS.[8] If the crypto asset was held for investment purposes, the taxpayer is allowed to deduct the adjusted basis in the tax year in which the loss was sustained.

In the case of individuals that are not engaged in a trade or business, the loss of a crypto asset is not allowed. For individual taxpayers engaged in a trade or business, if the taxpayer holds the crypto asset as part of the inventory, since they are subject to a cash basis accounting method, no deduction is granted for the loss of such asset, because the acquisition of it was already deducted.[9] If the crypto asset is held for investment purposes, then there is no deduction allowed for the loss of the crypto asset. This is true also if the taxpayer receives a crypto asset in a taxable transaction.

7. Article 120 of the MITL.
8. To identify the assets that are sold, they can elect to use any of the following accounting methods: (i) FIFO; (ii) identify the cost; (iii) average cost; and (iv) estimated costs.
9. Section 103 of the MITL.

(h) What are the income/capital gains tax consequences of a loss in value of crypto assets?

Because the Mexican income tax law requires a realization event to trigger any tax consequence related to assets, the loss in value of a crypto asset does not trigger any tax consequences.

It is important to mention that in the case of corporate taxpayers, the MITL only provides a deduction for physical inventory if the value of it has been lost, and the deduction is subject to compliance with certain conditions, such as filing a notice before the Mexican tax authority and destroying such inventory. Therefore, for intangible inventory it is not clear whether this deduction is available.

(i) What are the income/capital gains tax consequences of forks of crypto assets?

MITL does not provide a specific treatment for forks. However, a fork will not be a taxable event to the extent that the fork does not result in the creation of a new crypto asset. If the fork results in the creation of a new crypto asset, such fork can be considered as a taxable exchange, through which the taxpayer gives up the original asset and receives a new one. In such case, the rules applicable to taxable exchanges will be applicable (section b).

Since there are no regulations for these types of transactions, the technical issues pertaining to the fork become extremely important to determine whether the fork results in an exchange or an update. In the absence of any regulatory framework, we cannot anticipate what elements should be considered in order to determine in which cases a fork can derive in a variation of the same asset or in a completely different asset. Elements such as the change in the code, alterations in value, etc., might be taken into consideration.

(j) What are the income/capital gains tax consequences of airdrops of crypto assets? Are the tax consequences different if the airdropped tokens are unwanted?

If any type of taxpayer receives crypto assets free of charge, such airdrop will be a taxable event through which the taxpayer should recognize the fair market value of the crypto asset received as taxable income.[10] The acquisition cost for the crypto asset received is its fair market value included in the taxpayer's taxable income.[11]

It is important to note that if upon an airdrop the taxpayer is required to conduct any service or pay any amount, the transaction would be characterized as an acquisition. Therefore, these types of airdrops will be a taxable event to the extent that the fair market value of the crypto asset received exceeds the value of the price paid, or

10. Article 130 of the MITL.
11. Article 124 of the MITL.

the service rendered. In these cases, the price paid or the value of the services will be part of the acquisition cost of the crypto asset.[12] For individual taxpayers any difference of less than 10% does not trigger a taxable event,[13] and such difference should be included in the gross income of the taxpayer that received the crypto asset.

(k) *What are the income/capital gains tax consequences of (solo, pool, and cloud) mining?*

Mining is a taxable event, even though mining can be characterized either as compensation for services or as a taxable acquisition. In both cases, the taxpayer is required to recognize income at the fair market value of the crypto assets received from the mining activities, using such value as the acquisition cost for further transactions. If the taxpayer can show that its regular business activity is mining, it will be allowed to deduct all the expenses related to such activity; otherwise, no deduction will be allowed. It is important to note that although services might be considered as a trade or business, for income tax purposes, independent services (as opposed to labour services) fall into a separate tax regime.

In solo mining, the taxpayer should recognize the full value of the crypto asset received, while in pool mining, the taxpayer should recognize its allocable share of such value. The same rules apply to cloud mining. However, it is likely that in this case, the fees paid to the mining company can be deducted by the taxpayer.

(l) *What are the income/capital gains tax consequences of staking crypto assets?*

Staking would be a taxable event to the extent that the user receives a crypto asset. Like mining, staking can be characterized as compensation for services or as a taxable acquisition. In both cases, the taxpayer is required to recognize as income the fair market value of the crypto assets received from the mining/staking activities and such value will be the acquisition cost for further transactions. If the taxpayer can support that its regular business activity is staking, it will be able to deduct all the expenses related to such activity; otherwise, no deduction will be available.

(m) *What are the income/capital gains tax consequences of an indirect investment in crypto assets?*

The treatment will depend on the type of vehicle through which the investment is undertaken. In general terms we can classify the different types of investments as follows:

12. By taxing the airdrop in exchange for services rendered to the extent of the difference of the fair market value of the crypto asset over the fair market value of the services, the MITL is indirectly taxing the services.
13. Article 130, section I of the MITL.

(1) Mexican corporations. If the investment is conducted through shares of a Mexican corporation, for all tax purposes the investment will receive the treatment applicable to shareholders, meaning that any sale of such shares, except for buybacks, will be taxed on capital gains. Buybacks will be treated as a partial liquidation, and distributions from the corporation will be treated as dividends or capital redemptions.
(2) Controlled foreign corporations (CFCs). If the investment is conducted through a foreign corporation (a foreign entity with legal personality) treated as an opaque taxpayer and that is controlled by the taxpayer,[14] such taxpayer will be subject to an anti-deferral regime and will be obliged to recognize as taxable income the net taxable income of the relevant fiscal year. This regime does not apply if the relevant foreign corporation derives at least 80% of its gross income from business activities, so an analysis should be done on a case-by-case basis.
(3) Non-controlled foreign corporations. If the investment is conducted through shares of a foreign corporation for tax purposes, the investment will receive the treatment applicable to shareholders of a foreign corporation, meaning that any alienation of such shares, except for buybacks, will be taxed as a capital gain on the net capital gain. Buybacks will be treated as a partial liquidation, and distributions from the corporation will be treated as dividends or capital redemptions.
(4) Transparent foreign corporations and any other transparent entity. As with CFCs, if the investment is conducted through transparent vehicles, the relevant taxpayer is required to recognize as taxable income any income or gain derived through the investment vehicle. Unlike CFCs, where the taxpayer is required to anticipate the net taxable income derived by the vehicle in the relevant fiscal year, an investment trough transparent vehicles requires the taxpayer to recognize as a taxable event each transaction separately, as if directly conducted by the taxpayer.

From a Mexican perspective, each type of investment vehicle should be analysed and classified according to the prior classification. Hence, for example, an ETF can be characterized as either a transparent vehicle or a foreign corporation, depending on the tax laws of the country in which such ETF has its tax residency.

To determine whether a foreign vehicle will be treated as a foreign corporation or as a transparent entity or legal arrangement the following rules are applicable:

(1) Foreign corporation. All entities that have legal personality, in accordance with the laws in which they are incorporated, will be treated as foreign corporations.

14. Special rules for determining control are in force as of 1 Jan. 2020.

(2) Legal arrangement. All entities that lack legal personality, in accordance with the laws in which they are created, will be treated as transparent legal arrangements.
(3) Tax transparent entities. A foreign entity will be treated as tax transparent, to the extent it is not a taxpayer and that income derived by such entity is assigned to its members in accordance with the laws in which it was organized or in the country where it is effectively managed.

(n) How is income from crypto assets to be treated under double tax treaty law?

It is important to mention that according to MITL, aside from certain royalties, any other capital gains or profits deriving from the alienation of intangible assets, the sale of goods is not income sourced in Mexico. Consequently, a foreign tax resident without a permanent establishment in Mexico would not trigger any Mexican source income from trading with cryptocurrency.

Therefore, since the transfer of crypto assets is not sourced in Mexico for income tax purposes, it is not relevant to classify such deal under the relevant provisions of the tax treaty. For example, a non-Mexican tax resident selling a crypto asset to a Mexican tax resident will not be subject to income tax in Mexico and hence no tax treaty will be applicable.

On the other hand, if a non-Mexican tax resident renders services in Mexico (including mining and stalking) and receives crypto assets in payment for such services, such payment will be sourced in Mexico as a service, but the nature of such will remain as services income. It is important to note that, for income tax purposes there are no rules to determine in which cases any digital service is rendered within Mexico. Of course a physical presence in Mexico while the services (including mining and stalking) are rendered would be deemed to be rendered in Mexico, but there is still a lot of uncertainty in the MITL with respect to this type of digital services.

(o) What are the income/capital gains tax consequences of selling crypto assets in an ICO/STO/IEO?

ICO. Unlike IPOs, an ICO is a taxable exchange for the issuer, so all the proceeds from the sale of the crypto assets should be recognized as taxable income.

STO. The tax treatment depends on the underlying security that is traded. If the underlying security is stock or corporate bonds, the issuer should not recognize any income from the recipient of the funds.

For traders, selling crypto assets in an STO is treated as dealing with other types of securities. It is important to mention that, although the Fintech Law regulates Financial Technology Institutions, such entities are not part of the financial system for tax purposes. Consequently, such entities are not subject to the special tax regime applicable only to Financial Institutions, and hence, when dealing with crypto assets, the rules described below will also apply to Financial Technology Institutions and in general to any broker and dealer.

IEO. Like ICO, an IEO is a taxable exchange for the issuer, so all the proceeds from the sale of the crypto assets should be recognized as taxable income. For the crypto exchange company, dealings with crypto assets fall under the same rules previously described for sales or taxable exchanges.

1.1.3 *Other Taxes*

(a) *What are the value added tax/sales tax consequences of selling crypto assets?*

Like income tax, for Value Added Tax (VAT) purposes, crypto assets are treated as intangible property. Hence, receiving crypto assets as payment in consideration for a sale is treated as a taxable exchange of property. When services are paid with crypto assets, the service provider is receiving compensation in kind and the client is transferring an asset.

Now, Mexican VAT law taxes only the transfers of property conducted within Mexico. In the case of intangibles such as crypto assets, a sale is deemed to be performed within Mexico if both the transferor and transferee are Mexican tax residents. Hence, only transfers conducted between Mexican residents will be subject to 16% VAT. Please note that because paying to a merchant with crypto assets is a taxable exchange, such 'payment' will be subject to VAT to the extent that both parties are Mexican tax residents.

In addition, sales of intangible property such as crypto assets are subject to a 0% tax rate[15] to the extent that the transfer is conducted by a Mexican tax resident to a non-Mexican tax resident. Again, where a Mexican tax resident makes a payment with crypto assets to a foreign tax resident, a 0% VAT rate would be applicable.

(b) *Are payments in crypto assets subject to withholding taxes?*

There are no special withholding taxes or rates applicable to payments in crypto assets. However, the regular withholding tax rates for any federal tax will still apply even if the payment is made in kind. In this case, the Federal Tax Code provides that the recipient of the payment must provide to the withholding agent the funds required to pay the relevant tax.[16]

15. The 0% VAT rate does not trigger any economic burden to the taxpayer or the client, but allows the taxpayer to credit the input VAT related to the taxable transaction (which would not be creditable if the transaction were VAT exempted).
16. Section 6 of the Federal Tax Code.

(c) *Does payment of compensation in crypto assets give rise to payroll tax consequences?*

Payroll taxes are imposed by local states on employers. As of today there is no payroll tax imposed on employees. In most legislations, any compensation paid in kind is includable in the basis of the payroll tax. This should include payments in crypto assets. However, this assessment must be made by each local legislation.

(d) *Do transactions with crypto assets trigger any transfer taxes?*

Aside from income tax and value added tax, if any, no other Mexican taxes apply to crypto asset transactions.

(e) *Are firms operating in crypto space subject to digital service taxes?*

There is no digital services tax imposed in Mexico.

(f) *Are crypto assets subject to gift, inheritance, estate, or wealth taxes?*

Inheritances are exempt from income tax for both the decedent and the beneficiary. Beneficiaries receive a carryover basis in any property bequest.

For donor, gifts are not a taxable event for corporations for individuals, but the deduction of property gifted is not allowed. For the donee a gift will be taxed unless received from his/her spouse, descendants, or ascendants. Hence, in the presence of a taxable gift of a crypto asset, donee should recognize taxable income in the amount of the fair market value of such asset.

(g) *Are crypto assets subject to exit tax?*

Corporate taxpayers. MITL provides that upon the change of tax residence of a Mexican tax resident corporation, it is deemed that such corporation is liquidated and that it sold all its assets at a fair market value.[17] Hence, a corporation owning crypto assets upon migration to a different jurisdiction should recognize a gain or a loss for the difference of the acquisition cost of the crypto asset and its fair market value.
Individual taxpayers. MITL provides that upon the change of tax residence of a Mexican tax resident individual, any advance income tax payment is construed as definitive.[18] However, an individual would be deemed to be a Mexican tax resident for three years following a migration, if he/she migrates to a preferential tax regime (namely, a jurisdiction where an income tax is not imposed or its effective tax rate is

17. Section 12 of the MITL.
18. Section 90 of the MITL.

lower than the 75 % of the Mexican effective tax rate) with which Mexico does not have in place a broad exchange of information treaty.[19]

(h) Can mining trigger gambling tax?

Mexican Excise Tax Law[20] taxes only the person who organizes gambling activities and raffles that require governmental authorization and contests that require the use of electronic and visual images. Hence, because mining is a non-regulated activity that does not require any authorization from the government, and because mining does not require any visual image, mining activities are not subject to the Excise Tax.

1.1.4 Compliance and Documentation Obligations

(a) What documentation requirements exist for taxpayers regarding crypto assets and are there best practices in recordkeeping to support representations made in tax returns?

Aside from general tax documentation requirements, no specific documents are required for crypto assets. However, it is important to mention that to conduct any deduction or crediting of any VAT, all Mexican tax resident taxpayers should obtain from the relevant provider an electronic tax invoice if the provider is also a resident of Mexico or a tax invoice that contains certain specific information if the provider is not a Mexican tax resident.

(b) What is the evidentiary burden of supporting tax positions when a digital wallet address is lost or shared with other persons?

Taxpayers have the burden to prove any loss sustained. Now, given the nature of the asset, it is advisable to have an expert witness opinion that provides the technical explanations that support the loss of the wallet and the consequences of it. From a technical perspective, losing access to the crypto assets does not mean that the asset disappeared or that it no longer exists. Therefore, it is important to evidence that losing such access is equivalent to losing the asset.

(c) Are crypto asset exchanges and wallet providers subject to reporting obligations?

In September 2018, the Anti-Money Laundering Law was amended to consider the exchange and custody of crypto assets as vulnerable activities as of April 2020.[21] Consequently, all dealers and custodians of crypto assets conducting such activities

19. Section 9 of the Federal Tax Code.
20. Article 2, section II, subsection b) of the Mexican Excise Tax Law.
21. Article 17, section XVI of the Anti-Laundry Law.

within Mexico are required to set up a file of each of their clients and to file informative returns in a monthly basis. Among the information to be submitted, the Fintech Institutions must include the following:

(1) Information related to the Fintech institution (name, address, phone, etc.)
(2) Information related to the client (Name, tax ID, nationality, age, profession, etc.)
(3) Information related to the transaction:
   (a) name of the crypto asset;
   (b) exchange rate of the crypto asset in Mexican Pesos, at the moment of the transaction;
   (c) quantity of the operation;
   (d) operation hash;
   (e) date of the transaction; and
   (f) place of the transaction.

(d) Are taxpayers holding crypto assets subject to reporting obligations apart from the filing of income tax/capital gains tax returns?

Corporate taxpayers and individuals engaged in a trade or business are required to file their financial statements with the tax authority. For these taxpayers it is required to report any asset (including crypto assets) through their financial statements. Aside from this, there are no additional reporting obligations.

(e) Are crypto asset exchanges and wallet providers subject to CRS/FATCA reporting?

Although there is no special regulation for reporting crypto assets under the domestic legal framework implemented to comply with CRS and FATCA, if a financial institution for tax purposes offers investments in crypto assets, such financial institution is obliged to report this information to the Mexican tax authority. It is important to note that the Financial Technology Institutions are not part of the financial system for tax purposes, so according to the Federal Tax Code, such entities have no reporting obligation in the FATCA and CRS context.

1.1.5 Civil and Criminal Tax Enforcement

(a) What powers do the tax authorities have to compel the disclosure of information by third parties, such as exchanges or wallet providers, and have these been used in the past?

During an audit process the tax authorities have full powers to require third parties to disclose any transaction made with the relevant audited taxpayer. This power is broadly used by the tax authority. However, we do not know of any particular case in which the tax authority has required of a third party the disclosure of any information related to crypto assets.

(b) *What measures have the tax authorities undertaken in the past to ensure crypto tax compliance?*

In September 2018, the Anti-Money Laundering Law was amended to consider the exchange and custody of crypto assets as vulnerable activities as of April 2020.[22] Consequently, all dealers and custodians of crypto assets conducting such activities within Mexico are required to set up a file of each of their clients and file informative returns on a monthly basis.

(c) *Are the tax authorities cooperating with tax authorities in other jurisdictions on enforcement?*

In the context of CRS and FATCA, Mexico is very cooperative with other jurisdictions. However, as pointed out in section 1.1.4(e), there is no specific provision that requires special reporting for crypto assets.

22. Article 17, section XVI of the Anti-Laundering statute.

New Zealand

Barney Cumberland

1. COUNTRY GUIDES

1.1 New Zealand

1.1.1 Applicable Tax Law, Guidance, and Case Law

(a) Which laws, regulations, and other administrative guidance exist dealing with crypto assets?

Currently the New Zealand tax legislation – specifically the Income Tax Act 2007 (**ITA**), Goods and Services Tax Act 1985 (**GSTA**) and the Tax Administration Act 1994 – does not contain any specific provisions dealing with crypto assets. Accordingly, to date both the Inland Revenue Department (**IRD**) and taxpayers have been left to apply general tax rules to transactions involving crypto assets. IRD has released some guidelines[1] and public rulings,[2] which are referred to below, dealing with certain tax aspects of crypto asset transactions under current law. Further, in February 2020, IRD released a discussion document (**February Discussion Document**) recommending a number of statutory amendments to clarify the proper application of existing tax rules to crypto assets in situations where there is currently a degree of uncertainty.[3]

1. Inland Revenue Department 'Taxing cryptocurrency' www.ird.govt.nz, updated as at Aug. 2020.
2. *See* generally: Inland Revenue Department 'Income tax – salary and wages paid in crypto-assets' (27 Jun. 2019), 'Income tax – bonuses paid in crypto-assets' (27 Jun. 2019), 'Income tax – employer issued crypto-assets provided to an employee' (27 Jun. 2019) and 'Income tax – application of the employee share scheme rules to employer issued crypto-assets provided to an employee' (27 Jun. 2019), www.classic.ird.govt.nz.
3. Inland Revenue Department *GST policy issues – An officials' issues paper* (Feb. 2020), www.taxpolicy.ird.govt.nz.

(b) *Which court cases exist dealing with crypto assets?*

In April 2020, the High Court issued a (non-tax) judgment regarding Cryptopia Ltd, a New Zealand cryptocurrency trading exchange that went into liquidation in May 2019 after it was the victim of a serious hack.[4] The key issue before the Court was whether or not crypto assets are property that is capable of being held on trust. The Court held that crypto assets are items of intangible property that are capable of being held in trust.

1.1.2 *Income and Capital Gains Taxes*

(a) *How are crypto assets classified for income and capital gains tax purposes?*

New Zealand does not have a general capital gains tax.

For New Zealand income tax purposes, a crypto asset is generally regarded as a form of intangible personal property, susceptible to the application of general provisions in the ITA relating to dealing or trading in personal property.

A potential alternative treatment of crypto assets under the ITA is as 'financial arrangements'. 'Financial arrangement' is broadly defined as any arrangement under which a person receives money (which includes money's worth) in consideration for that person, or another person, providing money to any person at a future time or on the occurrence of a future event.[5] The financial arrangement rules are principally aimed at debt or debt-type instruments, and require parties to recognize for income tax purposes all gains and losses, whether realized or unrealized, under such arrangements on an accrual basis over their life. Many arrangements that would be captured by the broad definition of 'financial arrangement' but which would not be appropriate to tax on this basis are defined as 'excepted financial arrangements' so as to exclude them from the financial arrangement rules. Crypto assets are not currently included within excepted financial arrangements meaning conceptually the financial arrangements rules may apply to them.

In the February Discussion Document, IRD concluded that from a policy perspective, the nature of most crypto assets means that they should not be subject to the financial arrangement rules. As noted, the financial arrangement rules generally require taxpayers to spread realised and unrealised gains and losses from a financial arrangement over the life of an arrangement on an accrual basis. Such treatment would be inappropriate in relation to most crypto assets given the volatility in the value of crypto assets, illiquidity issues and other matters. As a result, IRD recommends defining most crypto assets as an 'excepted financial arrangement' retrospectively from 1 January 2009 (the date bitcoin, the first crypto asset, was launched),[6] with a savings

4. *Ruscoe v. Cryptopia Ltd (in liq)* [2020] NZHC 728.
5. Income Tax Act 2007, section EW 3.
6. Inland Revenue Department, *supra* n. 3, at 20.

provision for any taxpayer who has applied the financial arrangement rules to their crypto assets in this period.[7]

IRD noted, however, that the financial arrangement rules should apply to crypto assets that are, in fact, economically equivalent to debt instruments.[8] IRD gives the example of 'a token that is issued at $1 in value (in money, other tokens or services) and can be redeemed for $1.20 of value in two years' time'.[9] This will be achieved by excluding these kinds of crypto assets from the definition of crypto assets qualifying as excepted financial arrangements.

(b) *What are the income/capital gains tax consequences of selling crypto assets against fiat currency?*

The starting point is that invariably crypto assets will be 'revenue account property' of the holder under the ITA, meaning realised gains and losses from disposing of crypto assets will be taxable or deductible. Personal property acquired for the dominant purpose of sale or disposal is included as revenue account property. IRD has a published view that, by analogy with bullion, there is a presumption that taxpayers acquire crypto assets for the dominant purpose of disposal, because they typically do not provide any other income stream while held.[10] It is of course possible that a taxpayer could rebut this presumption if a particular crypto asset carries a dividend or interest-like feature, or in other circumstances.

A further distinction is then drawn between taxpayers who carry on a 'business' for the purposes of selling or exchanging crypto assets in the ordinary course of the business, so that their crypto assets are 'trading stock' (a subset of revenue account property) under the ITA, and non-business holders.

Non-business holders of crypto assets as revenue account property are taxed on disposal (whether the consideration is fiat currency or anything else) with a deduction allowed for the historic cost of the asset in the tax year of disposal (or when it ceases to exist). If a non-business holder cannot separately identify crypto asset units of the same type, they may adopt either a first-in, first-out or weighted average cost approach in order to allocate a cost to units sold. The last-in, first-out method is not permitted. Any gain on disposal will be taxable income in the tax year of disposal or any loss deductible in that year.

In the case of a business holder whose crypto assets are trading stock, the crypto assets will generally be revalued at the lesser of cost and market selling value at each tax year end. That value is then income for that year and a deduction in the following year. This may give rise to deductions for unrealised losses in a declining market. In the tax year of disposal, the disposal proceeds will be income, with a deduction for the deemed carrying value at the start of that year.

---

7. *Id.* at 16.
8. *Id.* at 16.
9. *Id.* at 16.
10. Inland Revenue Department 'Are proceeds from the sale of gold bullion income?' (20 Sep. 2017), www.classic.ird.govt.nz.

If the fiat currency paid or received for crypto assets is not New Zealand Dollars (**NZD**), for tax reporting purposes there would need to be a conversion into NZD at the exchange rate prevailing at the relevant time.

(c) What are the income/capital gains tax consequences of exchanging crypto assets against other crypto assets?

There is no distinction between exchanging crypto assets for fiat currency and exchanging crypto assets for other crypto assets (or any other form of consideration).[11] An exchange for another crypto asset is a disposal of the original crypto asset with the tax consequences described in the previous section. For tax reporting purposes the crypto asset received will need to be valued in NZD at the date of the exchange. If the crypto asset cannot be valued in NZD, then it would be necessary to take its USD or other fiat currency value and convert that into NZD at the relevant exchange rate.[12] Similarly, the NZD value of the crypto asset disposed of will be the cost base of the acquired crypto asset going forward.

(d) If a distinction is made between business assets and non-business assets, when does trading in crypto assets lead to a trade or business?

As noted above, as a general proposition, crypto assets will be treated as held on revenue (taxable) account, but with a distinction made between a holder that carries on business for the purpose of selling or exchanging crypto assets (as trading stock), and a non-business holder. In order to distinguish between these two categories of holder, the fundamental question is whether or not the holder is carrying on a business of trading in crypto assets.

'Business' is defined in the ITA as 'any profession, trade, or undertaking carried on for profit'.[13] The Court of Appeal in *Grieve v. CIR* held that in assessing whether or not a person is in business involves a two-step analysis, namely, looking first at the nature of the activity carried on and second at the intention of the taxpayer in engaging in that activity.[14] The inquiry into the nature of the activity will focus on its character in the circumstances, the taxpayer's commitment of time, effort, and money into the activity, the volume of transactions, and the financial results. The inquiry into the intention of the person will look at their actions and statements to assess whether profit-making is their predominant motive in undertaking the activity.

Overall, if a crypto trader is applying systematic processes with a view to undertaking a significant volume of transactions on a sustained basis in order to make a profit, he or she will likely be considered in business. A person undertaking more isolated transactions on a less organised or more opportunistic basis is less likely to be considered in business.

11. Inland Revenue Department, *supra* n. 1.
12. *Supra* n. 1.
13. Income Tax Act 2007, section YA 1.
14. *Grieve v. Commissioner of Inland Revenue* [1984] 1 NZLR 101 at 110.

(e) What are the income/capital gains tax consequences for an employee receiving wages or salaries in crypto assets?

IRD has issued a public ruling[15] to the effect that wages or salaries received in crypto assets are to be treated as part of normal remuneration and will generally be subject to New Zealand's employment income withholding tax regime – Pay As You Earn (**PAYE**).

Although the PAYE rules are generally directed at cash (fiat currency) remuneration, IRD views the concepts of 'salary' and 'wages' as broad enough to include both recurring remuneration,[16] and bonuses and other one-off payments[17] in the form of crypto assets. Conceptually there is a degree of tension between this position and the settled view that crypto assets are intangible assets, but not currency, for most tax purposes.

PAYE will always need to be paid in NZD fiat currency. If an employment agreement provides for the employee to be paid a fixed amount denominated in crypto assets, then the amount provided to the employee will need to be grossed up when calculating NZD PAYE payable.[18] Similarly, if the employment agreement provides for a net amount of crypto assets in NZD, then the amount provided will also need to be grossed up.[19] Otherwise, part of the crypto payment may be 'withheld', and exchanged for NZD in order to fund the PAYE due.

Crypto asset payments that are not denominated in NZD will need to have their NZD value calculated, for PAYE purposes, at the prevailing exchange rate on the date of transfer to the employee's wallet.

IRD notes that some crypto assets may be too dissimilar from cash to be treated as salary or wages, for PAYE and other purposes. Treatment as salary or wages requires the crypto asset to have the following features:[20]

- it must not be subject to a 'lock-up' period;
- it must be able to be converted into a fiat currency (on an exchange); and either
- a significant purpose of the crypto asset is to function like a currency; or
- the value of the crypto asset is pegged to one or more fiat currencies.

If the crypto asset is subject to a 'lock-up' period, i.e., the employee cannot convert or sell the asset for cash for a material period of time, then IRD views that payment as not sufficiently resembling a payment of salary or wages and is therefore not subject to PAYE rules.[21]

15. Inland Revenue Department 'Income tax – salary and wages paid in crypto-assets' (27 Jun. 2019), www.classic.ird.govt.nz.
16. *Id.* at 8.
17. Inland Revenue Department 'Income tax – bonuses paid in crypto-assets' (27 Jun. 2019), www.classic.ird.govt.nz.
18. Inland Revenue Department, *supra* n. 15, at 9.
19. *Id.* at 9.
20. *Id.* at 8.
21. *Id.* at 8.

Any crypto asset provided as remuneration that does not have the necessary features to fall within the PAYE rules will instead be a fringe benefit subject to the Fringe Benefit Tax (**FBT**) rules.[22] FBT is a tax payable by employers in relation to non-cash benefits provided to employees. It approximates the amount of PAYE that would be paid in order to deliver after-tax cash remuneration equivalent in value to the non-cash benefit.

Whether an employee who receives a crypto asset as remuneration and then holds the asset would then be taxable on any subsequent increase in value will depend on the facts and circumstances having regard to the principles discussed above at section 1.1.2(b). It may be possible for an employee in this position to assert that crypto assets received as remuneration are not revenue account property because they were not acquired for the purpose of disposal (or any purpose for that matter). However, asserting a non-purposive acquisition would be difficult where there is clear evidence of a deliberate decision to receive crypto assets in substitution for cash remuneration for speculative purposes.

(f) *What are the income/capital gains tax consequences for a merchant receiving payment in crypto assets?*

Crypto assets received as consideration for goods or services supplied by a merchant will be ordinary business income, and therefore taxable. For tax reporting purposes, the merchant will need to calculate the value of the crypto asset in NZD on receipt.

As to whether a merchant receiving payment in crypto assets who then holds the assets would be taxable on any subsequent increase in value, see the discussion with respect to employees receiving crypto assets as remuneration and retaining those assets in section 1.1.2(e) (above).

(g) *What are the income/capital gains tax consequences of a loss of crypto assets?*

For a non-business holder of a crypto asset as revenue account property, the loss of the asset will be treated as a disposal, meaning a deduction for the cost of the asset would be allowed in the tax year it is lost. A business holder of crypto assets as trading stock would revalue lost crypto assets at the end of the tax year concerned at nil, and so would be allowed a net deduction for the carrying value of the asset at the start of that tax year.

(h) *What are the income/capital gains tax consequences of a loss in value of crypto assets?*

An unrealised loss in value of crypto assets of a non-business holder will have no tax effect. A deductible loss will crystallise only at disposal.

22. *Id.* at 6.

A business holder of crypto assets as trading stock may enjoy an earlier deduction for unrealised losses given the ability to revalue trading stock at market selling value at tax year end (*see* above at section 1.1.2(b)).

(i) What are the income/capital gains tax consequences of forks of crypto assets?

In the event of a fork, the relevant provisions of the ITA should have sufficient flexibility to allow the cost of acquisition of the original crypto asset to be appropriately reallocated to both the original crypto asset and the newly created crypto asset according to the ratio of the assets' respective market values at the time of the fork. This will be the case for both business and non-business holders of crypto assets.

(j) What are the income/capital gains tax consequences of airdrops of crypto assets and are the tax consequences different if the airdropped tokens are unwanted?

For a non-business holder, there is no rule in the ITA that would treat the receipt of the crypto asset upon the airdrop as a tax event. Further, a non-business holder may be able to argue that airdropped crypto assets are not acquired for the purpose of disposal, meaning they are not revenue account property and so not taxable on a subsequent disposal.

For a business holder of crypto assets as trading stock, an airdropped crypto asset would likely be treated as an amount derived from the business such that its market value in NZD would be taxable on receipt.[23] Following receipt, the airdropped crypto asset would form part of the holder's trading stock in the normal course, with a base cost equating to its market value at the time of receipt. It is irrelevant whether the airdropped token is unwanted.

(k) What are the income/capital gains tax consequences of (solo, pool, and cloud) mining?

The IRD has a published view that mining is generally an income-earning activity rather than a hobby.[24] As a result, any mining-related fees or rewards are taxable income.[25]

For pool mining, the mining income is derived when the pool periodically distributes each miner's share, calculated individually by reference to its NZD market value at the time of distribution.[26] The IRD's published view does not extend to cloud mining, but there would seem to be little basis to treat it differently from pool mining.

23. Income Tax Act, section CB 1.
24. Inland Revenue Department, 'Mining Cryptocurrency', www.ird.govt.nz.
25. *Supra* n. 24.
26. *Supra* n. 24.

(l) *What are the income/capital gains tax consequences of staking crypto assets?*

The IRD in its published guidance expresses the view that staking is a consensus model (i.e., a way to achieve consensus on the blocks to add to the blockchain) and is therefore a type of crypto asset mining and would be taxed in the same way. *See* above at section 1.12(k).

(m) *What are the income/capital gains tax consequences of an indirect investment in crypto assets?*

New Zealand tax rules would generally apply to the instrument held by the taxpayer, without any look-through to underlying crypto assets. For example, if a taxpayer holds units in an investment fund, and the fund invests in crypto assets, the fund interest would be taxed under rules generally relevant to equity holdings, without any look-through to the crypto assets or any additional tax liability as a result of the fund holding the crypto. The exception would be if the investment entity were tax transparent (e.g., a general or limited partnership) in which case the partners would be treated as holding the underlying crypto assets directly. It is inherent in the legal concept of a partnership that the partners are in business. Accordingly, partners will be treated as business holders and the trading stock rules will apply.

(n) *How is income from crypto assets to be treated under double tax treaty law?*

None of New Zealand's double tax agreements (**DTAs**) directly addresses crypto assets.

The extent to which a non-New Zealand resident who is resident in a country with which New Zealand has a DTA may be taxable in relation to crypto asset transactions with a New Zealand connection would first depend on whether or not the income has a New Zealand source under the ITA. If the income does not have a New Zealand source, New Zealand would not assert any taxing right with respect to the income in the first place and the DTA would be irrelevant.

Taking the example of a non-resident in a New Zealand DTA jurisdiction trading crypto assets on a New Zealand exchange, there are two potentially relevant source rules. The first is income from the carrying on of a business, wholly or partly, in New Zealand.[27] It is unlikely that a non-resident who trades remotely through a New Zealand exchange would be characterised as carrying on business in New Zealand, even in part, but if the non-resident had a related New Zealand presence (including an automated presence such as a server) they would in all likelihood be treated as carrying on business in New Zealand. The second potentially relevant source rule is income

27. Income Tax Act 2007, section YD 4(2).

derived from the disposal of New Zealand situated property.[28] There is no established principle that crypto assets traded on a New Zealand exchange are New Zealand situated property. One can, however, foresee a potential IRD argument that the exchange is the 'locus' of the crypto assets traded through it.

Income may be more likely to have a New Zealand source if the transactions concern New Zealand-issued equity or asset-backed tokens. Under another source rule, income derived from shares in a New Zealand company is deemed to have a source in New Zealand. By analogy, IRD might argue that income derived from equity tokens issued by New Zealand companies has a New Zealand source. Similarly, proceeds received from the sale of asset-backed tokens where the underlying asset is located in New Zealand might be regarded as having a New Zealand source.

If the non-resident's crypto asset income were found to have a New Zealand source, DTA relief would very likely be available in the absence of a New Zealand permanent establishment, under the applicable business income[29] or alienation of property article.[30] New Zealand follows OECD guidelines in relation to the circumstances in which a server located in New Zealand may be a permanent establishment of an enterprise of the DTA counterparty.[31] Consequently, it is conceptually possible that if an enterprise of a counterparty state executes crypto-related transactions through a New Zealand located server owned or leased by the enterprise, the enterprise would be treated as having a New Zealand permanent establishment to which those transactions are attributable.

New Zealand taxes New Zealand residents on their worldwide income, with allowance for foreign tax credits up to the amount of New Zealand tax payable on each segment of foreign income. As such, New Zealand residents are taxable on foreign sourced crypto asset income, subject to any foreign tax credits that may be available for foreign tax paid on that income.

(o) What are the income/capital gains tax consequences of selling crypto assets in an ICO/STO/IEO?

IRD has provided some limited guidance on the tax treatment of an ICO. This states that the tax implications of an ICO will depend on the particular features of the crypto asset. IRD suggests that affected taxpayers apply for a binding ruling to obtain certainty on the issue.[32]

28. Section YD 4(12).
29. For example, Convention between Australia and New Zealand for the Avoidance of Double Taxation with respect to Taxes on Income and Fringe Benefits and the Prevention of Fiscal Evasion, Article 7.
30. Article 13.
31. OECD Committee on Fiscal Affairs 'Clarification on the Application of the Permanent Establishment Definition in E-Commerce: Changes to the Commentary on the Model Tax Convention on Article 5' (22 Dec. 2000), http://www.oecd.org.
32. Inland Revenue Department, *supra* n. 1.

Coins issued to employees in an ICO will likely be subject to FBT.[33]

Conceptually, if crypto assets are issued in order to raise funds to be invested as capital in a business, an argument could be made by the issuer that the issue of the crypto assets in the ICO is not itself a taxable transaction for the issuer. However, if the crypto assets are issued in order to raise revenue, then the proceeds would be taxable. This is likely to be the position for utility tokens since utility tokens do not provide an ownership stake in the issuer but rather represent a coupon for the supply of a particular good or service.

1.1.3 Other Taxes

(a) What are the value added tax/sales tax consequences of selling crypto assets?

As the GSTA currently stands, technically the supply of crypto assets in New Zealand is a taxable supply subject to GST, provided the supplier is a GST registered person.[34] The supply of crypto assets is the supply of a service, on the basis that 'service' is defined in the GSTA as 'anything which is not goods or money' (with 'money' restricted to fiat currency for this purpose).[35] Further, the supply of crypto assets does not fall within any existing exempt supply provision, including that applicable to financial services.[36] In practice, however, parties to crypto transactions have not viewed the trading of crypto assets as having GST implications and IRD itself has been inactive in enforcing GST obligations upon crypto asset suppliers given an apparent acceptance that crypto assets should be treated for GST purposes in line with either fiat currency (outside the GST net) or financial services (generally GST exempt locally and zero-rated if the recipient is a non-resident).

In the February Discussion Document, IRD expressly acknowledged this position and proposed amending the GSTA retrospectively from 1 January 2009 accordingly, with a savings provision for any taxpayer that has applied the GSTA according to its letter in the period before the amendment comes into force.[37] IRD favours treating crypto assets in the same way as money (i.e., completely outside the GST base) but consideration is also being given to the alternative of treating them as financial services (i.e., GST exempt/zero-rated).[38]

33. Inland Revenue Department 'Income tax – employer issued crypto-asses provided to an employee' (27 Jun. 2019), www.classic.ird.govt.nz. *See* above at section 1.1.2(e).
34. A person is liable to be registered for GST if they make supplies, in the course or furtherance of a taxable activity, of more than NZD 60,000 in a twelve-month period.
35. Goods and Services Tax Act 1985, section 2.
36. Section 14.
37. Inland Revenue Department, *supra* n. 2, at 20.
38. *Id.* at 17-18.

(b) Are payments in crypto assets subject to withholding taxes?

If a crypto asset is used to pay salary or wages, dividends, interest or royalties, there will in many cases be a withholding tax obligation under the ITA. The withholding tax will need in each case to be paid in NZD, requiring either a gross-up calculation or an exchange of 'withheld' coins into NZD.

(c) Does payment of compensation in crypto assets give rise to payroll tax consequences?

New Zealand does not have a payroll tax. For discussion on tax obligations in relation to the payment of an employee in crypto assets generally, *see* above at section 1.1.2(e).

(d) Do transactions with crypto assets trigger any transfer taxes?

New Zealand does not have any transfer taxes.

(e) Are firms operating in the crypto space subject to digital service taxes?

New Zealand does not, at this stage, have a digital services tax.

(f) Are crypto assets subject to gift, inheritance, estate, or wealth taxes?

New Zealand does not have gift, inheritance, estate, or wealth taxes.

(g) Are crypto assets subject to exit tax?

New Zealand does not have a specific exit tax regime, although companies that migrate from New Zealand are deemed to dispose of revenue assets at market value and then be liquidated at the moment of migration. Further, if a New Zealand company attributed existing crypto assets to its foreign permanent establishment, this would result in a deemed disposal (and reacquisition), for New Zealand tax purposes, at market value at the time of the attribution. As to general tax implications of disposing of crypto assets, *see* above at section 1.1.2(b).

(h) Can mining trigger gambling tax?

New Zealand does not have a gambling tax.

1.1.4 *Compliance and Documentation Obligations*

(a) What documentation requirements exist for taxpayers regarding crypto assets and are there best practices in recordkeeping to support representations made in tax returns?

There are no special rules for crypto assets. Taxpayers must generally retain, for a period of seven years, from the end of the tax year to which they relate, all financial and other records that are relevant to their tax positions.[39]

IRD recommends that holders of crypto assets should have access to their full transaction history (including transaction dates, the type and number of crypto assets per transaction and on hand at the beginning and end of each tax year, and NZD equivalent values) and be able to export it to a commonly used file, citing CSV as an example.[40] In some cases this may necessitate regularly downloading transaction histories, as exchanges may only maintain records for a short period of time. IRD also recommends taxpayers retain their bank statements and cryptocurrency wallet addresses for verification purposes.[41]

IRD recognizes the development of overseas software providers supplying accounting and tax reporting products. In relation to this, IRD recommends that the taxpayer ensures that the transactions are accounted for in a way that is in accordance with New Zealand tax law.[42]

(b) What is the evidentiary burden of supporting tax positions when a digital wallet address is lost or shared with other persons?

The crypto trader must hold sufficient, verifiable records to be able to prove to IRD that the investment was made and is now irrecoverable. In this circumstance, a deduction should be available (*see* the discussion above at section 1.1.2(g)).

(c) Are crypto asset exchanges and wallet providers subject to reporting obligations?

Crypto asset exchanges and wallet providers are under no positive reporting obligations. However, exchanges and wallet providers could be subjected to general information requests under IRD's broad investigative powers. Sections 16 and 17 of the Tax Administration Act 1994 allow IRD to request any information that is reasonably necessary for the enforcement of any tax rules.

Crypto assets bring with them an additional layer of complexity due to their often confidential and untraceable nature. As the crypto market develops, rules may well be introduced that require exchanges to identify transactions. In practice, this may place

39. Inland Revenue Department, *supra* n. 1.
40. *Supra* n. 1.
41. *Supra* n. 1.
42. *Supra* n. 1.

a constraint on the market given established expectations concerning confidentiality and anonymity.

(d) Are taxpayers holding crypto assets subject to reporting obligations apart from the filing of income tax/capital gains tax returns?

No. Taxpayers holding crypto assets are subject to the ordinary reporting cycle.

(e) Are crypto asset exchanges and wallet providers subject to CRS/FATCA reporting?

IRD has not expressed a view on whether crypto exchanges or wallet providers must report data under CRS/FATCA, but it seems unlikely crypto assets would be characterized as financial assets for the purposes of these regimes.

1.1.5 Civil and Criminal Tax Enforcement

(a) What powers do the tax authorities have to compel the disclosure of information by third parties, such as exchanges or wallet providers, and have these been used in the past?

See above at section 1.1.4(c). IRD has investigative powers under sections 16 and 17 of the Tax Administration Act 1994 to require the production of any information as long as it is reasonably necessary for the enforcement of any tax rule. The term 'reasonably necessary' has been interpreted generously, e.g., *Commissioner of Inland Revenue v. New Zealand Stock Exchange*. In that case, the Court upheld an IRD notice requiring the stock exchange to provide information regarding the identity and trading activity of share traders who had exceeded a certain volume of trades over a particular period.[43] By analogy, it would clearly be within IRD's powers to compel the disclosure of information concerning crypto asset holders or transactions from a New Zealand exchange or wallet provider. As noted above at section 1.1.4(e), there may be practical limitations on IRD's ability to obtain useful information given the anonymity of exchanges, but the looming policy question is whether exchanges should be required to obtain and hold information about their users.

Conceptually, IRD could also seek information beyond its jurisdiction under mutual assistance articles in DTAs and the Convention of Mutual Administrative Assistance in Tax matters (to which New Zealand is a signatory).

Whether IRD has used its powers to obtain information from crypto exchanges or wallet providers is not a matter that is in the public domain.

43. *Commissioner of Inland Revenue v. New Zealand Stock Exchange* (1990) 12 NZTC 7259 (CA).

(b) *What measures have the tax authorities undertaken in the past to ensure crypto tax compliance?*

Again, it is not in the public domain whether IRD has taken specific enforcement actions.

(c) *Are the tax authorities cooperating with tax authorities in other jurisdictions on enforcement?*

It is to date unclear whether, or to what degree, IRD has been cooperating with tax authorities in other jurisdictions on enforcement.

Norway

Joachim M. Bjerke & Benjamin J. Hamnes

1. COUNTRY GUIDES

1.1 Norway

1.1.1 Applicable Tax Law, Guidance, and Case Law

(a) Which laws, regulations, and other administrative guidance exist dealing with crypto assets?

Acquisition and sale of cryptocurrencies and tokens, as well as mining of cryptocurrencies, are not subject to specific rules or regulations with respect to taxation under Norwegian law. The tax treatment of crypto assets is determined based on the general rules in the Norwegian Tax Act[1] and the Norwegian Value Added Tax Act.[2] There has been limited administrative guidance on the direct tax treatment of crypto assets in recent years.[3] However, the Norwegian tax authorities have on their website stated that the taxation of crypto assets shall follow the general rules for taxation of income and wealth.[4] In relation to VAT, the Norwegian tax authorities published a statement in

1. The Norwegian Tax Act (*LOV-1999-03-26-14* (*skatteloven*)), as amended.
2. The Norwegian Value Added Tax Act (*LOV-2009-06-19-58* (*merverdiavgiftsloven*)), as amended.
3. Note that the Norwegian tax authorities issued a statement in 2013 where the general view was that bitcoins shall be treated as an asset subject to taxation once the bitcoin is realized for tax purposes. Taxable realization occurs once the bitcoin is disposed of, e.g., by way of a sale. Losses would be deductible insofar as capital gains would be taxable. This view is upheld in the guidance provided on the official website of the Norwegian Tax Administration as of May 2020.
4. The Norwegian Tax Administration, *Tax and VAT relating to Bitcoin and other virtual currencies*, official website (opened 24 May 2020), https://www.skatteetaten.no/en/business-and-organisation/reporting-and-industries/industries-special-regulations/internet/tax-and-vat-on-virtual-currencies/.

2018 on the VAT treatment of cryptocurrencies and the exemption for financial services.[5]

Pursuant to the general rules in the Norwegian Tax Act, individuals and companies tax resident in Norway are, as a starting point, taxable for their global wealth and income irrespective of whether the source state is Norway or a jurisdiction abroad.[6] Under domestic tax law, a non-resident person or company may have a limited tax liability to Norway on income derived from business activities in which the person or company engages or participates, provided the business activity is carried on in Norway or managed from Norway.[7] The right to tax a non-resident person or company for such income may be restricted under an applicable double tax treaty. It should be noted that computation of taxes is done in NOK, which entails that, e.g., assets denominated in a foreign currency must be converted to NOK for tax purposes.

With respect to the questions and comments in this chapter, we assume that the relevant subjects are tax resident in Norway.

(b) Which court cases exist dealing with crypto assets?

As of May 2020, there are to our knowledge no court cases in Norway dealing with the taxation or VAT treatment of crypto assets.

1.1.2 Income and Capital Gains Taxes

(a) How are crypto assets classified for income and capital gains tax purposes?

For income and capital gains tax purposes, crypto assets are classified as capital assets. The classification as a capital asset applies irrespective of whether the crypto assets are held in relation to a non-business activity (i.e., by individuals) or in relation to a business activity.[8] The consequence of classifying crypto assets as capital assets is that the rules on taxable realization of assets is applicable and may result in a taxable gain or in a deductible loss upon disposal of the crypto asset. Losses are deductible to the extent capital gains are taxable.

5. The Norwegian Tax Administration, *Utvinning av kryptovaluta – mval. § 3-6*, official website (17 Apr. 2018), https://www.skatteetaten.no/rettskilder/type/uttalelser/prinsipputtalelser/utvinning-av-kryptovaluta/.
6. *Cf.* section 2-1 (1), *cf.* (9), and section 2-2 (1), *cf.* (6), of the Norwegian Tax Act.
7. *Cf.* section 2-3 (1) b of the Norwegian Tax Act.
8. Note that the extent of acquisition and sale of crypto assets and the mining of crypto assets may affect whether the person (or persons) performing such activities should be deemed to undertake a business activity for tax purposes. Constitution of a business activity for tax purposes will impose additional registration and reporting requirements for the taxpayer.

(b) *What are the income/capital gains tax consequences of selling crypto assets against fiat currency?*

The income tax consequences of selling crypto assets against fiat currency are, as a starting point, the same irrespective of whether the crypto assets are held by individuals or a company as business assets: The taxpayer needs to compute capital gain or loss of crypto assets at the time of disposal. Capital gains are taxable and capital losses are deductible, both at a rate of 22%.[9] Capital losses are deductible against other sources of income of the taxpayer. If the activities performed by an individual represent trading, which constitutes a taxable business activity, the individual will be deemed to operate a sole proprietorship and can be taxed at a marginal rate of 49.6% (in 2020). There is no FIFO-principle (first in, first out) applicable when disposing of crypto assets. Instead, the taxpayer must determine which crypto asset is sold and compute the capital gain/loss based on the input value and output value of that specific crypto asset.

Capital gains and losses are computed as the difference between the input value (acquisition price plus transaction costs) and the output value (sales price minus transaction costs). Since crypto assets normally are settled in a foreign currency, the value of the crypto assets must be converted to NOK for tax purposes. The taxpayer must compute the value of the crypto assets in NOK at the date of the acquisition and subsequently at the date of disposal. The computation of the value shall be based on the relevant currency exchange rate at the date of acquisition and at the date of disposal (e.g., USD or EUR to NOK). The exchange rate should preferably be derived from the official quotations from Norges Bank (the central bank of Norway).

Capital gains or losses due to changes in currency rates in the ownership period are not computed separately, but form an integral part of the computation of the capital gain or loss of the crypto asset at the time of realization (a so-called consolidation principle).

(c) *What are the income/capital gains tax consequences of exchanging crypto assets against other crypto assets?*

In circumstances where one type of crypto asset (e.g., bitcoin) is exchanged against a different crypto asset (e.g., ether), a taxable realization of the original crypto asset is considered to have occurred. Computation of the capital gain or loss on the original crypto asset (e.g., bitcoin) follows the principles outlined in section 1.1.2(b) above.

Since an exchange of crypto assets occurs, the input value of the new crypto asset (e.g., ether) will equal the output value of the original crypto asset (e.g., bitcoin). If the new crypto asset (e.g., ether) is sold against fiat currency at a later stage this would constitute a taxable realization and a capital gain or loss would need to be computed for the sale of the ether.

9. *Cf.* section 5-1 and section 5-30, *cf.* section 9-2, of the Norwegian Tax Act.

(d) *If a distinction is made between business assets and non-business assets, when does trading in crypto assets lead to a trade or business?*

Whether the trading of crypto assets constitutes a 'business' for tax purposes must be assessed based on the criteria established through court case precedent:

- the activity must have a certain duration;
- the activity must have a certain scope;
- the activity must be likely to generate a profit (objectively); and
- the activity must be carried out at the taxpayer's own expense and risk.

Sporadic trading of crypto assets would normally not be sufficient to constitute a business activity. However, if the trading occurs routinely with completion of a significant amount of transactions, the trading would be more likely to constitute a business. There is no clear-cut standard for what should be considered as a 'significant amount of transactions'. This must be assessed on a case-by-case basis. If the taxpayer performs activities such as brokerage, reporting, and calculation of gain/loss as services on behalf of other persons or enterprises, these would be arguments for constituting a business activity.

(e) *What are the income/capital gains tax consequences for an employee receiving wages or salaries in crypto assets?*

If an employee receives wages or salaries in crypto assets, this would represent compensation in kind for the employee.[10] The tax treatment for the employee would be identical to the tax treatment had the wages or salaries been compensated in fiat currency. This entails that the employee will be subject to progressive taxation based on the value of the compensation in kind, with a minimum tax rate of 30.2% and with a marginal tax rate of approximately 46.4%.

Since the crypto assets represent compensation in kind, the assets must be valued at their fair market value at the time of the transfer (i.e., at the time the employee receives or has a right to receive the salary).[11] Crypto assets are normally denominated in a foreign currency, e.g., USD, and the value of the crypto assets must therefore be converted into NOK at the time of the transfer.

(f) *What are the income/capital gains tax consequences for a merchant receiving payment in crypto assets?*

The income tax consequences for a merchant receiving payment in crypto assets are identical to that of a merchant receiving payment for goods and services in fiat currency. The value of the goods or services sold by the merchant constitutes taxable income. Since the crypto assets represent compensation in kind, the crypto assets must

10. *Cf.* section 5-12 of the Norwegian Tax Act.
11. *Cf.* section 5-3 and section 14-3 of the Norwegian Tax Act.

be valued at their fair market value at the time of transaction (when the agreement is entered into). Crypto assets are normally denominated in a foreign currency, e.g., USD, and the value of the crypto assets must therefore be converted into NOK at the time of the transaction.

If the merchant at a later stage exchanges the received crypto assets into fiat currency or a different crypto asset, this would represent a new taxable transaction. Upon a disposal of the initially received crypto assets, the merchant would need to compute the capital gain or loss in NOK applying the same principles as described in section 1.1.2(b) above.

(g) What are the income/capital gains tax consequences of a loss of crypto assets?

A loss of crypto assets is considered as a realization for tax purposes, regardless of whether the taxpayer receives insurance payment or compensation for the loss.[12] Provided that no insurance or compensation is paid for the loss to the taxpayer, the assets would be realized with a tax deductible capital loss.[13] Capital losses are deductible against other sources of income of the taxpayer. If the taxpayer receives an insurance payment or compensation for the loss, this could result in the computation of a taxable capital gain provided that the received insurance payment or compensation exceeds the value of the loss.

(h) What are the income/capital gains tax consequences of a loss in value of crypto assets?

Any reduction in value of crypto assets will not be recognized for tax purposes before the crypto assets are realized (e.g., sold, exchanged, lost). Hence, a reduction or loss in value of crypto assets during the ownership period will have no immediate tax consequences for an individual holder of crypto assets or for a business holding crypto assets.[14]

(i) What are the income/capital gains tax consequences of forks of crypto assets?

No administrative guidance on the tax treatment of forks of crypto assets has been issued. Thus, the tax treatment must be determined based on the general rules in the Norwegian Tax Act. In this relation, we believe that it would be prudent to classify the newly received crypto asset resulting from the fork as a form of return on capital

12. *Cf.* section 9-2 of the Norwegian Tax Act.
13. *Cf.* section 6-2 of the Norwegian Tax Act.
14. Since crypto assets are regarded as capital assets, the actual value of crypto assets is reflected when computing the net wealth tax of individuals. If crypto assets lose their value, this will affect the computation of the net wealth tax although the crypto assets are not yet realized for tax purposes.

derived from the ownership of the original crypto asset. In such case, the value of the return (i.e., the new crypto asset) would need to be computed at the time of the fork. This value would also form the input value of the new crypto asset. An individual owning the original crypto assets would be taxed for such return on capital at the time of the fork, based on the new crypto asset's fair market value.[15] The same principles would apply if the forked crypto asset was owned by a business.

(j) What are the income/capital gains tax consequences of airdrops of crypto assets and are the tax consequences different if the airdropped tokens are unwanted?

Airdrops of crypto assets, i.e., a distribution of crypto assets free of charge for the recipient provided for promotional purposes, would be treated differently based on whether the parties to the transaction are individuals or businesses. Normally, airdrops would occur from a distributor carrying on a business for tax purposes. There are no regulations of airdrops in Norwegian law, thus, the tax treatment of the transaction must be assessed in accordance with the general rules. As a starting point, the following principles would apply:

- Provided that the airdrop is distributed from a business, the crypto assets (currency or tokens) would be classified as capital assets within the business. If assets are distributed free of charge from a business, they could represent a gift (gratuitous transfer), which is taxable at the hand of the business as if a sale was undertaken at fair market value.[16] Alternatively, the distribution of crypto assets through an airdrop may be viewed as a tax-deductible marketing cost in some instances. This would depend on an assessment of the distributor's business, purpose of the airdrop, etc.
- The gift would not be taxable for an individual being the recipient, but the individual would inherit the tax basis of the crypto assets and need to compute a capital gain or loss once the assets are disposed of.[17] If the recipient is a company carrying on a business activity, the gift would probably be required to be recognized as income (especially if a promotional service is provided in return). The company's input value on the crypto assets would equal the amount recognized as income upon receiving the crypto assets as a gift. If the crypto assets are disposed of later, the company would need to compute a capital gain or loss.

In the assessment, it is irrelevant whether the recipient, an individual or a company, wanted the crypto assets from the airdrop or not.

15. *Cf.* section 5-20 (1) of the Norwegian Tax Act.
16. *Cf.* section 5-2 (1) of the Norwegian Tax Act. Withdrawal of business assets for personal use is a taxable transaction for the business (equal to a transaction where the assets are sold at fair market value). However, an airdrop from a business with withdrawal of assets for personal use is unlikely to occur.
17. *Cf.* section 9-7 (3) of the Norwegian Tax Act.

(k) What are the income/capital gains tax consequences of (solo, pool, and cloud) mining?

Companies being tax resident in Norway are taxable on their income derived from solo, pool and cloud mining activities (verification of transactions within the blockchain). The income tax consequences for an individual undertaking solo, pool or cloud mining are affected by whether the performed mining activity constitutes a taxable business activity or not. The statements from the Norwegian tax authorities focus solely on solo mining, i.e., where a person performs mining by himself. Although the statements from the Norwegian tax authorities focus solely on solo mining, the assessment of whether an activity constitutes a taxable business activity equally applies in relation to pool mining and cloud mining arrangements.[18]

The Norwegian tax authorities have stated that, generally, the use of a private laptop to mine bitcoins is not considered a taxable business activity.[19] This would equally apply to other cryptocurrencies. Factors that may impact the business activity assessment are whether the taxpayer has made larger investment in computers and mining equipment, and the frequency of administrative follow-up performed on a daily or regular basis. According to the guidance from the Norwegian tax authorities, the '… decisive factor for deciding if the business activity requirement for mining is met is that the activity related to the follow-up of mining is carried out on a regular basis and is of a certain scope'.[20]

If the mining activity is not considered a taxable business activity, the individual performing the mining would not be required to recognise the received crypto assets as taxable income on an ongoing basis, but the actual value of the crypto assets is accounted for in the computation of the individual's net wealth. If the received crypto assets later are disposed of the individual would need to compute a capital gain or loss as the transaction would be a taxable realization.

Provided that the mining activity is considered to constitute a taxable business activity, the crypto assets received by performing the mining must be recognized as taxable income at their fair market value in NOK at the time they are received. If the crypto assets later are disposed of, this would constitute a taxable realization of the assets and a capital gain or loss would need to be computed. In cases of pool mining, it could be questioned whether the mining activities performed by all participants together could constitute a partnership for tax purposes.

18. *See also* section 1.1.1(d) above: The assessment of whether the solo mining, pool mining or cloud mining activity constitutes a business must be based on the conditions of whether the activity have certain duration, have a certain scope, is likely to generate a profit (objectively), and is carried out at the taxpayer's own expense and risk.
19. The Norwegian Tax Administration, *supra* n. 4.
20. *Ibid.*

(l) *What are the income/capital gains tax consequences of staking crypto assets?*

Proof of stake, as an alternative to proof of work, requires holders of the cryptocurrency to stake the blockchain, i.e., commit their cryptocurrencies to the blockchain and act as validators of the future transactions. Once the transactions are validated, the validator receives a corresponding fee. Proof of stake is by virtue of its mechanism a more passive activity than proof of work. Hence, performing an activity of validating transactions in the blockchain based on a proof of stake algorithm would require less work and thus would not likely fulfil the criteria of a taxable business activity. On the other hand, it could be argued that the taxpayer would have limited downside when performing the activity (mainly electricity costs), and thus the criteria that the activity must be likely to generate a profit could more easily be fulfilled.

Provided that staking crypto assets does not constitute a taxable business activity, the crypto assets received by the staking would only be taxable once they are realized in a later transaction. It could be questioned whether the fees received by validating transactions due to staking should be viewed as a form of interest payment (which would be taxable both for an individual and a business).

(m) *What are the income/capital gains tax consequences of an indirect investment in crypto assets?*

The income tax consequences of an indirect investment in crypto assets would be treated identically to indirect investments in other kinds of assets. The tax consequences would primarily be determined based on the object of the direct investment, and not the underlying asset being the indirect investment. Some examples may be:

- If one were to invest in units in an alternative investment fund trading in crypto assets, the investment fund units would represent capital assets for the investor whereby a capital gain or loss would need to be computed once the investment fund units are disposed of. If an individual were to sell units in an alternative investment fund trading in crypto assets, a capital gain would be taxable at a grossed up rate of 31.68% (22% x 1.44) and a loss would be deductible with 31.68%. If a company were to sell units in such an alternative investment fund, a capital gain could be exempted from taxation under the participation exemption method (provided the units are qualifying objects). Correspondingly, a loss would not be deductible. The participation exemption method entails that certain capital gains on shares, partnership interests, and financial instruments with shares as underlying object are not taxed at the time of realization. The method requires that the Norwegian owner of shares, partnership interests, and financial instruments with shares as underlying object is a qualifying subject under the method and that the asset disposed of is a qualifying object. Norwegian limited liability companies are qualifying subjects under the participation exemption method. Whether alternative investment fund units are qualifying objects must be assessed on a case-by-case basis, having regard to, *inter alia*, how the fund is structured and how its underlying investments are carried out. For investments outside the EU/EEA, there is a general requirement of 10% ownership and a two-year holding period.

- As an alternative, an investor could purchase derivatives having a cryptocurrency as its underlying asset. Provided that the derivative would be classified as a stand-alone capital asset separate from the underlying asset, disposal of such derivatives would follow the rules on taxation of capital gains or loss. Hence, capital gains would be taxed at 22% and losses would be deductible with 22%, both for an individual and for a business. Derivatives having cryptocurrency as underlying assets would probably not be a qualifying asset under the participation exemption method. Consequently, a business trading derivative having cryptocurrency as the underlying assets would need to compute a capital gain or loss on the derivatives once they are disposed of.

(n) How is income from crypto assets to be treated under double tax treaty law?

Neither the Norwegian tax authorities nor the Norwegian Ministry of Finance have provided any guidance with respect to crypto assets and their treatment under applicable double tax treaties. Normally, the classification of an income under domestic law would also provide the starting point for how the income should be treated under a double tax treaty. The majority of Norway's tax treaties are based on the OECD Model Tax Convention. Thus, it is likely that any development within the OECD and between OECD Member States in the area of crypto assets and double tax treaty law will be taken into account by the Norwegian tax authorities and the Norwegian Ministry of Finance.

According to Norwegian tax law it is likely that a non-resident company having a data centre mining crypto assets in Norway could be deemed taxable in Norway for the business carried on through that data centre.[21] Further, under the OECD Model Tax Convention, such data centre could qualify as a permanent establishment according to Article 5 of the Convention. If the criteria of limited tax liability according to the Norwegian Tax Act and the criteria of constituting a permanent establishment under Article 5 are fulfilled, the income arising from the activities of the data centre would be taxable in Norway. Income arising from the activities of the data centre would need to be allocated between the non-resident company and its permanent establishment in Norway according to Article 7 of the OECD Model Tax Convention.

Article 7 of the OECD Model Tax Convention, regulating the attribution of profits between an enterprise resident in one of the contracting states and the enterprise's permanent establishment in the other contracting state, would likely be of more relevance in the future in line with the globalization of mining communities and

21. *Cf.* section 2-3 (1) b of the Norwegian Tax Act.

trading activities of crypto assets. Many of Norway's double tax treaties have incorporated the Authorized OECD Approach (AOA) from 2010 as the relevant standard under an Article 7 profit allocation. One would expect that this principle would apply also for enterprises dealing with crypto assets.

(o) *What are the income/capital gains tax consequences of selling crypto assets in an ICO/STO/IEO?*

The Norwegian tax authorities have only briefly mentioned the tax consequences of ICOs, which, as with most taxation of crypto assets in Norway, are required to be assessed on a case-by-case basis. No statements have been made with respect to STO and IEO. There are no specific regulations applicable for ICOs, STOs, or IEOs and the general rules in the Norwegian Tax Act are given effect. ICOs are normally performed by companies as issuers and have been most popular the last years. Factors that may affect the tax treatment of the tokens distributed through ICOs, STOs and IEOs are, but are not limited to, the following:

- the smart contract being the basis for the tokens;
- whether the tokens are distributed free of charge or are purchased;
- whether the provided tokens are utility tokens or security tokens;
- whether the tokens provide the recipient with any rights;
- whether the value of the tokens are dependent on underlying assets' performance;
- how the tokens can be disposed of.

With respect to the VAT treatment of an ICO, the Norwegian tax authorities have stated that '[with] regards to VAT and ICOs, an individual assessment must be made of whether there is a supply of goods or services and if so, what has been supplied, including whether or not it can be considered a financial service'.[22]

1.1.3 *Other Taxes*

(a) *What are the value added tax/sales tax consequences of selling crypto assets?*

The Norwegian tax authorities' view is that use of cryptocurrency as a means of *payment* and services of *exchanging* cryptocurrency will often be subject to exemption from VAT based on the 'financial services' alternative in section 3-6 of the Norwegian Value Added Tax Act. This follows the stance taken by the Norwegian Ministry of Finance based on their comments to ECJ's ruling in Case No. C-264/14. The Norwegian

22. The Norwegian Tax Administration, *supra* n. 4.

Ministry of Finance also stated that the Norwegian VAT treatment of crypto assets should account for future developments within the EU.[23]

Further, it should be noted that the Norwegian tax authorities have issued administrative guidance with respect to the VAT implications of *mining* cryptocurrency, and concluded in 2018 that the mining activity should for VAT purposes be viewed as a VAT exempt activity under the 'financial services' alternative under section 3-6 of the Norwegian Value Added Tax Act.[24]

(b) Are payments in crypto assets subject to withholding taxes?

No, crypto assets are not subject to withholding taxes. However, if a Norwegian limited liability company resolves a dividend distribution in kind to its shareholders, with crypto assets being distributed as compensation, Norway would levy withholding taxes on the dividend distribution to non-resident recipients.[25] The domestic withholding tax rate is 25%, but the rate of the withholding taxes may be reduced based on an applicable tax treaty.

Norway has no rules on withholding tax for interest payments from a Norwegian entity to a non-resident recipient. The Norwegian Ministry of Finance has proposed the introduction of such rules, but the proposal requires a final legislative process to be effective, which is currently not actioned. If withholding tax on interest payments is introduced in the legislation, an interest payment with cryptocurrency as the functional currency could potentially be subject to the new rules.

(c) Does payment of compensation in crypto assets give rise to payroll tax consequences?

Compensation in crypto assets to an employee will represent compensation in kind, which is taxable as salary. This renders several payroll tax consequences for the employer. The employer is obliged to withhold tax from the employee's gross salary and pay an employer's national insurance contribution.[26] The employer's national insurance contribution is normally 14.1%, but can be lower. The consideration in kind must be reported by the employer to the tax authorities. Difficulties can arise when the employer shall withhold tax on behalf of the employee for the value of the crypto assets. For consideration in kind (i.e., crypto assets), the employer would withhold the computed tax by withholding the amount from other cash considerations to the employee. If the cash considerations to the employee do not provide sufficient cover for

23. The Norwegian Ministry of Finance, *Merverdiavgift – unntaket for finansielle tjenester*, official website (6 Feb. 2017), https://www.regjeringen.no/no/dokumenter/merverdiavgift---unntaket-for-finansielle-tjenester/id2538129/.
24. USKD-2018-14 in UTV-2018-739.
25. *Cf.* section 10-13 of the Norwegian Tax Act. However, note that there are several exemptions to the rules on withholding taxes for dividend distributions.
26. *Cf.* section 23-2 of the National Insurance Act.

the employer to withhold the computed tax for the consideration in kind, the employer would be obliged to contact the tax authorities.

(d) *Do transactions with crypto assets trigger any transfer taxes?*

Under the current rules, no transfer tax or stamp duty would apply to transactions with crypto assets.

(e) *Are firms operating in the crypto space subject to digital service taxes?*

Norway has currently no digital service taxes introduced in its legislation. Consequently, no digital service taxes would apply with respect to crypto assets.

(f) *Are crypto assets subject to gift, inheritance, estate, or wealth taxes?*

Norway does not have any gift or inheritance taxes. Estate tax will not be levied on crypto assets. Since crypto assets are regarded as capital assets for individuals, the value of crypto assets shall be accounted for in the computation of an individual's net wealth tax. The value of the crypto assets shall be based on their value in NOK per 1 January in the year after the income year. Net wealth tax may be levied towards individuals having a net wealth above NOK 1,500,000. The tax rate is 0.85%. Wealth taxes do not apply for companies.

(g) *Are crypto assets subject to exit tax?*

Yes, crypto assets will likely be covered under the current general rules on exit taxation. If the rules on exit taxation applies, capital gain on crypto assets would be taxable as if such assets were realized for tax purposes on the last day before the exit event, *see also* section 1.1.2(b) above.[27] Losses would be deductible to the extent capital gains are taxable. Payment of taxes for capital gains on assets may be deferred in some instances and under certain conditions.[28] Exemptions from exit taxation could apply in cases where a Norwegian company becomes resident in a different EEA jurisdiction.

(h) *Can mining trigger gambling tax?*

Norway has no specific rules on gambling tax. Incidental income arising from competition, games, lotteries, and similar activities are as a rule taxable provided the value of the prize exceeds NOK 10,000.[29] Although it could be argued that the effects

27. *Cf.* sections 9-14 and 10-71 of the Norwegian Tax Act.
28. *Cf.* section 9-14-1 to 9-14-4 in the regulations to section 9-14 of the Norwegian Tax Act.
29. *Cf.* section 5-50 of the Norwegian Tax Act.

of mining have a somewhat incidental character, since the 'prize' is received by solving cryptographic algorithms first, it is unlikely that the rules on incidental income would be applicable for mining activities.

1.1.4 *Compliance and Documentation Obligations*

(a) What documentation requirements exist for taxpayers regarding crypto assets and are there best practices in recordkeeping to support representations made in tax returns?

Pursuant to the general rules in the Norwegian Tax Administration Act, the taxpayer is obligated to provide correct and sufficient information when submitting his tax return.[30] In this regard, the taxpayer must act in good faith and in a loyal manner towards the tax authorities so that the taxation becomes correct in due course. This general rule applies to the disclosure of all representations made in the tax return.

With respect to crypto assets, the taxpayer should disclose information on current balances in his digital wallets with specified amounts for each crypto asset (tokens included). Additionally, the taxpayer should disclose information on acquisitions and sales throughout the income year, and an overview of crypto assets received due to mining and on which date.

There is no specific set of documentation requirements applying to crypto assets. In relation to bitcoins, the Norwegian tax authorities have stated on their website that the following documentation should be retained by the taxpayer:[31]

- transaction log/documentation of realized bitcoins from brokers/exchange agents with bitcoin addresses;
- documentation showing the date when the sold bitcoins are acquired, mined or purchased, including bitcoin addresses for these and the input value;
- mining log – overview of number of mined bitcoins and their realization date (pay-out address).

This guidance would equally apply to other kinds of cryptocurrencies and tokens. It is not required to submit the documentation together with the tax return, but the taxpayer should be able to provide this documentation upon request from the tax authorities. Since these documentation requirements are not incorporated by law, the Norwegian tax authorities would not be able to levy any surcharges if a taxpayer is not able to provide the above-mentioned documentation. The taxpayer must be able to support his tax positions, and it is important to assess what kind of documentation that is sufficient for the specific transactions. Regards must be had to the general rule of providing correct and sufficient information.

30. *Cf.* section 8-1 of the Norwegian Tax Administration Act.
31. The Norwegian Tax Administration, *supra* n. 4.

(b) *What is the evidentiary burden of supporting tax positions when a digital wallet address is lost or shared with other persons?*

The evidentiary burden of supporting a tax position in case a digital wallet address is lost or shared with other persons must be determined based on the specific burden of proof criteria established in the applicable tax rule. Normally, the tax authorities have the burden of proof; the tax authorities must evidence that it is more likely than not that the taxpayer's reported tax position is incorrect. If a digital wallet address is lost, i.e., that a user's public and private key is lost, the taxpayer could have difficulties extracting transaction logs, balances, etc. This would not mean that the tax authorities simply can presume that the tax positions are wrong upon inspection if the transaction logs are not available, but the taxpayer would need to support his tax positions with indicia (which could be more vulnerable for challenge).

(c) *Are crypto asset exchanges and wallet providers subject to reporting obligations?*

Crypto asset exchanges and wallet providers are not subject to any regulatory reporting obligations or reporting to the Norwegian tax authorities about their customers. However, *see also* comments in section 1.1.5(a) below.

(d) *Are taxpayers holding crypto assets subject to reporting obligations apart from the filing of income tax/capital gains tax returns?*

Except for the annual filing of their tax return, taxpayers owning crypto assets are not subject to any additional reporting obligations. Crypto assets owned but not realized by an individual taxpayer must be reported in the tax return as the assets are of relevance in the computation of the individual's net wealth tax.

(e) *Are crypto asset exchanges and wallet providers subject to CRS/FATCA reporting?*

Crypto asset exchanges and wallet providers are not explicitly subject to CRS or FATCA reporting in Norway.[32] The Norwegian tax authorities have not provided any guidance in this respect. The assessment of whether crypto asset exchanges and wallet providers are subject to CRS or FATCA reporting in Norway would depend on the functionality of the exchanges and wallet providers and whether they, after an interpretation of the relevant criteria for being a subject under CRS/FATCA reporting, should be deemed to be covered. This is likely not the case today, as the current rules are focused towards traditional financial institutions.

32. *Cf.* section 7-3 of the Norwegian Tax Administration Act.

1.1.5 *Civil and Criminal Tax Enforcement*

(a) What powers do the tax authorities have to compel the disclosure of information by third parties, such as exchanges or wallet providers, and have these been used in the past?

The Norwegian Tax Administration Act[33] promulgates that third parties are, upon request, obliged to provide the Norwegian tax authorities with information which may be of relevance for a taxpayer.[34] If third parties do not comply with such information request, the Norwegian tax authorities may levy charges such as daily fines for non-compliance.[35] These rules could apply to crypto asset exchanges and wallet providers upon further review.

Under the current rules, the Norwegian tax authorities have broad authority to perform inspection at the premises of a business being subject to the information disclosure rules for third parties.[36] This means that the Norwegian tax authorities in principle could perform inspection at the premises of a crypto asset exchange or a wallet provider and get access to, *inter alia*, archives, business assets, etc. If a third party does not comply with the rules on inspection of the premises, they could potentially receive fines and be sentenced to jail.[37]

There is no public information on whether the tax authorities have applied these rules towards crypto assets exchanges and wallet providers in the past.

(b) What measures have the tax authorities undertaken in the past to ensure crypto tax compliance?

There is no public information on what measures the Norwegian tax authorities have undertaken in the past to ensure crypto tax compliance, except for the administrative guidance provided in 2013[38], 2018,[39] and the current information on their official website.

(c) Are the tax authorities cooperating with tax authorities in other jurisdictions on enforcement?

It is not publicly known or confirmed whether the Norwegian tax authorities cooperate with tax authorities in other jurisdictions on the enforcement of taxation of crypto

33. The Norwegian Tax Administration Act (*LOV-2016-05-27-14* (*skatteforvaltningsloven*)), as amended.
34. *Cf.* section 10-2 of the Norwegian Tax Administration Act.
35. *Cf.* section 14-1 of the Norwegian Tax Administration Act.
36. *Cf.* section 10-4, *cf.* section 10-2, of the Norwegian Tax Administration Act.
37. *Cf.* section 14-13 of the Norwegian Tax Administration Act.
38. The Norwegian Tax Administration, *Bruk av bitcoins – skatte- og avgiftsmessige konsekvenser*, official website (11 Nov. 2013), https://www.skatteetaten.no/en/rettskilder/type/uttalelser/prinsipputtalelser/bruk-av-bitcoins--skatte--og-avgiftsmessige-konsekvenser/.
39. The Norwegian Tax Administration, *supra* n. 5.

assets. Generally, it should be noted that all of Norway's double tax treaties contain special provisions for the administrative cooperation on exchange of information in tax matters. Norway has also concluded separate agreements on the exchange of information for tax purposes with several jurisdictions.[40] Additionally, Norway is a signatory to the Multilateral Convention on Mutual Administrative Assistance in Tax Matters developed by the OECD and the Council of Europe. Further, Norway has entered into an agreement with the EU on the administrative cooperation combating fraud and recovery of claims in the field of value added tax.

40. The Norwegian Government, *Exchange of Information and other Agreements Regarding Mutual Administrative Assistance*, official website (1 Nov. 2019), https://www.regjeringen.no/en/topics/the-economy/taxes-and-duties/tax-treaties-between-norway-and-other-st/exchange-of-information-and-other-agreements-regarding-muteral-administrative-assistanse/id2576003/.

Poland

Joanna Prokurat

1. COUNTRY GUIDES

1.1 Poland

1.1.1 Applicable Tax Law, Guidance, and Case Law

(a) Which laws, regulations, and other administrative guidance exist dealing with crypto assets?

There is no single act regulating all crypto asset matters. The definition of crypto assets and general regulations related thereto are included in the Act on Countering Money Laundering and Terrorism Financing of 1 March 2018 (consolidated text: Journal of Laws of 2019, item 1115 – the 'AML Act').

Since 1 January 2019, amendments to the Polish Corporate Income Tax Act ('CIT Act') and Personal Income Tax Act ('PIT Act') have been introduced and specific regulations on income tax on transactions involving cryptocurrencies are now in place (new regulations are limited to cryptocurrencies – they do not apply to all crypto assets). Since there is a five-year statute of limitation period for taxes in Poland, the old rules apply to tax settlements made for 2018 and earlier tax years (in Poland, an entrepreneur's tax year does not have to be the same as the calendar year, in some cases the tax year may last up to twenty-three months. As the income tax rules binding from the first day of a given tax year apply to the whole tax year, the old income tax regulations may continue to apply even in 2020).

The amended CIT Act and PIT Act define cryptocurrencies by referring to the definition provided in the AML Act, which states that virtual currency shall be understood as a digital representation of value which is not:

(a) legal tender issued by the National Bank of Poland (NBP), foreign central banks or other public administration authorities;
(b) international unit of account established by an international organization and accepted by particular countries being members of that organization or cooperating with that organization;
(c) electronic money within the meaning of the Payment Services Act of 19 August 2011;
(d) financial instrument within the meaning of the Act on Trading in Financial Instruments of 29 July 2005;
(e) promissory note or cheque;

and which is convertible into legal tender in business transactions and is accepted as a mean of exchange, and which may be stored or transferred electronically or may be traded electronically.

No regulations have been introduced to deal with cryptocurrencies on the grounds of another tax than income tax. In particular, there are no Value Added Tax (VAT) regulations that would directly apply to crypto assets.

No administrative guidance or general tax ruling has been issued by the Polish tax authorities with respect to crypto assets on the grounds of the laws currently in force.

The Polish tax authorities have issued various individual tax rulings related to taxation of crypto assets. Almost all deal with cryptocurrencies. In Poland, individual tax rulings are issued upon taxpayer request and are binding for the tax authorities (under certain conditions, i.e., the description of facts or future facts must fully reflect the reality). The procedure of obtaining an individual tax ruling is quite easy and inexpensive.

(b) Which court cases exist dealing with crypto assets?

There have been various cases of the Polish Supreme Administrative Court or lower-instance administrative courts dealing with taxation of crypto assets. Most judgments refer to bitcoins and other cryptocurrencies and were issued on the grounds of the income tax law in force until 31 December 2018. There is no court judgment regarding cryptocurrencies issued on the basis of the CIT Act or PIT Act in force since 1 January 2019, when regulations specifically dealing with cryptocurrencies entered into force (this was mainly because of procedural reasons: the two-instance procedure before the tax administration authorities must be completed before an appeal to the administrative court may be filed and the period of waiting for the appeal procedure is relatively long; furthermore, some taxpayers decide not to file the case in court). These court judgments are expected in 2021 at the earliest (also depending on the impact of COVID-19 on the activity of the courts).

There are court judgments regarding the VAT treatment of cryptocurrencies – for example one related to the right to deduct input VAT on the distribution of cryptocurrency excavators (equipment used to mine cryptocurrencies). In principle, Polish courts that deal with VAT on cryptocurrencies follow the rationale of the judgment of the European Court of Justice (Fifth Chamber) of 22 October 2015 in case *Skatteverket v. David Hedqvist* (C-264/14).

1.1.2 Income and Capital Gains Taxes

(a) How are crypto assets classified for income and capital gains tax purposes?

The Polish income tax law provides for special rules of taxation of cryptocurrencies, but does not provide for a classification of crypto assets according to the accounting terminology (neither for business nor for private purposes).

Polish income tax regulations are different when it comes to cryptocurrencies as defined in the AML Act to which the CIT Act and the PIT Act apply and when it comes to other crypto assets. In the case of most popular crypto assets such as BTC, ETH, LTC, etc., there are no major problems with their classification as cryptocurrencies in the meaning of the AML Act. They are not depreciated for income tax purposes. In case of tokens, they should be examined from the perspective of the possibility of categorizing them as so-called security tokens (classified as securities), equity tokens (financial equity) or utility tokens (financial liability).

From the accounting perspective, crypto assets are usually deemed just as rights in property and therefore are classified as intangibles or current assets, depending on whether they are held for a long or a short term.

(b) What are the income/capital gains tax consequences of selling crypto assets against fiat currency?

Since 1 January 2019, gains from selling crypto assets that meet the criteria of cryptocurrency in the meaning of the AML Act are treated as a type of capital gains. This means that regardless of the amount of gains from selling such cryptocurrencies they are taxed at a flat rate of 19%. Importantly, it is not possible to offset the tax loss on cryptocurrencies against income from other capital gains (e.g., other crypto assets, shares, etc.) or other sources of income (in Poland, there are two possible sources of income applicable to CIT payers – capital gains and business income, and ten sources of income applicable to PIT payers, which include employment income, capital gains, business income, gains on alienation of real and other property, etc.).

The capital gain is a surplus of taxable revenue (which generally should reflect the market value of the crypto asset) over tax deductible costs. Since 1 January 2019, tax deductible costs are expenses incurred directly in purchasing cryptocurrencies and costs related to their disposal (e.g., sale, payment for goods/services, etc.). Expenses incurred indirectly on such actions are not tax deductible. By purchasing a cryptocurrency at an exchange, a taxpayer also has the right to recognize tax deductible costs (i.e., such expenses are tax deductible when they are actually incurred without the necessary of allocating them to the associated taxable revenues, and therefore FIFO,

LIFO or other methods of valuation are not required), provided that he/she is in possession of documents confirming the purchase.

Costs that are not deducted from revenues in a given year may be carried forward to subsequent years.

Costs of the purchase of crypto assets incurred before 2019 may be tax deductible only if disclosed in the annual tax return for 2018 (otherwise a correcting return should be filed or the costs will not be recognized as tax deductible at all).

The above rules apply irrespective of whether the cryptocurrency is alienated by a CIT or a PIT payer and whether as part of his/her business activity. However, gains on cryptocurrency earned as part of the business activity should be reported and accounted for separately from other economic activities.

The above does not apply to income on cryptocurrencies earned by entities mentioned in Article 2.2.14 of the AML Act (e.g., cryptocurrency exchanges and markets) that is deemed business income subject to the general rules of taxation. Such entities should declare taxable income on cryptocurrencies in accordance with the general rules. As concerns these entities, it is assumed that they are running a business and, therefore, their income on sales of cryptocurrencies should be deemed business income. CIT payers should recognize such income as business income subject to the 19% CIT. PIT payers may be liable to the 19% PIT (flat rate) or to progressive taxation (17% up to PLN 85,528 of taxable income p.a., and 32% above this threshold), depending on the PIT rate they chose in a given year for their business income.

The general rules of taxation applicable after 2019 to entities mentioned in Article 2.2.14 of the AML Act applied to all cryptocurrency transactions performed by any entity before 2019.

The same general rules applicable after 2019 to entities mentioned in Article 2.2.14 of the AML Act should apply to earnings on sales of crypto assets other than virtual currencies (e.g., tokens). However, in such case, PIT payers may generate earnings on sales of crypto assets within their business activity or outside their business. In the latter case, they would earn taxable income within the source of income named 'alienation of property and other rights' subject to progressive PIT (17% up to PLN 85,528 of taxable income p.a., and 32% above this threshold).

Apart from the above, since 2019, PIT payers may be liable to the additional 4% solidarity tax. This tax is due from all PIT payers whose annual income (total income from crypto assets, employment, business activities, etc.) exceeds PLN 1,000,000. An additional 4% solidarity tax is paid on the excess of this amount.

(c) What are the income/capital gains tax consequences of exchanging crypto assets against other crypto assets?

Since 1 January 2019, the exchange of one cryptocurrency for another should be tax neutral for a taxpayer unless he/she is an intermediary defined in Article 2.2.14 of the AML Act. In such case, the general rules of corporate or personal income taxation apply. In practice, both CIT and PIT payers that act as intermediaries should recognize taxable income equal to a surplus of the market value of the exchanged cryptocurrencies and the expenses incurred on their acquisition (in the part not yet deducted for income tax purposes). The same general rules of taxation applicable after 2019 to entities mentioned in Article 2.2.14 of the AML Act should apply to the exchange of crypto assets other than cryptocurrencies (in the meaning of the AML Act). In other words, exchange of crypto assets different than cryptocurrencies is not exempted from income tax.

Income tax neutrality of exchanges of cryptocurrencies means that there is no obligation to disclose revenues and costs resulting from exchanging one cryptocurrency for another in the annual tax return. The absence of income tax on cryptocurrency for cryptocurrency transactions does not mean that there is no need to record individual exchanges. Regardless of the tax rules, one is obligated to keep a record of transactions.

Before 1 January 2020, an exchange of crypto assets was treated as a sale subject to income tax.

(d) If a distinction is made between business assets and non-business assets, when does trading in crypto assets lead to a trade or business?

Such distinction should not be important for taxation of income generated on trading crypto assets classified as cryptocurrencies (in the meaning of the AML Act, as described above) by entities other than intermediaries (as defined in Article 2.14 of the AML Act, who generally are deemed to be conducting economic activities). In other words, in case of transactions on cryptocurrencies made by entities other than above-mentioned intermediaries, they are subject to the same rules (the new income tax regime of income taxation of cryptocurrencies adopted on 1 January 2019), whether conducted within or outside the business (i.e., whether classified as business or non-business assets).

Trading in other crypto assets can for tax purposes take place within the context of an economic activity (*działalność gospodarcza*) or outside of it. There are no clear-cut rules distinguishing these two types of activity, and certainly none applicable to crypto assets, and thus the general rules should apply.

Income tax regulations include their own definition of economic activity, i.e., a gainful activity:

(a) in manufacturing, building, trading or services;
(b) in prospecting, identifying and extracting or mining ore from deposits;
(c) in exploiting tangible property and intangible assets;

conducted on one's own behalf irrespective of the result, in an organized and continuous manner, the revenue from which is not attributed to revenue from other sources (e.g., employment, alienation of property rights, etc.). Simultaneously, none of these activities shall be recognized as non-agricultural activities if the following conditions are jointly met:

(1) liability to third parties for the result of these activities and their performance, excluding liability for committing torts, is incurred by the person who commissions them;
(2) they are performed under supervision and at the place and time determined by the person commissioning the activities;
(3) the person who performs the activities does not incur the economic risk related to the conducted activity.

There is a very limited practice of the Polish tax authorities in respect to classification of activities undertaken by entities trading in crypto assets (whether qualified as cryptocurrencies or not), so they need to be assessed on a case-by-case basis.

(e) What are the income/capital gains tax consequences for an employee receiving wages or salaries in crypto assets?

If a taxpayer (e.g., a miner) is remunerated in crypto assets for work carried out under an employment contract, irrespective of whether they are classified as cryptocurrency, taxable income from employment arises already at the point in time when crypto assets are received (thus, not only at the point in time when these crypto assets are exchanged into fiat currency). As a rule, the employer should add this income to the salary and (acting as the remitter) calculate, deduct, and pay PIT for the employee. Employment income is also subject to social security contributions and healthcare premiums.

Should taxpayers sell crypto assets received as their wage or salary, they should themselves recognize the taxable income on that sale. The costs of acquiring crypto assets should be equal to the value used for the purpose of calculating employment income (i.e., no double taxation should occur).

(f) What are the income/capital gains tax consequences for a merchant receiving payment in crypto assets?

A merchant's supply of goods or services paid in crypto assets is to be treated in exactly the same way as supply paid in fiat currency. In consequence, for income tax purposes, the fair market value of the goods or services constitutes the merchant's taxable income. The merchant's exchange of received crypto assets into fiat currency constitutes another taxable transaction.

(g) What are the income/capital gains tax consequences of a loss of crypto assets?

A loss of crypto assets (i.e., a loss of the private key associated with the address at which crypto assets are stored) is not relevant in case they were to qualify as non-business assets. A loss of business-related crypto assets may result in tax deductible costs, provided that the loss is definite. This fact should be confirmed with relevant documents issued by law enforcement agencies (e.g., by a decision to discontinue the proceedings due to a non-identification of the perpetrator) or the bailiff (e.g., by a decision to discontinue enforcement proceedings due to the lack of sufficient assets).

(h) What are the income/capital gains tax consequences of a loss in value of crypto assets?

A loss in value of crypto assets, which has not occurred as a result of a sale transaction, is normally not relevant for income tax purposes.

(i) What are the income/capital gains tax consequences of forks of crypto assets?

There exists no regulation or statement of the Polish tax authorities regarding forks. In practice, a fork itself is not deemed a taxable event postponed until new crypto assets are alienated. Although only expenses directly incurred on the acquisition of alienated crypto assets are tax deductible, there are arguments to claim that also historical expenses associated with the acquisition of the old crypto asset (subject to the fork) should qualify as tax deductible. There are no rules for the allocation of expenses among new crypto assets. In practice, tax authorities tend to accept the allocation based on the values of forked crypto assets on the fork date.

The above should apply equally to crypto assets held within and outside of an active trade or business.

(j) What are the income/capital gains tax consequences of airdrops of crypto assets and are the tax consequences different if the airdropped tokens are unwanted?

Tax consequences of airdrops (understood as crypto assets donated free of charge, presumably for marketing reasons) depend on whether these crypto assets are received (1) in return for a particular conduct (in particular for a service, e.g. a positive posting on social media) and (2) within or outside of regular economic activity.

In any case, crypto assets received within the economic activity should be recognized as taxable income equal to the market value of these crypto assets on the date of their receipt. Income associated with this event should be classified as business income. It is subject to the 19% CIT. In case of PIT, a progressive PIT (at the rate of 17% up to PLN 85,528 p.a. of total income subject to progressive taxation, including employment income, professional income, income on alienation of real estate, etc., and 32% above this threshold) or the 19% flat rate should apply, depending on which taxation type has been chosen for a given tax year by the PIT payer.

Crypto assets received outside the economic activity may be classified as one of the following:

(1) taxable income (if received in return for a particular conduct, in particular a service) classified as received from 'other sources' and subject to the progressive PIT at the rate of 17% up to PLN 85,528 p.a. of total income subject to progressive taxation, including employment income, professional income, income on alienation of real estate, etc., and 32% above this threshold; or
(2) Gift subject to the donation and inheritance tax, if the given crypto asset is executed in Poland (where the place of execution of a property right is in practice determined by the place of the performance of an obligation (*miejsce spełnienia świadczenia* - Article 454 of the Civil Code), i.e., outside of it, and if the receiving individual is a Polish citizen and the contract is concluded in Poland.

The applicable rate of the donation and inheritance tax depends on the personal relationship between the persons involved (circles) and is charged on the value of acquired items and property rights reduced by the value of debts and burdens.

The spouse, descendants, ascendants, stepchildren, siblings, stepfather, and stepmother may benefit from a donation and inheritance tax exemption. The only requirement that conditions benefitting from the exemption is that the event must be reported in a timely manner and that, in the case of a gift, the latter is properly executed and documented.

The marginal tax rate applicable to the first circle (if not exempted as specified above) - i.e., to the spouse, ascendants, descendants, stepchildren, sons-in-law, daughters-in-law, siblings, stepfather, stepmother and in-laws - is 7%, with the tax-free amount being PLN 9,637 (approximately EUR 2,400). The marginal tax rate applicable to the second circle - descendants of siblings, siblings of parents, descendants and spouses of stepchildren, spouses of siblings and siblings of spouses, spouses of siblings of spouses, spouses of other descendants - is 12%, with the tax-free amount being PLN 7,276 (approximately EUR 1,800). The marginal tax rate applicable to the third circle - others - is 20%, whereas the tax-free amount is PLN 4,902 (approximately EUR 1,200).

(k) What are the income/capital gains tax consequences of (solo, pool, and cloud) mining?

There are no straightforward regulations or official guidelines of the Polish tax authorities concerning taxation of income generated by miners of crypto assets, including cryptocurrencies. There are, however, some individual tax rulings issued by the tax authorities which confirm that receipt of crypto assets (specifically cryptocurrencies) within the mining activity is neutral for income tax purposes and that the income tax liability should arise only at the time of further exchange of the crypto asset for fiat currency, goods or services. Such income is taxed in accordance with the general rules of taxation of the alienation of crypto assets (described above). Since a sale of cryptocurrencies is subject to the same income tax regime whether performed within or outside business (except for intermediaries as defined in Article 2.14 of the

AML Act), the above should apply to the mining activity classified as a business activity as well.

Nonetheless, there is doubt whether expenses incurred by a miner of cryptocurrency may be tax deductible since only expenses directly connected with revenues may be treated as such. The tax authorities tend to exclude expenses incurred, for example, on excavators or energy from tax deductible costs.

(l) What are the income/capital gains tax consequences of staking crypto assets?

A proof of staking is understood as a consensus mechanism (an alternative to a proof of working), whereby transactions are validated by persons who have high holdings of this respective crypto asset and would therefore suffer the greatest damage from a blockchain with incorrect entries. Staking is like mining, but with hardly any use of resources and much more passive in appearance. There is no direct rule on income tax treatment of staking. We do not know of any individual tax ruling that has been issued in this respect. It seems that, because of its characteristics, it should be taxable as 'other income' in the case of PIT payers, unless received within the economic activity of a PIT or CIT payer (whether constituting a part of or the entire business activity of a PIT or CIT payer). In such case, either PIT or CIT should be due as if on business income.

(m) What are the income/capital gains tax consequences of an indirect investment in crypto assets?

There are no special rules on income taxation of indirect investments in crypto assets (including cryptocurrencies). Instead, the general rules of taxation applicable to particular investment instruments (e.g. bonds, investment units, investment certificates, etc.) should be applied.

In case of interest or discount on bonds (sale of a bond to the bond issuer), they are subject to the 19% CIT or PIT depending on the category of the investor. An income on such interest or discount on bonds cannot be decreased by a loss on other investments (e.g. in shares) made by a PIT payer. PIT is settled by the bond issuer or the entity holding the account (remitter). CIT is always settled directly by the CIT payer.

Income from sales of bonds to a third party (not the issuer) should qualify as a capital gain subject to the 19% CIT or PIT. It may be decreased by a loss incurred by the PIT or CIT payer on other investments in the same year or in 5 preceding years (subject to a limitation of 50% of tax losses incurred in one of 5 preceding years that can be utilized in one year). PIT and CIT should be settled directly by the taxpayer (there is no remitter). CIT is always settled directly by the CIT payer.

Income from a sale of investment units or investment certificates is also subject to the 19% CIT or PIT. In case an investment certificate is sold to a third party, PIT should be settled directly by the taxpayer. In other cases PIT is settled by the remitter. CIT is always settled directly by the CIT payer.

(n) *How is income from crypto assets to be treated under double tax treaty law?*

There are no straightforward rules regarding cross-border aspects of crypto asset taxation. Also, the Polish tax authorities have not issued any general instructions regarding the treatment of crypto assets under double tax prevention regulations.

Income earned in connection with sales of crypto assets can fall under various allocation rules of the OECD Model Convention and, therefore, also under double taxation prevention treaties concluded by Poland, depending mainly on the status of the taxpayer as an entrepreneur and potential presence in another jurisdiction that creates a permanent establishment. Namely:

(1) Pursuant to Article 7 of the OECD Model Convention, 'the profits of an enterprise of a Contracting State are taxable only in that State; however, if the enterprise carries on business in the other Contracting State through a permanent establishment situated therein, then the profits of that enterprise may be taxed in that other State but only those that are attributable to that permanent establishment.' Thus, for example, the profits of a cryptocurrency platform (enterprise) generated by a business carried on by a resident of Poland may only be taxed in Poland. However, if the cryptocurrency platform carried on business in the US through a permanent establishment situated in the US, then the profits attributable to that permanent establishment could be taxed in the US. If the same cryptocurrency platform carried on business in Belize through a permanent establishment situated in Belize, Poland would have the right to taxation since there is no double taxation prevention treaty between Poland and Belize.

(2) Pursuant to Article 13 paragraph 5 of the OECD Model Convention, 'gains from the alienation of any property, other than that referred to in preceding paragraphs, are taxable only in the Contracting State of which the alienator is a resident'. Thus, for example, an investor who is a tax resident in Poland and sells cryptocurrency through a crypto exchange located in Switzerland may be taxed only in Poland.

The above has been confirmed by the tax authorities in individual tax rulings.

(o) *What are the income/capital gains tax consequences of selling crypto assets in an ICO/STO/IEO?*

Those few sales of tokens launched in Poland (whether through ICO, STO, or IEO) have been carried out by corporations (rather than individuals) and, therefore, by CIT payers. Such sales of tokens result in the following tax consequences:

(1) Any tokens generated by the issuer should be capitalized at the acquisition cost (if any).

(2) The exchange of tokens should be tax neutral if they qualify as cryptocurrency (in the meaning of the AML Act). In the event of an exchange of other crypto assets, the value of remuneration (corresponding to its market value), whether fiat or not, should be recognized as taxable revenue.
(3) In the case of so-called utility tokens, where the issuer has a legal obligation to provide a certain service to the investor in the future (similar to the buyer of a voucher), it may be possible for the issuer to postpone the tax liability until he/she executes his/her obligation.
(4) Depending on their structure, so-called security tokens may be accounted for as equity capital or as debt capital, without creating any taxable profit for the issuer as of the day of receipt.

1.1.3 Other Taxes

(a) What are the value added tax/sales tax consequences of selling crypto assets?

The Polish tax authorities abide by the opinion of the ECJ expressed in its verdict C-264/14 (*Skatteverket v. David Hedqvist*) related to trading bitcoins. In consequence, the following applies:

(1) An entrepreneur who sells bitcoins in his own name through a website (i.e., pursuant to the same business model as Mr Hedqvist's) provides a service. If his customer is an entrepreneur, then such service is performed at the place from which the customer runs his business; otherwise, the service is performed at the place where the recipient has his residence, registered office or habitual place of stay. Should the place of performance of the service be in Poland, then the transaction should be exempted from VAT (a 0% VAT rate without the right to deduct input VAT should apply). Consequently, the entrepreneur who is selling bitcoins should normally not be entitled to a deduction of input VAT.
(2) An entrepreneur who sells bitcoins in his own name through a crypto ATM also carries out a service, namely at the physical location of that crypto ATM. Such service should be deemed to be supplied in Poland and therefore exempted from VAT (a 0% VAT without the right to deduct input VAT should apply), with no possibility for the entrepreneur to recover input tax (e.g., on the purchase price of the crypto ATM).
(3) An entrepreneur who operates an exchange and acts as an intermediary between sellers and buyers of bitcoins against consideration (without becoming an owner of bitcoins) should be deemed a supplier of financial intermediary services exempted from VAT (without the right to deduct input VAT), if supplied in Poland (in the meaning of VAT law).

The above should apply accordingly to other crypto assets, provided that they have been accepted by the concerned parties as a mean of payment alternative to legal tender and insofar as they do not serve any purpose other than a mean of payment. This should be examined on a case-by-case basis.

Otherwise, if a crypto asset is a security token, its sale should be outside the scope of VAT.

Sale of utility tokens should be deemed as subject to VAT at the standard rate (currently 23 %).

(b) *Are payments in crypto assets subject to withholding taxes?*

For the purpose of the applicability of withholding taxes, payments made by a debtor through a transfer of crypto assets are to be treated in the same manner as cash payments. For example, dividends paid outside Poland by a Polish entity are subject to a withholding tax of 19%, unless a double taxation prevention treaty or the EU Parent-Subsidiary Directive provide otherwise.

However, a Polish entity paying the dividend in crypto assets (*datio in solutum*) may be liable for income tax on a surplus of the current market value of crypto assets over acquisition costs (Article 14a of the CIT Act and Article 14.2e of the PIT Act).

(c) *Does payment of compensation in crypto assets give rise to payroll tax consequences?*

Compensation in crypto assets such as bitcoins does not give rise to any special payroll tax consequences and, therefore, is to be treated as any other payment in kind. Under the employment contract, the employer should act as an agent and calculate, deduct and remit PIT as well as social security contributions and healthcare premiums on the total wage put at the disposal of the employee, including in-kind benefits.

(d) *Do transactions with crypto assets trigger any transfer taxes?*

The civil-law activities tax (CLAT) is levied on certain civil law contracts and amendments thereto (specifically indicated in the CLAT Act), if they result in an increased CLAT base, such as contracts of sale and exchange of things and property rights and loan agreements, etc., if they concern rights executed in Poland or rights executed outside Poland, provided that the agreement is concluded in Poland and the acquirer is seated or has a place of habitual residence in Poland.

However, generally, a transaction is not subject to CLAT if at least one of the parties to it is a VAT payer or is exempt from paying VAT. The CLAT rate depends on the type of contract, i.e. loans are subject to 0.5% CLAT rate (except, for example, loans granted by shareholders to a capital company that is exempt from CLAT), acquisition of property rights is subject to 1% CLAT rate. There is a lot of controversy in Poland whether crypto assets may be classified as property rights in the meaning of civil law, and, if yes, whether they can be deemed as executed in Poland.

Since 13 July 2018, CLAT is not due on sales and loans of cryptocurrency based on the ordinance of the ministry of finance on discontinuing collection of CLAT in such cases. The government is working on amendments to the CLAT Act that will introduce an exemption of certain crypto asset transactions from CLAT (they are expected to enter into force in mid-2020).

(e) Are firms operating in the crypto space subject to digital service taxes?

At the moment there is no digital service tax (DST) in Poland. Although Poland had been considering implementing a national DST, the Polish Government has decided not to proceed with it. No legal framework for such tax has been created nor has the tax administration issued any official statements in this respect.

(f) Are crypto assets subject to gift, inheritance, estate, or wealth taxes?

Crypto assets are not subject to property taxes (real estate or agricultural) in Poland.

Donated or inherited crypto assets are subject to inheritance and donation tax in Poland, if property rights associated with such crypto assets are executed in the territory of Poland (where the place of execution of a property right is determined by the place of performance of an obligation (*miejsce spełnienia świadczenia* – Article 454 of the Civil Code) and is treated as the place of performance of an obligation) or received by individuals who are Polish citizens or have their habitual place of residence in Poland on the day of opening inheritance proceedings or concluding a donation agreement, respectively. There is a lot of controversy whether crypto assets may be deemed as executed in Poland (as defined above), however the tax authorities tend to confirm that they may.

The donation and inheritance tax applies only to individuals. Any donation or inheritance obtained by a CIT payer should increase its taxable income (i.e., business profits rather than capital gains).

The applicable tax rate depends on the family relationship between the persons involved (circles) and is charged on the value of acquired items and property rights reduced by the value of debts and burdens.

The spouse, descendants, ascendants, stepchildren, siblings, stepfather and stepmother may benefit from an exemption from the donation and inheritance tax. The only requirement associated with the right to benefit from the exemption is that the donation or inheritance ought to be reported in a timely manner, and in the case of a donation, it needs to be properly executed and documented.

The marginal tax rate for the first circle (if not covered by the above exemption) – applicable to the spouse, ascendants, descendants, stepchildren, sons-in-law, daughters-in-law, siblings, stepfather, stepmother and in-laws – is 7%, whereas the tax-free amount is PLN 9,637 (approximately EUR 2,400). The marginal tax rate for the second circle – applicable to descendants of siblings, siblings of parents, descendants and spouses of stepchildren, spouses of siblings and siblings of spouses, spouses of siblings of spouses, spouses of other descendants – is 12%, whereas the tax-free amount is PLN 7,276 (approximately EUR 1,800). The marginal tax rate for the third circle – others – is 20%, whereas the tax-free amount is PLN 4,902 (approximately EUR 1,200).

(g) *Are crypto assets subject to exit tax?*

The Polish exit tax covers most situations where, at the time of withdrawing the Polish tax residency, the CIT or PIT payer holds assets with built-in gains or where an asset with built-in gains is transferred from one tax jurisdiction to another. The following assets are covered: all rights and obligations in a partnership, shares in a company, shares and other securities, derivatives and titles to participate in investment funds. Exit tax applies when Poland loses the right to tax the built-in gain. With respect to natural persons, exit tax applies when the taxpayer has had a place of residence in Poland for at least five years in the past ten-year period prior to changing his tax residency and when the total value of transferred assets exceeds PLN 4 million (approximately EUR 1 million). Whether this threshold applies when a natural person changes residency is a matter of controversy. The exit tax rate is 19% for CIT payers or 19% and 3% for PIT payers (when no tax deductible costs are allowed). Since crypto assets as such are not listed as subject to exit tax, this tax should not apply when they are made to exit Poland. A taxpayer who acquires crypto assets and then leaves Poland should not be taxed when their value subsequently increases. Conversely, when a taxpayer holding crypto assets becomes a Polish tax resident, no step-up can be claimed for these assets.

(h) *Can mining trigger gambling tax?*

Although there has been some discussion on classifying mining as a game of chance (subject to the gambling tax), currently such classification is not made by the Polish tax authorities or in the legal doctrine.

1.1.4 Compliance and Documentation Obligations

(a) *What documentation requirements exist for taxpayers regarding crypto assets and are there best practices in recordkeeping to support representations made in tax returns?*

There are no specific documentation requirements for taxpayers holding crypto assets in Poland.

Therefore, these taxpayers are required to comply with general documentation requirements. In practice, the tax authorities should accept all reasonable documents. Therefore, a taxpayer should keep print screens or print-outs from the crypto asset exchange or ATM, bank account statements confirming payment of funds to the account of the crypto asset exchange, etc.

(b) *What is the evidentiary burden of supporting tax positions when a digital wallet address is lost or shared with other persons?*

A loss or misuse of a digital wallet outside a business is income tax neutral and, therefore, it seems that no specific actions need to be taken to prove the case. A similar event within a business may create tax deductible costs, provided that the loss is definite (it is formally determined that the digital wallet address cannot be recovered), which should be confirmed with relevant documents issued by law enforcement agencies (e.g., by a decision to discontinue proceedings due to non-identification of the perpetrator) or the bailiff (e.g., by a decision to discontinue enforcement proceedings due to the lack of sufficient assets).

(c) *Are crypto asset exchanges and wallet providers subject to reporting obligations?*

In Poland, crypto asset exchanges and wallet providers do not have to submit any periodic reports to the tax authorities regarding their customers. However, the tax authorities are empowered to obligate a person to provide information relevant to taxation of a third party (please refer to point 1.1.5(a) below).

(d) *Are taxpayers holding crypto assets subject to reporting obligations apart from the filing of income tax/capital gains tax returns?*

Polish taxpayers holding crypto assets do not have to submit any reports to the tax authorities apart from filing income tax/capital gains returns and annual financial statements (if required).

In particular, a taxpayer holding crypto assets who has not generated any taxable income in connection therewith is not obligated to disclose his/her crypto investments to the tax authorities.

(e) *Are crypto asset exchanges and wallet providers subject to CRS/FATCA reporting?*

The tax authorities have not issued any guidance on whether operators of crypto exchanges or providers of crypto wallets are obligated to report their customers' data under CRS/FATCA. There is no public information on the Polish tax authorities having the right to request such reports.

1.1.5 *Civil and Criminal Tax Enforcement*

(a) What powers do the tax authorities have to compel the disclosure of information by third parties, such as exchanges or wallet providers, and have these been used in the past?

The Polish Tax Ordinance empowers the tax authorities to request that legal persons, organisational units without legal personality and natural persons involved in economic activities prepare and submit the following information:

(1) At a written request of the tax authorities (in which the scope of and the deadline for submission are determined) – information on events under civil law relationships or labour law regulations that could lead to a tax obligation or affect the amount of the tax liability of persons or units that are parties to the contract;
(2) Without any specific request of the tax authorities – information on contracts concluded with non-residents within the meaning of the foreign exchange law (Article 82.1 of the Tax Ordinance).

Furthermore, the National Fiscal Administration may as a matter of performance of its statutory tasks process information, including personal data, of legal persons, organizational units without legal personality and natural persons who conduct economic activities concerning events that have an indirect influence on the creation or value of non-tax budgetary receivables, tax or customs liability, events resulting from acts in civil law or factual events that may influence the creation or rate of tax liability. It may also request such entities to present documents that contain the information, including personal data (Article 45.1 of the National Fiscal Administration Act). For example, based on that, the Polish tax authorities have requested Polish crypto asset platforms to provide the details of transactions made with their users, e.g. marks of the users and their corresponding data, particulars of non-verified users (e.g. bank account numbers, e-mail addresses, personal data), history of exchange of crypto assets, incoming and outgoing mail with corresponding user data, transaction date and user crypto address, platform crypto address, crypto addresses with corresponding user data, etc.

There have been no agreements concluded with crypto asset trading platforms regarding the transmission of data to verify taxable events.

(b) What measures have the tax authorities undertaken in the past to ensure crypto tax compliance?

On 4 April 2018, the Polish tax authorities published a communiqué (simplified guidelines) regarding taxation of transactions involving crypto assets consistent with the law binding in 2018 (amended since 1 January 2019). No measures supporting crypto tax compliance have been taken since then, especially after amendments to the

CIT and PIT Acts that introduced the rules of taxation of transactions involving crypto assets.

(c) *Are the tax authorities cooperating with tax authorities in other jurisdictions on enforcement?*

To ensure compliance by taxpayers holding crypto assets, the Polish tax authorities have several tools for obtaining information from abroad (for example, from crypto asset exchanges located outside Poland):

(1) Double taxation prevention treaties concluded by Poland contain provisions on the exchange of information between competent authorities.
(2) Poland has concluded tax information exchange agreements with some no-tax jurisdictions, e.g., Isle of Man.
(3) Under EU law, Poland may request information from other EU Member States that is reasonably relevant to the administration and enforcement of its domestic laws.
(4) Poland has also ratified the OECD/Council of Europe Convention on Mutual Administrative Assistance in Tax Matters, which also gives the Polish tax authorities access to information held abroad.

There is no public information on whether the Polish tax authorities cooperate on enforcement with the tax authorities in other jurisdictions and whether they have made use of various above-mentioned instruments at their disposal as concerns taxpayer crypto asset holdings.

Portugal

*Diogo Ortigão Ramos & João Pedro Russo**

1. COUNTRY GUIDES

1.1 Portugal

1.1.1 Applicable Tax Law, Guidance, and Case Law

(a) Which laws, regulations, and other administrative guidance exist dealing with crypto assets?

Currently, there are no laws or regulations (tax or otherwise) dealing specifically with crypto assets.[1]

However, the Portuguese Tax Authorities (PTA) have issued guidance on the treatment of certain taxable events involving cryptocurrency, relating to both Personal Income Tax (PIT) and Value Added Tax (VAT). No similar guidance has been issued relating to other crypto assets (i.e., asset-backed tokens,[2] utility tokens[3] and security tokens[4]) or for the purposes of any other tax (i.e., Corporate Income Tax or CIT).

---

* The authors acknowledge and thank Diogo Gonçalves Dinis, whose work and assistance was invaluable in preparing this country chapter.

1. For the purposes of this country chapter, crypto assets encompass cryptocurrency, asset-backed tokens, utility tokens and security tokens.
2. For the purposes of this country chapter, asset-backed tokens mean digital tokens that, in similar terms to an index, derive their value from something real and tangible, thus serving as a representation of ownership of the asset (e.g., natural resources such as oil or water).
3. For the purposes of this country chapter, utility tokens mean digital tokens that provide users with access to a product or service, from which the tokens derive their value. Utility tokens do not give holders ownership of a company's platform or assets and, although they might be traded between holders, they are not primarily used as a medium of exchange (but to gain access to a certain product or service).
4. For the purposes of this country chapter, security tokens mean digital tokens that, in terms similar to traditional securities, provide their holders with an economic stake in a legal entity: a right to

PIT

Regarding PIT, the PTA have argued[5] that cryptocurrency is technically not a currency with legal tender (fiat currency), but merely an asset that may be used as a medium of exchange in a barter transaction for fiat currency, goods and services.

Also, although to a limited extent, cryptocurrency may serve as a unit of account to measure the value of goods and services in the market; while its value fluctuates based on online demand for additional units, it is also true that the value of cryptocurrency may convert into a value expressed in a familiar unit of account, such as a fiat currency. Thus, crypto assets should be seen as assets susceptible of being used as a means of payment in the context of barter transactions for fiat currency. In turn, fiat currency denotes paper money or coins of no significant intrinsic value but with legal tender in any given jurisdiction.

Considering the above, as an asset, cryptocurrency may give rise to three types of PIT taxable income:

(1) Gains derived from the exchange of cryptocurrency with fiat currency (or vice versa).
(2) Income derived from the provision of services related to cryptocurrency (e.g., mining activities).
(3) Income derived from the provision of goods and services in exchange for cryptocurrency.

While recognizing the existence of the latter two income flows, the guidance produced by the PTA on the taxation of cryptocurrency relating to PIT solely concerned gains derived from exchanging cryptocurrency for fiat currency (or vice versa).

Under the guidance, these gains may only be subject to PIT if they result from an individual who is subject to PIT carrying out a professional or entrepreneurial trading activity aimed at obtaining a profit. However, any gains derived by individuals not professionally engaged in trading activities involving the exchange of crypto assets for fiat currency (or vice versa) should not be subject to PIT (or any other tax, as discussed below.

VAT

Regarding the VAT treatment of cryptocurrency, the PTA have published three official rulings relating to VAT treatment of cryptocurrency:

- Ruling No. 12904, of February 15, 2018: a Portuguese taxable person had intended to create a global e-commerce platform. This platform would have its own e-currency or token, based on the Blockchain Technology Ethereum, which would be the only currency accepted. This token is pre-sold. The PTA

receive cash or other financial asset in consideration of a future discretionary or mandatory event; the ability to vote in company's decisions or a residual interest in an entity.

5. Ruling no. 5717/2015, of 27 Dec. 2016.

were asked if the sale of the token is subject to VAT or if benefits from the domestic VAT exemption equivalent to Article 135(1)(e) of Council Directive 2006/112/EC of November 28, 2006, on the common system of value added tax ('VAT Directive').[6]

- Ruling No. 14763, of January 28, 2019: the PTA were asked about the VAT treatment of an activity consisting in buying and selling bitcoin, in particular, whether this activity may benefit from the domestic VAT exemption equivalent to Article 135(1)(e), of the VAT Directive.
- Ruling No. 14436, of July 3, 2019: A potential investor questioned the PTA regarding the VAT framework applicable to operations associated with cryptocurrency mining activity.

The PTA's conclusion in the three binding ruling requests was the same. Supported by the findings of the Court of Justice of the European Union (CJEU), Case C-264/14, *Skatteverket v. David Hedqvist*, of October 22, 2015, the PTA considered that, since in the cases at hand the cryptocurrency was used as 'means of payment', all the related transactions qualify as supply of services that benefit from the VAT exemption established in Article 135(1)(e) of the VAT Directive, which corresponds to article 9(27)(d) of the Portuguese VAT Code.

(b) Which court cases exist dealing with crypto assets?

There are no pending court cases or definitive case law specifically concerning crypto assets in the Portuguese judicial or arbitration courts.

1.1.2 Income and Capital Gains Taxes

(a) How are crypto assets classified for income and capital gains tax purposes?

For PIT and VAT purposes, the PTA have already argued that cryptocurrency is not a fiat currency, but merely an asset that may be used as a medium of exchange in a barter transaction and, to a limited extent, as a unit of account. No similar classification has been made public for other crypto assets or relating to any other taxes, namely CIT.

Nevertheless, considering their features and their underlying legal and regulatory regimes, one may assume that other types of crypto assets should also be seen as assets susceptible of being used as a means of payment in the context of barter transactions and, to a limited extent, as units of account, for the purposes of PIT, VAT, and all other applicable taxes under the Portuguese tax system (namely CIT).

6. Article 135(1)(e): '1. Member States must exempt the following transactions: (...) e) transactions, including negotiation, concerning currency, bank notes and coins used as legal tender, with the exception of collectors' items; that is to say, gold, silver or other metal coins or bank notes, which are not normally used as legal tender or coins of numismatic interest.'

(b) What are the income/capital gains tax consequences of selling crypto assets against fiat currency?

The tax consequences of the exchange of crypto assets for fiat currency depend on the type of taxpayer receiving the income (companies and other CIT taxpayers or individuals), the nature of the income (business or non-business), and on whether the taxpayer keeps accounting records.

Companies and CIT taxpayers

Companies and CIT taxpayers must keep mandatory accounting records.[7] Consequently, for these taxpayers, the CIT implications arising from the exchange of crypto assets for fiat currency depend, *prima facie*, on the accounting treatment given to these assets. There is no guidance on how these assets should be accounted for in Portugal, which means the Portuguese Generally Accepted Accounting Principles (GAAP) are applicable.

Under GAAP, the specific accounting treatment to be rendered to crypto assets depends on a number of factors, including the specific nature and features of the crypto assets, as well as the nature of the activities performed by their holders. Accordingly, these assets should be accounted for as one of the following:

- Intangible assets: Defined as identifiable and controllable non-monetary assets lacking physical substance and susceptible of generating future economic benefits for their holders. Generally subject to initial recognition at cost, these assets may be accounted for at fair market value (FMV), under a revaluation procedure. Treatment as intangible assets may apply to crypto assets that do not fulfil stricter requirements to be considered financial assets or inventories.
- Financial assets: Defined as (i) cash; (ii) equity instruments issued by another entity; (iii) contractual rights entitling their holder to receive cash or equity instruments issued by another entity or to trade financial assets and liabilities with another entity; (iv) a contract to be liquidated with equity instruments that are either: (a) non-derivative financial assets entitling their holder to receive a certain amount of equity instruments; or (b) derivative financial assets to be liquidated in a manner differing from the mere exchange against a fixed amount of cash or equity instruments. Generally subject to initial recognition at FMV, certain financial assets may, subject to certain requirements, be accounted for at cost. Regarding financial assets accounted for at FMV, any variations in the corresponding value may be reflected in their holders' yearly profits and losses accounts ('P&L accounts'). Treatment as financial assets may apply to certain crypto assets entitling their owner to receive cash or equity instruments issued by a third party pursuant to a future event (e.g., security tokens).

7. Article 17(1) of the CIT Code, *in fine*.

- Inventory: Defined, inter alia, as assets held for sale by taxpayers trading crypto assets, inventory is generally subject to initial recognition at cost or net realizable value, whichever the lower. Certain inventory held by qualifying traders may be valued at FMV, in which case, like financial assets, any variations in the FMV may be reflected in those traders' yearly P&L accounts. Treatment as inventory may apply to crypto assets held by a trading company exclusively with the intention of disposing them as part of its own corporate purpose.

Regarding crypto assets that, under the accounting rules referred to, qualify as intangible property or financial assets whose variations in the FMV are not reflected in their holders' P&L accounts, the capital gains and losses regime established in the CIT Code applies to any gains or losses arising from the exchange of crypto assets for fiat currency.[8]

The computation regime applicable to sales proceeds and losses applies to exchanges of crypto assets accounted for as inventory or financial assets whose variations in the FMV are reflected in their holders' P&L accounts, as any capital gains or losses arising from the exchange of these assets do not qualify as capital gains or losses, but as sales proceeds and losses.[9] Crypto assets treated as inventory under GAAP are accounted for under a first-in first-out (FIFO) method. No guidance has been provided regarding the accounting method applicable to financial assets and intangibles.

CIT capital gains and losses regime

Under this regime, capital gains (and losses) correspond to the positive (or negative) difference between a crypto asset's net realization value and its acquisition value, adjusted for any tax depreciation and imparity losses, among other amounts,[10] if applicable.[11]

In the case of crypto assets exchanged against fiat currency, the net realization value corresponds to the amounts of cash received, net of any expenditure necessary to ensure the exchange.[12] Where the fiat currency received as consideration in the sale is one without legal tender in Portugal, the net realization value should, to the extent possible, be accrued according to the exchange rate in force at the time of the sale.[13]

In addition, the CIT capital gains regime establishes a two-fold set of features specifically applicable to crypto assets qualifying as intangible assets:

8. Article 46(1) of the CIT Code.
9. Articles 18(9)(a)(b) and 46(1)(2) of the CIT Code, *a contrario*.
10. Article 46(2) of the CIT Code.
11. Crypto assets are not usually subject to depreciation.
12. Article 46(2) and (3)(g) of the CIT Code.
13. Article 46(10). Where it is not possible to determine this exchange rate, the last known exchange rate should be used.

- Computation of acquisition value: adjusted based on monetary inflation, for crypto assets held for at least two years before the sale.[14]
- Partial deduction: reduction of 50% of any reinvested capital gains arising from the sale of crypto assets held for at least one year before the sale. Eligible applications include the acquisition of other crypto assets qualifying as intangible assets.[15]

Capital gains computed under the regime referred to are included in the taxpayer's taxable profits for the corresponding year[16] and subject to CIT at a standard rate of 21%.[17] This standard rate may be potentially increased by the application of a two-fold set of surcharges:

- Municipal surcharge: Imposed on the taxpayer's taxable profits at rates that vary depending on the taxpayer's municipality(ies), up to a maximum of 1.5%.[18]
- State surcharge: Imposed on the taxpayer's taxable profits exceeding EUR 1.5 million, at rates of 3%, 5% and 9% applicable to any taxable profits between EUR 1.5 million and EUR 7.5 million, EUR 7.5 million and EUR 35 million and in excess of EUR 35 million, respectively.[19]

Capital losses arising from the exchange of crypto assets for fiat currency may be carried forward and deducted against a maximum of 70% of the taxable profits of the following five years.[20]

Computation regime applicable to sales proceeds and losses

Under the computation regime applicable to sales proceeds and losses, the adjustments referred to above relating to the CIT capital gains and losses regime and, more specifically, crypto assets qualifying as intangible assets, are not available, meaning that any tax proceeds and losses to be considered for tax purposes should match those resulting from the mandatory accounting records kept by the taxpayers.[21]

Regardless of the different computation regime, any sales proceeds or losses computed under this regime are still subject to the same overall CIT treatment,[22] meaning that:

- Sales proceeds are included in the taxpayer's taxable profits for the corresponding year and subject to CIT up to a maximum aggregate rate of 31.5%

14. Article 47 of the CIT Code.
15. Article 48 of the CIT Code.
16. Articles 17(1) and 18(1) of the CIT Code.
17. Article 87(1) of the CIT Code.
18. Exemptions are available, including for small and mid-sized enterprises.
19. Article 87-A(1)(2) of the CIT Code.
20. Article 52(1)(2) of the CIT Code.
21. Articles 47 and 48 of the CIT Code, *a contrario*.
22. Article 20(1)(a) of the CIT Code.

(resulting from the sum of the standard 21% rate with the maximum applicable rates of Municipal and State surcharges).
- Losses may be carried forward and deducted against a maximum of 70% of the taxable profits of the following five years.

Individuals

Non-business income derived by individuals from the sale of crypto assets against fiat currency should not be subject to PIT; however, (business) income derived by individual entrepreneurs professionally engaged in trading activities involving the exchange of crypto assets for fiat currency should be subject to PIT.

Concerning these individuals, the PIT implications that should be expected due to the exchange of crypto assets for fiat currency depend on whether these individuals keep accounting records of their crypto asset trading activities. Individual entrepreneurs deriving an annual amount of gross business income of more than EUR 200,000 must keep mandatory accounting records.[23] Individual entrepreneurs deriving less than this amount may still choose to keep accounting records of their activities, in which case the same PIT implications should be expected relating to their trading activities.[24]

Individual entrepreneurs that keep accounting records

Regarding both individual entrepreneurs required to keep mandatory accounting records of their crypto asset trading activities and those that choose to keep these records, according to the PIT Code, the computation of their business income should follow the rules of the CIT Code.[25]

As discussed above, the tax implications arising from the exchange of crypto assets for fiat currency depend, *prima facie*, on the accounting treatment given to these assets.

Without prejudice to the different computation regimes applicable to different situations, any taxable profits and losses computed according to their application are subject to the same overall PIT treatment, under which:

- Taxable profits are included in the taxpayer's taxable income for the corresponding year and subject to PIT at the general progressive rates established in the PIT Code, up to a maximum aggregate rate of 53% (for taxable income over EUR 250,000).[26]
- Losses may be carried forward and deducted against a maximum of 70% of the taxable profits of the following twelve years.[27]

23. Article 28(1)(2) of the PIT Code.
24. Article 28(3) of the PIT Code.
25. Article 32 of the PIT Code.
26. Articles 68 and 68-A of the PIT Code.
27. Articles 52(2) of the CIT Code and 55(1)(a) of the PIT Code.

Individual entrepreneurs that do not keep accounting records

Individuals that are not required to keep mandatory accounting records or choose not to keep accounting records are taxed under a simplified computation regime, which establishes the application of coefficients to the gains and losses accrued in the context of their crypto asset trading activities.[28]

The PTA have not addressed which coefficient should be applicable to crypto asset trading activities. However, we understand that, in the case at hand, the applicable coefficient should be 0.95, generally applicable to the positive balance between capital gains and losses computed in the context of a trading activity of a professional or entrepreneurial nature.[29]

With the application of this coefficient, the resulting taxable profits and losses are subject to the same overall PIT treatment as explained above, meaning that:

- taxable profits are subject to PIT at the general progressive rates, up to a maximum aggregate rate of 53%; and
- losses may be carried forward for twelve years.

(c) *What are the income/capital gains tax consequences of exchanging crypto assets against other crypto assets?*

The PTA have not issued any guidance on the tax implications to expect from the exchange of crypto assets for other crypto assets.

However, our comments in section 1.1.2(b), above, should apply here, with the following adjustments:

- The net realization value of the disposed crypto assets should correspond to the FMV of the crypto assets received in return, further increased by any amounts of additional cash received.[30]
- With regard to companies, other CIT taxpayers and individual entrepreneurs that keep accounting records, it would not be possible to benefit from the partial deduction of 50% of any reinvested capital gains arising from the sale of crypto assets held for at least one year before the sale.

(d) *If a distinction is made between business assets and non-business assets, when does trading in crypto assets lead to a trade or business?*

In the only ruling issued for the purposes of PIT[31], the PTA argued that any gains derived from the exchange of cryptocurrency for fiat currency may only be subject to

28. Articles 28(1)(a) and 31(1) of the PIT Code.
29. Article 31(1)(d) of the PIT Code.
30. Article 46(2) and (3)(a) of the CIT Code. Article 44(1)(a) of the PIT Code.
31. Ruling no. 5717/2015, of 27 Dec. 2016.

PIT if they result from a professional or entrepreneurial trading activity aimed at obtaining a profit.

Thus, any gains derived by individuals not professionally engaged in trading activities involving the exchange of crypto assets for fiat currency (or vice versa) should not be subject to taxation at the level of PIT (or any other tax).

There are no guidelines officially sanctioned by the PTA distinguishing one situation from the other, but the following criteria may suggest that a taxpayer is professionally involved in crypto asset trading activities:

- The taxpayer conducts the trading activities as his or her main occupation.
- The taxpayer maintains an office space and other material resources specifically for the purposes of these activities.
- The taxpayer resorts to previous consolidated professional experience for the purposes of discharging these activities.
- The taxpayer concludes a significant volume of transactions by resorting to technological means (e.g., trading bots).
- The taxpayer incurs debt financing to fund these activities.

(e) What are the income/capital gains tax consequences for an employee receiving wages or salaries in crypto assets?

The ruling issued by the PTA only relates to the taxation of capital gains derived by entrepreneurs professionally engaged in trading activities involving cryptocurrency.

However, the general rules of the PIT Code dictate that any payments in kind received by an employee on account of a labour relationship with its employer should be subject to PIT taxation.[32]

In light of the above, payments of wages and salaries received by an employee in crypto assets should be valued at FMV[33] and included in the taxpayer's taxable income for the corresponding year and be subject to PIT at the general progressive rates, up to a maximum aggregate rate of 53%.

(f) What are the income/capital gains tax consequences for a merchant receiving payment in crypto assets?

The PTA have not issued any guidance on the CIT and PIT implications arising from a merchant receiving payment in crypto assets. However, we understand that the tax treatment should be the same as if that merchant is paid with fiat currency, meaning that the following CIT and PIT tax implications apply:

32. Article 2(1) and (3)(b)(8) of the PIT Code.
33. Article 24(1)(e) of the PIT Code.

- **CIT:** Any sales proceeds derived by companies and other CIT taxpayers are included in that taxpayer's taxable profits for the year and subject to CIT up to a maximum rate of 31.5%; and
- **PIT:** Any sales proceeds derived by individual merchants are included in the taxpayer's taxable income for the year and subject to PIT at the general progressive rates up to a maximum aggregate rate of 53%.

The amount included in the P&L accounts and thus in taxable income is equal to the FMV of the crypto asset converted to fiat currency.

(g) *What are the income/capital gains tax consequences of a loss of crypto assets?*

For the purposes of this query, the loss of crypto assets denotes the loss of the private key associated with an address in blockchain in which the corresponding crypto assets are stored.

Similar to the exchange of crypto assets for fiat currency and other crypto assets, the tax implications associated with the loss of crypto assets depend on the type of taxpayer incurring the losses (companies and other CIT taxpayers or individuals), on the nature of the losses (business or non-business), and on whether the taxpayer keeps accounting records.

Companies and CIT taxpayers

Companies and CIT taxpayers must keep mandatory accounting records.

For these taxpayers, and regardless of the manner in which a crypto asset is accounted for (as either intangible asset, financial asset or inventory), the loss of crypto assets (as defined above) should also imply the write-off of these assets from the holders' accounts, with this write-off also being reflected in those taxpayers' P&L accounts as an expenditure in the amount of the FMV of the lost crypto assets at the time of the loss.

From a tax perspective, this expenditure is tax deductible, provided the loss of the private key is properly documented.[34]

Individuals

Any non-business expenditure incurred by individuals from the loss of crypto assets should not be deductible for PIT purposes.

Concerning individual entrepreneurs professionally engaged in trading activities, the PIT implications relating to the loss of crypto assets depend on whether those individuals keep accounting records of their crypto asset trading activities.

34. Articles 23(1) and (3) and 23-A(1)(b) *a contrario* of the CIT Code.

Individual entrepreneurs that keep accounting records

Regarding both individual entrepreneurs required to keep mandatory accounting records of their crypto asset trading activities and those that choose to keep these records, the PIT Code dictates that the computation of their business income should follow the rules of the CIT Code, meaning that the considerations referred to in section 1.1.2(b) apply here.

Individual entrepreneurs that do not keep accounting records

Individuals that are not required to keep mandatory accounting records or do not choose the option addressed above are taxed under a simplified computation regime for the application of coefficients to the gains and losses accrued in their crypto asset trading activities.

On account of the application of these coefficients to determine the taxable income, which relies on a certain amount of deemed expenditure, the deduction of any effective expenditure associated with the loss of crypto assets is not permitted.

(h) What are the income/capital gains tax consequences of a loss in value of crypto assets?

Similar to the losses addressed under section 1.1.2(g), above, the tax implications associated with losses in value of crypto assets depend on the type of taxpayer incurring the losses (companies and other CIT taxpayers or individuals), on the nature of the losses (business or non-business), and on whether that taxpayer keeps accounting records.

Companies and CIT taxpayers

Companies and CIT taxpayers must keep mandatory accounting records. Unlike losses of crypto assets, which always lead to a tax allowable write-off of the corresponding assets, the tax implications associated with losses in value in these assets depend, *prima facie*, on the accounting treatment given to these assets:

- Intangible assets: These assets are generally subject to initial recognition at cost, which means that any loss in value should be reflected in the taxpayer's balance sheet and P&L accounts. The same conclusion should be drawn for intangible assets accounted for at FMV, according to a revaluation procedure, meaning that any losses in value should also be reflected in the taxpayer's balance and P&L accounts. From a tax perspective, if properly documented, the tax deduction of this expenditure should also be permitted.
- Financial assets: Being generally accounted for at FMV, any losses in value should be reflected in this value according to a mandatory periodic revaluation procedure. When these variations are reflected in the P&L accounts of the holders of these assets, they should be tax deductible, provided they are

properly documented. The same treatment should apply to any losses in value of financial assets accounted for at depreciated cost.

- Inventory: Any losses in value of inventory accounted for at cost (which should be the rule) should be reflected in taxpayers' balance sheet and P&L accounts. The same conclusion should be drawn in respect of inventory accounted for at FMV, where any variations in the FMV are reflected in the corresponding P&L accounts. From a tax perspective, any losses in value incurred in any given year (or in previous tax years) should be tax deductible, provided they are properly documented and up to a maximum amount corresponding to the difference between the inventory's acquisition cost and its net realizable value.[35]

Individuals

Any non-business expenditure incurred by individuals from losses in value of crypto assets should not be deductible for PIT purposes.

Concerning individual entrepreneurs professionally engaged in trading activities, the PIT implications that should be expected to underlie the loss of crypto assets depend on whether these individuals keep accounting records of their crypto asset trading activities.

Individual entrepreneurs that keep accounting records

Regarding both individual entrepreneurs required to keep mandatory accounting records of their crypto asset trading activities and those that choose to keep these records, the PIT Code dictates that the computation of their business income should follow the rules of the CIT Code, meaning that the considerations referred to in section 1.1.2(b), above, apply here.

Individual entrepreneurs that do not keep accounting records

Individuals that are not required to keep mandatory accounting records, or those that choose not to, are taxed under a simplified computation regime, which applies coefficients to the gains and losses accrued in the context of their crypto asset trading activities.

On account of the application of these coefficients to determine the taxable income, which relies on a certain amount of deemed expenditure, the deduction of any effective expenditure associated with losses in value of crypto assets is not permitted.

35. Article 28(1) of the CIT Code.

(i) *What are the income/capital gains tax consequences of forks of crypto assets?*

A fork of crypto assets means the splitting of the value of a crypto asset into two or more other crypto assets, with no additional value being generated for their corresponding holders.

The PTA have not issued any guidance on the CIT and PIT treatment of forks of crypto assets.

Regardless, this treatment should not be expected to differ significantly from the case where a listed corporation spins-off assets into a separate entity: as the transaction does not generate any added value (the acquisition cost of the original (forked) assets is merely split between two or more crypto assets), the transaction should remain tax neutral, resulting in no CIT and PIT tax implications.

(j) *What are the income/capital gains tax consequences of airdrops of crypto assets and are the tax consequences different if the airdropped tokens are unwanted?*

An airdrop of crypto assets is a procedure through which a blockchain project distributes crypto assets for free among a group of active members of a blockchain community.

While the PTA have not issued any guidance on the CIT and PIT treatment of these airdrops, both taxes are imposed solely on capital gains derived from onerous transfers (i.e., transfers made in consideration of payment of any kind) of certain assets, not including gratuitous transfers, such as the one under analysis.

(k) *What are the income/capital gains tax consequences of (solo, pool, and cloud) mining?*

Solo, pool, and cloud mining are processes in which, in return for compensation (i.e., new crypto assets), transactions involving crypto assets are verified and added to a blockchain digital ledger by a crypto miner.

The tax consequences of crypto mining depend on the type of taxpayer receiving the resulting income (companies and other CIT taxpayers or individuals), the nature of the income (business or non-business), and whether the taxpayer keeps accounting records.

Companies and CIT taxpayers

For companies and other CIT taxpayers, any income derived from crypto mining activities should be accounted for in those entities' yearly P&L accounts and, consequently, be subject to CIT of up to 31.5%.

Losses arising from these activities (i.e., from the deduction of underlying expenditure) may be carried forward and deducted against a maximum of 70% of the taxable profits for the following five years.

Individuals

Any non-business income derived by individuals from crypto mining activities should not be subject to PIT; however, (business) income derived by individual entrepreneurs professionally engaged in crypto mining activities should be subject to PIT.

Concerning these individuals, the PIT implications that should be expected to underlie these taxable events depend on whether these individuals keep accounting records of their crypto mining activities.

Individual entrepreneurs that keep accounting records

Regarding both individual entrepreneurs required to keep mandatory accounting records of their crypto asset trading activities and those that choose to keep these records, the PIT Code dictates that the computation of their business income should follow the rules of the CIT Code, meaning that the considerations referred to in section 1.1.2(b), above, apply here.

Individual entrepreneurs that do not keep accounting records

Individuals that do not have to keep mandatory accounting records or choose not to keep these records are taxed under a simplified computation regime, which establishes the application of coefficients to any income and losses computed in the context of crypto mining activities.

The PTA have not addressed which coefficient should be applicable to crypto asset trading activities, but we understand that, in the case at hand, the applicable coefficient should be 0.35.[36]

According to the application of this coefficient, the resulting taxable profits and losses are subject to the same overall PIT treatment as explained above, as follows:

- Any taxable profits are included in the taxpayer's taxable income for the year and subject to PIT at the general progressive rates up to a maximum aggregate rate of 53%.
- Any losses may be carried forward and deducted against a maximum of 70% of the taxable profits of the following twelve years.

36. Article 31(1)(c) of the PIT Code.

(l) *What are the income/capital gains tax consequences of staking crypto assets?*

The staking of crypto assets refers to the proof of stake mechanism, a consensus mechanism under which transactions are validated by persons (i.e., stakeholders) who have high holdings of the relevant crypto asset and would suffer the greatest damage from a blockchain ledger containing incorrect entries. Staking is similar to mining in this regard, but with hardly any use of resources and much more passive in appearance.

The PTA have not issued any guidance on the CIT and PIT treatment applicable to the staking of crypto assets.

However, their treatment should not be expected to differ significantly from that applicable to crypto asset mining activities:

- For companies and other CIT taxpayers, any income derived from crypto mining activities should be accounted for in those entities' yearly P&L accounts and be subject to CIT up to a maximum aggregate rate of 31.5%
- For individuals, any non-business income derived from the staking of crypto assets should not be subject to PIT. On the other hand, any (business) income derived by individual entrepreneurs professionally engaged in staking activities should be subject to PIT. Regardless of whether accounting records are required to be kept, taxable profits are included in the taxpayer's taxable income for the year and subject to PIT at the general progressive rates up to a maximum aggregate rate of 53%.

(m) *What are the income/capital gains tax consequences of an indirect investment in crypto assets?*

An indirect investment in crypto assets denotes an investment held by an individual in a Portuguese company which, in turn, holds crypto assets.

For the tax implications to a company if the investment is held by a company or to partners if the investment is held by a partnership, *see* the previous sections, which address the tax implications applicable to multiple tax events for companies and other CIT taxpayers.

(n) *How is income from crypto assets to be treated under double tax treaty law?*

The PTA have not issued any guidance on how income derived from crypto assets should be treated under double tax treaty law, mainly under the double taxation treaties (DTT) concluded by Portugal.

Depending on the type of income and the nature of the activities performed by their beneficiaries, this income may fall under either of the following tax allocation regimes:

- **Business income:** Where the beneficiaries of the income hold the crypto assets for the purposes of discharging a profitable activity carried out professionally. According to Article 7 of most of the DTTs concluded by Portugal, this income may only be subject to taxation in the country in which the enterprise (i.e., the company or the individual) is resident for tax purposes, unless it is attributable to a permanent establishment of the same enterprise in the State in which the income is sourced, in which case that State is also entitled to tax this income;
- **Capital gains:** Applicable to any income arising from the disposal of crypto assets and derived by entities not professionally engaged in trading activities involving crypto assets. Generally, where this qualification is applicable, capital gains arising from the disposal of crypto assets should be subject to tax only in the State in which their beneficiaries are resident.
- **Other income:** Residual category, applicable if neither of the previous categories applies (e.g., income arising from the mere ownership of crypto assets). Where this qualification applies, exclusive taxing rights are generally attributed to the States in which the corresponding beneficiaries are resident for tax purposes.

(o) What are the income/capital gains tax consequences of selling crypto assets in an ICO/STO/IEO?

ICO, STO, and IEO denote Initial Coin Offerings, Security Token Offerings and Initial Exchange Offerings.

The tax implications associated with these taxable events should not be expected to differ from those addressed in section 1.1.2(b) and (c) above, concerning the tax implications arising from the exchange of crypto assets against fiat currency and other crypto assets. In other words, the tax implications depend on the type of taxpayer receiving the income (companies and other CIT taxpayers or individuals), the nature of the income (business or non-business), and on whether the taxpayer keeps accounting records.

1.1.3 Other Taxes

(a) What are the value added tax/sales tax consequences of selling crypto assets?

Regarding the VAT framework on cryptocurrency, the PTA follow the CJEU, namely C-264/14, *Skatteverket v. David Hedqvist*, of October 22, 2015 (*see* section 1.1.1(a), above). The guidance does not address other types of crypto assets.

In this sense, the sale of cryptocurrency is a VAT-exempt supply of services under Article 9(27)(d) of the Portuguese VAT Code, the place of supply of which will be Portugal if:

- both supplier and recipient of the services are established/domiciled in Portugal;
- the recipient, being a taxable person, is established in Portugal;[37] or
- the recipient, being a non-taxable person, is established/domiciled in the EU.[38]

Where the transactions are merely domestic, then the service provider must issue the corresponding invoice, indicating the reason why VAT will not be charged.[39] In a cross-border scenario, the transaction will not be located in Portugal. Hence, reference to the domestic rule equivalent to Articles 44 (B2B transaction)[40] or 59(e) (non-EU recipient)[41] of the VAT Directive must be included on the invoice.

If a Portuguese taxable person carries out exclusively exempt transactions, then it will be relieved from the obligation of filing periodic VAT returns.[42]

If the taxable person carries out both taxable transactions with the right to deduct input VAT and exempt transaction without such right, then the person will be qualified as a mixed taxable person and no longer will be relieved from the obligation to file periodic VAT returns.[43]

(b) Are payments in crypto assets subject to withholding taxes?

Payments in crypto assets should be generally subject to withholding taxes under the applicable regimes established in the CIT and PIT Codes.

To apply these withholding taxes, payments made by a debtor through the transfer of crypto assets should be treated in the same manner as payments made in cash, meaning that the payer of this income is obliged to withhold the tax due under the applicable rules and to remit it to the tax authorities.

Practically speaking, to do this, the value of the crypto assets must be converted into fiat currency with the withholding tax payable to be calculated based on the grossed-up amount.

(c) Does payment of compensation in crypto assets give rise to payroll tax consequences?

The Portuguese tax law does not impose a specific payroll tax.

However, an employer paying its employees in crypto assets should still withhold and remit any amounts of PIT due to the PTA.

37. Article 6(6)(a) of the Portuguese VAT Code.
38. In this case, by virtue of Article 6(6)(b) of the Portuguese VAT Code.
39. Article 9(27)(d) of the Portuguese VAT Code must be stated on the invoice.
40. Article 6(6)(a) of the Portuguese VAT Code.
41. In this case, the invoice issued by the supplier must state as a reason for not charging VAT the rule provided under Article 6(11)(e) of the Portuguese VAT Code.
42. Under Article 29(3) of the Portuguese VAT Code.
43. These transactions will have to be reported in Box 9 of the VAT return.

(d) *Do transactions with crypto assets trigger any transfer taxes?*

No transfer taxes should be triggered by any onerous or gratuitous transactions involving crypto assets.

(e) *Are firms operating in the crypto space subject to digital service taxes?*

The Portuguese tax law does not currently impose any digital service taxes.

(f) *Are crypto assets subject to gift, inheritance, estate, or wealth taxes?*

The Portuguese tax law does not impose any gift, inheritance, estate, or wealth taxes.

(g) *Are crypto assets subject to exit tax?*

The Portuguese CIT Code imposes an exit tax applicable to resident companies and other CIT taxpayers that transfer their tax residences abroad and non-resident companies and other CIT taxpayers that cease their activity in Portugal.

As the taxable basis of exit taxes includes all assets held by the exiting companies, regardless of their accounting treatment (or lack of accounting treatment), crypto assets are also subject to exit taxes.

(h) *Can mining trigger gambling tax?*

While the Portuguese tax law establishes a gambling tax, the scope of this tax is limited to entities operating websites and other facilities in which it is possible for the public to gamble. Thus, crypto mining activities are not subject to gambling tax.

1.1.4 Compliance and Documentation Obligations

(a) *What documentation requirements exist for taxpayers regarding crypto assets and are there best practices in recordkeeping to support representations made in tax returns?*

The Portuguese tax law does not impose any specific documentation requirements for taxpayers holding crypto assets, meaning that these taxpayers must comply with general documentation requirements under the general regimes.

Regarding CIT, any representations made in the applicable tax returns should be documented and accounted for; whereas, regarding VAT, the Portuguese invoicing requirements are aligned with those provided under the VAT Directive.

Supporting documentation for any given year, along with all books and records, must be kept for a minimum of ten years after the end of that tax year.

(b) *What is the evidentiary burden of supporting tax positions when a digital wallet address is lost or shared with other persons?*

If documented correctly, the loss of a digital wallet address may be tax deductible for CIT and PIT purposes.

Under the applicable general rules on allocating the burden of proof, the burden of proof of the facts constituting the rights of the PTA or of the taxpayers rests with the person or entity that invokes these facts,[44] meaning the burden of proof for the loss of a digital wallet address will rest with the taxpayers.

(c) *Are crypto asset exchanges and wallet providers subject to reporting obligations?*

No reporting obligations apply specifically to crypto asset exchanges and wallet providers vis-à-vis other entities operating in different sectors, meaning that these entities are all subject to the same reporting obligations, including (but not limited to) those resulting from anti-money laundering and terrorism financing laws.

(d) *Are taxpayers holding crypto assets subject to reporting obligations apart from the filing of income tax/capital gains tax returns?*

Under Portuguese law, taxpayers holding crypto assets are not required to fulfil any reporting obligations apart from filing CIT or PIT periodic returns, if there is any taxable income to report to the PTA.

(e) *Are crypto asset exchanges and wallet providers subject to CRS/FATCA reporting?*

In 2015, the Portuguese legislation implemented the FATCA regulation, based on Model 1, under which Portuguese financial institutions report information on US taxpayers' financial accounts to the PTA.

Regarding CRS, since 2016, financial institutions must identify their account holders as per the CRS identification requirements and report the financial account together with the information to the PTA, who then exchanges it with the foreign tax authorities.

The main question remains on considering crypto asset exchange and wallet providers under the scope of a financial account, which is considered to be a deposit account, a custody account, a monetizable insurance contract, a rent contract or a financial account held by an investment firm.

While an account holding crypto assets does not seem to fulfil the concept of financial account referred to above, the PTA have yet to provide any guideline on this,

44. Article 74(1) of the Portuguese General Tax Law (GTL).

so it is still not clear whether the FATCA/CRS framework applies to crypto asset exchanges and wallet providers.

1.1.5 *Civil and Criminal Tax Enforcement*

(a) What powers do the tax authorities have to compel the disclosure of information by third parties, such as exchanges or wallet providers, and have these been used in the past?

Under the Portuguese tax law, taxpayers have a duty to cooperate with the PTA.[45]

In addition, the PTA have the right to request information from a person to ascertain the tax liability of that person or a third party. These requests have to be complied with, and the information provided must be accurate and truthful.

The obligation to provide information includes the obligation to comply with any tax compliance obligations.

Either of these obligations is enforceable.

(b) What measures have the tax authorities undertaken in the past to ensure crypto tax compliance?

To the best of our knowledge, the PTA have not carried out any actions to ensure crypto tax compliance.

(c) Are the tax authorities cooperating with tax authorities in other jurisdictions on enforcement?

This new international context in terms of tax transparency has gradually been reflected throughout the Portuguese tax system.

On January 1, 2020, Portugal entered into income tax treaties with 79 countries (78 in force and 1 pending approval), including information on exchange tax information procedures.

Also, Portugal is part of the group of jurisdictions that has already implemented and exchanged information in compliance with the OECD Common Communication Standard.

However, regarding crypto assets exchange information, although the Portuguese Tax Authorities have these instruments, we do not have knowledge of whether they use them.

45. Article 59(1) of the GTL.

Russia

Daria E. Romanova

1. COUNTRY GUIDES

1.1 Russian Federation

1.1.1 Applicable Tax Law, Guidance, and Case Law

(a) Which laws, regulations, and other administrative guidance exist dealing with crypto assets?

Currently, Russian legislation on crypto assets is in state of dynamic, although somewhat turbulent development.

The key legislation in this area is as follows:

- The Tax Code;
- The Civil Code, esp. Articles 128 and 141.1;
- The Federal Law dd. 02.08.2019 No. 259-FZ on crowdfunding platforms.

A Bill No 419059-7 on Crypto Financial Assets was introduced in the Parliament in 2018 with the goal to provide a more comprehensive legal framework for crypto assets and transactions therewith. However, as of now the Bill is still under review. For instance, on 16 March 2020 the Central Bank of Russia proposed to add thereto a general ban on issue of and trading with cryptocurrencies in Russia.[1]

From the tax perspective, alongside with the Tax Code, there are several guidance letters issued by the Ministry of Finance and the Federal Tax Service on various issues related to crypto assets transactions (*see* below). While these guidance letters are not, strictly speaking, legally binding, they are treated as a persuasive authority as they reflect the regulator's view on how the law shall be construed and implemented.

1. https://www.rbc.ru/crypto/news/5e6f88da9a79478f579ddd01.

A new Russian Federal Law on financial crypto assets and crypto currency N 259-FZ (the Law) was signed on 31 July 2020. The Law will enter into force on 1 January 2021.

The Law, on one hand, acknowledges that cryptocurrency is a 'payment instrument' that is not fiat currency. On the other hand, the Law prohibits to receive payments in cryptocurrency to Russian companies, foreign companies' branches in Russia or individuals who spent more than 183 days in Russia during twelve consecutive months. Any claims that cryptocurrency's owners may have will be enforceable in court only if such owners have declared both cryptocurrency and all transactions therewith. Further amendments to tax legislation shall be introduced in order to determine how to file such declarations. Overall, the Law may significantly influence the approach to taxation of crypto currency transactions in Russia (as long as they are permitted), presumably by aligning them with fiat currency transactions.

It shall also be noted that the Law still uncovers many related areas, such as tokens or mining, so we may expect other legislative initiatives in the future.

(b) *Which court cases exist dealing with crypto assets?*

The majority of court cases in Russia that mention crypto assets are dealing with criminal law issues, rather than tax issues, owing to the infamous popularity of cryptocurrencies as means of payment in illegal transactions.

However, there are certain cases where courts have addressed the legal nature of crypto assets (cryptocurrencies in particular):

- Ninth Commercial Court of Appeal in Case No. 40-124668/2017 held that cryptocurrency should be treated as an asset for the purposes of Russian Civil law, despite the fact that the Civil Code at the time when the judgement was made had no express reference to crypto assets.
- The Moscow City Court in Case No. 7-4313/2018 held that cryptocurrency may not be viewed as a 'foreign currency' as this term is defined by the Russian currency control legislation. While this judgment dealt primarily with currency control issues, it may also be interesting from the tax perspective, because it demonstrates that Russian courts may be reluctant to treat crypto assets in the same way as fiat money.

1.1.2 Income and Capital Gains Taxes

(a) *How are crypto assets classified for income and capital gains tax purposes?*

This is still a controversial and unsettled issue. Russian financial and tax authorities in their guidance letters directly admit that the legal status of crypto assets, especially cryptocurrencies, is not yet defined by the Russian legislation.[2] As mentioned in section 1.1.1(a) above, it was planned that further legislation on the matter should have been passed. However, this has not happened yet.

To determine the legal nature of crypto assets, one may refer to the recently amended provisions of the Civil Code (Articles 128 and 141.1). The initial proposal was to include thereto rules on two types of assets: (1) cryptocurrencies and (2) crypto rights. However, only the latter were mentioned as a type of 'intangibles'.

While the definition of crypto rights provided by the Civil Code covers certain types of crypto assets (primarily, tokens), the legal status of many others, including such popular cryptocurrency as bitcoins, etc., is still not determined by legislation.

As mentioned above, it is currently unlikely that cryptocurrencies will be treated the same way as fiat currency in Russia, so the two main options available to taxpayers and tax authorities are to treat them either as goods[3] or as intangibles, based on the statutory definition of 'crypto rights'.

(b) *What are the income/capital gains tax consequences of selling crypto assets against fiat currency?*

The uncertainty of the legal status of crypto assets does not mean that transactions with them are not taxable in Russia. If crypto asset transactions lead to a monetary or in-kind economic benefit[4], such benefit is normally taxable with corporate tax or personal income tax applying, depending whether the taxpayer is a legal entity or an individual. In absence of any specific provisions on crypto assets in the Tax Code, Russian financial authorities issued guidance stating that general rules on corporate[5] and personal[6] taxation shall apply.

Corporate tax: Upon sale of goods not subject to depreciation or upon assignment of intangibles, the tax base is generally calculated as the difference between the sale proceeds and the acquisition costs. As of now, there is no guidance from Russian financial or tax authorities that would have challenged the possibility of such deduction.

The flat tax rate for corporate tax is 20%.

Personal income tax (PIT): In the absence of special tax provisions, the Ministry of Finance proposes that individual taxpayers may calculate the tax base upon the sale of cryptocurrency as the difference between the sale proceeds and the acquisition costs, provided that the latter are documentary evidenced and actually paid[7].

2. Letter of the Ministry of Finance 23.04.2018 No. 03-01-11/27036.
3. This term is defined as any type of movable (chattel) or immovable (real estate) asset.
4. Article 41 of the Tax Code.
5. Letter of the Ministry of Finance 28.08.2018 No. 03-03-06/1/61152.
6. Letter of the Ministry of Finance 24.08.2018 No. 03-04-05/60392.
7. Letter of the Ministry of Finance 17.05.2018 No. 03-04-07/33234 and the letter of the Federal Tax Service 04.06.2018 No. BS-4-11/10685@.

It is worth noting that the Ministry of Finance refers to Article 220 of the Tax Code, which deals with the sale of goods and not the assignment of intangibles[8]. Thus, if crypto assets are treated as intangibles, the taxpayer will have to rely on the court practice that allows deduction of acquisition expenses in case of sale of intangibles[9], rather than on express statutory provisions that do not address this issue in order to deduct such expenses.

A further implication of whether crypto assets are qualified as goods or intangibles is availability of a PIT tax relief on sale proceeds from the sale of goods (not intangibles, though!) owned for a certain period of time: three or five years depending on the type of acquisition (purchase, gift, etc.)[10]. However, the Ministry of Finance[11] has issued a guidance stating that until the legal status of the cryptocurrencies is defined by a statute, no such tax relief applies to their sale. The legal community has proposed granting tax relief to the sellers of crypto assets who owned them for one year or more[12], but that proposal has not been statutorily implemented yet.

The flat PIT tax rate is 13% for Russian tax residents[13].

(c) What are the income/capital gains tax consequences of exchanging crypto assets against other crypto assets?

In the absence of express statutory provisions, exchange of crypto assets should be treated for tax purposes in the same manner as any other exchange, swap or barter transaction. Namely, such exchange is equalled to two simultaneous sales and corresponding acquisitions of the crypto assets (intangibles).

Corporate tax: Any in-kind benefit of the corporate taxpayer (including the benefit from barter transactions[14]) should be accounted in accordance with the transaction price. The latter, in its turn, should be consistent with the fair market price of such transaction.

Personal income tax: In accordance with the guidance provided by the Ministry of Finance, individual taxpayers, while accounting their taxable benefits, should also consider the price(s) stipulated by the barter contract or, if there is no such price, fair market value of the in-kind benefit[15].

There is a presumption that a transaction price between non-affiliated parties is fair[16], but the tax authorities are nevertheless entitled to assess 'fairness'[17] of the

8. Intangibles are distinguished from other types of goods for taxation purposes in Russian tax legislation.
9. Ruling of the Supreme Court of Russia as of 22.07.2015 No 8PV15.
10. Article 217(17.1) of the Tax Code.
11. Letter of the Ministry of Finance 04.09.2018 No. 03-04-05/63144.
12. https://www.rbc.ru/crypto/news/5d40632c9a79472a8b9f4cd0.
13. PIT tax rate for non-residents is 30%. Please note that for the sake of simplicity it will not be specifically mentioned below.
14. Article 274(4) of the Tax Code.
15. Letters 11.01.2018 No. 03-04-05/547, 20.12.2017 No. 03-04-05/85244.
16. Article 105.3 of the Tax Code.
17. Review of Court Practice by the RF Supreme Court Presidium 16.02.2017.

transaction price. Thus, it may be advised for the parties to such transactions to carry an independent valuation of crypto assets to be exchanged.

Rules on tax deduction of the costs/expenses are similar to those described in section (b) above.

Sole traders and SME companies in Russia are entitled to apply Simplified Tax System (STS), which replaces the PIT/corporate tax, VAT and some other taxes by one unified tax. Interestingly, the Ministry of Finance issued a guidance that STS may not be applied to revenues from cryptocurrency transactions until the legal status of cryptocurrencies is defined by statute[18].

(d) If a distinction is made between business assets and non-business assets, when does trading in crypto assets lead to a trade or business?

Corporate taxation: Russian Tax Law and GAAP mainly distinguish between 'current' assets that are expected to be used (sold or consumed) within twelve months, including goods purchase for resale, and 'long-term/non-current' assets. However, regardless of how the corporate taxpayer decides to account for the particular crypto assets at hand, it is obliged to include revenues from their sale into the corporate tax base[19].

PIT taxation: The distinction between business or non-business assets might have been meaningful in case of sale of goods owned for three or five-year periods, as the PIT tax relief is available only in case of sale of long-owned non-business assets. Please note that any goods used by the individual in course of business (i.e., systematic activity aimed at generation of profit) may be treated as business assets. However, regardless of the above, fiscal Russian tax authorities assume that no such relief may be granted in any case until the legal status of crypto assets is further clarified.

(e) What are the income/capital gains tax consequences for an employee receiving wages or salaries in crypto assets?

Payment in crypto assets to the employee is likely to be treated as the receipt of a benefit in-kind. In this case, taxable income is calculated based on the fair market value of such asset at the moment when the legal title on it has been transferred to the employee.

If the employer is a Russian company or individual acting in course of their business as a sole trader, the employer shall act as a tax agent for the employees and is normally obliged to withhold 13 % PIT from any monetary payments to them. In case of in-kind distributions, the company should either withhold money from any other monetary payment made to the same person in the same tax period (with the limit of 50 % of such payment) or inform tax authorities that the tax was due but impossible to

18. Letter 14.11.2018 No. 03-11-11/81983.
19. Article 268 of the Tax Code.

withhold. In the latter case, the employee will have to declare income in an annual PIT tax return and pay the tax.

Please note that the Russian legislation restricts the portion of the salary which may be paid in-kind, so fully 'crypto' salary would be a violation of Labour law.

(f) What are the income/capital gains tax consequences for a merchant receiving payment in crypto assets?

Similar to section 1.1.2(e) above, payment in crypto assets to a merchant is likely to be treated as the receipt of a benefit in-kind, though in this case the counterparty will not act as a tax agent for the taxpayer, wherever the merchant is a company or an individual acting in a course of business as a sole trader.

Taxable income will be calculated at the fair market value of such asset. If the merchant applies the general tax regime (not the STS) and is a company or a so-called sole trader, such merchant is entitled to deduct 'reasonable' business expenses from revenues for the purpose of calculating the tax base for the corporate tax / PIT respectively[20].

(g) What are the income/capital gains tax consequences of a loss of crypto assets?

Corporate taxpayers may reduce their tax base by the expenses that meet the following criteria[21]:

- they are evidenced by documents;
- they are reasonable, i.e., they have an economic purpose.

Deductible expenses are divided into two major categories: so-called trade expenses and non-trade expenses, which include expenses per se and losses. The Tax Code provides an exclusive list of deductible losses[22], including losses from thefts and force majors.

In accordance with guidance issued by the Ministry of Finance[23], a corporate taxpayer who suffered a loss of an asset due to reasons not listed in the statute and received compensation (i.e., taxable income) for such loss, may argue that this loss is still deductible as 'non-trade expenses'. In theory, that might be applicable to those taxpayers who suffered the loss of crypto assets as well, but no actual cases are reported in media to either support or contradict this point of view.

20. Article 221 of the Tax Code.
21. Article 252 of the Tax Code.
22. Article 265(2) of the Tax Code.
23. Letters 19.06.2018 No. 03-03-07/41741, 27.08.2014 No. 03-03-06/1/42717.

(h) *What are the income/capital gains tax consequences of a loss in value of crypto assets?*

There is still no unified approach to how crypto assets shall be accounted for in accordance with Russian tax law and GAAP (Russian Accounting Standards, RAS). For instance, if crypto assets are treated as assets with a value denominated in a foreign currency, it is unclear how their cost should be translated into Russian Roubles in order to calculate forex gains or losses, which are taxable by corporate tax in Russia. Some practitioners proposed introduction of a unified cross exchange rate (e.g., bitcoins – USD – RUB), but there were no amendments in the statute and no guidance from the authorities.

As for gains or losses from fair market revaluation of crypto assets, it should be noted that, although assets' revaluations may be carried out in accordance with Russian GAAP, all arising gains and losses are dismissed for the Russian corporate tax purposes[24].

(i) *What are the income/capital gains tax consequences of forks of crypto assets?*

This issue has not been addressed yet by the Russian legislator, courts or tax authorities. In case of a hard fork, which creates a new crypto asset, the conservative approach would be to assume that the taxpayer has received, for no consideration, an in-kind benefit equal to the fair market value of such new asset, which would be a taxable event for the taxpayer based on general principles of the Tax Code as described above.

(j) *What are the income/capital gains tax consequences of airdrops of crypto assets and are the tax consequences different if the airdropped tokens are unwanted?*

The receipt of a crypto assets for no consideration (e.g., due to a marketing campaign) will be treated as receipt of an in-kind benefit by the taxpayer and will be taxable either by the corporate tax as the company's non-trade income or by the PIT as a gift to the individual. Although there are some cases when gifts are not taxable (e.g., if the grantor and the recipient are both individuals), they are not applicable to the majority of the 'airdrops'.

As mentioned above, the tax base in this case will be the fair market value of the crypto asset.

24. *See*, e.g., Article 257 of the Tax Code.

(k) *What are the income/capital gains tax consequences of (solo, pool, and cloud) mining?*

This issue is more relevant for individuals, rather than for companies, as the latter must include mining income in the non-exclusive list of non-trade incomes, which will be added in the overall corporate tax base.

However, tax and non-tax obligations are different for individuals acting as private persons or as sole traders. As of now, the state authorities admit that there is no legal certainty of how mining should be treated and taxed in Russia[25], and although some tax officials have provided informal comments to media that income from mining should be subject to the PIT, there is no formal guidance on this issue yet.

Interestingly, there are court decisions where the nature of mining is addressed, but not from the tax perspective. For instance, in one case[26] the court decided that mining is a business activity 'in the purest form'. As business activity is defined in Russia as any type of activity that is aimed at systematic generation of profit by using assets or trade in goods, works and services, the reasoning of the court seems quite clear. However, it remains to be seen how the tax authorities will react if the individual taxpayer claims the business expense deduction (available for sole traders under the general PIT rules) in relation to mining, e.g., rent of premises or electricity cost.

It is also worth noting that sole traders are eligible for some special tax regimes (such as STS, *see* above), and although currently the state authorities deny the possibility of their application to crypto asset transactions, there were some proposals to extend Russian patent tax regime to include mining operations. Under such regime, the miner will not need to declare an actual income/profit received. Rather than that, a 'potential' annual income from mining will be calculated and the miner will pay tax based on this calculation, which may be easier from the tax administering perspective.

(l) *What are the income/capital gains tax consequences of staking crypto assets?*

The conclusions provided above in section (k) in relation to mining would generally apply to staking as well, though a more 'passive' nature of staking might be considered as an argument against this being a business activity. Nonetheless, this is a matter to be addressed in the future by the legislator, courts and state authorities.

(m) *What are the income/capital gains tax consequences of an indirect investment in crypto assets?*

If one considers indirect investment through securities/derivatives, any transactions with such investment instruments will be taxed subject to general principles of corporate and personal taxation.

25. Letter of the Ministry of Finance 23.04.2018 No. 03-01-11/27036.
26. Judgment of Sverdlovsky Region Court (sitting as a court of appeal) 08.11.2019 No. 33-19533/2019.

In most cases, income[27]/capital gains derived from securities are taxed at 20% corporate tax rate or 13% PIT rate respectively.

Upon the sale of security, both corporate and individual taxpayers are allowed to deduct acquisition cost and other relevant expenses.

(n) *How is income from crypto assets to be treated under double tax treaty law?*

Although we were unable to find cases dealing with the application of double tax treaties (DTTs) to crypto assets in Russia, it seems that the following provisions may apply potentially to crypto assets transactions:

- Articles on capital gains - for sale or exchange of crypto assets;
- Articles on so-called other income - for all other possible types of income.

As the majority of DTTs executed by Russia fall in the line with OECD Model Tax Convention, generally gains from alienation of assets other than Russian real estate or corporate interest in real estate - rich companies, as well as 'other' income is taxed exclusively in the recipient's state of tax residence.

(o) *What are the income/capital gains tax consequences of selling crypto assets in an ICO/STO/IEO?*

Currently the only statutory act in Russia which governs public placement of crypto assets is the Law on crowdfunding, which only addresses 'utility crypto rights'[28] (to be distinguished from 'utility tokens') on certain crowdfunding platforms.

The 'utility crypto rights' are evidenced by crypto certificates, which are treated as securities. Therefore, it seems that any transactions with such certificates should be taxed in the manner similar to other security transactions.

1.1.3 Other Taxes

(a) *What are the value added tax/sales tax consequences of selling crypto assets?*

The sale of goods or the assignment of intangibles by a company or a sole trader in Russia is normally subject to VAT. While it is impossible to claim that crypto assets are physically located in Russia, treating them as intangibles opens the way to claiming that they are transferred into Russia for the VAT taxation purposes, as the assignment of intangibles is governed by the same rules as the provision of services[29] for the VAT

27. Dividends excluded.
28. A right of claim to the issuer to provide goods, IP, or services.
29. Letter of the Ministry of Finance 19.11.2019 No. 03-07-08/89137.

purposes. Thus, if the assignor ('service provider') is located in Russia[30], the transaction may be subject to Russian VAT.

Notably, some tax officials have provided informal comments to media that, due to the fact that cryptocurrencies have no definite legal status in Russia yet, they are not tradable goods at all, and their sale is not a VAT event. Such comments, however, seem inconsistent with the general provisions of civil and tax law, and as they are informal it may not be prudent for taxpayers to rely on them.

(b) Are payments in crypto assets subject to withholding taxes?

Russian tax law does not operate with a notion of 'withholding tax' per se, but in some cases certain Russian tax residents may be obliged to act as tax agents for their counterparties. The most notable examples are:

- when Russian companies/permanent establishments of foreign companies make payments to foreign counterparties that are taxable with corporate tax in Russia, they withhold the Russian corporate tax from the amounts paid to their counterparties;
- when Russian companies/permanent establishments of foreign companies or merchants make payments to individuals (e.g., employees) that are taxable with the PIT in Russia, they withhold the Russian PIT from the amounts paid to individuals.

Tax agents are obliged to withhold the relevant tax amount from the payments due to the counterparty[31]. However, there is a special withholding procedure for the PIT (described in more details in section 1.1.2(e) above) that imposes tax payment obligations on individuals themselves in case there are no monetary transactions (in fiat currency) between them and the tax agent during the tax period.

(c) Does payment of compensation in crypto assets give rise to payroll tax consequences?

There is no specific 'payroll tax' in Russia. Labour-related payments in crypto assets will be regarded as payments in-kind (as mentioned above, the portion of the salary which may be paid in-kind is limited by the Russian Labour Code), thus raising the obligation of the employer to withhold the 13% PIT from the employee's income (*see* section 1.1.2(e) above). Please note that any labour-related payments, in cash or in kind[32], must be considered while calculating the amount of social security contributions to be paid by the employer for the employee.

30. Article 148(1), subsection 5 of the Tax Code.
31. Article 226 and 310 of the Tax Code.
32. Article 421(7) of the Tax Code.

(d) *Do transactions with crypto assets trigger any transfer taxes?*

No, there are no transfer taxes or stamp duties in Russia.

(e) *Are firms operating in the crypto space subject to digital service taxes?*

There is no separate 'digital service tax' per se in Russia, though the so-called Google tax, which is a common nickname for certain amendments to VAT rules, was introduced in 2016.[33] These amendments imposed VAT on electronic services (such as hosting, advertising, providing access to internet search engines, online libraries, music stores, and so on) provided by foreign companies to Russian consumers. Since 2019, regardless of whether such consumers are individuals, merchants, or companies, foreign service providers are generally obliged to register with tax authorities in Russia and pay VAT on their own.

This may be relevant to firms operating in the crypto space if they would provide electronic services to clients located in Russia, which may be incidental to the crypto assets trading. Yet the 'pure' trading in crypto assets that is not connected with the provision of such electronic services does not fall under the scope of these rules. General VAT taxation rules will apply to such crypto asset transactions (*see* section 1.1.3(a) above).

(f) *Are crypto assets subject to gift, inheritance, estate, or wealth taxes?*

There is no separate inheritance tax and no gift tax in Russia.

If a company or an individual receives crypto assets for no consideration, it/they will be subject to the corporate tax or the PIT, unless other tax exemptions apply.

Inheritance income, whether monetary or in-kind, is expressly exempted from PIT taxation[34].

As for wealth taxes on individuals, Russian tax law only provides for taxation of real estate (separate taxes apply to land plots and other kinds of real estate, such as buildings or premises) and motorcars, while other assets and intangibles are out of the scope of taxation by wealth tax.

As for corporate property tax, since 2019 companies are obliged to pay it only on immovable assets (real estate), which does not include crypto assets.

(g) *Are crypto assets subject to exit tax?*

There is no exit tax in Russia.

Transfer of crypto assets to a foreign company or structure (trust, fund, etc.) controlled by a Russian resident may in some cases trigger application of Russian rules on Controlled Foreign Companies (CFCs). Under CFC rules, the profit earned by a CFC

33. Articles 148 and 174.2 of the Tax Code.
34. Article 217(18) of the Tax Code.

located in a low or no-tax jurisdiction may be attributed to its Russian controlling person and may be subject to corporate tax or PIT respectively.

(h) Can mining trigger gambling tax?

There is no gambling tax in Russia.

1.1.4 Compliance and Documentation Obligations

(a) What documentation requirements exist for taxpayers regarding crypto assets and are there best practices in recordkeeping to support representations made in tax returns?

Although there is no guidance from Russian authorities regarding crypto assets in particular, both corporate and individual taxpayers are advised to follow the best practices in this area, such as:

- income and expenses of the taxpayer must be supported by relevant documents. Electronic documents, while in theory admissible, are typically not considered as proper evidence by Russian courts or tax authorities; it is advisable to keep them in hard copies, preferably certified by a notary;
- documents issued abroad are advised to be certified by local authorities and apostilled, as otherwise they may not be accepted as an evidence by Russian court;
- documents made in a foreign language need to be translated into Russian and the translation certified by a notary;
- shall occur to be unfeasible or impractical to support an expense with the proper documents, it may be advisable to choose not to deduct the expense for the tax purpose;
- not only the amount of income/expenses but also the valuation dates are important, especially if the payments were made in foreign currency, so the taxpayer should check whether the documents duly reflect this information;
- if the taxpayer needs to establish the fair market value of an asset received or sold in order to determine relevant tax obligations, it is advisable to engage an independent appraiser to carry out a valuation and obtain relevant report which shall be kept by the taxpayer in a hard copy.

(b) *What is the evidentiary burden of supporting tax positions when a digital wallet address is lost or shared with other persons?*

Currently, no such cases have been reported. Although formally the burden of proof rests with the tax authorities[35] and all the uncertainties must be interpreted in favour of the taxpayer, in practice it would not be advisable to rely on this principle. A taxpayer needs to be prepared to prove their position by well-documented evidence, witness' statements and other evidence, preferably coming from independent third parties unrelated to the taxpayer.

(c) *Are crypto asset exchanges and wallet providers subject to reporting obligations?*

There are no specific reporting obligations for crypto assets exchanges or wallet providers. What is more, the legal status, rights, and obligations of crypto asset exchanges and wallet providers is not regulated by Russian law so far.

It is also worth noting that the claim of the Russian tax authorities that cryptocurrency transactions are subject to the same currency control rules and disclosure obligations as 'ordinary' foreign currency transactions was not supported by the court[36]. However, if crypto asset transactions include payments in fiat money, Russian currency control rules may still apply[37], so this issue requires case-by-case analysis.

(d) *Are taxpayers holding crypto assets subject to reporting obligations apart from the filing of income tax/capital gains tax returns?*

No such obligations in respect of crypto assets have yet been introduced in Russia, but corporate taxpayers need to keep records of the crypto assets that they hold in accordance with general tax and accounting rules and include their value in the annual financial statements filed with the Russian tax authorities.

(e) *Are crypto asset exchanges and wallet providers subject to CRS/FATCA reporting?*

Since Russian legislation in its current state still does not regulate the legal status of cryptocurrencies or the activities of crypto asset exchanges or wallet providers, any comments on this matter are confined to opinions. It is expected that the long-awaited Law on Crypto Financial Assets shall address, *inter alia*, rights and obligations of Russian crypto asset exchanges/wallet providers. Therefore, after its introduction, the regulation landscape in this area may change.

35. Article 108 of the Tax Code.
36. Judgment of the Moscow City Court 18.04.2018 case No. 7-4313/2018.
37. Letter of the Federal Tax Service 03.10.2016 No. -18-17/1027.

As of now, the Law on Financial Transaction with Foreign Citizens and Legal Entities contains an exclusive list of persons who are both entitled and obliged to make disclosure under FATCA rules[38], such as credit institutions, life insurers, brokers, etc. Crypto asset exchanges/wallet providers are not included in this list.

To the contrary, CRS rules incorporated into the Russian Tax Code[39] impose reporting obligations onto any 'financial market institutions'. This category includes all entities that obtain money and/or other financial assets from their clients for custody, management, investment, or transfers.

Financial assets are further defined as money, securities, derivatives, corporate interest in legal entities or interest in foreign structure without legal personality (e.g., trust), rights under insurance policy or any other financial instrument connected with the above-mentioned types of financial assets. No reference to crypto assets is made so far.

As mentioned above, crypto assets as a whole and cryptocurrencies in particular are not deemed to be equal to money (fiat currency) by the Russian legislator, courts or fiscal authorities. They are also not included in the list of securities set by civil legislation[40], with some minor exception for electronic certificates on crypto utility rights (tokens) issued for crowdfunding purposes (*see* section 1.1.2 above) and generally will not fall into the scope of derivatives or 'otherwise connected' financial assets.

Therefore, crypto asset exchanges or wallet providers may be potentially treated as 'financial market institutions' and be subject to reporting obligations under CRS rules, but only if they are to carry activities with financial assets expressly enlisted by Russian legislation, not purely with crypto assets.

1.1.5 Civil and Criminal Tax Enforcement

(a) What powers do the tax authorities have to compel the disclosure of information by third parties, such as exchanges or wallet providers, and have these been used in the past?

The tax authorities are entitled to request information and documents required for the performance of a tax audit (and, in certain cases, beyond the scope of the audit as well) both from the taxpayer and from third persons (e.g., counterparties of the taxpayer, banks and other financial institutions, etc.), if they assume that such persons hold relevant information and documents. A fine of RUB 200 may be imposed for each document that has not been presented in due course[41]. Furthermore, tax authorities have the power to seize the documents (or other evidence) required for the tax audit from the holder if they have the reason to believe that otherwise such documents will

38. Article 1 of the Federal Law 28.06.2014 No. 173-FZ.
39. Chapter 20.1 of the Tax Code.
40. Article 142 of the Civil Code.
41. Article 126 of the Tax Code.

be destroyed, amended, etc.,[42] and they may rely on police to enforce. They may also interview witnesses (who may decline to be interviewed only in certain circumstances expressly provided in the statute), etc.

The above-mentioned measures are widely used in practice during tax audits, although there are no publicly known cases of their application to crypto asset exchanges or wallet providers so far.

(b) What measures have the tax authorities undertaken in the past to ensure crypto tax compliance?

Due to the early stage of development the Russian legislation on crypto assets is currently in, not so many practical measures have been taken so far. For the most part, the tax and financial authorities limit themselves to providing informal statements to the media and guidance letters on various tax issues (many of them have been referenced above). However, even in such statements or guidance they take a very cautious approach and constantly underline the need for a more detailed statutory framework to regulate crypto assets in Russia.

(c) Are the tax authorities cooperating with tax authorities in other jurisdictions on enforcement?

Yes, Russia is a party to more than eighty DTTs, to the Convention on Mutual Administrative Assistance in Tax Matters and to some other treaties (e.g., among the members of Eurasian Customs Union) that provide for international tax cooperation and allow the Russian tax authorities to obtain fiscally relevant information from aboard both automatically and by request. A number of requests to foreign tax authorities were successfully made in the past, though we were unable to find any cases concerning crypto assets that had been disclosed to the public.

42. Article 94 of the Tax Code.

Singapore

Gurbachan Singh, Ban Su Mei, Alicia Lim & Foo Yong Lim

1. COUNTRY GUIDES

1.1 Singapore

1.1.1 Applicable Tax Law, Guidance, and Case Law

(a) Which laws, regulations, and other administrative guidance exist dealing with crypto assets?

The Singapore Income Tax Act (ITA)[1] is the main legislation dealing with the taxation of income. However, at present neither the ITA nor the subsidiary legislation issued under the ITA explicitly mention crypto assets or bitcoins. In terms of administrative guidance, the Inland Revenue Authority of Singapore (IRAS) has published on its website the position it takes in relation to the profits derived from trading in virtual currencies.[2] The IRAS has also published an e-Tax Guide titled *Income Tax Treatment of Digital Tokens* on 17 April 2020.[3] Crypto assets are referred to in the guide as 'digital tokens' (i.e., any cryptographically-secured digital representation of a value that can be transferred, stored, or traded electronically).

In relation to Goods and Services Tax (GST), the Singapore Goods and Services Act[4] ('GST Act') provides for a definition of 'digital payment token', and the Goods and Services Tax (Excluded Transactions) Order[5] sets out the GST treatment of the

1. Income Tax Act (Cap 134, 2014 Rev Ed).
2. *Income Tax Treatment of Virtual Currencies*, Inland Revenue Authority of Singapore.
3. *IRAS e-Tax Guide – Income Tax Treatment of Digital Tokens*, Inland Revenue Authority of Singapore (17 Apr. 2020).
4. Goods and Services Tax Act (Cap 117A, 2005 Rev Ed).
5. Goods and Services Tax (Excluded Transactions) Order (Cap 117A, O 2, 2001 Rev Ed).

provision of digital payment tokens as consideration in respect of transactions, other than a transaction for a supply of money or digital payment tokens.

The Payment Services Act was recently passed on 14 January 2019 to regulate the provision of payment services and is sufficiently broad to include payments made using crypto assets (*see* sections 1.1.4(c) and 1.1.5(b), below, for details).

(b) Which court cases exist dealing with crypto assets?

The court structure of Singapore includes the State Courts, the High Court and the Court of Appeal. In addition, a taxpayer who is aggrieved by an income tax or GST assessment issued upon him by the IRAS may take the assessment on appeal in the first instance to the Income Tax Board of Review or the GST Board of Review.

There is a Singapore Court of Appeal case which involved crypto assets.[6] However, the case dealt with crypto assets in the context of contract law and trust law. There is currently no court case or Board of Review case dealing with crypto assets in the context of tax laws or GST laws.

1.1.2 Income and Capital Gains Taxes

(a) How are crypto assets classified for income and capital gains tax purposes?

Crypto assets may be regarded as stock-in-trade or investments. Where a taxpayer is in the business of buying and selling crypto assets in the ordinary course of its business, the crypto assets would be regarded as stock-in-trade. On the other hand, where a taxpayer buys crypto assets for long-term investment purposes, the crypto assets may be regarded as investments.

6. In *Quoine Pte Ltd v. B2C2 Ltd* [2020] SGCA(I) 2, the appellant was an operator of a cryptocurrency exchange platform and also functioned as a market-maker on the platform. The appellant conducted its market-making trades through its 'Quoter Program'. The respondent was a trader on the platform and traded using an algorithmic trading software. Built into the algorithm was a fail-safe 'deep price' of 10 Bitcoin to 1 Ethereum which would be invoked should input data from the platform be unavailable. The appellant's oversight in making certain necessary changes to the platform's critical operating systems led to the Quoter Program's failure to generate new orders. This led to the 'deep price' in the trading software taking effect. The respondent's sell orders were eventually matched with the buy orders of two other traders. Eventually, 13 trades were concluded between the respondent and the two other traders at rates which were approximately 250 times the then going rate in the market. When the appellant became aware of the 13 trades, it unilaterally cancelled the trades and reversed the settlement transactions on the basis that the trades were concluded at highly abnormal rates. The respondent commenced proceedings against the appellant, alleging that its unilateral cancellation of the 13 trades and the reversal of the settlement transactions were in breach of contract or breach of trust. The Court of Appeal rejected the appellant's defences of unilateral mistake, common mistake and unjust enrichment. The Court of Appeal held that it was not necessary for it to decide whether cryptocurrency was a species of property that was capable of being held on trust as there was no express trust on the facts of the case. The Court of Appeal therefore dismissed the appellant's appeal on the breach of contract claim and allowed its appeal on the breach of trust claim. Given the decision that the 13 trades were valid and enforceable, the respondent was contractually entitled to the proceeds of the 13 trades from the appellant.

(b) *What are the income/capital gains tax consequences of selling crypto assets against fiat currency?*

For Singapore income tax purposes, taxpayers who buy and sell crypto assets in the ordinary course of their business will be subject to the existing income tax rules.[7] Taxpayers will be taxed on the income derived from trading in the crypto assets if the income was derived from or received in Singapore, or deemed to be derived from or received in Singapore. In ascertaining the gains on tokens previously acquired by the taxpayer over a period of time at different values, the IRAS accepts the 'first in first out' (FIFO) principle, or the weighted average cost methods of valuing the cost of the payment token disposed.

The IRAS has generally classified crypto assets into three broad categories:[8]

(1) **Payment Tokens:** The purchase of a payment token will not be regarded as a taxable event. However, when the taxpayer sells the payment token, the intention of the taxpayer when he purchased the token will be used to ascertain if the subsequent disposal of the token is a trading activity on revenue account.

(2) **Utility Tokens**: The purchase of a utility token is regarded a prepayment for the goods and services. If the purchase of the utility token was made in the course of a business, and redeemed for goods or services in accordance with its terms, the purchaser may claim a deduction at the time of redemption. If the purchaser then disposes of the token (instead of redeeming it), it is likely the IRAS would seek to tax any gains if the token was held on revenue account. From the issuer's perspective, the IRAS will regard the issuer as having earned the income upon redemption of the token (*see* section 1.1.2(o) for details).

(3) **Security Tokens:** These may be accounted for as a form of debt or equity, depending on the terms of the token, and any interest or dividend derived from the token will be subject to the usual income tax treatments. If the token is disposed of, the IRAS would seek to tax any gains if the token was held on revenue account.

As there is no capital gains tax in Singapore, the gains of taxpayers who buy crypto assets for long-term investment purposes and who can substantiate that the assets are held for long-term investment will not be subject to tax.

(c) *What are the income/capital gains tax consequences of exchanging crypto assets against other crypto assets?*

The taxability of a gain or loss from conversion of one payment token to another payment token will depend on whether the payment token is held on capital or revenue account. A taxpayer's profit from the exchange of crypto assets against other crypto assets in the ordinary course of their business would be subject to income tax.

7. *Income Tax Treatment of Virtual Currencies*, Inland Revenue Authority of Singapore, https://www.iras.gov.sg/irashome/Businesses/Companies/Working-out-Corporate-Income-Taxes/Specific-topics/Income-Tax-Treatment-of-Virtual-Currencies/.

8. *IRAS e-Tax Guide – Income Tax Treatment of Digital Tokens*, Inland Revenue Authority of Singapore (17 Apr. 2020),

In ascertaining the value of the crypto assets, the IRAS would allow taxpayers to use an exchange rate that best reflects the value of the tokens received, provided that the following two conditions are satisfied:

(1) The exchange rate must be reasonable and verifiable (e.g., determined using an average of exchange rates available on payment token exchanges). Where the exchange rate is not available on exchanges, taxpayers can use other means to support their claim that the basis of the exchange rate used is reasonable.
(2) The methodology used to determine the exchange rate should be consistently applied year on year.

As there is no capital gains tax in Singapore, taxpayers who buy crypto assets for long-term investment purposes and make capital gains from the disposal of such crypto assets will not be taxed on the capital gains. It is possible that taxpayers who exchange crypto assets held for long-term investment purposes against other crypto assets and make capital gains from such exchanges will not be taxed on the gains if it can be proven that the crypto assets were capital assets.

(d) If a distinction is made between business assets and non-business assets, when does trading in crypto assets lead to a trade or business?

In Singapore, a distinction is drawn between assets held as stock-in-trade and assets held as investments. In determining whether a person is carrying on a trade and, therefore, holding the asset as stock-in-trade, the IRAS and the Singapore courts will consider factors which are commonly referred to as the 'badges of trade'. The 'badges of trade' were introduced by the United Kingdom Royal Commission on the Taxation of Profits and Income[9] ('Report of the Royal Commission') and have been referred to with approval in Singapore.[10] All the badges of trade are considered as a whole, and the question of whether there is a trade is essentially a question of fact and law to be decided after taking into account all the surrounding circumstances and whether all the circumstances point to profit from a trade or the realization of an investment. Further, the clearest indication that an investment was acquired as a capital asset would be that the taxpayer intended to hold the investment as such for an indefinite period. The badges of trade, which were set out in the Report of the Royal Commission, are as follows:

(1) *The subject matter of realization.* Certain forms of property, such as commodities or manufactured articles, which are normally the subject of trading are only very exceptionally the subject of investment.

9. United Kingdom Royal Commission on the Taxation of Profits and Income (1955) Cmd 9474.
10. *See*, for example, *W Holdings Pte Ltd v. CIT* (1992) 1 MSTC 5,135 and *GRP Ltd v. CIT* (1995) 2 MSTC 5,207.

(2) *The length of period of ownership.* Generally, property meant to be traded is sold within a short time after purchase. In contrast, the longer one owns the property, the more likely the case that the disposal of the property is a realization of an investment.
(3) *The frequency or number of similar transactions by the same person.* It has been held that trading connotes 'habitual and systematic operations, a continuity or repetition of acts or similar operations'.[11] Accordingly, a high frequency of similar transactions is more indicative of trading than an isolated transaction.
(4) *Supplementary work on or in connection with the property realized.* If the property is worked on in any way to make it more marketable or if special exertions are made to fine or attract purchases, it is more likely that the subsequent disposal would be regarded as trading.[12]
(5) *The circumstances responsible for the realization.* Where there is an explanation for a quick sale, such as a sudden emergency or opportunity calling for ready money, that explanation may negate the idea that any plan of trading prompted the original purchase.[13]
(6) *Motive.* The question is whether the taxpayer acquired the asset with the intention to dispose of it at a profit at the time of acquisition or whether it was acquired as an investment.[14]

Other indicia of trading that may be considered are:

(1) *Financing.* Based on various Singapore Income Tax Board of Review decisions,[15] it would appear that the level of financing taken up by a taxpayer to purchase an asset is extremely important. The fact that the investment is highly geared and that holding onto the investment will produce a negative cash flow, is indicative of an intention to dispose of the asset quickly after acquisition.
(2) *Business of trading background.* The fact that the taxpayer may have a relevant background in a particular trade or business is also a factor to be considered.[16]
(3) *The taxpayer's accounts and constituting documents.* The taxpayer's accounts may be said to be an expression of the taxpayer's subjective intentions in relation to the asset. If the assets are reflected in the accounts as stock-in-trade, it is likely that they are acquired for disposal in a trade. Upon disposal, the gains may be regarded as trading gains. However, it is not necessarily the case that if an asset is reflected as a capital asset used in the business that it

11. *DEF v. CIT* [1961] MLJ 55 at 59.
12. *KE (S) Pte Ltd v. CIT* (1998) MSTC 5,235.
13. *KE (S) Pte Ltd v. CIT* (1998) MSTC 5,235.
14. *Simmons v. IRC* [1980] STC 350.
15. *See*, for example, *SCL Pte Ltd v. CIT* (1991) 1 MSTC 5,032; *C Ltd v. CIT* (1991) 1 MSTC 5,052; *W Holdings Pte Ltd v. CIT* (1992) 1 MSTC 5,135; *KE (S) Pte Ltd v. CIT* (1998) MSTC 5,235.
16. *SCL Pte Ltd v. CIT* (1991) 1 MSTC 5,032; *GRP Ltd v. CIT* (1995) 2 MSTC 5,207.

will be regarded as such.[17] It must also be borne in mind that the taxpayer's documents are not conclusive as the taxpayer is at liberty to draft the documents in any manner he wished.[18]

(4) *Organization*. The presence of an organizational set-up to facilitate the disposal of assets may be an indicium of trading.[19]

(e) *What are the income/capital gains tax consequences for an employee receiving wages or salaries in crypto assets?*

In general, all gains or profits derived from Singapore or received in Singapore from outside Singapore by an employee in respect of his employment are taxable unless they are specifically exempt from income tax or are covered by an existing administrative concession.[20]

The definition of 'gains or profits from any employment' in the Income Tax Act includes 'any wages, salary, leave pay, fee, commission, bonus, gratuity, perquisite or allowance...paid or granted in respect of the employment whether in money or otherwise'.[21] This definition is likely to be sufficient to cover wages or salaries to employees in crypto assets.

Wages paid in the form of crypto assets are taxable in the hands of the employee based on the value of the employment services performed by the employee. The IRAS would examine the terms of the employment contract to determine the taxable amount. Further, if a moratorium is imposed on the employee's disposal of the crypto assets, the payments in crypto assets will only be taxable when the moratorium is lifted as income is regarded as accruing to the employee only at the end of the moratorium.

(f) *What are the income/capital gains tax consequences for a merchant receiving payment in crypto assets?*

Tax consequences for the merchant

Crypto assets which constitute payment tokens are regarded as intangible property. Consequently, where merchants accept payment tokens as payment for goods or services rendered, the transaction is viewed as a barter trade. The value of goods or services transferred should be determined at the point of transaction and the merchant is expected to record the sale based on the open market value of the goods or services in Singapore Dollars or the functional currency adopted by the merchant's business.

17. In *C Ltd v. CIT* (1991) 1 MSTC 5,052 at 5,073, the Income Tax Board of Review ruled that the classification of the properties in the accounts was a neutral fact as to whether the taxpayer was trading.
18. *KE (S) Pte Ltd v. CIT* (1998) MSTC 5,235.
19. *Re AB Ltd* (1950-1985) MSTC 465; *DEF v. CIT* (1950-1985) MSTC 482.
20. Income Tax Act (Cap 134, 2014 Rev Ed) section 10(1)(b).
21. Income Tax Act (Cap 134, 2014 Rev Ed) section 10(2).

The merchant would be taxed on the value of the underlying goods or services performed.[22]

A business may choose to present its financial statements in Singapore Dollars or its chosen functional currency and will have to file its tax computation in the same functional currency as that chosen in the financial statements. The IRAS needs to be notified of the choice of functional currency adopted. At present, crypto assets is not an available option as a functional currency for purposes of filing tax computations. While a crypto asset may serve as a mode of payment, it is not a fiat currency as it is not issued by any government and is not legal tender. Regardless of the functional currency adopted in the financial statements and tax computations, businesses are required to file their tax returns in Singapore Dollars.

Tax consequences for the purchaser

Where the purchaser is a business and makes payment for goods or services using payment tokens, two implications arise:

(1) **Deduction**: Subject to the general rules on deduction under sections 14 and 15 of the Income Tax Act, the amount of deduction allowable would be determined with reference to the value of the underlying goods or services received. In ascertaining the value, the IRAS would examine the terms of the underlying contractual agreement.
   (a) If the contractual obligation is to pay an ***agreed value of fiat currency*** then notwithstanding that payment is effected with payment tokens (for example, SGD 100 to be paid in Bitcoins), the value for the purposes of deduction would be the amount of fiat currency.
   (b) If the contractual obligation is to pay an ***agreed number of payment tokens***, then the value for purposes of deduction may be determined to be the value of the payment tokens at the time the merchant becomes entitled to the tokens.

(2) **Gains or losses on disposal:** There will be no tax consequences for gains or losses on disposal if the purchaser holds the payment tokens on capital account. However, if the purchaser holds the said tokens on revenue account, then gains/losses will be taxable/deductible at the time of realization. The IRAS accepts the FIFO principle or the weighted average cost method of ascertaining the cost of tokens acquired over a period of time at different values.

22. *IRAS e-Tax Guide – Income Tax Treatment of Digital Tokens*, Inland Revenue Authority of Singapore (17 Apr. 2020).

(g) *What are the income/capital gains tax consequences of a loss of crypto assets?*

There is no specific guidance on the tax treatment of a loss of the crypto asset (for example, if the private key is lost or stolen). However, given that the IRAS has adopted the position to tax businesses on the gains on buying and selling crypto assets in the ordinary course of their business, and to regard the disposal of assets held for long-term investment purposes as a disposal of a capital assets, the IRAS is likely to apply general principles.

In this regard, it must first be determined whether the crypto asset which has been lost is stock-in-trade of the business or a capital asset. If it was a capital asset of the business, there will be no deduction for tax purposes.[23]

If the crypto asset was the stock-in-trade of a business and a deduction is sought in respect of the loss, the argument should be made that the occasion for the loss was the operation of the business in the normal way and such losses were a 'reasonable incidental' risk to the production of assessable income.[24] This is a question of fact. However, in the event the loss was caused by misappropriation by employees having 'overriding power or control', the lack of sufficient 'checks and balances' within the business to prevent abuse of overriding power would be detrimental to a claim for deduction.[25]

(h) *What are the income/capital gains tax consequences of a loss in value of crypto assets?*

The general rule is that neither profit nor loss may be anticipated,[26] and profit shall not be taxed until realized.[27] Crypto assets are volatile and carry the risk of a loss in value. Even if the value of the crypto asset falls significantly but continues to be held by the taxpayer, the taxpayer would not be able to obtain a deduction until the loss in value has been realized. The IRAS has confirmed that even if a change in fair value of the payment token is recognized in the financial statements for accounting purposes, such fair value gain/loss will not be taxable or deductible under current tax rules as the gain/loss is not realized.

However, if any particular crypto asset falls within the definition of a 'financial instrument' for the purposes of the Financial Accounting Standards (FRS), the tax treatment of such crypto asset may be aligned with the accounting treatment under the relevant accounting standard. Under FRS 32, a financial instrument is defined as any contract that gives rise to a financial asset of one entity and a financial liability or equity instrument of another entity.

23. Income Tax Act (Cap 134, 2014 Rev Ed) section 15(1)(c).
24. *Gold Bank Services Ltd v. Commissioner of Inland Revenue* (1961) NZLR 467.
25. *AQP v. CIT* [2013] 2 SLR 155.
26. *BSC Footwear Ltd v. Ridgway (Inspector of Taxes)* [1972] AC 544 at 560.
27. *Duple Motor Bodies Ltd v. Ostime* [1961] 1 WLR 739 at 751.

Pursuant to section 34A of the Income Tax Act, the tax treatment of financial assets is aligned with its accounting treatment under FRS 39. Any unrealized gain or loss recognized in a company's profit and loss account in respect of financial instruments held on revenue account would be taxable or allowable as a deduction. The aforesaid tax treatment applies to all companies except for companies that are temporarily exempt by the Accounting and Corporate Regulatory Authority (ACRA), or companies which have elected not to apply FRS 39 tax treatment under section 34A(3) of the Act.

FRS 109 replaced FRS 39 and applies to companies for financial years beginning on or after 1 January 2018.[28] Section 34AA provides for the tax treatment of financial assets to be aligned with accounting treatment under FRS 109. Under FRS 109, unrealized gains or losses may be recognized in the profit and loss account (P&L) or as Other Chargeable Income (OCI), depending on the classification of the financial asset. Where, in accordance with FRS 109, the unrealized gains or losses are to be recognized in the P&L (as opposed to under the OCI), such unrealized gains or losses would be taxable or allowable as a deduction.

If the crypto asset is a financial asset held on capital account, any gain or loss will neither be taxed nor deductible.[29]

(i) What are the income/capital gains tax consequences of forks of crypto assets?

A blockchain fork may occur due to a change in the underlying consensus rules of a blockchain which is partially adopted by some users but not all. This leads to a branching of the blockchain. In a fork which is permanent, the users holding crypto assets on the original blockchain would concurrently hold an equivalent number of crypto assets (the forked crypto assets) on the new blockchain branch. Crypto assets on both branches of the blockchain may have their own value.

The IRAS has issued guidance in this regard and taken the position that the new crypto assets can be viewed as a windfall to the recipient as the taxpayer had received the additional crypto assets without doing anything in return. Where it is regarded as a windfall, the fork would not be regarded as having given rise to a gain of an income nature and would not be taxable on the recipient at the point of receipt. However, it is not clear what circumstances the IRAS would take into consideration in deciding whether it is indeed a windfall. If it is not viewed as a windfall, then the usual principles (of ascertaining whether the taxpayer held the assets on revenue or capital account) will apply in determining whether the new crypto assets would be treated as income or capital.

---

28. *Adopting Financial Reporting Standard (FRS) 39 and 109 and its Tax Implications*, Inland Revenue Authority of Singapore, https://www.iras.gov.sg/irashome/Businesses/Companies/Working-out-Corporate-Income-Taxes/Specific-topics/Adopting-Financial-Reporting-Standard--FRS--39-and-109-and-its-Tax-Implications/.
29. Income Tax Act (Cap 134, 2014 Rev Ed) section 34AA(2).

Where the recipient is trading in crypto assets, the gains from the subsequent disposal of the crypto assets, including the disposal of any crypto assets received as a result of a fork, will not be treated as a windfall, and will be taxable. In other words, if the crypto assets are held by a taxpayer in the course of a business as stock-in-trade (*see* discussion in section 1.1.2(a) above), the IRAS will seek to tax any gains which may arise as a result of the fork.

What is uncertain is whether the gains are taxable at the time the fork occurred (i.e., when the taxpayer receives the forked crypto assets), or when the gains are actually realized (i.e., through a sale of the original or the forked crypto assets). A taxpayer may want to advance the argument that the gains should be taxed only upon realization. This is so especially if it is uncertain whether a market exists where the forked crypto assets would be recognized or sold. However, this must be considered in the light of section 34A (or section 34AA) relating to the applicability of FRS 39 (or FRS 109) which may treat crypto assets as financial assets (*see* discussion in section 1.1.2(h), above). This issue is unresolved.

For a taxpayer who is holding crypto assets on capital account, a hard fork should have no income tax consequences as there are no capital gains taxes in Singapore.

(j) What are the income/capital gains tax consequences of airdrops of crypto assets and are the tax consequences different if the airdropped tokens are unwanted?

An airdrop is the distribution of crypto assets without compensation. Airdrops are generally undertaken with a view to increasing awareness of a new token and to increase liquidity in the early stages of a crypto asset project. For income tax purposes, if the crypto asset is not received in return for any goods or services performed, it would not be regarded as income of the recipient. However, if the airdropped crypto asset is given in return for or in expectation of a service, then the gains from receipt of the crypto asset from an airdrop will be income and will be taxable.

In relation to GST, the IRAS has taken the position that there is no supply for GST purposes in an airdrop.[30]

(k) What are the income/capital gains tax consequences of (solo, pool, and cloud) mining?

Solo and pool mining involve miners contributing their computer's processing power to verify transactions on the blockchain network (referred to as 'mining'). Solo miners carry out mining operations on their own and are rewarded when a block is 'found'; pool miners undertake the mining operations collectively in a pool and upon 'finding'

30. *IRAS e-Tax Guide – GST: Digital Payment Tokens*, Inland Revenue Authority of Singapore (19 Nov. 2019).

a block, the reward is shared among all miners in the pool.[31] In cloud mining, the user does not contribute computer hardware, but signs a cloud mining contract with an operator with remote data centres. The user purchases the mining capacity of the hardware and the mining activities are carried on remotely in the cloud.

The profits derived by miners from the disposal of mined payment tokens will be taxable if the miner performs the mining activity with an intention to profit.[32] When a miner performs mining as a hobby or with the intention to hold the tokens mined as long-term investments, the IRAS has taken the position that the gains on disposal of the mined tokens are not taxable.

Please refer to section 1.1.2(d), above, for a discussion on the level of activity which amounts to trading. The IRAS has also taken the following positions as regards mining undertaken by companies and by individuals:

(1) **Companies**: A company is generally set up with a view to profit, so the IRAS would generally regard companies as carrying on a business in mining activities. Consequently, mining costs incurred from the date of commencement of business would be deductible. Indicators of commencement of a mining business include the purchase of mining equipment and sale of the mined digital tokens.
(2) **Individuals**: *Prima facie* an individual engaging in mining activities will be regarded as engaging in a hobby. However, if the individual shows habitual and systematic efforts to make a profit from the activities, then the IRAS may regard him as carrying on a vocation of a miner, and the profits from sale of the mined digital tokens are taxable.

The profits of mining will be taxed at the point of disposal of the token, not at the point in time where the token is successfully mined because the IRAS takes the view that no income is derived merely by holding the payment token.

Separately, where a miner is paid a fee to perform mining activities for another and where the mined tokens belong to the customer rather than the miner, the IRAS' position is to impose tax on the fees received by the miner as the miner is regarded as having received fees on the provision of a service.

(l) What are the income/capital gains tax consequences of staking crypto assets?

Crypto asset mining normally operates on a 'proof-of-work' model which is based on cryptography involving the use of intensive computing power to solve mathematical equations to validate transactions on the blockchain which is then posted to the public blockchain. The mining of crypto assets is therefore a more labour-intensive exercise.

31. Toshendra Kumar Sharma, *What is solo mining & how it works?* Blockchain Council (8 Aug. 2017), https://www.blockchain-council.org/blockchain/solo-mining-works/.
32. *IRAS e-Tax Guide – Income Tax Treatment of Digital Tokens*, Inland Revenue Authority of Singapore (17 Apr. 2020).

Crypto asset staking adopts an alternative model referred to as 'proof-of-stake' to validate transactions on the blockchain. The user has to put his or her coins into a specific wallet where the coins are frozen. The user's chance of successfully creating a new block on the blockchain (and earning the transaction fee) is proportionate to the amount staked.

Crypto asset staking is less labour-intensive than mining, and this would be a significant consideration in ascertaining if taxpayer is carrying out the staking in the course of a business.

(m) What are the income/capital gains tax consequences of an indirect investment in crypto assets?

Indirect investments in crypto assets may be effected by an investment in cryptocurrency funds. However, although there are various tax incentives in Singapore applicable to funds managed by fund managers in Singapore, the availability of the incentive is generally activity-centric and the fund has to meet all the qualifying conditions (including conditions on the nature of the underlying investment) before the incentive may be available. Where the conditions for such tax incentives are not met, the general tax rules will apply in respect of gains arising from indirect investments in crypto assets.

Further, if investments in crypto assets are made by persons not resident in Singapore through an agent in Singapore, and if the investment income is sourced in Singapore, the IRAS may resort to section 53 of the Income Tax Act under which the non-resident investor is subject to tax either directly, or in the name of his agent. Pursuant to section 53(2A) of the Income Tax Act, where a non-resident person and a resident person carry on business together, the non-resident person may be subject to tax in the name of a resident person as if the resident person was an agent of the non-resident person if there is a close connection between them and the non-resident person exercises substantial control over the resident person, such that the resident person receives either no profits or less than the ordinary profits expected to arise from the business carried out with the non-resident person.

(n) How is income from crypto assets to be treated under double tax treaty law?

In its administrative guidance, the IRAS has said that where a tax treaty is applicable, existing treaty rules would apply. As Singapore is a signatory to the OECD Model Tax Convention on Income and on Capital ('Model Tax Convention'), it is likely that income earned in connection with crypto assets would fall within the various allocation rules of the Model Tax Convention. Pursuant to Article 7 of the Model Tax Convention, profits of an enterprise of a contracting state are taxable only in that state. However, if the enterprise carries on business in the other contracting state through a permanent establishment situated therein, the profits that are attributable to the permanent establishment may be taxed in that other state.

(o) *What are the income/capital gains tax consequences of selling crypto assets in an ICO/STO/IEO?*

Tokens issued during an initial offering can be payment tokens, confer ownership rights or rights in respect of a business (security tokens), or rights in respect of products or services produced by the issuer (utility tokens).

Proceeds of the initial offering

The tax treatment of the proceeds of offering would depend on the terms of issue (as would be set out in the whitepaper or offer documents) of the token, and whether the proceeds for the issue of the token would in fact be capital in the books of the company or was in fact income.

The following sets out the general tax position of the initial offering proceeds of various types of digital tokens in the hands of the issuer:

(1) **Payment token proceeds**: Generally, payment tokens are not usually issued through an initial offering. However, the IRAS would review the facts of each case. If the issuer is a company, the IRAS is more likely to regard the company as carrying on a trade in payment tokens and the proceeds of the coin offering would be taxable. The transaction would be taxed at the point of issuance.
(2) **Utility token proceeds**: The IRAS has stated that the proceeds will generally be regarded as deferred revenue and taxable upon redemption of the token because the issuer would usually need to complete the development of its platform before it is able to fulfil its obligations under the token. In our view, it is correct to defer the recognition of revenue because neither profits nor losses may be anticipated. The proceeds should be taxed only when they can properly be counted as gains completely earned by the issuer without qualification.[33]
(3) **Security token proceeds**: If the tokens create a liability on the part of the issuer to repay a sum of money (i.e., in the nature of a loan), or if the tokens in fact represented equity in the issuer, it is possible that they would be characterized as capital, and not be subject to income tax. Further, if the tokens pay interest or dividends, the issuer may be able to claim deductions on the expenditure, subject to the rules on deductibility (i.e., sections 14 and 15 of the Income Tax Act). General withholding tax obligations apply to the dividend or interest paid to a non-resident owner of the token.

In all cases, the terms of issue of the particular crypto asset must be considered to ascertain the rights created therein.

33. *Arthur Murray (NSW) Pty Ltd v. FCT* 14 ADT 98.

Failed initial offering

A failure could occur if, for example, the issuer issues utility tokens but is subsequently unable to build and deliver the promised platform for which it is intended that the token holders would have access.

If the proceeds are refunded, the issuer will not be subject to tax on the refunded amounts. However, if the proceeds are not refunded, then the IRAS would evaluate if the proceeds are on capital or revenue account. Factors such as the issuer's business activities, reasons for the initial offering and contractual obligations arising from the issuance of the tokens would be considered.

Source

Another issue is whether the proceeds from the offering are considered sourced in Singapore or foreign sourced income. As Singapore has adopted a territorial system of taxation, income accruing in or derived from Singapore, or foreign sourced income received in Singapore would be taxed.

The fact that an initial offering may be executed digitally without a physical location or physical activities is a challenge in determining the source of the proceeds for issuance of payment tokens and utility tokens. The following are some factors which would be considered in determining whether the source of the offer proceeds is in Singapore:

(1) whether the issuer has a physical presence in Singapore;
(2) the manner in which the marketing and promotion of the offer is conducted;
(3) whether participants of the offer are predominantly based in or out of Singapore; and
(4) whether developers behind the technology are based in or out of Singapore.

As regards the question of source of offer proceeds in respect of the issuance of security tokens, the IRAS has taken the view that the usual source rules for interest and dividends will apply.

1.1.3 Other Taxes

(a) What are the value added tax/sales tax consequences of selling crypto assets?

The IRAS has set out the GST consequences of supplies of crypto assets in its e-Tax Guide titled *GST: Digital Payment Tokens* on 19 November 2019.[34] With effect from 1 January 2020, supplies of digital payment tokens will no longer be subject to GST. In particular, the use of digital payment tokens as payment for goods or services will no

34. *IRAS e-Tax Guide – GST: Taxing imported services by way of an overseas vendor registration regime*, Inland Revenue Authority of Singapore (26 Aug. 2019).

longer give rise to a supply of those tokens. In addition, a supply of digital payment tokens in exchange for fiat currency or other digital payment tokens, and the provision of any loan, advance or credit of digital payment tokens will be exempt from GST. With regard to crypto assets which do not qualify as digital payment tokens, the supply of such tokens continues to be regarded as taxable supplies of services, unless they fall under the prescribed list of exempt financial services under Part I of the Fourth Schedule to the GST Act.

Accordingly, the nature of the particular crypto asset would impact the GST consequences of the sale. A crypto asset may be a payment token (functioning as a medium of exchange), or could be security tokens (representing ownership rights) or a utility token (entitling the owner to services in future).

Payment Tokens

Previously, the supply of payment tokens was seen as a taxable supply of good or service for GST purposes because payment tokens (then referred to as 'virtual currencies') do not fit the definition of 'money' or 'currency'. However, the GST Act was amended in November 2019 with effect from 1 January 2020. The amendments introduced the concept of a 'digital payment token' in section 2A. A digital payment token has all of the following characteristics:

(1) it is expressed as a unit;
(2) it is designed to be fungible;
(3) it is not denominated in any currency, and is not pegged by its issuer to any currency;
(4) it can be transferred, stored or traded electronically; and
(5) it is, or is intended to be, a medium of exchange accepted by the public, or a section of the public, without any substantial restrictions on its use as consideration.

With effect from 1 January 2020, the use of virtual currencies which fall within the definition of a 'digital payment token' as consideration would not be treated as a supply of goods or services pursuant to Order 7 of the Goods and Services Tax (Excluded Transactions) Order.[35] However, this does not affect the usual GST treatment on the supply of the underlying goods and services by the GST-registered supplier (who received digital payment tokens as payment).

The exchange of digital payment tokens for currency or for other digital payment tokens, as well as the provision of any loan, advance, or credit of digital payment tokens is an exempt supply under the Fourth Schedule of the GST Act.

35. Goods and Services Tax (Excluded Transactions) Order (Cap 117A, O 2, 2001 Rev Ed).

Security Token

The crypto asset may be a security token which represents an ownership interest in a company or an asset, or may give the token-holder the rights to receive a sum of money from the issuer. In this regard, if the security token qualifies as 'equity security', 'debt security' or any other financial services set out in Part 1 of the Fourth Schedule, the supply of the security token may be an exempt supply under the GST Act.

An 'equity security' is defined in Part 3 of the Fourth Schedule to the GST Act as being 'any interest in or right to a share in the capital of a body corporate or any option to acquire any such interest or right but excludes a contract of insurance and an estate or interest in land, other than an estate or interest as mortgagee or chargeholder'.

A 'debt security' is defined as 'any interest in or right to be paid money that is, or is to be, owing by any person or any option to acquire any such interest or right but excludes a contract of insurance and an estate or interest in land, other than an estate or interest as mortgagee or chargeholder'.

Utility Token

Utility tokens generally give the token-holder a future right to utilize products or services which are being developed by the issuer. The particular product or services underlying the token has to be considered, and in this regard, potential GST issues in relation to the supply of digital services may arise (*see* section 1.1.3(e), below).

(b) *Are payments in crypto assets subject to withholding taxes?*

Withholding tax is a tax imposed at the source to ensure collection of the tax liability. Where a person in Singapore (the 'payer') makes payment of Singapore-sourced interest, royalties, management fees, or any of the amounts listed in section 12(6) and (7) of the ITA, to a person not known to him to be resident in Singapore (the 'payee'), sections 45 and 45A of the ITA requires the payer to deduct the amount of tax (as may be applicable) from the amount to be paid to the payee, and pay over to the Comptroller the amount of tax withheld.

At the moment, sections 45 and 45A of the Income Tax Act do not appear to provide any express guidance on situations when tax needs to be withheld on payments made using digital payment tokens. Said sections provide for tax at the applicable rates to be deducted from 'every dollar of the interest' and paid over to the Comptroller. Administratively, it is not clear how the provisions would be followed in the event of withholding tax on a payment made using digital payment tokens.

As an aside, we observe that there is a general provision in paragraph 11 of the Third Schedule of the GST Act which provides that 'where any sum relevant for determining value is expressed in a currency other than Singapore currency or in digital payment tokens, it is to be converted into Singapore currency at the selling rate of exchange prevailing in Singapore at the time when the supply takes place'. It remains to be seen whether a similar general provision will be adopted for the Income Tax Act as well.

We would highlight that a Singapore-based issuer of security tokens (characterized as debt) paying interest to the token holders under the terms of issue, would have withholding tax obligations under section 45 of the Income Tax Act in respect of interest payments made to non-resident holders of the said tokens.

(c) *Does payment of compensation in crypto assets give rise to payroll tax consequences?*

Singapore does not have any payroll tax. Employees are assessed an individual income tax on their employment remuneration.[36] It is likely that an employee receiving his wages or salary in crypto assets would similarly be assessed an income tax on the crypto assets, as the definition of 'gains or profits from any employment'[37] in the Income Tax Act is likely to be sufficiently broad to cover crypto assets.

In addition, where a foreign employee ceases employment in Singapore, goes on an overseas posting or plans to leave Singapore for more than three months, tax clearance is required. His employer must notify the IRAS at least one month in advance and withhold all monies due to the employee from the date the employer is aware of the impending cessation of employment or departure from Singapore. If the foreign employee has any unexercised stock options, under the 'deemed exercise' rule he is deemed to have derived gains from any unexercised stock options which he has at the time he ceases to work in Singapore with the employer which granted him the stock option.[38] The foreign employee will then be assessed an income tax on the gains he is deemed to have derived.

It remains to be seen whether any similar 'deemed exercise' rules would be introduced to cover a situation where a foreign employee leaves Singapore, holding wages received in the form of payment tokens subject to a moratorium.

(d) *Do transactions with crypto assets trigger any transfer taxes?*

Stamp duty is chargeable on the instruments prescribed by section 4 read with the First Schedule to the Stamp Duties Act (SDA).[39]

Chargeable instruments include transfer documents for shares, documents relating to immovable property as well as mortgage documents. There is presently no indication whether security tokens (which represent ownership interests in a property or a company or other chargeable property) or the blockchain ledger which records transactions involving such tokens could be considered an 'instrument' for the purposes of the SDA.

However, we note that sections 59–60 of the SDA were introduced in 2018 which provides for stamp duty to be levied on 'electronic instruments' effecting transfers of interest in immovable properties and in shares. It is not clear whether under these

36. Income Tax Act (Cap 134, 2014 Rev Ed) section 10(1)(b).
37. Income Tax Act (Cap 134, 2014 Rev Ed) section 10(2).
38. Income Tax Act (Cap 134, 2014 Rev Ed) section 10(6).
39. Stamp Duties Act (Cap 312, 2006 Rev Ed).

provisions security tokens can be viewed as instruments for purposes of the SDA, and it remains to be seen whether the IRAS or Parliament will seek to expressly extend the scope of the SDA to such security tokens which represent interests in immovable properties and shares.

(e) Are firms operating in the crypto space subject to digital service taxes?

Singapore has not imposed any specific digital service tax. However, the GST Act was amended in 2018 to extend the scope of GST to cover supplies of imported digital services with effect from 1 January 2020. The supply of digital services to a customer belonging in Singapore, by a taxable person belonging in a country other than in Singapore, is a taxable supply.[40]

'Digital services' under the GST Act refers to 'any service supplied over the Internet or other electronic network and the nature of which renders its supply essentially automated with minimal or no human intervention, and impossible without the use of information technology', and includes '(xii) any support service performed, through electronic means, for arranging or facilitating the completion of underlying transactions'.[41]

It is likely that services, such as the operation of remote data centres for the purposes of cloud mining and the operation of crypto asset exchanges, would fall within the scope of 'digital services' as envisaged by the GST Act.

An overseas supplier offering such 'digital services' to consumers in Singapore would be liable for registration under the Overseas Vendor Registration Regime,[42] if the value of its taxable supplies to customers belonging in Singapore exceeds SGD 100,000 and its global turnover exceeds SGD 1 million.

Further, a crypto asset exchange operator may potentially be treated as the supplier of the tokens through its exchange (assuming such tokens do not qualify as exempt supplies (*see* section 1.1.3(a), above), if the exchange operator:

(1) falls within the definition of an 'electronic marketplace' – a medium that (i) allows suppliers to make supplies available to customers by electronic means, and (ii) is operated by electronic means but exclude medium solely for processing payment of any supply;[43] and
(2) the operator:
    (a) authorizes the consideration for the supply to be charged to the customer;
    (b) authorizes delivery of the supply to the customer;
    (c) sets the terms and conditions under which the supply is made;

40. Goods and Services Tax Act (Cap 117A, 2005 Rev Ed) sections 8(1A) and (2A) and paragraph 3 of the Seventh Schedule.
41. Goods and Services Tax Act (Cap 117A, 2005 Rev Ed) paragraph 2 of the Seventh Schedule.
42. *IRAS e-Tax Guide – GST: Taxing imported services by way of an overseas vendor registration regime*, Inland Revenue Authority of Singapore (26 Aug. 2019).
43. Goods and Services Tax Act (Cap 117A, 2005 Rev Ed) paragraph 1 of Seventh Schedule.

(d) the documentation provided to the customer identifies the operator as making the supply; or
(e) the operator and overseas underlying supplier have agreed in writing that the operator is subject to tax on such supply.

If an overseas supplier offers 'digital services' to GST-registered persons in Singapore, the recipient would be responsible for accounting for GST on the basis of a 'reverse charge'. The IRAS has taken the position that the overseas supplier can rely on the GST registration number provided by the customers as proof of their GST registration, and the overseas supplier is required to maintain that information in its sales documentation for audit purposes. If the overseas supplier is otherwise unable to ascertain that the customer is GST-registered, the overseas supplier is required to charge GST.

(f) Are crypto assets subject to gift, inheritance, estate, or wealth taxes?

Estate duty has been removed in Singapore for deaths occurring on and after 15 February 2008.[44] Singapore does not impose gift, inheritance or wealth taxes.

However, in relation to gifts, it should be noted that a person declared as bankrupt must disclose to the Official Assignee all of the property that he disposed of prior to the bankruptcy or property disposed of by way of a gift or settlement within the five years preceding the bankruptcy, and such gifts may be voidable at the option of the Official Assignee.[45]

(g) Are crypto assets subject to exit tax?

Singapore does not impose exit tax except in very restricted circumstances relating to foreign employees (*see* above section 1.1.3(c), above).

(h) Can mining trigger gambling tax?

Gambling is regulated tightly through laws with the objectives of maintaining law and order as well as to minimise potential harm to society. Gambling activities are prohibited in Singapore unless they are exempted or licensed. The gambling-related legislation includes the Common Gaming Houses Act,[46] Betting Act,[47] Remote Gambling Act,[48] Private Lotteries Act,[49] and the Casino Control Act.[50] Neither the Singapore

44. Estate Duty (Abolition) Act 2008 (No. 13 of 2008).
45. Bankruptcy Act (Cap 20, 2009 Rev Ed) section 98.
46. Common Gaming Houses Act (Cap 49, 1985 Rev Ed).
47. Betting Act (Cap 21, 2011 Rev Ed).
48. Remote Gambling Act 2014 (No. 34 of 2014).
49. Private Lotteries Act (Cap 250, 2012 Rev Ed).
50. Casino Control Act (Cap 33A, 2007 Rev Ed).

legislature nor the Singapore courts have taken a stance on whether mining constitutes a form of gambling.

In Singapore, the following taxes are imposed on gambling activities:

(1) Betting and Sweepstakes Duties are levied on any amount received on bets by organizations (who receive approval from the Minister for Home Affairs) that operate or promote betting and sweepstake activities in Singapore.[51]
(2) Private Lotteries Duty is imposed on any lottery promoted by a club or society.[52] A private lottery is a lottery where the chance is offered for sale only to members of clubs or societies established for purposes not connected with gaming, wagering or lotteries. The promoter of the private lottery has to submit records and pay private lotteries duty to the IRAS.
(3) Casino tax is levied on the gross gaming revenue of two casinos in Singapore which are operated by the two integrated resorts, Marina Bay Sands and Resorts World Sentosa.[53]

The IRAS has taken the position that winnings from betting in Singapore are not taxable as they are windfalls and not regarded as income.[54]

1.1.4 Compliance and Documentation Obligations

(a) What documentation requirements exist for taxpayers regarding crypto assets and are there best practices in recordkeeping to support representations made in tax returns?

Taxpayers should keep proper records of transactions, which include supporting documents for the following:

(1) Date of transaction;
(2) Number of units of digital tokens received or sold;
(3) Value of digital token at the time of the transaction;
(4) Exchange rate used;
(5) Purpose of the transaction;
(6) Details of customers/suppliers (for buy-sell transaction);
(7) Details of the initial offering; and
(8) Receipts/invoices of business expenses.

51. Betting and Sweepstake Duties Act (Cap 22, 2012 Rev Ed) section 3.
52. Private Lotteries Act (Cap 250, 2012 Rev Ed) section 15.
53. Casino Control Act (Cap 33A, 2007 Rev Ed) section 146.
54. *Winnings (Toto, 4D etc.)*, Inland Revenue Authority of Singapore, https://www.iras.gov.sg/IRASHome/Individuals/Locals/Working-Out-Your-Taxes/What-is-Taxable-What-is-Not/Winnings--Toto--4D--etc--/.

(b) *What is the evidentiary burden of supporting tax positions when a digital wallet address is lost or shared with other persons?*

It is likely that the general principles regarding burden of proof would apply when a digital wallet address is lost or shared with other persons. Singapore has a state-assessment system where the IRAS is responsible for the assessment of tax. For example, with regard to income tax, where a person has delivered his tax return to the Comptroller of Income Tax, the Comptroller of Income Tax will generally accept the return and make the assessments accordingly.[55] In certain instances, however, the Comptroller of Income Tax can refuse to accept the return and will, to the best of his judgment, determine the person's chargeable income and make an assessment.[56] In addition, where a person has not delivered a return to the IRAS but, in the IRAS' opinion, the person is liable to pay tax, the Comptroller of Income Tax will determine the person's chargeable income according to the best of his judgment and make an assessment accordingly.[57]

If a taxpayer disputes an income tax or GST assessment issued on him, he may apply to the Comptroller of Income Tax or the Comptroller of GST respectively by notice of objection in writing within the prescribed time.[58] If the taxpayer disagrees with the decision of the respective Comptroller on his application for review and revision of the tax assessment, he may appeal to the Income Tax Board of Review or the GST Board of Review respectively.[59] The burden is then on the taxpayer to prove to the respective Board that, on a balance of probabilities, that the tax assessment made by the respective Comptroller is incorrect.

(c) *Are crypto asset exchanges and wallet providers subject to reporting obligations?*

In addition to the requirement to file annual tax returns, crypto asset exchanges could potentially be subject to licensing and regulation under the Payment Services Act (PSA). 'Payment services' include, *inter alia*, the provision of 'digital payment token services' namely any service of dealing in digital payment tokens, or any service of facilitating the exchange of digital payment tokens. The provision of 'payment services' can only be carried out by the holder of a license, or exempt persons (for example, banks, merchant banks and finance companies which are licensed under respective legislation).[60]

Pursuant to section 17 of the PSA, the holder of a license must submit such reports or returns on the licensee's business in the manner specified by the Monetary

55. Income Tax Act (Cap 134, 2014 Rev Ed) section 72(2)(a).
56. Income Tax Act (Cap 134, 2014 Rev Ed) section 72(2)(b).
57. Income Tax Act (Cap 134, 2014 Rev Ed) section 72(3).
58. Income Tax Act (Cap 134, 2014 Rev Ed) section 76; Goods and Services Tax Act (Cap 117A, 2005 Rev Ed) section 49.
59. Income Tax Act (Cap 134, 2014 Rev Ed) section 79; Goods and Services Tax Act (Cap 117A, 2005 Rev Ed) section 51.
60. Payment Services Act 2019 (No. 2 of 2019) section 5.

Authority of Singapore (MAS) in writing. Under section 37, the licensee's accounts, as well as the transactions related to the payment services provided by the licensee, are required to be audited annually. Further, the MAS has released Notice PSN02 to holders of payment services license (digital payment token service) setting out the due diligence measures and Anti-Money Laundering and Countering the Financing of Terrorism Steering risk assessment procedures which should be undertaken by licensees.[61]

If the crypto assets are security tokens instead, the crypto asset exchange may potentially be required to be registered as an 'approved exchange' or 'recognized market operator' under the Securities and Futures Act[62] if:

(1) the security token(s) to be traded on the exchange may be classified as a commodity (such as any index, right or interest in any produce, item, goods or article)[63] or a capital markets product (such as securities, units in a collective investment scheme, derivatives contracts) under the Securities and Futures Act; and
(2) the activities of the crypto asset exchange fall within the definition of an 'organized market' under the Securities and Futures Act. An 'organized market' is defined as a place at which, or a facility (whether electronic or otherwise) by means of which, offers or invitations to exchange, sell or purchase derivatives contracts, securities or units in collective investment schemes, are regularly made on a centralized basis, being offers or invitations that are intended or may reasonably be expected to result, whether directly or indirectly, in the acceptance or making, respectively, of offers to exchange, sell or purchase derivatives contracts, securities or units in collective investment schemes (whether through that place or facility or otherwise) or such other facility or class of facilities as the MAS may, by order, prescribe.[64]

An approved exchange is required to comply with various obligations under the Securities and Futures Act, including section 18 regarding the maintenance of a record of all transactions effected through its organized market in accordance with regulations prescribed by the MAS, as well as section 19 regarding the submission of periodic reports.

61. *MAS Notice PSN02 – Notice to Holders of Payment Service Licence (Digital Payment Token Service)*, Monetary Authority of Singapore (5 Dec. 2019), https://www.mas.gov.sg/-/media/MAS/Regulations-and-Financial-Stability/Regulatory-and-Supervisory-Framework/Anti_Money-Laundering_Countering-the-Financing-of-Terrorism/PSN02-Prevention-of-Money-Laundering-and-Countering-the-Financing-of-Terrorism--Digital-Payment-Toke.pdf.
62. Securities and Futures Act (Cap 289, 2006 Rev Ed).
63. Securities and Futures Act (Cap 289, 2006 Rev Ed) section 2.
64. Securities and Futures Act (Cap 289, 2006 Rev Ed) paragraph 1 of the First Schedule.

(d) *Are taxpayers holding crypto assets subject to reporting obligations apart from the filing of income tax/capital gains tax returns?*

Apart from income tax and GST returns which need to be filed, there are no other reporting obligations.

(e) *Are crypto asset exchanges and wallet providers subject to CRS/FATCA reporting?*

Singapore is a signatory to the multilateral competent authority agreement which implemented automatic exchange of information under CRS. Singapore has also signed an agreement with the United States of America to implement FATCA.

The reporting obligations[65] under both agreements apply to reporting Singaporean financial institutions (i.e., financial institutions tax resident or incorporated in Singapore, or the Singapore branch of a financial institution).

It is conceivable that a crypto asset exchange or wallet provider which provides (as a substantial portion of its business) custodial services holding crypto assets on the account of others could fall within the definition of a 'financial institution' provided that the crypto assets qualify as 'financial assets'.[66] While the relevant Singapore regulation implementing FATCA does not contain a definition of 'financial asset', under the regulation implementing CRS 'financial assets' are defined as 'a security (for example, a share of stock in a corporation;...note, bond, debenture or other evidence of indebtedness)...or any interest (including a futures or forward contract or option) in a security... [t]he term 'Financial Asset' does not include a non-debt, direct interest in real property.' It is possible that exchanges or custodial institutions holding security tokens which provide equity or debt interest in an entity similar to stocks or debentures could potentially be subject to CRS reporting requirements, although the position is far from certain.

1.1.5 *Civil and Criminal Tax Enforcement*

(a) *What powers do the tax authorities have to compel the disclosure of information by third parties, such as exchanges or wallet providers, and have these been used in the past?*

Under the Income Tax Act, the Comptroller of Income Tax has an extensive range of powers under section 65B of the Income Tax Act to enable him to obtain information for the purposes of the Income Tax Act. These include the power of full and free access

65. Income Tax (International Tax Compliance Agreements) (Common Reporting Standard) Regulations 2016 (S 621/2016), rule 16 and Income Tax (International Tax Compliance Agreements) (United States of America) Regulations 2015 (S 134/2015), rule 10.
66. Income Tax (International Tax Compliance Agreements) (Common Reporting Standard) Regulations 2016 (S 621/2016), rule 9 and Income Tax (International Tax Compliance Agreements) (United States of America) Regulations 2015 (S 134/2015), rule 4.

to all buildings, places, documents, computers, computer programs and computer software for any of the purposes of the Income Tax Act, and the power to inspect, copy, make extracts from or take possession of any such books, documents or papers. In addition, the Comptroller of Income Tax can demand any person to give oral or written information or information through the electronic service concerning his or any other person's income, assets or liabilities where such information is relevant for the purposes of the Income Tax Act. Accordingly, the Comptroller of Income Tax does have the power to compel the disclosure of information by third parties, such as exchanges or wallet providers.

If a taxpayer fails, neglects or refuses to comply with any notice or requirement of the Comptroller of Income Tax under section 65A or 65B of the Income Tax Act, or hinders or obstructs the Comptroller of Income Tax in the performance or execution of his duties under section 65B of the Income Tax Act, the taxpayer would be guilty of an offence and can be subject to a fine not exceeding SGD 10,000 or to imprisonment for a term not exceeding twelve months or to both and, in the case of a continuing offence, to a further fine not exceeding SGD 100 for every day or part of a day during which the offence continues after conviction.

An investigation into a taxpayer's affairs may include a surprise visit to the premises of any relevant third parties, interviews with any relevant third parties and the obtaining of information from or the verifying of information with other third parties such as banks and financial institutions.[67]

(b) What measures have the tax authorities undertaken in the past to ensure crypto tax compliance?

The Singapore authorities recognise the potential opportunities and applications for crypto assets and have adopted an approach which encourages innovation and growth of payment services as well as fintech.[68] In this regard, Parliament passed the PSA[69] on 14 January 2019, to regulate the provision of 'payment services' in Singapore. As discussed above in section 1.1.4(c), providers of 'payment services' need to be licensed,[70] and there are reporting obligations for the holders of such licences.[71]

The licensing and regulation of part of the crypto assets industry are steps which facilitate compliance by the license holder for tax purposes.

As regards measures taken by the Singapore tax authorities specifically, general administrative guidance on their position as regards income tax may be found on their webpage. The IRAS has also published an e-tax guide regarding the treatment of virtual currency following the amendments to the Goods and Services Tax Act.[72]

67. *Investigation by IRAS*, Inland Revenue Authority of Singapore, https://www.iras.gov.sg/irashome/Businesses/Companies/Getting-it-right/Tax-Evasion-or-Fraud/Investigation-by-IRAS/.
68. *Singapore Parliamentary Debates, Official Report* (14 Jan. 2019), vol. 94.
69. Payment Services Act 2019 (No. 2 of 2019).
70. Payment Services Act 2019 (No. 2 of 2019), section 5.
71. Payment Services Act 2019 (No. 2 of 2019), sections 17 and 37.
72. *Cf.* section 1.1.1(a).

(c) *Are the tax authorities cooperating with tax authorities in other jurisdictions on enforcement?*

The IRAS has several tools at its disposal for the obtaining of information from abroad. Singapore has signed Avoidance of Double Taxation Agreements (DTAs) with over ninety jurisdictions. Singapore also has Exchange of Information Arrangements ('EOI Arrangements') with Bermuda and the United States of America.

In general, Singapore's DTAs and EOI Arrangements include articles for the exchange of information between competent authorities for tax purposes (whether upon request, automatically, or spontaneously). The exchange of information may take place on request by a competent authority of a jurisdiction with which Singapore has a DTA or an EOI Arrangement. Alternatively, the exchange of information may take place automatically (for example, under the relevant multilateral competent authority agreement for CRS) or spontaneously (for example in the EOI Arrangement with the United States).

Singapore is a member of the Inclusive Framework for the global implementation of the OECD Base Erosion and Profit Shifting (BEPS) Project. Under the Inclusive Framework, Singapore has committed to spontaneously exchange information (on rulings relating to preferential regimes, unilateral APAs or other cross-border unilateral rulings on transfer pricing, cross-border rulings providing for downward adjustment of taxable profits, PE rulings and related party conduit rulings) with a jurisdiction if the jurisdiction meets the following conditions:

(1) the jurisdiction has a DTA or an EOI Arrangement with Singapore that provides for the spontaneous exchange of information;
(2) the jurisdiction has the necessary legal framework and safeguards to ensure confidentiality and appropriate use of the information exchanged; and
(3) the jurisdiction is similarly committed to compulsory spontaneous exchange of information under the Inclusive Framework.

In general, the spontaneous exchange of information on rulings will take place with the jurisdiction of residence of all related parties with which the taxpayer enters into transactions for which a ruling is granted or which gives rise to income from related parties benefitting from a preferential treatment. The spontaneous exchange of information on rulings will also take place with the jurisdictions of residence of the taxpayer's ultimate parent entity and the immediate parent entity, and in the case of rulings involving permanent establishments, the residence jurisdiction of the permanent establishment's head office.

In addition, Singapore may also obtain or provide international assistance in criminal matters, such as tax evasion, under the Mutual Assistance in Criminal Matters Act.[73] Under the said Act, the Attorney General of Singapore may request for assistance from other countries for assistance,[74] such as:

73. Mutual Assistance in Criminal Matters Act (Cap 190A, 2001 Rev Ed).
74. Mutual Assistance in Criminal Matters Act (Cap 190A, 2001 Rev Ed) sections 6 and 7.

(1) the provision and obtaining of evidence and things;
(2) the making of arrangements for persons to give evidence or assist in criminal investigations;
(3) the recovery, forfeiture or confiscation of property in respect of offences;
(4) the restraining of dealings in property, or the freezing of assets, that may be recovered, forfeited or confiscated in respect of offences;
(5) the execution of requests for search and seizure;
(6) the location and identification of witnesses and suspects; and
(7) the service of documents.[75]

The IRAS has not made available information in relation to whether they are cooperating with tax authorities in other jurisdictions on enforcement and whether they have made use of the various instruments mentioned above in respect of crypto asset holdings of taxpayers.

75. Mutual Assistance in Criminal Matters Act (Cap 190A, 2001 Rev Ed) section 3.

South Africa

Emil Brincker, Louis Botha & Louise Kotze

1. COUNTRY GUIDES

1.1 South Africa

1.1.1 Applicable Tax Law, Guidance, and Case Law

(a) Which laws, regulations, and other administrative guidance exist dealing with crypto assets?

The South African Income Tax Act[1] and Value Added Tax Act[2] were amended in 2018 to make provision for the tax treatment of cryptocurrencies in certain circumstances. In the Income Tax Act, cryptocurrencies have been incorporated either with direct reference thereto in the relevant sections of the Act; alternatively, incorporation has taken place indirectly by the inclusion of cryptocurrencies in the definition of 'financial instrument'. In the Value Added Tax Act, the definition of 'financial services' has been expanded to include specified activities pertaining to cryptocurrencies.

A media statement issued by the South African Revenue Service (SARS) on 6 April 2018 specified that the normal rules regarding income tax will apply to cryptocurrencies and that it is not regarded as recognized money. It stated that, at present, further elaboration on the taxation of cryptocurrencies is unnecessary as the existing South African taxation laws, regulations and jurisprudence are adequate to regulate the taxation thereof. On this basis, it was indicated in the media statement that gains and losses derived in respect of crypto assets will be categorized into three broad categories, specifically:

1. Income Tax Act, 1962 as amended.
2. Value Added Tax Act, 1991 as amended.

(1) the mining for crypto assets;
(2) the exchange of local currency for crypto assets; and
(3) the exchange of goods and services for crypto assets (a barter transaction).[3]

(b) Which court cases exist dealing with crypto assets?

To date there are no South African tax court cases that have dealt with cryptocurrencies or crypto assets.

1.1.2 Income and Capital Gains Taxes

(a) How are crypto assets classified for income and capital gains tax purposes?

The existing definition adopted by the South African tax framework refers to 'cryptocurrencies' and not to 'crypto assets', but South Africa's National Treasury have proposed amending the Income Tax Act to replace references to 'cryptocurrency' with 'crypto asset'. In any event, the Intergovernmental Fintech Working Group's (IFWG) Position Paper on Crypto Assets has indicated that the existing South African tax structure will be sufficient to deal with the tax treatment of crypto assets alongside cryptocurrencies.

For South African income tax and capital gains tax purposes, crypto assets and cryptocurrency are regarded as assets, which is defined in the Income Tax Act as property of whatever nature, whether movable or immovable, corporeal or incorporeal, and also includes any right or interest of whatever nature to, or in, such property. A utility token or security token will also be treated as an asset to the extent that it grants the owner thereof a right in such a utility token or security token.[4] This definition specifically excludes 'currency'. Even though 'currency' is not defined in the Income Tax Act, cryptocurrencies are not regarded as currency for tax purposes as it is not an official legal tender in South Africa, nor is it widely used and accepted in South Africa as a medium of payment.

Furthermore, crypto assets are deemed to be assets of an intangible nature, and there is no provision in the Income Tax Act that provides for any wear and tear allowance to be claimed in respect thereof.

3. One should note that in a South African context, the SARS is responsible to enforce tax legislation in South Africa. The statements made by it, including those in the media statement, are not binding and merely reflect its view regarding enforcement of tax provisions applicable to trading in cryptocurrency. Should a taxpayer wish to obtain certainty regarding the tax treatment applicable to a specific transaction involving crypto assets, such taxpayer can apply for an advance tax ruling, as provided for under the Tax Administration Act, 2011, which ruling would be binding on the taxpayer, if granted.
4. As 'cryptocurrency' also constitutes a 'financial instrument' under the Income Tax Act. The provisions applicable to financial instruments, including anti-avoidance provisions, would be applicable to crypto assets.

Whether crypto assets are classified as capital or revenue in nature will be dependent on the intention with which the crypto assets are acquired and held, and further dependent on the purposes for which they are applied. This classification will be done on a case-by-case basis, taking into account all relevant facts and circumstances. Case law has indicated that the primary intention with which an asset is acquired will be conclusive in determining whether the asset is held on capital or revenue account, barring the existence of other factors that may indicate a contrary intention. As such, crypto assets will be:

- revenue in nature if the proceeds are received as part of a business in carrying out a profit-making scheme or it is acquired for speculative purposes; proceeds will also be revenue in nature if the crypto assets are held as trading stock; or
- capital in nature if it is acquired for purposes of holding the crypto assets as an investment.

(b) What are the income/capital gains tax consequences of selling crypto assets against fiat currency?

The tax consequences associated with the sale of crypto assets against fiat currency are largely dependent on whether the crypto assets are held on revenue or capital account.

- Crypto assets held on revenue account

If the crypto assets are held on revenue account, the fiat currency against which the asset is sold will constitute income that is derived from the trade carried on by the taxpayer in respect of those crypto assets and will be included in the income of that taxpayer and subject to income tax. In the case of companies, the tax liability is calculated at 28% of taxable income. In the case of individuals, tax is calculated according to the progressive sliding scale tax tables, up to a rate of 45% of taxable income. All expenditures incurred pursuant to the profit-making scheme in terms of which crypto assets are traded may be claimed as a deduction against the income earned from the trading activities, provided that such deduction complies with the requirements set out in the Income Tax Act.

To the extent that the allowable deductions exceed the income earned, an assessed loss can be carried forward to the following year and may be used to set-off the income earned in that year if it meets the general deduction formula. The rules regarding the utilization of the assessed losses are dependent on whether the taxpayer who incurred the losses is an individual or a company. If the losses were incurred by an individual, the assessed losses may only be set-off against any future income derived from the trading in crypto assets. In other words, such losses are ring-fenced and may not be set-off against any other income derived by the individual taxpayer.[5] However, if a company incurs assessed losses in the course of trading in crypto assets,

5. Income Tax Act, section 20A.

it can set-off those losses against income derived by the company from other trades, provided it meets the requirements regarding the use of assessed losses.[6]

Transactions involving the arbitrage sale of crypto assets will be considered to derive income that is taxed on revenue account.

- Crypto assets held on capital account

If the crypto assets are held on capital account as an investment by a taxpayer, capital gains tax consequences will arise when the crypto asset is disposed of. The fiat currency against which the crypto asset is disposed of will constitute the proceeds of the sale and the gain or loss will be determined by subtracting from the proceeds the base cost of the crypto asset, which is determined in accordance with the provisions of the Eighth Schedule to the Income Tax Act. As a general rule, the base cost of the crypto asset will be the sum of all the costs associated with the acquisition of the crypto asset.

Subject to certain exclusions available to individuals, the gains or losses derived from the sale of the crypto assets will be included in taxable income at a rate of 40% for individuals and 80% for companies. The effective rate at which capital gains will be taxed is therefore maximum 18% for individuals and 22.4% for companies.

(c) *What are the income/capital gains tax consequences of exchanging crypto assets against other crypto assets?*

The exchange of crypto assets for other crypto assets will qualify under the third category identified by the SARS in its media statement, and the normal barter transaction rules will apply. Among these is the distinction between the capital and revenue nature of the cryptocurrencies held by a taxpayer that applies equally to barter transactions as to the sale of cryptocurrencies against fiat currency.

The amounts to be included in the income of a taxpayer include the value of every form of property that is received by, or has accrued to, the taxpayer. As such, where an asset has been exchanged or bartered for another asset, the value of the new asset constitutes an amount that has been received or accrued.[7] To the extent that the exchange constitutes a part of a profit-making scheme carried on by the taxpayer, the value of the crypto asset received by the taxpayer will be included in the taxpayer's income. This is so irrespective of whether the two crypto assets are similar or not.[8] The exchange of the crypto assets is thus a tax event.

Where the crypto asset that is exchanged was held as a capital asset, the value of the crypto asset that is received will constitute the proceeds in respect of which the capital gain or loss must be calculated and included in the taxable income of the taxpayer.[9]

6. Income Tax Act, section 20.
7. Silke on South African Income Tax – § 2.16 Barter and exchange transactions.
8. Silke on South African Income Tax – § 2.16 Barter and exchange transactions.
9. Paragraph 35 of the Eighth Schedule to the Income Tax Act.

The value to be attributed to the crypto asset received by a taxpayer in either of the above scenarios (being the amount that will be included in income or used to calculate a capital gain or loss) will be the market value thereof, being the fair price that would be received in an arm's length transaction between two unconnected persons in the open market. If a cryptocurrency were listed on a recognized exchange, the market value (for capital gains tax purposes) would be the price in respect of the crypto asset on that recognized exchange at close of business on the last business day before the date of disposal.[10] Although this provision is only included in the section of the Income Tax Act dealing with the sale of assets on capital account, where the market value of a cryptocurrency is determined for the profits realized on revenue account, the same principle would likely apply. The provision may also apply to the sale of crypto assets even if they are currently not expressly included in the definition of 'financial instrument'.

(d) *If a distinction is made between business assets and non-business assets, when does trading in crypto assets lead to a trade or business?*

In the South African Income Tax Act, 'trade' is defined to include every profession, trade, business, employment, calling, occupation, or venture.[11] It is not necessary for any of the aforementioned activities of a taxpayer to be the primary activity of that taxpayer in order for it to constitute a trade. In determining whether a taxpayer carries on a trade or business, it is necessary to take into account all of the surrounding facts and circumstances, including:

- the nature and scope of the activities;
- the presence or absence of a profit motive; and
- the continuity of activities.[12]

A taxpayer will generally be deemed to have a profit-making motive when the crypto assets are held on revenue rather than capital account. The Income Tax Act generally does not prescribe definitive criteria to be used in distinguishing whether an asset is capital or revenue in nature. The South African courts have, however, laid down the following principles that may be used in determining the nature of an asset that is similar to a crypto asset:

(1) The most relevant factor in the determination of the capital or revenue nature of an asset is the intention of the taxpayer at the time the assets were acquired and disposed of.[13] If the asset was purchased for the purpose of resale at a profit, the asset will be revenue in nature.

---

10. Paragraph 31 of the Eighth Schedule to the Income Tax Act. The provision applies to any 'financial instrument', which includes 'cryptocurrency'.
11. Section 1 of the Income Tax Act.
12. The Law of South Africa (LAWSA) – 570 Meaning of 'carrying on business'.
13. *Elandsheuwel Farming (EDMS) BPK v. Sekretaris Van Binnelandse Inkomste* 39 SATC 163.

(2) Profits derived from the sale of the assets that were not fortuitous but were purposefully sought out and worked for will be indicative that the asset was held on revenue account.[14]
(3) An occasional sale of such assets at a profit does not make the seller a dealer in them.[15]

It is unlikely that crypto assets that are acquired and held as long-term investments will constitute a trade. However, the SARS has indicated that crypto assets that are acquired through the process of mining will in all circumstances be held as trading stock by the person who mined the said crypto assets.

(e) *What are the income/capital gains tax consequences for an employee receiving wages or salaries in crypto assets?*

The receipt or accrual of crypto assets as a consequence of an employment relationship will be taxable in the hands of the recipient employee. Such a receipt or accrual will be subject to employees' tax. Employees' tax is a payroll tax that arises in respect of any remuneration that is received by an employee from an employer (or representative employer). The amount of employees' tax for which the employee is liable must be withheld by the employer and paid over to the SARS. In practice, the employees' tax paid will reduce the overall income tax liability of an employee for a particular year of assessment, pursuant to that employee submitting his income tax return for the year of assessment and being assessed for income tax.

Remuneration is defined in the Income Tax Act as any amount of income that is paid or is payable to any person by way of any salary or wage (among others), whether in cash or otherwise and whether or not in respect of services rendered.[16] From this definition, it is evident that the payment of salaries or wages in crypto assets will constitute remuneration for employees' tax purposes.

The value to be placed on the crypto assets must be determined in terms of the relevant provisions of the Seventh Schedule to the Income Tax Act, which provides that the value to be placed on the crypto assets is the market value thereof at the time that the crypto asset is acquired by the employee. However, if the crypto assets were held by the employer as trading stock prior to the acquisition thereof by the employee, the value to be placed thereon for employees' tax purposes must be the cost of the crypto asset to the employer. In this context, any unrealized gain as a result of an increase in the value of the crypto asset, before or after the employee has acquired the asset, will not be taxable in the hands of the employer or the employee. Only the capital gain realized on disposal of the crypto asset acquired by the employee will be taxed in the employee's hands. Alternatively, if the crypto assets were held as trading stock by the employer and the market value of the crypto assets has dropped to below the cost at the

14. *Commissioner For Inland Revenue v. Pick 'n Pay Employee Share Purchase Trust* [1992] 2 All SA 245 (A).
15. *Commissioner For Inland Revenue v. Middelman* [1991] 1 All SA 44 (C).
16. Paragraph 1 of the Fourth Schedule to the Income Tax Act.

date of acquisition by the employee, the value to be attributed to the crypto currency will be the market value thereof.

The value attributed to the crypto assets that is subject to employees' tax may later be used as the cost of acquisition of the crypto assets by the employee in the event that the crypto assets are sold at a later stage. In this way, double taxation is avoided.

The acquisition of an asset under these circumstances must be distinguished from the situation where an employee receives income pursuant to an employee incentive scheme. If pursuant to an employee incentive scheme (where an employee can generally receive shares in the company if he/she meets certain requirements), the asset, including a crypto asset, vests in the employee, and the accrual of such crypto asset would generally be on revenue account.

(f) What are the income/capital gains tax consequences for a merchant receiving payment in crypto assets?

The SARS has indicated that transactions in which goods and services are exchanged for crypto assets will constitute barter transactions. In effect, the receipt of crypto assets by a merchant will have substantially the same tax consequences as in the case where fiat currency is received by the merchant. The amount that must be included in the merchant's income and that will be subject to tax will be the market value of the crypto asset on the day that it has been received by the merchant.

The subsequent disposal of the crypto asset by the merchant will constitute a separate taxable transaction. Depending on the activities carried on by the merchant and the intention with which the crypto asset is held, the merchant will be taxed on the income generated through the sale of the crypto asset, alternatively a capital gain or loss will be included in the merchant's taxable income from the disposal of the crypto asset. In either case, the market value of the crypto asset that was included in the merchant's income when the asset was first acquired will constitute the cost of acquisition pursuant to the disposal of the crypto asset.

(g) What are the income/capital gains tax consequences of a loss of crypto assets?

The nature of the crypto assets held will inform the tax consequences arising from the loss thereof. In particular, if the crypto assets are held as trading stock, the holder will be entitled to claim a deduction from income of an amount equal to the cost of acquisition of the crypto assets that are lost. In this way, it is possible to generate a net loss for tax purposes. Losses can only be claimed if they constitute a loss actually incurred in the production of income for purposes of trade.

However, if the crypto assets are held as a capital investment, the loss thereof will constitute a disposal as defined in the Income Tax Act and the proceeds in respect thereof will be nil. As a result, a capital loss will be incurred, which may be set-off against any capital gains that have been realized in that year of assessment. However, an aggregate capital loss may not be used to set-off other income received by or accrued to the taxpayer and is therefore not capable of generating a net loss position for tax purposes. Such a capital loss may be carried forward to the succeeding year of assessment and may be used to set-off any capital gains realized in that succeeding year.

(h) What are the income/capital gains tax consequences of a loss in value of crypto assets?

In the absence of a disposal event (regardless of whether the crypto assets are held on revenue or capital account), a loss in value of crypto assets is not relevant for tax purposes.

Even though crypto assets may be held as trading stock, the provision in the Income Tax Act that allows for the impairment of trading stock specifically excludes from the scope of its application any financial instruments that are held as trading stock. As crypto assets constitute financial instruments under the Income Tax Act, no impairment deduction for the loss in value of the crypto assets may be claimed.

(i) What are the income/capital gains tax consequences of forks of crypto assets?

When a blockchain splits into two blockchains and the holder of crypto assets on the original blockchain subsequently holds an equal quantity of crypto assets on the new blockchain, it is likely that the value of the crypto assets on the new blockchain will constitute an accrual of income for tax purposes in the hands of the holder. This will be the case regardless of whether the crypto assets are held on revenue or capital account. The amount to be included in the holder's income will be the market value of the new crypto assets on the day that the fork takes place and the holder acquires the new crypto assets. At the same time, the market value of the crypto asset originally held and the crypto asset acquired as a result of the fork must be determined. If the result of the fork is a reduction in the market value of the crypto asset originally owned, the market value of the crypto asset will be the new cost (base cost for CGT purposes) to determine the tax consequences arising from any future sales or disposals. This would prevent double taxation where the original crypto asset is disposed of in future. The splitting is thus seen to be a tax event as one asset (or a portion of the asset) is exchanged for another.

Where the new crypto assets are held as trading stock, the holder may subsequently claim a deduction from income, equal to the market value at which the new crypto assets were acquired, at the beginning of the immediately succeeding year of assessment.[17] If the crypto assets are held on capital account, the value included in income at the time of accrual of the new crypto assets will constitute the base cost of the crypto assets. When these crypto assets are later disposed of, the difference

17. Section 22(2) of the Income Tax Act.

between the proceeds derived from the disposal and the base cost will constitute the capital gain or capital loss.

(j) What are the income/capital gains tax consequences of airdrops of crypto assets and are the tax consequences different if the airdropped tokens are unwanted?

Similar to the tax consequences associated with forks of crypto assets, the receipt of crypto assets by a taxpayer as a result of an airdrop will constitute a taxable receipt and will require that the value of the crypto assets received be included in income in the year of assessment during which the airdrop occurs. This will be the case regardless of whether the airdropped crypto assets are wanted or not. The value of the receipt to be taxed will be the market value of the crypto assets on the day that they are received. This value that was subject to income tax may then be claimed as a deduction (where the crypto assets are held as trading stock), or will constitute the base cost of the crypto assets (where they are held on capital account), when the crypto assets are sold or disposed of.

(k) What are the income/capital gains tax consequences of (solo, pool, and cloud) mining?

According to the SARS, crypto assets that are acquired through the crypto asset mining process will constitute trading stock in the hands of the taxpayer who mined, and subsequently owns, those crypto assets. This view should be understood against the backdrop of the particular aspects of the mining process (in particular that of solo and pool mining), being that equipment is acquired and subsequently put to use in order to generate rewards, while other expenses such as rent and electricity are incurred pursuant thereto.

Given the view of the SARS that all mining processes result in trading stock being held by the miner, it is unlikely that the tax consequences for each of the methods of mining will be substantially different. It is noteworthy that in the case of pool and cloud mining, each individual party involved therein will be regarded as participating in their own trade and will be responsible for accounting for the tax consequences thereof on an individual basis. To the extent that individuals form a partnership, which partnership then becomes involved in a mining pool, that partnership will have to account for tax. In South African law, partnerships do not have separate legal personality and for tax purposes, the income accrued or expenses incurred by the partnership, will be taxed in the hands of the partners, according to their partnership interests.[18] Even if a partnership is not formally established, and assuming the mining pool is not incorporated as a separate legal entity, if the mining pool meets the requirements of a

18. *See* section 24H of the Income Tax Act.

partnership under South African law and is carried on in partnership,[19] the mining pool would be treated as a partnership. The principles applicable to the taxation of partners of a partnership will apply to the tax consequences realized by the partners of the mining pool. If the partnership is trading, each individual partner will also be deemed to be trading.

The following tax implications will arise in the event that crypto assets are acquired by means of mining:

(1) The crypto assets acquired and held by the miner will be revenue in nature and classified as trading stock in respect of which a trade is carried on.
(2) The successful mining of a crypto asset will result in an immediate accrual for the miner and there will be an inclusion in income of an amount equal to the market value of the crypto asset on the date of acquisition. In the case of pool and cloud mining, only an amount equal to the proportionate share of that miner in the crypto asset that is acquired will be taxable.
(3) The amount that is included in income upon the accrual of the crypto asset (or portion thereof) will constitute the cost of acquisition of the crypto asset, which may be claimed as a deduction as and when the crypto asset is sold.
(4) As the miner is carrying on a trade, the expenses incurred pursuant to the mining of the crypto assets (e.g., electricity, rent, and salaries) will be allowed as a deduction from income in the year of assessment that they are incurred and to the extent that the expenses were incurred in the production of income. Regardless of the type of mining undertaken by a miner, the expenses that are claimable by the miner will be limited to the actual expenditure incurred by that miner in the mining process.
(5) Expenditure of a capital nature (e.g., the acquisition of computers and processing systems) that is actually incurred by the miner may be claimed by means of wear and tear or capital allowances, to the extent provided for in the Income Tax Act.
(6) The income generated through the sale of crypto assets will be included in the miner's income and will be subject to tax.
(7) Where an assessed loss is incurred by an individual taxpayer in respect of any crypto asset trading activities, that assessed loss will be ring-fenced and may not be set-off against taxable income that is generated from any other trade or occupation carried on by the miner in his individual capacity. If the miner is a company, the loss derived from mining activities may potentially be set-off against income derived from other trades, provided the rules for utilization of losses by companies are complied with.

19. Section 24H(2) of the Income Tax Act states where any trade or business is carried on in partnership, each member of such partnership shall, notwithstanding the fact that he may be a limited partner, be deemed for the purposes of this Act to be carrying on such trade or business.

(l) *What are the income/capital gains tax consequences of staking crypto assets?*

Although it is an alternative approach to mining, staking crypto assets also involves the validation of transactions that result in the acquisition of further crypto assets by the holder of the crypto assets involved in the staking. The only notable difference between staking and mining is the absence of equipment and other resources (apart from crypto assets) that are devoted to the acquisition of crypto assets in the staking process.

The media statement issued by the SARS does not provide guidance on the treatment of crypto assets acquired by means of staking. However, it is expected that there will also be an immediate accrual of income when a crypto asset is acquired in this manner, resulting in the imposition of tax.

The uncertainty that arises is how the crypto assets involved in the staking, and those acquired as a result thereof, will be classified and, specifically, whether these crypto assets should be classified as being revenue in nature.

It is likely that the crypto assets utilized in the staking process will be capital in nature as these assets must be held for extended periods of time and are used as the mechanism from which profits are derived.[20] This is analogous to the computers used by miners in the crypto asset mining process, which computers would undoubtedly be classified as capital assets.

On the other hand, the crypto assets acquired by means of the staking process will, in accordance with the views adopted by the SARS, likely be considered to be held on revenue account. Where these acquired crypto assets are subsequently used by the holder as part of the staking process, it could be argued that the intention with which the crypto assets are held has changed from revenue to capital in nature as these assets now constitute the mechanism through which profits are generated. A change in intention where trading stock is subsequently held as a capital asset will result in a deemed disposal and in an inclusion in income equal to the market value of the crypto assets on the date of the change in intention. This inclusion will, however, be accompanied by a deduction from income of an amount equal to the market value of the crypto asset on the date of acquisition. As such, should the newly acquired crypto asset be held as a capital asset immediately after it is acquired, the change in intention should have a tax neutral effect on the taxpayer.

(m) *What are the income/capital gains tax consequences of an indirect investment in crypto assets?*

An indirect investment in crypto assets will be treated in a manner similar to investments in unit trusts. The amount contributed by a taxpayer will be capital or revenue in nature depending on the intention of the taxpayer. Any growth in the value

20. In *Commissioner For Inland Revenue v. Visser* 8 SATC 271 at 276 it was explained that '"Income" is what "capital" produces, or is something in the nature of interest or fruit as opposed to principal or tree.'

will not be taxed if unrealized. However, proceeds are taxable as and when the investment is realized.

Where the return on investment is in the form of interest from a South African source, natural persons are exempt from income tax on interest earned up to ZAR 23,800 per annum, in the case of natural persons under the age of 65, and ZAR 34,500 per annum, in the case of natural persons who are 65 or older. This exemption does not apply to companies or trusts.

To the extent that an indirect investment in crypto assets is made by means of equity (shares) held in a company that invests in crypto assets, it is the company that will be subject to any tax consequences arising from the investment in crypto assets. The only tax consequences that arise for the holder of the equity in the company will be dividends tax (to the extent that the company makes a distribution to the holder of the equity) and income or capital gains tax consequences (to the extent that the holder disposes of the equity in the company).

(n) How is income from crypto assets to be treated under double tax treaty law?

The specific provisions of the double tax agreement (DTA) concluded between South Africa and another country will determine which country has the right to tax the income derived from transactions involving crypto assets. As these DTAs are generally drafted in accordance with the OECD Model Convention, the articles contained therein may be used as a basis for the tax treatment that is likely to be adopted.

Article 7 of the OECD Model Convention prescribes that the profits arising from an enterprise in one state may be taxed only in that particular state, unless the enterprise in question carries on business in another state through a permanent establishment that is situated in that other state. The profits attributable to that permanent establishment may be taxed in the state wherein the permanent establishment is situated. As such, to the extent that article 7 is incorporated into the relevant DTA, if crypto asset activities are carried on in South Africa through a permanent establishment therein, the income derived in respect thereof will be taxed in South Africa. However, if crypto asset activities are carried out in South Africa, as well as in another country by means of a permanent establishment in that other country, the entity will pay tax in South Africa on its worldwide income on the basis that it is a South African tax resident and that other state will be entitled to impose tax only on the profits emanating from the activities carried on in that other state. Depending on the specific circumstances, it is possible that mining activities that make use of substantial computer equipment may result in a permanent establishment in the country where the equipment is utilized.[21]

To the extent that Article 13(5) of the OECD Model Convention is adopted in the specific DTA, the capital gains derived from the disposal of crypto assets will be subject to tax only in the state where the seller is resident. South Africa's DTAs do not

21. Article 5(4)(b) of the Model Convention.

distinguish between the sale of equity, debt, or asset-backed tokens. In South Africa, residency is determined with regard to either the 'ordinarily resident' test (based on principles laid down by South African courts), the physical presence test (as prescribed in the Income Tax Act) or where the entity is effectively managed.

(o) What are the income/capital gains tax consequences of selling crypto assets in an ICO/STO/IEO?

To the extent that the ICO/STO/IEO is carried out for the purpose of capital-raising or fundraising, the income tax consequences arising therefrom will be similar, although not identical, to the income tax consequences arising from any other realization of crypto assets. Generally, the taxpayer will be seen to act on revenue account. Proceeds from the issue of crypto assets, including utility tokens, would generally be seen to be on revenue account if it occurs on a regular basis. If the arrangement is more akin to capital raising, the proceeds could be considered as held on capital account. Under the Income Tax Act, a 'share' is defined as 'in relation to any company, any unit into which the proprietary interest in that company is divided.' As such, if a crypto asset or utility token issued reflects a proprietary interest in the company concerned, that crypto asset can be treated as a share, that is, equity in the company, for income tax purposes.

1.1.3 Other Taxes

(a) What are the value added tax/sales tax consequences of selling crypto assets?

The South African Value Added Tax Act was amended in 2019 to clarify the value added tax (VAT) consequences associated with crypto assets. In particular, the definition of 'financial services' was expanded to include the 'issue, acquisition, collection, buying or selling or transfer of ownership of any cryptocurrency'.

As the Act provides that financial services constitute exempt supplies, a taxpayer who is a VAT vendor does not have to account for output VAT in respect of the supply of, or trade in, crypto assets. However, at the same time, a taxpayer who is a registered VAT vendor will be unable to claim input VAT incurred in the course of supplying crypto assets, as input tax can only be claimed to the extent that taxable supplies are made by the taxpayer.

However, any fee that is charged pursuant to the issue, acquisition, collection, buying or selling or transfer of ownership of any crypto asset will be subject to VAT at 15%, provided that the supplier is a registered VAT vendor. The supply of financial services for a fee constitutes a taxable supply. Any input VAT that is incurred by the supplier who is a registered VAT vendor in the course of making taxable supplies, including the supply of financial services in respect of cryptocurrency for a fee, may be claimed if it is directly attributable to the taxable supplies made.

(b) *Are payments in crypto assets subject to withholding taxes?*

The Income Tax Act makes provision for withholding taxes on:

- dividends;
- royalties paid to non-residents from a South African source;
- the disposal of immovable property by non-residents;
- payments made to foreign entertainers and sportspersons;
- interest paid to non-residents from a South African source; and
- service fees paid to non-residents from a South African source.

To the extent that payment is made in crypto assets in respect of any of the aforementioned instances, the person making the payment will be required to withhold a specified percentage of that payment as a withholding tax. It will then be incumbent on the person withholding the tax to make a Rand equivalent payment thereof to the SARS.

At present, there are no withholding taxes specifically applicable to crypto asset transactions where the crypto assets represent the subject of the transaction. Crypto assets are not recognized as legal tender in South Africa.

(c) *Does payment of compensation in crypto assets give rise to payroll tax consequences?*

There are no specific payroll tax consequences that arise when compensation is paid in crypto assets and the normal income tax rules will apply, as South Africa does not have a separate payroll tax, other than employees' tax referred to in section 1.1.2(e), above. As previously discussed, when crypto assets are used to remunerate employees, there will be employees' tax consequences, which employees' tax must be calculated and withheld by the employer paying the said remuneration.

(d) *Do transactions with crypto assets trigger any transfer taxes?*

In general, transactions undertaken with the use of crypto assets will not trigger any transfer taxes in South Africa. However, the transfer of immovable property in South Africa or the acquisition of any real rights in land or minerals will give rise to transfer duty that is levied on the value of the property or real right that is acquired. South Africa also imposes a tax on the transfer of shares in certain instances, known as securities transfer tax. Theoretically, it is possible for the transfer of a crypto asset to trigger the payment of securities transfer tax, if such crypto asset constitutes a 'share', that is, it represents the proprietary interest in a company. Transfer duty or securities transfer tax will have to be paid when crypto assets are used to make payment in respect of transactions subject to these taxes.

(e) Are firms operating in the crypto space subject to digital service taxes?

At present, South African taxation laws do not impose digital service taxes. However, the South African Parliamentary Budget Office published a document entitled *Tax Brief: Digital Economy and Taxation Policy Considerations* in June 2020, which indicates that the imposition of digital service taxes is being considered.

(f) Are crypto assets subject to gift, inheritance, estate, or wealth taxes?

Donations tax is imposed on residents of South Africa who make any gratuitous disposal of property, including any gratuitous waiver or renunciation of a right. For purposes of donations tax, property is defined to mean any right in or to property, whether movable or immovable, incorporeal or corporeal, and wherever situated. The donor is responsible for the payment of donations tax which is levied at a rate of 20% on the value of the gratuitous disposal if the aggregate of that value and the value of any other property donated by that person (from 1 March 2018) does not exceed ZAR 30 million. A tax rate of 25% will be used for donations in respect of which the aggregate value donated by that person during a specific year of assessment, exceeds ZAR 30 million. Certain donations are exempt from donations tax, including donations to spouses and to approved public benefit organizations. There are also annual exemptions in the amount of ZAR 10,000 for companies who make casual gifts, and ZAR 100,000 for donations made by individuals. Any crypto asset that is donated by a resident of South Africa will be subject to donations tax at a rate of either 20% or 25%. The tax will be calculated on the market value of the crypto asset on the date of donation, the Rand value of which must be paid to the SARS by the end of the month following the month during which the donation takes place.

Estate duty is a tax that is imposed on the wealth that a natural person has accumulated throughout their life. The Estate Duty Act[22] prescribes how the value of a deceased individual's estate must be calculated. It is the net value of the estate (determined in accordance with the provisions of the Estate Duty Act) that exceeds the ZAR 3.5 million exclusion available to every natural person that will be subject to tax:

- at a rate of 20% of the dutiable amount of the estate as does not exceed ZAR 30 million; and
- at a rate of 25% of the dutiable amount of the estate as exceeds ZAR 30 million.

Crypto assets that are held by a natural person will constitute property for purposes of estate duty, and the market value thereof at date of death must be included in the determination of the value of the estate. The deceased's estate is liable to pay to the SARS the estate duty that is imposed. However, it is possible that the testamentary writing provides that the legatees be held liable for their proportionate share of the estate duty payable.

22. Estate Duty Act 45 of 1955.

(g) *Are crypto assets subject to exit tax?*

Domestic South African tax law makes provision for 'exit charges' by means of capital gains taxes that are imposed when assets that would normally be subject to tax in South Africa are transferred abroad.[23] In particular, these exit charges arise when a taxpayer ceases to be a South African tax resident. The capital gains tax consequences that are imposed as an exit charge arise as a result of a deemed disposal by the taxpayer of all of its assets (excluding fixed property in South Africa), followed by an immediate reacquisition thereof. To this end, the proceeds from the disposal will be the market value of the assets on the date of deemed disposal.

As such, if the holder of crypto assets emigrates from South Africa, those crypto assets will be deemed to have been disposed of by the holder for an amount equal to the market value on that date and capital gains tax or income tax may be imposed to the extent that a gain is realized. The exit tax is only triggered in those instances listed in section 9H of the Income Tax Act.

In relation to permanent establishments, the principle pertaining to permanent establishments is only recognized for tax purposes. A permanent establishment does not per se constitute a legal person separate from the company whose activities abroad create a permanent establishment in that country. The transfer of a crypto asset to a permanent establishment is not deemed to be a disposal thereof. Equally, if that foreign permanent establishment uses an asset belonging to a South African resident company, it will not result in the exit tax being triggered. The South African resident company transferring the asset to the foreign permanent establishment is still taxed in South Africa on its worldwide income, including worldwide income derived with that asset, as the South African income tax system taxes entities and persons based on their residency. The principles set out in section 1.1.2(n), above, also apply here.

(h) *Can mining trigger gambling tax?*

While the possible introduction of gambling tax had been announced as early as 2011, and then again in 2019, South Africa's National Treasury has yet to publish legislation with the view of introducing gambling tax into the South African tax dispensation. As there is currently no gambling tax in South Africa, the mining of crypto assets will not trigger any gambling tax. Under South African law, the payment of taxes on gambling winnings is determined by the legislation passed by each of South Africa's provinces. Operators are subject to gambling tax at various rates and the payment of crypto assets as part of winnings could be taxed in the hands of professional gamblers under ordinary tax principles.

23. *See* section 9H of the Income Tax Act.

1.1.4 *Compliance and Documentation Obligations*

(a) What documentation requirements exist for taxpayers regarding crypto assets and are there best practices in recordkeeping to support representations made in tax returns?

While there are no special documentation requirements prescribed in respect of crypto assets, the Tax Administration Act[24] imposes an obligation on taxpayers to maintain records, books of account and any other documents that enable them to comply with all of the requirements under any of the South African Tax Acts. In this regard, it is also necessary to maintain these records to enable the SARS to be satisfied that all of these requirements have been complied with by the taxpayer. In general, these records must be kept for a period of five years from the date that a return is submitted. Where an audit or investigation is undertaken by the SARS, or where an objection or appeal against an assessment is lodged by a taxpayer, the records must be kept until the audit or investigation is concluded, or the objection or appeal is finalized.

(b) What is the evidentiary burden of supporting tax positions when a digital wallet address is lost or shared with other persons?

The South African Tax Administration Act prescribes that a taxpayer has the burden of proving the tax position adopted by it to the extent that it pertains to:

- whether an amount is exempt from income or is otherwise not subject to tax;
- whether an amount is deductible;
- the rate of tax applicable to a transaction, event, or class of taxpayer;
- whether an amount qualifies as a reduction of tax payable;
- the accuracy of a valuation; and
- whether a decision that is subject to objection and appeal is correct.

Where a taxpayer fails to respond to an audit enquiry with satisfactory evidence and supporting documentation, the SARS may issue an adjusted assessment on the basis that the taxpayer has failed to discharge its burden of proof. Despite this burden of proof that rests on the taxpayer, the SARS is obliged to adequately set out the grounds for the additional assessment so as to enable a taxpayer to satisfactorily respond thereto should an objection be lodged by the taxpayer.

A taxpayer who has lost its digital wallet address will have the duty to show, to the satisfaction of the SARS, the circumstances surrounding the loss and the resultant tax position adopted by the taxpayer.

24. Tax Administration Act 28 of 2011.

(c) Are crypto asset exchanges and wallet providers subject to reporting obligations?

The South African taxation laws do not impose specific reporting obligations on crypto asset exchanges and wallet providers.

(d) Are taxpayers holding crypto assets subject to reporting obligations apart from the filing of income tax/capital gains tax returns?

Neither the South African National Treasury nor the SARS have indicated any further reporting requirements (other than the filing of tax returns) that will be imposed on holders of crypto assets.

(e) Are crypto asset exchanges and wallet providers subject to CRS/FATCA reporting?

The South African Government has entered into an agreement with the Government of the United States of America to improve international tax compliance and to implement FATCA. However, the South African fiscal authorities have not issued any directives regarding whether or not crypto asset exchange platforms or crypto asset wallet providers are required to disclose the relevant information under FATCA.

In relation to CRS, the South African government has, under the Tax Administration Act, published the 'Regulations Specifying the Changes to the OECD Standard for Automatic Exchange of Financial Account Information in Tax Matters' ('CRS Regulations'). The obligation to comply with CRS reporting requirements will in all likelihood depend on whether crypto assets constitute 'financial assets' as defined under the CRS Regulations, and further whether these crypto asset platforms and wallet providers qualify as institutions that are subject to the CRS reporting obligations. The phrase 'financial assets' is defined to include any security (such as a share in a company), partnership interest, commodity, swap, 'insurance contract' or 'annuity contract', or any interest in a security, partnership interest, commodity, swap, 'insurance contract' or 'annuity contract'. It is not clear whether crypto assets form part of the definition of 'financial assets'. If they do, which is likely the case, and the crypto asset exchange or wallet provider's activities fall within the definition(s) of a 'custodial institution', 'depository institution' or 'investment entity' under the CRS Regulations, they would have to comply with the reporting obligations stipulated in the Regulations.

1.1.5 Civil and Criminal Tax Enforcement

(a) What powers do the tax authorities have to compel the disclosure of information by third parties, such as exchanges or wallet providers, and have these been used in the past?

Chapter 5 of the Tax Administration Act outlines the information gathering powers of the SARS. In terms thereof, and for purposes of administering a Tax Act in relation to a taxpayer, the SARS may require the taxpayer or another person to submit relevant material required by the SARS. A request for relevant material from a third party is limited to material that is kept, or should reasonably be kept, by that third party in respect of the taxpayer. The SARS is also empowered in respect of a field audit or criminal investigation to require a third party to make available at the third party's premises all relevant material specified in the prescribed notice in order to enable the SARS official to administer a Tax Act. There are, however, certain limitations on the SARS' information gathering powers, for example the disclosure of material that is covered by legal professional privilege cannot be compelled by the SARS.

Given the wide information gathering powers bestowed on the SARS, it has and will be able to compel South African crypto asset exchanges and wallet providers to disclose information relevant to South African taxpayers.

There have been instances where the enforcement division of the South African Reserve Bank, South Africa's central bank, has clamped down on trading in cryptocurrency to the extent that it contravenes South Africa's exchange control laws. It is possible that the SARS could have also taken steps to enforce payment of tax by such individuals, although this would not be public knowledge.

(b) What measures have the tax authorities undertaken in the past to ensure crypto tax compliance?

The general prohibition of disclosure of taxpayer information by the SARS means that any steps that may have been taken in the past to ensure crypto tax compliance is not in the public domain. No general programme has been instituted yet even though specific cases have arisen. The South African Tax Administration Act makes provision for voluntary disclosure programme (VDP) relief that taxpayers may apply for in order to disclose any profits or gains derived from crypto assets that they previously failed to disclose in accordance with their tax obligations. A successful VDP application will require the taxpayer to pay all taxes that are due on the previously undisclosed profits and gains, as well as interest thereon, but will allow the taxpayer to avoid having to pay penalties in respect of its past non-compliance with its tax obligations.

(c) Are the tax authorities cooperating with tax authorities in other jurisdictions on enforcement?

The double tax agreements concluded between South Africa and eighty other countries generally all contain provisions regulating the exchange of information between the fiscal authorities of each country, as well as provisions allowing for the assistance between countries in the collection of taxes. This assistance with the collection of taxes is also contained in the South African Tax Administration Act which empowers the SARS to recover tax on behalf of foreign governments.

Despite the existence of these mechanisms that allow for cooperation between jurisdictions, it is unknown whether SARS is cooperating with the tax authorities in other jurisdictions to ensure tax compliance in respect of crypto assets.

South Korea

Maria Chang

1. COUNTRY GUIDES

1.1 South Korea

1.1.1 Applicable Tax Law, Guidance, and Case Law

(a) Which laws, regulations, and other administrative guidance exist dealing with crypto assets?

Discussions around tax regulations involving crypto assets are still in the very early stages, as the 2018 regulation of crypto assets by the Korean Financial Services Commission (FSC) has discouraged development of laws and regulations relevant to crypto assets. In such respects, specific tax regulations dealing with crypto assets have not yet been implemented but are expected to develop quickly in the next year or so.

Korea's Ministry of Economy and Finance (MOEF) – the governmental authority responsible for developing and implementing national tax policy –has recently published a press release on taxation of crypto assets for non-residents,[1] in response to a large assessment handed down by the Korean tax authorities against Bitsum, one of the largest cryptocurrency exchanges in Korea ('Bitsum Assessment'). The MOEF has also issued a comprehensive plan for the taxation of cryptocurrency in its 2020 Tax Law Amendment Proposal issued on 22 July 2020.[2] If this proposed legislation passes the

1. Ministry of Strategy and Finance Press Release, 30 Dec. 2019, http://www.moef.go.kr/com/synap/synapView.do;jsessionid=QdmPFfdhpbCxrYQzTfKkXrKO.node40?atchFileId=ATCH_000000000010469&fileSn=1.
2. Ministry of Strategy and Finance Press Release, 22 Jul. 2020, http://www.moef.go.kr/nw/nes/detailNesDtaView.do?menuNo=4010100&bbsId=MOSFBBS_000000000028&searchBbsId1=MOSFBBS_000000000028&listType=1&searchSort=1&pageIndex=2&searchNttId1=MOSF_000000000041560&searchUseYn=0&searchMenu=4010100&searchNttId=MOSF_000000000041560.

National Assembly, the new legislation is expected to come into effect as of 1 October 2021.

Under the existing tax framework, the Korean Corporate Income Tax Act (CITA), the Individual Income Tax Act (IITA), and the Value Added Tax Act (VATA) are relevant.

(b) *Which court cases exist dealing with crypto assets?*

There are no tax-related decisions issued to date by the Korean courts dealing with crypto assets. The only existing guidance is in the form of ruling interpretations issued by the Korean tax authorities regarding the value added tax (VAT) implications of bitcoin transactions[3] and a recent decision by the Korean Tax Tribunal dealing with VAT issues in relation to mining of cryptocurrency.[4]

In the leading decision issued by the Korean Supreme Court on cryptocurrencies, the Court held that cryptocurrencies used in the context of criminal activity are deemed as intangible assets with property value and may be confiscated as criminal proceeds.[5] It is unclear whether and to what extent this decision will impact future tax-related decisions issued by the Supreme Court given the narrow scope of this decision.

1.1.2 Income and Capital Gains Taxes

(a) *How are crypto assets classified for income and capital gains tax purposes?*

The Korean tax laws had not provided any clear guidance on the appropriate classification of crypto assets for income and capital gains tax purposes until the 2020 tax amendment proposals were released in July 2020.

As a recent development, however, the Korean tax authorities conducted a tax audit against Bitsum, one of the biggest cryptocurrency exchanges in Korea, and in December 2019 issued the Bitsum Assessment in the amount of KRW 80.5 billion (approximately USD 65 million) for individual income tax withholding of Bitsum's non-resident customers by adopting the position that gross amounts withdrawn from the Bitsum exchange by non-residents of Korea are Korean assets subject to individual income taxation in the 'other income' category under the IITA.[6] The distinction between residents and non-residents was made in this case as non-residents may be taxed on all income tax categories unless specifically excluded under a relevant tax treaty, whereas residents may only be taxed on income categories specifically enumerated under the IITA. As a result, the Bitsum Assessment resulted in imposition of income tax only against non-residents trading in the Bitsum exchange. The assessment is meaningful in that the tax authorities seem to have taken the position – at least for

3. *Seomyeonbubgyugwa-920*, 25 Aug. 2014, *Seomyeon-2014-Buga-21616*, 29 Dec. 2015.
4. Tax Tribunal Decision *2019So0624*, 12 Feb. 2020.
5. Supreme Court Decision *2018Do3619*, 30 May 2018.
6. Article 119(12)(e) of the IITA.

purposes of this assessment – that crypto assets have value as property as opposed to currency.

The assessment raises questions as to the legality of this distinction between residents and non-residents. Another question raised by the Bitsum Assessment is whether the imposition of income tax on gross receipts is appropriate. Bitsum is expected to appeal this matter and as such, this case is likely to serve as an important precedent in the cryptocurrency-related tax space. In the meantime, there remained an equally relevant question as to how crypto assets held by Korean residents should be handled to ensure fairness in the crypto taxation scheme adopted by the Korean tax authorities.

In its 2020 tax amendment proposal, the MOEF proposes that income earned by Korean residents from the transfer of virtual assets under the Act on Reporting and Using Specified Financial Transaction Information be taxed in the category of 'other' income at the tax rate of 22% (inclusive of local income surtax). The tax base consists of the total gains and losses computed on an annual basis, based on the difference between the fair market value of the assets transferred and the acquisition price of such assets (along with incidental expenses). The proposal includes an annual minimum taxable threshold on gains derived from virtual assets of KRW 2.5 million (approximately USD 2000).

In the case of virtual asset transfers by non-residents or foreign corporation, gains are taxed as Korean-sourced 'other' income and subject to withholding by the payer of income at the time of transfer, loan or withdrawal of crypto assets from accounts held through a virtual asset business operator. The withholding agent is required to withhold on such transfers at the lesser of 11% of the transfer price or 22% of the capital gains, for payment with the tax office by the 10th day of the month following the transaction. Non-residents or foreign corporations eligible for tax exemption pursuant to a relevant tax treaty may claim treaty exemption by filing an Application for Tax Exemption with the withholding agent.

(b) *What are the income/capital gains tax consequences of selling crypto assets against fiat currency?*

The tax treatment of gains and losses from the sale of crypto assets against fiat currency has not yet been clearly defined. As discussed above, the tax authorities have treated gains incurred by non-Korean residents from the trading in the Bitsum exchange as domestic assets (*i.e.*, assets held and sold in Korea) subject to income tax in Korea. In issuing this assessment, the tax authorities rely on the 'domestic assets other than real property' category among the enumerated list of 'other income' categories as the appropriate classification of Bitsum. This categorization seems to indicate that the Korean tax authorities are likely to view crypto assets to consist of assets that are not real property but have similar characteristics as real property.

On the other hand, the MOEF has recently issued a press release addressing concerns on the Bitsum Assessment by indicating the view that Korean residents are not subject to income tax on gains arising from the sale of crypto assets given that Korean residents are only subject to taxation for enumerated income tax items listed under the IITA.[7] As crypto assets are not enumerated as taxable items under the Korean income tax laws, there are limitations under the existing tax laws for Korean resident taxpayers to be subject to taxes on sales of crypto assets. The 2020 proposed tax amendments provide more detailed guidance on the tax consequences of sales involving crypto assets, especially for those Korean resident taxpayers who have not been subject to tax on income/gains from the sale of crypto assets to date. As discussed above in 1.1.2(a), the gains incurred from the sale of crypto assets may be subject to tax in the "other" income category on the differential between the fair market value of the assets transferred and the acquisition price. The acquisition price of virtual assets acquired and held by a taxpayer prior to the implementation date of the tax legislation will be based on the greater of the actual acquisition price and the deemed acquisition price. The deemed acquisition price is computed based on the fair market value of such assets as of September 30, 2021.

(c) What are the income/capital gains tax consequences of exchanging crypto assets against other crypto assets?

Given the lack of guidance on the classification of crypto assets, it is unclear whether and how the exchange of crypto assets against other crypto assets will be treated for Korean income/capital gains tax purposes. The 2020 proposed tax amendments do not provide any additional guidance on this issue. For the sake of consistency with the Bitsum Assessment, it is presumable that any income generated from the exchange of crypto assets is likely to be categorized as 'other income'. If such exchange of crypto assets is deemed as a taxable exchange, valuation of income may be based on the valuation requirements for the exchange of unlisted shares, by computing the sales price at previously transacted prices and where such prices do not exist, at the fair market value of the assets exchanged.[8] Even if such exchange is deemed a taxable event subject to capital gains, valuation issues are also expected to arise in evaluating the value of the respective crypto assets involved in the exchange. Generally, the tax authorities will seek to use existing transactions as a reference to determine the value of such crypto assets. Where no such reference measurements exist, valuation methodologies stipulated under the Inheritance and Gift Tax Act (IGTA) are likely to apply.[9] If, on the other hand, the position adopted by the tax authorities in the Bitsum Assessment is implemented as tax law, the exchange is unlikely to be deemed a taxable event until there is a withdrawal of the crypto asset in the form of fiat currency.

(d) If a distinction is made between business assets and non-business assets, when does trading in crypto assets lead to a trade or business?

A distinction may be made between activities carried out on a non-recurring basis and activities being carried out on a continuous, recurring basis and independent basis for

7. Articles 16–22 of the IITA.
8. Article 100 of the IITA, Article 97-1 of the Basic Rules of the IITA.
9. Article 60 of the Inheritance and Gift Tax Act.

profit-making purposes under the Korean tax law. The Korean courts indicate that several factors are to be considered in light of social norms, such as whether continuous and recurring activities have a business purpose, the volume and importance of the activity, and the size of business.[10] Whereas non-recurring activities that are generally not regarded as business activities under social norms give rise to personal income for the taxpayer, activities that are carried out on a continuous and recurring basis independently for profit-making purposes are generally classified as business income[11]. For a taxpayer engaging in trading of crypto assets, this distinction may be important as continuous and recurring activity involving crypto assets would lead to characterization of the income arising from such trading of crypto assets to be deemed as business income. For the time being, the tax authorities do not seem to have made any such distinction for purposes of issuing their tax imposition against Bitsum, the leading case involving taxation of cryptocurrency in Korea to date.

(e) *What are the income/capital gains tax consequences for an employee receiving wages or salaries in crypto assets?*

There are no guidelines in place to address the tax consequences of an employee receiving wages or salaries in crypto assets. This form of compensation is unlikely to be widely adopted by Korean employers in the near future, given the complexities around valuation of crypto assets and the potential tax risks borne by the employer with respect to withholding of wages and payment of social contributions. Nonetheless, the most likely tax position is for the crypto assets received as wages or salaries to be subject to individual income taxation as employment income upon receipt of the income, because employment income consists of all economic gains earned by an employee in consideration for employment services, regardless of the formality of the designation given to the income, and includes salaries, wages, remuneration, allowances, bonus, and additional pay.[12]

In theory, there should be another taxable event on any gains or losses incurred on a subsequent exchange of the crypto asset for fiat currency. Under current tax laws, however, there is no legal basis for Korean resident taxpayers to be subject to taxation on the income/gains incurred on a sale of crypto assets.

(f) *What are the income/capital gains tax consequences for a merchant receiving payment in crypto assets?*

There is a lack of guidance on the tax treatment for merchants receiving payment in crypto assets, as this is not yet a widely used method of payment in South Korea. The assumption is that the income tax treatment for merchants receiving crypto assets as payment schemes will be subject to corporate income taxes on the income generated by

10. Seoul High Court Decision, *2018Nu59979*, 4 Dec. 2018.
11. Article 19 of the IITA.
12. Article 20 of the IITA, Article 38 of the Presidential Decree of the IITA.

characterizing the payments as taxable business income in the same manner as fiat currency payments. Although the value of the received crypto assets may, in theory, be the most accurate basis for determining the income base for the merchant receiving payment in crypto assets, it is foreseeable that the tax authorities are likely to accept the fair market value of the goods sold by the merchant to be the amount of income subject to tax.

To date, crypto payments are more prevalent in businesses engaging in illegal or criminal activities due to the strict regulation of cryptocurrency by the FSC and the relative anonymity offered when engaging in such activities using cryptocurrency as a currency medium.[13]

(g) *What are the income/capital gains tax consequences of a loss of crypto assets?*

To the extent the Bitsum Assessment is taken as a reference, the loss of crypto assets is not expected to give rise to any specific income tax consequences for non-residents. For Korean residents, the loss of crypto assets may qualify as deductible expenses for up to 60% of the income if the income is characterized as 'other income',[14] but due to the limitations present in the Korean tax laws, it seems unlikely that crypto assets of Korean residents will be treated as 'other income'.

Given the uncertainty in the income tax treatment of cryptocurrency for Korean residents, further guidance is necessary to better understand the income tax consequences where the keys to the address where crypto assets stored are lost.

(h) *What are the income/capital gains tax consequences of a loss in value of crypto assets?*

The loss in value of crypto assets is not relevant to non-residents, as it does not give rise to any specific consequences for income tax purposes. The Bitsum Assessment provides some insight into the current position of the tax authorities that the loss in value of crypto assets will not be considered in determining the taxable income base, to the extent taxable income is categorized as 'other income'. For Korean residents, in theory, it may be possible to recognize realized loss as a tax-deductible expense if the cryptocurrency activity generates business income.[15] It should be noted that depreciation is only allowed for tax deduction of fixed assets when expensed for book purposes.[16]

13. Supreme Court Decision *2018Do3619*, 30 May 2018.
14. Article 87(1-2) of the Presidential Decree of the IITA (PD-IITA).
15. Article 19(2) of the IITA.
16. Article 25 of the PD-IITA.

(i) *What are the income/capital gains tax consequences of forks of crypto assets?*

Given that the development of the tax framework on crypto assets is in its early stages, no reliable guidance exists on how forks should be treated. If income from a fork is also treated as 'other income', the fork itself is not expected to give rise to a taxable event at the time of the fork. Once the forked assets are sold, it may be possible for the value of the crypto asset – allocated based on fair market value of the original and new crypto assets – to be subject to income tax on the gross amount of the forked asset.

(j) *What are the income/capital gains tax consequences of airdrops of crypto assets and are the tax consequences different if the airdropped tokens are unwanted?*

Airdrops of crypto assets are likely to be taxable as gifts and subject to gift tax under the IGTA, under the assumption that crypto assets will be recognized as property with economic value.[17] The tax consequences are not expected to change even if the airdropped tokens are unwanted, as there are inherent challenges involved in evidencing the wishes of the taxpayer receiving airdrops of crypto assets. In such respects, the tax authorities are not likely to differentiate between airdrops of tokens that are wanted by the taxpayer and airdrops of tokens that are unwanted. Questions are likely to be raised as to the appropriate valuation of crypto assets for IGTA purposes.

(k) *What are the income/capital gains tax consequences of (solo, pool, and cloud) mining?*

Although only VAT issues associated with mining have been considered to date, mining should, in theory, be considered as leading to business income generated from engaging in business activity, unless the mining activity involves a single, non-recurring transaction without any business purpose.

(l) *What are the income/capital gains tax consequences of staking crypto assets?*

No clear guidance exists on the tax consequences of staking crypto assets. However, staking is likely to be considered as taxable in the 'other income' category since staking would generally not be considered business activity sufficient to be categorized as business income.

17. National Tax Service, press release, 5 Dec. 2017, https://www.nts.go.kr/news/news_01.asp?minfoKey=MINF8420080211204826&page=26&type=V.

(m) *What are the income/capital gains tax consequences of an indirect investment in crypto assets?*

Korean law does not expressly prohibit private funds from investing into crypto assets. However, these types of investments are not prevalent given the current position of the regulators that investment managers in Korea should not invest fund assets in cryptocurrencies until the regulatory framework on crypto assets is finalized.

In theory, indirect investments into crypto assets may be achieved through trust-type vehicles or through company-type funds. With respect to investments through trust vehicles, there is no taxation at the trust level and taxable income is only recognized once the income is distributed to the investors. Any income distributed by qualifying funds to individual investors is taxed as dividends whereas income distribution by funds that do not meet the requirement of qualifying funds is taxed according to the character of the income.

Company-type funds, such as investment companies and investment limited liability companies under the Korean Financial Investment Services and Capital Markets Act (FISCMA), are generally subject to corporate income tax on investment profits from investment operations. However, if 90% or more of the distributable income is paid out as dividends, this amount is deducted from the taxable income, which enables the fund to avoid double taxation at the fund level.

(n) *How is income from crypto assets to be treated under double tax treaty law?*

Despite the lack of guidance, the Bitsum Assessment provides insight into the tax authorities' position that non-residents of Korea should be eligible for taxation on all income categories – specifically under the 'other income' category under the IITA – pursuant to relevant tax treaties whereas residents may only be taxed on specifically enumerated list of tax items under the Korean tax laws. In such respect, certain tax treaties with non-discrimination clauses, such as the Korea-China tax treaty[18], may be invoked to prevent taxation of residents in those treaty countries given the current position of the Korean tax authorities that Korean residents are not subject to taxation on crypto assets. Additional questions arise as to whether non-residents may be taxed on gains from the sale of crypto assets under Article 13 of the OECD Model Convention, given that gains from the alienation of property other than real property, movable property and ships or aircrafts are subject to taxation in the country of residence.
Once the 2020 proposed tax amendments relevant to crypto assets taxation come into effect, however, a foreign corporation or non-resident entitled to the benefit of a tax treaty may be exempt from withholding taxation on capital gains, provided that the requisite application for tax exemption is filed with the withholding agent.

18. Article 24 of the Agreement between the Government of the Republic of Korea and the Government of the People's Republic of China for the Avoidance of Double Taxation and the Prevention of Fiscal Evasion with Respect to Taxes on Income.

Aside from the above, income may be treated as business profits under Article 7 of the OECD Model Convention to the extent crypto assets generate business income. Here, profits are taxable only in the country of residency unless the taxpayer has a permanent establishment in Korea through which the taxpayer carries on his/her business activity.

(o) What are the income/capital gains tax consequences of selling crypto assets in an ICO/STO/IEO?

ICO/STO/IEOs are generally not anymore banned in Korea since the FSC's announcement in early 2018 that ICOs that violate the FISCMA are banned.[19]

1.1.3 Other Taxes

(a) What are the value added tax/sales tax consequences of selling crypto assets?

The Korean tax authorities have issued broad tax interpretations indicating that VAT does not apply to the extent crypto assets are held as currency, whereas VAT applies to the extent crypto assets are held as goods with property value.[20] For tax purposes, no further guidance has been issued to address the question of whether and to what extent crypto assets should be regarded as currency or property.

(b) Are payments in crypto assets subject to withholding taxes?

Using the 2020 proposed tax amendments as a reference, it can be deduced that payments made in crypto assets are likely to trigger withholding taxes for non-residents of Korea as capital gains at the lesser of 11 % of the transfer price and 22 % of gains (including local surtax). Due to the practical difficulties in withholding and remitting taxes in cryptocurrency, the tax authorities are expected to require the cryptocurrency exchanges to remit withholding payment in fiat currency. Since withholding obligations do not arise where payments are made to Korean residents, a Korean resident receiving payment of crypto assets will likely bear tax its own reporting/payment obligations.[21]

19. FSC, Press Release, 4 Sep. 2017, https://www.fsc.go.kr/info/ntc_news_view.jsp?bbsid=BBS0030&page=2&sch1=subject&sword=%EA%B0%80%EC%83%81&r_url=&menu=7210100&no=32027.
20. *Seomyeonbubgyugwa-920*, 25 Aug. 2014, *Seomyeon-2014-Buga-21616*, 29 Dec. 2015.
21. Article 3 of the CITA.

(c) *Does payment of compensation in crypto assets give rise to payroll tax consequences?*

Compensation in crypto assets received by employees is likely to be treated as in-kind payment of wage income and gives rise to normal withholding obligations for the employer.[22]

(d) *Do transactions with crypto assets trigger any transfer taxes?*

There is some discussion around the treatment of crypto transactions as transfers subject to transfer taxes, similar to the Korean securities transaction tax applicable to the transfer of securities.[23] The primary reason for this group of thought is the comparative efficiency in levying transfer taxes as opposed to capital gains taxation.

(e) *Are firms operating in the crypto space subject to digital service taxes?*

Among the most recent changes to the tax law involving digital services tax, VAT applies to inbound business-to-consumer transactions involving advertisements, cloud computing services, and intermediation of goods and services.[24] These enumerated lists of digital services do not cover crypto-related services and would need to be amended in order for firms operating in the crypto space to be subject to digital services tax in Korea.

(f) *Are crypto assets subject to gift, inheritance, estate, or wealth taxes?*

In theory, gifts or inheritance of crypto assets may be subject to gift tax pursuant to the IGTA. During its Annual Forum in 2017, the tax authorities indicated in its preliminary assessment of taxation on cryptocurrencies that inheritance and gift tax would be taxable under the current law but that valuation standards would need to be developed to ensure transparency.[25] The 2020 proposed tax amendments stipulate that the valuation of crypto assets subject to gift tax or inheritance tax will be based on the

(g) *Are crypto assets subject to exit tax?*

Under the Korean tax law, the exit tax applies to majority shareholders of a Korean corporation leaving Korea to emigrate to a foreign country.[26] Aside from the above, corporations or entities with permanent establishment in Korea are not subject to any

22. Article 134 of the IITA.
23. Moon Sung Oh, Design of Fair and Innovative Taxes on Crypto Assets, 21 Feb. 2020.
24. Article 53-2 of the VATA.
25. National Tax Service, Press Release, 5 Dec. 2017, https://www.nts.go.kr/news/news_01.asp?minfoKey=MINF8420080211204826&page=26&type=V.
26. Article 118-9 of the IITA.

exit tax for expatriation under the existing tax laws. Due to the narrow scope of application and the lack of means available for residents to be taxed for crypto assets under the existing tax laws, crypto assets are not likely to be subject to exit tax under the current tax law.

(h) Can mining trigger gambling tax?

There has not been any indication by the Korean tax authorities that mining activity will trigger gambling tax. Winnings from gambling and lotteries are generally regarded as non-recurring taxable income of a taxpayer and taxed as 'other income'.[27] In such respects, based on information available to date, rewards generated from mining activity is expected to be treated as 'other income'.

1.1.4 Compliance and Documentation Obligations

(a) What documentation requirements exist for taxpayers regarding crypto assets and are there best practices in recordkeeping to support representations made in tax returns?

On 30 January 2018, the Korean Government introduced the Real Name Verification System. This system was implemented as an identification policy for accounts in cryptocurrency exchanges and requires cryptocurrency exchanges to cross-check user names and account numbers. Existing anonymous account users may only withdraw money and not make any further deposits whereas all new users are required to provide actual identification information in order to open cryptocurrency accounts. Aside from the above, no other specific documentation requirements exist for taxpayers regarding crypto assets. Overall, the trend has been for the tax authorities to target cryptocurrency exchanges and impose assessments against those exchanges, as is seen from the Bitsum Assessment.

(b) What is the evidentiary burden of supporting tax positions when a digital wallet address is lost or shared with other persons?

Under the Korean tax laws, the burden of proof to evidence a specific tax position varies depending on the issue involved. Based on the existing case law dealing with burden of proof, the general position of the courts is that the taxpayer has the burden of proving specific positions favourable to the taxpayer and in objecting to the imposition of tax must first make specific arguments regarding the illegality of the facts and the legal reasoning of the imposition.[28] Along these lines, it is expected that the Korean courts are likely to adopt the position that the taxpayer has the evidentiary burden of proving that a digital wallet address has been lost.

27. Article 21(2) and (14) of the IITA.
28. Supreme Court Decision, *2008Du12849*, 25 Sep. 2005.

(c) *Are crypto asset exchanges and wallet providers subject to reporting obligations?*

Crypto asset exchanges and wallet providers are not subject to any specific reporting obligations regarding their customers. Although the Real Name Verification System imposes obligations on crypto asset exchanges and wallet providers to collect information, the Bitsum Assessment indicates that the tax authorities are more likely to issue tax impositions against the exchanges and wallet providers themselves as opposed to seeking to collect individual taxpayer information for purposes of collecting taxes directly from individual customers. As Korea is in the early stages of crypto taxation, it remains to be seen whether specific tax-reporting schemes will be put in place for crypto asset exchanges and wallet providers to report customer activity.

(d) *Are taxpayers holding crypto assets subject to reporting obligations apart from the filing of income tax/capital gains tax returns?*

Korea has not yet implemented any specific reporting obligations associated with crypto assets. To date, individual taxpayers holding crypto assets have not been specifically required to disclose any activity related to crypto assets. The 2020 proposed tax amendments include offshore virtual asset accounts within the scope of foreign financial account reporting, requiring taxpayers with virtual asset accounts held outside of Korea to file a report disclosing such accounts with the Korean tax authorities.

(e) *Are crypto asset exchanges and wallet providers subject to CRS/FATCA reporting?*

Korea has not yet implemented any CRS/FATCA reporting requirements specific to crypto asset exchanges and wallet providers. The 2020 proposed tax amendments include foreign financial institutions engaging in crypto transactions to come within the scope of foreign financial institutions subject to reporting in Korea.

1.1.5 Civil and Criminal Tax Enforcement

(a) *What powers do the tax authorities have to compel the disclosure of information by third parties, such as exchanges or wallet providers, and have these been used in the past?*

Within the context of an audit, the tax authorities have broad authority to request not only information documents relevant to the taxpayer, but also information relevant to parties transacting with the taxpayer.[29] Therefore, theoretically, the tax authorities

29. Article 2(2) of the Regulation on Handling of Tax Audits.

could compel a third-party taxpayer to disclose information regarding its customers. However, as was seen with the Bitsum Assessment, the tax authorities are more likely to attempt taxation of the crypto exchanges or wallet providers themselves.

(b) What measures have the tax authorities undertaken in the past to ensure crypto tax compliance?

Due to the strict regulations in place to regulate crypto activity in Korea, the tax authorities have not aggressively sought tax compliance of crypto assets in the past. It is expected that the new tax plan for cryptocurrency expected to be unveiled in August 2020 will implement policies aimed at compliance.

(c) Are the tax authorities cooperating with tax authorities in other jurisdictions on enforcement?

Korea has tax treaties in place with ninety-one countries containing exchange of information clauses. In addition, Korea has also concluded Tax Information Exchange Agreements (TIEA) with numerous countries for the administration and enforcement of information exchange. Starting from 2017, Korea has exchanged with fifty-three countries, including the United Kingdom, Cayman Islands, British Virgin Islands, certain information on financial accounts and income according to the Multilateral Competent Authority Agreements (MCAA).[30] However, there is no publicly available information to indicate whether and to what extent the tax authorities are exchanging information on crypto assets.

30. Ministry of Economy and Finance, Press Release, 13 Mar. 2019, http://www.moef.go.kr/com/synap/synapView.do;jsessionid=QdmPFfdhpbCxrYQzTfKkXrKO.node40?atchFileId=ATCH_000000000010469&fileSn=1.

Spain

Álvaro de la Cueva & Juan Camilo Sánchez

1. COUNTRY GUIDES

1.1 Spain

1.1.1 Applicable Tax Law, Guidance, and Case Law

(a) Which laws, regulations, and other administrative guidance exist dealing with crypto assets?

In Spain, there are no specific laws or regulations that deal directly with transactions involving crypto assets. Therefore, the general tax system applies to such transactions.

However, from a tax perspective, the Spanish Tax Authorities (STA) have issued several binding rulings in which they have analysed the nature of crypto assets and their tax treatment.

From 2017 onwards, crypto assets and blockchain have become an official area of control and supervision by the STA.

(b) Which court cases exist dealing with crypto assets?

The main cases involving blockchain and bitcoin relate mostly to embezzlement crimes involving bitcoins.

From a tax perspective, there are no court cases yet.

1.1.2 Income and Capital Gains Taxes

(a) How are crypto assets classified for income and capital gains tax purposes?

Due to the lack of specific legislation in this regard, the STA has recognized crypto assets as 'virtual currency' and followed the EU definition as an 'unsecured digital representation of value that is often accepted as a means of payment'. In binding rulings V1604-18 and V1069-19, the STA described bitcoin as 'an intangible asset computable in units or fractions of units, which is not a legal tender, that can be exchanged for other goods including other virtual currencies, rights or services if accepted by the other party in the transfer, and which can generally be acquired or transferred in exchange for legal currency.'

Thus, crypto assets or tokens do not qualify as: (i) a 'financial asset' since they are not negotiated in any official financial market or as (ii) a legal tender or currency, as the Euro is the sole legal tender by law. The Supreme Court of Spain, in a judgment handed down on 20 June 2019, also stated that loss derived from crimes could only be compensated in Euro and not in bitcoins, since the latter could not be considered legal tender.

(b) What are the income/capital gains tax consequences of selling crypto assets against fiat currency?

These would depend on the following scenarios.

(i) Sale by an individual private investor

The transfer of crypto assets by individual private investors who do not carry out an economic or business activity would generate a capital gain or a capital loss calculated as the difference between the transfer value and the acquisition cost. Commissions of brokerage platforms, exchange houses, and other related expenses should be added to the acquisition cost or subtracted from the transfer value, as the case may be, according to binding rulings V0808-18 and V1604-18 by the STA.

The capital gain, if any, would be taxed under the individual's Personal Income Tax (PIT) at the special rates of 19% (up to EUR 6,000), 21% (up to EUR 50,000), and 23% (from EUR 50,000 onwards).

The capital loss could be offset against other capital gains obtained during the same fiscal year (FY) or during the subsequent four FYs, or even against other savings income (dividends, interest, etc.) under special rules.

For calculating the capital gain or loss, the FIFO (First in First Out) ordering convention must be applied, even if the crypto assets have been acquired from different exchange houses, according to binding ruling V1604-18 by the STA.

(ii) Sale by an intermediary ('**exchangers**')

a. Individuals:

Exchangers are intermediaries carrying out an economic activity through which they connect buyers and sellers of crypto assets, receiving a commission for their services. Both CIT and PIT Regulations establish that an economic or business activity is carried out when there is an organization of appropriate human and material means to perform the said activity. Therefore, exchangers are considered to be merchants when there is an organization of appropriate human and material means for trading crypto assets.

The commission received by the exchanger would be subject to PIT as an 'economic activity', at the general PIT rates (up to 48 %, depending on the region where the exchanger is resident).

If the exchanger transferred any crypto assets of its own, the income received would also be taxed as an 'economic activity' subject to the general PIT rates.

If the transfer of the crypto asset generated a loss, this could be offset against other income under the general PIT rules.

b. Companies:

Transfer of crypto assets by companies would generate a profit or a loss calculated as the difference between their transfer value and the (acquisition) tax value. The profit or loss would be added to the company's overall income and expenses for the fiscal year (FY).

The total income registered by the company, together with the commissions obtained, would be subject to Corporate Income Tax (CIT) at the general 25% rate.

The total loss obtained by the company, if any, could be offset in future FYs without time constraints although with certain quantitative limitations[1].

(iii) Sale by '**miners**'

Tax implications are described in section 1.1.2(k).

(c) What are the income/capital gains tax consequences of exchanging crypto assets against other crypto assets?

The exchange of crypto assets against other crypto assets should be treated as a barter, according to binding ruling V1149-18 by the STA.

If the crypto asset is transferred by an individual, a capital gain or loss could arise. In this regard, the capital gain (or loss) will be determined as the difference between (i) the acquisition value of the crypto asset and (ii) the higher of the following: (a) market value of the crypto asset transferred or (b) market value of the crypto asset received, in accordance with Article 37.1.h) of the PIT Law.[2]

The capital gain or loss obtained by an individual would be taxed at the special PIT rates (19%–23%) or at the general tax rate (up to 48%) depending on whether the individual is a private investor or a merchant carrying out an economic activity.

1. As a general rule, tax losses could be offset in future fiscal years up to 70% of the FY positive taxable base. Nevertheless, if the company or Group has a turnover of more than EUR 20 or EUR 60 million, higher restrictions (50% or 25%, respectively) could apply.
2. Law 35/2006, of 28 Nov. 2006, of Personal Income Tax and Partial Amendment of the Corporate Income Tax, Non-resident Tax and Wealth Tax Laws.

If the crypto asset is transferred by a company, the income or loss would be calculated as the difference between the market value of the crypto asset received and the acquisition cost of the crypto asset transferred.

(d) *If a distinction is made between business assets and non-business assets, when does trading in crypto assets lead to a trade or business?*

As mentioned, the PIT implications derived from the transfer of crypto assets would depend on the activity performed by the individual transferring the crypto assets.

On the one hand, if the transferor is a private investor who does not carry out an economic activity, the capital gain would be taxed at the special tax rates (19%–23%).

On the other hand, if the transferor is a merchant carrying out an economic activity, the profit obtained would be subject to PIT as an 'economic activity' at the general tax rates (up to 48% depending on the region of residence).

For CIT purposes, the tax implications would be the same regardless of whether the entity transfers business or non-business assets. In both cases, the profit, if any, would be subject to the general 25% CIT rate.

(e) *What are the income/capital gains tax consequences for an employee receiving wages or salaries in crypto assets?*

Crypto assets received by employees should be considered as a salary payment in kind earned at the time the employee receives the crypto assets (e.g., when the crypto assets are transferred to the employee's wallet), and quantified at the market value of the crypto asset, according to Article 43 of the PIT Law. In this case, the employer would be required to make payments on account (withholding) of the employee's PIT at progressive tax rates (up to 48%). If the company bears the payment of the withholding tax and it is not charged back to the employee, this would result in higher employment income for the employee.

(f) *What are the income/capital gains tax consequences for a merchant receiving payment in crypto assets?*

If a company or an individual merchant carrying out a business activity receives crypto assets as a means of payment, the company or the merchant would register a profit or a loss for the sale of goods or services, based on the fair market value of the crypto assets sold, regardless of whether the payment was made in crypto assets or Euro.

The crypto assets received by the company or merchant would be considered an intangible asset or inventory depending on recipient's core business, in accordance with ruling 38-14 issued by the Spanish Accounting and Audit Institute (ICAC) and with the interpretation given by the International Financial Reporting Standards (IFRS) Interpretation Committee:

- Intangible assets: when the company or merchant receives the crypto assets in order to maintain them on its balance sheet as an investment.
- Inventory: crypto assets might be integrated as inventory when the main business activity of the company or merchant is the purchase and sale of crypto assets.

(g) *What are the income/capital gains tax consequences of a loss of crypto assets?*

The CIT and the PIT laws do not regulate the loss of crypto assets due to the loss of a key or a wallet and there are no binding rulings either. In principle, if the taxpayer were able to justify and prove the loss of crypto assets, the loss would be deductible, although the Spanish Tax Authorities are very strict when allowing the deductibility of losses.

If the loss of crypto assets was due to bankruptcies or thefts, the loss could be included in the general component of taxable income, since it is not deemed generated on a transfer of assets, pursuant to Article 45 of the PIT Law. Therefore, this loss could only be offset against other capital gains included in the general component of taxable income or other general taxable items (e.g., salaries, business activities) with a 25% limit, according to Article 48 of the PIT Law.

However, the STA, in binding rulings V2603-15 and V1979-15, concluded that: (i) the loss derived from the bankruptcy of the exchange house or from a robbery would not be deductible until the credit has been definitively declared as non-recoverable by the courts, and (ii) the bitcoins stolen from a brokerage platform would only generate deductible capital losses under the following circumstances related to the exchange house or brokerage platform: (a) official debt-write off, (b) an arrangement of creditors, or (c) after the credit has been claimed before a court for a year.

The loss incurred by a company due to bankruptcies or thefts would be deductible only once it has become final (i.e., the debtor has been declared bankrupt or the obligations have been claimed in court or have been subject to an arbitration proceeding, according to Article 13 of the CIT Law).[3]

If these requirements are met, the loss would be added to the overall income and expense generated during the FY. The total loss obtained by the company, if any, could be offset in future FYs without time constraints although with certain quantitative limitations.

(h) *What are the income/capital gains tax consequences of a loss in value of crypto assets?*

For individuals and companies, the change in value of crypto assets due to market fluctuation is not relevant for tax purposes until they are transferred.

3. Corporate Income Tax Law 27/2014, of 27 Nov. 2014.

In the case of companies, an impairment expense could be recognized if the market value is lower, although this impairment would not generally be tax deductible. For instance, impairments losses on property, plant and equipment, investment property and intangible assets (including goodwill) are not deductible for CIT purposes. However, tangible and intangible assets can be depreciated based on their useful life stock (while inventory stock cannot be depreciated).

(i) What are the income/capital gains tax consequences of forks of crypto assets?

There is no official guidance from the STA in relation to forks of crypto assets.

In our opinion this could have tax consequences only if, when selling to a third party, there has been a change in the value of the crypto asset. If there is no change of value, no gain or loss would arise from the fork of crypto assets. The original acquisition cost, if any, should be allocated to all crypto assets derived from the split.

(j) What are the income/capital gains tax consequences of airdrops of crypto assets and are the tax consequences different if the airdropped tokens are unwanted?

With respect to the recipient, airdrops of crypto assets would be treated similarly to donations, if accepted. In this regard:

- Airdrops of crypto assets received by individuals could be subject to Inheritance and Gift Tax and to PIT. The mechanism of these Taxes is explained *infra* in section 1.1.3(f).
- Airdrops of crypto assets received by legal entities would be subject to the general 25% CIT rate.

As for the promoter, as a general rule, donations made by individuals and companies are non-deductible for tax purposes, unless given to special foundations and non-profit organizations.

(k) What are the income/capital gains tax consequences of (solo, pool, and cloud) mining?

Corporate Income Tax (Companies):

Crypto assets obtained through the mining process would be considered as inventory for the company as long as they are intended to be transformed into financial availability through sale as an ordinary business activity, as per Consultation 4 of the ICAC's Bulletin of 12 December 2019.

In this case, companies must value the crypto assets at their 'production cost' which may include the cost of electricity, equipment, etc., as per Resolution of 14 April 2015 issued by the ICAC.

The future sale of crypto assets by the company would trigger an income or loss that must be computed for CIT purposes. The resulting income, if any, would be subject to the general 25% CIT rate.

Personal Income Tax (Individuals):

If the individual miner acts as a merchant (i.e., with human and material means in order to create and trade them), and following the ICAC Resolution mentioned before[4], the crypto assets received would be considered as inventory, valued at their 'production cost' which may include the cost of electricity, equipment, etc. The future transfer of the crypto asset would generate a profit or loss for the difference between the transfer value and the inventory value. The profit, if any, would be subject to the general PIT rates (up to 48% depending on the region where the miner is resident).

If the individual miner does not carry out a business activity, the crypto assets received would be considered as a capital gain not derived from the disposal of assets and would be taxed at the general PIT rates (up to 48% depending on the region where the miner is resident) at the time the crypto assets were received.

Business Activities Tax:[5]

The STA confirmed in binding ruling V3625-16 that miners who perform their activity as a business (i.e., through human and material means) are subject to economic activities tax. Since trading with crypto assets is not on the list of regulated business activities, the STA have suggested registering under economic activities tax heading 831.1 'Other financial services' (when the miner obtains a commission and bitcoins for offering services, pursuant to binding ruling number V3625-16) or heading 969.7 'Other automatic machines' (when the miner's service is provided through automatic machines, according to binding ruling number V1028-15), as the case may be.

In any case, note that there are some exemptions for economic activities tax which apply to: (i) individual merchants (who are exempt from economic activities tax) and (ii) entities with a turnover below EUR 1 million, or during the first two years of a new activity, according to Article 82.1 of the Revised Local Finances Law.

(l) *What are the income/capital gains tax consequences of staking crypto assets?*

There is no official guidance from the STA in relation to staking crypto assets.

4. Although the ICAC resolution refers to companies, the same criterion should apply to the individuals carrying out a business activity through human and material means.
5. Local tax that should be paid by companies when they carry out a business activity, based on some parameters.

To the extent that staking crypto assets may give similar results to mining activities, the tax consequences should be similar.

(m) *What are the income/capital gains tax consequences of an indirect investment in crypto assets?*

Indirect investment in crypto assets is possible in many ways, but generally, it is done through investment funds dedicated to this kind of assets.

The tax implications that would derive from the investment in a fund that in turn invests in crypto assets would be the same as those derived from the investment in any other investment fund (i.e., there is no special regulation for investment funds acquiring crypto assets). Generally, a transfer of participations in a fund qualifies as a capital gain (or loss) taxable as savings income at reduced rates.

(n) *How is income from crypto assets to be treated under double tax treaty law?*

The STA has not issued any binding rulings on the treatment of crypto assets under double tax treaties. Nevertheless, income generated from crypto assets could fall under Articles 7 (business profits) or 13 (capital gains) of the OECD Model Convention, depending on the nature of the income.

(o) *What are the income/capital gains tax consequences of selling crypto assets in an ICO/STO/IEO?*

The regulation of ICOs in Spain is mostly undefined and the authorities are opting for regulating this practice by analogy to other crowdfunding methods. The National Securities Market Commission (CNMV) provided some considerations about ICOs in its publication of 8 February 2018, stating that ICOs should have a similar treatment as IPOs. In this regard, the CNMV also stated that tokens issued in an ICO could be considered negotiable securities since they have a similar content to shares, bonds or other financial assets.

Although there are no laws or rulings regulating the tax implications that would derive from utility tokens and security tokens, in our opinion the tax treatment would be as follows:

- The ICO of utility tokens should be considered as anticipated income in account for the future obligation to provide services or products to the investor. In this sense, this anticipated income will be taxable for CIT purposes. Nevertheless, the allocation of this income should be imputed proportionally to the services rendered in each fiscal year.
- In case of security tokens, they should be considered as capital contributions and, therefore, no taxable income will arise for CIT purposes.

The tax implications for the investor derived from transferring the crypto assets are the same as those described in section 1.1.2(b).

1.1.3 *Other Taxes*

(a) *What are the value added tax/sales tax consequences of selling crypto assets?*

VAT application is harmonized at the EU level due to the transposition of European Directives into Spanish legislation. In this regard, the STA have followed the European Court of Justice (ECJ) criteria regarding the VAT implications of crypto assets.

Transfer of bitcoins against other currencies:

Although the STA have considered that these transactions are subject to but exempt from VAT, over the years the STA have been changing their criterion regarding the qualification of crypto assets for VAT purposes, bringing it into line with CJEU case law.

At first, the STA concluded that the transfer of crypto assets was subject to but exempt from VAT arguing that 'bitcoins act as a means of payment and, due to their very features, they should be included in the concept of "other bills of exchange"'.[6] Therefore, the STA understood that the exemption provided in the Spanish VAT Law for transactions with bills of exchange.[7]

Nevertheless, in October 2015, the CJEU handed down a judgment on *David Hedqvist* (C-263/14) concluding that the transfer of crypto assets against other currencies was a 'supply of services for consideration' where both parties accept the swap of traditional currency for virtual currency and the miner collects a small margin for its work. The CJEU considered bitcoin as a 'virtual currency' with no other purpose than to be a means of payment. In this case, the CJEU established that these services should be subject to but exempt from VAT according to the exemption provided for transactions concerning currency, bank notes, and coins used as legal tender.

As a result of the CJEU judgment, the STA modified its criterion in binding rulings V1748-18, V2034-18, and V1274-20 and concluded that the exemption for transactions concerning currencies, regulated in Article 20.One.18, j) VAT Law, applied to bitcoins.

(b) *Are payments in crypto assets subject to withholding taxes?*

This depends on the nature of the underlying transaction. Generally, if it is subject to withholding tax, the payer will be obliged to make the relevant withholdings regardless of whether the payment is made in cash, in kind or through crypto assets.

6. STA binding rulings V1028.15, V1029-15, V2846-15.
7. Value Added Tax Law 37/1992, of 28 Dec. 1992, Article 20.One.18. h) and i).

(c) Does payment of compensation in crypto assets give rise to payroll tax consequences?

As previously mentioned in section 1.1.2(e), crypto assets received by employees must be considered as payments in kind, quantified at the market value of the crypto asset.

(d) Do transactions with crypto assets trigger any transfer taxes?

Transactions with crypto assets do not necessarily trigger transfer taxes. Rather, the application of these taxes depends on the nature of the underlying transaction itself, regardless of whether the payment is made through crypto assets or in other currencies.

As for the transfer of crypto assets itself:

- If made by entities or individuals carrying out a business activity (deemed to be employers or professionals for VAT purposes), the transfer would be subject to but exempt from VAT.
- If made by non-merchants, and following the CJEU interpretation, according to which crypto assets are 'virtual currencies' with no other purpose than to be a means of payment, it could be argued that the transaction is subject to but exempt from transfer tax since the payment of crypto assets would constitute the price of goods or the payment for personal services[8].

(e) Are firms operating in the crypto space subject to digital service taxes?

Digital service tax in Spain is undergoing review by Parliament and has not been approved yet.

(f) Are crypto assets subject to gift, inheritance, estate, or wealth taxes?

Crypto assets received by individuals as a result of a gift or an inheritance would be subject to inheritance and gift tax. The taxable base would generally be the market value of the crypto assets, according to Article 9.b) of Inheritance and Gift Tax Law, regardless of subsequent reductions and deductions that may apply depending on the autonomous region.

Crypto assets received by entities would be subject to CIT and taxed at the general 25% rate.

Inter vivos gifts may also trigger a capital gain or loss for the donor if the market value of the crypto asset is higher than its acquisition cost. The capital gain, if any, would be subject to the special PIT rates (19%–23%).

8. Legislative Royal Decree 1/1993, of 24 Sep. 1993, Article 45.1.B.4 of the ITP-AJD Law, approving the Revised Transfer and Stamp Tax Law.

The Spanish wealth tax depends on the autonomous region of the taxpayer. Taxpayers who are obliged to pay this tax will have to report their crypto assets portfolio annually. The STA stated in binding ruling V0590-18 that crypto assets must be reported for wealth tax purposes as if they were investments in foreign currency (i.e., at their market value expressed in Euro on 31 December).

(g) Are crypto assets subject to exit tax?

Spanish exit tax is charged on unrealized gains on units or shares held in, among others, entities or collective investment institutions when taxpayers change their tax residence, in accordance with Article 95 *bis* of the PIT Law.

The STA confirmed in binding ruling V1149-18 that bitcoins and Iota are not included within the scope of exit tax since they are considered as intangible assets and, in no case, shares or units representing equity. The consequences for other crypto assets should be the same as long as their nature is similar to bitcoins and Iota.

(h) Can mining trigger gambling tax?

Gambling tax is levied on the holding or organizing of competitions, contests, games, bets, or raffles in which money or other valuable goods are risked. Therefore, it involves a certain component of randomness, chance, or luck. Although the STA have not issued a binding ruling in this regard, we understand that mining would trigger gambling tax if it involved holding or organizing competitions, contests, games, bets, or raffles in the specific sense of its regulations. Gambling tax rate varies depending on the specific gambling activity that is being carried out and ranges from 15% to 25%. Taxable base also depends on the kind of activity carried out: for most activities, the taxable base will be the income received due to the people's participation in the game, while for random combinations, the taxable base will be the value of prizes or advantages offered to contestants.

1.1.4 Compliance and Documentation Obligations

(a) What documentation requirements exist for taxpayers regarding crypto assets and are there best practices in recordkeeping to support representations made in tax returns?

Spanish domestic tax law does not provide for any specific formal obligation regarding the ownership or trade of crypto assets. However, general formal obligations will apply for taxpayers holding crypto assets as merchants. In this regard, Article 29 of the General Tax Law establishes that these taxpayers must keep a record of their assets: having accounting books and keeping them for a potential tax inspection. In this regard, it will be important to record crypto assets in an appropriate way in the accounting books and value them using the correct criteria.

(b) *What is the evidentiary burden of supporting tax positions when a digital wallet address is lost or shared with other persons?*

As previously explained in section 1.1.2(g), the loss or theft of bitcoins will only be recognized for legal effects when the credit is final or declared irrecoverable by a court.

(c) *Are crypto asset exchanges and wallet providers subject to reporting obligations?*

Under Spanish tax law, there is no specific reporting obligation for wallet providers to inform about crypto asset exchanges occurred in their platforms. Nevertheless, the STA can require employers and parties connected to a taxpayer to provide specific information if necessary.

(d) *Are taxpayers holding crypto assets subject to reporting obligations apart from the filing of income tax/capital gains tax returns?*

Spanish taxpayers must inform about the ownership of certain assets or accounts held abroad. In particular, taxpayers must declare: (i) bank accounts in financial institutions, (ii) securities, assets, or titles representing share capital or equity of all types of entities, and (iii) real estate, when their value is higher than EUR 50,000 (this threshold is computed for each category). This information must be reported to the STA through tax Form 720. This form must also be filed in subsequent FYs when the value of the assets varies by more than EUR 20,000 from one fiscal year to the next.

The STA stated in binding ruling V1149-18 that bitcoins and iota cannot be considered as participation shares, or securities of any entity. Thus, in principle crypto assets (including *security* and *utility tokens*) should not be included in the scope of this information obligation. Nevertheless, the Spanish Draft Law on Prevention and Fight against Tax Fraud does envisage the inclusion of a new category to declare in tax Form 720 'crypto assets located in foreign territory' along with other information obligations regarding crypto assets. These measures have not been approved yet.

(e) *Are crypto asset exchanges and wallet providers subject to CRS/FATCA reporting?*

The Spanish authorities have implemented the CRS reporting obligations in Spanish tax legislation with few changes, i.e., the regulation and content of CRS reporting (tax Form 289) is a direct implementation of the OECD guidelines with no further development.

On the other hand, regarding FATCA reporting (tax Form 290), unless crypto asset exchange houses and virtual wallets start to be legally considered as financial institutions and financial accounts, respectively, no obligation should arise.

1.1.5 *Civil and Criminal Tax Enforcement*

(a) *What powers do the tax authorities have to compel the disclosure of information by third parties, such as exchanges or wallet providers, and have these been used in the past?*

As mentioned in section 1.1.4(c), Article 93 of the General Tax Law establishes the obligation for taxpayers to provide information to the STA regarding other taxpayers with whom they have a professional, economic, or financial relationship.

As already mentioned, since 2017 the STA have been publishing their concerns regarding blockchain and virtual money in their Annual Tax Control Plans. The STA have already started requesting information about these transactions from brokerage platforms, exchange houses and all kinds of intermediaries dealing in crypto assets that perform their activities in Spain.

(b) *What measures have the tax authorities undertaken in the past to ensure crypto tax compliance?*

During 2019, based on the information collected through information requests, the STA started sending warning alerts to certain taxpayers as a reminder to include in their PIT returns the capital gains or income that they may have obtained from transactions with crypto assets.

Given the STA's focus on risks derived from blockchain and crypto assets, in the years to come, there is likely to be a big increase in information requests and the implementation of new control measures.

(c) *Are the tax authorities cooperating with tax authorities in other jurisdictions on enforcement?*

Spain has concluded double tax treaties and numerous information exchange agreements with many countries. Available information is shared between different jurisdictions.

Switzerland

Nils Harbeke

1. COUNTRY GUIDES

1.1 Switzerland

1.1.1 Applicable Tax Law, Guidance, and Case Law

(a) Which laws, regulations, and other administrative guidance exist dealing with crypto assets?

Switzerland is a tax ruling jurisdiction. This means that explicit Swiss tax legislation would typically cover only the general principles. While administrative guidelines issued by the Swiss tax authorities have a higher level of detail, such guidelines will often also still be principle-based. In Switzerland, however, it is possible and common practice to file advance private tax ruling requests. A tax ruling confirmation will be binding on the Swiss tax authorities on the basis of the facts presented in the ruling request. Neither tax ruling requests nor tax ruling responses are made public.

Swiss tax laws do not expressly mention crypto assets in general or bitcoins in particular. In terms of administrative guidance, the Swiss Federal Tax Administration (FTA) has issued guidelines on cryptocurrencies addressing (corporate) income tax, wealth tax, withholding tax, and stamp tax issues. In addition, the FTA's VAT guidelines address certain tax aspects relating to crypto assets.

(b) Which court cases exist dealing with crypto assets?

In Switzerland there are currently no published court cases dealing with tax aspects of crypto assets. Because crypto assets bring up new tax issues, court cases may, however, be expected in the future.

1.1.2 *Income and Capital Gains Taxes*

(a) *How are crypto assets classified for income and capital gains tax purposes?*

For purposes of Swiss income and capital gains taxation, crypto assets (including cryptocurrencies) are not classed as domestic legal tender. Swiss tax law distinguishes between private assets and business assets. Capital gains on (movable) private assets are tax-exempt. Capital gains on business assets are subject to (corporate) income tax at the standard tax rates. For movable assets, the tax treatment is the same regardless of the type of asset (i.e., regardless of the classification of the asset as, for example, a currency or an intangible asset). However, if the asset is held as a business asset, the classification of the asset can be relevant for valuation purposes.

An individual can have both private assets and/or business assets. An individual's crypto assets will be considered private assets unless the assets are primarily used for the purposes of a business run by that individual, or the individual is considered a 'professional securities trader' as defined in Swiss tax practice.

Assets held by legal entities will be characterised as business assets. As a rule, the same will usually hold true for assets held by partnerships, notwithstanding partnerships being treated transparent for purposes of Swiss income taxation. Taxation of businesses follows statutory accounting. Crypto assets can qualify as fixed assets or as current assets, and crypto assets may qualify as intangible assets or as other kinds of assets. Valuation rules applying to fixed assets may differ from valuation rules applying to current assets, and valuation rules applying to intangible assets may differ from valuation rules applying to other kinds of assets.

(b) *What are the income/capital gains tax consequences of selling crypto assets against fiat currency?*

Capital gains on (movable) private assets are tax-exempt.

Capital gains on business assets are subject to (corporate) income tax at the standard tax rates. Taxable capital gains are determined on the basis of the Swiss statutory stand-alone accounts of the business and are taxed as part of the overall annual profit (i.e., no separate taxation of capital gains and no separate tax rates for capital gains).

For individuals, the federal and, in general, the cantonal rates are progressive. The federal rate is between 0% and 11.5%, and the cantonal rate ranges between 0% and about 34.5%.

For corporations, the federal corporate income tax rate is 7.83% of profits before tax. Cantonal rates vary and are often flat. The maximum combined (federal and cantonal) effective tax burden varies between approx. 11.7% and 22% of profits before taxes.

(c) What are the income/capital gains tax consequences of exchanging crypto assets against other crypto assets?

The same principles of taxation apply as those applicable when selling crypto assets against fiat currency. As in the case of selling crypto assets against fiat currency, the exchange of one crypto asset against another crypto asset also constitutes realization of income. Such an exchange of assets involves both an acquisition and a disposal. The sales value of the asset disposed of constitutes the acquisition cost of the asset acquired. For tax purposes, valuation relies on statutory accounting (i.e., no separate tax accounting).

(d) If a distinction is made between business assets and non-business assets, when does trading in crypto assets lead to a trade or business?

Assets held by partnerships or legal entities will be characterized as business assets. Taxation of a business follows statutory accounting requirements.

An individual can have both private assets and/or business assets. An individual's crypto assets will be considered private assets unless the assets are primarily used for the purposes of a business run by that individual, or the individual is considered a 'professional securities trader' as defined in Swiss tax practice.

Assets primarily used for the purposes of a business run by the individual need to be recorded as business assets either under statutory accounting rules or else in separate documentation maintained for tax purposes.

As regards the notion of a 'professional securities trading', the Swiss tax authorities have issued guidance setting out safe harbour thresholds (with traditional securities trading in mind). In terms of a safe harbour rule, an individual will not be considered a 'professional securities trader' provided all the following criteria are met:

- the assets sold have been held for at least six months;
- the total transaction volume (i.e., the sum of all purchase price payments and sales proceeds) in the calendar year does not exceed five times the total value of relevant assets held at the beginning of the year;
- it is not necessary for the individual to rely on capital gains to cover personal living expenses or compensate for loss of other income items; the tax authorities will usually consider this test to be met if the capital gains realized account for less than 50% of the net income in the calendar year;
- the individual either does not use any debt at all to fund personal investments, or the taxable income from investments (e.g., interest, dividends) is more than the pro-rata interest expense on debt (note: this test was introduced before the current low interest/negative interest environment emerged); and
- if derivatives are used, this is only done to hedge the individual's other assets.

(e) What are the income/capital gains tax consequences for an employee receiving wages or salaries in crypto assets?

If an employee receives wages or salaries in crypto assets, the employee realizes taxable income from employment. This employment income is deemed realized at the point in time at which the crypto assets are received (as opposed to the point in time of the exchange of such crypto assets into fiat currency).

For the employer, the value of the crypto assets given to the employee constitutes cost of employment and is therefore a deductible business expense. As a consequence, the employer should not experience a taxable exchange.

Income tax owed by the employee is levied in the form of wage source tax to be withheld by the employer (only) if:

- the employer is an entity in Switzerland (including a Swiss permanent establishment) and the employee is subject to taxation as a non-resident in Switzerland (i.e., as opposed to taxation as a resident in Switzerland); or
- the employee holds neither Swiss citizenship nor a Swiss permanent-residence permit type 'C' and is not married to a person holding either Swiss citizenship or a Swiss permanent-residence permit type 'C'.

Income tax (including wage source tax to be withheld by the employer) must be paid to the tax authorities in fiat currency (as opposed to cryptocurrency), at the times applicable under local legislation for (wage source) tax payment.

(f) What are the income/capital gains tax consequences for a merchant receiving payment in crypto assets?

If a merchant receives payment in crypto assets, the merchant realizes taxable income. By default, the merchant's taxable income should equal the fair market value of the merchant's goods or services, unless a different value can be established as being the market value of the crypto assets. Once the merchant exchanges the crypto assets, another taxable transaction will occur.

(g) What are the income/capital gains tax consequences of a loss of crypto assets?

Swiss tax law distinguishes between private assets and business assets. A loss of a private asset (including e.g., misplacing or theft) is not tax deductible, while a loss of a business asset is deductible (at the lost asset's fair value or, if different, tax value).

(h) *What are the income/capital gains tax consequences of a loss in value of crypto assets?*

Swiss tax law distinguishes between private assets and business assets. A loss in value of a private asset is not tax deductible. If a business asset loses value, then that asset (following statutory accounting rules, which dictate the applicable tax values) may (or must) be written down and the cost of amortization will be tax deductible.

(i) *What are the income/capital gains tax consequences of forks of crypto assets?*

The Swiss tax authorities' administrative guidance does not expressly address the tax treatment of forks. If the crypto assets are held as private assets (as opposed to business assets), a fork of the crypto assets should not be a taxable event. For crypto assets held as business assets, the general principles governing taxation in Switzerland allow arguments to claim that occurrence of the fork alone should not constitute a taxable event. Instead, the newly received crypto assets should inherit the tax values of the previous assets.

(j) *What are the income/capital gains tax consequences of airdrops of crypto assets and are the tax consequences different if the airdropped tokens are unwanted?*

For private individuals, Swiss tax law provides that 'any income' (with the exception of capital gains on private assets other than Swiss real property) is taxable income, regardless of the nature of the income. For a business, any income item that must be recognized as income under statutory accounting rules constitutes an income item for tax purposes. On this basis, airdrops of crypto assets will generally constitute taxable income. For private individuals, there are arguments to claim that airdrops of crypto assets may constitute a donation rather than income. This view would rely on the argument that the individual has not caused the airdrop. A donation received by a private individual in Switzerland (with few exceptions, e.g., in the canton of Ticino) is usually out of scope of Swiss taxation if the donor (i.e., the person or entity responsible for the airdrop to occur) is resident outside of Switzerland. If the donor is resident in Switzerland, then Swiss gift tax may apply (subject to the local tax legislation of the Swiss canton in which the donor is resident).

(k) *What are the income/capital gains tax consequences of (solo, pool, and cloud) mining?*

Partnerships or legal entities engaged in mining realize taxable income to the extent they receive benefits that must be recognized as income items under statutory accounting rules.

Individuals engaged in mining may be considered to perform a self-employed activity generating taxable income. In their assessment of the individual case, the Swiss tax authorities would check if the general criteria constituting a self-employed activity are met (systematic approach, offering on the market, own organization run at own risk). Whether or not a self-employed activity exists is, however, mainly relevant for social security purposes. Benefits received by an individual from mining should constitute 'income' in terms of Swiss income tax law and thus be taxable in any case. The reason is because under Swiss tax law generally any income of an individual is taxable, at tax rates not depending on the nature of the income, whereas social security charges (levied in addition to tax) vary depending on the characterization of the gainful activity performed by the individual.

(l) What are the income/capital gains tax consequences of staking crypto assets?

Partnerships or legal entities realize taxable income to the extent they receive benefits that must be recognized as income items under statutory accounting rules.

For private individuals, guidance issued by the Swiss VAT authorities provides for arguments to claim that staking does not involve a relevant level of gainful activity that would constitute a self-employed activity. As in the case of mining, the question of whether or not a self-employed activity exists is, however, mainly relevant for social security purposes. Benefits received by an individual from staking should constitute 'income' in terms of Swiss income tax law and thus be taxable in any case.

(m) What are the income/capital gains tax consequences of an indirect investment in crypto assets?

The same principles of taxation apply as those applicable to direct investments.

Income received from instruments held to create indirect exposure will be taxable. Private capital gains will be tax-exempt.

Thus, indirect (as opposed to direct) investment in crypto assets is not a means per se to escape income taxation. Income taxation may, however, be delayed or diluted. For example, financial instruments (e.g., structured products, investment fund units) may be accumulating or distributing and may be treated as fiscally transparent or opaque.

Legal entities other than (most) investment fund vehicles are taxed as separate entities (subject to the general anti-abuse test). For individuals, dividend income is taxable income (possibly taxed at a reduced rate, in the case of a qualifying shareholding quota) whereas a private capital gain on the shares is tax-exempt. Corporate shareholders may be able to get tax relief under the Swiss participation relief.

Legal entities with their statutory seat outside Switzerland are subject to Swiss corporate income taxation if they have a permanent establishment or their place of effective management in Switzerland.

(n) *How is income from crypto assets to be treated under double tax treaty law?*

Income items will need to be characterized according to the treaty rules, and then allocated to the contracting states for taxation. Use of hardware located in a specific jurisdiction may constitute a permanent establishment in that jurisdiction and thus trigger income allocation.

(o) *What are the income/capital gains tax consequences of selling crypto assets in an ICO/STO/IEO?*

For the issuer, the proceeds from the sale of crypto assets constitute income unless the asset sold is a debt instrument. At the same time, however, the issuer can defer the income if the issuer has accepted obligations with the asset sale that require funding or yet need to be fulfilled in order for the issuer to earn the proceeds from the asset sale. In such cases, it can be possible for the issuer to defer the income from the asset sale by treating the sales proceeds as customer prepayment or by setting aside a provision for anticipated project cost. With this approach, the issuer may be able to balance the total proceeds. Only under special circumstances, for example, in the case of non-tax-exempt foundations set up to serve a purpose in a commercial project, can the tax authorities tax the issuer on a minimum margin. Any return owed by the issuer to the investors is generally a tax-deductible cost for the issuer. Limitations and anti-avoidance rules may apply if investors are related parties (e.g., shareholders may be deemed to earn dividend income, thus preventing the company from deducting the payment as an expense item). Only to hold crypto assets should not make an investor a related party in this sense, regardless of the economic features of the crypto asset.

1.1.3 Other Taxes

(a) *What are the value added tax/sales tax consequences of selling crypto assets?*

Switzerland levies VAT on the supply of goods and services.

The use of payment tokens as a means of payment for a supply is treated the same as use of fiat currency. Thus, the transfer of the payment tokens to the supplier of the goods/services does not constitute a separate supply for VAT purposes. The situation is different for asset tokens and utility tokens. If asset tokens or utility tokens are used to pay for a supply, this constitutes a barter transaction and can trigger VAT.

For transactions in payment tokens (purchase or sale of payment tokens), a VAT exemption without input VAT credit applies. The VAT treatment of a sale of asset tokens or utility tokens will generally follow the VAT treatment (characterization of the underlying supply as supply of goods versus supply of services, place of supply rules, VAT exemptions) of a sale of the asset or use possibility incorporated by the token. VAT is triggered if prepayment is received (for a forthcoming supply that can already be determined) or else when the supply is made.

For ICOs/STOs/IEOs, or if crypto assets are used to pay an employee, the same principles apply (i.e., the VAT treatment of a sale of crypto assets will depend on the characterisation of the crypto assets sold or given to the employee).

(b) *Are payments in crypto assets subject to withholding taxes?*

There is no withholding tax that would apply specifically to payments in crypto assets. Where withholding tax applies to payments in fiat currency, similar payments made in crypto assets would equally be subject to withholding tax. In particular, salaries, dividends or interest can be liable for Swiss tax withholding. As a general rule, the crypto assets' fair value at the point in time the tax is triggered, and expressed in fiat currency, will determine the amount of withholding tax payable in fiat currency. Any withholding tax payment to the Swiss tax authorities will need to be made in fiat currency.

(c) *Does payment of compensation in crypto assets give rise to payroll tax consequences?*

Income tax owed by an employee is levied in the form of wage source tax to be withheld by the employer if:

- the employer is an entity in Switzerland (including a Swiss permanent establishment) and the employee is subject to taxation as a non-resident in Switzerland (i.e., as opposed to taxation as a resident in Switzerland); or
- the employee holds neither Swiss citizenship nor a Swiss permanent-residence permit type 'C' and is not married to a person holding either Swiss citizenship or a Swiss permanent-residence permit type 'C'.

If any of these situations applies, the employer owes wage source tax whether fiat currency or crypto assets are used to pay the employee. Any tax payment to the Swiss tax authorities will need to be made in fiat currency.

(d) *Do transactions with crypto assets trigger any transfer taxes?*

Transactions with crypto assets will usually be out of scope of Swiss transfer taxes.

If an asset token constitutes a debt instrument in the form of a 'bond-like' instrument as defined in the relevant guidelines issued by the Swiss Federal Tax Authorities, then secondary market transactions can trigger Swiss securities transfer tax if a Swiss securities dealer (as defined in Swiss tax law) is involved as a party or an intermediary in the transaction. Transfers of non-Swiss bonds (including 'bond-like' instruments) to a non-Swiss buyer or from a non-Swiss seller are exempt (then 50% of the tax will not be levied, while another 50% charge continues to apply, unless the other party is also an exempt investor).

Crypto assets other than asset tokens constituting a debt instrument in the form of a 'bond-like instrument', however, are generally not taxable securities unless the crypto asset references any other specific taxable security.

A Swiss 'securities dealer' may be, e.g., a domestic bank, Swiss securities broker, or a Swiss corporation holding balance sheet assets in taxable securities in excess of CHF 10 million. The tax is owed by the Swiss securities dealer. If the Swiss securities dealer acts as an agent or on behalf of a customer, market practice is such that the Swiss securities dealer charges the tax to the customer. The tax is levied on the consideration agreed by the parties for the transfer of the securities. If the consideration is agreed to be made in crypto assets, then the crypto assets' fair value, expressed in fiat currency, will be the tax base. For securities issued by a Swiss issuer, the tax rate is 0.15%. For securities issued by a non-Swiss issuer, the tax rate is 0.3%.

Sales of crypto assets by the direct shareholder to the company in exchange for consideration below market value can constitute a 'hidden contribution' subject to a 1% Swiss share issuance stamp duty (the tax applies irrespective of the fact that no shares are actually issued).

(e) *Are firms operating in the crypto space subject to digital service taxes?*

In Switzerland, there is currently no digital service tax.

The Swiss government has recently set up a working group to come up with considerations as to how Switzerland shall respond to the pending 'OECD Pillar 1' proposal on taxation of the 'digital economy'. Thus, while so far in Switzerland there is no 'digital services' tax, it is possible that in the future Swiss tax legislation providing for 'market nexus'-based taxation is introduced.

(f) *Are crypto assets subject to gift, inheritance, estate, or wealth taxes?*

Provided Swiss gift, inheritance, estate, or wealth taxes are triggered according to the general principles of taxation, these taxes also capture crypto assets. As a general rule, the tax base is the fair value of the taxable asset at the point in time tax is triggered.

(g) *Are crypto assets subject to exit tax?*

In Switzerland, exit tax legislation applies only to corporate entities subject to corporate income tax. In particular, private individuals are not subject to exit taxation in Switzerland.

Provided exit taxation is triggered, the tax also captures crypto assets.

(h) Can mining trigger gambling tax?

No, only (licensed) gambling houses are subject to Swiss gambling tax.

1.1.4 Compliance and Documentation Obligations

(a) What documentation requirements exist for taxpayers regarding crypto assets and are there best practices in recordkeeping to support representations made in tax returns?

In Switzerland, there are no special documentation requirements for taxpayers holding crypto assets. Thus, such taxpayers must comply with the general documentation requirements. Taxpayers running a business are required to maintain books under statutory accounting rules (also used for taxation) or (if statutory accounting rules do not apply) to keep other records for tax purposes.

(b) What is the evidentiary burden of supporting tax positions when a digital wallet address is lost or shared with other persons?

As a starting point, the taxpayer is obliged to declare all taxable positions in the tax return and to provide all information that the tax authorities may reasonably request to audit the taxpayer. If relevant facts remain unclear or unknown, the tax authorities may make a reasonable estimate. The tax authorities must not, however, simply assume the existence of taxable positions. If the taxpayer has fulfilled the declaration/information obligations, the burden of proof for taxable positions yet unclear lies with the tax authorities. If it is known, or likely, that a digital wallet existed and it is known what positions (broadly) were (likely) held in the wallet, then, e.g., based on general market development and information from other taxpayers, the tax authorities may make a reasonable estimate of taxable positions in that wallet. If, however, access to the wallet is permanently lost so that the taxpayer has factually lost the assets in the wallet, then it should not be possible any more to fiscally impute taxable wallet positions on the taxpayer. The burden of proof for circumstances reducing the tax burden is with the taxpayer. To show that access to the wallet is permanently lost, the taxpayer can use/offer any means of information, provided the information presented supports the taxpayer's position and can be verified by the tax authorities.

(c) Are crypto asset exchanges and wallet providers subject to reporting obligations?

Under Swiss domestic tax law, neither crypto asset exchanges nor wallet providers are subject to any special obligations vis-à-vis the tax authorities to report crypto positions of their customers.

(d) *Are taxpayers holding crypto assets subject to reporting obligations apart from the filing of income tax/capital gains tax returns?*

Apart from the filing of income (and wealth) tax returns, Swiss tax law does not require taxpayers holding crypto assets to report their assets/income items to the tax authorities.

(e) *Are crypto asset exchanges and wallet providers subject to CRS/FATCA reporting?*

Whether or not an asset qualifies as an asset liable for automated reporting under treaty law (e.g., as a 'financial asset') will be determined primarily by the provisions of the applicable treaty, rather than executing Swiss domestic law. In the area of CRS/FATCA, it should be fair to say that Switzerland is reluctant to establish a domestic practice on its own, but places importance on duly considering the views and reasonable expectations of the treaty counterparty concerned, and in any case will act in line with applicable international standards.

1.1.5 *Civil and Criminal Tax Enforcement*

(a) *What powers do the tax authorities have to compel the disclosure of information by third parties, such as exchanges or wallet providers, and have these been used in the past?*

Third-party providers may be obliged to issue statements to their customers (as opposed to the tax authorities) confirming information relevant for taxation. Only in qualifying cases (e.g., where an income item is subject to withholding tax, or where legal title to an asset is held by a third party together with the taxpayer and so on) do the Swiss tax authorities have the possibility to request information directly from third-party providers. In the tax assessment of a taxpayer, the Swiss tax authorities may, however, also use information found in a tax audit of a third party.

(b) *What measures have the tax authorities undertaken in the past to ensure crypto tax compliance?*

On various occasions (e.g., at seminars) representatives of the tax authorities have addressed compliance issues with a particular focus on crypto assets. It is also possible to approach the tax authorities with an advance private tax ruling request (e.g., for crypto-based employee benefit plans).

So far, the Swiss tax authorities have not started audit or enforcement activities specifically focussing on tax issues related to crypto assets. Tax audits, however, are not uncommon in Switzerland, and the tax authorities look at crypto assets as part of their standard audit procedures.

(c) Are the tax authorities cooperating with tax authorities in other jurisdictions on enforcement?

As part of its treaty policy, Switzerland follows the Article 26 OECD-MC exchange of information standard. Exchange of information is different from, and does not include, debt enforcement (e.g., seizure of assets). While under double tax treaty law tax authorities abroad can request information from the Swiss tax authorities, tax authorities abroad are generally not able to enforce tax debts in Switzerland.

The Netherlands

Pepijn Pinkse & Margriet Lukkien

1. COUNTRY GUIDES

1.1 The Netherlands

1.1.1 Applicable Tax Law, Guidance, and Case Law

(a) Which laws, regulations, and other administrative guidance exist dealing with crypto assets?

There are no tax laws specifically aimed at crypto assets. All regular tax laws that are applicable to individuals and companies apply to crypto assets to the extent possible. This includes – among others – the Corporation Income Tax Act 1969,[1] the Income Tax Act 2001,[2] the Dividend Withholding Tax Act 1965,[3] Turnover Tax Act 1968,[4] Inheritance Tax Act 1956,[5] Wage Tax Act 1964[6] and all decrees and regulations pertaining to these tax acts.

To date the Dutch Government only published one single document – a letter – to shed some light on its views on the taxation of crypto assets.[7] This letter however only deals with cryptocurrency (like bitcoin) and does not distinguish token-style crypto assets such as utility tokens and security tokens.

1. *Wet op de vennootschapsbelasting 1969.*
2. *Wet inkomstenbelasting 2001.*
3. *Wet op* de *dividendbelasting 1965.*
4. *Wet op de omzetbelasting 1968.*
5. *Successiewet 1956.*
6. *Wet op de loonbelasting 1964.*
7. Letter of the State Secretary of Finance dated 28 May 2018 addressed to the permanent commission of finance of the senate.

(b) *Which court cases exist dealing with crypto assets?*

There are currently no Dutch court cases dealing with crypto assets from a corporate or personal income tax perspective. There is however a civil law lower court case dealing with the qualification of bitcoins which can be considered relevant for the Dutch tax treatment of crypto assets.[8] The lower court held that bitcoins do not qualify as 'money' within the meaning of the Dutch Civil Code. The court found however that this may be the case in the future, if bitcoins progress towards a tolerated means of regular payment. However, as the Dutch Government has indicated that it does not regard bitcoins as lawful currency, this is currently not the case. The Dutch State Secretary concurs with this qualification for Dutch tax purposes.[9]

From a VAT perspective there is a court case which is related to crypto assets. In a Dutch court ruling dated 22 February 2019[10] the Dutch VAT treatment of the provider of an e-wallet was discussed. In that case, the claimant exploited a mobile phone application – the e-wallet – which enabled its users to purchase electronic money that could then be used to make payments. The claimant was not licensed for the handling of the electronic payments and thus outsourced this activity to another party. The court ruled that the claimant was entitled to VAT recovery as its services could not be considered to be an activity that falls within the scope of a (financial) exemption for VAT purposes.

Furthermore, there is currently a Dutch lower court case regarding a bitcoin mining company pending in which the lower court has asked prejudicial questions to the Dutch Supreme Court regarding the VAT implications of the fact that the mining company cannot identify (the residence country of) its customers.

1.1.2 *Income and Capital Gains Taxes*

(a) *How are crypto assets classified for income and capital gains tax purposes?*

In the Netherlands, there are no specific tax laws on the qualification and taxation of crypto assets. The tax treatment is based on general principles and guidance issued by the Dutch tax authorities. For purposes of applying the various Dutch tax laws, crypto assets should be broken down roughly into three categories: cryptocurrencies, security tokens, and utility tokens. Whether a specific crypto asset qualifies for any of these categories will strongly depend on the terms and conditions pertaining to the crypto asset.

Broadly speaking, cryptocurrencies can be defined as crypto assets which do not establish any kind of relationship between the issuer and the holder. Although cryptocurrencies are a means of payment, they are not formally treated as 'money' or

8. *Rechtbank Overijssel* 14 May 2014, ECLI:NL:RBOVE:2014:2667.
9. Letter of the State Secretary of Finance dated 28 May 2018 addressed to the permanent commission of finance of the senate.
10. *Rechtbank Noord-Holland* 22 Feb. 2019, EU:NL:RBNHO:2019:1290.

liquid assets in the Netherlands. This position has explicitly been taken by the Dutch Minister of Finance and the Dutch National Bank.[11] Cryptocurrencies are treated as (current) tangible assets for Dutch tax purposes.

Utility tokens could roughly be defined as crypto assets which establish a relationship between the issuer and the holder, resulting in non-monetary obligations between them. The holder of the utility token may for example request a service from the issuer. Another way of thinking of a utility token is of a 'coupon' which is only valuable within the context of the relevant company, and gives certain rights to the holder. No specific rules exist for the Dutch tax treatment of such tokens. This means the existing tax law framework has to be applied. In general it can be expected that for the issuer, payments received for utility tokens can be qualified as advance payments for Dutch tax purposes. For the holder, utility tokens would likely be treated as (current) assets.

Security tokens can be used to raise money from capital markets from various investors. These tokens may generally be qualified as equity or debt, depending on the characteristics of the token.[12] It can generally be stated that if a token contains a repayment obligation, it could be considered as debt for Dutch corporate law purposes. However, Dutch tax law may still qualify such debt instruments as equity for Dutch tax purposes. Dutch Supreme Court case law prescribes three specific cases in which a repayment obligation formally exists, but is disregarded for tax purposes resulting in an equity qualification. Most notably this is the case if a debt instrument has a profit-dependent interest rate, no maturity date or a maturity date after more than fifty years and is junior to all other debt. The other two cases are the so-called sham loan (equity is actually intended) and the so-called bottomless pit loan (it is immediately apparent that no repayment will ever take place). In such cases Dutch tax law recharacterizes such corporate law debt instruments into equity. Conversely, if no repayment obligation is included in the terms of the security token, it is likely qualified as equity for both Dutch corporate and tax law purposes.

(b) What are the income/capital gains tax consequences of selling crypto assets against fiat currency?

The Dutch tax consequences vary significantly depending on whether the crypto assets are sold by an individual or a corporate entity. It is noted that the tax consequences described in this chapter solely relate to Dutch tax resident individuals and corporate entities and not to individuals and companies resident outside of the Netherlands.[13]

11. Letter of the Minister of Finance dated 8 Mar. 2018 addressed to the Dutch parliament.
12. For the qualification Dutch law only looks at the characteristics of the token itself, not at the underlying assets.
13. As a general comment, foreign tax resident individuals may be subject to personal income tax in the Netherlands in various circumstances; most commonly, if they own real estate in the Netherlands, operate a business in the Netherlands, or hold an interest of 5% or more in a Dutch tax resident company. Foreign tax resident companies may be subject to corporate income tax in the Netherlands, for example, if they operate a business in the Netherlands through a

Individuals may be subject to personal income tax when selling crypto assets. The effective tax rate varies depending on the facts and circumstances in relation to the crypto assets sale. In most cases the crypto assets will be taxed on a net wealth basis, taking into account the net value of all relevant assets of an individual on 1 January of a year. The effective tax rate varies between approximately 0.54% and 1.6% (2020). This means that the actual profits derived from the sale of crypto assets are not taxed.

However, crypto assets which can be attributed to a so-called source of income may be taxed progressively up to 49.50% (2020) as 'miscellaneous income'. A source of income is considered present if an individual enters into economic transactions and strives to obtain a profit which can reasonably be expected. Whether a source of income is present depends on the facts and circumstances of a specific case. However, it can be noted that speculation is normally not seen as a reasonable expectation of profit.

If crypto assets can be attributed to a source of income, and in addition, the individual qualifies as an entrepreneur carrying out a business enterprise, general tax incentives may apply, effectively lowering the progressive tax rate below 49.50% (2020).[14] A business enterprise is defined as a sustainable organization of capital and labour, which aims at realizing a profit by entering into economic transactions and such profit can be reasonably expected. Whether individuals can be seen to carry out a business enterprise depends on the facts and circumstances and as such is to a certain extent a grey area.

For individuals, there is another category of taxation in which crypto assets could fall. In the rare case an individual holds (security) tokens which can be regarded as profit-sharing certificates, which entitle such an individual to 5% or more of the annual profit of the issuing company, crypto assets can qualify as a so-called substantial interest. A substantial interest is taxed with 26.25% (2020) personal income tax at the time a gain is realised or if the issuer makes payments to the holder, i.e., profit appropriation. The gain is calculated at the difference between the transfer price and the cost price. Since it is such a rare situation that crypto assets constitute a substantial interest, we will not address this in the rest of this chapter.

Conversely, a corporate entity is deemed to carry out a business enterprise with all its assets by way of fiction.[15] Crypto assets therefore are considered part of the business enterprise of the corporate entity (irrespective of the business it operates). This means that in principle gains realised upon sale are taxed and losses are tax deductible. The corporate income tax rate is 25% (2020, as of 2021 expected to be

permanent establishment, if they own real estate in the Netherlands, or if they own an interest of 5% or more in a Dutch resident company under specific circumstances.

14. These are a broad range of incentives, such as a lump sum deduction, investment allowances, depreciation allowances, R&D deductions, and so on. These incentives are of a general nature and hence not specifically linked to crypto assets.
15. In very specific circumstances the tax authorities may dispute whether certain assets and results belong with the corporate entity, or should be allocated to the shareholder(s). This predominantly relates to assets held for the personal motives of the shareholder (e.g., racing horses, private jets).

lowered to 21.7%), with a lower rate of 16.5% (2020, expected to be lowered to 15% in 2021) for the first EUR 200,000 of profit.

The profit resulting from the sale of crypto assets for both corporate entities and individuals generating business income/miscellaneous income is calculated by the fair market value (typically the sale price) minus the book value. As crypto assets are generally considered current assets or inventory, they are ordinarily valued at cost price or lower market value, however other valuation methods may be acceptable as well. As taxpayers may hold large amounts of crypto assets, it could be cumbersome to record the cost prices of all crypto assets. In some cases an average cost price may be calculated. If cost prices can be recorded accurately, upon sale of crypto assets methods such as first in, first out (FIFO) or last in, first out (LIFO) could be applicable.

In very specific circumstances a corporate entity may apply an exemption to gains realised upon the sale of security tokens. This would be the case if a token holder owns an interest of 5% or more in the nominal capital of the issuer (i.e., of the regular shares) and the security token gives a profit entitlement mirroring it to a profit-sharing certificate.

For the tax treatment of both corporate entities and individuals it is in any case irrelevant whether the consideration for the sale is in cash (fiat currency) or in kind (such as other crypto assets).

(c) What are the income/capital gains tax consequences of exchanging crypto assets against other crypto assets?

Reference can be made to section 1.1.2(b), above. In principle it is irrelevant whether a consideration in cash or in kind (such as other crypto assets) is received. The difference between the fair market value (typically the sales price) and the book value will be treated as taxable profit for corporate income tax purposes (for corporate entities) and personal income tax purposes (for individuals, however please note the comments in section 1.1.2(b)).

The most difficult issue when exchanging crypto assets for other crypto assets is determining the fair market value of the consideration. Because taxpayers file their tax return in euros,[16] the fair market value of the consideration (the crypto assets received) needs to be calculated in euros on the day of the exchange. Determining the correct conversion rate may be difficult as trading platforms may offer crypto assets at (slightly) different prices. The Dutch Government takes the position that, as there are currently no official guidelines for determining the correct exchange rate, the exchange rate of the trading platform executing the transaction should be used.[17] This will be the book value of the newly obtained crypto assets.

16. Under certain conditions, a functional currency request can be approved by the Dutch tax authorities, allowing a taxpayer to calculate its taxes in a fiat currency other than the euro. Please note however that the actual amount of tax due is always in euro.
17. Letter of the State Secretary of Finance dated 28 May 2018 addressed to the permanent commission of finance of the senate.

(d) If a distinction is made between business assets and non-business assets, when does trading in crypto assets lead to a trade or business?

As mentioned under section 1.1.2(b), above, this is only relevant for individuals as corporate entities are deemed to carry out a business enterprise with all their assets by way of fiction. For individuals this is a grey area. Non-business assets are only taxed on a net wealth basis against an effective tax rate which varies between approximately 0.54% and 1.6% (2020). Business assets (or assets qualifying as a source of miscellaneous income, see the last paragraph of this section) are taxed against a progressive tax rate up to 49.50% (2020). Crypto assets qualify as business assets if they can be allocated to a sustainable organization of capital and labour, which aims at realizing a profit by entering into economic transactions and such profit can be reasonably expected. In practice, the Dutch tax authorities look at, for example, the labour intensity, number of customers, risks, liability for debts, capital, and presentation. General tax incentives are available to individuals carrying out a business enterprise as an entrepreneur (effectively lowering the tax rate).[18]

Income from crypto assets can also be qualified as income from pseudo business assets, being assets which generate so-called miscellaneous income. Income from crypto assets can fall into this category if an individual participates in economic transactions and can expect a profit of these transactions. Miscellaneous income is taxed against the progressive tax rate up to 49.50% (2020). However, the tax incentives applying to entrepreneurs carrying out a business enterprise will not apply.

(e) What are the income/capital gains tax consequences for an employee receiving wages or salaries in crypto assets?

It has been specifically mentioned by the Dutch Government in the letter[19] regarding crypto assets that if wages are paid out in crypto assets, this will be treated as wages in kind. Wage tax should be withheld by the employer on the fair market value in euro on the day the wage is received.

(f) What are the income/capital gains tax consequences for a merchant receiving payment in crypto assets?

The tax consequences will depend on whether the merchant carries out a business enterprise as an individual or through a corporate entity. In both cases however, the payment will be recorded as a regular payment in kind of which the fair market value calculated in euro will be counted as income for purposes of either personal income tax (for individuals) or corporate income tax (for corporate entities). To the extent a

18. These are a broad range of incentives such as a lump sum deduction, investment allowances, depreciation allowances, R&D deductions, and so on. These incentives are of a general nature and hence not specifically linked to crypto assets.
19. Letter of the State Secretary of Finance dated 28 May 2018 addressed to the permanent commission of finance of the senate.

taxable profit is realised over a tax year, the individual will be taxed progressively up to 49.50% (2020) and a corporate entity between 16.5% and 25% (2020, expected to be lowered to 15% and 21.7% in 2021).

(g) *What are the income/capital gains tax consequences of a loss of crypto assets?*

The Dutch tax consequences vary significantly depending on whether the crypto assets are lost by a corporate entity or an individual, and whether the crypto assets can be attributed to a business enterprise/miscellaneous income of an individual.

For individuals whose crypto assets do not qualify as business assets or as assets generating so-called miscellaneous income, the loss of crypto assets – meaning the loss of the private key associated with an address at which crypto assets are stored – will not be tax deductible for personal income tax purposes. However, the loss will decrease the total net wealth position of that individual, which is taxed with personal income tax at an effective rate between approximately 0.54% and 1.6% (2020).

For individuals whose crypto assets qualify as part of their business enterprise or miscellaneous income, a loss of their crypto assets may be tax deductible.

For corporate entities, a loss of crypto assets is in principle tax deductible. However, if the crypto assets fall under a specific exemption[20] a loss is not deductible (however, such an exemption will likely not apply). Refer to section 1.1.2(b), above.

(h) *What are the income/capital gains tax consequences of a loss in value of crypto assets?*

For individuals whose crypto assets do not qualify as business assets or as assets generating so-called miscellaneous income, a loss will not be tax deductible for personal income tax purposes. However, a decrease in value of the crypto assets will count towards the total net wealth, taxed with personal income tax at an effective rate between approximately 0.54% and 1.6% (2020).

For individuals whose crypto assets qualify as part of their business enterprise or miscellaneous income, a loss in value of crypto assets upon disposal is in principle tax deductible.

For corporate entities a loss in value of crypto assets upon disposal is in principle tax deductible. However, if crypto assets fall under a specific exemption[21] a loss is not deductible (and a gain not taxed). Refer to section 1.1.2(b), above.

If a loss in value occurs during the time an individual or corporate entity holds the crypto asset, the loss may not be taken into account in all circumstances. Whether a loss can be taken into account is governed by the Dutch principle of sound business practice. This principle allows various valuation methods. Once a method is chosen it

20. This regards the Dutch participation exemption which may apply to shareholdings of 5% or more in the nominal capital of a company, under certain conditions.
21. This regards the Dutch participation exemption which may apply to shareholdings of 5% or more in the nominal capital of a company, under certain conditions.

should be applied consistently. If crypto assets are valued at cost price or lower market value, a loss can be taken into account. If for example market value is elected, losses and gains will impact the taxable profit. If however crypto assets are valued at cost price, no loss can be taken into account unless the loss can be considered permanent. Considering the volatility of crypto assets, it may be difficult to ascertain this. However, considering facts and circumstances (especially for utility tokens and security tokens) it may nevertheless be plausible.

(i) What are the income/capital gains tax consequences of forks of crypto assets?

The Dutch Government has not issued any guidance on the tax treatment of (hard) forks, meaning cases where a blockchain splits into two blockchains, so that a taxpayer holding crypto assets on the original blockchain now additionally holds the same number of crypto assets on the new blockchain.

The base case will likely be that the fair market value of the newly obtained crypto assets qualifies as taxable income for either corporate income tax purposes or personal income tax purposes (if the new crypto assets can be attributed to a source of income, please refer to section 1.1.2(b), above). The book value of the new crypto assets would – going forward – be set at this fair market value. In specific circumstances, it may be possible to take the position that the new crypto assets replace the old crypto assets, which could mean that the book value of the old crypto assets would be rolled over to the new crypto assets. Consequently, no taxable income would be taken into account as a result of the fork. It should be noted that if the old crypto assets would be sold subsequently, the taxable gain would be higher as the book value of these old crypto assets would be zero (as it is transferred to the new crypto assets).

(j) What are the income/capital gains tax consequences of airdrops of crypto assets and are the tax consequences different if the airdropped tokens are unwanted?

For individuals, the tax consequences of airdrops, meaning cases where crypto assets are given free of charge, depend on the personal tax position of that individual. If the crypto assets can be attributed to a so-called source of income (refer to section 1.1.2(b), above), the fair market value in euro of the tokens received is taxable at a progressive rate of up to 49.50% (2020). This could for example be the case if the individual is a freelance developer which receives the crypto assets for marketing purposes (and not as payment for his services).

If an individual receives free crypto assets without performing any economic activity in connection with the crypto assets received, the value of the crypto assets would be taxed only on a net wealth basis, effectively at a rate between approximately 0.54% and 1.6% (2020).

For corporate entities the airdropped tokens would be part of their taxable income taxed with corporate income tax at a rate between 16.5% and 25% (2020, expected to be lowered to 15% and 21.7% in 2021).

It is of no relevance whether the airdropped tokens are wanted or unwanted; if the airdrop is accepted it is treated as described above.

(k) What are the income/capital gains tax consequences of (solo, pool, and cloud) mining?

The Dutch tax consequences vary significantly depending on whether the mining is undertaken by a corporate entity or an individual, and whether the mining constitutes a business enterprise/miscellaneous income of an individual.

For individuals, profits realised with mining (meaning income minus costs connected to the mining activity) are only taxed with personal income tax if there is a source of income which is connected to a business enterprise or leads to so-called miscellaneous income. Please refer to section 1.1.2(b), above. For a source of income in this respect, an individual should enter into economic transactions and strive to obtain a profit and can reasonably expect a profit with regard to these transactions. The Dutch Government has stated that in the current mining climate, it is highly unlikely that an individual can expect a profit from mining, considering that currently costs of mining are so high that only large-scale mining can be profitable.[22] However, whether a profit can be reasonably expected should be judged on a case-by-case basis. For the sake of completeness, we note that any crypto assets derived by individuals from the mining activities will subsequently be included in the net wealth base on which yearly personal income tax is levied at an effective rate of between approximately 0.54% and 1.6% (2020).

Corporate entities are deemed to carry out a business enterprise with all of their assets by way of fiction. Mining income is therefore considered part of the business enterprise of a corporate entity (irrespective of the business it operates). Profits generated by corporate entities are taxed with corporate income tax. The corporate income tax rate is 25% (2020, as of 2021 expected to be lowered to 21.7%), with a lower rate of 16.5% (2020, expected to be lowered to 15% in 2021) for the first EUR 200,000 of profit.

(l) What are the income/capital gains tax consequences of staking crypto assets?

Where miners in a Proof of Work consensus mechanism (bitcoin, ether) need to invest in equipment to increase their chances of obtaining block rewards, in a Proof of Stake consensus mechanism (dash, NEO) forgers need to invest in the relevant tokens to

22. Letter of the State Secretary of Finance dated 28 May 2018 addressed to the permanent commission of finance of the senate.

increase their chance of obtaining a transaction fee. These staked tokens are locked and can be considered the working capital of such forgers.

For individuals, income from staking crypto assets (i.e., the transaction fee) is only taxed with personal income tax if there is a source of income (please refer to section 1.1.2(b), above). For a source of income in this respect, an individual should enter into economic transactions and strive to obtain a profit and can reasonably expect a profit with regard to these transactions. This may not be the case as staking is a relatively passive activity. However, this should be judged on a case-by-case basis. Particularly in cases of (very) substantial stakes it is possible that there could be a source of income. Such income is taxed progressively up to 49.50% (2020). Conversely, if there is no source of income, the stake of crypto assets will be taxed as part of the net wealth of the individual, taxed at an effective rate between approximately 0.54% and 1.6% (2020).

Corporate entities are deemed to carry out a business enterprise with all of their assets by way of fiction. The transaction fees generated by corporate entities are taxed with corporate income tax. The corporate income tax rate is 25% (2020, as of 2021 expected to be lowered to 21.7%), with a lower rate of 16.5% (2020, expected to be lowered to 15% in 2021) for the first EUR 200,000 of profit. It should be noted that also the changes in value of the staked crypto assets (calculated in euro) could be taxed with corporate income tax. However, considering the fact that the stake is required to obtain the transaction fees (i.e., generate business income) there may be possibilities to lock the value of the stake for Dutch corporate income tax purposes, thereby postponing capital gains or losses of the stake until the stake is withdrawn.

(m) What are the income/capital gains tax consequences of an indirect investment in crypto assets?

The Dutch tax aspects of investing in crypto assets indirectly will be strongly dependent on the specific structure through which the investment is made. To a large extent, only the qualification of the direct investment is relevant for Dutch personal income tax and corporate income tax purposes. The underlying assets are irrelevant, except for specific circumstances (for example if these are Dutch based real estate). Examples of indirect investments in crypto assets and their Dutch tax treatment are the following.

One example consists of bonds which are issued at nominal value, which may or may not pay interest and which are repaid at maturity in an amount based on the performance of one specific crypto asset, of a basket of several crypto assets or of a crypto asset index. For individuals such bonds would likely be taxed on a net wealth basis at an effective rate between approximately 0.54% and 1.6% (2020), as these would be considered a passive investment not attributable to a business enterprise. For corporate entities the income and gains on these bonds would be taxed with corporate income tax at a rate of 25% (2020, as of 2021 expected to be lowered to 21.7%), with a lower rate of 16.5% (2020, expected to be lowered to 15% in 2021) for the first EUR 200,000 of profit.

Another possibility would be to purchase units in an investment fund, which in turn invests in crypto assets. For individuals the interest in the investment fund would likely be taxed on a net wealth basis, similar to the tax treatment described above. However, if the interest in the fund would be 5% or more, income and gains pertaining to the investment in the fund would be taxed with 26.25% (2020) personal income tax, provided the investment fund is opaque from a Dutch tax perspective. For corporate entities they are in principle taxed as mentioned above, however if they hold an interest of 5% or more in the nominal capital or membership rights of the investment fund, any income and gains derived from the fund could be exempt under the Dutch participation exemption.[23]

(n) *How is income from crypto assets to be treated under double tax treaty law?*

The Dutch tax authorities have not issued any guidance on the application of double tax treaties. It will have to be analysed on a case-by-case basis how a tax treaty would apply to income or capital gains derived from crypto assets. In general it can be noted that if an item of income is not defined in a tax treaty, it should be qualified according to the domestic legislation of the country applying the tax treaty. With regard to the Netherlands, there is no specific guidance on the qualification of crypto assets. This means that it is conceivable that income from crypto assets qualifies for a range of tax treaty articles depending on the facts and circumstances.

As an example, if the income from crypto assets (e.g., transaction fees) can be considered part of a business enterprise, Article 7 of the (relevant tax treaty article similar to the) OECD Model Convention would grant taxation rights to the Netherlands if a company would be resident in the Netherlands, unless it carries on (part of) its business through a permanent establishment in another state. Alternatively, if income from security tokens held by a Dutch resident could be qualified as dividends, Article 10 of the (relevant tax treaty article similar to the) OECD Model Tax Convention could grant taxation rights to the Netherlands but allow the state of the token issuer to tax the dividends up to a specific percentage. As a final example, capital gains obtained from selling crypto assets could be taxed by the Netherlands pursuant to Article 13(5) of the (relevant tax treaty article similar to the) OECD Model Convention, if the seller is resident of the Netherlands (whether an individual or corporate entity).

(o) *What are the income/capital gains tax consequences of selling crypto assets in an ICO/STO/IEO?*

A company issuing tokens in an ICO/STO/IEO will usually receive consideration from the acquirers. This consideration may be in cash or in kind (e.g., other crypto assets). As companies are deemed to carry out a business enterprise with all their assets by way

23. It is noted that very specific conditions should be met in order to apply the Dutch participation exemption.

of fiction, the received consideration is in principle taxed with corporate income tax. The corporate income tax rate is 25% (2020, as of 2021 expected to be lowered to 21.7%), with a lower rate of 16.5% (2020, expected to be lowered to 15% in 2021) for the first EUR 200,000 of profit.

However, if the crypto assets can be regarded as equity of the company for tax purposes, the consideration would not be taxable at the level of the issuer, but rather entered on the balance sheet as capital. Whether crypto assets can qualify as such will depend on the terms and conditions of the crypto assets. This may for example be the case if crypto assets grant entitlement to a profit-dependent return for the holder, do not have a maturity date or a maturity date of more than fifty years and is subordinated to all other creditors.

If crypto assets should be considered debt, for example because the issuer has a repayment obligation to the holder, the consideration may also not lead to a taxable profit, but rather a liability should be entered on the balance sheet of the issuer.

Lastly, if utility tokens are issued, the issuer may be required to perform a service in the future in return for the utility token. An example is that holders can acquire stage tickets with their tokens. In such case profit realization can be postponed by entering the consideration on the balance sheet of the issuer as an advance payment. The consideration received in return for the issuance of the utility tokens will become taxable once the service has been rendered to the holder.

For completeness sake it is noted that the tax consequences for the investor/recipient of the tokens in an ICO/STO/IEO are described in section 1.1.2(b), above.

1.1.3 Other Taxes

(a) What are the value added tax/sales tax consequences of selling crypto assets?

As a general rule, the supply of goods and services for consideration by a taxable person, taking place in the Netherlands, is subject to Dutch VAT. The question arises whether a person trading in crypto assets could be considered a taxable person for VAT purposes and whether the sale of crypto assets could qualify as a supply of services (as the supply of goods, in principle, merely refer to tangible goods). In this respect, there is little to no guidance on a Dutch national level. To determine the Dutch VAT consequences of selling crypto assets the specifics of the crypto assets should therefore be carefully analysed on a case-by-case basis.

As mentioned earlier, broadly speaking, crypto assets can roughly be broken down into (i) cryptocurrencies, (ii) security tokens, and (iii) utility tokens.

In respect of (i) cryptocurrencies, the ECJ ruled in the *Hedqvist* case (C-264/14)[24] that the exchange of traditional currency for bitcoin (i.e., cryptocurrencies), or vice versa, qualifies as a service within the scope of VAT. However, this service should,

24. ECJ 25 Oct. 2015, *Skatteverket v. David Hedqvist*, C-264/14.

according to the ECJ, fall within the scope of the VAT exemption for financial transactions, including negotiation, concerning currency, bank notes, and coins used as legal tender. An important factor appears to be that bitcoins serve no other purpose than being a means of payment. Although this ruling has not (yet) been confirmed by national courts in the Netherlands, the *Hedqvist* case should, as national law should be interpreted in accordance with EU law, which means for Dutch VAT purposes that the sale of bitcoins and other cryptocurrencies, for which the sole purpose is to be used as a means of payment, should be exempted from Dutch VAT.

With regard to (ii) security tokens, it should further be noted that, in the *Hedqvist* case, the ECJ also considered whether bitcoin transactions could fall within the scope of the VAT exemption for transactions in shares, interests in companies or associations, debentures and others securities. The ECJ ruled against this, as bitcoins are not securities conferring a property right to its owner. However, it is possible that a security token would have characteristics of a security and fall within the VAT exemption. In that case, the sale of such security token could qualify as a service which is potentially exempted from VAT.

Lastly, with respect to (iii) utility tokens, a utility token can be regarded as a token that establishes a relationship between the issuer and the holder, resulting in non-monetary obligations between them. The VAT treatment of the sale of a utility token therefore depends on the obligations it represents. Under certain conditions, a utility token may be considered to be a 'voucher' for VAT purposes, which entitles the owner of the utility token to procure goods or services upon redemption. It should be noted that if a utility token qualifies as a voucher, the Dutch VAT treatment of selling such utility token depends on its qualification as either a 'single purpose voucher' – defined as a voucher in respect of which the place of supply as well as the VAT amount payable is already known upon issuance – or a 'multi-purpose voucher' – defined as all vouchers, not being single purpose vouchers. If a utility token qualifies as a single purpose voucher, the sale of such utility token is deemed to be a supply of the underlying goods or services that can be obtained upon redemption of that token and the Dutch VAT treatment should be determined accordingly. If a utility token qualifies as a multi-purpose voucher, the sale of such token is not a taxable event for VAT purposes. Instead, the taxable event takes place upon redemption of the utility token, at which time the Dutch VAT treatment should be determined accordingly.

Given the versatile application of crypto assets, and the scarcity in guidance, the Dutch VAT treatment of the sale of crypto assets depend on the facts and circumstances at hand and especially on the characteristics of the crypto asset concerned.

Besides VAT, no other sales taxes should apply under Dutch law.

(b) Are payments in crypto assets subject to withholding taxes?

Payments made in cash or in kind (such as crypto assets) are treated similarly for purposes of applying the Dutch withholding tax rules. Currently, the Netherlands only levies a withholding tax on dividend payments at a rate of 15%. In case the party that receives the dividends holds a stake of 5% or more, an exemption could be applied, unless certain anti-abuse measures are triggered.

Beginning in 2021, a new withholding tax on intra-group interest and royalty payments will be introduced. However, this new withholding tax will have a limited scope as only (in)direct intra-group payments to low-tax jurisdictions or to hybrid entities will be taxed.

As such, payments in crypto assets could be subject to withholding taxes in case it could be considered dividend payments or, from 2021 onwards, also if it could be considered an intra-group interest or royalty payment. For completeness sake, it is noted that any taxes due should be paid in euro.

We also would like to note that, if crypto assets themselves qualify as equity (or as from 2021 also as debt or licensed intellectual property) for Dutch tax purposes, payments made by the issuer to the holder may give rise to withholding tax.

(c) Does payment of compensation in crypto assets give rise to payroll tax consequences?

Compensation in crypto assets such as bitcoins does not give rise to any special payroll tax consequences and thus is to be treated as any payment in kind. Normally, the employer will have to calculate and remit wage withholding tax and various social security contributions. The employer has the obligation to withhold wage tax (and if applicable, national insurance contributions) on the fair market value of the crypto assets.

(d) Do transactions with crypto assets trigger any transfer taxes?

No. The only transfer taxes applicable in the Netherlands relate to real estate. We note that, if it would become possible for tokens to represent ownership of real estate, transfer tax could be applicable at 6%, unless the real estate could be considered a dwelling, in which case the rate is 2%.

(e) Are firms operating in the crypto space subject to digital service taxes?

No, the Netherlands currently does not levy a digital service tax nor are there any indications that such a tax would be introduced.

(f) Are crypto assets subject to gift, inheritance, estate, or wealth taxes?

Like all regular assets, crypto assets can be subject to gift and inheritance tax. Gift and inheritance tax is levied on assets gifted by or inherited from individuals residing in the Netherlands, irrespective of where the recipients or assets are located. The tax is levied on the recipient, based on the value of the assets[25] and the relation to the grantor/deceased. Transfers up to a certain value are exempt, depending on the relation between the recipient and the grantor/deceased. The gift and inheritance tax will be levied at a rate of 10%–20% for spouses and straight descendants (i.e., children, grandchildren, etc.) and 30%–40% for all other recipients. The tax is levied in case something is received from a Dutch resident or a person with the Dutch nationality that has lived in the Netherlands in the past ten years.[26]

Crypto assets which do not pertain to a source of income for personal income tax purposes are taxed on a net wealth basis, taxed effectively at a rate between approximately 0.54% and 1.6%.

(g) Are crypto assets subject to exit tax?

Like all regular assets, crypto assets can be subject to an exit charge when an individual or corporate entity migrates from the Netherlands. For corporate entities, corporate income tax is due on realised and unrealised profits (hidden reserves and goodwill) at the time of exit. The corporate income tax rate is 25% (2020, as of 2021 expected to be lowered to 21.7%), with a lower rate of 16.5% (2020, expected to be lowered to 15% in 2021) for the first EUR 200,000 of profit. The taxable amount is calculated at the time of migration and is formalised in an assessment. If the new place of residence is within an EU/EEA Member State, payment of the tax due may, on request, be deferred. In such a case the exit charge may be paid in five annual instalments, but no later than the time of sale of the crypto assets. The corporate entity will have to comply with certain administrative requirements and may be required to provide security in order to obtain the deferral. Moreover, collection interest is calculated at 4% of the amount of tax for which a deferral is granted.

For individuals, an exit charge can be levied if the crypto assets form part of a business enterprise or a so-called source of income. At the time of exit, personal income tax is due on realised and unrealised profits (hidden reserves and goodwill). A progressive tax rate of up to 49.50% (2020) applies. A protective assessment is imposed of which payment can be deferred until the moment of realisation. Security may need to be provided if the new place of residence is outside the EU/EEA. It should also be noted that an exit charge can apply indirectly to crypto assets if they are held by an individual through a Dutch corporate entity of which that individual holds an interest of 5% or more.

(h) Can mining trigger gambling tax?

Dutch Gambling Tax is levied upon prices awarded as a result of a game of chance. To qualify as a game of chance the designation of the winners must be made by means of

25. At the time of the gift or the decease.
26. It is noted that in specific cases Dutch gift and inheritance tax can also apply, for example if a grantor migrates tot the Netherlands and dies within 180 days of making the gift.

any clauses of chance over which the participants generally have no control. Miners do have in general some control; they strengthen the system and deliver actual input. As a consequence, no Dutch Gambling Tax should be triggered for miners.

1.1.4 Compliance and Documentation Obligations

(a) What documentation requirements exist for taxpayers regarding crypto assets and are there best practices in recordkeeping to support representations made in tax returns?

In the Netherlands, there are no specific documentation requirements for taxpayers holding crypto assets. Thus, such taxpayers must comply with the general documentation requirements. As a general requirement, all taxpayers should set up their administration in such a way that all their rights and obligations, as well as any other information relevant to the levy of taxes, can be clearly demonstrated and checked by the Dutch tax authorities. All documents and information which could be relevant should be kept in the administration for at least seven years. Notwithstanding this general requirement, various specific documentation requirements may apply to a taxpayer with regard to transfer pricing or to support certain tax positions. These are however not specific to owners of crypto assets and depend on the specific facts and circumstances of the taxpayer.

(b) What is the evidentiary burden of supporting tax positions when a digital wallet address is lost or shared with other persons?

In general, the burden of proof lies with the party asserting a fact or making a claim. This means, for example, that if the Dutch tax authorities wish to disallow the deduction of a loss originating from the loss of a digital wallet, the burden of proof lies with them. This can, however, be different in various cases. An important example is that the burden of proof will lie with the taxpayer if his record keeping is faulty. Another important example is that the burden of proof will shift to the taxpayer if he has not filed an adequate tax return. This is considered the case if a substantial amount in relative and absolute terms is incorrectly omitted from the tax return.

(c) Are crypto asset exchanges and wallet providers subject to reporting obligations?

Under Dutch tax law, crypto asset exchanges and wallet providers are not subject to any periodic reporting obligations vis-à-vis the Dutch tax authorities regarding their customers. It should be noted that from a regulatory perspective, it is expected that legislation will enter into force in 2020 which provides that, among others, crypto asset exchanges (unless only crypto-to-crypto exchanges are facilitated) and wallet providers will fall under the supervision of the Dutch National Bank (DNB). This will mean that such companies should register with the DNB, board members should meet certain qualifications, transactions should be monitored and reported if unusual, and certain Know-Your-Client checks should be performed.

(d) *Are taxpayers holding crypto assets subject to reporting obligations apart from the filing of income tax/capital gains tax returns?*

Under Dutch tax law, taxpayers holding crypto assets are not subject to any reporting obligations vis-à-vis the tax authorities apart from regular reporting obligations which apply to all taxpayers. Therefore, no specific report needs to be filed to disclose detailed information regarding any crypto assets held. Notwithstanding, the tax authorities do have the power do request detailed information which may be relevant for the tax position of a taxpayer or a third party (please refer to sections 1.1.4(a) and 1.1.5(a)).

(e) *Are crypto asset exchanges and wallet providers subject to CRS/FATCA reporting?*

The Dutch Government has not yet issued specific guidelines in respect of crypto asset exchanges and wallet providers. Based on the very broad definitions of the term financial institutions for FATCA and CRS purposes, it is however conceivable that both crypto asset exchanges and wallet providers may fall under the scope of the FATCA and CRS rules. This is certain if they accept fiat currency in addition to crypto assets. Due to the fact that the general definition of the term financial asset is also very broad and includes commodities and commodity swaps (with the exception of a commodity that is a physical good), crypto assets might be considered financial assets as well.

1.1.5 Civil and Criminal Tax Enforcement

(a) *What powers do the tax authorities have to compel the disclosure of information by third parties, such as exchanges or wallet providers, and have these been used in the past?*

Under Dutch law, in addition to providing documents and information with respect to their own taxation, persons required to keep records are also obliged to provide the Dutch tax authorities with documents and information relevant for the taxation of third parties.[27] The requested information should be provided clearly, accurately and completely.[28] This also includes information that is easily available to the person required to keep records (e.g., by asking a question to a person '*in its surroundings*'),

27. Articles 53 State Taxes Act (*Algemene Wet inzake Rijksbelastingen*). This obligation does not apply to private persons. It does also apply to foreign taxpayers, to the extent relevant for the Dutch state taxes, and to entities whose capital is divided in shares of which a person or body that is not a Dutch resident holds 50% or more (in situations where the body or person is no resident of a country with which information is already exchanged based on international law).
28. Articles 47 and 49 State Taxes Act.

but does not go as far as having to conduct further investigations or having to make complicated calculations. As a rule, a person required to keep records relevant to its own taxation is not obliged to keep additional records which may only be relevant for the taxation of third parties. Notwithstanding, as mentioned above any records that are held should be made available upon request. In addition, the person required to keep records is obliged to provide the Dutch tax authorities access to property for an on-site observation upon request.[29] The general principles of proper administration apply to these information requests, e.g., the request should be necessary, reasonable, proportionate and appropriate. The obligation to provide information with regard to the taxation of third parties does not end when a legal procedure is brought before the court.

When no or insufficient information is provided, this can lead to criminal sanctions.[30] In addition, the Dutch tax authorities can enforce cooperation by means of civil law preliminary relief proceedings, in which the civil court can impose an incremental penalty payment on the person obliged to keep records if it does not provide the requested information.

As crypto asset exchanges and wallet providers are seen as persons required to keep records under Dutch law, the Dutch tax authorities have the power to compel the disclosure of information regarding their Dutch customers. Whether such information has been requested from cryptocurrency exchanges or wallet providers has not been publicly disclosed.

(b) *What measures have the tax authorities undertaken in the past to ensure crypto tax compliance?*

To improve the insight in crypto assets, the Dutch tax authorities have started to educate their (auditing) employees on this matter and to develop technical devices.[31] In addition, the Dutch tax authorities have updated the information for the general public on their website.

(c) *Are the tax authorities cooperating with tax authorities in other jurisdictions on enforcement?*

The Dutch tax authorities cooperate with other tax authorities in order to ensure the exchange of information in various ways. First, a large number of bilateral treaties containing clauses on the exchange of information are in place.[32] In addition, the Netherlands is bound by the EU Common Reporting Standards, aimed at the exchange

29. Article 50 State Taxes Act.
30. Article 68 State Taxes Act.
31. Annex 1 to Letter to parliament advising regulators on the regulation of cryptos ('*Kamerbrief advies toezichthouders regulering van crypto's*'), Minister of Finance, 18 Jan. 2019, https://www.rijksoverheid.nl/documenten/kamerstukken/2019/01/18/antwoorden-op-kamervragen-advies-toezichthouders-regulering-crypto-%E2%80%99s.
32. Overview of treaties in the field of direct taxation per 1 Jan. 2020 (in Dutch), https://www.rijksoverheid.nl/documenten/circulaires/2020/01/01/verdragenoverzicht-per-1-januari-2020.

of information which is foreseeably relevant to the administration and enforcement of its domestic laws. Finally, the Netherlands is a party to the Convention on Mutual Administrative Assistance in Tax Matters (a joint initiative of the OECD and the Council of Europe).Whether the Dutch tax authorities have made use of these possibilities with regard to crypto asset holdings of taxpayers, is not public information.

United Kingdom

Ben Fryer & Bridget English

1. COUNTRY GUIDES

1.1 United Kingdom

1.1.1 Applicable Tax Law, Guidance, and Case Law

(a) Which laws, regulations, and other administrative guidance exist dealing with crypto assets?

At present, the tax law of the UK does not explicitly address the taxation of crypto assets. Their taxation is therefore determined in accordance with the general body of UK tax law governing the taxation of income, gains and transactions (itself a combination of statute and case law). Her Majesty's Revenue and Customs (HMRC), the UK tax authority, has, however, issued (non-binding) guidance setting out how it considers such laws apply to transactions involving crypto assets which are exchange tokens.[1,2] The guidance expressly does not cover the taxation of utility tokens or security tokens, which HMRC has stated will be addressed in future guidance.[3]

1. HMRC policy papers 'Cryptoassets: tax for individuals' and 'Cryptoassets: tax for businesses' (both updated 20 Dec. 2019).
2. Exchange tokens are intended to be used as a means of payment and include 'cryptocurrencies' like bitcoin. They do not provide the holder with any rights to any underlying property or access to goods or services. Their value is based on their use as a means of exchange or investment.
3. In contrast to exchange tokens, the value of utility tokens and security tokens derives from the holder's right to an underlying asset (or interest therein). Utility tokens provide the holder with (current or future) access to particular goods or services. They are issued by businesses or groups of businesses who commit to accepting the tokens as payment for the particular goods or services in question. Security tokens have some characteristics in common with traditional securities such as shares or notes; they provide the holder with a particular interest in a business, such as a share in the issuer's profits or rights akin to debt instruments.

The guidance highlights that the tax treatment of exchange tokens is fact-specific. Nevertheless, HMRC confirms that exchange tokens are not considered to constitute currency or money, and would instead be considered assets in their own right. The specific tax treatment which may apply to these assets is considered in further detail below.

It is worth noting that HMRC has expressly stated that its 'views may evolve further as the sector develops', and so its contents are not necessarily definitive. The guidance also clarifies that, when assessing the tax treatment of crypto assets, terminology will not be determinative, and HMRC will 'look at the facts of each case and apply the relevant tax provisions according to what has actually taken place'.

(b) Which court cases exist dealing with crypto assets?

At the date of writing, no judgements have been given in UK courts or tribunals specifically regarding the taxation of crypto assets. There is, however, one decision of the European Court of Justice (ECJ) regarding the value added tax treatment of certain transactions in bitcoins.[4] This decision would be binding in the UK even after the end of the Brexit transitional period (during which the UK and the EU Member States have agreed to treat the UK as though it is a Member State of the EU), unless it is subsequently overruled by domestic UK legislation or the UK Supreme Court decides to depart from the ECJ's decision.[5] The UK Government has not given any indication that it intends to legislate on the subject.

1.1.2 Income and Capital Gains Taxes

(a) How are crypto assets classified for income and capital gains tax purposes?

As mentioned above, HMRC considers that exchange tokens constitute neither money nor currency. This means that specific UK tax rules relevant to such assets (such as the foreign exchange currency rules, the 'disregard' rules relating to exchange gains and losses, and rules governing designated currency elections) will not apply. Exchange tokens will therefore be taxed as assets in their own right.

Subject to certain exceptions (including those discussed below), the tax treatment of exchange tokens will depend on whether they are characterized as capital assets or non-capital assets (e.g. trading assets).[6] Given that HMRC has noted in its

4. ECJ 22 Oct. 2015, C-264/14, *Hedqvist*.
5. Any decision by the UK Supreme Court to depart from retained EU case law would be subject to the same rules which apply to Supreme Court departures from its own previous case law. In Jul. 2020, the UK Government launched a public consultation regarding the possibility of allowing lower UK courts and tribunals to depart from retained EU case law (as to which, *see* 'Retained EU Case Law – Consultation on the departure from retained EU case law by UK courts and tribunals', dated 2 Jul. 2020).
6. Crypto assets could be non-capital assets without necessarily being trading assets. For example, receipts in respect of a crypto asset could be characterized as 'miscellaneous income' (*see* further

guidance that it similarly considers that other crypto assets are neither currency nor money, it is expected that the same would generally be true of such crypto assets (although that point is not expressly dealt with in HMRC's guidance).

Whether crypto assets are considered to be held by a taxpayer as non-capital assets (such that receipts in respect thereof are characterized as income subject to income tax or corporation tax) or capital assets (such that receipts in respect thereof would be subject to capital gains tax or corporation tax on chargeable gains)[7] will be decided based on general principles. This is a fact-specific question, generally dependent on whether the taxpayer is carrying on a business in the nature of a trade vis-à-vis the crypto assets in question or holding the crypto assets as a capital asset (*see* further below).

Notwithstanding the above, in determining the applicable tax treatment, in some cases it would not be necessary to consider whether crypto assets are held by a taxpayer as capital assets or non-capital assets. For corporation taxpayers, specific tax regimes apply to certain kinds of assets, such as loan relationships,[8] or intangible fixed assets.[9] Broadly, assets within the scope of these special regimes are taxed by reference to the debits and credits recognized for accounting purposes in respect thereof in the taxpayer's (GAAP-compliant) profit and loss statement, and the applicable tax treatment does not generally depend on the asset's characterisation as a capital or non-capital asset.

HMRC considers that:

- Exchange tokens would not be within the scope of the special tax regime applying to loan relationships, because the exchange tokens would not constitute 'loan relationships' (i.e., 'money debts arising from a transaction for the lending of money').[10] This is because arrangements governing the mere holding of exchange tokens do not, given the lack of a counterparty, give rise to a debt.
- Exchange tokens may, depending on the circumstances, constitute 'intangible fixed assets', and hence may fall to be taxed in accordance with the special tax regime applying thereto. Broadly, to be characterized as 'intangible fixed assets', crypto assets would need to be *both*:
  (i) Intangible assets for (generally accepted) accounting purposes.[11] Generally, crypto assets would not meet this test if they are held for sale

supra n. 35) or employment income (*see* section 1.1.2(e)). Nevertheless, for simplicity our discussion of the tax treatment of non-capital assets herein is generally limited to trading assets.

7. Corporation taxpayers pay corporation tax on chargeable gains. The amount payable is generally calculated in the same way as for capital gains tax. Accordingly (unless otherwise stated), references in this chapter to the capital gains tax should be read, for corporation taxpayers, as corporation tax on chargeable gains.
8. *See* Part 5 of the Corporation Tax Act 2009.
9. *See* Part 8 of the Corporation Tax Act 2009.
10. *See* Parts 5 and 6 of the Corporation Tax Act 2009.
11. *See* IFRS Interpretations Committee tentative agenda decision of Mar. 2019 and IFRS Staff Paper on 'Holdings of Cryptocurrencies' of Jun. 2019.

in the ordinary course of business (i.e., inventory for accounting purposes).[12]

(ii) Acquired or created by the company for use on a continuing basis in the course of the company's activities (effectively, a 'fixed' asset for accounting purposes). HMRC has confirmed that merely holding crypto assets, even in the course of the company's activities, would not be sufficient to meet this test.

Although not expressly stated in HMRC's guidance, crypto assets which are stock in trade, and crypto assets held solely for investment purposes, should not, therefore, generally qualify as intangible fixed assets.

As mentioned above, the tax treatment of utility tokens and security tokens has not been addressed by HMRC. As with exchange tokens, it can be expected that the tax treatment will be fact specific and will depend on whether the circumstances are such that the crypto assets in question (i) meet the criteria for taxation under a special tax regime (such as the intangible fixed assets regime[13]) or failing which, (ii) fall to be taxed in accordance with the general capital/non-capital asset distinction described above. For these reasons, the responses to the questions below do not consider the position if HMRC were to take the view that such assets are characterized as anything other than: (i) capital assets (not subject to any special tax regime), (ii) non-capital assets (not subject to any special tax regime) or (iii) intangible fixed assets.

(b) What are the income/capital gains tax consequences of selling crypto assets against fiat currency?

The tax treatment of gains and losses from the sale of crypto assets against fiat currency depends on whether (i) (for corporation taxpayers) such crypto assets are 'intangible fixed assets' and (ii) if not (and for non-corporation taxpayers generally), whether they are capital or non-capital assets. HMRC does not consider that the holding of exchange tokens is a speculative venture akin to gambling (the proceeds of which are free from tax). It seems likely that HMRC would take the same view with utility tokens and security tokens.

Capital asset

Generally, if such assets are held as capital assets, then chargeable gains (or allowable losses) will arise on disposal. A chargeable gain will typically be taxable at a rate of 10% or 20% for individual capital gains taxpayers (depending on the amount of their taxable income in the relevant year) or 19% for corporation taxpayers. The chargeable gain (or allowable loss) will, broadly, be calculated as: (i) the consideration received

12. Finance leasing of intangible fixed assets is expressly brought within the regime by the Corporation Tax (Finance Leasing of Intangible Assets) Regulations 2002, even if the assets being leased are accounted for as financial assets. However, an exclusion applies where the lessee within the charge to income tax uses the assets in the course of a trade or business.
13. *See supra* n. 8.

for the disposal less (ii) the consideration paid for the crypto assets, and allowable incidental costs such as transaction fees and legal and valuation costs.[14] Where the crypto assets disposed of were mined, HMRC does not consider that the costs incurred in such mining can be deducted. Irrespective of whether a disposal is between related parties, if it is not on arm's length terms, then the market value of the crypto assets disposed of will be substituted for the consideration received.[15] Individuals may be able to apply their capital gains tax annual allowance (of up to GBP 12,300 per person for the 2020/21 year) against any gain.

Capital losses can generally be offset against capital gains in the current period or carried forward for offset against capital gains in future periods (but not carried back to offset gains in past periods).[16] For corporation taxpayers, from April 2020, restrictions have been placed on the quantum of carried forward losses capable of offsetting capital profits in any period.[17]

Under UK capital gains tax rules, fungible assets are generally required to be ring-fenced and 'pooled' (i.e. effectively treated as a single asset) for the purposes of calculating the capital gain realized on their disposal. If any fungible assets forming part of the same 'pool' are sold, that is considered a part-disposal of the single asset that is the pool. Deductible costs in respect of fungible assets in the same pool (which would include acquisition costs, improvements costs and incidental disposal costs incurred) are considered on an aggregate basis, and an appropriate proportion of the deductible costs can be deducted in calculating the gain on disposal of any assets within the pool (i.e. a part-disposal of the single asset that is the pool).[18] Exceptions to this 'pooling' treatment may apply (for example, where fungible assets are acquired shortly after a disposal). HMRC considers that exchange tokens are fungible with other exchange tokens *of the same kind*, but are not generally fungible (for example, bitcoins are fungible with other bitcoins, but not with ether or litecoins). Provided that exchange tokens of the same kind are in fact fully fungible, they should be considered part of the same pool for this purpose, even if they are held in different wallets. However, whether exchange tokens are so fungible would be a question of fact.

Trading asset

If crypto assets are held as trading assets, then any profit made on their disposal will form part of the taxpayer's trading profit, and will be subject to corporation tax at a rate of 19% or for sole traders and other income taxpayers, income tax at a rate of 20%, 40% or 45% (depending on their total taxable profits for the period). Individuals can benefit from an annual allowance (of GBP 1,000 for the 2020/2021 tax year) below which trading (and miscellaneous) income would not be subject to tax.[19]

14. Section 38 of the Taxation of Chargeable Gains Act 1992.
15. Section 17 of the Taxation of Chargeable Gains Act 1992.
16. Sections 1, 1E and 2A of the Taxation of Chargeable Gains Act 1992.
17. *See* Finance Bill 2019/2021 (published in Jul. 2019 and Mar. 2020).
18. Sections 104–110 of the Taxation of Chargeable Gains Act 1992.
19. Sections 783A–783A Income Tax (Trading and Other Income) Act 2005

In calculating the profits of the trade for a period, the starting point is the profit recognized in the (GAAP-compliant) accounts for that period.[20] There is no market value override. Total taxable profits would be calculated by subtracting total deductible expenses (adjusted, for tax purposes, to add back any expenses not incurred wholly and exclusively for the purposes of the trade) from total income. Since April 2017, subject to certain restrictions (including as to quantum), corporation taxpayers can set off trading losses against other taxable profits or capital gains from current, past or future periods. For income taxpayers, (again, subject to certain restrictions) trading losses can be offset against other current year profits or capital gains and carried forward to offset against future trading or other profits (but cannot be carried back to offset against past profits).

A taxpayer need not necessarily trade *in* crypto assets for them to constitute trading assets. Crypto assets used in the course of a taxpayer's trade could, in some circumstances, be trading assets. For example, if a security token acquired by a taxpayer entitled the taxpayer to services which it intended to use in the course of its trading business (such that the expenditure on the token was incurred wholly and exclusively for the purposes of its trade), it is possible that the security token would constitute a trading asset.

Intangible fixed asset

For the purposes of the intangible fixed assets regime, tax broadly 'follows the accounts'. A disposal will only be taxable if: (i) there is a 'realisation', which broadly requires that the asset ceases to be recognized on the balance sheet, or its balance sheet value is reduced (a 'part-realisation') and (ii) a profit (or loss, as applicable) is recognized in the taxpayer's (GAAP-compliant) profit and loss statement.[21] The amount taken into account for tax purposes is the difference between (i) the proceeds of the realisation (i.e. the amount recognized as the proceeds in the accounts, less the amounts recognized as incidental costs of realization), and (ii) the tax written down value of the asset prior to realisation. However, if the sale is between related parties, the realisation is, for such purpose, treated as having taken place at market value.[22]

(c) What are the income/capital gains tax consequences of exchanging crypto assets against other crypto assets?

Such an exchange will, as a general matter, constitute a taxable event, involving both a disposal and an acquisition for each of the relevant taxpayers.

If the assets exchanged are capital assets, HMRC considers that such an exchange would constitute a 'barter' transaction.[23] There would be a taxable disposal of crypto assets by both parties. This would be taxed as described in section 1.1.2(b) above, with

20. Section 46 of the Corporation Tax Act 2009, and section 1127(4) Corporation Tax Act 2010.
21. *See* Chapter 4 of Part 8 of the Corporation Tax Act 2009.
22. Section 845 of the Corporation Tax Act 2009.
23. HMRC Capital Gains Tax Manual, paragraphs CG12100 and CG78310.

the proviso that, for the purposes of calculating the taxable gain, the consideration received for the disposal would (if the bargain is at arm's length) be the value, in pounds sterling, of the crypto assets received on the date of exchange. On a subsequent disposal of the assets acquired, the allowable acquisition cost would similarly be the value of the crypto assets disposed of, in pounds sterling, on the date of exchange. Holdover or rollover relief would not generally be available.[24]

The consequences of disposing of trading assets, and intangible assets, are discussed in section 1.1.2(b) above. On an exchange of intangible fixed assets, however, rollover relief may be available.[25] As with a disposal, the tax consequences of acquiring trading or intangible fixed assets will depend on the impact the acquisition has in the profit and loss statement, and whether any debits recognized therein are incurred wholly and exclusively for the purposes of the trade. For intangible fixed assets, if the acquisition is capitalized for accounting purposes (i.e., reflected in the balance sheet), annual amortisation relief should also be available.

(d) *If a distinction is made between business assets and non-business assets, when does trading in crypto assets lead to a trade or business?*

As discussed in section 1.1.2(a) above, the tax treatment of crypto assets will often depend on whether the crypto assets are trading assets or capital assets. This would be the case, for example, where the crypto assets are not subject to any special tax regime, such as the intangible fixed assets regime. In such circumstances, it will be necessary to consider whether the taxpayer is carrying on a trade vis-à-vis the particular crypto assets.

Whether taxpayers are carrying on a trade vis-à-vis crypto assets will be determined based on UK case law, and in particular, an assessment of whether the so-called 'badges of trade' (i.e., indicia of trading) are present in the taxpayer's activities. There is no bright-line test, and different indicia may weigh in different directions. Some of the factors to be considered are the degree and frequency of the taxpayer's activities, the taxpayer's level of organisation, the taxpayer's motive, the commerciality of the transactions and the interval between purchase and sale.[26]

HMRC notes in the draft guidance that the approach in determining whether a taxpayer is trading in exchange tokens will be similar to that taken when considering whether a taxpayer is trading in shares and securities. Generally, it is considered more difficult to prove the existence of a trade in such assets.

HMRC considers that in the majority of cases, individuals will not be holding exchange tokens for trading purposes, and they will instead constitute capital assets.

24. Rollover relief might be available if the assets disposed of were capital assets used in the taxpayer's trade, and the proceeds are reinvested in assets to be put to the same use (as to which, *see* section 152 of the Taxation of Chargeable Gains Act 1992).
25. Section 754 of the Corporation Tax Act 2009.
26. HMRC's Business Income Manual, paragraph BIM20200 onwards.

(e) What are the income/capital gains tax consequences for an employee receiving wages or salaries in crypto assets?

Such earnings would generally be subject to tax as employment income, in the same way as cash earnings. The applicable income tax, employer's national insurance contributions, and employee's national insurance contributions payable in respect of such employment income would, broadly, be calculated based on the value of the crypto assets on the date of payment.

How such income tax and national insurance contributions will be accounted for to HMRC will depend on whether the crypto assets can be readily converted into their monetary value (so-called readily convertible assets). HMRC considers that, for exchange tokens, this will typically be the case. In such circumstances, a UK employer will need to account to HMRC for the applicable income tax and national insurance contributions, based on its best estimate of the value of the assets received. The employee will need to 'make good' or reimburse the employer within a certain period for the income tax and employee national insurance contributions (or such payment by the employer will itself be treated as similar to a taxable bonus payment to the employee).[27]

If the crypto assets received could not, for whatever reason, be readily converted into their monetary value (such that they are not 'readily convertible assets'), then the employee would have to report such earnings to HMRC as part of its self-assessment return, and pay the applicable income tax to HMRC itself. In such circumstances, for employer's national insurance contribution purposes, the crypto assets would be treated as a 'benefit in kind', subject to slightly different rules (although the amount of the contribution payable would not typically differ).

The above applies equally if the crypto assets are provided by a third party by reason of the individual's employment. However, in such a case, there are circumstances where the employer's national insurance contributions may be payable by the third party, rather than the employer.

If the employee subsequently disposed of the crypto assets received, typically, any gain would be subject to capital gains tax. In calculating the gain, it would be expected that the value of the crypto assets used, on acquisition, for income tax purposes would be treated as the acquisition cost for capital gains tax purposes.

(f) What are the income/capital gains tax consequences for a merchant receiving payment in crypto assets?

If a person carrying on a trade accepts payments from its customers in crypto assets (being 'money's worth'), the tax consequences are the same as they would be if the customer had paid in fiat currency. The value of the crypto assets received (in pounds

27. Section 222 of the Income Tax (Earnings and Pensions) Act 2003.

sterling, on the date of receipt) would be a taxable trading receipt (even if not recognized in the taxpayer's profit and loss statement).[28]

If the merchant subsequently disposed of the crypto assets received (e.g., in exchange for fiat currency) that would constitute another taxable transaction. Unless the taxpayer is trading in crypto assets, the crypto assets received from customers are unlikely to be held as trading assets (such as inventory). Instead, they are likely to be characterized as capital assets, such that their disposal would be subject to capital gains tax (*see* section 1.1.2(b) above). In such circumstances, the allowable acquisition cost would be the value of the services for which the crypto assets were provided as consideration (such services being 'money's worth'),[29] which should generally equate to the value of the crypto assets brought into account for income tax purposes on receipt.

(g) *What are the income/capital gains tax consequences of a loss of crypto assets?*

Crypto assets may be lost if the private key associated with an address at which crypto assets are stored is lost.

For capital gains tax purposes, HMRC does not consider that there has been a disposal, as the crypto assets continue to exist. However, if a taxpayer can show that there is no prospect of recovering the key or accessing the crypto assets, the taxpayer can make a 'negligible value' claim. If successful, the taxpayer would be treated as having disposed of and re-acquired the relevant crypto asset, allowing the loss to be crystallized. Such a claim could only be made in respect of a 'pool' of fungible crypto assets (*see* section 1.1.2(b) above).

If the crypto assets lost are held as trading stock, the tax impact of the loss would generally depend on whether it resulted in the recognition of a debit or credit in the taxpayer's profit and loss statement.[30] For tax purposes, the loss of stock 'in the normal course of trading' would generally be allowed as a deductible expense. HMRC guidance specifically confirms that 'the loss of stock-in-trade ... by ... negligence of an employee is, in the ordinary course of events, an allowable deduction.' The same principle may apply where the crypto assets cannot be accessed because the key has been lost.[31]

If the crypto assets are intangible fixed assets, then the loss may be crystallized at the end of the accounting period if the value of the asset is written down in the balance sheet of the taxpayer (or the asset is removed from the balance sheet entirely), such that there is a realisation or part-realisation.

28. Section 49A of the Corporation Tax Act.
29. Section 38 of the Taxation of Chargeable Gains Act 1992.
30. *See* section 46 of the Corporation Tax Act 2009.
31. HMRC Business Income Manual, paragraph BIM45850 and BIM45851.

(h) What are the income/capital gains tax consequences of a loss in value of crypto assets?

For capital gains tax purposes, a loss in value will not normally have any tax impact unless it is crystallized through a disposal. The exception is where a negligible value claim (discussed in section 1.1.2(g) above) can be made.

Where the crypto assets are held as trading stock or intangible fixed assets, a loss in value in the course of a taxable period will be crystallized at the end of the period, if the loss is reflected in the profit and loss statement for the period.

(i) What are the income/capital gains tax consequences of forks of crypto assets?

Blockchains are governed by a protocol which users of the chain (i.e., the holders of crypto assets) agree to abide by. When users want to make changes to that protocol, a 'fork' occurs. The changes are effectively a kind of software update.

A 'soft fork' occurs when all the users of the chain agree to adhere to the new changes. In that circumstance, no new asset is created, and there are no tax consequences.

In contrast, a 'hard fork' occurs when only a portion of the users of an existing blockchain wish to adhere to the proposed changes. They agree to create a second 'branch' of the original blockchain which would be subject to the revised protocol. In that circumstance, a new crypto asset, compatible with the new blockchain branch is created. Such holders retain the same number of crypto assets on the original blockchain. In addition, they receive an equal number of crypto assets on the new blockchain.

Broadly speaking, the fork itself does not create a taxable event. However, the new crypto assets and the old crypto assets are not fungible with each other. As a result, for capital gains tax purposes, a new 'pool' of assets would be created. HMRC considers that the value of the new crypto assets is derived from the value of the original crypto assets. The allowable costs available in respect of the latter must therefore be split between the two pools 'on a just and reasonable basis'.[32]

If a person holds crypto assets on an exchange, they can only be disposed of if the exchange recognises the crypto asset. After a fork, if an exchange decides not to recognise the new or the original crypto assets such assets can become 'trapped', and their value reduced accordingly. In such circumstances, HMRC 'will consider cases of difficultly as they arise'. Although not expressly confirmed by HMRC, in such circumstances, the taxpayer may be able to make a 'negligible value' claim (*see* section 1.1.2(g) above).

If the crypto assets are held as trading stock, the impact of the fork may be reflected in the 'cost of goods sold' figure in the profit and loss statement, and hence

32. Sections 42(4) and 43 of the Taxation of Chargeable Gains Act 1992.

may impact the taxable profits for the period.[33] If the crypto assets are intangible fixed assets, then whether the fork has any tax impact would depend on whether the fork gave rise to a debit or credit in the profit and loss statement for accounting purposes (e.g., because of a revaluation).[34]

(j) *What are the income/capital gains tax consequences of airdrops of crypto assets and are the tax consequences different if the airdropped tokens are unwanted?*

An 'airdrop' occurs when a person receives crypto assets free of charge (e.g., as part of a marketing or advertising campaign). The airdropped crypto assets will generally have an infrastructure (e.g., a blockchain, or distributed ledger technology) which is new and operates independently of existing crypto assets. As such, it is not fungible with existing crypto assets. The tax consequences of an airdrop will not differ on the basis of whether the airdropped tokens are wanted or unwanted.

For capital gains tax purposes, the airdropped crypto assets will therefore need to form their own pool (which will include any other crypto assets of that specific kind already held, or subsequently acquired, by the taxpayer). The allowable acquisition cost when the airdropped crypto assets are sold should be nil.

Irrespective of whether the taxpayer is trading in crypto assets, an airdrop would not be characterized as a taxable trading receipt unless it is in fact consideration for a service provided by the taxpayer in the course of their trade. However, the airdropped crypto assets may nevertheless be added to the taxpayer's trading stock, and the proceeds of their subsequent disposal would be a taxable trading receipt.

The tax consequences of an airdrop of crypto assets treated as intangible fixed assets would generally depend on whether the airdrop had any impact on the taxpayer's profit and loss statement or (for amortisation purposes) its balance sheet.

(k) *What are the income/capital gains tax consequences of (solo, pool, and cloud) mining?*

'Miners' are persons awarded crypto assets (or fees) in return for verifying additions to the ledger. Where the individual acts alone, this is described as 'solo' mining. Whether such mining constitutes a trade (such that the crypto assets awarded or fees received

---

33. For accounting purposes, the cost of goods sold can be calculated as 'the value of opening stock, less the cost of stock acquired, less the value of closing stock'. HMRC considers that the only two bases of valuation acceptable for tax purposes are 'the lower of cost and the net realisable value' or 'mark to market (as to which, *see* HMRC Business Income Manual, paragraph BIM33115). If the former approach is chosen, any increase in the value of closing stock deriving from the fork would not have any impact on the calculation of taxable profits, because such increase in value did not come at any cost to the taxpayer.
34. Our understanding is that the accounting treatment of forks was not addressed in the materials referred to in *supra* n. 9 (as to which, *see* the 'Supplemental Issues' paper of 25 Sep. 2019 from the European Financial Reporting Advisory Group).

constitute taxable trading receipts) will depend on whether the badges of trade are present in the taxpayer's activities (*see* section 1.1.2(d) above).

HMRC's crypto asset guidance includes an example of a person using a home computer which has spare capacity to mine tokens, and concludes that this would not normally amount to a trade. In such circumstances HMRC considers that the taxpayer's activities would be taxed as 'miscellaneous income'[35] (being a charge to tax levied on certain income receipts which are not trading receipts). The fee received or the value of the token received (as applicable), less the costs incurred in mining, would be taxable. As mentioned above, an individual's first GBP 1,000 of miscellaneous (and trading) income is tax-free. Any crypto assets received are likely to constitute capital assets. Their subsequent disposal would therefore be subject to capital gains tax. Although not expressly stated in the HMRC guidance, the allowable acquisition cost for this purpose would likely be the market value of the mining services provided (which should, in an arm's length transaction, be the value of the crypto asset, in pounds sterling, on the day of receipt). In this respect, HMRC has expressly stated that 'capital gains tax does not need to be paid on the value of the tokens that [a taxpayer] has already paid income tax on', but 'capital gains tax would be chargeable 'on the gain [the taxpayer makes after they have] received them'. Accordingly, allowable costs on the subsequent disposal cannot include costs which have already been deducted against profits for income tax, or mining costs.[36] It is unclear whether the income tax or corporation tax paid on acquisition of the crypto asset (as applicable) may itself be deductible as an 'incidental cost' of acquisition.[37]

In contrast, HMRC considers that 'a taxpayer purchasing a bank of computers to mine tokens for an expected net profit (taking account of the cost of equipment and electricity) would probably constitute trading activity'. Although the taxpayer's trade is the mining of crypto assets, rather than dealing in crypto assets, HMRC appears to contemplate that exchange tokens mined can form part of trading stock. The value of the tokens, in sterling, on the day of receipt would therefore constitute a trading receipt, while mining costs may be deductible if incurred wholly and exclusively for the purposes of the trade. The tax treatment on disposal of trading stock is discussed above.

The above treatment applies equally to cloud mining, where the miner does not own the equipment and software necessary to mine, but instead rents the computing

---

35. For income taxpayers, *see* sections 687–689 of the Income Tax (Trading and Other Income) Act 2005 and for corporation taxpayers, *see* sections 979–981 of the Corporation Tax Act 2009.
36. HMRC Guidance 'Check if you need to pay tax when you sell Cryptoassets': https://www.gov.uk/guidance/check-if-you-need-to-pay-tax-when-you-sell-cryptoassets. Although not expressly stated, the same principle should, we consider, apply to corporation taxpayers subject to a miscellaneous income charge in respect of mining activity.
37. By way of analogy, when an employee disposes of employment related securities, any income tax charged on the disposal constitutes an allowable expense against the portion of the disposal proceeds subject to capital gains tax (as to which, *see* section 120 of the Taxation of Chargeable Gains Act). HMRC also accepts that both the stamp duty paid on the acquisition of shares and any irrecoverable value added tax on transaction expenses constitute deductible incidental expenses (*see* HMRC's Capital Gains Tax Manual, paragraph CG15250 and Statement of Practice D7).

power from a provider. Any crypto assets mined (or fees received) would belong to the miner, rather than the provider. In such circumstances, the position described above would apply equally (albeit that the level of organisation required may be an indication of a trading activity). The rental costs incurred would constitute either a deductible trading expense, or an allowable deduction for capital gains tax purposes (as applicable).

Sometimes miners work collectively, distributing tasks among the group. This is referred to as 'pool' mining. The tax treatment of pool mining in particular has not been covered in the HMRC crypto assets guidance. Broadly, the position in such circumstances should be as described above - albeit that, again, the level of organisation would seem to indicate a trading activity. However, members of the pool may be 'carrying on a business in common with a view to a profit',[38] such that the pool would constitute a partnership for UK tax purposes (even if not formally registered as such). If so, members of the pool would (as applicable) be taxed on their proportionate share of the pool's profits (computed at the level of the partnership and attributed to the partners)[39] and their portion of the pool's capital gains (as though the members had each disposed of their proportionate interest in the relevant pool assets).[40]

(l) What are the income/capital gains tax consequences of staking crypto assets?

Transactions on a blockchain are validated by crypto asset holders participating in the chain. Such persons often compete to be chosen to validate transactions by 'staking' a portion of the crypto assets they hold; the more assets staked by a person, the more likely that the person will be chosen as a validator. No new crypto assets are created as part of the process, and validators instead receive a fee for their work. If a person is chosen as a validator and does not complete the validation work, or validates a fraudulent transaction, the crypto assets they have 'staked' are forfeited.

Staking is not dealt with in HMRC's crypto asset guidance. However, validation activities are unlikely to constitute trading. The fees earned are therefore likely to be taxable as miscellaneous income (*see* section 1.1.2(k) above).

If the crypto assets staked were trading assets, then the tax consequences of the forfeiture would depend on whether, for accounting purposes, any debits or credits were recognized in the profit and loss statement. If the crypto assets staked were held as capital assets, then any forfeiture is likely to constitute a taxable disposal. Notwithstanding that the holder obtains no consideration, the taxable gain would likely be

38. Section 1(1) of the Partnership Act 1890.
39. The computation of profits at the level of the partnership will differ depending on whether the pool member is an individual subject to income tax (as would typically be the case) or a corporate partner subject to corporation tax. For individual partners, *see* section of the 849 Income Tax (Trading and Other Income) Act 2005 and HMRC Business Income Manual, paragraph BIM82210. For corporate partners, *see* section 1259 of the Corporation Tax Act 2009 and HMRC's Company Taxation Manual, paragraph CTM36510.
40. HMRC Statement of Practice D/12, as set out in HMRC Capital Gains Tax Manual, paragraph CG27170.

calculated as the market value of the assets forfeited less allowable costs (such as their acquisition cost). It seems unlikely that HMRC would consider the activity sufficiently speculative to constitute gambling (such that the forfeiture of capital assets would not have any tax consequences).[41] If the crypto assets staked were intangible fixed assets, the forfeiture would likely result in the asset being removed from (or written down in) the taxpayer's balance sheet, thereby leading to a 'realisation' or 'part-realisation' for tax purposes (the consequences of which are described in section 1.1.2(g) above).

(m) What are the income/capital gains tax consequences of an indirect investment in crypto assets?

Investors may wish to gain exposure to crypto assets without directly holding crypto assets. Such investors could instead invest in the assets described below:[42]

- Shares in companies investing in crypto assets:
  - Dividends received by UK corporation taxpayers are frequently exempt from corporation tax,[43] but this should be examined on a case-by-case basis. Individuals benefit from an annual tax-free dividend allowance (GBP 2,000 for the 2020/21 tax year).[44] Dividends received in excess of the allowance are subject to tax at reduced rates of 7.5%, 32.5% or 38.1% (depending on the taxpayer's total taxable income for the year).
  - For UK corporation taxpayers, broadly, the disposal of shares may benefit from a participation exemption (the so-called 'substantial shareholding exemption') if the taxpayer has held at least 10% of the ordinary share capital in the investee company for at least a consecutive 12-month period in the six years prior to disposal, and the company is a trading company). If these conditions are not met, the disposal would generally be taxed in the same manner as a disposal of crypto assets.[45] For individuals, the same tax treatment applies on the disposal of shares as the disposal of crypto assets (and, in limited circumstances, qualifying individuals may be able to reduce their capital gains tax liability under the business asset disposal relief (formerly, entrepreneurs' relief) rules).
- Units in investment funds (in the form of open ended investment companies and/or authorized unit trusts) investing in crypto assets:

41. *See* HMRC's Capital Gains Tax Manual, paragraph CG12100, which discusses 'highly speculative transactions'.
42. A full discussion of the tax consequences of investing in such assets is beyond the scope of this chapter. The response accordingly represents a brief, high-level summary of the consequences of such investment, assuming that the assets are held as investment (rather than trading) assets.
43. Part 9A of the Corporation Tax Act 2009.
44. Section 6 of the Income Tax Act 2007.
45. Reorganization relief might be available in certain circumstances (subject to meeting certain conditions) if the shares were exchanged for shares in another company.

- For income taxpayers, income distributions will be taxed in the same way as dividends received from shares.[46] For corporation taxpayers, special rules apply, such that the tax treatment of the distribution is dependent on the source of the funds being distributed: any portion of the distribution which itself derives from distributions received by the fund will be taxed in the hands of the corporation taxpayer in the same way as a dividend. However, any remaining portion of the dividend will be subject to withholding tax at a rate of 20% (without any entitlement to a refund or credit).[47]
- On disposal, the capital gains tax treatment would generally be the same as that applying on the disposal of crypto assets.

- Bonds paying a return which tracks the performance of any crypto asset (or any basket of crypto assets):
  - If an income or corporation taxpayer's return (i.e., interest or the redemption amount) tracks the performance of crypto assets impacting the performance of any part of the issuer's business (e.g., crypto assets held by the issuer), interest may be treated as a distribution and taxed in the same way as a dividend on shares.[48] However, the annual dividend allowance would not apply for individuals. If the interest tracked the performance of crypto assets which did not in any way impact the issuer's business, interest should be respected as such[49] (to the extent it represents a reasonable commercial return on the principal lent).
  - On disposal, for income taxpayers, the capital gains tax treatment would generally (subject to certain limited exemptions)[50] be the same as that applying on the disposal of crypto assets. For corporation taxpayers, the bond would likely constitute a 'loan relationship', and hence would generally be taxed on the basis of the amounts recognized in the profit and loss statement.

Generally, individuals can invest an amount each year (no more than GBP 20,000 for the 2020/2021 tax year) in certain kinds of 'individual savings accounts', including a 'stocks and shares individual savings account' (a 'stock ISA'). The above shares, units, and bonds could be placed in such a stock ISA. Distributions from investments in a stock ISA are tax-free, and no capital gains tax is payable on disposal of the relevant investments.

46. Regulation 22 of the Authorised Investment Funds (Tax) Regulations 2006 (SI 2006/964).
47. Regulations 48-50 of the Authorised Investment Funds (Tax) Regulations 2006 (SI 2006/964).
48. Section 1000 of the Corporation Tax Act 2010, section 383 of the Income Tax (Trading and Other Income) Act 2005 and HMRC's Company Taxation Manual, paragraph CTM15120 and Savings and Investment Manual, paragraph SAIM5030.
49. For examples of securities likely to give rise to distribution treatment on this basis, *see* HMRC's Company Taxation Manual, paragraph CTM15520.
50. Sections 116 and 117 of the Taxation of Chargeable Gains Act 1992.

(n) *How is income from crypto assets to be treated under double tax treaty law?*

HMRC has not issued any guidance as to how it intends to treat crypto assets for the purposes of the double tax treaties to which the UK is party. Nevertheless, it seems likely that:

- Income from crypto assets would fall within the scope of (the relevant equivalent of) Article 7 of the OECD Model Convention. Article 7 provides that profits of an enterprise resident in a contracting state are taxable only in that state. However, if the enterprise carries on business in the other contracting state through a permanent establishment situated therein, the profits attributable to the permanent establishment may be taxed in the other state. The UK's treaties generally do not diverge from this position. Whether activities in a state constitute a permanent establishment would be decided on the basis of general principles (a discussion of which goes beyond the scope of this chapter); there are no rules specific to crypto assets.
- The disposal of capital assets would be taxed pursuant to (the relevant equivalent of) Article 13(5) of the OECD Model Convention. Article 13(5) provides that gains from the alienation of moveable property are generally taxable only in the contracting state of which the alienator is resident at the time of disposal. One exception is where the alienated property is part of the business property of a taxpayer's permanent establishment; in that circumstance, the jurisdiction in which the permanent establishment is located would have taxing rights. The UK's treaties generally do not diverge from this position. However, some double tax treaties to which the UK is party give taxing rights to a contracting state in which the taxpayer was resident during a specified period *prior to* the alienation.[51]

(o) *What are the income/capital gains tax consequences of selling crypto assets in an ICO (initial coin offering) / STO (security token offering) / IEO (initial exchange offering)?*

ICOs are a means of fundraising. They are not dissimilar to initial public offerings, except that tokens are offered, rather than shares. The tokens offered can be exchange tokens, utility tokens or security tokens. In consideration for the tokens offered, investors typically give the issuer tokens in other cryptocurrencies (rather than cash). IEOs are merely ICOs which take place on an exchange.

Irrespective of how such offerings are described, their terms may vary widely. Some offerings will involve the packaging together of existing crypto assets, whereas some will involve the creation of new assets (e.g. a bundle of contractual rights which the purchaser acquires). For some offerings, the obligations of the issuer will be complete once the assets being offered are transferred to the purchasers (as would

51. *See* HMRC's International Tax Manual, paragraph INTM153150.

typically be the case in the context of exchange token offerings), whereas in other offerings the issuer will remain subject to future obligations owed to the purchaser, such as the obligation to perform certain future services (as would typically be the case in the context of utility token offerings).

HMRC's guidance does not confirm how these offerings would be treated for tax purposes. As a result, the particular facts and circumstances, including the applicable contractual terms, would need to be analysed on a case-by-case basis. As part of this process, taxpayers may, for example, need to consider:

- Whether the offering involves a taxable disposal by the issuer (*see* sections 1.1.2(b) and (c) above). This could be the case if the offering involves either (i) the transfer of existing assets or (ii) the creation of new assets (e.g. the tokens) and their on-sale to subscribers (rather than the mere issuance of new assets to subscribers without any transfer).
- If there is a disposal:
  - What, as a legal matter, is being disposed of? This could, for example, be the token itself, the bundle of contractual rights to which the purchaser of the token is entitled or a right to an interest in underlying assets (as could perhaps be the case with certain security token offerings).
  - Whether the disposal constitutes the disposal of a capital asset or the disposal of a non-capital asset, such as a trading asset. This may depend, for example, on whether the issuance is a standalone issuance, or one of a series (such that the issuer could potentially be said to be trading in the tokens). If the offering involves the disposal of an interest in an underlying asset, the tax treatment would depend on the characterisation of the underlying asset, and the tax rules applicable to its transfer.
- The applicable accounting treatment. This would be particularly relevant where the assets being offered are within the scope of the special tax regimes mentioned above (e.g. the intangible fixed assets regime), such that their tax treatment is generally determined by reference to debits and credits recognized in the taxpayer's (GAAP-compliant) profit and loss statement. For example, an offering which subjects the issuer to future obligations (such as certain utility token or security token offerings) could conceivably (depending on the circumstances and the applicable accounting treatment) give rise to the recognition of a liability in the issuer's profit and loss statement.

1.1.3 Other Taxes

(a) What are the value added tax/sales tax consequences of selling crypto assets?

In *Hedqvist,*[52] the ECJ held that the VAT exemption at Article 135(1)(e) of the VAT Directive,[53] which broadly applies to transactions concerning legal tender, can apply to transactions in bitcoin (provided that bitcoins are accepted by the parties as a means of payment and are not used by the parties for other purposes). HMRC therefore takes the position that when exchange tokens are exchanged for goods and services, no VAT is due on the supply of the exchange token itself. However, this does not mean that the supply of the goods or services paid for in crypto assets would be exempt. Supplies subject to VAT which are paid for in exchange tokens would attract VAT in the normal way - with the consideration subject to VAT being the value of the exchange tokens, in pounds sterling, on the date the transaction takes place.

As a result of the above finding, the court in *Hedqvist* held that the service of exchanging bitcoin constituted an exempt supply under Article 135(1)(e).[54] In the UK, HMRC has extended this slightly, by confirming that 'a supply of *any services required to exchange* tokens for legal tender (or other exchange tokens) and vice versa, would be exempt' (emphasis added).[55] In a similar vein, arranging transactions in exchange tokens will be exempt from VAT,[56] provided, broadly, that the arranger is acting in an intermediary capacity (i.e., bringing together someone seeking an exchange token service with someone providing that service).[57]

HMRC has also confirmed that the receipt of bitcoin and similar exchange tokens in consideration for mining activities falls outside the scope of VAT, on the basis that (i) the activity does not constitute an economic activity for VAT purposes, because there is an insufficient link between any services provided and any consideration and (ii) there is no customer for the mining service.

HMRC does, however, note that the treatment set out in their guidance is 'provisional pending further developments; in particular in respect of the regulatory and EU VAT positions'. This may perhaps indicate that, even after the end of the Brexit transitional period, the UK intends to keep step with the EU regarding the VAT treatment of transactions involving exchange tokens.

---

52. *See supra* n. 4.
53. Council Directive 2006/112/EC of 28 Nov. 2006 on the common system of value added tax, as amended.
54. Under Article 135(1)(e) of Council Directive 2006/112/EC of 28 Nov. 2006 on the common system of value added tax, as amended.
55. Under Item 1 of Group 5 of Schedule 9 to the Value Added Tax Act 1994, which applies to 'the issue, transfer, receipt of, or any dealing with, money, any security for money or any note or order for the payment of money'.
56. Under Item 5 of Group 5 in Schedule 9 to the UK Value Added Tax Act 1994, which applies to 'the provision of intermediary services in relation to any transaction comprised in (amongst other categories) item 1 ... (whether or not any such transaction is finally concluded) by a person acting in an intermediary category).'
57. *See* HMRC's VAT Finance Manual, paragraph VATFIN7200.

As mentioned above, HMRC's guidance covers neither (i) the VAT treatment of utility tokens or service tokens nor (ii) ICOs, IEOs and STOs. As with direct taxes, the treatment will likely turn on the relevant contractual terms and circumstances, and what exactly is being provided between the parties. Matters which may need to be considered include:

- Whether the offering could be considered to involve the provision of goods or services subject to VAT.
- If so, whether an exemption from VAT may apply. For example, depending on the circumstances, it is conceivable that certain offerings could perhaps benefit from exemptions applying to the provision of certain financial services,[58] such as the UK VAT exemption applying to 'the issue, transfer or receipt of, or any dealing with, money, any security for money or any note or order for the payment of money'.[59]
- If VAT is payable, when it may be required to be accounted for. It may be necessary to consider, for example, whether subscription for a token could be characterized as a prepayment for the future delivery of goods or services subject to VAT (as could perhaps be the case for certain offerings of utility tokens). If so, the 'tax point', triggering the obligation to account for the relevant VAT to a tax authority, may be accelerated.[60]

(b) Are payments in crypto assets subject to withholding taxes?

In the UK, the payment of normal company dividends does not attract withholding tax. However, subject to certain exemptions, payments which do attract withholding tax include (i) payments of UK source interest on debts intended to remain outstanding for one year or more;[61] (ii) certain 'annual payments' made by non-individuals pursuant to contractual obligations, which are income, and 'pure profit', in the hands of the recipient[62] and (iii) certain royalty payments.[63]

HMRC has not made any statement regarding the withholding tax position if such payments are made in crypto assets, and in particular in exchange tokens. However, it is reasonable to assume that the same withholding tax principles would apply, notwithstanding that payment was made in 'money's worth' rather than cash. For the purposes of calculating the amount to be withheld and accounted for to HMRC, it seems likely that HMRC would consider that the amount paid would be the value of the crypto assets, in pounds sterling, on the date of payment.

58. *See* Group 5 in Schedule 9 of the Value Added Tax Act 1994.
59. In light of HMRC's view that exchange tokens do not constitute money, this particular exemption is unlikely to be available for exchange token offerings.
60. *See* section 6(4) of the Value Added Tax Act 1994 and HMRC's VAT Time of Supply Manual, paragraph VATTOS5120.
61. Section 874 of the Income Tax Act 2007.
62. Section 901(4) of the Income Tax Act 2007.
63. Sections 903 and 906 of the Income Tax Act 2007.

The UK tax code contains specific rules where, broadly, payments subject to withholding tax are satisfied through the issuance of bonds.[64] These rules require a certain portion of the bonds to be withheld, and enable the person withholding to satisfy its obligation to account to HMRC by transferring the bonds to HMRC. In the absence of equivalent rules to accommodate crypto assets, it should be assumed that HMRC would require the obligation to account to be satisfied in cash.

(c) Does payment of compensation in crypto assets give rise to payroll tax consequences?

Please *see* section 1.1.2(e) above.

(d) Do transactions with crypto assets trigger any transfer taxes?

UK stamp duty applies on transfers of stock or marketable securities (and interests in partnerships holding stock or marketable securities).[65] UK stamp duty reserve tax (SDRT) applies to agreements to transfer 'chargeable securities' (which is, broadly, defined similarly).[66] HMRC considers it unlikely that exchange tokens currently existing would constitute either stock or marketable securities, or chargeable securities. If that is the case, transactions in exchange tokens themselves should not be subject to such transfer taxes. However, HMRC has noted that this would need to be considered on a case-by-case basis, by reference to the characteristics and nature of the particular exchange token. Unsurprisingly, transactions in exchange tokens themselves will not be subject to UK stamp duty land tax (which broadly applies to transfers of interests in UK land).[67]

However, transactions where exchange tokens are given in consideration for stock or marketable securities, chargeable securities, or interests in UK land, would need to be considered separately. When calculating a stamp duty charge, HMRC has stated that exchange tokens given in consideration for stock or marketable securities will not be counted as part of the consideration subject to stamp duty, as they do not fall under the meaning of 'money', 'stock or marketable securities', or 'debt' for stamp duty purposes. The transfer may therefore escape charge entirely (depending on whether any other 'stampable consideration' is given). In contrast, for SDRT and stamp duty land tax, any consideration in the form of 'money's worth' will be subject to charge. This will include exchange tokens (with the charge calculated by reference to their value, in pounds sterling, on the date of the transaction).

HMRC has not considered in its published guidance to date the stamp duty, SDRT or stamp duty land tax implications of transfers of (or agreements to transfer) other crypto assets such as utility tokens or security tokens. Care would need to be taken, in

64. Section 939 of the Income Tax Act 2007.
65. Schedule 13 of the Finance Act 1999 and section 122 of the Stamp Act 1891.
66. Section 87 and 99 of the Finance Act 2003.
67. Part 4 of the Finance Act 2003.

particular, regarding the transfer of security tokens granting interests in, or rights over, stock or marketable securities, chargeable securities or UK land.

(e) *Are firms operating in the crypto space subject to digital service taxes?*

A new UK digital services tax took effect from 1 April 2020.[68] The tax applies to online search engines, social media platforms, and online marketplaces. Transactions in crypto assets, and those providing services in respect thereof, should not therefore generally be within scope. In any event, the charge only applies to businesses generating global annual revenue of more than GBP 500 million from such activities (in circumstances where at least GBP 25 million of such revenue derives from UK users). These thresholds are unlikely to be exceeded by crypto businesses.

(f) *Are crypto assets subject to gift, inheritance, estate, or wealth taxes?*

The UK does not have wealth taxes. However UK inheritance tax may apply to the estate of a deceased person, certain lifetime gifts and certain trust arrangements.[69] Subject to certain exceptions, these taxes will mainly be of relevance to individuals.

In some circumstances, assets outside the UK may escape charge (e.g., if the individual is not domiciled in the UK).[70] However, HMRC's position is that (i) exchange tokens are assets for this purpose and (ii) subject to the terms of any relevant double tax treaty,[71] their situs is wherever the holder is resident. Inheritance tax cannot, therefore, be circumvented by investing in assets on a non-UK exchange.

Broadly, inheritance tax only applies to the assets of a person's estate if the value of the estate (excluding assets which will pass to the person's spouse, civil partner or charities) exceeds GBP 325,000.[72] Any excess is subject to tax at a rate of 40%.

For inheritance tax purposes, lifetime gifts do not generally attract a charge at the time of transfer. However, the value of gifts made in the last three years prior to death will count towards the GBP 325,000 threshold mentioned above (as will a proportion of the value of gifts made in the last four years prior to that). Certain lifetime gifts constitute 'exempt gifts', including any gifts to a spouse or charity, gifts out of income, and any gifts of less than GBP 250.[73] In addition, each person has an annual allowance of GBP 3,000.

68. Part 2 of the Finance Act 2020.
69. Where assets are placed in a discretionary trust, or a trust subject to a contingency, a charge of up to 6% will apply when the assets are removed from the trust, or if later, on each ten-year anniversary of the trust (*see* further Part 3 of Chapter 1 of the Inheritance Tax Act 1984). Depending on the circumstances, these provisions may capture commercial trust and escrow arrangements.
70. Section 6(1) of the Inheritance Tax Act 1984.
71. The UK has double tax treaties covering inheritance tax with the Republic of Ireland, the Netherlands, France, Sweden, Italy, Switzerland, India, Pakistan, South African and the US.
72. Sections 4 and 7–9 of the Inheritance Tax Act 1984. This limit can be increased to GBP 500,000 (for the 2020–2021 tax year) if the assets include the deceased's home, which is to pass to his/her children or grandchildren.
73. Part 2 of Chapter 1 of the Inheritance Tax Act 1984.

Lifetime gifts of crypto assets which are capital assets may also give rise to a capital gains tax charge. This is because such gifted assets will generally be treated as having been disposed of for their market value.[74] Exemptions apply for gifts to spouses and civil partners[75] and gifts to charities.[76] Relief from the charge may also be available for gifts of capital assets which are business assets.[77]

A gift of crypto assets which constitute trading assets or intangible fixed assets would not generally give rise to a tax charge, as it would not be expected to generate a credit in the donor's profit and loss statement.[78] Subject to the fulfilment of certain conditions, a donation of crypto assets which are trading assets to charity may in fact *generate* tax relief capable of being offset against taxable profits.[79] Equivalent relief would not be available in respect of a gift of crypto assets which are intangible fixed assets.

(g) Are crypto assets subject to exit tax?

UK exit charges apply where (i) a company ceases to be resident in the UK or (ii) a non-resident company ceases to carry on a trade in the UK through a permanent establishment. Broadly, the intent is to bring certain unrealized profits or gains into the charge to tax.

Exit charges apply in respect of (among other categories of assets) the company's capital assets, trading stock and intangible fixed assets. The exit charge would, therefore, apply to any crypto assets held by the taxpayer. How the charge is calculated will vary slightly as between the relevant assets. Broadly, the effect will be to bring into the charge to tax (i) any difference between the base cost of capital assets and their market value;[80] (ii) the market value of closing trading stock;[81] and (iii) the difference between the carrying value and market value of intangible fixed assets.[82] Subject to certain conditions, the payment of the exit charge can be deferred, and paid in instalments.[83] At the end of the Brexit transactional period, these deferment provisions (which derive from EU law)[84] will be retained, unless specifically repealed or amended

74. Section 17 of the Taxation of Chargeable Gains Act 1992.
75. Section 58 of the Taxation of Chargeable Gains Act 1992.
76. Section 257 of the Taxation of Chargeable Gains Act 1992.
77. Gift holdover relief effectively allows the recipient to take over the donor's capital gains tax position in respect of the asset, without a charge arising for the donor (*see* further section 165 of the Taxation of Chargeable Gains Act 1992).
78. However, where the gift is to a related party, transfer pricing rules may be in point, and (for intangible fixed assets) a market value override would apply in calculating the profit on realization (as to which, *see* sections 845–849 of the Corporation Tax Act 2009).
79. For corporation taxpayers, *see* sections 105–108 of the Corporation Tax Act 2009. For income taxpayers, *see* section 108 of the Income Tax (Trading and Other Income) Act 2005.
80. Sections 25, 185 and 187 of the Taxation of Chargeable Gains Act 1992.
81. Sections 41 and 162 of the Corporation Tax Act 2009 (by virtue of section 41(2)(b), CTA 2009).
82. Section 859 of the Corporation Tax Act 2009.
83. Schedule 3ZB to the Taxes Management Act 1970.
84. EU Council Directive (EU) 2016/1164 laying down rules against tax avoidance practices that directly affect the functioning of the internal market (known as ATAD).

by the legislature. The British government has not given any indication that it intends to do so.

Exit charges do not apply to any other category of taxpayer.

(h) Can mining trigger gambling tax?

In the UK, any rewards from gambling activities are not subject to tax. HMRC has not made any statement as to whether mining activities may constitute gambling. However, in light of HMRC's statement that investment in exchange tokens would not be characterized as gambling,[85] it seems unlikely that HMRC would be willing to adopt a different approach for mining.

1.1.4 Compliance and Documentation Obligations

(a) What documentation requirements exist for taxpayers regarding crypto assets and are there best practices in recordkeeping to support representations made in tax returns?

There are no legislative documentation requirements specific to crypto assets. The overriding obligation on taxpayers is to keep records (in hard copy or digital form) sufficient to the support the position taken in their tax returns. How long the records must be kept for varies as between different categories of taxpayer. Generally, for any tax return:

- relating to income or gains:
  - of individuals not carrying on a business, it is 22 months from the end of the period to which the return relates;
  - of individuals trading (or in partnership), it is five years from 31 January following the end of the period to which the return relates; and
  - of companies, it is six years from the end of the accounting period to which the return relates;
- relating to VAT, it is six years from the end of the relevant reporting period; and
- relating to employee income tax withholding (so-called 'Pay As You Earn' or 'PAYE' withholding) and employee and employer national insurance contributions, it is three years from the end of the relevant reporting period.[86]

85. *See* 'Cryptoassets: tax for individuals', referred to in *supra* n. 1.
86. *See* sections 12B and 12C and Schedule A1 of the Taxes Management Act 1970, paragraph 21 of Schedule 18 of the Finance Act 1998, paragraph 6 of Schedule 11 of the Value Added Tax Act 1994, regulations 33–33B of the Value Added Tax Regulations 1995 (SI1995/2518) and the Income Tax (Pay As You Earn) Regulations 2003 (SI 2003/2682).

Breach of these obligations will generally result in a fine of up to GBP 3,000, and more practically, may impact the amount of tax ultimately payable if the taxpayer's position in the return cannot be substantiated.

For individuals, HMRC has, however, provided guidance regarding record keeping obligations in the context of transactions in exchange tokens. The guidance notes that crypto asset exchanges may only keep records for a limited period of time or may no longer be in existence by the time a person is required to submit their tax return to HMRC. It therefore stresses that the onus is on the taxpayer to keep records of each crypto asset transaction, and that these must include '(a) the type of crypto asset; (b) the date of the transaction; (c) whether the assets were bought or sold; (d) the number of units [subject to the transaction]; (e) the value of the transaction in pounds sterling; (f) the cumulative total of investment units held; and (g) bank statement and wallet addresses'.

In addition, guidance applying to both individuals and businesses specifies that for capital gains tax purposes, individuals and businesses must keep records of the 'allowable cost' for any pool (*see* further section 1.1.2(b) above).

Noting the requirement that profits, gains and losses must generally be reported to HMRC in pounds sterling, and that many crypto asset exchanges do not use pounds sterling, HMRC has confirmed the following:

- for transactions which do not have a value in pounds sterling (e.g. where one kind of exchange token is exchanged for another), an appropriate exchange rate must be established to convert the transaction into pounds sterling;
- reasonable care should be taken to arrive at an appropriate valuation for transactions using a consistent methodology; and
- records should be kept of such valuation methodology.

(b) *What is the evidentiary burden of supporting tax positions when a digital wallet address is lost or shared with other persons?*

As discussed above, for capital gains tax purposes, where an exchange token is lost (e.g. because the key to the wallet in which the token is held has been lost), taxpayers may be able to make a negligible value claim. The claim will need to state (i) the asset which is the subject of the claim, (ii) the amount for which the asset should be treated as disposed of (which may be GBP 0) and (iii) the date that the asset should be treated as disposed of. Appropriate valuations may have to be agreed with HMRC.[87]

When, as a result of such loss, the taxpayer submits a tax return claiming a deductible expense in respect of trading or intangible fixed assets, or makes a negligible value claim in respect of capital assets, the burden of proof is no different than that which applies to any other return in which such expense or relief is claimed; the burden of proof falls on the taxpayer to establish that the conditions for the deduction or relief have been met. The applicable standard of proof is the balance of probabilities.

87. *See* HMRC's Capital Gains Tax Manual, paragraph CG13120P onwards.

(c) *Are crypto asset exchanges and wallet providers subject to reporting obligations?*

Crypto asset exchanges and wallet providers are not subject to any *specific* obligation to report information regarding their customers to HMRC. However, HMRC has powers to compel the provision of information relating to UK taxpayers from exchanges and wallet providers (*see* section 1.1.4(a) for individual taxpayers recordkeeping obligations).

If such exchanges and providers are themselves within the scope of UK tax, standard reporting obligations applicable to UK taxpayers would apply.

(d) *Are taxpayers holding crypto assets subject to reporting obligations apart from the filing of income tax/capital gains tax returns?*

UK taxpayers holding crypto assets would not be subject to any particular additional filing obligations.

If a UK taxpayer is merely holding crypto assets, this would not generally have to be reported in tax returns until the holding of, or transactions in, such assets had an impact on the amount of capital gains/losses or income/expenses to be reported in such returns.

Similarly, if exchange tokens were (i) used to pay for goods or services subject to VAT, (ii) given in consideration for an acquisition of an interest in UK land subject to stamp duty land tax, or (iii) given as employment remuneration, then the usual reporting obligations relevant to such transactions would apply (irrespective of the form of payment).

(e) *Are crypto asset exchanges and wallet providers subject to CRS/FATCA reporting?*

Broadly, pursuant to FATCA/CRS reporting requirements, 'financial institutions' (being 'investment entities', 'depositary institutions' and 'custodial institutions') are required to conduct due diligence on certain customers who have 'financial accounts' with them, and report on the same to tax authorities.[88] The information reported is then automatically exchanged between tax authorities.

HMRC has not given any indication as to its views on whether crypto exchanges or wallet providers would constitute financial institutions for the purposes of CRS/FATCA reporting. As a result, the particular services offered by a crypto asset exchange or wallet provider, and the nature of the crypto assets in respect of which such services are provided, would need to be analysed on case-by-case basis.

---

88. *See* the International Tax Compliance Regulations 2015 (as amended) (SI 2015/878).

1.1.5 Civil and Criminal Tax Enforcement

(a) What powers do the tax authorities have to compel the disclosure of information by third parties, such as exchanges or wallet providers, and have these been used in the past?

HMRC can compel third parties to provide information and documents about UK taxpayers if such information is 'reasonably required for the purpose of checking the taxpayer's tax position'.[89] Such obligation is limited to information or documents in the 'possession or power' of the third party.[90] However, HMRC's requests need not be limited to specific documents, and can require third parties to create new documents. In the absence of consent from the relevant taxpayer, HMRC would need judicial approval to make such a 'third-party request'.[91] Broadly, for approval to be granted, the relevant tribunal must be satisfied that HMRC has reasonable grounds for making the request. Third parties who do not comply can be subject to daily penalties and in some cases, tax-based penalties.

Indeed, it has been reported that HMRC has sent such third-party notices to certain crypto asset exchanges.[92] In response to a freedom of information request from a crypto asset publication, HMRC is reported to have said that 'These exchanges can retain information on their clients and the transactions that they have completed. These transactions may result in potential tax charges and HMRC has the power to issue notices requiring exchanges to provide this information.'

(b) What measures have the tax authorities undertaken in the past to ensure crypto tax compliance?

HMRC has published guidance (described above) clarifying how certain existing UK tax laws apply to exchange tokens. Beyond that, it is not known what (if any) additional steps HMRC has taken to ensure crypto tax compliance.

As mentioned above, it has been reported that HMRC has asked cryptocurrency exchanges, including Coinbase, CEX.IO, and eToro, for details about their customers' transaction history.[93] However, this has not been confirmed, because HMRC is generally subject to privacy obligations regarding steps taken in respect of specific taxpayers.[94] Although HMRC does have the power to publish information regarding deliberate tax defaulters,[95] it is not possible to ascertain, from the details published, whether any such defaults relate to the holding of, or transactions in, crypto assets.

89. *See* paragraph 2 of Schedule 36 of the Finance Act 2008.
90. *See* paragraph 18 of Schedule 36 of the Finance Act 2008.
91. *See* paragraph 3 of Schedule 36 of the Finance Act 2008.
92. *See* https://www.coindesk.com/british-tax-authority-seeks-customer-data-from-crypto-exchanges-in-search-of-tax-evaders.
93. *Ibid.*, coindesk.com.
94. *See* section 19 of the Commissioners for Revenue and Customs Act 2005 and HMRC's Compliance Handbook, paragraph CH207323.
95. *See* section 94 of the Finance Act 2009.

More generally, if HMRC was to introduce specific measures targeting cryptocurrency compliance, this would typically be preceded by a public consultation. In this respect, nothing has been announced to date. However, a 2018 report from the 'Cryptoassets Taskforce' of HM Treasury, the UK Financial Conduct Authority and the Bank of England notes that 'both [HM Treasury and HMRC] recognise the risks of tax avoidance and evasion arising from the increased use of crypto assets and are continuing to review the range of enforcement tools and approaches at HMRC's disposal.'[96]

(c) *Are the tax authorities cooperating with tax authorities in other jurisdictions on enforcement?*

In order to ensure compliance by taxpayers holding crypto assets, HMRC has a number of means available to request information from abroad (e.g., from foreign tax authorities in respect of crypto asset exchanges and other providers of services in respect of crypto assets located outside the UK):

- Over 100 of the double tax treaties to which the UK is party contain (an equivalent of) Article 26 of the OECD Model Convention, providing for the exchange of information between contracting states' competent authorities.
- The UK is party to a number of bilateral 'Tax Information Exchange Agreements' with certain jurisdictions with which the UK does not have a tax treaty, including Bermuda, BVI, Guernsey, Jersey and the Isle of Man.
- The UK has, together with 136 other jurisdictions, signed up to the OECD Convention on Mutual Administrative Assistance in Tax Matters, which facilitates the exchange of information between signatory states.

Broadly, for HMRC to request information pursuant to the above instruments, the information would need to be foreseeably relevant to the administration and enforcement of the UK's laws concerning the taxes covered therein.

In addition, during the Brexit transitional period, the UK has remained subject to, and benefitted from, the rights and obligations of EU Member States regarding the collection and exchange of certain information which may be relevant from a tax perspective.[97] Specifically, as with other EU Member States, the UK has been required to: (a) collect, and automatically exchange, information regarding beneficial ownership collected pursuant to anti-money laundering processes and (b) implement legislation requiring information regarding certain cross-border arrangements (including, but not limited to, those with a main benefit of obtaining an EU tax advantage) to be

96. *See* 'Cryptoassets Taskforce: final report' (at https://assets.publishing.service.gov.uk/government/uploads/system/uploads/attachment_data/file/752070/cryptoassets_taskforce_final_report_final_web.pdf).
97. Council Directive 2011/16/EU of 15 Feb. 2011 on administrative cooperation in the field of taxation, as amended.

reported to, and exchanged between, the tax authorities of EU Member States.[98] Once the transitional period has ended, the UK's obligations to collect this information, and provide it to EU Member States, will be retained as part of domestic UK law, unless expressly repealed by the UK Government. It is not yet clear whether EU Member States will grant the UK reciprocal access to such information they have collected. Nevertheless, information could still be requested from EU Member States under the multilateral and bilateral agreements mentioned above.

It is not publicly known whether HMRC has exercised its powers under the above instruments to seek information regarding UK taxpayer's holdings of crypto assets, and if so, whether HMRC has been successful in gaining access to such information.

98. The International Tax Enforcement (Disclosable Arrangements) Regulations 2020 (25/2020). Originally, such information would have been reported to HMRC from Jul. 2020 and exchanged between the tax authorities of EU Member States from 31 Oct. 2020. However, in light of the COVID-19 pandemic, certain Member States, including the UK, agreed to defer the dates for first reporting, and first exchanges between tax authorities, by six months.

United States of America

Lisa Zarlenga[*]

1. COUNTRY GUIDES

1.1 United States of America

1.1.1 Applicable Tax Law, Guidance, and Case Law

(a) Which laws, regulations, and other administrative guidance exist dealing with crypto assets?

There are no tax laws that specifically deal with crypto assets in the United States (US). Instead, general tax rules contained in the Internal Revenue Code of 1986, as amended, and the regulations promulgated thereunder will apply.[1]

The US Department of Treasury ('Treasury') and the Internal Revenue Service (IRS) (collectively referred to as the 'IRS')[2] have issued some administrative guidance regarding the tax treatment of convertible virtual currency. Specifically, Notice 2014-21[3] generally treats convertible virtual currency as property for tax purposes and states that general tax principles applicable to property transactions apply to transactions involving convertible virtual currency. The Notice defines virtual currency as 'a digital representation of value that functions as a medium of exchange, a unit of account, and/or a store of value'.[4] Virtual currency is convertible if it 'has an

* Lisa would like to thank Steptoe attorneys David Fruchtman, Beth Tractenberg, Jasmine Campirides, and John Cobb for their contributions to this chapter.

1. Unless otherwise specified, all section references are to the Internal Revenue Code of 1986, as amended (the 'Code'), and all references to 'Treas. Reg. §' are to the Treasury Regulations thereunder.
2. Treasury and the IRS issue regulations and other administrative guidance jointly, but the IRS is responsible for enforcement of the tax laws.
3. 2014-16 I.R.B. 938 (25 Mar. 2014), https://www.irs.gov/pub/irs-drop/n-14-21.pdf.
4. *Id.* at § 2.

equivalent value in real currency, [or] acts as a substitute for real currency', such as bitcoin.[5]

The IRS subsequently issued frequently asked questions (FAQs) elaborating on the treatment of convertible virtual currency as property for individuals who hold cryptocurrency as a capital asset and are not engaged in the trade or business of selling cryptocurrency.[6] Although FAQs are not formal guidance on which taxpayers can rely to avoid penalties, and they can be revised without notice, they do provide some general insight into how the IRS approaches these questions.

Finally, the IRS issued Revenue Ruling 2019-24,[7] which provides guidance on the tax treatment of hard forks. The ruling concludes generally that a taxpayer has ordinary income as a result of an airdrop of a new cryptocurrency following a hard fork if the taxpayer receives units of new cryptocurrency.[8]

(b) Which court cases exist dealing with crypto assets?

There exist no tax cases dealing with crypto assets. However, there are a couple of district court decisions holding that bitcoin is a commodity for purposes of regulation by the Commodities Futures Trading Commission ('CFTC').[9] As discussed further in sections 1.1.2(d) and 1.1.4(c) and (d), below, classification of crypto assets as a commodity may have some relevance for tax purposes.

1.1.2 Income and Capital Gains Taxes

(a) How are crypto assets classified for income and capital gains tax purposes?

The IRS has indicated that convertible virtual currency is treated as property for tax purposes, and not as foreign currency.[10] However, it did not define what kind of property. Therefore, existing IRS guidance does not directly address the classification of crypto assets.

The classification is further complicated by the fact that the regulatory agencies in the US have taken differing positions on how crypto assets are classified. For example, bitcoin is treated as property by the IRS, as a commodity by the CFTC,[11] and

5. *Id.*
6. Frequently Asked Questions on Virtual Currency Transactions, https://www.irs.gov/individuals/international-taxpayers/frequently-asked-questions-on-virtual-currency-transactions (hereinafter 'IRS FAQ').
7. 2019-44 I.R.B. 1004 (28 Oct. 2019), https://www.irs.gov/pub/irs-drop/rr-19-24.pdf.
8. *See also* IRS FAQ, at Q&A 22.
9. *See Commodity Futures Trading Comm'n v. My Big Coin Pay, Inc.*, No. 18-10077-RWZ (D. Mass. 26 Sep. 2018); *Commodity Futures Trading Comm'n v. McDonnell*, No. 1:18-cv-00361 (E.D.N.Y. 6 Mar. 2018).
10. *See* Notice 2014-21, at § 4 Q&A 1 and 2; IRS FAQ, at Q&A 2.
11. *See* Testimony of CFTC Chairman Timothy Massad before the US Senate Committee on Agriculture, Nutrition and Forestry (10 Dec. 2014), http://www.cftc.gov/PressRoom/SpeechesTestimony/opamassad-6. This position has been upheld by US federal courts. *See supra* note 9.

as money by the Treasury's Financial Crimes Enforcement Network ('FinCEN').[12] In addition, the Securities and Exchange Commission ('SEC') has said that bitcoin and ether do not constitute securities, but other tokens could.[13] Specifically, a crypto asset should be analysed to determine whether it has the characteristics of a 'security' under the federal securities laws, which may include an 'investment contract', as well as other instruments such as stocks and bonds. Thus, while a security token that would be characterized as debt or equity would likely be a security, certain utility or payment tokens could also be treated as securities if they constitute an investment contract. The SEC applies the 'Howey' test, named after a US Supreme Court case,[14] to find an investment contract when there is the investment of money in a common enterprise with a reasonable expectation of profits to be derived from the efforts of others. This often depends on where the token is in its life cycle. For example, the SEC has concluded that where investors in a token rely on the managerial efforts of a sponsor or developer to develop the platform and market the token, the token may be an investment contract, but where the token and platform are developed, and the token may be used to consume goods and services on the platform, it may not be an investment contract.[15]

(b) *What are the income/capital gains tax consequences of selling crypto assets against fiat currency?*

In general, selling crypto assets for fiat currency will be a realization event giving rise to taxable gain or loss.[16]

The character of the gain or loss generally depends on whether the crypto asset is a capital asset in the hands of the taxpayer.[17] A taxpayer generally realizes capital gain or loss on the sale or exchange of virtual currency that is a capital asset in the hands of the taxpayer.[18] Property held for investment, such as stocks and bonds, is generally treated as a capital asset. Property used in a trade or business is generally not a capital asset, including:

12. FinCEN has taken the position that convertible virtual currency substitutes for currency and, thus, can make someone a 'money transmitter' (31 C.F.R. § 1010.100(ff)(5)(i)(A)). *See also* FinCEN Guidance, Application of FinCEN's Regulations to Persons Administering, Exchanging, or Using Virtual Currencies, FIN-2013-G001 (18 Mar. 2013); FinCEN Guidance, Application of FinCEN's Regulations to Certain Business Models Involving Convertible Virtual Currencies, FIN-2019-G001 (9 May 2019).
13. Specifically, the SEC has said that bitcoin and ether, in their present decentralized state, are not securities, but that certain tokens issued in initial coin offerings may be securities. *See* William Hinman, *Digital Asset Transactions: When Howey Met Gary (Plastics)*, Remarks at the Yahoo Finance All Markets Summit: Crypto (14 Jun. 2018), https://www.sec.gov/news/speech/speech-hinman-061418; *see also* SEC, *Framework for 'Investment Contract' Analysis of Digital Assets*, https://www.sec.gov/corpfin/framework-investment-contract-analysis-digital-assets.
14. *SEC v. W.J. Howey Co.*, 328 U.S. 293 (1946).
15. *See* SEC, *Framework for 'Investment Contract' Analysis of Digital Assets*, https://www.sec.gov/corpfin/framework-investment-contract-analysis-digital-assets#_ednref5.
16. Code § 1001. *See* IRS FAQ, at Q&A 4.
17. *See* Notice 2014-21, at § 4 Q&A 7.
18. *See* Code § 1222.

(1) inventory or other property held primarily for sale to customers in a trade or business, or
(2) property of a character which is subject to the allowance for depreciation or real property used in a trade or business.[19]

In addition, certain self-created assets are treated as non-capital assets, namely certain copyrights, literary, musical, or artistic compositions, letters or memorandums, or similar property.[20] As discussed further in section 1.1.2(d), crypto assets held by a dealer in crypto assets would be treated as inventory and thus ordinary under (1) above. However, because crypto assets are not tangible assets, they likely would not be subject to depreciation under (2) above.

In general, gain or loss on the sale or exchange of a capital asset is treated as long-term capital gain or loss when the capital asset has been held for longer than one year, or short-term capital gain or loss when the capital asset has been held for less than one year.[21] Long-term and short-term capital gains and losses are treated as follows for tax purposes:

- For individual taxpayers, a long-term capital gain is taxed at preferential rates (generally a maximum rate of 20%).[22] A short-term capital gain is taxed at ordinary income rates (up to a maximum rate of 39.6%, or 37% for taxable years beginning after 31 December 2017 and before 1 January 2026).[23] Capital losses are deductible to the extent of capital gains; plus individuals may deduct up to USD 3,000 of net capital losses.[24] Individuals may carry forward unused capital loss indefinitely, but they retain their character as long-term or short-term losses.
- Corporations pay the same marginal rate of tax on ordinary or capital gains (i.e., 21%). Net capital losses incurred by corporations cannot be currently deducted.[25] Instead, net capital losses generally can be carried back for three taxable years and carried forward for ten taxable years.[26]

The amount of gain or loss is computed by subtracting the taxpayer's cost basis from the amount realized. This amount must be reported on the federal income tax

19. Code § 1221(a). Section 1231 allows gain or loss from the disposition of property that is used in a trade or business and is of a character subject to the allowance for depreciation under section 167 or any real property used in a trade or business to be treated as capital, provided that it is held more than one year, notwithstanding it would otherwise be ordinary under section 1221.
20. *See* Code § 1221(a). For dispositions after 31 Dec. 2017, self-created patents, inventions, models or designs (whether or not patented), and secret formulas or processes also will generally not be treated as capital assets. Pub. L. No. 115-97 § 13314.
21. Code §§ 1(h), 1222. *See* IRS FAQ, at Q&A 5.
22. For individuals with incomes above USD 250,000 for married couples filing jointly and USD 200,000 for single people, there is an additional 3.8% tax on net investment income, including capital gains (Code § 1411).
23. Code § 1(a), (j), added by Pub. L. No. 115-97 (22 Dec. 2017).
24. Code § 1211(b).
25. Code § 1211(a).
26. Code § 1212(a).

return in US dollars.[27] When the crypto asset is sold for fiat currency, the amount realized is the amount of cash received. The IRS has provided some guidance on the computation of cost basis for sales of convertible virtual currencies. In general, cost basis is equal to the amount spent to acquire the virtual currency, including fees, commissions, and other acquisition costs, expressed in US dollars.[28] More specifically:

- The basis of virtual currency received as payment for goods or services is equal to the fair market value of the virtual currency in US dollars when the virtual currency is received.[29]
- The basis of virtual currency received in exchange for property is equal to the fair market value of the virtual currency when it is received.[30]

With respect to the fair market value of virtual currency, Notice 2014-21 provided that if a virtual currency is listed on an exchange, then the value of such virtual currency generally could be determined using the exchange rate, in a reasonable manner that is consistently applied.[31] The subsequent FAQs, however, appear to call for a more restrictive approach to valuation:

- If a taxpayer receives cryptocurrency in a transaction facilitated by a cryptocurrency exchange, the value of the cryptocurrency is the amount that is recorded by the cryptocurrency exchange for that transaction in US dollars (or would have been recorded if it had been an on-chain transaction).[32]
- If a taxpayer receives cryptocurrency in a peer-to-peer transaction or some other transaction not facilitated by a cryptocurrency exchange, the fair market value of the cryptocurrency is determined as of the date and time the transaction is recorded on the distributed ledger, or would have been recorded on the ledger if it had been an on-chain transaction.[33]
- The IRS will accept as evidence of fair market value the value as determined by a cryptocurrency or blockchain explorer that analyses worldwide indices of a cryptocurrency and calculates the value of the cryptocurrency at an exact date and time. If a taxpayer does not use a value determined by an explorer, the taxpayer must establish that the value used is an accurate representation of the cryptocurrency's fair market value.[34]
- When a taxpayer receives cryptocurrency in exchange for property or services, and that cryptocurrency is not traded on any cryptocurrency exchange and

27. IRS FAQ, at Q&A 6.
28. IRS FAQ, at Q&A 7.
29. Notice 2014-21, at § 4 Q&A 4, IRS FAQ, at Q&A 12.
30. IRS FAQ, at Q&A 20.
31. Notice 2014-21, at § 4 Q&A 4.
32. IRS FAQ, at Q&A 25.
33. IRS FAQ, at Q&A 26.
34. IRS FAQ, at Q&A 26. The IRS appears to mean a global pricing index rather than an explorer, which as typically used in the industry, would not include pricing information.

does not have a published value, then the fair market value of the cryptocurrency received is equal to the fair market value of the property or services exchanged for the cryptocurrency when the transaction occurs.[35]

If a taxpayer owns multiple units of one kind of virtual currency, which were acquired at different times and have different basis amounts, the taxpayer may specifically identify the units that are deemed disposed of.[36] The taxpayer can do this by:

(1) documenting the specific unit's unique identifier such as a private key, public key, and address;
(2) by records showing the transaction information for all units of a specific virtual currency held in a single account, wallet, or address; or
(3) although not specified in the guidance, presumably transaction identifiers, as opposed to wallet identifiers, such as transaction IDs, transaction hashes, or UTXOs.[37]

If specific identification is not used, then first-in-first-out ('FIFO') accounting should be used.[38]

(c) What are the income/capital gains tax consequences of exchanging crypto assets against other crypto assets?

Because crypto assets are treated as property for US federal tax purposes, when a taxpayer exchanges one crypto asset for another one, the taxpayer is engaging in both an acquisition and a disposition. Thus, the taxpayer generally recognizes a gain or loss equal to the difference between the fair market value of the crypto asset received and the taxpayer's adjusted basis in the crypto asset disposed. In addition, the acquired crypto asset may generate a taxable gain or loss upon a later disposition to the extent of any future appreciation or depreciation.

Some investors took the position that an exchange of one crypto asset for another crypto asset was a tax-deferred like-kind exchange under pre-2018 law.[39] Section 1031 provides an exception to the general rule of recognition in the case of certain like-kind exchanges of business or investment property.[40] Like-kind property is property of the same nature, character or class.[41] It is not clear whether the IRS would agree that crypto assets may be of like-kind to other crypto assets. Nonetheless, the Tax Cuts and Jobs

35. IRS FAQ, at Q&A 27.
36. IRS FAQ, at Q&A 38.
37. IRS FAQ, at Q&A 39.
38. IRS FAQ, at Q&A 40.
39. *See* Code § 1031, prior to amendment by Pub. L. No. 115-97 (22 Dec. 2017).
40. Instead the taxpayer takes a carryover basis in the property received, which means that the taxpayer's gain effectively is deferred until the taxpayer disposes of the property received in a taxable transaction.
41. Treas. Reg. § 1.1031(a)-1(b).

Act[42] limited like-kind exchanges under section 1031 to exchanges of certain real property, so crypto assets can no longer qualify for tax-deferred treatment under section 1031.

Crypto assets can be used to acquire goods and services, much like cash. Because crypto assets are treated as property, this is generally treated as a barter transaction, giving rise to gain or loss equal to the difference between the fair market value and adjusted basis of the crypto asset.[43]

(d) If a distinction is made between business assets and non-business assets, when does trading in crypto assets lead to a trade or business?

Different US federal income tax rules apply to investors, traders, and dealers. Traders and dealers are considered to be in a trade or business; investors are not. Generally, to be engaged in a trade or business, the taxpayer must be involved in the activity with continuity and regularity and that the taxpayer's primary purpose for engaging in the activity must be for income or profit.[44] Note that corporations are generally deemed to be engaged in a trade or business.

The distinction between investors, traders, and dealers is based on the facts and circumstances, which considers: (1) the frequency, extent, and regularity of transactions, (2) the taxpayers' investment intent, and (3) the nature of the income derived from the activity.[45]

Investor: An investor purchases crypto assets to profit from income (such as interest and dividends) and capital appreciation over a longer investment horizon, as opposed to seeking profits from short-term price swings.[46] Investors are not treated as engaged in a trade or business, even if the investor engages in a high volume of transactions.[47] As a result, any gain or loss on the sale of crypto assets by an investor will be capital in nature,[48] and expenses are generally deductible only as a miscellaneous itemized deduction (that is, only to the extent the aggregate of such deductions exceeds 2% of adjusted gross income).[49] However, the Code was amended to disallow a miscellaneous itemized deduction for taxable years beginning after 31 December 2017 and before 1 January 2026.[50]

Trader: A taxpayer may be a trader in crypto assets if its trading activities are substantial enough to rise to the level of a trade or business. Traders buy and sell crypto assets for their own accounts rather than for customers. A trader's activities must be

42. Pub. L. No. 115-97 (22 Dec. 2017).
43. *See, e.g.*, IRS FAQ, at Q&A 13, 15, 18.
44. *See, e.g.*, *Comm'r v. Groetzinger*, 480 U.S. 23 (1987); *Whipple v. Comm'r*, 373 U.S. 193 (1963).
45. *See, e.g.*, *Higgins v. Comm'r*, 312 U.S. 212 (1941); *Estate of Yaeger v. Comm'r*, 889 F.2d 29 (2d Cir. 1989).
46. *See, e.g.*, *Moller v. United States*, 721 F.2d 810 (Fed. Cir. 1983); *Mayer v. United States*, 32 Fed. Cl. 149 (1994).
47. *Whipple v. Comm'r*, 373 U.S. 193 (1963).
48. Code § 1221(a).
49. Code § 67(a). This does not apply, however, to fees, commissions, and other costs to acquire crypto assets, which are added to cost basis. *See* IRS FAQ, at Q&A 7.
50. Code § 67(h), added by Pub. L. No. 115-97 (22 Dec. 2017).

directed to short-term trading, not the long-term holding of crypto assets, and income must be principally derived from the sale of investments rather than from dividends and interest paid on those investments.[51] A trader may deduct expenses from gross income (except for commissions and fees to acquire crypto assets, which are added to the cost basis).[52] Traders in crypto assets may be able to make an election to mark-to-market open positions at the end of each year, if the crypto assets are properly characterized as securities[53] or commodities.[54] This mark-to-market gain or loss is treated as ordinary, so it may be netted against other income.[55]

Dealer: Generally, dealers are engaged in the trade or business of making a market in an asset class, by being willing to buy or sell such asset at certain prices, seeking to profit from bid-ask spreads.[56] Dealers generally do not seek to profit from appreciation on investments or short-term market swings. Thus, dealers in crypto assets have inventories of crypto assets that they hold for sale to customers in the ordinary course of their trade or business. If the crypto assets are properly characterized as securities, dealers must mark them to market at the end of each year, and if the crypto assets are properly treated as commodities, dealers may elect to mark them to market, in either case recognizing ordinary gain or loss.[57] In addition, a dealer may deduct expenses from gross income.[58]

(e) What are the income/capital gains tax consequences for an employee receiving wages or salaries in crypto assets?

Payment of wages or salaries in crypto assets is taxed in the same as any other payment in kind, which means that such compensation payments generally will be subject to income tax.[59] Specifically, the service provider is required to include the fair market value of the crypto asset, in US dollars, when received (which, in an on-chain transaction, is on the date and at the time the transaction is recorded on the distributed ledger).[60] In addition, the payment in crypto assets would be subject to payroll or self-employment tax depending on the nature of the employment, and reportable on

51. *See* cases cited *supra* note 46.
52. Code § 162; IRS FAQ, at Q&A 7.
53. For this purpose, the term 'security' means stock in a corporation; interest in publicly traded partnership; a note, bond, debenture, or other evidence of indebtedness; a notional principal contract; a derivative in one of the foregoing or in currency, including an option, forward contract, or short position; and any hedge with respect to one of the foregoing. Code § 475(c)(2).
54. Code § 475(f)(1), (2). For this purpose, the term 'commodity' means personal property of a type that is actively traded. Code § 475(e)(2)(A). Actively traded personal property includes any personal property traded on an established financial market, such as an interdealer market. Treas. Reg. § 1.1092(d)-1(a). Assuming that crypto asset exchanges are interdealer quotation systems, crypto assets may be treated as commodities for purposes of the mark-to-market election.
55. Code § 475(f)(1)(D).
56. Code § 475(c). *See generally* T.D. 9328 (11 Jun. 2007).
57. Code § 475(a), (d)(3), and (e).
58. Code § 162.
59. *See* Notice 2014-21, at § 4 Q&A 3; IRS FAQ, at Q&A 8.
60. IRS FAQ, at Q&A 11. This appears to have narrowed the rule set forth in Q&A 3 of Notice 2014-21, which refers only to the date of the transaction, not the specific time.

information returns (e.g., IRS Forms W-2, *Wage and Tax Statement*, or 1099-MISC, *Miscellaneous Income*).[61]

Further, the use of the crypto asset to pay for services would be treated as a taxable exchange of the crypto asset, and the person making the payment will recognize gain or loss on the exchange.[62]

(f) *What are the income/capital gains tax consequences for a merchant receiving payment in crypto assets?*

A merchant who receives payment in crypto assets for goods or services must include the fair market value of the crypto assets, measured in US dollars, when received (which, in an on-chain transaction, is on the date and at the time the transaction is recorded on the distributed ledger).[63]

In addition, third-party settlement organizations (generally, persons who make settlement payments between merchants and their customers) are required to report such settlement payments, even if made in the form of crypto assets, to such merchants on IRS Form 1099-K, *Payment Card and Third Party Network Transactions*, if, for the calendar year, both (1) the number of transactions settled for the merchant exceeds 200 and (2) the gross amount of payments made to the merchant exceeds USD 20,000.[64]

(g) *What are the income/capital gains tax consequences of a loss of crypto assets?*

In general, a deduction is allowed for losses if the taxpayer has not been compensated for the loss by insurance.[65] To be deductible, losses must be evidenced by closed and completed transactions, fixed by identifiable events, and actually sustained during the taxable year.[66] For individual taxpayers, deductible losses are limited to losses: (1) incurred in a trade or business, or (2) incurred in any transaction entered into for profit.[67] In addition, theft and casualty losses are deductible, regardless of whether incurred in a business or transaction entered into for profit.[68]

An exchange or wallet provider could be hacked and any private keys held by that company could be stolen. If a taxpayer's crypto assets are stolen through a hacking or otherwise, the victim may claim a loss for theft in the year the theft was discovered.[69] However, if the taxpayer merely loses his or her private key, thus becoming unable to

61. IRS FAQ, at Q&A 9, 10; Notice 2014-21, at § 4 Q&A 10, 11, 13.
62. *See* IRS FAQ, at Q&A 13.
63. IRS FAQ, at Q&A 11, 18. This appears to have narrowed the rule set forth in Q&A 3 of Notice 2014-21, which refers only to the date of the transaction, not the specific time.
64. Notice 2014-21, at § 4 Q&A 15.
65. Code § 165(a).
66. Treas. Reg. § 1.165-1(b).
67. Code § 165(c)(2).
68. Code § 165(c)(3), (e), (h). If the theft losses relate to a transaction entered into for profit, they may be deducted under section 165(c)(2), which contains fewer limitations on the amount that may be deducted. *See* Rev. Rul. 2009-9, 2009-14 I.R.B. 735.
69. Code § 165(e).

access the associated wallets, it is unlikely to result in a deductible loss.[70] It may be possible to claim a deductible loss if the taxpayer abandons his or her private key, but proving abandonment generally requires a clear intent to abandon the property and an overt act of abandonment, such as writing to the custodian of the private key (e.g., the exchange or wallet provider) that the taxpayer intends to abandon the private key.[71]

(h) *What are the income/capital gains tax consequences of a loss in value of crypto assets?*

If a crypto asset loses value, an investor may recognize a capital loss upon the sale or exchange of that crypto asset at a loss.[72] If the taxpayer is a dealer or a trader that has elected the mark-to-market accounting method for crypto assets that are treated as securities or commodities as discussed in section 1.1.2(d), above, losses are recognized at the end of each year, even if no sale or exchange occurs. In addition, any losses will be treated as ordinary.[73]

However, unlike deductions for theft or abandonment losses, holders of crypto assets may not be able to claim a deduction for worthlessness. In general, holders may be able to claim a loss for securities that are capital assets and that become worthless during the taxable year.[74] For this purpose, security means stock, rights to acquire stock, or a debt instrument with interest coupons or that is in registered form,[75] so this deduction likely is only possible for crypto assets that would otherwise be treated as meeting this definition of a security.

(i) *What are the income/capital gains tax consequences of forks of crypto assets?*

Revenue Ruling 2019-24[76] provides guidance on the tax treatment of hard forks. The ruling concludes first that a taxpayer does not have gross income as a result of a hard fork of a cryptocurrency the taxpayer owns if the taxpayer does not receive units of a new cryptocurrency.[77] Thus, if the taxpayer holds its cryptocurrency in a third-party wallet that does not support the forked currency, the taxpayer generally would not have income.

However, the ruling concludes that a taxpayer does have ordinary income if the taxpayer receives units of new cryptocurrency as a result of an airdrop of a new cryptocurrency following a hard fork.[78] Specifically, the IRS reasoned that, when the

70. *See, e.g., Bakewell v. Comm'r*, 23 T.C. 803 (1955); *Sava-Goiu v. Comm'r*, 9 T.C.M. 128 (1950).
71. *See, e.g., Beus v. Comm'r*, 261 F.2d 176 (9th Cir. 1958); Rev. Rul. 2004-58, 2004-1 C.B. 1043.
72. *See* Code § 1211.
73. *See* Code § 475(d)(3), (f)(1)(D).
74. Code § 165(g)(1).
75. Code § 165(g)(2).
76. 2019-44 I.R.B. 1004.
77. *See also* IRS FAQ, at Q&A 21.
78. *See also* IRS FAQ, at Q&A 22. The ruling contemplates that a forked currency is received via airdrop, although the reasoning seems to apply to the receipt of any forked currency.

taxpayer receives units of the new cryptocurrency, the taxpayer has an accession to wealth, which is treated as income.[79] The income arises once the taxpayer has dominion and control over the forked currency, which the IRS concludes is at the time it is recorded on the distributed ledger, because the taxpayer immediately has the ability to dispose of forked cryptocurrency.[80] The amount of the income is the fair market value of the new cryptocurrency at the time it is received.[81] This is true even if the hard fork results in a reduction in value of the original cryptocurrency; if that happens, the taxpayer may recognize a loss on the original cryptocurrency when he or she disposes of it.

The recipient would take a cost basis in the forked cryptocurrency equal to the amount included in income, so the recipient may recover his or her investment upon the later use or conversion of the cryptocurrency.[82]

A soft fork, on the other hand, does not result in a split of the blockchain into two crypto assets and does not result in the creation of a new native token. As a result, it does not generate a taxable event.[83]

(j) *What are the income/capital gains tax consequences of airdrops of crypto assets and are the tax consequences different if the airdropped tokens are unwanted?*

The IRS has not yet provided any guidance on the tax treatment of an airdrop, whereby crypto assets are deposited in the recipient's wallet for no consideration, typically to market a new crypto asset. Although Revenue Ruling 2019-24 refers to airdrops following hard forks, the guidance only addresses the treatment of hard forks and does not specifically address airdrops. However, the reasoning applied to hard forks[84] would likely result in income when the airdrop is received. The value of the airdropped crypto asset could be treated as income from the performance of services of the recipients if the recipients had to do something to obtain it (such as promoting it on social media), or it could be treated as a taxable accession to wealth if unsolicited (generally analogous to free samples or prizes or awards).[85] Either way, it should be considered ordinary income to the recipient, as opposed to capital gain.[86]

---

79. Code § 61; *Comm'r v. Glenshaw Glass Co.*, 348 U.S. 426 (1955).
80. *See also* IRS FAQ, at Q&A 22.
81. *See* Rev. Rul. 2019-24; IRS FAQ, at Q&A 23.
82. *See* IRS FAQ, at Q&A 24.
83. *See* IRS FAQ, at Q&A 29.
84. *See supra* section 1.1.2(i).
85. *See, e.g.*, Treas. Reg. § 1.61-14(a) (property found by the taxpayer is gross income in an amount equal to its value when reduced to 'undisputed possession'); *Comm'r v. Glenshaw Glass Co.*, 348 U.S. 426 (1955) (taxpayer recognizes income on windfalls when they represent 'undeniable accessions to wealth, clearly realized, and over which the taxpayers have complete dominion'); *Haverly v. US*, 513 F.2d 224, 226 (7th Cir.), *cert. denied*, 423 U.S. 912 (1975) (sample textbooks sent by publishers to principal of public school and donated by him to school library; held, 'intent to exercise complete dominion over unsolicited samples is demonstrated by donating those samples to a charitable institution and taking a tax deduction therefor,' and their value was thus gross income).
86. A sale or exchange is generally required for a gain to be a capital gain. *See* Code §§ 1222, 1231, 1234A.

In addition, the recipient would likely take a cost basis in the airdropped crypto asset equal to the amount included in income, so the recipient may recover his or her investment upon the later use or conversion of the crypto asset.[87]

(k) *What are the income/capital gains tax consequences of (solo, pool, and cloud) mining?*

Crypto asset transactions using a proof-of-work validation protocol are verified by miners who solve complex math problems and are either awarded crypto assets for successful mining efforts or are paid a transaction fee in crypto assets. Thus, miners may be considered as receiving crypto assets in exchange for providing a service. Notice 2014-21 provides that a taxpayer who mines virtual currency must include the fair market value of the virtual currency received in gross income as of the date of receipt.[88] If the mining activity is carried on as a trade or business[89] and the miner is not conducting those activities as an employee, the earnings from the mining activity (net of allowable business expense deductions) constitute self-employment income, which are subject to self-employment tax.[90] If a miner conducts mining activities as an employee, the value of the crypto assets received are considered wages, which is subject to federal income tax withholding by employers as well as employment taxes.[91]

In addition, the miner would take a cost basis in the crypto asset received equal to the amount included in income, so the miner may recover his or her investment upon the later use or conversion of the crypto asset.[92] A miner that is engaged in a trade or business may deduct fees and expenses (e.g., electricity or home office) incurred in connection with the mining business, and claim depreciation or amortization deductions with respect to computer equipment and software.[93] If a miner's activities do not rise to the level of a trade or business, but are considered a hobby, expenses incurred in connection with the mining activities would be deductible as hobby losses to the extent of income derived from the hobby.[94] If the mining activity is an investment, as discussed above in section 1.1.2(d), expenses are generally deductible only as a miscellaneous itemized deduction.[95]

In addition to solo mining, miners may pool their resources and join a mining pool. The miner pays a fee to the pool and shares in rewards or transaction fees

87. *Compare* IRS FAQ, at Q&A 24.
88. Notice 2014-21, at § 4 Q&A 8.
89. As discussed above in section 1.1.2(d), whether a taxpayer is engaged in a trade or business is based on the facts and circumstances.
90. Notice 2014-21, at § 4 Q&A 9. *See also* Notice 2014-21, at § 4 Q&A 10 (virtual currency received by an independent contractor is subject to self-employment tax); IRS FAQ, at Q&A 9 (same).
91. Notice 2014-21, at § 4 Q&A 11; IRS FAQ, at Q&A 10.
92. Notice 2014-21, at § 4 Q&A 4; IRS FAQ, at Q&A 12.
93. Code §§ 162(a), 167, 197. It is also possible to take advantage of special tax provisions that temporarily allow taxpayers to deduct the entire cost of equipment in the year it is placed in service. *See* Code §§ 168(k), 179.
94. Code § 183.
95. Code § 67(a). However, the Code was amended to disallow a miscellaneous itemized deduction for taxable years beginning after 31 Dec. 2017 and before 1 Jan. 2026. Code § 67(h), added by Pub. L. No. 115-97 (22 Dec. 2017).

received by the pool. The IRS has not provided any guidance on the treatment of mining pools. However, it is possible that a mining pool is treated as a constructive or de facto partnership for tax purposes, even if it is not formally organized as a partnership. A partnership includes 'a syndicate, group, pool, joint venture, or other unincorporated organization through or by means of which any business, financial operation, or venture is carried on, and which is not, within the meaning of [the Internal Revenue Code], a corporation or a trust or estate'.[96] It has been held that if persons join together for the present conduct of an undertaking or enterprise (such as by making a capital contribution to the enterprise and sharing in net profits), they should be treated as partners in a partnership.[97] Characterizing these relationships as partnerships would create significant practical problems for participants. For example, partnerships are required to file a tax return and furnish a Schedule K-1, *Partner's Share of Income, Deductions, Credits, etc.*, to each partner, and these parties may not be easily identified. In addition, partners must recognize income earned by the partnership regardless of whether the income is distributed to the partners.[98]

Cloud mining allows miners, instead of using their own machines, to buy mining power of the hardware placed in remote data centres. The mining is done in the cloud, without having to deal with offline issues, such as electricity, hosting, or installation and maintenance. Although the actual expenses incurred are different, the tax consequences should generally be the same as with solo mining. Cross-border cloud mining by non-US persons may raise novel issues, because it is not clear under what circumstances this mining income would be treated as income sourced within the US.

(l) What are the income/capital gains tax consequences of staking crypto assets?

In a proof-of-stake protocol, validators must stake a balance of the crypto asset and may be selected by the protocol to attest to the validity of the transactions in the block (called 'forging' or 'minting'). The selected validator receives additional crypto assets (known as 'staking rewards'). The protocol imposes rules (known as 'slashing rules') that cause a validator to forfeit its stake if it validates a fraudulent transaction or engages in other behaviour that is detrimental to the protocol. The forfeiture of the stake should be treated as a disposition of the crypto asset, giving rise to gain or loss at that time. Because validators may increase their chances of being selected by staking more crypto assets, validators may form a staking pool to increase their staking capacity. Similar to a mining pool discussed in section 1.1.2(k) above, this could result in the creation of a constructive or de facto partnership for tax purposes.

The differences between mining and staking raise the question of whether staking rewards should be treated differently than mining rewards. The IRS has not provided guidance on staking rewards, though it seems reasonable to conclude that

96. Code § 761(a).
97. *See, e.g., Comm'r v. Culbertson*, 337 U. S. 733 (1949); *Luna v. Comm'r*, 42 T.C. 1067 (1964).
98. *See* Code § 702(a).

staking rewards represent an accession to wealth similar to mining rewards.[99] However, staking seems more like a passive investment activity, whereas mining is more like the provision of a service. Thus, the nature of the income may be more like a dividend or other return on investment rather than compensation. As such, it may not be subject to employment taxes.

(m) What are the income/capital gains tax consequences of an indirect investment in crypto assets?

There are no specific rules governing the treatment of an indirect investment in crypto assets, and the treatment of an indirect investment will depend upon the form that this investment takes. For example, an investor may make an indirect investment in crypto assets through an investment fund that is treated as a partnership for tax purposes and that, in turn, invests in crypto assets. Any taxable income of the investment fund from its transactions in crypto assets generally would be allocated to the partners in the partnership under general partnership tax principles and the partnership agreement of the fund.[100] Partners must recognize income earned by the partnership regardless of whether the income is distributed to the partners.[101]

Indirect investments may also be made through a regulated investment company ('RIC'),[102] such as a mutual fund or exchange traded fund ('ETF'). A RIC allows investors to own an interest in a portfolio of securities. An individual taxpayer who is an investor in a RIC may receive distributions from the fund that are ordinary income, capital gain, tax-exempt income, or return of capital. Upon the sale, exchange, or redemption of RIC shares, a taxpayer generally realizes capital gain or loss. The main difference between a mutual fund and an ETF is that ETFs are bought and sold like stocks; mutual fund shares are acquired directly from the RIC and are disposed of by surrendering them to the RIC for redemption.

Similarly, investments in options, futures, or other derivatives based on the performance of a crypto asset generally would be subject to tax under the complex rules that apply to such derivative investments. For example, when the special rules of section 1256 do not apply, writing and buying options generally are subject to open transaction treatment. Under open transaction treatment, the premium is not recognized by the writer until a sale, exchange, or expiration of the option itself or upon a closing transaction.[103] Similarly, the option buyer is not allowed a deduction for the premium and recognizes gain or loss upon a sale, lapse, or termination of the option equal to the amount realized (if any) minus the premium.[104] If the option is exercised, the buyer recognizes no gain or loss and adds the premium to its basis in the property

99. *See e.g., Comm'r v. Glenshaw Glass*, 504 U.S. 229 (1992); Notice 2014-21, at § 4 Q&A 8.
100. *See* Code §§ 702, 703, 704.
101. *See* Code § 702(a).
102. Code § 851.
103. *See, e.g., Burnet v. Logan*, 283 U.S. 404 (1931).
104. Rev. Rul. 78-182, 1978-1 C.B. 265.

acquired.[105] Special mark-to-market rules apply to options covered by section 1256. These rules generally apply to options (other than a right to acquire stock from the issuer) that are traded on (or subject to the rules of) a qualified board or exchange, including a national securities exchange which is registered with the SEC, or a domestic board of trade designated as a contract market by the CFTC.[106] As a result, section 1256 may apply to certain options in crypto assets, but no guidance has been provided in this area.

(n) How is income from crypto assets to be treated under double tax treaty law?

In general, the US employs the foreign tax credit[107] to prevent double taxation and supplements this policy through treaty provisions. These treaty protections generally only apply to residents of a country with which the US has entered into an income tax treaty. Other limitations on treaty benefits also may apply.[108]

There are no specific rules governing the treatment of crypto assets for purposes of double tax treaty law in the US, and the terms of each tax treaty entered into by the US vary.

Most US tax treaties provide that effectively connected income associated with the active conduct of a trade or business is not taxed in the host country unless that income is derived through a permanent establishment or fixed place of business in that country.[109] Thus, the business profits of a taxpayer's US trade or business are not taxed if they are not attributable to the taxpayer's permanent establishment maintained in the US. In addition, most US tax treaties provide for an exemption or a reduced rate of withholding on dividends, interest, or royalties arising in one country to a person resident in the other country.[110] Finally, most US tax treaties provide that gains from the transfer of property are generally taxed by the country of the transferor's residence, except that business gains may be taxed by the other country if attributable to a permanent establishment in that country, and gains from real estate are taxed where the real estate is located.[111] Thus, the treatment of crypto assets under double tax treaties will depend on how they are characterized.

In general, a US resident for purposes of a US income tax treaty can request assistance from the US competent authority if he or she thinks that the actions of the US, a treaty country, or both, cause or will cause double taxation or taxation otherwise inconsistent with the treaty.[112]

105. Rev. Rul. 88-31, 1988-1 C.B. 302.
106. *See* Code § 1256(b)(1)(C), (g)(3), (g)(5), and (g)(7).
107. Code §§ 901-906.
108. *See, e.g.*, US Model Income Tax Convention, art. 22 (Limitation on Benefits).
109. US Model Income Tax Convention, art. 7(1).
110. US Model Income Tax Convention, arts. 7(1), 10(2), 11(1), (2).
111. US Model Income Tax Convention, art. 13.
112. *See* Competent Authority Assistance, https://www.irs.gov/individuals/international-taxpayers/competent-authority-assistance.

(o) What are the income/capital gains tax consequences of selling crypto assets in an ICO/STO/IEO?

An initial coin offering ('ICO') or a securities token offering ('STO') is similar in many ways to an initial public offering of stock in a corporation. Crypto assets, or tokens, are offered to investors in exchange for fiat currency or other crypto assets to fund the creation and growth of the underlying business model. An initial exchange offering ('IEO') is conducted by a crypto asset exchange on behalf of the company that seeks to raise funds with its newly issued tokens. The token issuers pay a listing fee along with a percentage of the tokens sold during the IEO.

Crypto assets are treated as property for federal income tax purposes, but the IRS has not indicated what type of property, nor has the IRS provided any guidance on token offerings more specifically. The issuance of the tokens may result in income to the issuer. The tax consequences depend in part on what type of property the crypto assets are.

Many issuers have asserted that the tokens they are issuing are utility tokens to avoid classification as a security by the SEC.[113] If the token can be used to obtain a good or service on a platform, the issuance of utility tokens may be treated as a prepaid sale of a good or service by the issuer.[114] If the token may be used for payment, similar to other cryptocurrencies, the token could be treated as a commodity or simply as property. Either way, if the tokens are held primarily for sale to customers in the ordinary course of the issuer's business, then the sale of the tokens would give rise to ordinary gain or loss. On the other hand, if the tokens are held as investment assets, their issuance would give rise to capital gain or loss.[115] If the token issuer is a foreign subsidiary, the income generated may be subject to tax as subpart F or global intangible low-taxed income.[116]

A securities token may or may not be treated as equity for tax purposes. Generally, to be treated as equity for tax purposes, the token would have to convey rights of an equity holder, such as voting and sharing in the profits.[117] If the token is treated as equity for tax purposes, the issuance by the issuer should not be taxable, although reporting and other complications could arise from this characterization.[118]

The purchase of the token, itself, is not a taxable transaction to the investor; instead, it results in cost basis and any gain or loss would be recognized upon the later

113. *See* section 1.1.2(a), above, for further discussion on SEC classification of tokens.
114. Advanced payments for goods or services are generally taxable upon receipt of the payments. *See* Treas. Reg. § 1.451-5; *Schlude v. Comm'r*, 372 U.S. 128 (1963); *American Automobile Ass'n v. US*, 367 U.S. 687 (1961); *Automobile Club of Michigan v. Comm'r*, 353 U.S. 180 (1957). However, in certain circumstances, a taxpayer may elect to defer inclusion of advanced payments to the next taxable year if such payments are deferred for financial accounting purposes. *See* Code § 451(c) (effectively codifying Rev. Proc. 2004-34, 2004-1 C.B. 991).
115. *See* section 1.1.2(b), above for a discussion of the different treatment of ordinary and capital gains and losses.
116. *See* Code §§ 951, 951A.
117. *See, e.g., John Kelley Co. v. Comm'r*, 326 U.S. 521 (1946); *Fin Hay Realty Co. v. United States*, 398 F.2d 694 (3d Cir. 1968).
118. *See, e.g.,* Code § 1032.

sale or exchange of the token. If the investor transfers crypto assets or other property in exchange for the token, he or she would realize gain or loss on that transfer. However, if the token is treated as equity, the investor may qualify for tax-deferred treatment on the transfer of any cryptocurrency or other property.[119]

Many issuers pre-sell their tokens under 'simple agreements for future tokens', or SAFTs. The typical SAFT provides that the holder, in exchange for a price paid in fiat or cryptocurrency, has the right to receive a certain number of tokens (typically priced at a discount from the anticipated token offering price). If the token offering does not go forward, and the issuer dissolves, the SAFT provides that the holder may receive the purchase price back, to the extent the company has assets remaining. The SAFT typically does not provide for dividend or voting rights or provide for the payment of any interest.

The IRS has not provided any guidance on the appropriate tax treatment of a SAFT, though the intended tax treatment of income received by the issuer of a SAFT is to defer recognition until the tokens are issued, similar to a forward contract - indeed, many SAFTs state that the parties will treat the agreement as a forward contract. Case law typically has treated a traditional forward contract as having no tax effect at the time of its issuance, because the contract is merely executory.[120] Instead, the transaction is held 'open' for tax purposes, and a taxable event only occurs when the property to be sold under the forward contract is delivered and the contract is no longer executory. Although the IRS has sanctioned open transaction treatment in the case of a prepaid forward contract where, similar to a SAFT, the purchase price is paid at the time the forward contract is issued,[121] open transaction treatment generally is disfavoured by the IRS.[122] It is also possible that the IRS could view the SAFT as a debt instrument and impute taxable interest payments over the term of the SAFT.[123]

119. *See, e.g.*, Code § 351. To qualify for tax-deferred treatment, one or more persons must transfer property to a corporation solely in exchange for stock of the corporation, and immediately after the transfer, such persons must be in control of the corporation (within the meaning of Code section 368(c)).

120. *See, e.g.*, *Lucas v. North Tex. Lumber*, 281 U.S. 11 (1930) (taxpayer notice of intent to exercise option did not give rise to income until actual delivery because notice created executory contract only); *Rich Lumber Co. v. U.S.*, 237 F.2d 424 (1st Cir. 1956) (executory sale not closed until settlement); *S.C. Johnson & Son, Inc. v. Comm'r*, 63 T.C. 778, 786 (1975) (no income to donor on donating appreciated forward contracts, because he had no right to gain until delivery under the contract).

121. Rev. Rul. 2003-7, 2003-5 I.R.B. 363 (involving a prepaid forward contract for stock where certain requirements were satisfied, including the number of shares to be delivered varied based on value and the taxpayer was not economically compelled to deliver the pledged shares and could deliver cash instead). Courts have also treated partially or fully prepaid forward contracts as open transactions. *See, e.g.*, *Comm'r v. Segall*, 114 F.2d 706 (6th Cir. 1940) (no sale on date executory contract formed; sale occurred on performance); *McKelvey v. Comm'r*, 148 T.C. No. 13 (2017); *Modesto Dry Yard v. Comm'r*, 14 T.C. 374 (1950) (partially prepaid forward contract to buy raisins did not transfer ownership until delivery).

122. Treas. Reg. § 1.1001-1(a) (stating that the open transaction doctrine should only apply 'only in rare and extraordinary cases'). *See also* Notice 2008-2, 2008-2 I.R.B. 252 (stating that the IRS was considering the tax policy issues raised by the treatment of prepaid forward contracts, including whether parties to a prepaid forward contract should be required to accrue income or expenses during the term of the contract).

123. *See* Code § 483, 1274.

1.1.3 Other Taxes

(a) What are the value added tax/sales tax consequences of selling crypto assets?

The US does not impose a value added tax. However, throughout the US, transaction taxes are a leading source of receipts for state and local (subnational) governments. Sales and use taxes are the most widely known of these taxes, and are imposed by forty-five states and thousands of localities.

In general, sales and use taxes are due whenever an end-user purchases goods or specified services from a retailer. Because almost every such purchase in the US involves an exchange of dollars for goods or services, valuation is not an issue and sales tax is determined based on the dollars transferred. However, even transactions not involving dollars may be subject to sales tax. Thus, barter exchanges involving goods or specified services may be taxable, the only additional issue being the value of the sold items in US dollars. States may classify purchases made with crypto assets as barter transactions.

Sales of Cryptocurrency: In general, states do not treat sales of crypto assets as being a sale of goods or services. Therefore, no sales tax is imposed on such sales.[124]

Purchases Using Cryptocurrency: In general, states treat purchases of goods or services by an end-user using virtual currency as taxable transactions. As such, sales tax is due on the value paid for the goods or services. For example, the Washington Department of Revenue has provided the following question and answer:

> [Q:] If a vendor receives payment in exchange for goods or services in the form of bitcoin, is there a taxable transaction?
> [A:] Yes. Bitcoin is treated as consideration for the purchase of goods or services.[125]

Similarly, New York has provided the following example:

> An online retailer registered for New York State sales tax purposes accepts convertible virtual currency from a customer as payment for home decor items that will be delivered to the customer's location in New York State. In effect, the customer has purchased the home decor items in exchange for the convertible virtual currency, and the retailer has purchased the convertible virtual currency in exchange for the home decor items.
>
> Because home decor items are taxable, the customer owes sales tax based on the taxable receipt for the purchase of the items. The taxable receipt is the fair market value of the convertible virtual currency in US dollars at the time of the

124. *See e.g.*, New York State Department of Taxation TSB-M-14(17)S (5 Dec. 2014) (hereinafter 'NYS') ('For sales tax purposes, convertible currency is intangible property. Since the purchase or use of intangible property is not subject to sales tax, any convertible currency received by a party to a barter transaction is not subject to sales tax.'). *See also* Wisconsin Sales and Use Tax Report 1-14 (Mar. 2014) (hereinafter 'Wisconsin') ('The sales price from the sale of virtual currency is not taxable because virtual currency represents an intangible right.').
125. *See e.g.*, Washington Department of Revenue, Interim Statement Regarding Bitcoin: Payments, Mining, and Investment Income (20 Aug. 2019) (hereinafter 'Washington').

> transaction. However, because convertible virtual currency is intangible property, the retailer does not owe any sales tax on its exchange of home decor items for the convertible virtual currency.
>
> The retailer must record in its books and records the amount of the sale and the sales tax collected in US dollars, and report the sale and remit the sales tax due in US dollars when filing its periodic sales tax returns.[126]

In general, the value of the bitcoins is determined at the time of the transaction (this is the amount that will be used to determine sales tax due). This is true even if the bitcoins are not immediately converted into US dollars.

However, as cautioned by the Washington Department of Revenue, if a crypto asset has features (or restrictions) that change its valuation, the sales tax treatment of its purchase or use might change as well:

In this guidance, we address the taxability of bitcoin related activities. Information in this guidance may be relevant for addressing other cryptocurrency business activities, depending on the facts in each case. However, please note that other forms of cryptocurrency may have different features that may lead to different tax results, and thus businesses should be aware that the Department will review other cryptocurrencies based on the facts applicable to those cryptocurrencies.[127]

(b) *Are payments in crypto assets subject to withholding taxes?*

Yes, payments in crypto assets are subject to withholding taxes to the same extent as any other in-kind payments. For example, the medium in which remuneration for services is paid is immaterial to the determination of whether the remuneration constitutes wages for employment tax purposes. Consequently, the fair market value of virtual currency paid as wages is subject to federal income tax withholding, as with any other wages.[128] Similarly, payments to non-US persons made using crypto assets generally will be subject to withholding to the same extent as payments made in any other medium.[129]

In addition, payments made using virtual currency are subject to backup withholding to the same extent as other payments made in property.[130] Therefore, payors making reportable payments using virtual currency must solicit a taxpayer identification number ('TIN') from the payee. The payor must backup withhold from

126. NYS, *supra* note 124.
127. Washington, *supra* note 125. Wisconsin provides a comparable caution ('If the sale of virtual currency represents the sale of a specific identifiable product or service that is subject to tax (such as an admission to an amusement event, digital music, or other digital good), the sale is taxable as the sale of the specific identifiable product.'). Wisconsin, *supra* note 124.
128. Code § 3402; Notice 2014-21, at § 4 Q&A-11. *See also* Publication 15 (Circular E), Employer's Tax Guide, for information on the withholding, depositing, reporting, and paying of employment taxes.
129. *See* Code §§ 1441, 1442, 1446; Notice 2014-21, at § 4 Q&A-13. *See also* Publication 515, Withholding of Tax on Nonresident Aliens and Foreign Entities.
130. Code § 3406; Notice 2014-21, at § 4 Q&A 14. *See also* Publication 1281, Backup Withholding for Missing and Incorrect Name/TINs, for more information on backup withholding.

the payment if a TIN is not obtained prior to payment or if the payor receives notification from the IRS that backup withholding is required.

Note that, because taxes generally cannot be paid in crypto assets, sufficient crypto assets must be liquidated to pay the withholding taxes, which will give rise to taxable gain or loss.

(c) *Does payment of compensation in crypto assets give rise to payroll tax consequences?*

In general, if an employee or independent contractor is paid in convertible virtual currency, the fair market value of the virtual currency (in US dollars) must be included in income.[131] In addition, the payment of wages to an employee in convertible virtual currency would be subject to federal income tax withholding, Federal Insurance Contributions Act tax, and Federal Unemployment Tax Act tax.[132] Similarly, the payment of compensation to an independent contractor in convertible virtual currency would be subject to self-employment taxes.[133] Such payments to employees or independent contractors are also reportable on information returns (e.g., IRS Forms W-2, *Wage and Tax Statement*, or 1099-MISC, *Miscellaneous Income*).[134]

Although one could assume that similar rules apply for other crypto assets, the IRS has not provided guidance beyond the receipt of convertible virtual currency.

(d) *Do transactions with crypto assets trigger any transfer taxes?*

The US does not currently impose a federal transfer tax apart from the gift and estate taxes discussed below in section 1.1.3(f).

(e) *Are firms operating in the crypto space subject to digital service taxes?*

The US does not currently impose a federal digital service tax.

(f) *Are crypto assets subject to gift, inheritance, estate or wealth taxes?*

The US imposes a gift tax on transfers during life and an estate tax on transfers at death, which are to be paid by the donor or the donor's estate at the time of the transfer. In general, transfer taxes are imposed if the donor or decedent is a US citizen or domiciled in the US, or if he or she transferring US situs assets. The IRS has provided limited guidance on how a donee treats gifts of convertible virtual currency but has not provided specific guidance on the on the gift or estate tax consequences of transfers of crypto assets. However, because crypto assets are generally treated as property for

131. *See* Notice 2014-21, at § 4 Q&A 3; IRS FAQ, at Q&A 8.
132. Notice 2014-21, at § 4 Q&A 11; IRS FAQ, at Q&A 10.
133. Notice 2014-21, at § 4 Q&A 10; IRS FAQ, at Q&A 9.
134. Notice 2014-21, at § 4 Q&A 11, 13; IRS FAQ, at Q&A 10.

federal tax purposes, they are likely subject to gift or estate taxes just like any other transfer of property by gift or at death.[135] Although gift taxes are not generally imposed on gifts of intangible property by a non-resident that is not a citizen of the US, estate taxes are.[136] However, the IRS has not provided guidance on the situs of crypto assets.

The gift tax generally is imposed on the donor of gifts of property exceeding a USD 10,000 threshold, which is adjusted annually for inflation (for 2020, the threshold is USD 15,000) during the taxable year. A donor can double the amount of gift he or she is able to make tax-free by electing to 'split' the gift with his or her spouse (so the married couple can make tax-free gifts of USD 30,000 based on the 2020 threshold).[137] Gifts may be made between spouses without incurring a gift tax.

A gift of virtual currency is not included in the income of the donee until the donee disposes of the virtual currency.[138] The basis of the virtual currency received as a gift differs depending on whether the donee will have a gain or loss when he or she disposes of the virtual currency. For purposes of determining any gain, the donee's basis is equal to the donor's basis, plus any gift tax paid by the donor.[139] For purposes of determining any loss, the donee's basis is equal to the lesser of the donor's basis or the fair market value of the virtual currency at the time the gift was received.[140] The donee's holding period for the virtual currency received as a gift includes the time the virtual currency was held by the donor, as long as the donee has documentation of the donor's holding period.[141]

The estate tax is imposed on the transfer of a person's property at the time of that person's death.[142] The amount of tax is determined by applying the relevant tax rates to the taxable estate – the gross estate reduced by any deductions. The gross estate includes the value of all property, whether real or personal, tangible or intangible, wherever situated.[143]

There is a credit allowed against gift and estate taxes of each person (known as the applicable credit) equal to USD 5 million (USD 10 million for tax years 2018–2025), which is adjusted annually for inflation (for 2020, the applicable credit is USD 11.58 million).[144]

Taxpayers may also make charitable donations of crypto assets. The IRS guidance provides that a taxpayer does not recognize income, gain, or loss on the donation of convertible virtual currency to a charitable organization, and may deduct the fair market value of the virtual currency at the time of donation, if it has been held for at

135. *See* Notice 2014-21, at § 4 Q&A 1; IRS FAQ, at Q&A 2.
136. Code § 2501(a)(2).
137. The election is made on the gift tax return (Form 709, *United States Gift (and Generation-Skipping Transfer Tax Return)*).
138. *See* Code § 102; IRS FAQ, at Q&A 30.
139. This of course implies that gifts of virtual currency are subject to gift taxes.
140. *See* Code §1015(a); IRS FAQ, at Q&A 31.
141. IRS FAQ, at Q&A 32.
142. Code § 2001.
143. *See* Code §§ 2033-2045.
144. *See* Code § 2010(c). Spouses can essentially combine their applicable credit so that a couple has USD 22.16 million for 2020.

least one year.[145] If the taxpayer held the virtual currency for less than one year prior to the charitable donation, the deduction is equal to the lesser of the taxpayer's basis or the fair market value of the virtual currency.[146] The documentation and reporting requirements applicable to charitable donations also applies to donations of virtual currency, including the requirement to obtain an appraisal for donations of property worth more than USD 5,000.[147]

(g) Are crypto assets subject to exit tax?

The US imposes a one-time mark-to-market tax on the net unrealized gain in the property of covered expatriates.[148] The tax is determined on the gain that would have been taken into account, as if the sale of the property had occurred on the day before the expatriation date, to the extent that the gain exceeds USD 600,000, which is adjusted annually for inflation (for 2020, the amount is USD 737,000). A covered expatriate is any US citizen who relinquishes citizenship, or any long-term resident who ceases to be a lawful permanent resident of the US, if the individual meets any of the following requirements:

(1) the individual has an average annual net income tax liability for the five tax years ending before the expatriation date that exceeds USD 124,000, which is adjusted annually for inflation (for 2020, the amount is USD 171,000);
(2) the individual has a net worth of USD 2 million or more on the expatriation date; or
(3) the individual fails to certify under penalties of perjury that he or she has complied with all US tax obligations for the five tax years preceding the tax year that includes the expatriation date or fails to submit evidence of compliance as required by the Secretary.[149]

Although the IRS has not provided guidance on whether crypto assets are subject to the exit tax, there is no reason to believe they would be excluded.

(h) Can mining trigger gambling tax?

The US does not currently impose a federal gambling tax apart from the general income tax. In other words, income from gambling is subject to income tax like any other

145. The deduction for charitable contributions is subject to certain income limitations and limitations based on the type of charity the asset is donated to (Code § 170(b)). For example, contributions of appreciated capital gain property (other than qualified appreciated stock) to private foundations are limited to basis.
146. IRS FAQ, at Q&A 33, 34.
147. *See* IRS FAQ, at Q&A 35, 36.
148. Code § 877A.
149. Code §§ 877A(g)(1), 877(a)(2).

income.[150] The US imposes special reporting and withholding rules on certain gambling winnings, but these rules do not appear to apply to mining crypto assets.[151]

1.1.4 *Compliance and Documentation Obligations*

(a) What documentation requirements exist for taxpayers regarding crypto assets and are there best practices in recordkeeping to support representations made in tax returns?

There are no specific documentation requirements for taxpayers holding crypto assets. Instead, such taxpayers must comply with the general documentation requirements, which require taxpayers to maintain records that are sufficient to establish the amount of gross income, deductions, credits, or other matters required to be shown by such person in any tax return.[152] The IRS has confirmed this in the context of transactions in convertible virtual currency, noting that records should document receipts, sales, exchanges, or other dispositions of virtual currency and the fair market value of the virtual currency.[153]

(b) What is the evidentiary burden of supporting tax positions when a digital wallet address is lost or shared with other persons?

There are no specific rules governing the evidentiary burden of supporting tax positions relating to crypto assets (though as discussed in section 1.1.2(g), above, the loss of a digital wallet address likely does not give rise to a deduction). In general, the IRS' deficiency determination is presumed to be correct, which places the burden of proof and the burden of going forward with the evidence upon the taxpayer.[154] Once the taxpayer establishes a prima facie case, the burden of going forward with the evidence generally is shifted to the IRS to refute the evidence or show offsetting items, as long as the taxpayer has complied with all of the documentation and substantiation requirements and has cooperated with the IRS.[155] The IRS has the burden of proof, however, for penalties assessed on individuals or concerning an item of income that the IRS reconstructed using statistical information with respect to unrelated taxpayers.

150. *See* Code § 61.
151. *See* Treas. Reg. §§ 1.6041-10(a) (information reporting of payments of reportable gambling winnings); 31.3402(q)-1 (withholding requirements for certain gambling winnings); 31.3406(g)-2(d) (backup withholding for payments of reportable gambling winnings).
152. Code § 6001; Treas. Reg. § 1.6001-1(a).
153. IRS FAQ, at Q&A 45.
154. *Welch v. Helvering*, 290 U.S. 111 (1933).
155. Code § 7491(a)(1).

(c) *Are crypto asset exchanges and wallet providers subject to reporting obligations?*

The IRS has provided some limited guidance on the application of US tax information reporting requirements with respect to certain crypto asset transactions. Specifically, the guidance provides that payment of wages in virtual currency must be reported by the employer on IRS Form W-2, *Wage and Tax Statement*, and payment of compensation of USD 600 or more to an independent contractor must be reported on IRS Form 1099-MISC, *Miscellaneous Income*.[156]

In addition, 'third-party settlement organizations' (generally, persons who make settlement payments in the form of virtual currencies between merchants and their customers) are required to report such settlement payments to the merchants on IRS Form 1099-K, *Payment Card and Third Party Network Transactions*, if, for the calendar year:

(1) the number of transactions settled for the merchant exceeds USD 200, and
(2) the *gross* amount of payments made to the merchant exceeds USD 20,000.[157]

Some of the larger crypto asset exchange platforms (e.g., Coinbase) have determined that they are subject to these reporting requirements and have provided Form 1099-K to certain users.[158]

However, the guidance does not refer to other reporting requirements, so it is unclear whether and how they apply. For example, the IRS could potentially apply the information reporting requirements applicable to brokers, dealers, barter exchanges, and certain other middlemen – who annually report information about securities or commodities sold by their customers on IRS Form 1099-B, *Proceeds from Broker and Barter Exchange Transactions* – to crypto asset transactions.[159] Specifically, brokers must report:

(1) the gross proceeds from the disposition of, among other assets, securities and commodities;[160] and
(2) the adjusted basis of 'specified securities' that are sold by the broker on behalf of a customer.[161]

156. Notice 2014-21, at § 4 Q&A 11, 13; IRS FAQ, at Q&A 10.
157. Notice 2014-21, at § 4 Q&A 15.
158. *See, e.g.*, Coinbase.com, *1099-K Tax Forms FAQ for Coinbase Pro, Prime, Merchant*, https://support.coinbase.com/customer/en/portal/articles/2721660-1099-k-tax-forms-faq-for-coinbase-pro-prime-merchant.
159. Code § 6045.
160. Code § 6045(a); Treas. Reg. § 1.6045-1(a)(9).
161. Code § 6045(g); Treas. Reg. § 1.6045-1(d). The term 'specified security' generally covers stock, debt, and options and securities futures contracts on stock or debt. Treas. Reg. § 1.6045-1(a)(14)-(15).

While some technical arguments exist that cryptocurrency brokers, dealers, or exchanges may already be covered by these rules,[162] it would appear to require amendments to the regulations to extend Form 1099-B reporting to crypto assets. The IRS has not yet issued any guidance in this area; however, this guidance is part of the IRS's priority guidance plan for 2019–2020.[163]

(d) Are taxpayers holding crypto assets subject to reporting obligations apart from the filing of income tax/capital gains tax returns?

Taxpayers holding crypto assets are currently subject to a few reporting obligations:

- Gains or losses from disposing of or spending virtual currency is reported on IRS Form 8949, *Sales and Other Dispositions of Capital Assets* (which is then summarized on Form 1040, Schedule D, *Capital Gains and Losses*).[164]
- Ordinary income from virtual currency is reported on Form 1040 along with other similar types of income (e.g., wages on line 1, self-employment income on Schedule C).[165]
- Form 1040, Schedule 1, *Additional Income and Adjustments to Income*, includes a new checkbox on the 2019 tax return, which asks, '[a]t any time during 2019, did you receive, sell, send, exchange, or otherwise acquire any financial interest in any virtual currency?'

It is not clear whether taxpayers are required to report foreign crypto asset wallets on Form 114, *Reports of Foreign Bank and Financial Accounts (FBAR)*, or on Form 8938, *Statement of Foreign Financial Assets*.

- US persons must file an FBAR with Financial Crimes Enforcement Network ('FinCEN') if the person has a financial interest in, or authority over, any financial account outside of the US where the aggregate maximum value of the account(s) exceeds USD 10,000 at any time during the calendar year. A 'financial account' includes bank, securities, commodity futures, and options accounts, insurance policies with a cash value, mutual funds or similar pooled funds or any other accounts maintained in a 'foreign financial institution' or a person 'performing the services of a financial institution'. Certain crypto asset

162. The term 'commodity' is defined for these purposes in Treas. Reg. § 1.6045-1(a)(5)(i) as '[a]ny type of personal property or an interest therein (other than securities as defined in paragraph (a)(3)), the trading of regulated futures contracts in which has been approved by the Commodity Futures Trading Commission.' Commentators have noted that crypto assets might fall within this definition because contracts relating to certain crypto assets are traded on both the Chicago Board Options Exchange and Chicago Mercantile Exchange and have been approved by the CFTC.
163. *See* Treas. Reg. § 1.1065-1(a)(5), (9) (defining sale to include dispositions of commodities and defining commodities to include any other personal property that the Secretary determines is treated as a commodity).
164. IRS FAQ, at Q&A 42.
165. IRS FAQ, at Q&A 43.

exchanges and custodial services could be treated as 'foreign financial institutions' for these purposes – if so, any account holders that are US persons generally would be subject to the FBAR reporting rules. FinCEN has indicated informally, however, that the FBAR Regulations do not currently define cryptocurrency held in an offshore account as a type of reportable account, but that FinCEN and the IRS continue to evaluate whether cryptocurrency should be incorporated into the FBAR reporting regime.[166]

- In addition, US persons must report 'specified foreign financial assets' the aggregate value of which exceeds USD 50,000 on the last day of the taxable year or USD 75,000 at any time during the taxable year on Form 8938, which is attached to the specified person's US federal tax returns.[167] Although the term 'specified foreign financial assets' is defined broadly for these purposes, it is not clear whether this reporting regime covers crypto assets, and the IRS has not provided guidance.

(e) Are crypto asset exchanges and wallet providers subject to CRS/FATCA reporting?

The Foreign Account Tax Compliance Act ('FATCA') generally requires foreign financial institutions ('FFIs') to register with the IRS and to comply with certain information reporting, withholding, and due diligence requirements with respect to 'financial accounts' maintained by US persons.

Generally, an FFI includes any non-US entity that is a custodial institution, an investment entity, or a depository institution.[168] A key question in this analysis, which has not been answered by the IRS, is whether crypto assets would qualify as a 'financial asset'. IRS guidance classifies convertible virtual currency as property, and not currency, for tax purposes,[169] though the guidance does not elaborate on what type of property. An FFI must identify and report certain information regarding its 'financial accounts' maintained by US persons. A 'financial account' includes any depository or custodial account maintained by an FFI as well as any equity or debt interest in an FFI (other than interests that are regularly traded on an established securities market).[170]

The IRS has not released any guidance on the circumstances under which a crypto asset intermediary would be treated as an FFI or a crypto asset investment would be treated as a 'financial account'. Nonetheless, applying the current definitions in the regulations, it is possible to conclude, depending on their activities, that centralized cryptocurrency exchanges taking custody of private keys, custodial wallet

166. US Government Accountability Office, 'Virtual Currencies – Additional Information Reporting and Clarified Guidance Could Improve Tax Compliance,' GAO-20-188 ('GAO Report'), February 2020, at pp. 31, 42.
167. The term 'specified person' is defined in Treas. Reg. § 1.6038D-1(a)(2) to include any US citizen.
168. Treas. Reg. § 1.1471-5(e)(1).
169. Notice 2014-21, at § 4 Q&A 1; IRS FAQs, at Q&A 2.
170. Treas. Reg. § 1.1471-5(b)(1).

providers, and cryptocurrency investment funds could be viewed as FFIs providing financial accounts to their customers.

1.1.5 Civil and Criminal Tax Enforcement

(a) What powers do the tax authorities have to compel the disclosure of information by third parties, such as exchanges or wallet providers, and have these been used in the past?

The IRS has the authority to issue a summons to third parties to compel disclosure of information about taxpayers.[171] The IRS must notify the taxpayer of the issuance of the summons, and the taxpayer can initiate a judicial proceeding to quash the summons.[172] If the third party does not comply, the IRS can initiate a proceeding to enforce the summons, and the taxpayer can intervene in that proceeding.[173] Generally, the summons must identify the taxpayer about whom information is sought, but in certain circumstances, the IRS may issue a 'John Doe' summons that does not identify a particular taxpayer, if the IRS establishes in a court proceeding that:

(1) the summons relates to a particular person or ascertainable group of persons;
(2) there is a reasonable basis to believe that such persons may have failed to comply with the tax law;
(3) the information sought is not readily available from another source; and
(4) the information sought is narrowly tailored to information that pertains to the failure (or potential failure) of the person or group to comply with the tax law.[174]

In November 2016, the IRS filed to serve a 'John Doe' summons on all US Coinbase customers who transferred bitcoin from 2013–2015. Coinbase challenged the summons, and the scope was narrowed by the IRS to customers with transactions at least USD 20,000 and narrowed further by the court to include only:

(1) taxpayer ID numbers;
(2) names;
(3) birth dates;
(4) addresses;
(5) records of account activity, including transaction logs or other records identifying the date, amount, and type of transaction (purchase/sale/exchange), the post-transaction balance, and the names of counterparties to the transaction; and

171. Code § 7609.
172. Code § 7609(a), (b)(1).
173. Code §§ 7604, 7609(b)(1).
174. Code § 7609(f).

(6) all periodic statements of account or invoices (or the equivalent).[175]

The request resulted in Coinbase turning over records for approximately 13,000 account holders.

(b) *What measures have the tax authorities undertaken in the past to ensure crypto tax compliance?*

In July–August of 2019, the IRS sent letters to approximately 10,000 taxpayers with regard to cryptocurrency transactions.[176] In the letters, the IRS provided 'educational' material and a hotline number for questions related to the letters, promising a response within three business days. There were three different form letters, with varying levels of sternness:

- Letter 6173 is the harshest letter. It indicates that the IRS knows that the taxpayer owns cryptocurrency, but did not report any income with respect to that cryptocurrency on his/her income tax return. It requires a response from the taxpayer.
- Letter 6174 seems a bit less harsh than Letter 6173. The language indicates that the IRS knows that the taxpayer owns cryptocurrency, but that the IRS might not necessarily know whether the taxpayer has unreported/underreported income related to cryptocurrency transactions. The letter instructs the taxpayer to review some 'educational' material, and then to amend or to file if reporting was not properly performed. Otherwise, no response is necessary.
- Letter 6174-A seems to be the least harsh of the three letters. The language indicates that the IRS knows that the taxpayer reported cryptocurrency transactions on his/her income tax return, but potentially reported those transactions incorrectly. For example, the taxpayer may have reported transactions on the wrong schedule. The letter provides similar instructions to those provided with Letter 6174.

(c) *Are the tax authorities cooperating with tax authorities in other jurisdictions on enforcement?*

In July 2018, tax authorities from the US joined forces with tax authorities from four other countries to form the Joint Chiefs of Global Tax Enforcement (known as the 'J5'), which targets transnational tax crime through increased enforcement collaboration.

175. *United States v. Coinbase Inc.*, No. 3:17-cv-01431 (N.D. Cal. 2017). The court held that such information as user profiles, user preferences, use security setting and history, user payment methods, and other information related to the funding sources used for their account were 'broader than necessary'.

176. IR-2019-132 (26 Jul. 2019), https://www.irs.gov/newsroom/irs-has-begun-sending-letters-to-virtual-currency-owners-advising-them-to-pay-back-taxes-file-amended-returns-part-of-agencys-larger-efforts.

The J5 comprises the Australian Criminal Intelligence Commission and ATO, the Canada Revenue Agency, the Netherlands Fiscale Inlichtingen- en Opsporingsdienst, U.K. HMRC, and US IRS Criminal Investigation.[177]

Furthermore, the US is a party to income tax treaties, which contain provisions regarding the exchange of information, and tax information exchange agreements with a number of countries. In addition, the US is one of the 136 jurisdictions that has signed the OECD Convention on Mutual Administrative Assistance in Tax Matters, which facilitates the exchange of information between signatory states.

177. *See* Joint Chiefs of Global Tax Enforcement, https://www.irs.gov/compliance/joint-chiefs-of-global-tax-enforcement.

www.ingramcontent.com/pod-product-compliance
Lightning Source LLC
LaVergne TN
LVHW020649300926
849161LV00004B/873
* 9 7 8 9 4 0 3 5 2 3 5 0 7 *